WOMEN ON WAR

2006 nurturing for community First United Methodist Church United Methodist Women Faith

(Counts - 2 Books)
UMW Reading Program

2006
Community

WOMEN ON WAR

AN INTERNATIONAL ANTHOLOGY OF WOMEN'S WRITINGS FROM ANTIQUITY TO THE PRESENT

Edited and with an Introduction
by Daniela Gioseffi

The Feminist Press at the City University of New York
New York

Published by the Feminist Press at the City University of New York
365 Fifth Avenue, New York, NY 10016
www.feministpress.org

Second edition, 2003

Library of Congress Cataloging-in-Publication Data

Women on war: an international anthology of women's writings from antiquity to the
    present / edited and with an introduction by Daniela Gioseffi.—2nd ed.
        p. cm.
    Includes bibliographical references and index.
    ISBN 1-55861-408-7 (alk. paper) — ISBN 1-55861-409-5 (pbk. : alk. paper)
        1. Women and peace. 2. Women and war. I. Gioseffi, Daniela.

JZ5578.W665 2003
303.6'6—dc21   2003042407

This publication was made possible, in part, by public funds from the New York State Council on
the Arts, a state agency, and the National Endowment for the Arts.

Publication of this book was also made possible, in part, by support from the Ploughshares Fund.

The Feminist Press would also like to thank Laura Brown, Mariam Chamberlain, Johnnetta B. Cole,
Blanche Wiesen Cook, Helene D. Goldfarb, Florence Howe, Barbara Grossman, Nancy Hoffman,
Yolanda T. Moses, and Shirley Mow for their generosity in supporting this publication.

Text design and composition by Dayna Navaro.
Printed on acid-free paper by Transcontinental Printing.
Printed in Canada.

09 08 07 06 05 04 03   5 4 3 2

Contents

PART 1: PROPHECIES AND WARNINGS

Dedication and Acknowledgments

This book is dedicated especially to my beloved daughter, Thea Dora, and to my stepdaughters, Amy, Nina, and Tanya, and niece, Dana, with hope in their futures and their childrens' futures. It is dedicated with love to my sisters, Camille Gioseffi, and Theresa Bowen; and my husband, Lionel B. Luttinger, for their humanity and understanding of the issues.

It is also dedicated to all women of peace and war resistance, everywhere, and to children of our blessed planet Earth who need to believe in empathy, equality, tolerance, and unity among all peoples in order to survive into the future.

There is special thanks due to Sally Lillienthal of the Ploughshares Fund, a World Peace Foundation of Fort Mason, California, for an award grant that made the original edition possible, and for help with this new edition. Without the encouragement from the Ploughshares Fund, Women's Leadership Development Division, this book and its new edition would not have been possible.

Gratitude is also due to the Before Columbus Foundation, which awarded the first edition of this compendium an American Book Award, 1990.

I wish to express my gratitude to the authors herein, who contributed their works, some very generously, to make this project possible. I also thank Jean Casella, Publisher/Director of the Feminist Press, for her valuable advice, and Amanda Hamlin, Dayna Navaro, and Lissa Fox for their contributions to the publication process.

D.G.

While I drew and wept along with the terrified children I was drawing,
I really felt the burden I am bearing. I felt that I have no right to withdraw
from the responsibility of being an advocate. It is my duty to voice the sufferings
of humankind, the never-ending sufferings heaped mountain-high.
This is my task, but it is not an easy one to fulfill."
—KÄTHE KOLLWITZ, (1867–1945)
world-renowned German antiwar artist, from *Diaries* (1920)

Introduction

CASSANDRA'S DAUGHTERS

"You can no more win a war than an earthquake!" said the first woman ever elected to the United States Congress, peace activist Jeannette Rankin. Her words resonate as prophetically as those of ancient Troy's Cassandra. The terrors of war that have long inhabited human nightmares have become more terrifying still with the technological development of weapons of mass destruction, which threaten not only individual but global annihilation. Since the first edition of this book appeared in 1988, and the subsequent end of the so-called Cold War (which raged hot in Korea, Vietnam, Cambodia, Central America, Angola, Afghanistan, and so many other areas of the globe), the threat of total war has only increased. Even those partial agreements to control nuclear, biological, and chemical weapons have been deserted of late by the ultimate military power, the United States, which has undermined any blossoming international accords meant to enhance global survival. "People rarely win wars, governments rarely lose them. People get killed. Governments molt and regroup, hydra-headed. They first use flags to shrink-wrap peoples' minds and suffocate real thought, and then as ceremonial shrouds to cloak the mangled corpses of the dead," wrote Arundhati Roy of India in her essay "War Is Peace" (www.Outlook.com, October 29, 2001). Roy is only one of the many vital writers added to this new edition of *Women on War*.

Sensibilities like those of Jeannette Rankin and Arundhati Roy are desperately needed everywhere in the world today, but the fact remains that few women hold powerful political office, even in the industrialized countries of the world. When Rankin cast her vote in 1917 and again in 1941 against the United States' entry into war, she is said to have wept with passionate conviction. Many have never forgiven her for what to them was a lapse of judgment, just as Cassandra was maligned for displaying emotion. Yet to weep, even to be hysterical (from the Greek word for "womb") is to be appropriately human and, therefore, rational in the deepest sense of the word. Cool logic has brought us to the brink of what disarmament activists call omnicide, a word coined to designate an act of homicide combined with suicide and even more terrible than the many acts of genocide in our common history—the complete destruction of all life on Earth forever.

Terrorism and Genocide, Wars Past and Present, and the Importance
of Women's Political Know-How

The 2001 terrorist attacks in New York and Washington, D.C., are said to have changed the world forever for Americans living in the United States. But much of the rest of the world has lived with the terrors of war—insurgent, colonial, invasive, civil, or world war—for much of human history. In the later years alone, Rwandans have murdered one another in a huge civil strife that reflects the legacy of colonialism in a war that killed nearly a million people in the space of a few months in 1994. The killing fields of Bosnia ran with blood closely upon the sorrows of Nicaragua and El Salvador, Cambodia and Vietnam. Civil strife, very much a legacy of colonial destruction, rages on in the Congo as "drug wars" kill untold civilians in Colombia, and as civilian casualties rise in the so-called war on terrorism in Afghanistan, Iraq, Israel, and Palestine. The United States has had a hand in a disturbing number of conflicts. Since the end of World War II alone, the United States has intervened overtly, or covertly by instigating wars of civil conflict, in China (1945–46 and 1950–53), Korea (1950–53), Guatemala (1954 and 1967–69), Indonesia (1958), Cuba (1959–60), Belgian Congo (1964), Peru (1965), Laos (1964–73), Vietnam (1961–73), Cambodia (1969–70), Angola (1975–91), El Salvador (1978–92), Nicaragua (1979–90), Grenada (1983), Libya (1986), Panama (1989), Iraq (1991), Bosnia (1995), Sudan (1998), Kosovo (1999), and Afghanistan (2001–02).

Facts like these must be understood by U.S. citizens who live in the most powerful nation of the world and by the citizens of their allies. Americans, after terrorist attacks against the World Trade Center and the Pentagon, asked, "Why do they hate us?" The conventional reply was that they are "jealous of our way of life and our freedoms." But many of the women in this compendium point to U.S. foreign policy and U.S. responsibility to the world community as the paramount issue in the struggle for peace and an end to the age of terrorism in which we now live. No historical explanation can excuse the terrorist murder of civilians. But as Michelle Chihara writes in this collection, true love of country must be what she calls "tough love," which also demands that we speak out against injustices carried out by our own government.

The United States is by no means the only superpower that has dodged its responsibilities to the world community. The USSR has never fully redressed the horrors of the reign of Stalin, which some estimate caused the deaths of more than 20 million people and destroyed the lives of countless others. In the post–World War II period, the USSR crushed democratic movements in Eastern Europe, intervened in civil wars in Angola and elsewhere, and fought in Afghanistan for more than a decade. It, like the United States, has never addressed the problem of its polluting nuclear and biological warfare manufacture. Today, post–Soviet Russia remains the second-largest holder of such weapons of mass destruction, which are in their very existence "war crimes." This behavior by the United States and former USSR makes it impossible to redress any human rights abuses on the part of the People's Republic of China.

Major powers remain locked in a deadly competition, pointing fingers of accusation at one another, instead of cooperating to save the planet's ecosystems.

The People's Republic of China, in the same postwar period, witnessed a bloody civil war arising out of the despair caused by a despotic empire, leading to the Communist takeover, as well portrayed in *Wild Swans*, a memoir dealing with three generations of Chinese women by Jung Chang. Since 1959, China has been responsible for the deaths of more than a million Tibetans in its military domination of that small mountain country. Tibetans are known to have perished by starvation, execution, imprisonment, and armed conflict, and thousands more, including their spiritual and political leader, the Dalai Lama, have been driven into exile. Ani Pachen, a Tibetan nun, explains in her memoir, *Sorrow Mountain*, excerpted herein, what she had to survive at the hands of the Chinese. Human rights abuses are rampant, while the Tibetans' rich mineral resources have been plundered from their land and its ecosystem devastated.

Japan today is a largely demilitarized nation, but has yet to acknowledge and apologize for its war crimes in the early part of the century, when approximately 20 million Chinese civilians died under Japanese imperialism. Neither has Japan paid reparations to its "Comfort Women," mentioned later in this introduction. Instead, the Japanese government has attempted to revise the history of its horrific conduct during World War II by issuing school textbooks that deny the imperialist aggression, and make war heroes of the commanders who ordered or sanctioned the commission of war crimes. Similar revisionist histories are used by other superpowers. The United States, now Japan's staunch ally, has also refused to support reparations for the "Comfort Women."

These examples of evildoing by militarized superpowers constitute facts that must be realized by their citizens. But citizen opinion is too often shaped by major media conglomerates owned by multinational corporations, which themselves are interested in the oil, nuclear, and military industries. These same industries have close links to the government. There is an obvious conflict of interest involved when, for example, as reported by the *Wall Street Journal* in October 2001, the elder George Bush works as a consultant for the infamous Carlyle Group on Wall Street, dealing in military contracts, as his son President Bush Junior wages a war in Afghanistan. Vice President Dick Cheney, meanwhile, is a former member of the Board of Directors of the defense contractor Lockeed-Martin, which acquired a major new contract to build bombers following the attacks of September 11. Numerous government officials have come from the high ranks of the oil industry, which has already invested heavily in a pipeline to carry oil from the Caspian Sea through Afghanistan—now the site of what we are told is purely a continuing "war on terrorism." And the next target of war is oil-rich Iraq.

These are the hard-nosed political realities that all citizens must face. The nitty-gritty "politics of destruction" must be adequately addressed and understood. The profit motive of corporate military industrialists needs to be fully exposed, rather than be hidden behind moral, religious, and nationalist motives for war. Corporate greed lies menacingly beneath the surface of armed strife everywhere across the globe and throughout history. Without confronting such issues, all peace initiatives are doomed to powerlessness, and a book like this would be merely decorative. We women, in particular, need to supply ourselves with political know-how if we are to help in saving the children and our planet. Mere sloganeering about peace cannot suffice.

One might say that powerful male leaders of militarized nations behave like terrorists, holding ordinary people in a state of fear and danger as they expand their arsenals because of greed. Often they cloak their motives in the rhetoric of Christian, Muslim, Buddhist, Jewish, Hindu, or other types of patriarchal fundamentalism. Men have killed and maimed in the name of God, with the idea that "He" is on their side, throughout history—but always, there are other hidden agendas: to dominate or to steal the rights and resources of others. And the uncompromising fundamentalisms themselves have little to do with the religious teachings of their prophets.

Barbara Erhenreich's essay, "The Religion of War," from her book *Blood Rites*, explains well the religious type of fervor that can be stirred by false patriotism. Much earlier in the century, Emma Goldman presaged Erhenreich's analysis in "Patriotism as a Cause of War," in which she identifies patriotism as a "superstition" whose purpose it is to rationalize war. Today, in the United States, it is also being used to rationalize a McCarthy-style erosion of civil liberties under the shrewdly named USA-Patriot Act. But war is not rational. It cannot be justified by religion, by patriotism, or by the need to uphold truly democratic ideals or freedom. "Operation Enduring Freedom" cannot ultimately be won with armaments. Killing far more Afghan civilians than the numbers who died in the 9/11 attacks is not the answer to finding justice for the dead Americans, contend such women of wisdom as Arundhati Roy and Barbara Kingsolver in the pages of this book. Only humanitarian diplomacy and a kinder, gentler commitment to a global community can end international terrorism. Only steps to promote greater economic justice, fair labor practices, and sound environmental policies can move us toward a safe and peaceful world.

The Age of International Terrorism Today?

The world stands at the head of a new era, the age of international terrorism, which at this juncture in 2002 threatens only to worsen because of the lack of cooperation on the part of the most powerful nations toward the developing world's community. Prior to the first edition of *Women on War* in 1988, Helen Caldicott warned us that "the end of the world could come next year," and, unfortunately, that fact has not changed but become even more pronounced, as her vital new book, *The New Nuclear Danger*, excerpted herein, explains. We live in a world where 50,000 children die every year from malaria, because multinational drug corporations have no interest in developing a cure for it. Since the wealthy nations do not suffer to any extent from this disease, there is no profit motive to cure it. But at the same time, there is multibillion-dollar profit in war weaponry manufacture and the selling of arms to promote civil strife in such developing nations where malaria is a problem.

The United Nations Children's Fund, or UNICEF, tells us that approximately 25 million children around the globe die of starvation and malnutrition every year, as they are doing now in the Congo, Afghanistan, Iraq, and many other countries. Moreover, the population of the earth is doomed to rise to 24 billion in the lifetime of young adults of today. The ecosystems of the planet cannot support such a population. The dangers of this population explosion is ignored as religious leaders and politicians debate the so-called right to life, and the Bush administration bans funds for international family planning. Nor is nearly enough done to alleviate the suffering of children already here. Millions of children, fully conscious and in pain—feeling, living, breathing beings beloved of their mothers—are condemned to death by the misery and famine that follows war and civil strife.

Women, who as Virginia Woolf explained should see themselves as citizens of the world, need to be aware of the enormity of genocide during the twentieth century and of the development of human rights laws and diplomatic institutions in response. As writers like Eleanor Roosevelt explain herein, international bodies like the United Nations and international laws enforced by world tribunals are the best instruments we have for lessening suffering and quelling war. The United States, along with other powerful nations, has a legacy of slavery, colonialism, and the destruction of indigenous peoples. Such a history carries with it "blowback"—or a "curse," as Alice Walker, citing Zora Neal Hurston, declares in these pages. Against the pattern of nuclear and biological warmongering and cruel colonialism, innumerable women activists and social critics throughout the globe, many of them represented herein, have demonstrated solidarity.

Human Rights, Women's Rights, and War Crimes

After World War II and the Holocaust, the words "never again" were widely used to designate that such genocide should never again be allowed to happen. But since 1945, genocides, or ethnic cleansings, have happened "ever again"—most recently and dramatically in the former Yugoslavia and in Rwanda. The wars of ethnic cleansing in the former Yugoslavia during the 1990s made the world more aware than ever of the ways in which women's bodies are used as instruments of conquest in such conflicts. This realization propelled initiatives to have the mass rape and sexual enslavement of women declared war crimes. The trial of Bosnian Serb commanders in 2000, convened in the Hague by the International Criminal Tribunal for the Former Yugoslavia (ICTY), was a landmark case for war crimes prosecution and a precious step in the struggle for women's human rights worldwide. On June 12, 2002, the UN Court of Appeals upheld the sentences of three Bosnian Serbs for their part in the gang rape and torture of Muslim women in the 1992–95 Bosnian conflict. As the first sexual enslavement prosecution in an international court, the so-called Foca Case set a powerful precedent that bodes well for future prosecutions of war crimes against women.

According to a report issued by the UN Economic and Social Council, an estimated 20,000 to 50,000 women were assaulted during the conflict in Bosnia-Herzegovina ("Rape and Abuse of Women in the Former Yugoslavia,"

1994). Compelling novels like *S.* by Slavenka Drakulic, excerpted herein—along with other published memoirs and oral histories, as well as the efforts of activists—have helped to educate the international community on the prevalence of war crimes against women. Although the conflict in the former Yugoslavia brought widespread attention to the issue of rape as an instrument of warfare, in actuality, this crime has been a part of war throughout ancient and modern times.

At the end of the twentieth century, the world became more cognizant, too, of the huge numbers of Korean and Filipina women enslaved, raped, and tortured as prostitutes by the Japanese Imperial Army during World War II. Maria Rosa Henson, a Filipina survivor, describes in her memoir *Comfort Woman* the miseries she endured as a fifteen-year-old girl.

Just a few years later in the century, during the 1947 partition of India, it is estimated that more than 75,000 women were brutally abducted and raped in the civil conflict following years of British rule, a conflict in which more than 1 million people died, 12 million were displaced, and countless children disappeared. The world in 2002 still reaps the horrors of Partition in the disputed Kashmir territory on the border between India and Pakistan, two volatile nuclear powers. Urshashi Butalia of the Indian feminist press Kali for Women has collected oral histories of the survivors of those massacres in her book *The Other Side of Silence*. These testimonies reveal an additional horror: many women were murdered or urged to commit suicide by their own male relatives to prevent their falling into enemy hands.

The sprawling brothel-slums outside U.S. military bases in the Philippines and worldwide attest to another kind of sexual slavery wrought by poverty—often the result of colonialism.

Rape is considered a war crime under the Geneva Conventions, but until the Akayesu Decision of the International Criminal Tribunal for Rwanda (ICTR), addressing the rape and genocide in Rwanda in 1994, sexual assault by military forces had been treated as a violation of the laws and customs of war. This was a lesser charge than "crimes against humanity." Now, as a result of the labors of feminist activists throughout the world, even a single incident of rape has the potential to be tried as a war crime. In the case of Akayesu, the communal leader who publicly provoked and supervised attacks on Tutsi women during Rwanda's civil war, the classification of rape as an individual crime was forced into reexamination under the overwhelming evidence that sexual abuse was both systematic and carried out on a massive scale. Charlotte Lindsey, who worked for the British Red Cross and who is responsible for the International Red Cross's Project on Women and War, has written: "Thousands of women all over the world suffer the traumas of war—widowed, displaced, detained, separated from loved ones, victims of violence and injury. Usually civilians caught in the crossfire, women very often show resourcefulness and resilience in coping with the loss and destruction of their lives. International law provides extensive protection for women in war, whether as civilians or captured combatants. If these rules were better observed, the suffering of women in war would be much less."

The modern idea of universal human rights was popularized after World War II through the Universal Declaration of Human Rights (1948) and the creation of a United Nations Commission on Human Rights. The project was to a large extent inspired and propelled by the tireless work of Eleanor Roosevelt, who chaired the writing of the declaration. Supported by women delegates from India, China, the Soviet Union, and Lebanon, Eleanor Roosevelt was able to argue for gender-neutral terms, avoiding such phrases as *mankind* in favor of universal terms such as *the human person.*

The movement for women's human rights still struggles to be fully realized, but grew in emphasis around the second World Conference on Human Rights in Vienna in 1993. In Vienna, the issues of gender-based violence, rape, female genital mutilation, infanticide, and sexual slavery were emphasized as a human rights crisis not adequately addressed by the human rights community in general, and by war crime prosecutions in particular. The UN Fourth World Conference on Women, held in Beijing in 1995, reflected a movement that had evolved over the preceding decade—one still struggling—to the point that the new World Court conceded to seek justice for gender-based crimes committed against women as a part of the systemic violence of wars.

War, Women Refugees, and Children's Rights

According to the UN High Commissioner for Refugees, the world in 2002 still contained 50 million or more people displaced by war and civil strife and its resultant famines. Of the estimated 22.3 million for whom the UN Commission cares, 10 million were children under the age of eighteen, and the majority of the rest were women. Women and children together constitute approximately 75 percent of the world's refugees. A particular problem faced by women refugees in combat zones like those currently in Afghanistan is sexual abuse, even by some members of UN peacekeeping forces. Too often, food distributors at refugee camps force women to exchange sex for food for their family's survival. As Cynthia Enloe documents in the excerpt from her 2000 book *Maneuvers* and Beverly Allen corroborates in her 1996 study *Rape Warfare,* even members of UN peacekeeping forces are sometimes guilty of such coercive practices and transgressions. The end of armed conflict brings improvement to women's lives only when specific efforts are made to empower women in the postwar leadership. For example, after East Timor's bloody war of independence from Indonesia ended, and a new state was established in 2002, women managed to be elected to 27 percent of congressional offices (twice the ratio of women in the U.S. Congress). East Timor's new constitution contains provisions against slavery and forced sexual trafficking and provides for maternity leave. Such progressive moves reflect the work of UN nongovernmental agencies in East Timor, which worked to discover grassroots women community leaders.

Unfortunately, far more typical is the situation in Kosovo, which became riddled with exploitation of women and children after the war with Serbia ended. Jasmina Tesanovic's essay gives a Serbian view of the situation for women that follows in the wake of war. As Vandana Shiva explains in her books *Monocultures of the Mind* and *The Hijacking of the World's Food Supply*—and according to the International Labour Office in London, as well as Women for Women (www.womenforwomen.org) the global financial ruling class of the new century is greatly responsible for the rise in fundamentalist movements worldwide. As local ruling classes were overwhelmed by international institutions, room was made for fundamentalist leaders to move in and capture people's minds and means of survival. According to many world observers of economic trends, the real struggle is between the forces of globalization and the grassroots forces that have sprung up to oppose them. The problem is not "globalization" in the sense of nations blending their efforts at trade and production, so much as the lack of decent labor laws and environmental protections that go along with the undermining of local governments, labor unions, and land and water rights by profit-driven multinational corporations accountable to no one. Central to such militant movements as, for example, Serbian nationalism or Taliban despotism is the control of women's labors, livelihoods, and bodies. The anger over the global elitist control of resources and livelihood everywhere is creating a horrific backlash against women's rights in the pecking order of societies throughout the world.

In addition, more than 500,000 youths currently are serving as child soldiers—many under the age of ten years old. Most girl soldiers are forced into sexual slavery, as well. The 1989 Convention on the Rights of the Child is the most important legal framework for the protection of children worldwide. Of all UN conventions it has been ratified by the highest number of nations—in fact, every country except the United States has ratified the treaty.

In the year 2000 the Convention on the Rights of the Child approved two new protocols, one condemning the sale of children and child pornography and another on establishing age eighteen as the minimum age for participation by children as soldiers or military workers in hostilities, but, still, the United States has not ratified.

The New Nuclear Peril and the Macho Threat to Peace

World peace activists had greatly hoped that the dissolution of the Soviet Union and the end of the Cold War would be followed by a lessening of the nuclear threat. But as Theresa Hitchens, vice president of the nonprofit Center for Defense Information (founded by top retired U.S. military personnel) in Washington, D.C., explains, the nuclear peril has only grown since the 1980s. Countries like Pakistan and India have gained nuclear capabilities as tensions have increased between them. The breakup of the Soviet Union left nuclear weapons in the hands of volatile nations like Kazakhstan. Security for nuclear weapons in the former Soviet bloc appears in many cases to be dangerously lax. And the world's only remaining superpower, the United States, in December 2001 abandoned the landmark Treaty on Anti-Ballistic Missile (ABM) Systems in favor of developing a whole new arsenal of deadlier-than-ever nuclear weaponry. The U.S. plan resembles the widely discredited "Star Wars" program. Disguised as "national missile defense," the plan calls for placement of a large nuclear reactor in outer space by the year 2003 to power the system. Even nuclear-free Japan, disturbed by the U.S. policy shift, has made innuendos about ending its ban on producing and harboring nuclear weapons.

The biggest threat to world peace lies in this U.S resumption of the nuclear arms race, which will not only bankrupt a world economy already overly militarized, but also force Russia and China to respond with new nuclear weapons programs. Even if—and that is a big if—nuclear wars are not fought, war industries pollute the earth and bankrupt the resources needed to sustain life on the planet. As Dr. Helen Caldicott of Australia and Dr. Rosalie Bertell of Canada explain herein, the new Star Wars will bring the nuclear arms race and its deadly filth to outer space to hang over all life on Earth like a sword of Damocles. This endeavor, promoted in the name of security, will make all life on Earth more vulnerable than ever. And this unilateral U.S. initiative, purported to protect Americans, will only make the United States less secure and more unpopular in a world community that universally condemns the plan.

This huge ballistic missile buildup is particularly ill-advised given that the real nuclear threat lies in terrorism. A small nuclear device or radiation-releasing "dirty bomb" is what needs to be addressed. More funding is needed for homeland security, detection, verification, and inspection everywhere across the globe. The United States has spent hundreds of billions on ballistic missile programs since 1983. The cost of the new Star Wars system now proposed is estimated by the Congressional Budget Office to be more than $60 billion in just the upcoming year or two—while diplomacy and homeland security remain in dire need of funding. The Federation of American Scientists, and internationally renowned scientists like Vera Kistiakowsky of the United States and Dorothy Crowfoot Hodgkin of the United Kingdom, have denounced the plan as unworkable and insane, yet the Bush administration has been forging ahead with this folly.

Perhaps just as frightening is the prospect of U.S. deployment of "bunker busters," which burrow their nuclear warheads deeply into enemy hideouts and caves. The Federation of American Scientists warns that these "small" nuclear weapons would cause untold amounts of civilian deaths as a result of the environmental disasters they would cause. They would go on killing for decades to come as radioactive craters are exploded in the earth and radioactive dirt rains down on local regions, creating an especially intense fallout that would eventually be blown across the surface of the earth and permeate its groundwaters and oceans. This new generation of nuclear weapons makes the use of radioactive bombs in conventional warfare more likely and their use could easily lead to an all-out nuclear catastrophe.

The United States, having abandoned the ABM treaty, and having begun to develop and test such new nuclear weapons, is reneging on its public pledge to end the arms race. The 2002 treaty signed by President George W. Bush and Russian premier Vladimir Putin to reduce their nuclear arsenals has little impact. According to disarmament experts worldwide, it does little more than pledge to store some aging warheads a decade from now. While developed nations were building their nuclear arsenals, nonaligned nations such as Norway and Sweden were furthering the defensive technologies that detect nuclear and chemical warfare agents, leaving no excuse—other than military profiteering—for not implementing protocols and treaties that would allow for inspection and disarmament. Such protocols can be used in place of MAD—mutually assured destruction. The irrationality of using polluting nuclear weapons as deterrence can come to an end if military-industrial technocrats and their puppets are prevented by international law from running powerful governments.

The United States has also deserted its commitment to the 1972 Biological Weapons Convention, which was ratified by 144 nations, including the United States. In July 2001, the United States walked out of a London conference held to discuss a 1994 protocol designed to strengthen the convention by providing for on-site inspections, even as it accuses Iraq, among other countries, of violating the convention. The United States was the only nation to oppose the United Nations Agreement to Curb the International Flow of Illicit Small Arms in July 2001. The Land Mine Treaty (of which Princess Diana was one notable global champion), signed in Ottawa in December 1997 by 122 nations, was refused by the United States, along with Russia, China, India, Pakistan, Iran, Iraq, Vietnam, Egypt, and Turkey. Land mines kill and maim thousands of children, farmers, and other civilians worldwide every year. President Bill Clinton rejected the treaty, claiming that mines were needed to protect South Korea against North Korea's "overwhelming military advantage." He stated that the United States would "eventually" comply, in 2006, but this idea was disavowed by President Bush in August 2001.

These new deadly war perils bespeak irrational madness on the part of the mostly male leaders who hold all our lives in the balance. Several of the writers in this book analyze archetypal masculine logic, devoid of feminine feeling, as a dangerous mode of thinking that must be avoided by both sexes if we are to survive as a species. Psychologist Carol Cohn's essay, "Sex and Death and the Rational World of Defense Intellectuals," is an astute analysis of U.S. military contractors and legislators that explains just how irrational is the world they dominate with their need for macho prowess as they contend to produce the biggest phallic-shaped missiles. Helen Caldicott recounts in her autobiography, *A Desperate Passion*, how the only way she was able to get a group of Australian labor leaders to listen to her talk on radiation was to mention how the penis is affected by such invincible poison from military industries.

During the last decades of the Cold War, the U.S. nuclear air force swept into action several times on "red alert," because of the failure of a twenty-nine-cent computer chip—a fact reported in the *New York Times* and throughout the European press. Accidental or deliberate nuclear and biological war is a grave possibility. Missile reaction time has grown exceedingly short, and small tactical weapons or cruise missiles with the blast power of sixteen Hiroshima bombs—or mere dirty bombs carried by individual terrorists—can cause monumental destruction of life and Earth's ecosystems. Yet we live in relative apathy, even with these facts known. Petra Kelly, who fostered the West German Green party, wrote: "Fallible computers and men, sometimes found to be on drugs, hold our futures in their hands." She warned us in the 1990s that the world expenditure on the arms race was well over a thousand million dollars per day. But she also told us of a growing network of women—and the camaraderie among them—as they assert themselves in the international peace movement.

The Rwandan Genocide and International Racism

A horrendous example of genocide rooted in the legacy of colonialism—in this case, Belgian and German colonialism particularly affected the lives of Rwandan women and their children—occurred in the space of a few months in the spring of 1994 in Rwanda. More than half a million Rwandans were killed and innumerable refugees fled over borders. Just as in Nazi Germany, propaganda, racial hatred, and violence were promoted by the government before it carried out the destruction of targeted groups. The state-directed slaughter and at least 250,000 rapes were directed against innocent, selected civilians. On one single day in May 1994, 250,000 people crossed into Tanzania from Rwanda to form the largest refugee camp in the world. In July, a million refugees fled to Zaire and settled around the town of Goma. A great majority of fleeing refugees died later for lack of food, water, and sanitation while the world's response was slow and unempathetic. The United Nations, because of a lack of international community, ignored the warnings that were clearly given. In one of the great historical betrayals of conscience, the Security Council, led by the United States at the urging of Belgium, voted to withdraw the peacekeepers, leaving a small contingent of 270 in Kigali who protected some refugees in a stadium and who assisted with the protection of expatriates.

Amnesty International stated in its 1994 report *Forsaken Cries*, "The flight out of Rwanda had begun for anyone who could escape." The U.S. State Department did not publicize the fact that genocide was taking place, mainly because it was reluctant to participate in a United Nations peacekeeping mission—many speculate because no oil or other important resource was to be protected, as in the Afghan war. During a few days in Goma, 50,000 people died of cholera while the world's powerful nations hesitated to send in aid or respond, in what came to look like a racist brand of neglect. Tens of thousands of refugees continued to die in Rwanda even after the violence was finally halted, as the international humanitarian community attempted to create a massive aid operation.

Rwanda and bordering Burundi are regions where, two decades earlier, major genocide had occurred—giving plenty of reason to understand what might happen. Rwanda is located in the middle of east-central Africa, bordered by Uganda, Tanzania, Burundi, and the Congo—one of the most densely populated areas in Africa. The rapid pace of the genocide in Rwanda is a horrible lesson that explains why international means of preventing such conflicts, as well as enforceable international laws and courts, are so necessary. Yet the United States and Japan are among a handful of countries that have undermined the power of international tribunals rather than upheld them—as feminist dignitary Eleanor

Roosevelt had hoped they would in her undying struggle to create international human rights laws.

Signed in Rome in July 1998 and approved by 120 countries, the treaty creating the International Criminal Court (ICC)—to be set up in the Hague to try political leaders and military personnel charged with war crimes and crimes against humanity—was opposed by only seven countries, including the United States. In October 2001, Great Britain became the forty-second nation to sign. In December that year, the U.S. Senate added an amendment to a military appropriations bill that would keep U.S. military personnel from being subject to the jurisdiction of the ICC. Clearly the United States did not wish to be responsible to the world community for its own war crimes. In 1986, the International Court of Justice at the Hague ruled that the United States was in violation of international law for "unlawful use of force" in Nicaragua, through its actions and those of its contra proxy army. The United States refused to recognize the court's jurisdiction. A UN resolution calling for compliance with the court's decision was approved 94 to 2 with only the United States and Israel voting no.

The United Nations established an International Criminal Tribunal for Rwanda, and a small number of people have been tried for war crimes and genocide. Slaughter continued in Sierra Leone and other countries after the Rwandan massacre. The Rwandan genocide still has economic, political, and social repercussions throughout central Africa. Jean Kadaliki Uwankunda of Pro Femme explains in these pages the impact of the Rwandan genocide on women, who suffered disproportionately during its occurrence, and now bear a disproportionate share of the burden of rebuilding the country.

Africa, a continent extremely rich in natural resources, suffers the greatest poverty of all continents. This poverty stems from more than a century of European colonialism and is enforced by colonialism's present-day legacies and the greed of many of Africa's own ruling elites. No doubt racism is a factor in the continued suffering of African nations. It also seems clearly a factor in the response—or lack of response—by the developed nations to genocides like Rwanda's. According to the United Nations special representative for Africa in 2002, "Africa is still the poorest continent in the world, the biggest sufferer of HIV and AIDS, the continent with the most external debts and the least foreign investment." The operations of the World Bank and the International Monetary Fund, which are known for funding Third World "development" that benefits the rich nations that dominate these institutions, are crucial elements in understanding why misery and famine continue to unfold in many areas of Africa today. The roots of these sufferings are in the racist colonization of African countries by European armies and business interests. Prior to colonization, there were droughts, but such vast numbers of people did not starve as they do today. There were wars, but genocides did not occur on the huge levels they do now, when the destruction has been increased exponentially by the introduction of European and American armaments.

Stereotypical reactions to "the other," the stranger—the one whose language or color, religion or custom, costume or hair, is different—were an intrinsic part of colonialism and continue to play a role in the foreign policies of the developed nations toward the developing world. In general, the enemy—or the civilian casualty of another nation—must be thought to have no real humanity, or she could not so easily be murdered in the hate that is war. The idea, for example, that a Rwandan, Afghan, Palestinian, or Iraqi civilian's death is not as sorrowful an event as an American civilian's death is a presumption of imperialism, not democracy. As cited by James Ridgeway in the *Village Voice* in August 2002, Marc Herold, a University of New Hampshire professor who has been tracking civilian casualties in Afghanistan, compared the compensation given to victims of the U.S. military in various countries. The United States paid $2 million in compensation for each of the Italian citizens killed in 2001 after a U.S. military plane accidentally destroyed a tramway at a ski resort. The NATO bombing of the Chinese embassy in Belgrade resulted in $150,000 in compensation for each victim. For each of the civilian deaths in Afghanistan, the price tag is a mere $100.

In the UN Human Rights Commission, the United States, the richest and most powerful nation in the world, stood virtually alone in opposing resolutions supporting lower-cost access to HIV/AIDS drugs, acknowledging a basic human right to adequate food, and calling for a moratorium on the death penalty. In April 2001, the United States was not reelected to the Human Rights Commission, after years of withholding dues to the UN. In the year 2001 alone, the United States refused to sign or participate in numerous international initiatives aimed at improving life in the world community. In February 2001, the United States refused to join 123 nations that pledged to ban the use and production of antipersonnel bombs and mines, the deployment of which spread widely during the Cold War era.

The Kyoto Protocol of 1997, for controlling global warming—which all major climatologists agree is definitely upon us—was declared "dead" by President Bush in March 2001 as he rolled back many environmental policies. The protocol would have forced higher standards on the United States, which is the world's biggest air polluter and destroyer of the ozone layer. In May 2001, the United States refused to participate in talks in Paris with the Organization for Economic Cooperation and Development, which deals with ways of cracking down on offshore and other tax and money-laundering havens that blossomed in the Cold War years.

In September 2001, just prior to the attacks on the World Trade Center and the Pentagon, the Conference on Racism, bringing together 163 countries, was held in Durban, South Africa. The United States walked out of it. In July, the United States was the only nation to oppose the International Plan for Cleaner Energy, devised by the G8 group of industrial nations (the United States, Canada, Japan, Russia, Germany, France, Italy, and the United Kingdom). In the UN in October 2001, the General Assembly passed a resolution, for the tenth consecutive year, calling for an end to the illegal U.S. embargo of Cuba, by a vote of 167 to 3 (the United States, Israel, and the Marshall Islands were the only ones in opposition). In November 2001, the United States forced a vote in the UN Committee on Disarmament and Security to demonstrate its opposition to the Comprehensive Nuclear Test Ban Treaty. The Test Ban

Treaty, which was signed by 164 nations and ratified by 89, including France, Great Britain, and Russia, was signed by President Clinton in 1996—but rejected by the Senate in 1999 by a very slim margin. The United States is one of thirteen nonratifiers among countries that have nuclear weapons or nuclear power programs.

In addition to other UN conventions like CEDAW and the Convention on the Rights of the Child, the United States has yet to ratify the UN International Covenant on Economic, Social and Cultural Rights of 1966, covering a wide range of rights to be monitored by the Committee on Economic, Social and Cultural Rights. The United States signed this covenant in 1977 but has not ratified it. As to the 1948 UN Convention on the Prevention and Punishment of the Crime of Genocide, the United States finally ratified in 1988, adding several "reservations" to the effect that the U.S. Constitution and the "advise and consent" of the Senate are required to judge whether any "acts in the course of armed conflict" constitute genocide. These imperial reservations were rejected by Britain, Italy, Denmark, the Netherlands, Spain, Greece, and others.

The 1989 UN International Covenant on Civil and Political Rights, Optional Protocol, is aimed at abolition of the death penalty and contains a provision banning the execution of those under eighteen. The United States has neither signed nor ratified, and specifically exempts itself from, the latter provision, making it one of only five countries that still execute juveniles, joining Saudi Arabia, the Democratic Republic of the Congo, Iran, and Nigeria. China abolished the practice in 1997, Pakistan in 2000.

There is a myth afoot among Americans that the United States is a generous giver of humanitarian aid to less fortunate countries. The truth is that many developed nations give a much larger percentage when measured against their gross national product (GNP). Denmark gives 1.01 percent of its GNP, Norway gives .91 percent, and the Netherlands .79 percent. Among the lowest contributors are the United States with .10 percent; the United Kingdom with .23 percent; and Australia, Portugal, and Austria with .26 percent each. The United States would be not only a more just nation, but also a safer one, were it to become "a kinder, gentler nation" with a humane foreign policy toward the world community. The women of the most militarized superpower, more than any other community of peace activists on Earth, need to face these facts squarely because we have a more powerful responsibility to address the effects of our government policies on the lives of women everywhere. If Eleanor Roosevelt were alive today, she would be resolutely facing them. She would be calling for women of the United States to be more politically aware of where their nation stands in its responsibility to the world community.

Women and Major-Media Bias

One of the biggest stumbling blocks to ending war globally is the lack of factual information readily available to citizens, particularly women, even in the most powerful nations of the world. For example, according to alternative U.S.

media and all reputable press outside the United States, the bombardments of Afghanistan caused far more civilian casualties, and suffering among women and children, than most major U.S. media reported. We are lulled into a false sense of security by nightly news broadcasts that seldom look beyond the information found in government press releases, and distracted by a glut of entertainment commercials, and sports, leaving us ignorant of our own governments' foreign policies—the very policies that shape and determine the quality and durability of our lives and our children's lives. The political historian Barbara Tuchman explained during the Reagan years: "As the world grows more complex and more in need of expert handling in foreign relations, we must not rest content with persons who merely look good on television. Our electoral choices now become crucial, and one hopes they will be founded on a basis more mature than the televised—Tele-Prompter, artificial images picked by professional fund raisers and advertising companies."

It is, again, particularly interesting for feminists to note how the plight of Afghan women was widely cited by pro-war politicos and covered by major media only after the onset of the war on terrorism and the invasion of Afghanistan, though feminists had been attempting for years to acquire media attention for the oppression of Afghan women. Many feminists believed that this sudden attention was used to help shore up support for the war in Afghanistan by gaining the support of women.

In fact, women's voices are given very little play on major media throughout the world. A recent study of news from powerful U.S. networks was reported by Ina Howard, the research director of Media International in the June 2002 issue of *Extra,* the newsletter of Fairness and Accuracy in Reporting, a not-for-profit media-watch organization based in New York. The research study, which monitored the major network newscasts, showed that women experts and authorities were given less than 18 percent coverage by these networks—NBC, ABC, and CBS. Shockingly, even in coverage of gender-related issues, women were given less then .2 percent of major network television news time. People of color were also highly underrepresented as authorities with opinions. During the study year, 2002, 92 percent of the experts asked opinions were white, and the great majority were from the Republican, right-wing Bush administration, with the Democratic opposition given only less than one-quarter of the time afforded administrative incumbents. This was the latest of many studies that disprove the popular myth of a liberal major media in the United States. When women do appear in major media, it is likely to be in the context of a sexual scandals like the Chandra Levy or Monica Lewinsky cases, rather than on vital topics of the day, including gender-based issues, the feminization of poverty, or the occurrence of rape as a crime of war. Likewise, the voices of disarmament activists are virtually never heard in the United States, and issues of such paramount importance as the nuclear arms buildup are extremely underplayed.

In 1984, the United States quit UNESCO, the UN Educational, Scientific and Cultural Organization, and ceased its payments for UNESCO's budget, because of the New World Information and Communication Order (NWICO), designed to lessen world media dependence on the "big four" wire agencies: AP,

UPI, Agence France-Presse, and Reuters. The United States charged UNESCO with "curtailment of press freedom," as well as mismanagement and other faults, despite a 148 to 1 vote in favor of NWICO in the UN. UNESCO terminated NWICO in 1989, but the United States nonetheless refused to rejoin until Bush sought a resolution for a war on Iraq in September 2002. In 1995, the Clinton administration had proposed rejoining, but the move was blocked by a Republican-dominated Congress. In February 2000, the United States finally paid some of its dues in arrears to the UN—but had excluded UNESCO.

Citizens of the world, particularly women, should be very wary of believing the slanted sound-bites offered by the old-boy circuit of network television and radio and the big-four news wire outlets, which to a large degree control world opinion.

Women need to understand that while they are given little say in government and their voices are not much heard by major media, they must nonetheless listen to one another and join together in the struggle against self-destruction. Constructive choices must be made now, before no other choices remain. Together we can actualize the dream of peace and a better quality of life throughout the world community.

The Hope of a Growing Worldwide Women's Peace Movement

A hopeful element in all this sorrow and folly is a still-burgeoning world peace and disarmament movement, largely organized by women who understand the importance of a human response like that of Jeannette Rankin, when she said, "You can no more win a war than an earthquake." Rankin, like so many great women activists, held her strong convictions throughout her life, and at the age of eighty-eight, led a 1968 march of women on Washington against the Vietnam War. Today's growing, multi-national network Women in Black, founded in Israel by both Israeli and Palestinian women and vigilant in the Yugoslavian conflict, among others, is just one example of the many women's organizations working for peace and social justice and helping refugee women and children throughout the world today. Descriptions of these many organizations can be found on the interactive resource list on the Feminist Press web site. Go to www.feministpress.org and click on "Special Projects."

Another example of grassroots women's antiwar activism is the Third Global Women's Strike, held on March 8, 2002, International Women's Day, with the motto "Invest in Caring, Not Killing." Women from around the world united to push for "a world which values all women's work and every life and to end America's new war and all wars." The women of this movement charge that "never before has there been so much wealth—yet so many of us with so little." Women's Strike is one of many international collectives resisting the cruelly dehumanizing effects of globalization and the insanely destructive militarization of the world economy. These groups insist that it is flatly wrong to prioritize the production of things over enforcing humane labor laws, and to threaten human life and the life of the planet with polluting military industrialization. The Strike calls for a total change of social and economic priorities for the whole society, beginning with women. Global Women's Strike demands protection and asylum from all violence and persecution as well as freedom of movement, including the right to immigration and asylum. It also demands that so-called Third World debt not be paid. Their slogan, "We owe nothing, they owe us," is based on acknowledging how hard women work, and for how little monetary reward, around the globe. According to the UN, women do two-thirds of the world's work, and two-thirds of this work for no wages. The Strike also argues that war machine economics destroys and takes priority over women's important labors of nurturing life—which it surely does.

For the past two years, women and girls in more than sixty countries have joined the Strike to "Stop the World and Change It"—often with dramatic results. All sorts of creative nonviolent protests have been planned around the globe for March 2003. More men and women than ever are interested in what women have to say about the most baffling, challenging, and tragic issues facing all of life. As Nobel scientist Dorothy Crowfoot Hodgkin of the United Kingdom has said, "Though cool headedness may be necessary in the laboratory, the scientist must learn to respond with more consideration to the consequences of what is discovered or invented there." The problem for the scientist, however, is that laboratory work is most often owned and funded by corporations that have only one ethic in mind—that of "capitalist fundamentalism," which places the profit motive above all quality-of-life issues. Multinational corporate accountability is one of the most important issues of our time.

One way in which citizens of the United States, the most powerful of militarized nations, are protesting their government's policies is by refusing to pay taxes that finance war. The National War Tax Resistance Coordinating Committee, an organization based in Ithaca, New York, that links fifty groups opposing war or weapons, has witnessed a surge in interest since the attacks of September 11, 2001.

In the tradition of Jeanette Rankin, Congresswoman Barbara Lee of California was the only member of the U.S. House of Representatives to oppose the war on Afghanistan. Lee said, "There are many ways to get at the root of this problem, economic, diplomatic, legal, and political. A rush to launch precipitous military attacks runs too great a risk that more innocent men, women and children will be killed." Her prophecy proved correct. Independent sources estimate that well more than four thousand Afghan civilians died in the ironically dubbed "Operation Infinite Justice," as did several U.S. soldiers. It was for this very reason that many had urged the use of UN ground forces in Afghanistan, as an alternative to unilateral U.S. carpet bombings.

A stance in opposition to that war was also taken by the Worldwide Sisterhood Against Terrorism and War, an organization of leading feminists from Central Asia. Such prominent U.S. feminists as Alice Walker, Gloria Steinem, and Susan Sarandon also opposed the attacks on Afghanistan, signing a petition under the heading "Not in Our Name," which stated,"We will not support the bombing or U.S invasion of Afghanistan, for it would only punish suffering people and increase the hatred on which terrorists feed." These women were not fooled by the sudden flood of media attention given to Afghan women's rights, for which organizations like the Feminist Majority Foundation had been working for years. It is essential that women activists see through such tactics and remember that in spite of its misogynistic practices, the Taliban was quite recently funded by the United States in its not-so-covert war against the Soviets, as well as in the so-called war on drugs. Likewise feminists have pointed out that the Northern Alliance, with which the United States collaborated in the war on terrorism, has been no better in their record on women's rights or human rights than the Taliban. Despite the Bush administration's lip service to empowering Afghan women, only one expatriate woman was finally given a seat in the newly formed government of Afghanistan. It is worthwhile, once again, to remember that the United States actually joins Afghanistan among only four nations that have failed to ratify CEDAW, the UN Convention on the Elimination of Discrimination Against Women.

War Resistance: "Patriotism in Its Highest Significance."

As Jesse Wallace Hughan (1876–1955), an American pacifist organizer who devoted her life to the antiwar cause, wrote, "The strength of war resistance is patriotism in its highest significance. A war is not like an earthquake or a tornado—it's an act of men and women. Wars will cease when men refuse to fight and women refuse to approve and allow. Do not allow people to lead you to think for a moment that war is a necessary institution." She goes on to explain that war resisters base their action on reason, on the desire to prevent hysterical officials from plunging their country into certain disaster and destruction. They stand on the solid ground of reason, humanity, and patriotism in its highest significance. In a sense they are like Electra or Cassandra, who refuse to participate in an immoral lie or to avoid the consequences of telling the truth. The purpose of war resistance is not merely the satisfaction of individual conscience, as important as that is, but also to break down the war system and its psychology by building up an ever stronger international majority who refuse unconditionally to give their personal support to the violence of war.

This collection offers evidence that many women are assertive war resisters, actively linking hands around the globe, doing their best to save the children, as women have always done throughout herstory. The growing awareness of planetary citizenship is a reality among women scholars, writers, and activists of the world, as attested in these pages. Having begun the first edition of *Women on War* sometime prior to the 1986 International PEN congress in New York—which I attended as a member of American PEN—I was all the more inspired to complete it. That newsmaking congress of writers showed that, once again, the vast accomplishment of women in the fields of literature and intellectual endeavor was underrepresented, undermined, or forgotten. Even after the ardent feminism of the decade prior, which witnessed the advent of women's studies scholarship throughout developed countries, women were once again made to feel invisible on the male-proposed theme of that congress: "The imagination of the writer versus the imagination of the state." And this despite the fact that some of the finest writers on the subject, from Rosa

Luxemburg to Jane Addams, Emma Goldman to Simone Weil, Chi'u Chin of China to Sappho of ancient Greece, Christa Wolf of Germany to Nadine Gordimer of South Africa, have been women. As here suggested, a rich literature exists and needs only to be highlighted. This compendium of "Cassandra's Daughters," a mere sampling, could be called *The Feminine Imagination Versus the Irrationality of the Patriarchal State.*

Everywhere, throughout history and today—sometimes in the name of "freedom," often a cloak for corporate greed—innocent people are tyrannized by war and its companions—torture, famine, exile, oppression, and death. Right or Left rhetoric rots in the mouths of the more than 300 million souls who have died in wars in the twentieth century alone. Angelica Balabanoff, an activist for democracy who traveled freely between Moscow and other major European cities in the days preceding and following the Russian Revolution and who worked untiringly in the international peace movement, wrote: "History has been falsified without shame by the Fascists and, unfortunately, also, by the Bolsheviks. The truth was never more necessary than it is today."

Whether the women herein write of the massacre of Jews, Palestinians, Poles, Rwandans, Salvadorans, Afghans, Armenians, Indians, Vietnamese, or Tibetans, of Holocaust victims or Hiroshima victims, it's the same nightmare of history from which we must awaken. Always the war horrors are accompanied by women's stories of courage, comforting love, resistance, and transcendence, and these are the subjects of this collection, too. Whether we read of medieval Inquisitions in which witches—mostly women—were burned by religious zealots; Nero's Praetorian Guard or Mao Tse-tung's Red Guard; Miskuito Indians caught between Sandinistas and Contras; Ukranians caught between Communists and Fascists; Afghans, Israelis, Iraqis, or Palestinians caught in the cross fire of "oil wars," the Hitlers or Stalins among us deserve the same ignominious infamy in our shared horror story. They never work alone, but are surrounded by a network of evil supporters and administrators. No nation is free of ancient tribal blood rivalries or the guilt of wars, yet no people has ever chosen to reap the misery of war. Always, war has been initiated by powerful leaders—rarely women—who hold military might and who are often insane, ignorant, or misguided puppets of military and corporate profiteers who support their election. It is ordinary people, more than their leaders hiding in bunkers, who are the sufferers and victims of war. And as the Romanian writer Ileana Malancioi's poem "Antigone" herein illustrates, it is women who are left to bury the bodies and mourn the dead.

In 1945, Edna St. Vincent Millay, a poet who sacrificed her energies in the cause of justice, wrote: "I am disgusted by the hollow talk of disarmament. We put wreaths on the grave of the Unknown Soldier, who's pretty damn well known by now as a symbol of the next war." Wars have persisted into the twentieth-first century, even though the threat of total annihilation has outmoded all ideologies and justifications for war. There are many means of finding solutions for conflict and of producing disarmament agreements in our sophisticated times. Science has made nuclear disarmament completely verifiable by technologies of various kinds and combinations. The irony remains that while wars and revolutions are fought in the name of freedom versus tyranny, we all of us are hostages to the greatest tyranny civilization has ever known. As Italian educator Maria Montessori long ago explained, "The people of the world who profess to want to get rid of war as the worst of scourges are, nevertheless, the very ones who concur in the arming and starting of wars."

Cynthia Enloe, professor of government at Clark University and one of the finest scholars writing on how militarization affects women's lives, explains that women, in particular, suffer poverty throughout the world because of militarized economies. Increased military spending has lowered the standard of living for billions of people around the globe. By far the largest percentage of people living below the poverty line is found among families headed by single women, and their numbers are steadily increasing due in part to the carnage and displacement that men commit upon one another in wars. The horrendous increase in poverty around the world—especially among women—is paralleled by the largest military buildup in history. Militarism creates misery everywhere, but women are especially hard hit by its economic violence. We are conditioned, often in subtle ways, into accepting the militarization of our economy without understanding its human impact.

Even those of us who seem to live in peace in developed countries suffer from the huge emphasis on building weapons of mass destruction. Scientists Rosalie Bertell, a biological epidemiologist, and Dr. Helen Caldicott, an eminent founding physician of International Physicians for Social Responsibility, tell us that one out of two of us will contract cancer, and the increase in this disease is in large part a direct result of the military and chemical industries that are poisoning our air and waters and destroying our environment everywhere. The quest for military might has actually destabilized the delicate natural balances of Earth's ecosystems and caused widespread devastation. Bertell explains that in the aftermath of the Gulf War, experts predicted that the smoke from burning oil fields would warm the lower atmosphere throughout South Asia, causing the monsoon to arrive earlier and more forcefully than usual. In 1999, a huge typhoon struck Bangladesh on May 1, killing 100,000 people. Depleted uranium ammunition was used in the Gulf War, though the United States was loath to admit it had done so. These weapons spread a lethal radioactive dust through the region and beyond.

As warfare and its means have become more technologically sophisticated, the long-term health and environmental effects have become more insidious. Though it is easy to see the visible aftermath of war, it is difficult to evaluate the long-term cost of the poverty, famine, sickness, and environmental devastation wrought by it. Each year governments waste monumental sums of money and human resources on deadly military endeavors that could be put to humane uses to better our lives on the planet and create a more peaceful existence. Always, ironically, we are murdered and poisoned in the name of defense.

This environmental and social devastation calls for an entirely new approach to what is called national security. It shows the need for world diplomacy for a solution to global problems. Eleanor Roosevelt pointed out the importance of such world organizations as the United Nations, despite its imperfect powers and the undermining of its world tribunals by superpowers like the United States, which holds too much sway over its policies and operating budget.

Where people escape being killed by bombs or bullets, they may not escape famine or disease, which always follows or appears alongside war. In countries not seemingly involved in war, in various ways people are deprived of resources, both material and human, which are absorbed by military activities. The fact that the Japanese economy thrived most markedly when Japan was deprived of all military endeavors proves the point that peacetime development would win the economic argument for those nations duped by their military profiteers. In Britain, for example, it costs nearly 2 million pounds to train a fighter pilot, the Pledge for Peace in London tells us. Betty Lall, who was one of the world's experts on the arms race and a director of the Council for Economic Priorities in the United States, was adept at putting monumental military spending in statistics that made such spending comprehensible. She wrote: "It costs about the same to arm and train one soldier as it does to educate eighty children for a lifetime career; to build one modern bomber as it did to wipe out smallpox over a ten-year period; to launch the latest nuclear missile submarine as it does to build 450,000 homes for the poor." Indeed, the entire food-stamp program to help feed hungry people in the United States does not cost the markup overhead—just the overhead—on one nuclear bomber! What will it take to awaken the military industrial fathers to the fact that their profits are literally killing their children and heirs and destroying their nation?

Understanding Ways and Means to Peace

Despite a few token women leaders who have existed in a man's world throughout the history of warfare everywhere, it is men who mainly hold the political power and have been making the decisions about national priorities for all of us right up until today. The U.S. economy, among other economies around the world, is dependent on a military-industrial complex from which only a small minority of people, mainly military contractors and government officials, benefit. According to the War Resisters League, the overwhelming majority of the U.S. fiscal budget, for example—more than 65 percent of it— is proposed for the military, while only approximately 20 percent is actually earmarked for human needs. The few corporate executives or party bureaucrats who profit from this status quo—and who have now stockpiled, as the Center for Defense Information tells us, the explosive power for more than fifty tons of TNT for every human on the globe—are most often the last to pay taxes or suffer the poverty and deprivation they cause.

Everywhere one looks, old men, mostly white—like Sophocles' stubborn Creon—cause the death of the young and idealistic Antigones of the planet. These men decide our fate, while women and people of color have little voice in their own fate or their children's. Angelica Balabanoff of the Ukraine echoed Jane Addams's sentiments when she said, "Where are your husbands, your brothers, your sons? Why must they destroy one another and all that they, and we, have created? Who benefits by this bloody nightmare? Only a minority of war profiteers. Since the men can't speak, you must. Working women of the warring countries, unite!"

Christa Wolf, an East German writer admired by women of the international peace movement worldwide for her book *Cassandra*, has pointed out that many who are very skeptical about the survival of the race have a conviction that nations and their economies can be governed only by competition, rather than cooperation. Wolf notes, too, that even the youthful Japanese of today have little sense of the suffering of Hiroshima victims. The reality or memory of the suffering of war is absent from the lives of many people in developed countries and that, also, is a raison d'être of this collection—to create a global communality concerning war in the light of our universal fate.

As Simone Weil wrote in *The Illiad: Poem of Force* during World War II, "Pain and suffering are a kind of currency passed from hand to hand until they reach someone who receives them but does not pass them on." And as Virginia Woolf wrote in *Three Guineas*, "The outsider will say I have no country. As a woman, my country is the world."

Helen Keller understood the power of propaganda when she said, "We the people are not free. Our democracy is but a name. We vote? What does that mean? It means that we choose between Tweedledee and Tweedledum. We elect expensive masters to do our work for us, and then blame them because they work for themselves and their class."

We are always told—especially as women—that to be polite at a party or gathering, we should never discuss religion or politics; but that rule was invented to keep everyone in their unquestioning place. There is really nothing more important than our sociopolitical orientation to the world and the salvation of the children and our Earth, itself, from pillaging by a huge war-machine economy. For those who say they want nothing to do with politics, the Nobel laureate poet of Poland, Wislawa Szymborska, answers with her poem included in this collection: "We are the children of the epoch. / The epoch is political." There is no escape from politics. There is only the act of washing one's hands of responsibility for the destruction of innocent lives.

Women everywhere want to educate themselves to the situation that keeps them and their families enslaved to the terror of annihilating forces. When profiteers of the military-industrial complex own the major media, women have to look to alternative media—socially conscious presses and magazines, or books from nonprofit presses such as this—for truth. The final nuclear, biological, or chemical sword of Damocles hangs over all of us, destroying the peaceful paradise our gorgeous Earth could be, while many are oblivious to the precariousness of planetary life. If that final sword falls, it means death to us and to all we love, our children and our children's children, our music and poetry and art, along with the magnificent snow leopard and the blue heron. It means death to the giant sequoia, red rose, purple lotus, and black orchid. It means death to all the wondrous creation pulsing from what may be the only teardrop of human life and laughter afloat in cold dark space.

There are many ways and means of promoting peace and minimizing civilian suffering: Insisting on diplomacy for conflict resolution. Promoting an appreciation of cultural diversity. Passing international laws for corporate accountability to human rights. Strengthening the World Court. Making it unlawful for former CEOs and members of corporate boards of the oil, nuclear, and military industries to be elected to public office with their obvious conflicts of interests. Promoting cooperation rather than competition in the world marketplace. Creating enforceable, humane labor laws and environmental protection statutes as a necessary component of "globalization." Decentralizing the International Monetary Fund and World Bank. Insisting on United Nations forces to quell armed conflicts and genocide, rather than the use of unilateral national force. Using UN peacekeeping ground troops instead of carpet bombing to stop genocide and capture terrorists. Making far better use of intelligence for security against international terrorism, without destroying civil liberties.

One small note of hope is found in the passage of UN Security Council Resolution 1325, which was approved unanimously on October 31, 2000. This was the first resolution ever passed by the Security Council that specifically addresses the impact of war on women. The eighteen-point resolution urges member states to ensure increased representation of women at all decision-making levels and encourages the UN Secretary General to implement action calling for an increase in the participation of women in conflict resolution and peace processes. It also calls for the protection of women and girls in war. This is only a resolution, and it was long overdue. Still, it is groundbreaking, and deserves mention here.

As Käthe Kollwitz, the German Lutheran antiwar artist (celebrated herein in a poem by Muriel Rukeyser, the American Jewish antiwar poet), wrote in her diary: "Pacifism simply is not a matter of calm looking on; it is work, hard work. Those lovely small apples out there, everything, could be so beautiful if it were not for the insanity of war! One day, a new idea will arise and there will be an end to all wars. People will have to work hard for that new state of things, but they will achieve it. At such times when I feel I'm working with an international society opposed to war, I'm filled with a warm sense of contentment." Kollwitz was able to say this after having lost both a son and a grandson to World Wars I and II. Even after the Nazi regime destroyed her studio and much of her work, she persisted in her war resistance activities and art.

Women and men need to celebrate the heroines and heroes of nonviolence instead of the false heroes of war. Women need to join organizations promoting international peace work, and insist that our governments truly support the United Nations and the Geneva Accords, as well as other international peace-making efforts. Those of us in superpower nations need to call and write our federal representatives and make our voices heard in support of peace and nuclear disarmament. We need to support women of conscience who run for political office. Each of us can make a difference. As Helen Keller, a woman who triumphed over darkness and silence, said, "I am only one; but still I am one. I cannot do everything, but still I can do something. I will not refuse to do something I can do."

This Book and Its Arrangement

These warnings and prophecies, testimonies to survival, essays, excerpts from diaries, poems, and stories of the causes of war and the ways and means to peace, exchanged among women of the world, are arranged chronologically according to the birthdate, or approximate birthdate, of the authors within each section. Part 1: Prophecies and Warnings, Part 2: Violence and Mourning, Part 3: Courage and Resistance, and Part 4: Hope and Survival take us on a journey through women's <u>herstory</u>, offering communion for those who understand and inspiration for those who wish to avert psychic numbing.

The first edition of *Women on War* was published in 1988 and won the 1990 American Book Award in its third printing. This new edition contains a great deal of new and different material. Although women are still underrepresented in translation and publication, there is more women's writings from around the world—especially from the developing world—available now than there was a decade or two ago. Of course this collection reflects the fact that fewer texts were available in ancient and bygone years than currently. It also reflects women's experience of war in the past fourteen years, and the growing awareness of such sad realities as rape as a widespread war crime and the sufferings of girl soldiers and women refugees.

The acknowledgments at the back of the book, arranged in alphabetical order, serve as an index and easy accessibility to the text, which offers the many men who want to listen an opportunity to hear an international sampling of women's thoughts and reactions to war. There is an ample bibliography for further reading provided for scholars, students, and the general reader at the end of the volume. An interactive resource list, including women's peace organizations, can be accessed at www.feministpress.org under "Special Projects."

These voices of Cassandra's sisters, the mothers and daughters of our faltering planet, our common homeland, need to be heeded as much as the maligned but clairvoyant Cassandra. "Surely the earth can be saved by all the people who insist on love," the distinguished African American author Alice Walker, has said. May her conviction prove true as women everywhere link hands to save Earth, our universal mother—blue marbled globe afloat in endless space—from the deadly war machine.

Daniela Gioseffi
New York City
December 2002

PART 1:
PROPHECIES AND WARNINGS

If the first woman God ever made was strong enough to turn the world upside down, these women together ought to be able to turn it back and get it right-side up again.
—SOJOURNER TRUTH (c.1797–1883),
African American suffragist and abolitionist

I'm certain that if women in every country would clearly express their conviction, they would find that they spoke not for themselves, alone, but for those men for whom war has been a laceration —an abdication of the spirit.
—JANE ADDAMS (1860–1935),
first American women to win the Nobel Peace Prize

To refuse to countenance a war that dares not speak its true name . . . you can no longer mumble the old excuse, "We didn't know"; and now that you do know, can you continue to feign ignorance or content yourselves with mere token utterance of horrified sympathy?
—SIMONE DE BEAUVOIR (1908–1986),
French feminist author and activist

The idea of missile defense in outer space. . . . is monstrously expensive, and offensive, and it won't work, so it's a total waste of money which is needed elsewhere. I think if you want to get rid of nuclear weapons, you just get rid of them!
—DOROTHY CROWFOOT HODGKIN (1910–1994),
British scientist and activist, 1964 winner of the Nobel Prize for Chemistry

ENHEDUANNA

Lament to The Spirit of War ✔

Enheduanna (circa 2300 B.C.E.), a Sumerian poet/priestess, is the first known poet, man or woman, of prehistory. She can also be thought of as one of the earliest known war protesters in history: her works, preserved on artifact from an ancient civilization, lament the same horrors of war known to modern women.

■

You hack everything down in battle. . . .
God of War, with your fierce wings
you slice away the land and charge
disguised as a raging storm,
growl as a roaring hurricane,
yell like a tempest yells,
thunder, rage, roar, and drum,
expel evil winds!
Your feet are filled with anxiety!
On your lyre of moans
I hear your loud dirge scream.

Like a fiery monster you fill the land with poison.
As thunder you growl over the earth,
trees and bushes collapse before you.
You are blood rushing down a mountain,
Spirit of hate, greed and anger,
dominator of heaven and earth!
Your fire wafts over our land,
riding on a beast,
with indomitable commands,
you decide all fate.
You triumph over all our rites.
Who can explain why you go on so?

Translation adapted by Daniela Gioseffi

EMMA GOLDMAN

Patriotism as a "Menace to Liberty"

Emma Goldman (1869–1940) was born in Russia and immigrated to Rochester, New York, in 1886. She worked in clothing factories and, after a few years became active in the anarchist movement. Her speeches to improve labor rights, including within the kind of sweatshop conditions still prevalent today, attracted attention throughout North America. Goldman was imprisoned in 1893 for "inciting a riot." In 1916, she was imprisoned for public advocacy of birth control and in 1917 for obstruction of the draft. Goldman was deported in 1919 to Russia, but voluntarily left that country in 1921 because of her disagreement with the Bolshevik government. Allowed reentry to the United States in 1924, but forced to refrain from public lectures on political issues, she still managed to take an active role on the issue of the Spanish Civil War. A brilliant intellect, she published the anarchist journal *Mother Earth* as well as many books, among them *Anarchism and Other Essays* (1911), in which this speech on the dangers of patriotism appears.

■

What is patriotism? Is it love of one's birthplace, the place of childhood's recollections and hopes, dreams and aspirations? Is it the place where, in childlike naïveté, we would watch the floating clouds and wonder why we, too, could not run so swiftly? In short, is it love for the spot, every inch representing dear and precious recollections of a happy, joyous, and playful childhood?

If that were patriotism, few American men of today would be called upon to be patriotic, since the place of play has been turned into factory, mill, and mine, while deepening sounds of machinery have replaced the music of the birds. No longer can we hear the tales of great deeds, for the stories our mothers tell today are but those of sorrow, tears, and grief.

What, then, is patriotism? "Patriotism, sir, is the last resort of scoundrels," said Dr. Johnson. Leo Tolstoy, the greatest anti-patriot of our time, defines patriotism as the principle that will justify the training of wholesale murderers.

Indeed, conceit, arrogance, and egotism are the essentials of patriotism. Let me illustrate. Patriotism assumes that our globe is divided into little spots, each one surrounded by an iron gate. Those who have had the fortune of being born on some particular spot consider themselves nobler, better, grander, more intelligent than those living beings inhabiting any other spot. It is, therefore, the duty of everyone living on that chosen spot to fight, kill, and die in the attempt to impose his superiority upon all the others.

The inhabitants of the other spots reason in the like manner, of course, with the result that from the early infancy the mind of the child is provided with bloodcurdling stories about the Germans, the French, the Italians, Russians, et cetera.

Thinking men and women the world over are beginning to realize that patriotism is too narrow and limited a conception to meet the necessities of our time. The centralization of power has brought into being an international feeling of solidarity among the oppressed nations of the world; a solidarity which represents a greater harmony of interests between the working man of America and his brothers abroad than between the American miner and his exploiting compatriot; a solidarity which fears not foreign invasion, because it is bringing all the workers to the point when they will say to their masters, "Go and do your own killing. We have done it long enough for you."

The proletariat of Europe has realized the great force of that solidarity and has, as a result, inaugurated a war against patriotism and its bloody spectre, militarism. Thousands of men fill the prisons of France, Germany, Russia and the Scandinavian countries because they dared to defy the ancient superstition.

America will have to follow suit. The spirit of militarism has already permeated all walks of life. Indeed, I am convinced that militarism is a greater danger here than anywhere else, because of the many bribes capitalism holds out to those whom it wishes to destroy.

The beginning has already been made in the schools. Children are trained in military tactics, the glory of military achievements extolled in the curriculum, and the youthful mind perverted to suit the government. Thus innocent boys are morally shanghaied into patriotism, and the military Moloch strides conquering through the nation.

When we have undermined the patriotic lie, we shall have cleared the path for the great structure where all shall be united into a universal brotherhood—a truly free society.

ROSA LUXEMBURG

Militarism as a Province of Accumulation

Rosa Luxemburg (1870–1919) is one of the great figures of the people's world revolutionary movement. A nonviolent activist, she was born in Russian-ruled Poland in 1870. She studied law and economics in Zurich, and in 1896 settled in Germany, where she became one of the leading writers and theorists of international socialism in the period preceding World War I. She broke with the Second International early in the war because much of the leadership supported the war effort in their countries, at the expense of the worker. She joined with Karl Liebknecht, people's martyr and founder of the Spartacus League, who was assassinated in 1919 by right-wing militarists. Rosa Luxemburg was murdered soon after by the same faction. This excerpt from her economic treatise, *The Accumulation of Capital,* is an explanation of militarized economies just as valid today as when she wrote it.

■

Militarism serves a very definite function in the history of capital, accompanying as it does every historical phase of accumulation. In the period of so-called "primitive accumulation," it was a means of conquering the New World and the spice-producing countries of India. Later, it was employed to subjugate modern colonies, to destroy the social organizations of non-industrialized societies in order to appropriate and compel their means of production. It was used to introduce commodity trade in countries where the social structure had been unfavorable to it, and to change the natives into a proletariat by forcing them to work for slave wages in their own lands or starve. It is responsible for the creation and expansion of spheres of capital interest for Europeans in non-European regions, for stealing railway monopolies in underdeveloped countries, and for enforcing the claims of superpower governments as benevolent international lenders. Finally, militarism is a weapon in the competitive struggle between nations for areas of underdeveloped or non-industrialized lands.

Also, militarism has still another important function. From the purely economic point of view, it is a pre-eminent means for the realization of surplus value; it is in itself a means of accumulation. In examining the question who should count as a buyer for the mass of products containing the capitalized surplus value, we forever refuse to consider the state and its bureaucrats as consumers. Since the state's income is derivative, bureaucracies were all taken to belong to the special category of those who live from surplus value (or partly on the wage of labor), together with the liberal professions and the various parasites of present-day society: rich tax evaders, kings, dictators, presidents, party chieftains, mercenaries or industrial militarists. . . . When the monies concentrated in national treasuries by taxation are used for the production of armaments, the bill of militarism is paid for mainly by the working classes and the small family farmers.

Translation adapted by Daniela Gioseffi with L.B. Luttinger

EDNA ST. VINCENT MILLAY

O Earth, Unhappy Planet
Born to Die

Edna St. Vincent Millay (1892–1956) is one of the best-known poets of U.S. literature and among the finest sonneteers of modern English. She lived for many years in upper New York State, where her farm home is now a colony devoted to working artists. A poet of humane conscience, Millay publicly protested the unjust trial and murder of Sacco and Vanzetti, victims of hatred against immigrant labor rights. She was a strong voice for peace and social justice throughout her life. Her sonnet is from a sequence titled "Epitaph for the Race of Man"—amazingly prophetic considering it was written before our current age of nuclear proliferation and environmental anxiety.

■

O Earth, unhappy planet born to die,
Might I your scribe and your confessor be,
What wonders must you not relate to me
Of Man, who when his destiny was high
Strode like the sun into the middle sky
And shone an hour, and who so bright as he,
And like the sun went down into the sea,
Leaving no spark to be remembered by.
But no; you have not learned in all these years
To tell the leopard and the newt apart;
Man, with his singular laughter, his droll tears,
His engines and his conscience and his art,

Made but a simple sound upon your ears:
The patient beating of the animal heart.

MARTHA GELLHORN

From The Face of War

Martha Gellhorn, (1908–1998) was a noted war correspondent, journalist, and essayist whose career spanned many wars. Her classic book *The Face of War,* from which this excerpt of the introduction comes, covered fifty years of accounts of the bloody twentieth century. Her earliest articles were written in 1937 concerning the Spanish Civil War, and began a series that encompassed Finland, China, and, ultimately, all of Europe during another eight years of slaughter. Though Gellhorn states, "War is a horrible repetition," she manages to have a genius for the awful task of reporting the horrors of war. She courageously continued her accounts in Java, Vietnam, the Middle East, and Central America. Martha Gellhorn witnessed the hideous refinements of weaponry, including the birth and proliferation of nuclear madness, but she never gave into hopelessness. She was among the first to celebrate the advent of the antinuclear movement, stating clearly and simply, "There has got to be a better way to run the world and we better see that we get it."

■

It took nine years, and a great depression, and two wars ending in defeat, and one surrender without war, to break my faith in the benign power of the press. Gradually I came to realize that people will more readily swallow lies than truth, as if the taste of lies was homey, appetizing: a habit. (There were also liars in my trade, and leaders have always used facts as relative and malleable. The supply of lies was unlimited.) Good people, those who opposed evil wherever they saw it, never increased beyond a gallant minority. The manipulated millions could be aroused or soothed by any lies. The guiding light of journalism was no stronger than a glow-worm.

I belonged to a Federation of Cassandras, my colleagues the foreign correspondents, whom I met at every disaster. They had been reporting the rise of Fascism, its horrors and its sure menace, for years. If anyone listened to them, no one acted on their warnings. The doom they had long prophesied arrived on time, bit by bit, as scheduled. In the end we became solitary stretcher-bearers, trying to pull individuals free from the wreckage. If a life could be saved from the first of the Gestapo in Prague, or another from behind the barbed wire on the sands at Argelès, that was a comfort but it was hardly journalism. Drag, scheming, bullying and dollars occasionally preserved one human being at a time. For all the good our articles did, they might have been written in invisible ink, printed on leaves, and loosed to the wind.

After the war in Finland, I thought of journalism as a passport. You needed proper papers and a job to get a ringside seat at the spectacle of history in the making. In the Second World War, all I did was praise the good, brave generous people I saw, knowing this to be a perfectly useless performance. When occasion presented, I reviled the devils whose mission was to deny the dignity of man; also useless. I took an absurd professional pride in getting where I intended to go and in sending my copy to New York on time; but I could not fool myself that my war correspondent's work mattered a hoot. War is a malignant disease, an idiocy, a prison, and the pain it causes is beyond telling or imagining; but war was our condition and our history, the place we had to live in. I was a special type of war profiteer; I was physically lucky, and was paid to spend my time with magnificent people.

After the victory in World War II, I hung on in the climate of war for another year, since peace was uneasy and unconvincing. At last in Java I saw the postwar new-style little war, and knew I never wanted to see any more of it again anywhere. Probably that pathetic murderous mess in the East Indies was inevitable. The tall white men had been conquered and debased by short yellow men; why should anyone accept the white man as master again? The Dutchmen of the Indies returned, like skeletons and ghosts, from Japanese prisons and from building the Japanese death railway through the jungle; their sick, starved women and children emerged from years in Japanese concentration camps on Java; and immediately they were set upon by the natives they had tried to rule with care and decency. Both the Indonesians and the Dutch needed time to heal from the war and find a just plan for their lives. There was no time. Nothing anybody wrote was going to shorten this torment, nor save one victim, white or brown.

Journalism at its best and most effective is education. Apparently people would not learn for themselves, nor from others. If the agony of the Second World War did not teach them, whatever would? Surely the postwar world is a mockery of hope and an insult to all those who died so that we should survive. . . .

Until the invention of the A-bomb, the H-bomb, the Cobalt bomb, or whatever next, we could reasonably consider human history to be a giant interminable roller coaster, going up and down. The ceaseless but temporary riders on the roller coaster changed their clothes, carried new luggage, talked in varying jargons, yet remained me, women and children, constant in their humanity. The unique possession anyone on the roller coaster had, as far as I could see, was his own behavior while making the mysterious journey. For his own behavior each one is responsible, but no behavior is final. It shapes human destiny—any behavior, all behavior—but it makes no last decision. Victory and defeat are both passing moments. There are no ends; there are only means.

Journalism is a means; and I now think that the act of keeping the record straight is valuable in itself. Serious, careful, honest journalism is essential, not because it is a guiding light but because it is a form of honorable behavior, involving the reporter and the reader. I am no longer a journalist; like all other private citizens, the only record I have to keep straight is my own.

Despite official drivel about clean bombs and tactical nuclear weapons, anyone who can read a newspaper or listen to a radio knows that some of us mortals have the power to destroy the human race and man's home on earth. We need not even make war; only by preparing, by playing with our new weapons, we poison the air, the water, the soil of our planet, damage the health of the living, and weaken the chances of the unborn. How can anyone, anywhere, discount the irreversible folly of testing our nuclear bombs, or the promise of extinction if we use them in war?

The world's leaders seem strangely engaged in private feuds. They hurtle in airplanes on their Olympian business; they meet each other, always each other; or they deliberate in the various palaces of government; and they talk and talk, incessantly, for publication. Their talk sounds as if they believed nuclear war to be a thing that can be won or lost, and probable; any minute now, without warning, we may find ourselves in it. (Be calm. We will slay the enemy with our superspace, supersonic, triple-intercontinental, X-ray-guided, anti-offensive-defensive missiles. Do not fear. We will burn the foe with our best smallest deadliest fission-unfission-defission-profission bombs. Meanwhile, my comrades, my people, fellow citizens, loyal subjects, your service is civil defense; dig a little blast proof hole in your backyard and wait for the Apocalypse.)

The world's leaders appear to have lost touch with life down here on the ground, to have forgotten the human beings they lead. Or perhaps the led—so numerous and mute—have ceased to be quite real, not living people but calculated casualties. For we are led and must follow whether we want to or not; there is no place to secede to. But we need not follow in silence; we still have the right and duty, as private citizens, to keep our own records straight. As one of the millions of the led, I will not be herded any farther along this imbecile road to nothingness without raising my voice in protest. My *NO* will be as effective as one cricket chirp.

We hardly remember who fought the Wars of the Roses or why, yet those wars lasted for thirty years and must have been a deep dark night for the combatants and civilians trapped in them. Still, we are here: the natural world remained healthy, nourishing and lovely; the race continued, uninfected in its bones, its blood, its minds. From the earliest wars of men to our last heartbreaking world-wide effort, all we could do was kill ourselves. Now we are able to kill the future. And we are so arrogant that we dare to prepare for this, insane pygmies menacing the very existence of nature. Five hundred years from now our East-West quarrel will seem as meaningless as the Wars of the Roses. Who are we that we presume to *end* anything?

At this point I hear loud and angry voices, as passionate as mine, saying: survival is not all. If men will not fight against tyrants and slavery, life is worthless and civilization should perish. Et cetera. I cannot understand this argument, although I have tried. I do not see how the human spirit, housed in the human body, will be able to cherish freedom, revere the rights of others, and practice its highest talent, love, when the earth is sterile from man-made poisons, the air tainted, and the race sick and dying. I do not see what human values can be defended when all humanity is lost, the good and the evil together.

If we make or allow war, we deserve it; but we must limit our weapons and our locales, and keep our crime under control. We will have to satisfy the madness that is in human nature with small non-nuclear wars of a type we are getting more and more used to. It is in our ancient tradition to murder each other; but only we, in the present, should pay the price for our abominable stupidity.

Nothing that concerns us, in our brief moment of history, gives us the right to stop time, to blot out the future, to end the continuing miracles and glories and tragedies and wretchedness of the human race. . . .

There is a single plot in war; action is based on hunger, homelessness, fear, pain and death. Starving wounded children, in Barcelona in 1938 and in Nijmegen in 1944, were the same. Refugees, dragging themselves and whatever they could carry away from war to no safety, were one people all over the globe. The shapeless bundle of a dead American soldier in the snow of Luxembourg was like any other soldier's corpse in any other country. War is a horrible repetition.

I wrote very fast, as I had to; and I was always afraid that I would forget the exact sound, smell, words, gestures which were special to this moment and this place. I hope I learned to write a bit better as the years passed. The point of these articles is that they are true; they tell what I saw. Perhaps they will remind others, as they remind me, of the face of war. We can hardly be reminded too much or too often. I believe that memory and imagination, not nuclear weapons, are the great deterrents.

GWENDOLYN BROOKS

The Progress

Gwendolyn Brooks (1917–2000) was a pioneer of the blossoming of Black literature in America in the second half of the twentieth century. Brooks was born of working-class parents in Chicago. Her father was the son of a runaway slave. She won the Pulitzer Prize for poetry in 1950 for *Annie Allen*, poems about African American life in Chicago. She was the first African American woman to win a Pulitzer. Her other works include *A Street in Bronzeville* (1945), *Maud Martha* (1953), *The Bean Eaters* (1960), *Selected Poems* (1963), *In the Mecca* (1968), and *The World of Gwendolyn Brooks* (1971). With Broadside Press she published *We Real Cool* (1966), *The Wall* (1967), *Riot* (1969), *Family Pictures* (1970), *Aloneness* (1971), and *Black Steel* (1971). A writer concerned with human rights issues, Brooks served for many years as a professor or guest writer at many colleges and universities throughout the country, and edited *Black Position,* a magazine of essays and commentary.

■

And still we wear our uniforms, follow
The cracked cry of the bugles, comb and brush
Our pride and prejudice, doctor the sallow
Initial ardor, wish to keep it fresh.
Still we applaud the President's voice and face.
Still we remark on patriotism, sing,
Salute the flag, thrill heavily, rejoice
For death of men who too saluted, sang.
But inward grows a soberness, an awe,
A fear, a deepening hollow through the cold.
For even if we come out standing up
How shall we smile, congratulate: and how

Settle in chairs? Listen, listen. The step
Of iron feet again.   And again.   wild.

CARILDA OLIVER LABRA

Declaration of Love

Carilda Oliver Labra (b. 1922) is a premier poet of Cuba and one of the island's first feminist poets to champion women's right to an erotic life without the constraints of Catholicism. She became celebrated among the youth of Cuba for her love poems, but she has also written *Song to Martí* in praise of the revolutionary hero. Born in Matanzas, she graduated with a degree in civil law from the University of Havana. She won the National Prize for poetry in 1950 as a result of her popular and notorious book, *At the South of My Throat (Al sur de mi garganta)* (1949). She has published numerous volumes of poetry, among them *Dust Disappears.* Her work has been widely translated and recognized all over Europe, especially in Spain. This poem was written in response to the 1963 Cuban Missile Crisis, which brought the world to the brink of nuclear war.

■

I ask if I'm wise
when I awaken
the danger between his thighs,
or if I'm wrong
when my kisses prepare only a trench
in his throat.

I know that war is probable;
especially today
because a red geranium has blossomed open.

Please, don't point your weapons
at the sky:
the sparrows are terrorized,
and it's springtime,
it's raining, the meadows are ruminating.
Please,
you'll melt the moon, only night-light of the poor.

It's not that I'm afraid,
or a coward,
I'd do everything for my homeland;
but don't argue so much over your nuclear missiles,
because something horrible is happening:
and I haven't had time enough to love.

Translation by Daniela Gioseffi with Enildo A. Garcia

GRACE PALEY

Is There a Difference Between Men and Women *and* What If (This Week)

Grace Paley (b. 1922) was born Grace Goodside in New York City to a family of Russian Jewish immigrants and attended Hunter College. Well known as a peace and social justice activist, Paley was a part of the Women's Pentagon Action, and one of the White House Lawn Eleven arrested for antinuclear protests. She has worked closely with the War Resisters League and many other groups committed to the cause of human rights and has been arrested many times for nonviolent civil disobedience. On the board of PEN American Center, Grace Paley served as chairperson of a Women's Committee, formed to promote women's literature in a spirit of cross-cultural exchange. She has been awarded a National Endowment for the Arts Senior Fellowship and been elected for a term as a New York State Writer. She has taught creative writing at many institutions, including Columbia University, the City University of New York, and Sarah Lawrence College. She currently lives in Vermont. Paley's witty, poetic stories, which often center around conversations between women, have led her to be dubbed "the Chekhov of New York." Her three volumes of stories have been united in *Collected Stories* (1994), her nonfiction writing in *Just As I Thought* (1998), and her poetry in *Begin Again: Collected Poems* (2000).

■

IS THERE A DIFFERENCE BETWEEN MEN AND WOMEN

Oh the slave trade
    the arms trade
death on the high seas
    massacre in the villages

    trade in the markets
        melons mustard greens
    cloth shining   dipped in
        onion dye beet grass
    trade in the markets   fish
        oil   yams   coconuts   leaves
    of water spinach leaves
        of pure water   cucumbers
    pickled   walking back
        and forth along the stalls
    cloth bleached to ivory
        argument from stall to stall
    disgusted and delighted
        in the market

    oh the worldwide arms trade
        the trade in women's bodies
    the slave trade
        slaughter

oranges coming in from
the country in one
basket on the long
pole   coconuts
in the other   on the
shoulders of women
walking   knees slightly bent
scuffing   stumbling
along the road   bringing
rice into the city
hoisting the bundles of dry
mangrove for repair
of the household   trade
in the markets on
the women's backs and shoulders
yams   sometimes peanuts

oh the slave trade
the trade in the bodies of women
the worldwide unending arms trade
everywhere man-made slaughter

What If (This Week)

What if this century doesn't end
what if the Serbs continue their snarling self-loving wrath
and the Kosovars their hopeless arming
and the Hutus their vengeful slaughtering rage
and the American armed mullahs of Afghanistan their devout
exclusion of the joyful life of women
and the landowners of the world their terrible return again
and again to what is unrightfully theirs
and the darker people burning with insult and pride
of population
and the Americans and their deliberate impoverishment of
Vietnam in order to win the lost war
and the Russians continue their hard job of giving up old
badness just to be bad like everyone else
and the Irish unstrung on the lyres of history
and the Somalis clanned and unclanned
and the Turks their habitual attacks on the Kurds
and the Iraqis their habitual attacks on the Kurds

What if my friend never stops saying   if I had six sons I'd
give them all

what if I scream   horror
and she explains the idealistic politics of sacrificing sons

What if the thirty-six just men who repair the world year
                         after year feel their frailty
and petition that One to increase their number
what if there is no answer from time-creating heaven
no sound   no interest   not a turning away   suddenly   absence
what if there is no child   male or female   white or black
no mother   no child

WISLAWA SZYMBORSKA

Children of the Epoch

Wislawa Szymborska (b. 1923) received the Nobel Prize for Literature in 1996. Born in Kornik, in western Poland, where she continues to live, she was educated at the Jagiellonian University in Cracow, in Polish literature and sociology. She has been poetry editor of the prominent weekly journal *Literary Life* and has received many coveted awards for her sixteen collections of poems. Szymborska is also a translator of French poetry. This poem answers all who suppose it is possible to be apolitical in precarious times.

■

We are the children of the epoch.
The epoch is political.

All my daily and nightly affairs,
all your daily and nightly affairs,
are political affairs.

Whether you want it or not,
your genes have a political past,
your skin a political tone,
your eyes a political color,
What you say resounds,
what you don't say is also
politically significant.

Even coming through the rye,
you walk with political steps
on political ground.

Apolitical poems are also political,
and in the sky there's a moon
that's no longer moonlike.

To be or not to be, that is a question.
Oh darling, what a question, give a suggestion.
A political question.

You don't have to be human
to acquire a political meaning.
It's enough to be petroleum,
cattle fodder, raw material.
Or just a conference table whose shape
was disputed for months.

In the meantime, people were killed.
Animals died,
houses burned,
fields grew wild,
as in distant
and less political epochs.

Translation by Austin Flint

MAXINE KUMIN

The Nightmare Factory

Maxine Kumin (b. 1925) is the author of eleven books of poetry. Her 1972 collection, *Up Country,* received the Pulitzer Prize for poetry, and she has won numerous other awards and fellowships. She has also written a memoir, *Inside the Halo and Beyond: The Anatomy of a Recovery* (2000), four novels, stories, essays, and children's books. The volume in which this poem appeared, *The Long Approach* (1986), is an elegiac odyssey that takes the reader on a trip around the world through Europe, the Middle East, and Japan as it displays an international conscience deeply concerned with the nuclear threat and omnicide. Kumin lives in New Hampshire.

■

these are the dream machines
the dream machines
they put black ants in your bed
silverfish in your ears
they raise your father's corpse

they stick his bones in your sleep
or his stem or all thirty-six
of his stainless steel teeth
they line them up
like the best orchestra seats

these are the nightmare tools
down the assembly line
they send an ocean of feces
you swim in and wake from
with blood on your tongue
they build blind sockets
of subways and mine pits

for you to stop in
the walls slick as laundry soap
swelling and shrinking

these are the presses
they hum in nine languages
sing to the orphans
who eat pins for supper
the whole map of Europe
hears the computers click
shunting the trains you take
onto dead sidings
under a sky that is
packed full of blackbirds

night after night in
the bowels of good citizens
nazis and Cossacks ride
klansmen and judases
postmen with babies
stuffed in their mailsacks
and for east Asians
battalions of giants
dressed in g i fatigues
ears full of bayonets

here on the drawing board
fingers and noses
leak from the air brush
maggots lie under
if i should die before
if i should die
in the back room
stacked up in smooth boxes
like soapflakes or tunafish
wait the undreamt of

CHRISTA WOLF

From Cassandra

Christa Wolf (b. 1929) is a literary critic, novelist, and essayist and one of the leading writers to come out of the German Democratic Republic. Born in Landsberg (now in Poland), she grew up under the Third Reich, an experience she later wrote about in her fourth novel, *A Model Childhood* (1982). She studied literature at the universities of Leipzig and Jena, and then began her career as a reviewer. Her earliest published books won her a position as a preeminent state-sanctioned writer. While she remained committed to socialism, her later work reflects disillusionment with the corruption and totalitarianism of the East German system. Her novel *The Quest for Christa T.* (1966), which reflects these feelings, was banned from publication in the GDR. All of Wolf's work strikingly combines elements of fiction, autobiography, and social commentary. Her more recent works include *Accident/A Day's News* (1989), a response to the Chernobyl disaster; *What Remains and Other Stories* (1993); and *Medea: A Modern Retelling* (1996). Her earlier retelling of an ancient myth, *Cassandra* (1983), was much admired among feminists and antiwar activists. In it she interweaves reflections on current events with the story of Cassandra, daughter of Priam, the king of Troy. Cassandra was given the gift of prophecy, along with the curse that she would never be believed. She was imprisoned and raped during the Trojan War, which she had warned against to no avail. This excerpt comes from a section of Wolf's book entitled "A Work Diary, About the Stuff Life and Dreams Are Made Of," written during a period of especially high Cold War tensions.

■

Meteln, April 29, 1981. My interest in the Cassandra figure: to retrace the path out of the myth, into its (supposed) social and historical coordinates.

Television: program about the storage of American poison gases in the West German Federal Republic. The giant depot at Pirmasens [Center of the West German chemical industry in the Rhine Palatinate—Trans.] A small amount of gas is said to have already escaped in an uninhabited area of one of the U.S. states and killed thousands of sheep. You see pictures of the paralyzed animals dragging themselves forward on their knees. Rabbits are kept as measuring devices in the underground poison depots . . . (What difference is there between them and the sacrificial animals of the ancients? The progress it meant when people switched from human to animal sacrifice.) A new poison-gas rocket is being developed in the United States. The American says it is intended for the potential battlefield; and that happens to be Europe.

After that we see the protest actions of Protestant Christians, to whom politicians reply by pointing out that the Sermon on the Mount is not, after all, a guide to concrete political action. A young woman says: "I would not like it if later on my children had to ask me—the way we ask our parents and grandparents—Why didn't you speak up at the time?" She is one of a human type that has come into being, alike or identical in East and West: a slim hope.

In Priam's day, when kings ruled smaller realms (and enjoyed the additional protection of being considered divine), perhaps they were not screened off from normal everyday life as totally as today's politicians, who arrive at their decisions not on the grounds of personal observation and sensory experiences but in obedience to reports, charts, statistics, secret intelligence, films, consultations with men as isolated as themselves, political calculation, and the demands of staying in power. Men who do not know people, who deliver them to destruction; who by inclination or training can endure the icy atmosphere at the tip of the pyramid. Solitary power affords them the protection they have not received, and could not receive, from everyday life, where they would rub shoulders and skins with normal people. Banal, but that's how it is.

The carefully filtered, serviceably built, and abstracted image of reality that is assigned to these politicians. Is it "realistic" to try to neutralize the hierarchical male reality principle—or is it, though necessary, an unrealistic endeavor? Moreover, to what extent can the man of letters, and can literature, go on supporting this "reality principle" by its total remoteness from the sensory experience of everyday life? . . .

Meteln, April 30, 1981. Yesterday, the pictures the Americans took when they liberated Dachau concentration camp. Piles of bones, piles of corpses. Germans from Dachau energetically throwing the corpses onto farm wagons that are taking them away to be buried. The faces of well-nourished Americans underneath their helmets—figures from another world. This constellation—conquerors and conquered, the humiliated and the triumphant—is a basic constellation in human history. The conquest of Troy is one of the first cases we know of, and was itself an artist's composite of the conquests of dozens of cities which took place in those times. But no doubt it has happened only once that the victors came across stigmas like Auschwitz, like Dachau. A word like "inhuman" says nothing because it covers up rather than reveals. Aren't the emotional insensibility and antlike industriousness which signalize such frenzied atrocities also symptoms of a leaning to self-destruction that stems from a malignant, long-term frustration of the ability to act? Isn't it inevitable that a dearth of action such as that imposed on progressive forces over vast stretches of German history will lead to atrocities? Must it not turn on its head the contrasting pair "empty of deeds and full of thoughts"?

Meteln, May 1, 1981. To prevent wars, people must criticize, in their own country, the abuses that occur in their own country. The role taboos play in the preparation for war. The number of shameful secrets keeps growing incessantly, boundlessly. How meaningless all censorship taboos become, and how meaningless the consequences for overstepping them, when your life is in danger.

About reality. The insane fact that in all the "civilized" industrialized nations, literature, if it is realistic, speaks a completely different language from any and all public disclosures. As if every country existed twice over. As if every resident existed twice over: once as himself and as the potential perceiver of an artistic presentation; second, as an object of statistics, publicity, agitation, advertisement, political propaganda.

As for turning things into objects: Isn't that the principal source of violence? The fetishizing of vital, contradictory people and processes, within public notifications, until they have rigidified into ready-made parts and stage scenery: dead themselves, killing others.

To what extent is there really such a thing as "women's writing"? To the extent that women, for historical and biological reasons, experience a different reality than men. Experience a different reality than men and express it. To the extent that women belong not to the rulers but to the ruled, and have done so for centuries. To the extent that they are the objects of objects, second-degree objects, frequently the objects of men who are themselves objects, and so, in terms of their social position, unqualified members of the subculture. To the extent that they stop wearing themselves out trying to integrate themselves into the prevailing delusional systems. To the extent that, writing and living, they aim at autonomy. Autonomous people, nations, and systems can promote each other's welfare; they do not have to fight each other like those whose inner insecurity and immaturity continually demand the demarcation of limits and postures of intimidation.

Shouldn't an experiment be made to see what would happen if the great male heroes of world literature were replaced by women? Achilles, Hercules, Odysseus, Oedipus, Agamemnon, Jesus, King Lear, Faust, Julien Sorel, Wilhelm Meister.

Women as active, violent, as knowers? They drop though the lens of literature. People call that "realism." The entire past existence of women has been unrealistic.

Meteln, May 7, 1981. But why do I feel uneasy when I read so many publications—even in the field of archaeology, ancient history—which go under the title of "women's literature"? Not just because I know by experience the dead end into which sectarian thinking—thinking that rules out any points of view not sanctioned by one's own group—invariably leads. Above all, it is because I feel a genuine horror at that critique of rationalism which itself ends in reckless irrationalism. It is not merely a dreadful, shameful, and scandalous fact for women that women were allowed to contribute virtually nothing to the culture we live in, officially and directly, for thousands of years. No, it is, strictly speaking, the weak point of culture, which leads to its becoming self-destructive—namely, its inability to grow up. But it does not make it any easier to achieve maturity if a masculinity mania is replaced by a femininity mania, and if women throw over the achievements of rational thought simply because men produced them, in order to substitute an idealization of prerational stages in human history. The tribe, the clan, blood-and-soil—these are not values to which men and women of today can adhere. We Germans, of all people, should know that these catchwords can supply pretexts for hideous regressions. There is no way to bypass the need for personality development, for rational models of the resolution of conflict, and thus also for confrontation and cooperation with people of dissident opinions and, as it goes without saying, people of different sex. Autonomy is a task for everyone, and women who treat their femininity as a value they can fall back on act fundamentally as if they were trained to act. They react to the challenge which reality poses to them as whole persons with a large-scale evasive maneuver.

Translation by Jan Van Heurck

ROSALIE BERTELL

From Planet Earth: The Latest Weapon of War

Canadian Rosalie Bertell (b. 1929) has a doctorate in biomedics and is an epidemiologist who has worked in the field of environmental health since 1969. She has been involved in the founding of several organizations, including the International Institute of Concern for Public Health in Toronto, of which she is president. She led the Bhopal and Chernobyl Medical Commissions, has undertaken collaborative research with numerous organizations, and is the recipient of the Right Livelihood Award, the World Federalist Peace Prize, the United Nations Environment Programme (UNEP) Global 500 Award, and five honorary doctorates. Bertell is a member of a Roman Catholic religious congregation, the Grey Nuns of the Sacred Heart. The following is the introduction to her 2000 book, which is a critical study of the military and the environment.

■

I felt the piercing cold and saw the clear blue sky and magnificent sun. It was an unreal experience, this winter day at the top of Beckley Hill in Vermont. I was more used to a winter filled with overcast, cold and dreary days, and had formed a close mental association between sunny and warm.

The sunny cold of Vermont made me think more generally about deceptive appearances and how misleading a "first look" can be. My mother always looked well, even at the age of 95, and this was probably because of the twinkle in her eyes and the fact that her spirit was still fully alive. Some of my friends with cancer could have walked in a beauty pageant and no one would ever have noticed that they were sick. It made me think about the Earth and the delicately balanced natural processes that regulate it. If the Earth were damaged or suffering from some "illness," would we be able to recognise the problem early on, when it might be possible to reverse the process?

On this Vermont day, the birch trees were stripped of their leaves, standing naked in seasonal repose. But this bareness was normal, natural, and in the spring, the delicate green leaves would appear again to clothe the trees in elegance. Obviously one must understand the complete life cycle of a natural organism in order not to mistake a dormant period for death or deterioration. The Earth itself has cycles, and our human ancestors have faithfully marked the passing of the seasons and the weather for some 150 years. However, our knowledge of how these cycles function and how they interact is, as yet, incomplete. We do not know how resilient the Earth is, nor can we gauge its capacity to heal itself

On a clear cold day, the Earth looks wonderful, the air feels refreshing and it can be hard to believe the warnings that we have seriously compromised its health. Yet, since the United Nations Conference on the Environment in 1972, it has become obvious that the Earth faces serious problems: trees dying, species becoming extinct, contamination and depletion of drinking water, soil erosion, deforestation, smog, reduction of fish stocks, poverty and overcrowding. More recently, the incidence of violent weather has been increasing at an alarming rate and there is evidence that many so-called "natural" disasters are linked to human activities. All of our attempts to restore the health of the planet by changing our lifestyle, reducing dependence on fossil fuels, "reusing, recycling and reducing" seem not to have stemmed the tide. In fact in September 1999 the United Nations Environment Program announced that the environmental crisis is deepening not receding.

It is my belief that we have been treating the symptoms but not the cause of the disease of the Earth. We have been abusing Earth's natural systems, the way it regulates temperature and water supply, recycles waste and protects life. For me, some of the most fundamental abuses have occurred because of our continued reliance on the military.

Wars result in immediate deaths and destruction, but the environmental consequences can last hundreds, often thousands of years. And it is not just war itself that undermines our life support system, but also the research and development, military exercises and general preparation for battle that are carried out on a daily basis in most parts of the world. The majority of this pre-war activity takes place without the benefit of civilian scrutiny and therefore we are unaware of some of what is being done to our environment in the name of "security."

While there is a legitimate need for a police force in the global community, there can be no rationale for a military force. Blowing up a neighbourhood suspected of harbouring a criminal has never been seen as a civilised way of promoting domestic order. Nor is destruction of a nation and contamination of its food, air and other resources a means of achieving global peace. Of course, the inability to wage war does not eliminate regional disputes—it merely guarantees that the disputes will be submitted to negotiated settlement rather than violence. Large political and trade coalitions, such as the Organization of African States (OAS) and the European Union, can be formed through legal discussions rather than coming together through force.

In fact, I believe that our definition of global security has become outdated. Military security has its foundations in either the protection of wealth, land and privilege or the desire to confiscate the wealth and land of others. Modern society seems to have an unhealthy dependency on economic gain, and this has resulted in a widening gap between the haves and the have nots of the world. This is a major destabilising factor that actually causes global insecurity, not security. It also distorts a market economy towards catering for the wealthy whilst the needs of the poor go unanswered. This cannot be the basis of true democracy.

I also believe we have been confused by the struggle between communism and capitalism, which has been the dominant dialogue among thinkers for many years. This is basically a conflict over how to manage the excess in an economy. The essence of the dispute is whether accumulation of wealth should be held by government, which claims to use it for the benefit of the masses through funding of social programmes, or by private entrepreneurs, who think they can more wisely "build the economy" thereby providing jobs and a better standard of living for the people.

The problem with both systems is that they have focused on economic stability at the expense of ecological and social stability, when it has become increasingly clear that these three are interdependent. The most urgent problem facing us at the moment is how to sustain Earth, our life-support system, not how to redistribute wealth (although I think if we learn how to do the former we will be forced to recognise the wisdom of the latter). A meeting of the G7 to decide on interest rates cannot rectify the over-stretching of our natural resources and the manipulation of Earth's restorative power! Life thrives on balance, not on a singular focus on the economic "bottom line."

However, this goal of balanced social planning requires that we first provide a new job description for the military in order that they truly fulfil their purpose of serving and protecting the interests of the people. In order to do this, we have to look beyond the model of global dominance through force towards more gentle, cooperative solutions to the problems we face. To many, this may seem idealistic in a world dominated by what I would call a hard and unbending capitalism. But it is only by envisaging ideal solutions that we can begin the process of change.

Already there are signs of hope. The women's movement and the growing awareness of human rights, animal rights and Earth rights are all signs of profound transformations in societal structures and in the way inequalities and conflict are addressed. The United Nations is undergoing a period of reform and can now benefit from fifty years of experience. The stewardship of the land exercised for centuries by indigenous people is slowly being recognised and their ability to live in the midst of plenty without exploiting or destroying that abundance is a lesson for those who aspire to global management. The present crisis is a global one and in order to solve it, we must seek global solutions. . . .

In understanding our history, we can better see the implications of today's preparations for war and find a new path into the future.

But war itself is only one side of the military coin. Equally destructive to the health of our planet is the military experimentation and research which exploits our natural resources and destabilises a balanced ecology. . . . The tendency to experiment first and ask questions later characterises the search for ever-more sophisticated weaponry, especially in the race towards "Star Wars.". . .

At present, the greatest threat to our security is not invasion by "the enemy"; it is the destruction of the natural resources upon which we all rely for life and health. Without efficient use and responsible management of these resources, the fabric of civilisation will disintegrate and we will be reduced to fighting with each other over basics such as clean air and water. In order to provide future generations with what I have called "ecological" security, we need to work on both a global and a local level. . . .

I see the single focus of the military and the environmental or social scientist as one of the greatest menaces to the survival of the planet. If the environmentalists begin to look at the impact and implications of military exercises, the international policy experts begin to think about the survival of the planet, and the military strategists realise that they are capable of making this beautiful Earth unlivable, then my [work] will have met its goal.

But it is not just the experts who have a role to play—we all need to rethink our responses to the main problems of the day in order to avoid ecological collapse and we must adopt practices that will be beneficial to the future of our planet.

One of the greatest barriers to civilian action is the secrecy that surrounds military projects. [I have] sometimes felt overwhelmed with anger at the abuse of our Earth and sadness for our widespread ignorance of the affairs and undertakings of our own countries and allies. It should not be necessary to have to explain in detail all of the intrigue and ill-conceived experiments which have been undertaken by the governments of democratic countries. Responsibility for national actions and policy rests with the people, and keeping the people ignorant undermines the very meaning of democracy.

However, it is not only the civilian community who have been kept in the dark. Young politicians today know almost nothing about the atmospheric nuclear testing of the 1950s, and less than nothing about the history of military ionospheric experiments. (I'm sure very few politicians choose the *Astrophysics Journal* as bedtime reading!) Therefore we do not have an historical context in which to understand the present: and we do not have the language to interpret military plans for the future. . . .

We must set up a cooperative relationship with the Earth, not one of dominance, for it is ultimately the gift of life that we pass on to our children and the generations to follow.

ADRIENNE RICH

From Dark Fields of the Republic: Six Narratives

Adrienne Rich (b. 1929) was still an undergraduate at Radcliffe College when she published her first book of poems, *A Change of World,* which won the Yale Series of Younger Poets Award in 1950. Since then she has published numerous volumes of poetry and several nonfiction books, including such classic works of feminist cultural analysis as *Of Woman Born: Motherhood as Experience and Institution* (1976), and *On Lies, Secrets, and Silence* (1979). She has also written extensively on the relationship between poetry, literature, and politics. Her definition of a revolutionary poet is a "relayer of possibility." Rich's many awards include the Lifetime Achievement Award from the Lannan Foundation, the Academy Fellowship, the Ruth Lilly Poetry Prize, the Lenore Marshall Poetry Prize, the National Book Award, and a MacArthur Fellowship. In 1999, she was elected a Chancellor of the Academy of American Poets. She lives in northern California. She has said, "I came out first as a political poet . . . under the taboo against so-called political poetry in the US, which was comparable to the taboo against homosexuality. In other words, it wasn't done. And this is, of course, the only country in the world where that has been true. Go to Latin America, to the Middle East, to Asia, to Africa, to Europe, and you find the political poet and a poetry that addresses public affairs and public discourse, conflict, oppression, and resistance. That poetry is seen as normal. And it is honored." The following is excerpted from a long 1994 poem that appeared in the book *Dark Fields of the Republic.*

■

5

I was telling you a story about love
how even in war it goes on speaking its own language

Yes you said but the larynx is bloodied
the knife was well-aimed into the throat

Well I said love is hated   it has no price

No you said   you are talking about feelings
Have you ever felt nothing? that is what war is now

Then a shadow skimmed your face
Go on talking in a normal voice   you murmured
Nothing is listening

6

You were telling a story about war   it is our story
an old story   and still it must be told
the story of the new that fled the old
how the big dream strained and shifted
the ship of hope shuddered on the iceberg's breast
the private affections swayed and staggered
So we are thrown together   so we are racked apart
in a republic shivering on   its glassy lips
parted   as is the fundamental rift
had not been calculated from the first into the mighty scaffold.

JAYNE CORTEZ

Stockpiling

Poet and performance artist Jayne Cortez (b. 1936) was born in Fort Huachuca, Arizona. Her books of poetry include *Somewhere in Advance of Nowhere* (1997), *Coagulations: New and Selected Poems* (1982), *Poetic Magnetic* (1991), *Firespitter* (1982), *Mouth on Paper* (1977), *Scarifications* (1973), and *Piss-Stained Stairs and The Monkey Man's Wares* (1969). Her work has been translated into twenty-eight languages. Cortez has also released a number of recordings, many with her band the Firespitters, including *Taking the Blues Back Home* (1997), *Cheerful and Optimistic* (1994), *Everywhere Drums* (1991), and *Maintain Control* (1986). In 1964, she founded the Watts Repertory Company, and in 1972, she formed her own publishing company, Bola Press. Her awards include fellowships from the National Endowment for the Arts and the New York Foundation for the Arts, the International African Festival Award, and the American Book Award. Cortez has performed, lectured, and taught at many universities, museums, and festivals.

She lives in New York City. "Stockpiling" is from *Coagulations*, which also contains many other poems on the nuclear threat and causes of war.

■

The stockpiling of frozen trees
      in the deep freeze of the earth
The stockpiling of dead animals
      in the exhaust pipes of supersonic rockets
The stockpiling of desiccated plants
      on the death root of an abscessed tooth
The stockpiling of defoliants
      in the pine forest of the skull
The stockpiling of aerosols
      in the pink smoke of a human corpse
Stockpiles
      of agent orange agent blue agent white acids
      burning like the hot hoof of a race horse on
                          the tongue
Look at it
      through the anti-bodies in the body
      through the multiple vaccines belching in the
                        veins
      through the cross-infection of viruses
                stockpiled
                in the mouth
      through the benzine vapors shooting
                into the muscles of the
                stars
      through the gaseous bowels of military
                fantasies
      through the white radiation of delirious
                dreams
Look
      this stockpile marries that stockpile
      to mix and release a double stockpile of
                fissions
exploding
      into the shadows of disappearing space
Global incapacitations
Zero
      and boom
This is the nuclear bleach of reality
the inflated thigh of edema
the filthy dampness in the scientific pants
                of a peace prize
the final stockpile of flesh dancing in
the terrible whooping cough of the wind

And even if you think you have a shelter
that can survive this stockpiling
                    of communal graves
                    tell me
Where are you going
with the sucked liver of mustard flint
the split breath of hydrogen fumes
the navel pit of invisible clams
the biological lung of human fleas
the carcinogenic bladder of sponges
lips made of keloid scars
poems in the numb section of the chromosomes
            Just where do you think you're going
                    with that stockpile of
                    contaminated stink

Listen
When I think of the tactical missiles plunging
            into the rancid goiters of the sun
The artillery shells of wiretapping snakes hissing and
                            vomiting
            into the depths of a colorless sky
The accumulation of fried phosphoric pus graffitied
            on the fragile fierceness of the moon
The pestering warheads of death-wings stockpiling
                    feathers upon feathers
                    in the brain
And the mass media's larval of lies stockpiled
                    in the plasma of the ears
And the stockpiling of foreign sap in the fluxes
                    of the blood
And the stockpiling of shattered spines
                    in chromium suits
                            under
                            polyurethane
                            sheets
        I look at this stockpiling
at this rotting vegetation
and I make myself understand the target
That's why I say I'm into life
        preservation of life now
        revolutionary change now
before the choking
        before the panic
            before the penetration
                    of apathy

            rises up
        and spits fire
    into the toxic tears
        of this stockpile

BELLA AKHMADULINA

Words Spoken by Pasternak During a Bombing

Bella Akhmadulina (b. 1937), born in Moscow, was considered to be one of the most daring poets writing in the USSR. Her poetry was first published in 1954. In 1960 she graduated from the Gorky Literary Institute. Also a translator and an essayist, she was barred from the Writers' Union for many years for writing poems thought to be "too personal and superfluous," in a time and place in which to write an intimate love poem rather than a poem of socialist realism was a revolutionary act of freedom. ("If the East is dumb, then the West is deaf," was an internationally known aphorism among worldly writers of the Cold War period. Though U.S. poets seemed free to express radical politics, most of their compatriots did not hear their voices.) Akhmadulina's first marriage was to the well-known poet Yevgeny Yevtushenko, her second was to Youri Nagibin, and in 1974 she married the famous Russian artist Boris Messerer. In this poem, Akhmadulina took on a male persona, basing the text on a wartime event in the life of the great poet Boris Pasternak.

■

In olden times in forever
What was I then, a cloud, a star?
Unawakened yet by love,
A mountain stone, transparent as water?

Summoned from eternity by desire,
I was torn from darkness and born.
As a man, now, I'm a singing dome,
Round and inexplicable as a hull.
I've experience now and aptitude in art.
That day I implored: Oh earth!
Give me shelter, even the smallest bush
to forgive and shade me!

There in the sky, the bombsight shone
intractable so that I could taste
the vulnerability of a speck of creation
held in its target line.

I'm on my knees in doom up to my waist.
I writhe in quicksand, breathless.
Oh, crazed boy, wake up!
Don't sight me in your fateful line!

I'm a man, a valuable nugget
Lies in my soul. But I don't want to glow,
And gleam—I'm a mountain stone,
Worn and smooth, desiring invisibility!

The steady roaring faded;
The bush breathed and grew and I sighed
Beneath it. The merciless modern angel
Flew away, loathing my inconsequence.

Into this world of new senses,
Where things turn golden with light,
Where things sing and sparkle, I bore my body,
an intimate and breakable thing.

I wept, feeling intimate with all that lives,
breathing, pulsing, alive.
Oh my supplication, lowly, but still lofty,
I repeat your gentle whisper.

Death, I've seen your blank,
Lonely features and carried myself
Away from them as a strange child
Who hardly looked myself.

I'm not begging for a long life!
But, as in that hour in gray silence,
For some human flame-like unfolding
that accidentally lived in me.

It survived, and above the water
I stood for a long, long time, tired.
I wished to be a cloud, a star,
A mountain stone transparent as water.

Translation by Daniela Gioseffi with Sophia Busevska

HELEN CALDICOTT

From The New Nuclear Danger

Helen Caldicott (b. 1939) is founder and president emerita of Physicians for the Prevention of
Nuclear War, the international group that won the Nobel Peace Prize in 1985. She is a pediatri-
cian and a renowned activist in the cause of nuclear disarmament. She was the original driving
force behind the citizens' organization known as WAND, or Women's Action for Nuclear

Disarmament. More recently, she has been most concerned with the danger of accidental nuclear war due to high-tech missile-launching systems or terrorist acts—a danger that continues to escalate. Caldicott has received many prizes and awards for her work, including nineteen honorary degrees, and was personally nominated for the Nobel Peace Prize by Linus Pauling, himself a Nobel laureate. She has written for numerous publications and has authored five books, *Nuclear Madness* (1979), *Missile Envy* (1984), *If You Love This Planet: A Plan to Heal the Earth* (1992), *A Desperate Passion: An Autobiography* (1996), and the book from which this excerpt of the introduction was taken, *The Nuclear Danger: George Bush's Military Industrial Psychosis and Its Dangerous Consequences* (2002). She is establishing a new nonprofit organization called the Institute for Common Sense in the Nuclear Age, to be based in California. Its purpose is to educate through the media and to mobilize a mass movement of concerned citizens throughout the United States to oppose current nuclear policies, on the issues of both Star Wars and nuclear power.

■

On September 11, before much of the world was even aware of what happened in New York, Washington, and Pennsylvania, the Bush administration had raised the country's nuclear alert codes from defcon 6 to defcon 2—the highest state of alert before the launch code is operable.[1] [Author's note: It is not known how long this situation was maintained.] Russia, the country with the second largest nuclear arsenal in the world, almost certainly responded in kind. As a result, thousands of nuclear weapons stood poised on hair-trigger alert, ready to be launched by the president of either country with a decision time of just three minutes. The intercontinental nuclear-armed ballistic missiles controlled by these codes have a thirty-minute transit time from Russia to America or vice versa. They cannot be recalled. And they pose an ever-present threat of global nuclear holocaust.

In the months since the terrorist attacks, Secretary of Defense Donald Rumsfeld and others in the administration have also used September 11 to justify everything from pursuit of a missile-defense shield (even though such a shield would be utterly useless against suicidal men armed with boxcutters and plane tickets) and abandonment of long-standing weapon-control treaties, to massive increases in defense spending. While most Americans desire an increased sense of security in a newly destabilized world, many do not realize that the new "security" measures and the "conventional" war the United States has waged against Afghanistan are intimately connected to the enormous nuclear threat posed by the current American posture. Aggressive militarization under the rubric of defense against terrorism threatens to provoke a chain reaction among nuclear nations, big and small, that, once set in motion, may prove impossible to control. No military confrontation anywhere in the world is free from this ominous and ever-present danger.

The U.S.'s own behavior in Afghanistan has veered frighteningly close to deployment of nuclear weapons, which could easily have engendered a nuclear response. In addition to deploying the most horrific conventional weapons known to man (even though there were very few targets of military significance), the defense department recommended the use of tactical nuclear weapons,[2] while some members of Congress strongly advised the use of small nuclear "bunker busters."[3] Bush advisors, including Stephen Hadley, Deputy National Security Advisor Stephen Cambone, and William Schneider, also advocated the use of nuclear weapons.[4] The founder of the neutron bomb, Samuel Cohen, even postulated that his weapon might be appropriate for Afghanistan.[5] (The neutron bomb has a relatively small blast effect compared with its radiation, hence it tends to kill large numbers of people with horrendous radiation illness while leaving buildings intact.) Although the U.S. has previously been clear that it would attack only nuclear-armed countries with nuclear weapons, Secretary of Defense Rumsfeld consistently refused to rule out the use of nuclear weapons in Afghanistan, which is not nuclear-armed.[6]

Some of the conventional weapons America used to support the Northern Alliance during their advances on the Taliban were so powerful that they are described by the Pentagon as "near nuclear" weapons. They are as follows:

15,000-POUND FUEL AIR EXPLOSIVES (FAEs): In military jargon these are referred to as "Daisy Cutters." The Foreign Military Studies Office at Fort Leavenworth says, "A fuel air explosive can have the effect of a tactical nuclear weapon without the radiation."[7] There are many different varieties of FAEs, but they typically consist of a container of fuel and two separate explosive charges. Dropped by parachute from a huge MC-130 Combat Talon plane, they detonate just above the ground, creating a wide area of destruction.[8] The first explosion bursts the container at a predetermined height, disbursing the fuel, which mixes with atmospheric oxygen. The second charge then detonates this fuel-air cloud, creating a massive blast that kills people and destroys unreinforced buildings. Near the ignition point people are obliterated, crushed to death with overpressures of 427 pounds per square inch, and incinerated at temperatures of 2500 to 3000 degrees centigrade. Another wave of low pressure—a vacuum effect—then ensues. People in the second zone of destruction are severely burned and suffer massive internal organ injuries before they die. In the third zone, eyes are extruded from their orbits, lungs and ear drums rupture, and severe concussion ensues. The fuel itself—ethylene oxide and propylene oxide—is highly toxic.[9] Up to 200 civilians died 20 miles away from the cave complex in Afghanistan where Osama bin Laden was thought to be hiding at Tora Bora when U.S. planes attacked. They suffered blast trauma—ruptured lungs, blindness, arms and hands blown off, almost certainly from FAEs.[10]

CLUSTER BOMBS: They have been used extensively in Afghanistan by the U.S. Terrifyingly and deadly, each bomb is composed of 202 bomblets, which are packed with razor-sharp shrapnel dispersed at super-high speed over an area of 22 football fields, ripping into human bodies. These weapons are prohibited by the Geneva Protocol.[11] Civilians were inevitably killed throughout Afghanistan by these illegal and dreadful weapons. On one documented occasion, the U.S. bombed a mosque in Jelalabad during prayer and while neighbors were digging out 17 victims, additional bombs killed more than 120 people.[12]

Historically, between 5 and 30 percent of these bomblets fail to explode initially, lying around the countryside as mines that explode with violent force if touched, tearing their victims to pieces. Tragically, the bomblets are colored yellow and shaped like a can of soft drink, and therefore attractive to children.[13] The food parcels containing peanut butter, Pop Tarts, rice, and potatoes dropped throughout Afghanistan by the U.S. are also yellow and the same size and shape as the munitions. (Some of these food drops themselves went astray, destroying houses and killing more people.[14]) Human Rights Watch estimates that over 5000 unexploded cluster bomblets may be littered across Afghanistan, adding to the hundreds of thousands of mines left after the Russian-American war of 1979 to 1989.[15] Afghanistan is currently the most heavily mined country in the world.

GUN SHIPS: These lumbering C-130 planes built by Lockheed Martin have been converted to airborne gunships, capable of firing a fearsome array of weapons, inflicting the most devastating damage, and leveling an area of several football fields, with up to 2000 rounds per minute.[16] They are armed with 25mm Gattling guns, which fire 1800 rounds per minute; 40mm Bofors cannons, which fire 120 rounds per minute; and 105mm Howitzer cannons, which fire 8 to 10 rounds per minute. Secretary of Defense Rumsfeld said Afghanistan is not a "target rich" area, and many analysts felt that these attacks far exceeded their expectations. On October 22nd, in the village of Chowkar-Karez, scores of civilians were mown down by these gunships. CNN quoted an "unnamed" Pentagon official as saying, "The people are dead because we wanted them dead."[17] Almost certainly, many civilians therefore were wounded and killed.[18, 19]

BUNKER BUSTERS: Dropped from B-1 or B-2 planes, these 5000-pound behemoths are made from the gun barrels of retired naval ships and are so heavy that they burrow 20 to 100 feet into the ground before their high explosive materials detonate. Most are laser guided, but some use Global Positioning satellites for guidance.[20]

CARPET BOMBING: This means dropping tons of bombs from B-52 planes at a 40,000-foot altitude: high enough to protect pilots but too high to protect civilians. This is indiscriminate bombing, and the pilots have no idea on whom their bombs are landing. In 1969 carpet bombing used in Cambodia by Kissinger and Nixon during the Vietnam War induced the total destruction of the ancient irrigation system and water supply and most of the rice-growing areas of the country and, as a secondary effect, caused the absolute disintegration of Cambodia's culture. The bombing runs were called "breakfast," "lunch," and "supper."[21]

UNMANNED DRONES: These are pilotless planes armed with Hellfire missiles, guided by the Global Positioning System, allowing the military to reduce the time between "identification and destruction of a target."[22] Clearly these planes pose no threats to pilots but terrible threats to civilians on the ground, who may live next to or within a certain "military target," which could be a factory, an electricity generator, or a railway station.

The U.S. has not announced whether or not it used depleted uranium weapons in Afghanistan (as it has done elsewhere in recent wars), but it is quite possible that it did. We will not know for sure until independent sources can enter the war zones and test for this radioactive element.

During the first four weeks of the war, half a million tons of bombs were dropped on Afghanistan, 20 kilos for every man, woman, and child.[23] During eight and a half weeks of U.S. bombing, a documented 3,763 civilians were killed.[24]

What Are the International Ramifications of This Behavior Likely to Be?

Pakistan has been deeply involved in Afghanistan since the 1979-1989 U.S.–Russian war, when America channeled weapons, training, and funding through the Pakistani military and intelligence services to the mujahadeen, the Taliban, and Osama bin Laden to fight the Russians. After September 11, America changed sides, pressuring Pakistan to ally with the U.S. against their previous friends and allies, the Taliban, bin Laden, and al-Qaeda, because the U.S. needed Pakistani airports to fight their war—a move that was anathema to thousands of Pakistani supporters of bin Laden and the Taliban. These supporters include many members of the Pakistani military, who could well rebel and gain control of the army and its 20 to 50 nuclear weapons, passing these on to the Taliban and al-Qaeda in Afghani-stan or to their global networks.

The use of Pakistani nuclear weapons could trigger a chain reaction. Nuclear-armed India, an ancient enemy, could respond in kind. China, India's hated foe, could react if India used her nuclear weapons, triggering a nuclear holocaust on the subcontinent. If any of either Russia or America's 2,250 strategic weapons on hair-trigger alert were launched either accidentally or purposely in response, nuclear winter would ensue, meaning the end of most life on earth.

Other Nuclear Threats

Terrorist Nuclear Weapons
Up to 100 small suitcase Russian nuclear weapons have been lost over some years. Al-Qaeda network may now possess several of these, which could well be smuggled into America on a small boat or overland, from Canada or Mexico, in a truck. Nuclear Oklahoma Cities are not beyond question. Immediate deaths would number in the tens of thousands, while tens of thousands of cancers would incubate quietly among the survivors over decades. Britain, Europe, and Australia, among other places, will not remain immune.

Dirty Nuclear Devices
Hundreds of highly carcinogenic plutonium and enriched uranium stand unguarded in Russia. From 1993 to 2000, the UN International Atomic Energy Agency—which monitors nuclear security—documented 153 confirmed cases

of theft of nuclear materials.[25] Some of this material could be obtained by terrorists to make primitive nuclear weapons, or "dirty" bombs. There would be no nuclear explosion, but conventional explosives would be used to scatter plutonium or uranium across a wide area, contaminating all in the pathway with these carcinogenic elements. Other radioactive elements from reprocessed nuclear fuel, such as cesium-137, strontium-90, and cobalt-60, could also be deployed.[26]

Terrorists could, with some difficulty, manufacture their own nuclear devices from stolen plutonium or uranium. The design for a primitive weapon can be found on the Internet. The possibilities for nuclear terrorism seem endless.

Nuclear Meltdowns

Terrorists do not actually need nuclear weapons. They have been conveniently supplied with 103 nuclear power plants scattered throughout the United States (438 of these deadly facilities exist throughout the world).[27] A planned meltdown at one of these facilities would make the World Trade Center attacks seem like child's play. The massive concrete containers protecting the reactors are not strong enough to withstand the impact of a jumbo jet.

Alternatively, an infiltrator working as an operator could engineer a meltdown by taking over the control room, as the hijackers on September 11 took over the planes. They could also disrupt the water supply (one million gallons a minute is needed to cool a reactor core) or the external electricity supply. Either event would induce a meltdown within hours. The spent-fuel cooling pools adjacent to the reactor contain 20 to 30 times more long-lived radiation than the actual reactor core.[28] (A 1000 megawatt nuclear reactor contains as much long-lived radiation as that released by the explosion of 1000 Hiroshima-sized bombs).

Here is the medical description of the meltdown of a 1000-megawatt nuclear power plant near New York City (there are two reactors at Indian Point, 35 miles north of Manhattan):

> With ten million people at risk, 3300 people would die from severe radiation damage within several days; 10,000 to 100,000 would develop lethal acute radiation sickness within 2 to 6 weeks of exposure; 45,000 would become short of breath from lung damage caused by inhalation of intensely radioactive gases; 240,000 would become hypothyroid, with accompanying symptoms of weight gain, lassitude, slow mental functions, loss of appetite, constipation, and absent menstruation; 350,000 males would be rendered temporarily sterile, while the remaining sperm would be genetically mutated; 40,000 to 100,000 women would stop menstruating, many permanently. Up to 100,000 babies would be born as cretins, mentally retarded, as radioactive iodine destroys their thyroid glands (imperative for neurological development), and there would be 3000 deaths in utero. Five to sixty years later, 270,000 people would develop cancers of various organs, and there would be an estimated 28,000 cases of thyroid malignancy.[29]

Apart from the nuclear power plants, there are many military-related nuclear facilities in the United States with massive quantities of nuclear waste, all vulnerable to terrorist attacks.

Since September 11, the FAA banned all aircraft flying within 12 miles of any nuclear facility. The Nuclear Regulatory Commission (NRC) advised all reactors to go on the highest state of alert,[30] and for the first time, the NRC is investing 800,000 dollars to stockpile massive quantities of potassium iodide tablets to be made available to the public in case of a meltdown. Specific states will need to request the tablets, and this medicine must be taken within hours of a meltdown to block the uptake of radio-iodine by the thyroid gland. (This measure may not be adequate, however, because over one hundred different deadly radioactive elements are also released during a meltdown, and these concentrate in other bodily organs.[31])

Political Implications

The scope of U.S. retaliation for September 11 may be as important a factor in international response as the nature of the weapons the U.S. employs. In Washington, the Bush administration is experiencing its own internecine warfare around this topic. On the one hand, Secretary of State Colin Powell and the state department put together a harmonious if tenuous international coalition with Europe, Russia, China, and the Arab nations to "battle" terrorism in Afghanistan only. But the defense department has been taken over by unreconstructed, Reagan-era Cold War warriors, intent on moving the war from Afghanistan to other states.[32]

This policy is extremely dangerous. Vice President Cheney has listed fifty states or countries that could be targeted by the U.S. for military, financial, or diplomatic action, including North Korea, Somalia, Yemen, Iran, the Sudan, Libya, Syria, Lebanon, Indonesia, the Philippines, Saudia Arabia, and countries in South America. Victoria Clarke, a Pentagon spokeswoman, warned, "The war on terrorism neither begins nor ends with Afghanistan. The president will decide the next target."[33]

Iraq tops the list. Ever since the U.S.-Iraqi war in 1991, when America "failed to eliminate Hussein," a right-wing putsch has been eager to finish the job. The excuse: Iraq will not allow weapons inspectors to enter the country, barring them since December 1998 from checking for nuclear, biological, or chemical weapons activities. (However, Iraq's foreign minister, Naji Sabri, said in late November 2001, "We will consider a return of monitoring [of weapons] after the lifting of sanctions."[34]) Deputy Secretary of Defense Paul Wolfowitz is spearheading the Iraqi attack movement along with his close colleague Richard Perle, who was Reagan's undersecretary of defense.

Perle chairs an unofficial bipartisan group called the Defense Policy Board, which is vigorously promoting the overthrow of Hussein, even though there is no evidence linking him to the September 11 attacks.[35, 36] (The Defense Policy Board meets in a room adjacent to the secretary of defense's office, and includes such luminaries as Henry Kissinger, former secretary of state; Harold Brown, former secretary of defense; Newt Gingrich, former house majority leader; and R. James Woolsey, former director of the CIA. The group has assumed a quasi-official status with the imprimatur of Secretary Rumsfeld.) This attitude seems to be prevailing within the administration, and Powell appears to be losing his authority, although the international community is outraged by these proposals.

An attack on Iraq would infuriate Arab populations, the U.S.-led alliance against al-Qaeda[37] would dissolve, and the world would descend into a terror-ist-ruled-chaos. A veteran of the CIA's Directorate of Operations said, "The agency as an institution would never offer up a view of these people [Perle, et al.], but if you ask individuals, they think these guys are more than a little nuts." Another longtime case officer at the CIA said, "Attack these places and there will be consequences that we simply will not be able to deal with. But Perle and Wolfowitz are absolutists, and they're stupid."[38]

Meanwhile, other destabilizing plans are afoot in the Bush administration:

- The administration will aggressively pursue testing of its missile defense system, a.k.a. Star Wars, even though Russia and China are adamantly opposed. After the cordial Bush-Putin meeting at Crawford Ranch in Texas in November 2001, National Security Advisor Condoleezza Rice said, "The timeline has not really changed. The president continues to believe that he has got to move forward with the testing program in a robust way, so that we can really begin to evaluate the potential for missile defenses." What she meant was the U.S. withdrawal from the seminal Anti Ballistic Missile Treaty (ABM) with six months notice.[39] That move destabilized global arms control and the associated treaties, and induced a massive new nuclear arms race.

- The Bush administration boycotted the Comprehensive Test-Ban Treaty Conference (CTBT) at the United Nations in November 2001 and had the audacity to remove its nameplate from its seat in the conference room. A week before, at a General Assembly meeting, the U.S. was the only country to vote against placing the CTBT on the General Assembly's agenda for 2002. Washington has signed, but the Senate has not ratified, the treaty, which would ban all above- and below-ground nuclear testing. As a group of non-government organizations said, "Failure to act may lead to a cascade of proliferation events that will enable future terrorists to use nuclear weapons."[40]

- There is a strong move by Bush's people to resume nuclear testing at the Nevada Test site because, as Secretary of Defense Rumsfeld said, "we may need to develop new nuclear weapons." This could stimulate Russia, China, India, and Pakistan, among others, to resume nuclear testing, leading to a new nuclear arms race.[41]

- In July 2001, the U.S. prevented the UN conference on curbing small-arms exports from convening by insisting that it was a threat to the Second Amendment.

- Also in July 2001, after ten years of negotiations, the U.S. refused to endorse a protocol on a compliance to ban biological weapons, saying it would put at risk national security and confidential business information.

- In February 2001, the U.S. delegate at a UN debate to combat terrorism said such a conference would have no practical benefits.[42]

- In November 2001, Congress cut 69 million dollars from a program designed to safeguard Russian nuclear materials in order to prevent terrorists stealing plutonium and enriched uranium to build their own nuclear bombs. Bush wanted to reduce the program still further by 29 million dollars.[43]

- Simultaneously, Congress increased the funding for U.S. nuclear weapons by 300 million dollars and granted 8.3 billion dollars for missile defense.[44] As Joseph Cirincione of the Carnegie Endowment for International Peace said, "Tragically some are using the terrible tragedy [September 11] to justify their existing programs, slapping an 'anti-terrorist' label on missile defense and military budget increases.[45]

- The terrorist attack has provided a great fillip for the military-industrial complex. The military budget is expected to reach 373 billion dollars in 2001, a 66 billion dollar increase from 2001, and Deputy Secretary of Defense Paul Wolfowitz said that these appropriations will "just be a down-payment" toward the major long-term increases the Pentagon will need to fight its new kind of war,[46] which Vice President Cheney says "may not end in our lifetimes."[47]

- The war in Afghanistan is costing 1 billion dollars a month,[48] while two thirds of the world's children are malnourished and starving.

Loren Thompson, defense analyst from the Lexington Institute, said, "The whole mind set of military spending changed on September 11. The most fundamental thing about defense spending is that threats drive defense spending. It's now going to be easier to fund almost anything." Indeed, Lockheed Martin stocks rose from $39.39 on September 11 to $48.11 by November 12, 2001. The Pentagon is to receive 20 billion dollars of the 40 billion dollars allocated by Congress for antiterrorist activities, an amount to be added to 343.2 billion dollars for fiscal 2001, already the largest military budget since Reagan's at the height of the cold war—greater than 50% of all discretionary funding for domestic needs. Among the firms already benefiting from this extraordinarily extravagant and unnecessary largess are Lockheed Martin, Grumman, Raytheon, and Boeing. Most of this money will not be used for the war in Afghanistan, but for new fighter planes like the F/A-18E/F, the F-22, and the Joint Strike fighter, for a new Virginia class submarine designed to trail now-extinct Soviet subs around the globe, and for 12 more Trident D5 submarine ballistic missiles. In this context it is interesting to note that the Afghanis had very few planes to speak of, and that these were destroyed by massive U.S. bombing within the first few days of the war. Paul Nisbet, another defense analyst said, "With the [Bush] administration, we will see a rebuilding of the military to bring it back to where it was eight years ago. We will see a considerable appreciation in defense stocks as we saw in the Reagan years."[49, 50]

People may feel reassured that President Bush, meeting in Texas in November 2001 with President Putin, offered to reduce America's stockpile of strategic weapons from some 7000 down to 2220–1700 over the next ten years. But this offer was made without the guarantee of any formal written treaty and can therefore be abandoned or reversed at any time. Without verification, it will be impossible to confirm that cuts are actually carried out, while the ten-year duration gives much latitude for reversal and change.

In fact, although the cuts look good on paper, they mean nothing. The U.S. will still have plenty of weapons to maintain its first-strike winnable nuclear war policy, and none of the weapons will be dismantled, but will be stored, awaiting possible future use. The reductions do not include the removal of multiple warheads on missiles required by the STARTII Treaty (the Russians have a monstrous ten-warheaded SS-18 missile, code named "Satan"). And the U.S. Trident submarine fleet, with their invulnerable first-strike arsenal, will be exempt, as will weapons on long-distance bombers being overhauled, and all tactical nuclear weapons.[51]

In truth, if Russia comes to the party, such bilateral reductions will make it easier for the U.S. to win a nuclear war against Russia, because there will be fewer targets, and the missile-defense system now under construction will mop up any Russian missiles that escape the initial surprise attack. U.S. antisatellite weapons under construction will also be necessary to destroy the "eyes and ears" of the Russian early-warning system. This is a terrifying but realistic scenario, a logical extension of the Pentagon's current policy to "fight and win" a nuclear war.

So Bush's unilateral reductions proposal is a ploy to divert the world's attention away from his Star Wars project, which Simon Tisdall of the London *Guardian* called "a reckless act of weapons proliferation," which will provoke an international arms race, entangle third parties such as Britain and Australia, and as this book makes clear, lead directly to the militarization of space if it does not cause nuclear winter first.

Tisdall warns that "the highly contentious military and geostrategic foundations of the 21st century are being laid—and hardly anybody is watching."[52]

Notes

1. Situation Reports, STATFOR.com (September, 11, 2001).

2. "Pentagon Recommends the Use of Nuclear Weapons," *Japan Today* (September 19, 2001).

3. Jeffrey St. Clair, "Trigger Happy, Bush Administration Hawks Want to Deploy 'Mini-nukes' Against Osama Bin Laden," www.inthesetimes.com/issue/25/26/news2.shtm.

4. Dana Milbank, "U.S. Pressed on Nuclear Response, a Policy of Less Ambiguity, More Pointed Threat Is Urged," *The Washington Post* (October 5, 2001).

5. Wes Vernon, "Father of Neutron Bomb: Use It on Osama," www.af.mil/vision (September 25, 2001).

6. James Carroll, "Bombing with Blindfolds On" *The Boston Globe* (November 11, 2001).

7. Nigel Chamberlain and Dave Andrews, "Thermobaric Warfare," www.cnduk.org/briefing/thermo.htm (January 11, 2001).

8. Andrew Maykuth and Jonathan S. Landay, "U.S. Intensifies Attacks with BLU-82s," Knight Ridder Newspapers (November 6, 2001).

9. "Backgrounder on Russian Fuel Air Explosives (Vacuum Bombs)," Human Rights Watch, www.hrw.org/pres/2000/02/chech0215b (February 2000).

10. Tim Weiner, "U.S. Bombs Strike 3 Villages and Reportedly Kill Scores," *The New York Times* (December 1, 2001).

11. "Protocol 1, Relating to the Protection of Victims of International Armed Conflicts, Article 51."

12. Geov Parrish, "Where the Bodies Are," www.workingforchange.com (October 22, 2001).

13. "Unexploded Cluster Bombs Pose Threat to Civilians, Dawn, Pakistan," Centre for Research on Globilisation, www.globalresearch.ca/articles/DAW111B (November 15, 2001).

14. Amy Waldman, "Food Drops Go Awry, Damaging Houses," *The New York Times* (November 21, 2001).

15. "Unexploded Cluster Bombs Pose Threat to Civilians."

16. USAF, www.aviationzone.com/facts/ac130.

17. "International Action Center Factsheet: The Truth About the U.S. War in Afghanistan," [www.iacenter.org] *Toronto Globe and Mail* (November 3, 2001).

18. Michael R. Gordon, "U.S. Hope to Break the Taliban with Pounding From the Air," *The New York Times* (October 17, 2001).

19. Thom Shanker and Stephen Lee Myers, "U.S. Sends in Special Plane with Heavy Guns," *The New York Times* (October 16, 2001).

20. "Bunker Busters Brought into Use," *The Daily Camera*, Camera Wire Services; and Raymond Whitaker, "Attack on Afghanistan: Washington's Fearsome Arsenal," *The Independent* (November 4, 2001).

21. Dr. Helen Caldicott, *Missile Envy* (New York: William Morrow, 1984).

22. "Afghan War Will Shape Future U.S. Military Structure," www.stratfor.com (November 23, 2001).

23. Dr. Farrukh Saleem, "Stop the Bombing Please," *JANG*, Pakistan, www.jang.com.pk/thenews/index (November 4, 2001).

24. Professor Marc Herold, "A Dossier on Civilian Victims of United States' Aerial Bombing of Afghanistan," www.cursor.org/stories/civilian_deaths.htm (December 6, 2001).

25. Bil Nichols and Peter Eisler, "The Threat of Nuclear Terror is Slim but Real," *USA Today* (November 28, 2001).

26. Ibid.

27. Louis Charbonneau, "Experts Warn of Low Grade Nuclear Terror Attack," Reuters (November 2, 2001).

28. Mathew Wald, "Reactors and Their Fuel Are Among the Flanks U.S. Needs to Shore Up," *The New York Times* (November 4, 2001).

29. Dr. Helen Caldicott, *Nuclear Madness* (New York: W.W. Norton, 1994).

30. Michael Grunwald and Peter Behr, "Are Nuclear Plants Secure?" *The Washington Post* (November 3, 2001).

31. Mathew Wald, "Agency Weighs Buying Drug to Protect Against Radiation-Induced Ailments," *The New York Times* (November 29, 2001).

32. Efward Luttwak, "New Fears, New Alliance," *The New York Times* (October 2, 2001).

33. Barbara Slavin, "Pentagon Builds Case to Bomb Iraq," *USA Today* (November 11, 2001).

34. "Iraq Says to Consider Return of Weapons Monitoring," Reuters (November 21, 2001).

35. Elaine Scolino and Alison Mitchell, "Calls for New Push into Iraq Gain Power in Washington," *The New York Times* (December 3, 2001).

36. Anton La Guardia, "Iraq 'Not Linked to September 11,'" *The Telegraph* (November 11, 2001).

37. Barbara Slavin, "Pentagon Builds Case to Bomb Iraq," *USA Today* (November 19, 2001).

38. Jason Vest, "Beyond Osama: The Pentagon's Battle with Powell Heats Up," *The Village Voice* (November 20, 2001).

39. Sandra Sobieraj, "U.S. to Pursue Missile Test Plans," The Associated Press (November 16, 2001).

40. Jim Wurst, "U.S. Supports Weapons Cut While Opposing International Agreements," *News World Communications Inc.* (November 14, 2001).

41. "N-Testing to Resume?" Opinion/Editorial, www.downwinders.org.

42. Jim Wurst, "A Call to Arms Control," *The Washington Times* (November 12, 2001).

43. "Action on Threat Reduction," andrew@californianpeaceaction.org (November 9, 2001).

44. Ibid.

45. William D. Hartung, "Bush's War on Terrorism: Who Will Pay and Who Will Benefit?" www.motherjones.com (September 27, 2001).

46. William D. Hartung, "The War Dividend," www.motherjones.com (September 28, 2001).

47. John Pilger, "The Truths They Never Tell Us," *The New Statesman* (November 26, 2001).

48. James Dao, "U.S. Is Expecting to Spend $1 Billion a Month on War," *The New York Times* (November 12, 2001).

49. Frida Berrigan, "The War Profiteers: How Are Weapons Manufacturers Faring in the War," World Policy Institute (December 17, 2001).

50. "The Military Budget Up, Up, and Away," Arms Trade Resource (December 20, 2001).

51. Michael R. Gordon, "U.S. Arsenal: Treaties vs. Nontreaties," *The New York Times* (November 14, 2001).

52. Simon Tisdall, "How the Future Was Shanghaied," *The Guardian* (October 21, 2001).

MARGARET ATWOOD ✓

Bread

Margaret Atwood (b. 1939), internationally known Canadian novelist and poet, was born in Ottawa, Ontario, and attended Victoria College, University of Toronto; she did graduate work at Radcliffe College and Harvard University. Atwood is the author of many books of poetry, several collections of stories and essays, and ten novels. Her 1985 novel, *The Handmaid's Tale*, which portrays a chillingly misogynistic future, won her international renown. Her more recent novels include *Alias Grace* (1996) and *The Blind Assassin* (2000), and her latest collection of poetry is *Eating Fire: Selected Poems, 1965–1995*. She has received many literary awards, and has served as president of the Canadian Writers Union and PEN Canadian Centre. In her prose poem *Bread*, she helps us to understand the basic desperation and primal reality that can lead to war.

■

Imagine a piece of bread. You don't have to imagine it, it's right here in the kitchen, on the bread board, in its plastic bag, lying beside the bread knife. The bread knife is an old one you picked up at an auction; it has the word BREAD carved into the wooden handle. You open the bag, pull back the wrapper, cut yourself a slice. You put butter on it, then peanut butter, then honey, and you fold it over. Some of the honey runs out onto your fingers and you lick it off. It takes you about a minute to eat the bread. This bread happens to be brown, but there is also white bread, in the refrigerator, and a heel of rye you got last week, round as a full stomach then, now going mouldy. Occasionally you make bread. You think of it as something relaxing to do with your hands.

•

Imagine a famine. Now imagine a piece of bread. Both of these things are real but you happen to be in the same room with only one of them. Put yourself into a different room, that's what the mind is for. You are now lying on a thin mattress in a hot room. The walls are made of dried earth and your sister, who is younger than you are, is in the same room with you. She is starving, her belly is bloated, flies land on her eyes; you brush them off with your hand. You have a cloth too, filthy but damp, and you press it to her lips and forehead. The piece of bread is the bread you've been saving, for days it seems. You are as hungry as she is, but not yet as weak. How long does this take? When will someone come with more bread? You think of going out to see if you might find something that could be eaten, but outside the streets are infested with scavengers and the stink of corpses is everywhere.

Should you share the piece of bread or give the whole piece to your sister? Should you eat the piece of bread yourself? After all, you have a better chance of living, you're stronger. How long does it take to decide?

•

Imagine a prison. There is something you know that you have not yet told. Those in control of the prison know that you know. So do those not in control. If you tell, thirty or forty or a hundred of your friends, your comrades, will be caught and will die. If you refuse to tell, tonight will be like the last night. They always choose the night. You don't think about the night however, but about the piece of bread they offered you. How long does it take? The piece of bread was brown and fresh and reminded you of sunlight falling across a wooden floor. It reminded you of a bowl, a yellow bowl that was once in your home. It held apples and pears; it stood on a table you can also remember. It's not the hunger or the pain that is killing you but the absence of the yellow bowl. If you could only hold the bowl in your hands, right here, you could withstand anything, you tell yourself. The bread they offered you is subversive, it's treacherous, it does not mean life.

•

There were once two sisters. One was rich and had no children, the other had five children and was a widow, so poor that she no longer had any food left. She went to her sister and asked her for a mouthful of bread. "My children are dying," she said. The rich sister said, "I do not have enough for myself," and drove her away from the door. Then the husband of the rich sister came home and wanted to cut himself a piece of bread; but when he made the first cut, out flowed red blood.

Everyone knew what that meant.
This is a traditional German fairy-tale.

·

The loaf of bread I have conjured for you floats about a foot above your kitchen table. The table is normal, there are no trap doors in it. A blue tea towel floats beneath the bread, and there are no strings attaching the cloth to the bread or the bread to the ceiling or the table to the cloth, you've proved it by passing your hand above and below. You didn't touch the bread though. What stopped you? You don't want to know whether the bread is real or whether it's just a hallucination I've somehow duped you into seeing. There's no doubt that you can see the bread, you can even smell it, it smells like yeast, and it looks solid enough, solid as your own arm. But can you trust it? Can you eat it? You don't want to know, imagine that.

BARBARA EHRENREICH

From Blood Rites: The Religion of War

Barbara Ehrenreich (b. 1941) is a leading feminist and democratic socialist thinker who has written extensively on the feminization of poverty. A Ph.D. in biology from Rockefeller University, she has published articles and essays in major newspapers around the country and has written regularly for *Mother Jones, The Progressive, In These Times,* and *The Nation.* Her ten books include *The Hearts of Men: American Dreams and the Flight from Commitment* (1983), *Fear of Falling,* and, most recently, the best-selling *Nickeled and Dimed: On (Not) Getting By in America* (2001). This excerpt is from *Blood Rites*—an original treatise on "the origins and history of the passions of war," which takes the reader on a journey from the elaborate human sacrifices of the ancient world to the carnage and holocaust of twentieth-century "total war"—the greatest threat to human life. The section excerpted here is entitled "The Religion of War."

■

Not only warriors are privileged to undergo the profound psychological transformation that separates peace from war. Whole societies may be swept up into a kind of "altered state" marked by emotional intensity and a fixation on totems representative of the collectivity: sacred images, implements, or, in our own time, yellow ribbons and flags. The onset of World War I, for example, inspired a veritable frenzy of enthusiasm among noncombatants and potential recruits alike, and it was not an enthusiasm for killing or loot or "imperialist expansion" but for something far more uplifting and worthy.

In Britain, the public had been overwhelmingly opposed to involvement until the moment war was declared, at which time screaming crowds poured into the streets and surrounded Buckingham Palace for days. In Berlin, the crowds poured out, "as though a human river had burst its banks and flooded the world."[1] In St. Petersburg a mob burned the furnishings of the German embassy while women ripped off their dresses and offered them to soldiers in the middle of a public square.[2] When the United States entered the war, on April 6, 1917, the audience at the New York Metropolitan Opera House stood up, and greeted the announcement with "loud and long cheers."[3]

Hardly anyone managed to maintain their composure in the face of the oncoming hostilities. Rainer Maria Rilke was moved to write a series of poems extolling war; Anatole France offered to enlist at age seventy; Isadora Duncan recalled being "all flame and fire" over the war. Socialists rallied to their various nations' flags, abandoning the "international working class" overnight. Many feminists, such as England's Isabella Pankhurst, set the struggle for suffrage aside for an equally militant jingoism, and contented themselves with organizing women to support the war effort. "The war is so horribly exciting but I cannot live on it," one British suffragette wrote. "It is like being drunk all day."[4] Even pacifists like the German novelist Stefan Zweig felt a temptation to put aside their scruples and join the great "awakening of the masses" prompted by war.[5] In India, young Gandhi recruited his countrymen to join the British army; even Freud . . . briefly lost perspective, "giving all his libido to Austria-Hungary."[6]

But Freud failed to reflect on his own enthusiasm; otherwise he would never have hypothesized that men are driven to war by some cruel and murderous instinct. The emotions that overwhelmed Europe in 1914 had little to do with rage or hatred or greed. Rather, they were among the "noblest" feelings humans are fortunate enough to experience: feelings of generosity, community, and submergence in a great and worthy cause. There was little difference, in fact, between the fervor that greeted the war and the emotional underpinnings of the socialist movement, which promised land (or bread) and *peace*. As historian Albert O. Hirschman has written:

> [For] important sectors of the middle and upper classes . . . the war came as a release
> from boredom and emptiness, as a promise of the longed-for community that would
> transcend social class.[7]

Just after the war, the American psychologist G. E. Partridge observed that the mood of war had been, above all—and despite the war's acknowledged horrors—one of "ecstasy." Drawing on the work of early-twentieth-century German psychologists, he enumerated, in a way that can now only seem quaint, the various "ecstasies" associated with war: that of heroism, of "taking part in great events," or of victory ("Siegestrunkenheit"); the "joy of overcoming the pain of death"; and, summing up all the other ecstasies, the "social intoxication, the feeling on the part of the individual of being a part of a body and the sense of being lost in a greater whole."[8] The thrill of being part of a vast crowd, of abandoning ordinary responsibilities in order to run out into the streets, of witnessing such "great events" as declarations of war: This was "ecstasy" enough for the millions who would never see actual combat.

It was the sense of self-loss, Partridge opined, of merger into some "greater whole," which showed that war was an attempt to meet the same psychological needs otherwise fulfilled by "love, religion, intoxication, art."[9] A historian of our own time, Roland Stromberg, would agree, writing of the men who volunteered to fight in World War I:

> Doubtless they found hell, but they did not go seeking it; rather than an itch to kill, hurt, or torture their fellow men, as Freud claimed, they felt something much more akin to love.[10]

The mass feelings inspired by war, many noted right after World War I, are eerily similar to those normally aroused by religion. Arnold J. Toynbee, the British historian, had been caught up in World War I like most of his peers, and produced several volumes of "atrocity propaganda" as his contribution to the war effort.[11] Later, repenting for that brief burst of militarism, he argued that war had in fact become a religion, moving in to fill the gap left as traditional forms of worship lost their power over people. "Man," he wrote, requires "spiritual sustenance," and if man was now less inclined to find it in a church, he would find it in the secular state and express it as a militant nationalism in which "the glorification of War [is] a fundamental article of faith."[12]

To say that war may be, in an emotional sense, a close relative of religion is not to pass moral judgment on either of these ancient institutions. We are dealing with a very basic level of human emotional experience, which can be approached just as well at, say, a labor rally as at a nationalist gathering or a huge outdoor mass. Coming together in a large crowd united by some common purpose, people feel sure of collective strength, and they may project this sense of power onto God, the Nation, or the People. *El pueblo unido*, goes the left-wing chant, *jamas sera vencido* (The people united cannot be defeated). As the nineteenth-century theorist of crowd psychology, Gustave Le Bon, observed, somewhat haughtily:

> In crowds the foolish, ignorant, and envious persons are freed from the sense of their insignificance and powerlessness, and are possessed instead by the notion of brutal and temporary but immense strength.[13]

Individually we are weak, but with God, or through "the fatherland" or "the working class," we become something larger than ourselves—something indomitable and strong. Even those of us who will never experience battle, or for that matter, God, can know the thrill of being swept along with a huge and purposeful crowd.

This is one of humankind's great natural "highs," and is, perhaps paradoxically, as likely to be experienced at an anti-war demonstration as at a pro-war rally. But it is a high that can be most reliably experienced in contemplation of an enemy—the Viet Cong or, for that matter, the military-industrial complex—which both excites our adrenaline and serves to unite us. All "minor" differences (as, for example, of class) disappear when compared to the vast differences (construed as moral, cultural, and sometimes racial) that supposedly separate us from the "jerries," the Communists, the Arabs, or the Jews.

Through the mass rally or the spontaneous gathering in the streets, large numbers of people can experience something analogous to the transformation that makes a man into a warrior. Just as the ancient warrior fasted, took drugs, danced all night, and even became a monster, the crowd, too, leaves mundane things behind and transmutes itself into a new kind of being, larger than the sum of its parts, more powerful than any single individual. Consider the British psychologist Roger E. Money-Kyrle's eyewitness description of a Hitler rally:

> The people seemed gradually to lose their individuality and become fused into a not very intelligent but immensely powerful monster, which was not quite sane and therefore capable of anything. Moreover, it was an elementary monster . . . with no judgment and few, but very violent passions. . . . [W]e heard for ten minutes about the growth of the Nazi Party, and how from small beginnings it had now become an overpowering force. The monster became self-conscious of its size and intoxicated by the belief in its own omnipotence.[14]

But there is more to the "religion" of war than the thrill of the mass rally or of the battle itself. In between wars, there are ample reminders of the collective high induced by the threat or actuality of war. The tribal war chieftain had his collection of skulls or similar trophies to contemplate in times of peace; the ancient emperor had his stelae commemorating victories, his temples to Mars or Minerva. In the modern European world, according to historian George Mosse, war cemeteries and monuments serve as the "sacred spaces of a new civil religion"[15]—lovingly tended and solemnly redecorated year after year. The grave of the "unknown soldier" is an especially stirring reminder of the moral transcendency of war: in war the individual may be entirely obliterated for the higher cause, made nameless as well as dead. Yet even in this abject condition, he, or at least some remnant of the "glory" associated with his passing, lives on forever, symbolized by a perpetual flame.

By the twentieth century, war, and the readiness for war which is so much a part of nationalism, had become the force unifying states and offering individuals a sense of transcendent purposefulness. Today, even in peacetime, the religious side of war is everywhere manifest. No important state function can go forward without the accompaniment of drumrolls and soldiers at attention. The inauguration of presidents, the coronation of monarchs, the celebration of national holidays—these events require everywhere the presence of the soldier as a "ceremonial appurtenance."[16] Where there are no true soldiers, exclusively ceremonial ones may be maintained: Even the Vatican—which, one might imagine, needs no further embellishment with quasi-religious pompery—has its Swiss Guard.

The word "sacrifice" summed up the religious passion of war for generations of Europeans and Americans. In the rhetoric of religious militarism, killing the enemy was almost an incidental outcome of war compared to making "the supreme sacrifice" of one's own life. Dying in war was not a mishap inflicted on the unfortunate, but the point, almost, of the whole undertaking.

"Happiness," the German poet Theodor Korner declared at the time of the Napoleonic Wars, "lies only in sacrificial death."[17] Mosse has commented on the extensive "cooptation of Christian symbolism and ritual to sanctify the life and death of the soldier" in World War I.[18] The war was compared to the Last Supper, the soldier's death to the martyrdom of Christ—in, for example, post-cards showing angels hovering over handsome, contented-looking, and apparently unwounded corpses.[19]

Not all Europeans, at all times, have seen war as an occasion for a beautiful, sacrificial death, of course, but the notion is a widespread one and not only among urban, industrialized cultures. In his groundbreaking study of "primitive" war, the American anthropologist Harry Turney-High offered numerous examples of similar sacrificial fervor among tribal peoples. He reports dryly that on Mangaia, for example, in Polynesia,

> [the] high-born, noble Tiora did not shrink when informed by the war priests that their god demanded his sacrificial death at the enemy's hands. He went against the foe alone and they obligingly killed him, unaware that his immolation was intended to accomplish their own defeat.[20]

Caesar reported that the Aquitanians had an elite society of fighters called *solidurii*, or "bound-by-duty," who were sworn to share one another's deaths in battle or else to kill themselves.[21] There were similar "no retreat" societies among North American Indian tribes. A Crow could "vow his body to the enemy," which meant he was prepared to die in an attack against hopeless odds.[22]

Self-sacrifice is perhaps the least "rational" of all human undertakings. Anthropologists may debate whether it is rational, in a self-serving sense, to fight for land or women or to avenge some wrong. But there is no straightforward biological calculation that could lead a man to kill himself, like one of the *solidurii*, or to die—possibly unwed and childless, like the Crow warrior—because he has sworn a vow. "At bottom, the reason why fighting can never be a question of interest," the military theorist Martin van Creveld writes, "is—to put it bluntly—that dead men have no interests."[23]

A cynic might dismiss the religiosity of war as a mystification of its mundane, ignoble aims, all the rhetoric of "sacrifice" and "glory" serving only to delude and perhaps intoxicate otherwise unwilling participants. At some level, the cynic would be right: The results of war—the burned villages, bombed cities, sobbing orphans and captives—are the same whether the war was driven by less worthy motives, like vengeance or greed. Thus most scholars have no doubt felt themselves justified in slighting the high-flown rhetoric and rituals of war to concentrate on its technology and impact. Of all the volumes on war listed in the bibliography of this book, only a half-dozen at most concern themselves directly with the passions that have made war, to so many of its participants, a profoundly religious undertaking.[24]

But there are at least two reasons to take seriously the religious dimension of war. First, because it is the religiosity of war, above all, which makes it so impervious to moral rebuke. For millennia, and long before the Enlightenment or even the teachings of Jesus, people have understood that war inverts all normal morality; that it is, by any sane standard, a criminal undertaking. Buddhism, arising in the fifth century B.C., condemned war, and one of the most bluntly reasoned anti-war arguments ever made comes to us from the Chinese philosopher To Ti in the fourth century B.C.:

> When one man kills another man it is considered unrighteous and he is punished by death. Then by the same sign when a man kills ten others, his crime will be ten times greater, and should be punished by death, ten times. . . . Similarly if a small crime is considered crime, but a big crime such as attacking another country is applauded as a righteous act, can this be said to be knowing the difference between righteousness and unrighteousness?[25]

But war, as Mo Ti must have realized, enlists passions which feel as "righteous" to those who experience them as any of the arguments against it.

The other reason to study the religiosity of war is for what it has to say about us as a species, about "human nature," if you will, and the clichéd "problem of evil." Other creatures, including our near relatives the chimpanzees, have also been known to kill their own kind with systematic zeal; certain species of ants even do so on a scale and with a tactical ingenuity fully deserving of the label "war." But of course no other species exhibits behavior we recognize as "religious," and none can be said to bring exalted passion to their acts of intraspecies violence.

So, we might well ask of ourselves: What is it about our species that has made us see in war a kind of sacrament? Not all wars, of course, have excited the kind of passion aroused by World War I. But does the fact that humans *can* and often do sacralize the act of killing mean that we are more vicious than any other creature? Or is it the other way around, with our need to sacralize the act of killing proving that we are, deep down, ultimately moral creatures? Which are we: beasts because we make war, or angels because we seek so often to make it into something holy?

A psychologist might offer one sort of answer, based on the anxieties that seem built into the individual life cycle, but here I am interested in another kind of answer drawn from efforts to reconstruct our collective biography as a species, our history, and prehistory. Since the search for prehistoric "origins" has become distinctly unfashionable among contemporary anthropologists, I should explain, first, that the kind of origin I seek is not a hypothetical event, or "just-so" story, like the mythical rebellion, in Freud's *Totem and Taboo*, of the "primal horde" against its patriarchal leader. "Antecedent" may be a better word for what we are after here: Hunting is an antecedent of war, almost certainly predating it and providing it with many valuable techniques: here we seek a similarly long-standing antecedent to the *sacralization* of war.

Second, it should be acknowledged at the outset that to know the origin of something is not, of course, to know why it persists or plays itself out, over and over. But in the case of repetitive, seemingly compulsive patterns of behavior, the first step to freedom may be to know how it all got started. Like a psychologist facing an individual patient, we need to uncover the original trauma.

We begin, in the next chapter, with the most clear-cut case of sacralized violence that human cultures have to offer: religious rituals of blood sacrifice. Even in times of peace, the religions of many traditional cultures were hardly aloof from the business of violence. In fact, their rituals have very often centered on the act of killing, either mimed or literally enacted, of humans or animals. As René Girard emphasized in his classic *Violence and the Sacred*, violence was, well into the historical era, at the very core of what humans define as sacred, and the first question we will address is *why*.

In the conventional account of human origins, everything about human violence is explained as a result of our species' long prehistoric sojourn as hunters of animals. It is the taste for meat and the willingness to kill for it that supposedly distinguish us from other primates, making us both smart and cruel, sociable and domineering, eager for the kill and capable of sharing it. We are, in other words, a species of predators—"natural born killers" who carried the habit of fighting into the era of herding and farming. With the Neolithic revolution, wild ungulates were replaced as prey by the animals in other people's herds or the grain stored in other villages' fortresses: and the name for this new form of "hunting" was war. In this account, the sacralization of war arises only because the old form of hunting, and probably also the sharing of meat, had somehow been construed as sacred for eons before.

No doubt much of "human nature" was indeed laid down during the 2 million years or so when *Homo* lived in small bands and depended on wild animals and plants for food. But it is my contention that our peculiar and ambivalent relationship to violence is rooted in a primordial experience that we have managed, as a species, to almost entirely repress. And this is the experience, not of hunting, but of being preyed upon by animals that were initially far more skillful hunters than ourselves. In particular, the sacralization of war is not the project of a self-confident predator, I will argue, but that of a creature which has learned only "recently," in the last thousand or so generations, not to cower at every sound in the night.

Rituals of blood sacrifice both celebrate and terrifyingly reenact the human transition from prey to predator, and so, I will argue, does war. Nowhere is this more obvious than in the case of wars that are undertaken for the stated purpose of initiating young men into the male warrior-predator role—a not uncommon occurrence in traditional cultures. But more important, the anxiety and ultimate thrill of the prey-to-predator transition color the feelings we bring to all wars, and infuse them, at least for some of the participants, some of the time, with feelings powerful and uplifting enough to be experienced as "religious." . . .

[I] will consider the sacralization of war in historical times, and its evolution from an elite religion observed by a privileged warrior caste to the mass religion we know today primarily as nationalism. It is in our own thoroughly "modern" time, we will see, that the rituals and passions of war most clearly recall the primitive theme of resistance to a nonhuman threat.

Notes

1. Roland Stromberg, *Redemption by War: The Intellectuals and 1914* (Lawrence: University of Kansas Press, 1982), 20

2. Ibid, 233

3. Lawrence LeShahn, *The Psychology of War: Confronting Its Mystique and Its Madness* (Chicago: Noble Press, 1992), 67

4. Quoted in Johanna Alberti, *Beyond Suffrage: Feminists in War and Peace, 1914–1928* (New York: St. Martin's Press, 1989), 50.

5. George L. Mosse, *Confronting the Nation: Jewish and Western Nationalism* (Hanover and London: Brandeis University Press, 1993), 64

6. Quoted in Stromberg, 2.

7. Albert O. Hirschman, *Shifting Involvements: Private Interest and Public Action* (Princeton, NJ: Princeton University Press, 1982), 5.

8. G. E. Partridge, *The Psychology of Nations: A Contribution to the Philosophy and History* (New York: Macmillan, 1919), 23.

9. Ibid, 22.

10. Stromberg, 190.

11. Ibid, 53.

12. Arnold J. Toynbee, *A Study of History*, abridged and edited by D.C. Somevell (London: Oxford University Press, 1957), 18.

13. Gustave Le Bon, *The Crowd: A Study of the Popular Mind* (Atlanta: Cherokee Publishing, 1982), 34.

14. Quoted in Franco Fornari, *The Psychoanalysis of War,* translated by Alenka Pfeiffer (Bloomington: Indiana University Press, 1975) 151.

15. Mosse, 32.

16. Alfred Vagts, *A History of Militarism: Civilian and Military* (New York: Free Press, 1959), 21.

17. Quoted in Mosse, 70.

18. Ibid, 25.

19. Ibid, 74–75.

20. Harry Holbert Turney-High, *Primitive War: Its Practice and Concepts* (Columbia: University of South Carolina Press, 1949), 214.

21. Ibid, 215.

22. Ibid, 213.

23. Martin Van Creveld, *The Transformation of War* (New York: Free Press, 1991), 158.

24. I would include in this category LeShahn, Mosse, Fornari, Partidge, and Dudley Young, *The Origins of the Sacred: The Ecstasies of Love and War* (New York: HarperPerennial, 1992), as well as many others.

25. Auoted in Sun Tzu, *The Art of War,* translated and with an introduction by Samuel B. Griffith (London: Oxford University Press, 1971), 22.

MOLLY PEACOCK

Among Tall Buildings

Molly Peacock (b. 1947) is poet-in-residence at the Cathedral of St. John the Divine in New York City. She is the author of *How to Read a Poem and Start a Poetry Circle* (1999) as well as a memoir, *Paradise Piece by Piece* (1998). As part of her wide-ranging interests, she has edited a collection of essays called *The Private I: Privacy in a Public World* (2001). Former president of the Poetry Society of America, she is one of the originators of Poetry in Motion, which places poems on the nation's subways and buses. Her newest volume of poetry, *Cornucopia: New and Selected Poems* (2002), includes this poem, written as a vision of a postnuclear city, which has striking new resonance after September 11.

■

And nothing, not even the girl you love
with the mole on her arm, will be left. Huge
trenches will be dug just beyond the stove
the whole northeast corridor will become
and the dead will be piled in each rude gouge,
even that girl whose left ear always sticks
slightly out beyond her hair. To fix
the names of who died on tape won't be done
since they'll dig quick to prevent disease. Nobody
likes to hear this kind of talk. I always
hated to hear it myself until I began
loving the mortar between blocks, that cruddy
pocked cement holding up buildings so a man
and a woman can embrace in the maze
of what they've built on the errors of their ways.

ROCHELLE RATNER

Borders

Rochelle Ratner (b. 1948) is a poet, novelist, editor, and critic living in New York City. Her many books include *Practicing to Be a Woman: New and Selected Poems* (1982), *Someday Songs* (1992), and *Zodiac Arrest* (1995) and the novels *Bobby's Girl* (1986) and *The Lion's Share* (1991). Most recently, she edited the landmark anthology *Bearing Life: Womens' Writings on Childlessness* (2000), which won the Susan Koppelman Award. She is executive editor of the *American Book Review* and a former board member of the National Book Critics Circle and reviews frequently for *Library Journal* and other publications. She recently edited a special feature, "Focus 9/11," for www.PoetsUSA.com/.

■

1.

Just before a storm
we sit on the porch.
You have been picking berries.
Soon we will go to dinner.

While the others are inside
I ask you how it felt
to grow up in Berlin
with the Wall dividing you

and in broken English
you try to explain
how you lived in East Berlin
and were on vacation
when it happened

you were among the lucky ones
who had a choice:
give up home, job,
possessions, friends,
go live with relatives

your father knew then
those in the West
might be allowed to visit,
those who stayed in the East
might never leave

so at ten years old
you started over.
At ten, at twelve, at fourteen
even walls were natural.

2.

We sit on the porch.
You speak in broken English
because, I say,
I want to understand.
Under my breath I am speaking
of Israel.

I barely know you.
Two days later
you'll ask my friend
if I'm Jewish, when I'd hoped
you wouldn't understand.

3.

The image of us sitting there:
Jew born three years
after the war,
German born eight years after.
We do not speak of prejudice.

I tell you, instead,
of my father

how he had a business
how the Blacks who worked
minimum wage there
unionized against him
how, when I was ten years old,
I stood by helpless
while a loved one's hate grew.

You explain it happened
bit by bit:
first they set up
separate currencies,
then a new police force;
though the Wall was unexpected
all the bricks were laid.

You say thank God
there was no fighting
after the first months, that is

and I thank God
we did not live in the South
where there were riots
and my father would have been
among the first attacked.

I am thinking of Israel,
how what Jews say of Arabs

sounded so familiar,
how what began as pride
got out of hand

and I wonder
whether to tell you this.
Uwe, what I should have said was
the borders are inside us.

WENDY ROSE

The Fifties

Wendy Rose (b. 1948), author of *Bone Dance* (1993), *Going to War with All My Relations* (1995), *Itch Like Crazy* (2002), and several other volumes of verse, is a poet and artist of the Hopi Nation. The Hopi are known for their ecological intelligence and gift for prophecy. This verse comes from *Nuke Chronicles*, an antinuclear anthology. A study completed in August 2001 by the U.S. Centers for Disease Control and Prevention suggests that for all Americans born after 1951, "all organs and tissues of the body have received some radiation exposure from nuclear testing." The study reported that the global fallout could eventually be responsible for more than 11,000 cancer deaths in the United States alone. Most of the U.S. nuclear tests carried out from the 1940s until above-ground tests were barred in 1963 took place at the notorious test site in Nevada, close to the homeland of the Hopi in the southwestern United States.

■

full of concrete caves
dug by frightened men
who cast searchlights
to restricted city skies
for Russian bombers
sure to come sooner or later,
they said. I was little,
easily fit beneath
my desk at school,
listened to the British teacher
tell of the blitz
with long shudders of her arm
showing how the planes had come
like insects out of Germany.
I looked the part
of a war-humbled refugee,
open-mouthed in the air-raid shelter
and tuning into Conelrad,
practicing how to die
in a foetal position. 1980 now

and my bones have burrowed
deeply into this world,
my tongue has traveled
its many highways
crossing mountains and seasons
and once again
we drill under tables,
store food and water
in bottles and cans—pure enough
for a century or more
of mutating under the sun.
Once again
we scan our western expanse of sky
not for bombers and Russians
but for a thing more final
than antique atom bombs.
Like earthquakes
crawling up the Richter scale
the ghosts of our future
are unpredictable
and out of control.

This is a weather report:
who knows what will end
in the fury of the storm?

January 1980.
Berkeley.

ANN DRUYAN

At Ground Zero in Hiroshima

Ann Druyan (b. 1949) is an author, lecturer, and television and movie producer who is also working to help reverse the nuclear arms race. Druyan played a key role in establishing an American seismic network in the Soviet Union to monitor Soviet compliance with their unilateral moratorium on underground nuclear tests, a joint U.S.-Soviet scientific study of implementing and verifying massive nuclear disarmament, and a U.S.-Soviet project to design a legally and scientifically viable treaty banning chemical and biological warfare that the United States has never deserted. On February 5, 1987, Druyan was arrested for the third time at the Nevada test site while protesting continuing U.S. nuclear testing in the face of a Soviet moratorium. She has described her actions in her lecture "Why We Can't Wait: The Need for a Comprehensive Nuclear Test Ban." Druyan is the widow of the distinguished American astronomer and world peace activist Carl Sagan. She has co-authored several books, including *Comet,* and her articles have appeared in numerous periodicals. She was co-writer of the Emmy and Peabody Award–winning television series *Cosmos*.

■

At ground zero in Hiroshima there is a plaque that soothes: "Rest in Peace for It Shall Not Happen Again." The desire to salvage some meaning from such a cataclysm is understandable. However, when we consider the reality of our global situation that reassurance seems the emptiest of promises.

During World War II we murdered fifty million of our own. But somehow we were left unsatisfied. Before the killing stopped we were already hard at work on streamlining the process. Our knowledge, our genius, and enormous amounts of our wealth were deployed to invent weapons that could transform whole cities into crematoria, whole continents into gas chambers. We pored over the photographs of the immolated and irradiated victims of the thirteen-kiloton Hiroshima bomb and at the very same time that we were lamenting their suffering, we were building those bombs bigger and bigger, all the way up to a sixty-megaton model. Now they come in all sizes and we have fifty thousand of them. Clearly, we are not yet serious about preventing it from happening again.

Despite this, I have hope. I believe I know what we must do. We have to stop letting the boys get away with murder by asserting our equality with them in the governance of this planet. We have to denude violence of its phony glory. We have to expose the delusion of nationalism for what it is, one of the early symptoms of the onset of the mass psychosis of war. We have to know what we are talking about so that no bomb salesman can intimidate us with the jargon of science or technology. We must arouse ourselves from our complacency towards the billion of us who have nothing. We must work for social and economic progress everywhere so that nonviolent avenues to justice remain open.

Can these things be done? As women of this era we have personal experience with the radical change that is possible when the conditions are right and there is a unity of political will. Our liberation gives me reason to believe in humanity's future. We *will* redeem the promise made at ground zero and thereby honor the heroic struggles of the 40,000 generations of life-giving women who came before us.

LILLIAM JIMÉNEZ

To the Soldiers of El Salvador
Who from 1931 to 1980 Have Ruled the Country
Through a Military Dictatorship

Lilliam Jiménez (b. circa 1950) a Salvadoran poet, has suffered imprisonment for her political convictions. A journalist who now resides in Mexico, she has published several books of poetry and a treatise on the economic and social realities of her homeland. According to the U.S. Committee in Solidarity with the People of El Salvador, Jiménez's country has experienced the loss of a huge percentage of its population to death squads, terrorism, and the poverty that results from political turmoil and economic injustice. Though her poem speaks for the dead of El Salvador, it is universally applicable to the innocent civilian victims of all wars everywhere.

■

All flesh and bone are thus betrayed,
these sons of dogs who cover life with tar
attempting to darken the Sun.

Look at them standing before History
the universal truth,
before the living and the dead
who speak from the graves and attest to their deeds.

Behind their uniforms
thousands of skeletons are crying
who are calmly awaiting with hope their appointed hour.
There is a chill that causes the earth to tremble
and frightens the birds from the forest.

The military men
are a sophism and simultaneously a dialect,
products without reason of the reason of class.
They are men
without authentic manhood.

But tomorrow
Even without desiring it,
they will have to see what must be seen.
They will have to pay
for the horrible fate of each victim,
for all the lips they silenced,
for all the dreams they ripped out of our breasts.

Tomorrow, in the center of their eyes,
the coffins will open up.
They will see face to face
all those whom they have assassinated,
all the luminous immortal fallen.

The thousands and thousands of tortured
and slain
will rise as a rising tide against them.

Translation by Mary McAnally

Carol Cohn

Sex and Death and the Rational World of Defense Intellectuals

Carol Cohn (b. 1951) has served as a senior research fellow at the Center for Psychological Studies in the Nuclear Age in Cambridge, Massachusetts. She has been a research associate in psychiatry at the Harvard Medical School. Previously, she was on the faculty of Seminar College at the New School for Social Research in New York City. She has researched and written extensively on the language and thinking of nuclear defense intellectuals, under a grant from the MacArthur Foundation. A longer version of this article—which made quite a stir in feminist intellectual circles during the dangerous days of the Cold War—can be read in the summer 1987 issue of *Signs: A Journal of Women in Culture and Society*. It holds just as true today, in the age of a renewed nuclear buildup and "Star Wars" program.

■

My close encounter with nuclear strategic analysis started in the summer of 1984. I was one of 48 college teachers attending a summer workshop on nuclear weapons, strategic doctrine, and arms control that was held at a university containing one of the nation's foremost centers of nuclear strategic studies, and that was cosponsored by another institution. It was taught by some of the most distinguished experts in the field, who have spent decades moving back and forth between academia and governmental positions in Washington. When at the end of the program I was afforded the chance to be a visiting scholar at one of the universities' defense studies center, I jumped at the opportunity.

I spent the next year immersed in the world of defense intellectuals—men (and indeed, they are virtually all men) who, in Thomas Powers's words, "use the concept of deterrence to explain why it is safe to have weapons of a kind and number it is not safe to use." Moving in and out of government, working sometimes as administrative officials or consultants, sometimes in universities and think tanks, they create the theory that underlies U.S. nuclear strategic practice.

My reason for wanting to spend a year among these men was simple, even if the resulting experiences were not. The current nuclear situation is so dangerous and irrational that one is tempted to explain it by positing either insanity or evil in our decision makers. That explanation is, of course, inadequate. My goal was to gain a better understanding of how sane men of goodwill could think and act in ways that lead to what appear to be extremely irrational and immoral results.

I attended lectures, listened to arguments, conversed with defense analysts, interviewed graduate students throughout their training, obsessed by the question, "How *can* they think this way?" But as I learned the language, as I became more and more engaged with their information and their arguments, I found that my own thinking was changing, and I had to confront a new question: How can *I* think this way? Thus, my own experience becomes part of the data that I analyze in attempting to understand not only how "they" can think that way, but how any of us can.

This article is the beginning of an analysis of the nature of nuclear strategic thinking, with emphasis on the role of a specialized language that I call "technostrategic." I have come to believe that this language both reflects and shapes the American nuclear strategic project, and that all who are concerned about nuclear weaponry and nuclear war must give careful attention to language—with whom it allows us to communicate and what it allows us to think as well as say.

I had previously encountered in my reading the extraordinary language used to discuss nuclear war, but somehow it was different to hear it spoken. What hits first is the elaborate use of abstraction and euphemism, which allows infinite talk about nuclear holocaust without ever forcing the speaker or enabling the listener to touch the reality behind the words.

Anyone who has seen pictures of Hiroshima burn victims may find it perverse to hear a class of nuclear devices matter-of-factly referred to as "clean bombs." These are weapons which are largely fusion rather than fission and they release a somewhat higher proportion of their energy as prompt radiation, but produce less radioactive fallout than fission bombs of the same yield.

"Clean bombs" may provide the perfect metaphor for the language of defense analysts and arms controllers. This language has enormous destructive power, but without emotional fallout; without the emotional fallout that would result if it were clear one was talking about plans for mass murder, mangled bodies, human suffering. Defense analysts don't talk about incinerating cities: they talk about "countervalue attacks." Human death, in nuclear parlance, is most often referred to as "collateral damage"; for, as one defense analyst said, with just the right touch of irony in his voice and a twinkle in his eye, "the Air Force doesn't target people, it targets shoe factories."

Some phrases carry this cleaning up so far as to invert meaning. The MX missile will carry ten warheads, each with the explosive power of 300 to 475 kilotons of TNT: *one* missile is the bearer of destruction approximately *250* to *400* times that of the Hiroshima bombing. Ronald Reagan has christened the MX missile "the Peacekeeper." While this renaming was the object of considerable scorn in the community of defense analysts, some of these very same analysts refer to the MX as a "damage limitation weapon."

Such phrases exemplify the astounding chasm between image and reality that characterizes technostrategic language. They also hint at the terrifying way in which the existence of nuclear devices has distorted our perceptions and redefined the world. "Clean bombs" as a phrase tells us that radioactivity is the only "dirty" part of killing people.

It is not hard to feel that one function of this sanitized abstraction is to deny the uncontrolled messiness of the situations one contemplates creating. So that we not only have clean bombs but also "surgically clean strikes": "counterforce" attacks that can purportedly "take out"—that is, accurately destroy—an opponent's weapons or command centers, without causing significant injury to anything else. The image is unspeakably ludicrous when the surgical tool is not a delicately controlled scalpel but a nuclear warhead.

Feminists have often suggested that an important aspect of the arms race is phallic worship; that "missile envy," to borrow Helen Caldicott's phrase, is a significant motivating force in the nuclear buildup. I have always found this an uncomfortably reductionist explanation and hoped that observing at the center would yield a more complex analysis. Still, I was curious about the extent to which I might find a sexual subtext in the defense professional's discourse. I was not prepared for what I found.

I think I had naively imagined that I would need to sneak around and eavesdrop on what men said in unguarded moments, using all my cunning to unearth sexual imagery. I had believed that these men would have cleaned up their acts, or that at least at some point in a long talk about "penetration aids," someone would suddenly look up, slightly embarrassed to be caught in such blatant confirmation of feminist analyses.

I was wrong. There was no evidence that such critiques had ever reached the ears, much less the minds, of these men. American military dependence on nuclear weapons was explained as "irresistible, because you get more bang for the buck." Another lecturer solemnly and scientifically announced, "To disarm is to get rid of all your stuff." A professor's explanation of why the MX missile is to be placed in the silos of the newest Minutemen missiles, instead of replacing the older, less accurate missiles, was "because they're in the nicest hole—you're not going to take the nicest missile you have and put it in a crummy hole." Other lectures were filled with discussion of vertical erector launchers, thrust-to-weight ratios, soft lay downs, deep penetration, and the comparative advantages of protracted versus spasm attacks—or what one military adviser to the National Security Council has called "releasing 70 to 80 percent of our megatonnage in one orgasmic whump."[1]

But if the imagery is transparent, its significance may be less so. I do *not* want to assert that it somehow reveals what defense intellectuals are really talking about, or their motivations; individual motives cannot necessarily be read directly from imagery, which originates in a broader cultural context. The history of the atomic bomb project itself is rife with overt images of competitive male sexuality, as is the discourse of the early nuclear physicists, strategists, and members of the Strategic Air Command.[2] Both the military itself and the arms manufacturers are constantly exploiting the phallic imagery and promise of sexual domination that their weapons so conveniently suggest. Consider the following, from the June 1985 issue of *Air Force Magazine*: Emblazoned in bold letters across the top of a two-page advertisement for the AV-8B Harrier II—"Speak Softly and Carry a Big Stick." The copy below boasts "an exceptional thrust-to-weight ratio," and "vectored thrust capability that makes the . . . unique rapid response possible."

Another vivid source of phallic imagery is to be found in descriptions of nuclear blasts themselves. Here, for example, is one by journalist William Laurence, who was brought by the Army Air Corps to witness the Nagasaki bombing.

Then, just when it appeared as though the thing had settled down into a state of permanence, there came shooting out of the top a giant mushroom that increased the size of the pillar to a total of 45,000 feet. The mushroom top was even more alive than the pillar, seething and boiling in a white fury of creamy foam, sizzling upward and then descending earthward, a thousand geysers rolled into one. It kept struggling in an elementary fury, like a creature in the act of breaking the bonds that held it down. [3]

Given the degree to which it suffuses their world, the fact that defense intellectuals use a lot of sexual imagery is not especially surprising. Nor does it, by itself, constitute grounds for imputing motivation. The interesting issue is not so much the imagery's possible psychodynamic origins as how it functions—its role in making the work world of defense intellectuals feel tenable. Several stories illustrate the complexity.

At one point a group of us took a field trip to the New London navy base where nuclear submarines are home-ported, and to the General Dynamics Electric Boat yards where a new Trident submarine was being constructed. The high point of the trip was a tour of a nuclear-powered submarine. A few at a time, we descended into the long, dark, sleek tube in which men and a nuclear reactor are encased underwater for months at a time. We squeezed through hatches, along neon-lit passages so narrow that we had to turn and press our backs to the wall for anyone to get by. We passed the cramped racks where men sleep, and the red and white signs warning of radioactive materials. When we finally reached the part of the sub where the missiles are housed, the officer accompanying us turned with a grin and asked if we wanted to stick our hands through a hole to "pat the missile." *Pat the missile?*

The imager reappeared the next week, when a lecturer scornfully declared that the only real reason for deploying cruise and Pershing II missiles in Western Europe was "so that our allies can pat them."

Some months later, another group of us went to be briefed at NORAD (the North American Aerospace Defense Command). On the way back, the Air National Guard plane we were on went to refuel at Offut Air Force Base, the Strategic Air Command headquarters near Omaha, Nebraska. When word leaked out that our landing would be delayed because the new B-1 bomber was in the area, the plane became charged with a tangible excitement that built as we flew in our holding pattern, people craning their necks to try to catch a glimpse of the B-1 bomber in the skies, and climaxed as we touched down on the runway and hurtled past it. Later, when I returned to the center I encountered a man, who, unable to go on the trip, said to me enviously, "I hear you got to pat a B-1."

What is all this patting? Patting is an assertion of intimacy, sexual possession, affectionate domination. The thrill and pleasure of "patting the missile" is the proximity of all that phallic power, the possibility of vicariously appropriating it as one's own. But patting is not only an act of sexual intimacy. It is also what one does to babies, small children, the pet dog. The creatures one pats are small, cute, harmless—not terrifyingly destructive. Pat it, and its lethality disappears.

Much of the sexual imagery I heard was rife with the sort of ambiguity suggested by "patting the missiles." The imagery can be construed as a deadly serious display of the connections between masculine sexuality and the arms race. But at the same time, it can also be heard as a way of minimizing the seriousness of militarist endeavors, of denying their deadly consequences. A former Pentagon target analyst, in telling me why he thought plans for "limited nuclear war" were ridiculous, said, "Look, you gotta understand that it's a pissing contest—you gotta expect them to use everything they've got." This image says, most obviously, that this is about competition for manhood, and thus there is tremendous danger. But at the same time it says that the whole thing is not very serious—it is just what little boys or drunk men do.

Sanitized abstraction and sexual imagery, even if disturbing, seemed to fit easily into the masculine world of nuclear war planning. What did not fit was another set of words that evoked images that can only be called domestic.

Nuclear missiles are based in "silos." On a Trident submarine, which carries 24 multiple-warhead nuclear missiles, crew members call the part of the sub where the missiles are lined up in their silos ready for launching "the Christmas tree farm." In the friendly, romantic world of nuclear weaponry, enemies "exchange" warheads; weapons systems can "marry up." "Coupling" is sometimes used to refer to the wiring mechanisms of warning and response, or to the psychopolitical links between strategic and theater weapons. The pattern in which a MIRVed missile's nuclear warheads land is known as a "footprint." These devices are called "reentry vehicles," or "RVs" for short, a term not only totally removed from the reality of a bomb but also resonant with the image of the recreational vehicles of the ideal family vacation.

These domestic images are more than simply one more way to remove oneself from the grisly reality behind the words; ordinary abstraction is adequate to that task. Calling the pattern in which bombs fall a "footprint" almost seems a willful distorting process, a playful, perverse refusal of accountability— because to be accountable to reality is to be unable to do this work.

The images evoked by these words may also be a way to tame the uncontrollable forces of nuclear destruction. Take the fire-breathing dragon under the bed, the one who threatens to incinerate your family, your town, your planet, and turn it into a pet you can pat. Or domestic imagery may simply serve to make everyone more comfortable with what they're doing. "PAL" (permissive action links) is the carefully constructed, friendly acronym for the electronic system designed to prevent the unauthorized firing of nuclear warheads. The president's annual nuclear weapons stockpile memorandum, which outlines both short- and long-range plans for production of new nuclear weapons, is benignly referred to as "the shopping list." The "cookie cutter" is a phrase used to describe a particular model of nuclear attack.

The imagery that domesticates, that humanizes insentient weapons, may also serve, paradoxically, to make it all right to ignore sentient human beings. Perhaps it is possible to spend one's time dreaming up scenarios for the use of massively destructive technology, and to exclude human beings from that technological world, because that world itself now includes the domestic, the human, the warm and playful—the Christmas trees, the RVs, the things one pats affectionately. It is a world that is in some sense complete in itself; it even includes death and loss. The problem is that all things that get "killed" happen to be weapons, not humans. If one of your warheads "kills" another of your warheads, it is "fratricide." There is much concern about "vulnerability" and "survivability" but it is about the vulnerability and survival of weapons systems, rather than people.

Another set of images suggests men's desire to appropriate from women the power of giving life. At Los Alamos, the atomic bomb was referred to as "Oppenheimer's baby"; at Lawrence Livermore, the hydrogen bomb was "Teller's baby," although those who wanted to disparage Teller's contribution claimed he was not the bomb's father but its mother. In this context, the extraordinary names given to the bombs that reduced Hiroshima and Nagasaki to ash and rubble—"Little Boy" and "Fat Man"—may perhaps become intelligible. These ultimate destroyers were the male progeny of the atomic scientists.

The entire history of the bomb project, in fact, seems permeated with imagery that confounds humanity's overwhelming technological power to destroy nature with the power to create: imagery that converts men's destruction into their rebirth. Laurence wrote of the Trinity test of the first atomic bomb: "One felt as though he had been privileged to witness the Birth of the World." In a 1985 interview, General Bruce K. Holloway, the commander in chief of the Strategic Air Command from 1968 to 1972, described a nuclear war as involving "a big bang, like the start of the universe."

Finally, the last thing one might expect to find in a subculture of hard-nosed realism and hyper-rationality is the repeated invocation of religious imagery. And yet, the first atomic bomb test was called Trinity. Seeing it, Robert Oppenheimer thought of Krishna's words to Arjuna in the *Bhagavad Gita*: "I am become death, destroyer of worlds." Defense intellectuals when challenged on a particular assumption, will often duck out with a casual, "Now you're talking about matters of theology." Perhaps most astonishing of all, the creators of strategic doctrine actually refer to their community as "the nuclear priesthood." It is hard to decide what is most extraordinary about this: the arrogance of the claim, the tacit admission that they really are creators of dogma; or the extraordinary implicit statement about who, or rather what, has become god.

Although I was startled by the combination of dry abstraction and odd imagery that characterizes the language of defense intellectuals, my attention was quickly focused on decoding and learning to speak it. The first task was training the tongue in the articulation of acronyms.

Several years of reading the literature of nuclear weaponry and strategy had not prepared me for the degree to which acronyms littered all conversations, nor for the way in which they are used. Formerly, I had thought of them mainly as utilitarian. They allow you to write or speak faster. They act as a form of abstraction, removing you from the reality behind the words. They restrict communication to the initiated, leaving the rest both uncomprehending and voiceless in the debate.

But being at the center revealed some additional, unexpected dimensions. First, in speaking and hearing, a lot of these terms are very sexy. A small supersonic rocket "designed to penetrate any Soviet air defense" is called a SRAM (for short-range attack missile). Submarine-launched cruise missiles are referred to as "slick'ems" and ground-launched cruise missiles are "glick'ems." Air-launched cruise missiles are magical "alchems."

Other acronyms serve in different ways. The plane in which the president will supposedly be flying around above a nuclear holocaust, receiving intelligence and issuing commands for where to bomb next, is referred to as "Kneecap" (for NEACP—National Emergency Airborne Command Post). Few believe that the president would really have time to get into it, or that the communications systems would be working if he were in it—hence the edge of derision. But the very ability to make fun of a concept makes it possible to work with it rather than reject it outright.

In other words, what I learned at the program is that talking about nuclear weapons is fun. The words are quick, clean, light; they trip off the tongue. You can reel off dozens of them in seconds, forgetting about how one might interfere with the next, not to mention with the lives beneath them. Nearly everyone I observed—lecturers, students, hawks, doves, men, and women—took pleasure in using the words; some of us spoke with a self-consciously ironic edge, but the pleasure was there nonetheless. Part of the appeal was the thrill of being able to manipulate an arcane language, the power of entering the secret kingdom. But perhaps more important, learning the language gives a sense of control, a feeling of mastery over technology that is finally not controllable but powerful beyond human comprehension. The longer I stayed, the more conversations I participated in, the less I was frightened of nuclear war.

How can learning to speak a language have such a powerful effect? One answer, discussed earlier, is that the language is abstract and sanitized, never giving access to the images of war. But there is more to it than that. The learning process itself removed me from the reality of nuclear war. My energy was focused on the challenge of decoding acronyms, learning new terms, developing competence in the language—not on the weapons and wars behind the words. By the time I was through, I had learned far more than an alternate, if abstract, set of words. The content of what I could talk about was monumentally different.

Consider the following descriptions, in each of which the subject is the aftermath of a nuclear attack:

> Everything was black, had vanished into the black dust, was destroyed. Only the flames that were beginning to lick their way up had any color. From the dust that was like a fog, figures began to loom up, black, hairless, faceless. They screamed with voices that were no longer human. Their screams drowned out the groans rising everywhere from the rubble, groans that seemed to rise from the very earth itself.[4]
>
> [You have to have ways to maintain communications in a] nuclear environment, a situation bound to include EMP blackout, brute force damage to system, a heavy jamming environment, and so on.[5]

There is no way to describe the phenomena represented in the first with the language of the second. The passages differ not only in the vividness of their words, but in their content: the first describes the effects of a nuclear blast on human beings; the second describes the impact of a nuclear blast on technical systems designed to secure the "command and control" of nuclear weapons. Both of these differences stem from the difference of perspective: the speaker in the first is a victim of nuclear weapons, the speaker in the second is a user. The speaker in the first is using words to try to name and contain the horror of human suffering all around her; the speaker in the second is using words to insure the possibility of launching the next nuclear attack.

Technostrategic language articulates only the perspective of the users of nuclear weapons, not the victims. Speaking the expert language not only offers distance, a feeling of control, and an alternative focus for one's energies; it also offers escape from thinking of oneself as a victim of nuclear war. No matter what one deeply knows or believes about the likelihood of nuclear war, and no matter what sort of terror or despair the knowledge of nuclear war's reality might inspire, the speakers of technostrategic language are allowed, even forced, to escape that awareness, to escape viewing nuclear war from the position of the victim, by virtue of their linguistic stance.

I suspect that much of the reduced anxiety about nuclear war commonly experienced by both new speakers of the language and longtime experts comes from characteristics of the language itself: the distance afforded by its abstraction, the sense of control afforded by mastering it, and the fact that its content and concerns are those of the users rather than the victims. In learning the language, one goes from being the passive, powerless victim to being the competent, wily, powerful purveyor of nuclear threats and nuclear explosive power. The enormous destructive effects of nuclear weapons systems become extensions of the self, rather than threats to it.

It did not take long to learn the language of nuclear war and much of the specialized information it contained. My focus quickly changed from mastering technical information and doctrinal arcana, to an attempt to understand more about how the dogma I was learning was rationalized. Since underlying rationales are rarely discussed in the everyday business of defense planning, I had to start asking more questions. At first, although I was tempted to use my newly acquired proficiency in technostrategic jargon, I vowed to speak English. What I found, however, was that no matter how well informed my questions were, no matter how complex an understanding they were based upon, if I was speaking English rather than expert jargon, the men responded to me as though I were ignorant or simpleminded, or both. A strong distaste for being patronized and a pragmatic streak made my experiment in English short-lived. I adopted the vocabulary, speaking of "escalation dominance," "preemptive strikes," and one of my favorites, "sub-holocaust engagements." This opened my way into long, elaborate discussions that taught me a lot about technostrategic reasoning and how to manipulate it.

But the better I became at this discourse, the more difficult it became to express my own ideas and values. While the language included things I had never been able to speak about before, it radically excluded others. To pick a bald example: the word "peace" is not a part of this discourse. As close as one can come is "strategic stability," a term that refers to a balance of numbers and types of weapons systems—not the political, social, economic, and psychological conditions that "peace" implies. Moreover, to speak the word is to immediately brand oneself as a soft-headed activist instead of a professional to be taken seriously.

If I was unable to speak my concerns in this language, more disturbing still was that I also began to find it harder to even keep them in my own head. No matter how firm my commitment to staying aware of the bloody reality behind the words, over and over I found that I could not keep human lives as my reference point. I found I could go for days speaking about nuclear weapons, without once thinking about the people who would be incinerated by them.

It is tempting to attribute this problem to the words themselves—the abstractness, the euphemisms, the sanitized, friendly, sexy acronyms. Then one would only need to change the worlds: get the military planners to say "mass murder" instead of "collateral damage," and their thinking would change. The problem, however, is not simply that defense intellectuals use abstract terminology that removes them from the realities of which they speak. There *is* no reality behind the words. Or, rather, the "reality" they speak of is itself a world of abstractions. Deterrence theory, and much of strategic doctrine, was invented to hold together abstractly, its validity judged by internal logic. These abstract systems were developed as a way to make it possible to, in Herman Kahn's phrase, "think about the unthinkable"—not as a way to describe or codify relations on the ground.

So the problem with the idea of "limited nuclear war," for example, is not only that it is a travesty to refer to the death and suffering caused by any use of nuclear weapons as "limited," or that "limited nuclear war" is an abstraction that obfuscates the human reality beneath any use of nuclear weapons. It is also that limited nuclear war is itself an abstract conceptual system, designed, embodied, and achieved by computer modeling. In this abstract world, hypothetical, calm, rational actors have sufficient information to know exactly what size nuclear weapon the opponent has used against which targets, and adequate command and control to make sure that their response is precisely equilibrated to the attack. No field commander would use the tactical nuclear weapons at his disposal at the height of a losing battle. Our rational actors would have absolute freedom from emotional response to being attacked, from political pressures from the populace. They would act solely on the basis of a perfectly informed mathematical calculus of megatonnage. To refer to limited nuclear war is to enter a system that is de facto abstract and grotesquely removed from reality. The abstractness of the entire conceptual system makes descriptive language utterly beside the point.

This realization helped make sense of my difficulty in staying connected to concrete lives as well as some of the bizarre and surreal quality of what people said. But there was still a piece missing. How is it possible, for example, to make sense of the following:

> The strategic stability of regime A is based on the fact that both sides are deprived of any incentive ever to strike first. Since it takes roughly two warheads to destroy one enemy silo, an attacker must expend two of his missiles to destroy one of the enemy's. A first strike disarms the attacker. The aggressor ends up worse off than the aggressed.[6]

The homeland of "the aggressed" has just been devastated by the explosions of, say, a thousand nuclear bombs, each likely to be at least 10 to 100 times more powerful than the bomb dropped on Hiroshima, and the aggressor, whose homeland is still untouched, "ends up worse off"?

I was only able to make sense of this kind of thinking when I finally asked myself: Who—or what—is the subject? In technostrategic discourse, the reference point is not human beings but the weapons themselves. The aggressor ends up worse off than the aggressed because he has fewer weapons left; any other factors, such as what happened where the weapons landed, are irrelevant to the calculus of gain and loss.

The fact that the subjects of strategic paradigms are weapons has several important implications. First, and perhaps most critically, there is no real way too talk about human death or human societies when you are using a language designed to talk about weapons. Human death simply is collateral damage—collateral to the real subject, which is the weapons themselves.

Understanding this also helps explain what was at first so surprising to me: most people who do this work are on the whole nice, even good, men, many with liberal inclinations. While they often identify their motivations as being concern about humans, in their work they enter a language and paradigm that precludes people. Thus, the nature and outcome of their work can utterly contradict their genuine motives for doing it.

In addition, if weapons are the reference point, it becomes in some sense illegitimate to ask the paradigm to reflect human concerns. Questions that break through the numbing language of strategic analysis and raise issues in human terms can be easily dismissed. No one will claim that they are unimportant. But they are inexpert, unprofessional, irrelevant to the business at hand. The discourse among the experts remains hermetically sealed. One can talk about the weapons that are supposed to protect particular peoples and their way of life without actually asking if they are able to do it, or if they are the best way to do it, or whether they may even damage the entities they are supposedly protecting. These are separate questions.

This discourse has become virtually the only response to the question of how to achieve security that is recognized as legitimate. If the discussion of weapons was one competing voice in the discussion, or one that was integrated with others, the fact that the referents of strategic paradigms are only weapons might be of less note. But when we realize that the only language and expertise offered to those interested in pursuing peace refers to nothing but weapons, its limits become staggering. And its entrapping qualities—the way it becomes so hard, once you adopt the language, to stay connected to human concerns—become more comprehensible.

Within a few weeks, what had once been remarkable became unnoticeable. As I learned to speak, my perspective changed. I no longer stood outside the impenetrable wall of technostrategic language and once inside, I could no longer see it. I had not only learned to speak a language: I had started to think in it. Its questions became my questions, its concepts shaped my responses to new ideas. Like the White Queen, I began to believe six impossible things before breakfast—not because I consciously believed, for instance, that a "surgically clean counterforce strike" was really possible, but because some elaborate piece of doctrinal reasoning I used was already predicated on the possibility of those strikes as well as on a host of other impossible things.

My grasp on what I knew as reality seemed to slip. I might get very excited, for example, about a new strategic justification for a no-first-use policy and spend time discussing the ways in which its implications for the U.S. force structure in Western Europe were superior to the older version. After a day or two I would suddenly step back, aghast that I was so involved with the *military* justifications for not using nuclear weapons—as though the moral ones were not enough. What I was actually talking about—the mass incineration of a nuclear attack—was no longer in my head.

Or I might hear some proposals that seemed to me infinitely superior to the usual arms control fare. First I would work out how and why these proposals were better and then ways to counter the arguments against them. Then it might dawn on me that even though these two proposals sounded different, they still shared a host of assumptions that I was not willing to make. I would first feel as though I had achieved a new insight. And then all of a sudden, I would realize that these were things I actually knew before I ever entered this community and had since forgotten. I began to feel that I had fallen down the rabbit hole.

The language issues do not disappear. The seductions of learning and using it remain great, and as the pleasures deepen, so do the dangers. The activity of trying to out-reason nuclear strategists in their own games gets you thinking inside their rules, tacitly accepting the unspoken assumptions of their paradigms.

Yet, the issues of language have now become somewhat less central to me, and my new questions, while still not precisely the questions of an insider, are the questions I could not have had without being inside. Many of them are more practical: Which individuals and institutions are actually responsible for the endless "modernization" and proliferation of nuclear weaponry, and what do they gain from it? What role does technostrategic rationality play in their thinking? What would a reasonable, genuinely defensive policy look like? Others are more philosophical, having to do with the nature of the "realism" claimed for the defense intellectuals' mode of thinking and the grounds upon which it can be shown to be spurious. What would an alternative rationality look like?

My own move away from a focus on the language is quite typical. Other recent entrants into this world have commented that while the cold-blooded, abstract discussions are most striking at first, within a short time you get past them and come to see that the language itself is not the problem.

I think it would be a mistake, however, to dismiss these early impressions. While I believe that the language is not the whole problem, it is a significant component and clue. What it reveals is a whole series of culturally grounded and culturally acceptable mechanisms that make it possible to work in institutions that foster the proliferation of nuclear weapons, to plan mass incinerations, of millions of human beings for a living. Language that is abstract, sanitized, full of euphemisms; language that is sexy and fun to use; paradigms whose referent is weapons; imagery that domesticates and deflates the forces of mass destruction; imagery that reverses sentient and nonsentient matter, that conflates birth and death, destruction and creation—all of these are part of what makes it possible to be radically removed from the reality of what one is talking about, and from the realities one is creating through the discourse.

Close attention to the language itself also reveals a tantalizing basis on which to challenge the legitimacy of the defense intellectuals' dominance of the discourse on nuclear issues. When defense intellectuals are criticized for the cold-blooded inhumanity of the scenarios they plan, their response is to claim the high ground of rationality. They portray those who are radically opposed to the nuclear status quo as irrational, unrealistic, too emotional— "idealistic activists." But if the smooth, shiny surface of their discourse—its abstraction and technical jargon—appears at first to support these claims, a look below the surface does not. Instead we find strong currents of homoerotic excitement, heterosexual domination, the drive toward competence and mastery, the pleasures of membership in an elite and privileged group, of the ultimate importance and meaning of membership in the priesthood. How is it possible to point to the pursuers of these values, these experiences, as paragons of cool-headed objectivity?

While listening to the language reveals the mechanisms of distancing and denial and the emotional currents embodied in this emphatically male discourse, attention to the experience of learning the language reveals something about how thinking can become more abstract, more focused on parts disembedded from their context, more attentive to the survival of weapons than the survival of human beings.

Because this professional language sets the terms for public debate, many who oppose current nuclear policies choose to learn it. Even if they do not believe that the technical information is very important, some believe it is necessary to master the language simply because it is too difficult to attain public legitimacy without it. But learning the language is a transformative process. You are not simply adding new information, new vocabulary, but entering a mode of thinking not only about nuclear weapons but also about military and political power, and about the relationship between human ends and technological means.

The language and the mode of thinking are not neutral containers of information. They were developed by a specific group of men, trained largely in abstract theoretical mathematics and economics, specifically to make it possible to think rationally about the use of nuclear weapons. That the language is not well suited to do anything but make it possible to think about using nuclear weapons should not be surprising.

Those who find U.S. nuclear policy desperately misguided face a serious quandary. If we refuse to learn the language, we condemn ourselves to being jesters on the sidelines. If we learn and use it, we not only severely limit what we can say but also invite the transformation, the militarization, of our own thinking.

I have no solutions to this dilemma, but I would like to offer a couple of thoughts in an effort to push it a little further—or perhaps even to reformulate its terms. It is important to recognize an assumption implicit in adopting the strategy of learning the language. When we outsiders assume that learning and speaking the language will give us a voice recognized as legitimate and will give us greater political influence, we assume that the language itself actually articulates the criteria and reasoning strategies upon which nuclear weapons development and deployment decisions are made. This is largely an illusion. I suggest that technostrategic discourse functions more as a gloss, as an ideological patina that hides the actual reasons these decisions are made. Rather than informing and shaping decisions, it far more often legitimizes political outcomes that have occurred for utterly different reasons. If this is true, it raises serious questions about the extent of the political returns we might get from using it, and whether they can ever balance out the potential problems and inherent ones.

I believe that those who seek a more just and peaceful world have a dual task before them—a deconstructive project and a reconstructive project that are intimately linked. Deconstruction requires close attention to, and the dismantling of, technostrategic discourse. The dominant voice of militarized masculinity and decontextualized rationality speaks so loudly in our culture that it will remain difficult for any other voices to be heard until that voice loses some of its power to define what we hear and how we name the world.

The reconstructive task is to create compelling alternative visions of possible futures, to recognize and develop alternative conceptions of rationality, to create rich and imaginative alternative voices—diverse voices whose conversations with each other will invent those futures.

Notes

1. General William Odom, "C³I and Telecommunications at the Policy Level," incidental paper from a seminar, *Command Control, Communications and Intelligence* (Cambridge, Mass.: Harvard University Center for Information Policy Research, Spring 1980), 5.

2. See Brian Easlea, *Fathering the Unthinkable: Masculinity, Scientists and the Nuclear Arms Race* (London: Pluto Press, 1983).

3. William L. Laurence, *Dawn over Zero: The Study of the Atomic Bomb* (London: Museum Press, 1974), 198–99.

4. Hisako Matsubara, *Cranes at Dusk* (Garden City, N.Y.: Dial Press, 1985).

5. General Robert Rosenberg, "The Influence of Policy Making on C³I," speaking at the Harvard seminar, *Command, Control, Communications and Intelligence*, 59.

6. Charles Krauthammer, "Will Star Wars Kill Arms Control?" *New Republic*, January 21, 1985, 12–16.

VANDANA SHIVA

Bioterror and Biosaftey

Vandana Shiva (b. 1952) is a world-renowned physicist, philosopher, and ecofeminist. She is director of the Research Foundation for Science, Technology and Ecology, New Delhi, and vice president of the Third World Network. Her books include *Water Wars: Privitization, Pollution, and Profit* (2002), *Stolen Harvest: The Hijacking of the Global Food Supply* (1999), and *Biopiracy: The Murder of Nature and Knowledge* (1997). She wrote this essay on bioterror and biosafety for *The Hindu* newspaper of New Delhi on October 19, 2001.

■

The reports of anthrax cases in Florida and New York (Fall, 2001) have put a renewed focus on bioterror—the risks and hazards posed by biological agents. From the U.S. to India, Governments are on high alert. Even the World Health Organisation has issued warnings. Americans and Europeans have been stockpiling gas masks and antibiotics, and images of policemen and investigators in biohazard suits have started to make front-page appearances in newspapers and magazines.

The panic and fear being spread about biohazards in the post–September 11 period is so different from the complacency earlier, even though the threat to public health and the environment from hazardous biological agents is not new. If we have to respond adequately and consistently to bioterror, we need to take two basic issues into account. Firstly, infective biological agents cause disease and kill, irrespective of who spreads them and how they spread. The current paranoia arises from the fear that they could get into terrorist hands.

However, terrorists can get them because they are around. And they pose hazards even if they are not in terrorist hands. As Vaclav Havel, President of the Czech Republic, said in his opening remarks of Forum 2000 in Prague on 14th October, "Bin Laden did not invent bacterial agents." They were invented in defence or corporate labs. Anthrax has been part of the ascent of biological warfare of the very states which are today worried about bioterrorism. And genetic engineering of biological organisms, both for warfare and food and agriculture, is creating new biohazards, both intended and unintended. Secondly, it is fully recognised that stronger public health systems is the only response to bioterrorism. However, precisely at a time when public health reports are needed most, they are being dismantled under privatisation and trade liberalisation pressures. Bioterrorism should help governments recognise that we desperately need strong biosafety regulation and public health systems.

The global citizens movement and the movement of concerned scientists for biosafety have been alerting Governments to the ecological and health risks of genetic engineering and therefore the imperative to test, assess and regulate the release of genetically modified organisms (GMOs) into the environment. This basic conflict over the need to assess GMOs for biohazards was at the heart of negotiations that stretched over a decade under the aegis of the United Nations Convention on Biological Diversity and were finally concluded in February 2000 in Montreal in the Protocol on Biosafety.

There are two major concerns for potential risks of biohazards from GMOs. Firstly, the vectors used for introducing genes from one organism to another to make a GMO are highly infectious and virulent biological agents. It is, in fact, their infectious nature which makes them useful as vectors to introduce alien genes into biological organisms. The risks of the use of virulent vectors for engineering novel life forms have not been assessed. And their use for bioterrorism becomes easier as they spread commercially around the world.

Secondly, since GMOs are novel organisms which have not existed in nature, their impact on the environment and on human health is not known. Ignorance of the impact is being treated as proof of safety, a totally unscientific approach. This has been called a "don't look, don't see" approach to biosafety.

Biowarfare or bioterrorism is the deliberate use of living organisms to kill people. When economic policies based on trade liberalisation and globalisation deliberately spread fatal and infectious diseases such as AIDS, TB and malaria, by dismantling health and medical systems, they too become instruments of bioterror. This is the way citizens groups have organised worldwide against the TRIPS (Trade Related Intellectual Property Rights) Agreement and GATS (General Agreement on Trade in Services) of the WTO. TRIPS imposes patents and monopolies on drugs, taking essential medicines beyond the reach of the poor.

For example, AIDS medicine, which costs $200 without patents, costs $20,000 with patents. TRIPS and patents on medicines become recipes for spreading disease and death because they take cure beyond people's reach. Similarly, privatisation of health systems as imposed by the World Bank under SAPS (Structural Adjustment Programmes) and also proposed in GATS, spreads infectious diseases because low cost, decentralised public health systems are withdrawn and dismantled. These are also forms of bioterror. They are different from the acts of terrorists only because they are perpetrated by the powerful, not the marginalised and the excluded and they are committed for the fanaticism of the free market ideology, not fundamentalist religious ideologies. But in impact they are the same. They kill innocent people and species by spreading disease.

Stopping the spread of bioterror at all these levels requires stopping the proliferation of technologies which create potentially hazardous biological organisms. It also requires stopping the proliferation of economic and trade policies which are crippling public health systems, spreading infectious diseases and leaving societies more vulnerable to bioterrorism.

JOAN SMITH

From Misogynies: Crawling from the Wreckage

Joan Smith (b. 1953) is a London-born journalist who now lives near Oxford. She worked at the *Sunday Times* from 1979 to 1984. She is the author of *Clouds of Deceit*, an investigation of Britain's early nuclear weapons industry, and of three acclaimed mysteries featuring her feminist academic-detective, Loretta Lawson: *A Masculine Ending, Why Aren't They Screaming?* and *Don't Leave Me This Way*. She is presently at work on a major examination of the romantic hero in

British culture. Her book *Mysogynies: Reflections on Myths and Malice* (1991) was reviewed by U.S. feminist author Marilyn French as a collection of essays that are "brilliant and unerring" in their observations and analyses.

■

You have to pity the poor USAF bomber pilot. There he is in his flying suit, his reflecting aviator glasses, and his multimillion dollar machine, all dressed up and nowhere to go. Until nuclear war breaks out, he is condemned to fly on endless manoeuvres in which he is forbidden to do the very thing he's trained for: kill people. Sorties like the one against Libya in 1986 are, for political reasons, pretty rare. Meanwhile, all he has to do is wait; wait, think, and dream. Sometimes he is moved to write down his dreams, as did a group of pilots from the USAF 77th Tactical Fighter Squadron stationed at Upper Heyford in Oxfordshire. They published their work in the form of a pamphlet called the *Gambler's Song Book*, named for the squadron's nickname. The introduction, which ends with a quotation from the German First World War flying ace, the Red Baron, reads:

> This book is our thoughts, our songs and our games. Lesser individuals who have never strapped their asses to a piece of flaming metal will consider these of little or no redeeming social value. Because of this, the songs contained in this book are held sacred by those of us who have. These people do not know, nor will they ever know, what it means to be a FIGHTER PILOT. The book is not for them . . . it is for us. The GAMBLERS is a collection of over 75 years of tradition. A tradition that will never die as long as enemy aggression challenges for supremacy of the skies and free men rise to defeat them. "Anything else is rubbish."[1]

The first thing to note is that these are essentially the *private* thoughts of American pilots; far from being a public relations exercise, this is what they really think. (The fact that the book was on sale at an open day at Upper Heyford in 1987 was later described by the U.S. Air Force as a mistake.) It is clear from the introduction that the men who compiled it, all pilots of F1-11 nuclear fighter-bombers, consider themselves an elite, the inheritors of an honourable tradition which is unlikely to be understood by "lesser" individuals, people who are differentiated from the authors by their implied cowardice and inaction. The songs in the book are "sacred"—set apart, entitled to veneration, dedicated to something which is not defined but which is clearly connected to the defense of the skies by "free men" against "enemy aggression." For the pilots, then, they are the songs of freedom. What do they tell us about their preoccupations?

The tone is set by the squadron's theme tune, "Heyford's Own Victor Alert Song"[2] which was written to be sung to "My Favourite Things" from *The Sound of Music*. The first verse reads:

> Reading our porno and picking our asses
> Checking our forms out and passing our gasses

Silver sleek B-61's slung below
Nuclear war and we're ready to go.

The pilot's two main concerns, sex and war, are instantly revealed; the first activity occupies their time, even in the vicarious form of reading pornography, until the second takes over. Sex and death form a continuum. A couple of verses later, the enemy is identified:

Leaving the orbit our pits start to sweat
We'll asshole the fuckers and that's a sure bet
Burn all those Ruskies [sic] and cover 'em with dirt
That's why we love sitting Victor Alert.

The sexual imagery now carries over into combat itself: the Russians, "those fuckers," will be "assholed" in turn; here the enemy's preoccupation with sex, far from being an admirable trait as it is in the American pilots, is a sign of his degeneracy and will be punished by the humiliation of buggery. (The very next stanza opens with the aside that thinking about "fagots" [sic] "scares the shit out of me." The song's final verse and chorus are as follows:

Nearing the target, our nerves they are STEADY
Switches are thrown and we got us a READY
Bay doors are open the jobs [sic] almost done
Killing those Commies, we're having some fun

When the shit fills up your flight suit
And you're feeling had, just simply remember that
Big mushroom cloud, and then you won't feel SO BAD.

The sexual imagery persists in the form of an undertone: the ambiguous phrase "we got us a READY" could apply equally to a state of preparedness for sex or for war. The chorus is similarly ambiguous. The pilot, suddenly overwhelmed by terror, is exhorted to remember that "Big mushroom cloud," the after-effect of detonation which, streaming unstoppably upwards and outwards, could well stand as a metaphor for orgasm. But the song expresses above all else a powerful mixture of bravado in the face of the enemy, and fear. The paradox of these men's existence is that the job they are trained to do—dropping nuclear bombs on the enemy, who is variously described as the "Commies," "Persian-pukes" and, in the older songs, the "Viet Cong"—is likely to cost them their lives. They exist in a state of anticipation, fuelled by simplistic right-wing politics, in which the longed-for event is also the final mission: what they are waiting for, longing for, dreaming of, is death. It is hardly surprising, then, that death—violent death—haunts the fifty-two pages of the book; yet it is also the case that the enemy who is the probably instrument of their own destruction is dealt with in an almost perfunctory way. The song "Phantom Flyers in the Sky"[3] stands out from the rest of the book in that the notional enemy *is* addressed, and addressed directly in its three short verses; its loathing of the Muslims, and in particular the Iranians, suggests it is a response to a specific event, the holding of hostages in the American embassy in Tehran. The first stanza runs:

> Phantom flyers in the sky,
> Persian-pukes prepare to die,
> Rolling in with snake and nape,
> Allah creates but we cremate.

The emotions behind the lyric, crude racism and a thirst for revenge, are relatively uncomplicated. Not so those which inspire the bulk of the songs in the book. They tend, as I said before, to be on the subjects of sex or death or, more often, sex-and-death. More specifically, they are about women and death. Time and time again, woman is the image chosen to represent death, as in the following song whose tune will immediately be evident from its title, "Ghost Fuckers in the Sky:"[4]

> An old cowpoke went riding out
> One dark and windy day
> Stopped beneath a shady tree
> And paused to beat his meat
> When all at once a slant-eyed bitch
> Came ridin' down the trail
> He stopped her and asked her
> How 'bout a piece of tail?
>
> Her tits were all a floppin'
> Her cunt ate out with clap
> Her socked it to her anyway
> And gave her ass a slap
> She shit, she moaned
> She groaned
> She threw him from her crack
> He rolled across the desert
> And broke his fucking back.

The song describes exactly the state of the F1-11 pilot's psyche as he sets off on the final mission: at long last (he is an "old cowpoke," he has been waiting for this) he sees the enemy, who both allures him and repels him ("a slant-eyed bitch came ridin' down the trail"), sees his own death embodied there ("Her cunt ate out with clap"), but his desire, fuelled by years of self-denial, is too strong ("He socked it to her anyway"). The attack, which is visualized as rape, results in his own death ("broke his fucking back"). The song is fatalistic; the protagonist unquestioningly accepts his fate.

This is not the case throughout the book. The most extraordinary and disturbing song in it is baldly entitled "I Fucked a Dead Whore;"[5] it runs as follows:

I fucked a dead whore by the road side,
I knew right away she was dead.
The skin was all gone from her tummy,
The hair was all gone from her head.

As I lay down there beside her,
I knew right away that I had sinned.
So I pressed my lips to her sweet pussy,
And sucked out the wad I'd shot in.

Sucked out, sucked out,
I sucked out the wad I'd shot in, shot in,
Sucked out, sucked out,
I sucked out the wad I'd shot in.

These lines, which bring irresistibly to mind the crimes of the Yorkshire Ripper, are very different in tone from "Ghost Fuckers in the Sky." Here, far from acquiescing in his own destruction, the protagonist triumphantly cheats death. He begins by willingly involving himself with it ("I knew right away she was dead"), even reveling in the manifestations of decay, yet refuses to pay the price of the encounter ("I knew right away that I had sinned"), withdrawing not only himself, but his life force—his sperm. It is a fantasy in which the pilot goes into battle, experiences the sexual thrill of killing, *and still manages to escape with his life*. Both songs raise the question of what the pilots see in a woman that leads them to use her as their chief image for death.

One clue lies in the way in which women's bodies appear to provoke both excitement and disgust in the pilots. Even in the song just quoted, the corpse's "pussy" is sweet, and the act of retrieving sperm provides the protagonist with an opportunity for the covert performance of a sexual act—cunnilingus—which is often construed as humiliating for men. (The song also hints at the breaking of an even greater taboo, that of homosexuality; when the protagonist sucks back his own sperm from the corpse, his part in the proceeding is analogous to that of the passive partner in the act of fellatio.) Other songs in the book are straightforward tirades directed at women's bodies in which no attempt is made to disguise the contempt the pilots feel for them, and particularly for their sexuality. The intense loathing which inspires a song called "These Foolish Things (Remind Me of You)"[6] makes this point crystal clear.

Ten pounds of tittie in a loose brassiere,
A twat that twitches like a mouses [*sic*] ear,
Ejaculation in my glass of beer
These foolish things remind me of you.

A pubic hair upon my breakfast roll,
A bloody Kotex in my toilet bowl,

The smelly fragrance of your fat asshole,
These foolish things remind me of you.

A sloppy blowjob in a taxicab,
A cunt that's covered with syphilitic scabs,
These foolish things remind me of you.

In this song, as in some of the others mentioned above, the protagonist feels a powerful and confusing blend of attraction and repulsion for the woman he is addressing. He simultaneously desires and despises both the manifestations of her sex and the feelings she provokes in him. Because the desire is strong, it seems unlikely that the woman's vagina is really "covered with syphilitic scabs"; this is a *wish* on the pilot's part, the punishment he would like to impose on her, not a description of what he can actually see. A similar image crops up in "The Ballad of Lupe,"[7] a song about a Mexican prostitute, but is this time taken further. The woman Lupe is praised at the beginning of the song for her skill at fellatio, only to wind up "dead in her tomb, while maggots crawl out of her decomposed womb" at the end. This is an important indicator of what is going on in the pilots' minds here: here death and decomposition are the woman's punishment for the pleasurable feelings she has stirred up in the protagonist. It is not a huge step from wanting women dead, thinking that they deserve to die, to appropriating them as an image for death itself. But not just for death; although the transformation is never directly acknowledged, women fulfil a further role for the pilots in that they take the place of the distant, unseen, and unknowable enemy. Indeed, it is clear from the songs that in some sense women *are* the enemy.

Why should American pilots regard women as the real enemy? The U.S. is often described as a matriarchal society, whatever that means, and it would be possible to construct an answer to the question which used that classification—the idea that the men's loathing is a response to a particular sort of power structure—as a starting-point. Such an answer would, however, be specific to one time and place, obscuring the fact that we are dealing with a phenomenon which has been observed in other, unrelated military units. Klaus Theweleit, a German academic, has studied the literature of the *Freikorps*, the private right-wing death squads which roamed Germany after the First World War, many of whose members were later recruited by the Nazis. (Rudolf Höss, commandant of Auschwitz, was a member of the *Freikorps* commanded by a man called Gerhard Rossbach and was sent to prison for five years for murder in 1923.) In his book about members of the *Freikorps, Male Fantasies,*[8] Theweleit examines a mass of material, including their novels and autobiographies. There are obvious differences between these writings and the Upper Heyford songs; for one thing, the *Freikorps* literature is much greater in volume than our little songbook. For another, most of the German material was written specifically for publication, for propaganda purposes, and its sexual content is correspondingly circumscribed by its wider market. Nevertheless, we still find passages of sexual sadism in which women undergo humiliation as a punishment for their supposed sexual activities in a manner reminiscent of the "whores" in the USAF songbook. *Riders in the German Night* by Hanns Heinz Ewers (1932) is a long, complicated novel whose *Freikorps* hero, First Lieutenant Gerhard Scholz, is incestuously loved by his sister, Käte. In order to save Scholz from prison, Käte gives herself to a Belgian colonel and gains a reputation as a whore. She is captured by a group of German youths, admirers of Scholz, who put her on trial, cut off her hair, force her to take a laxative, and march her off into the woods:

> "Jump to it, sweetheart," their leader says. "You'll find a pig's wallow down there—the sort of place a prize slut like you belongs!"
>
> She stood there on the country road, helpless, immobile.
>
> "Get a move on, fairy princess!" the leader warned.
>
> "Into the woods with you. A bit of movement will soon warm you up. A sight for sore eyes, you are—with your bald head and shit all over your dress!" The other boy gave her a whack across her fanny with his switch. "Move it, you whore, before I have to do it for you!"
>
> She turned around and felt a second lash across her left breast. The pain bit into her. She let out a shrill scream.[9]

Käte's captors leave her to wander through the woods, too ashamed of her condition to approach anyone and ask for help. Eventually she dies of pneumonia. There is a striking parallel between Käte the "whore," bald and shit-smeared, and the "dead whore" whom the USAF airman found by the roadside. Each woman is punished for her sexuality—the whore for being a whore (how did he know that's what she was, by the way? Because *all* women are whores?), Käte because of her incestuous passion and her relationship with the Belgian colonel, even though the purpose of the latter was her brother's freedom. Scholz himself understands this perfectly: in Theweleit's words, "he finds the lads'" action above reproach; indeed he commissions his own attorney to take over the defense of his sister's murderers.

What the *Freikorps* writings lack in descriptions of sex they make up for in those of violence. At first glance this differentiates them from the USAF songs, in which women tend to be already dead when the action begins or progress to that state without obvious violence; one explanation for this is that the *Freikorps* men were seasoned fighters, familiar with cavalry charges and street battles in a way that airmen, engaging in combat only at long distance, are not (this is particularly true of the Upper Heyford pilots, few of whom have ever been in action). Favourite targets for the *Freikorps* fighters are the Red Army riflewomen, fantasy monsters who, according to E. F. Berendt's National Socialist Primer, a propaganda publication from 1935, "were the sort of cruel furies only Bolshevism could devise. While the heart of one of the men of the Red Army might be moved to pity at the sight of suffering innocents, those women were bestialized and devoid of all human feelings."[10] In other words, we are back with the idea that, no matter who the ostensible enemy might be, women always constitute the group who are most to be feared. Theweleit quotes a passage from Edwin Dwinger's novel *Die letzten Reiter* ("The Last Riders," 1935) in which one of these Red Army women, Marja, falls into *Freikorps* hands and is murdered by assassins hired by the hero, Pahlen:

> Pahlen pulls out a wallet that still gleams with the imprint of a seven-pointed crown, its edges worn smooth with use, and hands them a large bill. "There's nothing to be afraid of. It's not against orders. She's murdered so many people that this is simply a punishment for her crimes."
>
> "A rifle-woman then?" the first one asks.
>
> "A genuine rifle-woman!" Pahlen nods absent-mindedly.
>
> The first man nods and licks his lips. "Then everything's in order. We'd have done it even without the bill. One of the famous rifle-women, is she?" He repeats, shaking his head as he stares at her. Then they bend down again, grab her by her shattered arms, and haul her brutally away. Pahlen takes one look at her face; she seems fully conscious, yet it is distorted by an animal hatred. Curses spring from her protruding lips, pouring forth with every breath she takes.[11]

A few minutes later, Pahlen's squadron moves off. He passes a stream packed with the bodies of dead Bolsheviks:

> The last body they ride past seems to be that of a woman. But it's very hard to tell, since all that's been left is a bloody mass, a lump of flesh that appears to have been completely lacerated with whips and is now lying within a circle of trampled, reddish slush.[12]

Although Pahlen has not witnessed the killing himself, he relives it vicariously in this passage—first the whipping, then the trampling into "reddish slush." In another Dwinger novel, *Auf halbem Wege* ("Only Half Way," 1939), his *Freikorps* hero Donat is confronted by a mob of shouting, howling women and shoots one of them:

> Everything turns suddenly to frenzied flight. Yet Donat sees nothing of this. He sees only the woman who was standing there before him a moment ago. It threw her onto her back, as if she had been blown over by some gigantic wind. Is that thing at his feet really her? That person without a face? The head isn't really a head anymore, just a monstrous, bloody throat. "I warned her," Donat thinks to himself, trembling. "I warned her . . ."[13]

The *Freikorps* men's attempts to justify their attacks on women have a subtle parallel in the Upper Heyford songbook. Here we find an emphasis not on women's guilt in being allied with the actual enemy (and in being even more barbarous than he happens to be), but on their sexual infidelity and their proclivity to use up men. Several of the songs about sexually active women warn of their insatiability: "She'll suck out your guts." In a song called "No Balls At All"[14] the theme is female conspiracy; a woman who has married a man "with a very short peter and no balls at all" bemoans her husband's sexual incapacity to her mother and is advised to take lovers. The result is a bouncing baby foisted on the cuckolded husband. "Masturbating Man,"[15] a complaint about the untrustworthiness of women, begins with the line:

Melinda was mine, til [*sic*] the time that I found her, sucking Jim, blowing him.

The song ends with the protagonist's averral that:

. . . until I can find me,
A girl who'll lay and won't play games behind me,
I'll be what I am a Masturbating Man.

These complaints have a manufactured air, just as do the *Freikorps* fantasies about wild-eyed, barbarous rifle-women; we are faced with the question of why these diverse groups of military men should detest women to so great a degree and take pleasure in their destruction. Klaus Theweleit's perceptive observation about the *Freikorps* men seems equally true of both groups:

The women's crime seems to be that they excite the men too much and that the men cannot stand this inner turmoil.[16]

He backs it up with a revealing passage *from Der Berg der Rebellen* ("The Mountain of the Rebels," 1937) by Kurt Eggers:

With their screams and filthy giggling, vulgar women excite men's urges. Let our revulsion flow into a single river of destruction. A destruction which will be incomplete if it does not also trample their hearts and souls.[17]

Military men, probably more than any others, spend their lives in a state of repressed emotion. Normal human reactions to dangerous situations must be kept at bay if they are to carry out their function. Women pose a particular threat, since love and affection could force a chink in the men's armour which would then allow in unwanted feelings—fear and the urge to flee instead of fight. (The characters in some *Freikorps* novels boast openly of their imperviousness to female charms.) But this is not in itself the whole answer. It is clear that the men are also afraid of women's sexuality, both because it disgusts them and because they cannot cope with the intense feelings it arouses in them. The reaction is partly explained by the fact that most Judaeo-Christian societies hate sex, and the men in them have inherited a tradition which projects on to women the bad feelings that accompany their own arousal. By obliterating the women they hope to avoid having the feelings in the future; that is why Eggers, in the passage quoted above, is determined that the annihilation of women should be complete, that it should "trample their hearts and souls"—vague terms which nevertheless refer to the repressed feelings and sensibility which, in a curious reversal, the women are seen to have projected on to the men rather than the other way round. But the fear of women expressed by both sets of men is so overwhelming that it cannot simply be sexual, and I think the final answer is this: men who are part of a macho, swaggering culture, as are the USAF pilots at Upper Heyford and as were the proto-Nazis of the *Freikorps*, have placed themselves in a position where they constantly have to prove their masculine identity. A key element of this identity is their distance, their separateness, from women. One of the characteristics that differentiates them from the other sex is their prized absence of feeling (men who *do* feel emotion are dismissed as sissies). Having thus built up their defences, they are unused to coping with intense urges or desires. When they are suddenly caught unawares, whether by love or lust or pity or rage, they have no experience to fall back on, nothing to guide them or tell them how to cope. They are swept back helplessly to the one period in their lives when the barricades against emotion were still down, the earliest days of their existence when they were in a close symbiotic relationship with their mothers. That is a lost paradise: no matter how happy they were at that time, nestled in women's arms and reliant on them for affections and sustenance, they have since learned to despise themselves for their involuntary acquiescence to female power and for their "feminine" acceptance of feeling. Even worse, it was a time when they lacked the vaunted masculine identity, when they were half merged with the female, not knowing the boundary between the fledgeling selves and their mothers' accommodating bodies. Now, as outwardly tough but secretly vulnerable adult men, their greatest fear is a return to that humiliating state, a return which threatens every time they are confronted by intense feeling. For them, emotion is truly overwhelming, a threat to their carefully constructed masculine existence; is it surprising that the dreams of such men are dreams of dead women?

Notes

1. *Gamblers' Song Book*, USAF 77th Tactical Fighter Squadron, Upper Heyford, Oxon; compiled by Capt. George 'Kelmaniac' Kelman, Capt. Thomas "Tunes" Theobald, Capt. Mike "Boomer" Clowers, Capt. Tom "Grunt" Carmichael, SRA John "The Kid" Galletta.

2. Ibid., 1.

3. Ibid., 30.

4. Ibid., 21

5. Ibid., 13.

6. Ibid., 32.

7. Ibid., 14.

8. Klaus Theweleit, *Male Fantasies* (London: Polity Press and Minneapolis: University of Minnesota Press, 1987).

9. Ibid., 119.

10. Ibid., 76.

11. Ibid., 188

12. Ibid., 189

13. Ibid., 179–80.

14. *Gamblers' Song Book*, 7.

15. Ibid., 27.

16. Theweleit, 180.

17. Ibid., 180.

JASMINA TESANOVIC

Women and Conflict: A Serbian Perspective

Jasmina Tesnaovic (b. 1954) was born in Belgrade, Yugoslavia. She attended English elementary and high schools while living in Egypt and Italy, and graduated from the University of Milan. Living in Rome, she worked on several films and as a correspondent for various news media. In 1978, she was one of the three organizers of the first feminist conference in eastern Europe, in Belgrade. Returning to Belgrade in 1979, she worked for TV Belgrade and translated books from the Italian and English. In 1994, together with two other women, she founded the first women's publishing house in Serbia, Feministicka 94. She teaches creative writing at Women's Studies of Belgrade and is a full-time freelancer publishing in major papers in Yugoslavia and Italy as well as in *Index on Censorship*, the *Philadelphia Inquirer*, the *Washington Post*, and the *Guardian*. She is one of the most prominent writers of her country, her fiction including *The Invisible Book*, *In Exile*, *A Women's Book*, and *The Mermaid* (Borislav Pekic Award). Stories by Jasmina Tesanovic have been translated and published in Italy, Austria, Hungary, and the United States. Her non-fiction works include *The Suitcase: Refugee Voices from Bosnia and Croatia* (edited with J. Mertus), *On Normality: A Moral Opera by a Political Idiot*, a diary of daily life in Belgrade from 1998 to 1999, excerpted in *Granta* and published in the United States as *Diary of a Political Idiot*. It has also been translated and published in Spanish, Portuguese, Italian, Swedish, Bulgarian, Albanian, and Russian and adapted into a film for German television. *Me and My Multicultural Street*, a book of war essays in which this piece appears, was published in 2001. Current projects include *Matrimony*, a diaristic vigil following the year after her mother's death from lack of medicine during sanctions, and *The Globalization with Evil*, a Baghdad-Belgrade correspondence with Iraqi artist and writer Nuha al-Radi.

■

In 1991 when the war started in the former Yugoslavia I was sitting in a restaurant called Srpska Kafana in downtown Belgrade with two men and another woman when two policemen came to our table. At that time we had many checkpoints because the military police were trying to find men who were dodging the draft—70 percent (inoffical data) of men from Belgrade refused to participate in the war. The men showed the police their identity cards, they were checked and thanked politely. I handed them my document. They looked at me in a very strange way and said: "These men are answering for you. This is a matter of life and death. This is war!"

I am ashamed to say that my first reaction to the war, which I knew was a dirty war, was a gender reaction and not a pacifist one. Why, I wondered indignantly, in matters of life and death are women excluded like second-class citizens? Why is it nobody asks me if I want to fight in the war? If you take up a gun and you kill or risk being killed, you are in a completely different position than if you don't take up a gun and you don't kill. This is a man's war in a man's world.

This paper attempts to deal with the difference of the experiences of men and women in war, differences that are completely defined by gender and sex, and particularly with the experiences of women. Men, even if they came from prison camps with scars on their bodies, are eager to talk about the ideology of the war, to quote the politicians, and to have their own nebulous explanations about history, graves or whatever other symbols they fought for, instead of telling their own stories. In contrast, their wives say: "We know nothing; it was they who fought the war." Yet it is the personal stories of women that really show the complexities of the war and tell what really happened.

I will refer to a book, *The Suitcase: Refugee Voices from Bosnia and Croatia* (University of California Press, Berkeley 1997), a collective work of peaceful people, mostly women, and we did this work during the worst years of war in the former Yugoslavia. Doing this book was, for me, a healing process. I am a writer and I cannot change the world by writing; I couldn't really do anything useful when the war started and destroyed my life along with everybody else's. I tried to understand what was going on and to give an answer through writing about the war, through the innocent witnesses of this war. 95 percent of those killed in this war were civilians and only 5 percent were soldiers, which is completely the opposite of what happened in the First World War. Since there were many wars going on in the former Yugoslavia—a nationalist war, an ethnic war, a religious war, a civil war—all people from the former Yugoslavia became refugees at a certain point by being forced in one way or another to make a decision about which side they belonged to, what their nationality was, even if they were from mixed marriages, as most were, and without any political or national conscience, as most people born after World War II were, being Yugoslavs. And looking back now at this book that was finished in 1995, I can say this book is a nostalgic and romantic book. Nearly all the refugees we spoke to at that time, before the Dayton treaty, were claiming that they would go back home and start their lives anew as soon as the war was finished. Now, there is no way to go back, because the same states and policies that expelled them are not letting them go back.

National, state and public identity in women are a secondhand identity. Women take their name from their father, they change it to their husband's, and very often they are supported or protected by a son after their spouse's death, or adopt a new identity with the next husband. Their bond to their society or its credo is completely—philosophically, legally and psychologically—of a different kind and nature compared to men's. They construct their identity in support of their men more than in support of their nation or state. This is as true now as it was in ancient Greece, when women could at any time be sent back from their husband's home to their father's without their children. This explains both how women can be stateless and how they can be nationalistic, adopting the allegiances of the man who is currently the source of their support.

I will tell you a very typical story of a woman refugee, from the book *The Lawbreakers*. A Serbian women married to a Croat lived in the Muslim-dominated city of Bugojno in Bosnia. At the outbreak of the war her husband decided to stay because there was an alliance between Croats and Muslims, but when this alliance started to break he decided that they should leave for Croatia. They were a middle-aged couple with three grownup children. Now this woman was only ethnically a Serb. She was married to a Croat, she took his surname, she even converted to Catholicism when she married. Her citizenship was Bosnian, like her husband's and her children's, and her family was from Bugojno for many generations. When they came to the border of Croatia, heading toward Germany, the Croats wouldn't let her in because she wasn't ethically Croatian. Her husband and her children were admitted, and she was sent away. She couldn't go back to her city in war without a husband—being a Serb she would be killed—so for the first time in her life she headed toward Serbia where she ethnically belonged, with serious doubt that she would be admitted with her Bosnian passport and Croatian surname. Arriving at the Hungarian border without proper documents, she was arrested and put in prison with common criminals. She had a hard time proving that she was a refugee, but after a week they released her, gave her refugee papers, put her in a refugee camp at the border, and asked her to pay for her prison stay. As a refugee, she is not provided for by the state as a criminal would be. Only by paying can she get her refugee status because she cannot claim direct national, ethnic, or state protection that is provided only for men and their children, because only men are bearers of legality or ethnic purity in old fashioned states.

The problem is that she has no single, one-way identity. She has a multiple identity that is only exposed by a critical situation. Hannah Arendt writes that in modern society women are the biggest minority; they are a majority in number but they are treated as any minority, legally speaking. Arendt adds that very often minorities are only recognized by the law when they break it.

During the war, misogyny becomes very apparent in political life, particularly in the dividing line between heroes and traitors. The Yugoslav official policy approves of neither Radovan Karadzic nor Biljana Plavsic—the two leaders in the Serbian part of Bosnia. But when they mention Mr. Karadzic, they respectfully call him a psychiatrist and a poet, while Plavsic is called an ugly baba, an old lady who should stay at home and take care of her grandchildren. Today Plavsic is called a traitor because she collaborates with "the foreigners," the peace-keeping troops. People who voted for "Sloba" (Milosevic) often hate his wife, Mira Markovic. They call her a raven, a witch, a crazy and ugly woman, who makes him do all these bad things. Maybe, the logic goes, the war is something his wife put him up to and is therefore responsible for and not him or the foreign powers!

This is a typical social exorcism of evil through women, so well-known in the past in the branding of women as witches. The (re)construction of women during wars, especially nationalistic wars, can be defined with three words: instrumentalization, naturalization, and traditionalization. Instrumentalization is when women in emergency situations like war are used in the place of men for men's goals. Like working in factories and then being kicked out when the men come back, even if they perform their jobs better. Naturalization is when women, as well as men, become degraded from their politically and socially constructed social selves, to their functions dictated by the construct of "Nature": those who give birth, who breastfeed, bury the dead. The concept of natural born women denies women the right to emancipation and the status of persons. Traditionalization is a conservative political tool of gender in society. Again in an emergency situation as the war is, women are asked to perform their traditional duties in traditional ways: to be mothers, wives, to dress and act as the traditional society prescribes. Antiabortion politics with a strong Catholic flavor surfaced in Croatia, as did a pro-life nationalist policy in Serbia. In other words, any free space for women ceases to exist. Once again, women carry the loot of nations on their backs, and women who refuse to accept this are traitors and witches.

Because it is a movement when society becomes totemistic, every nationalism, positive or negative, is based on a differently constructed man-woman relationship in which there is one point in common: the emergence of manliness in men and the subordination of women. Gender roles take extremes of masculinity and femininity. Women have to become the angels of their homes and take on all family duties. But that includes traditionally male work such as engineers, workers, miners and doctors while men are presumably saving the world or their lives. Many women eagerly accept this contradictory demand because they get the public space that is often denied them in peace time.

In this role, women are again used as instruments for men's goals. I heard of two villages on the frontline of Bosnia that were very close: one was Muslim-dominated and the other populated by Serbs. Every day men from the villages would take up their arms and go to the frontline to shoot, while the women would presumably stay at home. Food was only available through the black market shared by the warring parties. So women went to the frontline as well and exchanged goods while their men were shooting over their heads. They then returned home and never spoke of where they had been. Although the men knew about the black market, and knew where their cigarettes and food had come from they kept their honor by not mentioning the collaboration with the enemy. The deal was to keep them silent and stick to their roles: heroes fight and angels stay at home.

Another true story is one of an ethnically divided city in Croatia in which, during the war, the Serbian part had water and the Croatian part electricity. After some time the women became angry about trying to do the washing, so they brought their washing machines and their laundry to the dividing line between the two parts of the city. They attached the machines to the electricity on one side and the water on the other and chatted together and exchanged information while washing the clothes, each staying on their proper side. But this emergence of women into the public sphere lasts only as long as the war lasts. Women are thrown back into the private sphere the moment the warriors come back home. We saw this after World War II in the USA and in Europe, when women were once again denied the freedom of a complete life, after having proven that they could do everything men could do and sometimes better. Traditionalization of society comes as a consequence of this phenomenon of extreme reversal: women sent back home become wives who tend to occupy themselves with petty things all day long.

Muslim women suffered most from traditionalization because being a Muslim in Bosnia was mostly a religious identity and not a strong cultural identity. Muslim refugees were sometimes sent to fundamentalist Arab countries, for example, Pakistan, where modern girls in miniskirts were told to wear veils and their husbands were free to take more wives.

Another conflict women face in war is whether to support state or private interests, that is, the lives of their men. Women who refuse to take part in the war and support the main dominant ideology are so-called traitors. In past centuries they were called witches and were burned and hanged. At the beginning of the war in the former Yugoslavia, when the JNA federal army tried to occupy Slovenia, the mothers of mobilized soldiers made demonstrations, just as in ancient Greece when the first demonstration of soldiers' mothers occurred, for the same reasons. Immediately they were called traitors and this word continued to be attached to women throughout the war.

Women in wartime also suffer a gender-violence that in war comes with all its contradictory moments. I am referring to rape. This is a true story: She was a 19-year-old girl who lived in Bosnia with her family. When the war began her brothers fought on the Serbian side, while she huddled in cellars in the part of the city occupied by the army. She was raped by soldiers and became pregnant. When her father discovered that she was pregnant and by whom he decided that she could not go on living with them. So she ran away to another city. Before the baby was born she received this message from her father: "If you have a boy you can come back home, but if you have a girl, we don't want you." She delivered a girl and gave up the baby for adoption. She returned home because she needed her family emotionally; she was still more a child than a mother. However, over the next few months she suffered a terrible sense of guilt and she decided to go back and get her baby. Helped by women's groups, she got her baby, got a flat, and tried to live a normal life. She managed for a few months. And then one night, purely by chance, she was found standing on the ledge of her window by a friend as if she were in a trance, ready to jump. After coming in off the window ledge she explained what had happened to her; it was night, the moonlight was very strong lighting the beautiful face of her sleeping baby. As she gazed at her little angel she realized who the father was. The face of the person she loved most in the world—her baby—was also the face of the person she hated most in the world—her rapist. She had an impulse to kill her baby but decided to kill herself instead. When reality splits in this way, one's mind splits as well.

Judith Lewis Herman, in her book *Trauma and Recovery*, draws a parallel between the survivors of domestic violence (such as rape or battering) and soldiers surviving heroic wars, as the same kind of trauma and violence, whether private or public. It is a lifelong scar that heals but never fades. This is one way that men's and women's experiences of war are actually quite similar, though they are seldom seen as such. Women bear shame, public and personal, while men are regarded as heroes. But then on the contrary, women's trauma is recognized and treated as such while men's is frequently kept secret: the price of being a hero.

The bodies of these women were used and abused as if they were territory to be conquered or abandoned. If women were used for the purpose of ethnic cleansing, if raping women was a way of sealing a territory and planting a flag on it, it proves that these women were tortured as women, and that the crime of rape is clearly a gender crime. That is valid from women's point of view, but not from men's. To a raped women, the primary trauma is her rape; it is less important, if at all, whether the rapist was a man from her community or not. For men, the main point is the patriarchal right over the property of the woman's body, so that the ethnically "other" perpetrators become more important than the victim, just as to the rapist, the otherness of the victim excused the crime. Once again women are invisible. In order to prosecute a crime, there has to be a law that makes this crime visible and transparent as a crime against gender.

With hard work, international feminists have made sure that rape is no longer a normal practice in war, nor less important than killing and torture. Victims of rape are not covered by official witness protection programs. They cannot stay anonymously until the trial or be given a shelter. Women have to testify that they were raped, sign the indictment, and then go back to their homes where publicity becomes an additional trial to bear among family and friends. If they admit the rape, women cannot protect their children born from rape from suffering social stigma. So these women are driven to silence and the crime to invisibility.

Trauma takes other forms than the specific abuse of rape and has many effects. Very often in speaking to women who had suffered the violence of war I saw that they had a terrible sense of guilt and depression. Yet, these women hadn't committed any violent act, indeed many had been raped. But they felt they should have done more to protect their men, their village or their country. They took the responsibility directly into their bodies, suffering painful symptoms of depression and guilt because of this big thing they had nothing to do with, from which, on the contrary, they were excluded. A woman refugee in Switzerland, safe in exile, developed a toothache. She had refugee status that covered her health care, but she didn't go for treatment. Her face swelled and she suffered because she wanted to feel the pain, because she couldn't see her face in the mirror otherwise: a typical symptom of hysteria. She believed that if she went to the doctor, he would realize how guilty she was for the war and that she didn't have the right to be treated. She believed that the pain she suffered was proof that she was alive and, at the same time, a punishment for staying alive. Victims of trauma often have a sense of guilt for something else that is really guilt for staying alive. From this sense of guilt I would directly identify the source of the notion of a collective guilt. I definitely do not believe collective guilt exists but I am sure that a collective sense of guilt exists, and it is mainly a feminine body of guilt. Women are the designated psychological bearers of the collective conscience of a community. Luckily enough, from this collective sense of guilt comes a personal sense of guilt, and then out of that comes a vital moment that survivors recovering from trauma need: a strong sense of duty, a need to survive, to save the values of life and civilization, of morals, and to do something against the war, against violence.

Women refugees from the former Yugoslavia, from this guilt-inspired sense of duty, developed a women's solidarity during the war as a constant everywhere. Women helped each other throughout the war, recognizing in each other a more similar position than in that of their men, unrelated to their ethnic or national state. They protected each other with false names and nationalities, risked lives, wrote letters, gave promises and kept them. In the new Yugoslavia, 70 percent of new groups—feminist, conflict resolution, Women in

Black, opposition parties—were made of women. Even if they had a man as a formal leader, they were created and energized by women.

As a war survivor, and as a political idiot, I say that this is the only politics I still believe in, politics without heroes, big ideas, big words or big promises. I believe only in anonymous heroines. I don't think anybody can save me anymore or fulfill my needs unless I do it myself with my own means and language. On the other hand, my enemy is no longer a bad hero, nor a politician, nor a person in power, but the culture that makes such primitive people possible and empowers them. Such people can ruin your personal life and take away years of normality that may never return. Even worse, in so doing, they changed the world, they changed our country, our children. Our children are children of nationalism, if not nationalists themselves. They have no other identity except for the Serbian one: claustrophobic, xenophobic, and biased against the rest of the world. These young people grew up in war, cut off from the rest of the world and from the exchange of information and ideas. These children belong more to nationalist policy than to us, mothers who bear a sense of guilt for only staying alive without protecting altogether our values and culture, for not making the world a better home.

BARBARA KINGSOLVER

A Pure, High Note of Anguish

Barbara Kingsolver (b. 1955) was raised in eastern Kentucky. She attended DePauw University in Indiana, where she majored in biology and became active in anti–Vietnam War protests, and pursued graduate studies in biology and ecology at the University of Arizona in Tucson. A position as a science writer for the University of Arizona soon led her into feature writing for journals and newspapers. Her articles and essays have appeared in a variety of publications, including the *Nation*, the *New York Times*, and *Smithsonian*. Her first novel, *The Bean Trees* (1988), was enthusiastically received by critics. For Kingsolver, writing is a form of political activism. When she was in her twenties she discovered Doris Lessing. "I read the Children of Violence novels and began to understand how a person could write about the problems of the world in a compelling and beautiful way." She has also written *Homeland and Other Stories* (1989), the novels *Animal Dreams* (1990) and *Pigs in Heaven* (1993), the essay collection *High Tide in Tucson: Essays from Now and Never* (1995), the collection of poetry *Another America: Otra America* (1992), and the nonfiction book, *Holding the Line: Women in the Great Arizona Mine Strike of 1983* (1989). Her novel *The Poisonwood Bible* (1998) earned worldwide praise; *Prodigal Summer* (2000) is a novel set in southern Appalachia; and *Small Wonder* (2002) presents twenty-three essays wherein she praises nature, family, literature, and the joys of everyday life while analyzing war, violence, and poverty. This article first appeared in the *Los Angeles Times* on September 23, 2001.

■

TUCSON—I want to do something to help right now. But I can't give blood (my hematocrit always runs too low), and I'm too far away to give anybody shelter or a drink of water. I can only give words. My verbal hemoglobin never seems to wane, so words are what I'll offer up in this time that asks of us the best citizenship we've ever mustered. I don't mean to say I have a cure. Answers to the main questions of the day—Where was that fourth plane headed? How did they get knives through security?—I don't know any of that. I have some answers, but only to the questions nobody is asking right now but my 5-year-old. Why did all those people die when they didn't do anything wrong? Will it happen to me? Is this the worst thing that's ever happened? Who were those children cheering that they showed for just a minute, and why were they glad? Please, will this ever, ever happen to me?

There are so many answers, and none: It is desperately painful to see people die without having done anything to deserve it, and yet this is how lives end nearly always. We get old or we don't, we get cancer, we starve, we are battered, we get on a plane thinking we're going home but never make it. There are blessings and wonders and horrific bad luck and no guarantees. We like to pretend life is different from that, more like a game we can actually win with the right strategy, but it isn't. And, yes, it's the worst thing that's happened, but only this week. Two years ago, an earthquake in Turkey killed 17,000 people in a day, babies and mothers and businessmen, and not one of them did a thing to cause it. The November before that, a hurricane hit Honduras and Nicaragua and killed even more, buried whole villages and erased family lines and even now, people wake up there empty-handed. Which end of the world shall we talk about? Sixty years ago, Japanese airplanes bombed Navy boys who were sleeping on ships in gentle Pacific waters. Three and a half years later, American planes bombed a plaza in Japan where men and women were going to work, where schoolchildren were playing, and more humans died at once than anyone thought possible. Seventy thousand in a minute. Imagine. Then twice that many more, slowly, from the inside.

There are no worst days, it seems. Ten years ago, early on a January morning, bombs rained down from the sky and caused great buildings in the city of Baghdad to fall down—hotels, hospitals, palaces, buildings with mothers and soldiers inside—and here in the place I want to love best, I had to watch people cheering about it. In Baghdad, survivors shook their fists at the sky and said the word "evil." When many lives are lost all at once, people gather together and say words like "heinous" and "honor" and "revenge," presuming to make this awful moment stand apart somehow from the ways people die a little each day from sickness or hunger. They raise up their compatriots' lives to a sacred place—we do this, all of us who are human—thinking our own citizens to be more worthy of grief and less willingly risked than lives on other soil. But broken hearts are not mended in this ceremony, because, really, every life that ends is utterly its own event—and also in some way it's the same as all others, a light going out that ached to burn longer. Even if you never had the chance to love the light that's gone, you miss it. You should. You bear this world and everything that's wrong with it by holding life still precious, each time, and starting over.

And those children dancing in the street? That is the hardest question. We would rather discuss trails of evidence and whom to stamp out, even the size and shape of the cage we might put ourselves in to stay safe, than to mention the fact that our nation is not universally beloved; we are also despised. And not just by "The Terrorist," that lone, deranged non-man in a bad photograph whose opinion we can clearly dismiss, but by ordinary people in many lands. Even by little boys—whole towns full of them it looked like—jumping for joy in school shoes and pilled woolen sweaters.

There are a hundred ways to be a good citizen, and one of them is to look finally at the things we don't want to see. In a week of terrifying events, here is one awful, true thing that hasn't much been mentioned: Some people believe our country needed to learn how to hurt in this new way. This is such a large lesson, so hatefully, wrongfully taught, but many people before us have learned honest truths from wrongful deaths. It still may be within our capacity of mercy to say this much is true: We didn't really understand how it felt when citizens were buried alive in Turkey or Nicaragua or Hiroshima.

Or that night in Baghdad. And we haven't cared enough for the particular brothers and mothers taken down a limb or a life at a time, for such a span of years that those little, briefly jubilant boys have grown up with twisted hearts. How could we keep raining down bombs and selling weapons, if we had? How can our president still use that word "attack" so casually, like a move in a checker game, now that we have awakened to see that word in our own newspapers, used like this: Attack on America.

Surely, the whole world grieves for us right now. And surely it also hopes we might have learned, from the taste of our own blood, that every war is both won and lost, and that loss is a pure, high note of anguish like a mother singing to any empty bed. The mortal citizens of a planet are praying right now that we will bear in mind, better than ever before, that no kind of bomb ever built will extinguish hatred.

"Will this happen to me?" is the wrong question, I'm sad to say. It always was.

THERESA HITCHENS

Why Missile Defense Will Not Make Us Safer

Theresa Hitchens (b. 1959) is vice president of the Center for Defense Information (CDI), a non-profit, Washington-based security think tank. She has had a long career in defense and foreign policy analysis, spending more than a decade as a defense journalist in Washington and Brussels, including two years as editor of the international defense trade journal *Defense News*. Prior to joining CDI in mid-2001, Hitchens was research director at the British American Security Information Council, a transatlantic security research organization with headquarters in Washington and London. Hitchens sits on the editorial board of the *Bulletin of the Atomic Scientists,* and is a member of Women in International Security and the Institute for Strategic and International Studies.

■

In the wake of the national tragedy of September 2001, it is now certain that the United States will aggressively pursue a national missile defense program.

President George W. Bush has informed his Russian counterpart, Vladimir

Putin, that the United States intends, no matter Russian concerns, to scrap the long-standing Anti-Ballistic Missile Treaty in order to do so. Congress has quietly gone along with an $8.3-billion boost in the missile defense budget—loathe to challenge the president as he leads the U.S. war on terrorism.

But even if a missile shield can be made to work—and that is a big, big if—it is unlikely to make us any safer. And, for a number of troubling reasons, we can only hope that it will not make us less so.

Many smart people in U.S. leadership circles have been mesmerized by the "Star Wars" dream. It isn't hard to see why. Today's world is a scary place. A number of countries, and even terrorist groups such as Osama bin Laden's al Qaeda, have been trying to obtain nuclear, biological, and chemical weapons. Because of the rapid pace and spread of technology, long-range missiles to deliver such weapons are easier for our enemies to build. If there is some chance we could put up a technological shield to protect us, why wouldn't we want to try?

The logic of this argument is seemingly simple. Unfortunately, the world is complex. And the Star Wars dream offers only false hope—hope of an America no longer insulated from the rest of the teeming world by its oceans, but newly safe in a bubble of technological and military superiority.

The first problem with missile defense is precisely that of technology. It doesn't exist. Yes, there has been progress on some fronts and maybe we will someday be able to develop that technology. But that someday is a long, long way away.

While they don't readily admit it in public, even the fiercest missile defense proponents know the likelihood is exceedingly slim that a truly impenetrable missile shield, as envisioned by Ronald Reagan, could ever be built. It would require space-based weapons that we have yet to figure out how to build, launch, or maintain on orbit. It would require an antimissile system of 100 percent reliability—something never achieved by any weapon.

So instead, proponents talk about a "limited defense" against "rogue" states or terrorists, based on interceptor missiles (or lasers) launched from ground, air, or sea. To be sure, the technology needed for such a missile defense system is still elusive, but it is far more doable over the next two or three decades than anything based in space.

However, it is also a missile defense that, even if working to perfection, may well miss some incoming missiles, especially if the enemy builds enough of them or is smart enough to use spoofing techniques (many already available) against our own antimissile missiles. And "one nuclear, biological, or chemical weapon can ruin your whole day," to paraphrase the famous bumper sticker.

The second problem is cost. Although in the throes of the antiterror campaign no one in Washington is worrying about the price tag of anything on the Pentagon's wish list, the projected cost of missile defense is a serious mid- and long-term problem. In any configuration, it will be expensive, costing hundreds of billions of dollars. Where will that money come from?

This is not simply a traditional "guns versus butter" question, but a dire national security issue. Because if September 11 taught us anything, it is that we are vulnerable to all kinds of terrorist attacks, and that most of those threats don't require much in the way of high technology.

In fact, the National Intelligence Estimate for 2002, put together by the CIA and all of the nation's other intelligence agencies, says missile attack is less likely than an act of terror using ships, trucks, or airplanes. Such methods of delivering a nuclear, biological, or chemical weapon are less expensive than missiles, and can be developed and used covertly and without identifying the attacker, according to the study.

So ought we not be spending more money securing the safety of our borders, ports, roads, rail networks, and airlines than on missile defense? Our borders and ports remain woefully porous, as every U.S. leader and politician readily admits, and the agencies responsible for their security woefully underfunded and undermanned. The FBI's computer tracking and communications capabilities necessary for finding suspected terrorists are outdated and inadequate.

Even many military leaders privately question whether money ought better be spent on ways to take out missile launchers before they are used to shoot missiles at us, rather than on efforts to knock missiles out of the sky after they are launched.

The outcome of this "guns versus guns" budgetary debate will determine if we are safer in the future than we were on September 11, and than we are now. If missile defense is allowed to siphon money from higher-priority homeland defense needs, it will surely make us less safe.

Lastly, and perhaps more importantly, it is difficult to see any positive international political consequences of an obsessive U.S. pursuit of missile defense. As hard as we may try, America cannot withdraw from the world the way it can withdraw from international treaties. Other countries are frightened by what they see as an attempt by the U.S. at global military domination.

Even our closest friends and allies continue to caution us about disengaging from multinational efforts to secure worldwide peace and security and undertaking a "go-it-alone" effort to secure the spectral vision of American invulnerability. As the world's biggest economic and military power, America cannot escape the world, anymore than the world can escape it—with or without missile defense.

ARUNDHATI ROY

The Algebra of Infinite Justice

Arundhati Roy (b. 1961) was born in Bengal and grew up in Kerala. She trained as an architect at the Delhi School of Architecture, but became better known for her complex, scathing film scripts. She wrote and starred in *In Which Annie Gives It Those Ones* and wrote the script for Pradip Kishen's *Electric Moon*. Media attention came when she spoke out in support of Phoolan Devi, who she felt had been exploited by Shekhar Kapur's film *Bandit Queen*. The controversy escalated into a court case, after which she retired to private life to work on her first book, *The God of Small Things*, published in 1997. As the daughter of Mary Roy, the woman whose court case changed the inheritance laws in favor of women, she was closely acquainted with the Syrian Christian traditions that feature prominently in the book. She says, "A feminist is a woman who negotiates herself into a position where she has choices." *The God of Small Things* won Britain's premier book prize, the Booker McConnell, in 1997. She is the first nonexpatriate Indian author and the first Indian woman to have won this prize. Since then, in keeping with her longtime interest in social issues, she has immersed herself in causes such as the antinuclear movement and has been involved in the Narmada Bachao Andolan and the International Rivers Network. Her two major essays, "The End of Imagination" and "The Greater Common Good" are available online as well as from South End Press. Her personal fame has drawn attention and donations to these causes, and she has also made significant monetary contributions herself. This essay first appeared in the *Guardian* on September 29, 2001.

■

In the aftermath of the unconscionable September 11 suicide attacks on the Pentagon and the World Trade Center, an American newscaster said: "Good and Evil rarely manifest themselves as clearly as they did last Tuesday. People who we don't know massacred people who we do. And they did so with contemptuous glee." Then he broke down and wept.

Here's the rub: America is at war against people it doesn't know, because they don't appear much on TV. Before it has properly identified or even begun to comprehend the nature of its enemy, the U.S. government has, in a rush of publicity and embarrassing rhetoric, cobbled together an "international coalition against terror," mobilized its army, its air force, its navy and its media, and committed them to battle.

The trouble is that once America goes off to war, it can't very well return without having fought one. If it doesn't find its enemy, for the sake of the enraged folks back home, it will have to manufacture one. Once war begins, it will develop a momentum, a logic and a justification of its own, and we'll lose sight of why it's being fought in the first place. What we're witnessing here is the spectacle of the world's most powerful country reaching reflexively, angrily, for an old instinct to fight a new kind of war. Suddenly, when it comes to defending itself, America's streamlined warships, cruise missiles and F-16 jets look like obsolete, lumbering things. As deterrence, its arsenal of nuclear bombs is no longer worth its weight in scrap. Box-cutters, penknives, and cold anger are the weapons with which the wars of the new century will be waged. Anger is the lock pick. It slips through customs unnoticed. Doesn't show up in baggage checks.

Who is America fighting? On September 20, the FBI said that it had doubts about the identities of some of the hijackers. On the same day President George Bush said, "We know exactly who these people are and which governments are supporting them." It sounds as though the president knows something that the FBI and the American public don't.

In his September 20 address to the U.S. Congress, President Bush called the enemies of America "enemies of freedom." "Americans are asking, 'Why do they hate us?'" he said. "They hate our freedoms—our freedom of religion, our freedom of speech, our freedom to vote and assemble and disagree with each other." People are being asked to make two leaps of faith here. First, to assume that The Enemy is who the U.S. government says it is, even though it has no substantial evidence to support that claim. And second, to assume that The Enemy's motives are what the U.S. government says they are, and there's nothing to support that either.

For strategic, military and economic reasons, it is vital for the U.S. government to persuade its public that their commitment to freedom and democracy and the American Way of Life is under attack. In the current atmosphere of grief, outrage and anger, it's an easy notion to peddle. However, if that were true, it's reasonable to wonder why the symbols of America's economic and military dominance—the World Trade Center and the Pentagon—were chosen as the targets of the attacks. Why not the Statue of Liberty? Could it be that the stygian anger that led to the attacks has its taproot not in American freedom and democracy, but in the U.S. government's record of commitment and support to exactly the opposite things— to military and economic terrorism, insurgency, military dictatorship, religious bigotry and unimaginable genocide (outside America)?

It must be hard for ordinary Americans, so recently bereaved, to look up at the world with their eyes full of tears and encounter what might appear to them to be indifference. It isn't indifference. It's just augury. An absence of surprise. The tired wisdom of knowing that what goes around eventually comes around. American people ought to know that it is not them but their government's policies that are so hated. They can't possibly doubt that they themselves, their extraordinary musicians, their writers, their actors, their spectacular sportsmen and their cinema, are universally welcomed. All of us have been moved by the courage and grace shown by firefighters, rescue workers and ordinary office staff in the days since the attacks.

America's grief at what happened has been immense and immensely public. It would be grotesque to expect it to calibrate or modulate its anguish. However, it will be a pity if, instead of using this as an opportunity to try to understand why September 11 happened, Americans use it as an opportunity to usurp the whole world's sorrow to mourn and avenge only their own. Because then it falls to the rest of us to ask the hard questions and say the harsh things. And for our pains, for our bad timing, we will be disliked, and perhaps eventually silenced.

The world will probably never know what motivated those particular hijackers who flew planes into those particular American buildings. They were not glory boys. They left no suicide notes, no political messages; no organization has claimed credit for the attacks. All we know is that their belief in what they were doing outstripped the natural human instinct for survival, or any desire to be remembered. It's almost as though they could not scale down the enormity of their rage to anything smaller than their deeds. And what they did has blown a hole in the world as we knew it.

In the absence of information, politicians, political commentators and writers (like myself) will invest the act with their own politics, with their own interpretations. This speculation, this analysis of the political climate in which the attacks took place, can only be a good thing. But war is looming large. Whatever remains to be said must be said quickly.

Before America places itself at the helm of the "international coalition against terror," before it invites (and coerces) countries to actively participate in its almost godlike mission—called Operation Infinite Justice until it was pointed out that this could be seen as an insult to Muslims, who believe that only Allah can mete out infinite justice, and was renamed Operation Enduring

Freedom—it would help if some small clarifications are made. For example, Infinite Justice/Enduring Freedom for whom?

Is this America's war against terror in America or against terror in general? What exactly is being avenged here? Is it the tragic loss of almost 7,000 lives, the gutting of five million square feet of office space in Manhattan, the destruction of a section of the Pentagon, the loss of several hundreds of thousands of jobs, the bankruptcy of some airline companies and the dip in the New York Stock Exchange? Or is it more than that?

In 1996, Madeleine Albright, then the U.S. Ambassador to the United Nations, was asked on national television what she felt about the fact that 500,000 Iraqi children had died as a result of U.S.-led economic sanctions. She replied that it was "a very hard choice," but that, all things considered, "we think the price is worth it." Albright never lost her job for saying this. She continued to travel the world representing the views and aspirations of the US government. More pertinently, the sanctions against Iraq remain in place. Children continue to die.

So here we have it. The equivocating distinction between civilization and savagery, between the "massacre of innocent people" or, if you like, "a clash of civilizations" and "collateral damage." The sophistry and fastidious algebra of infinite justice. How many dead Iraqis will it take to make the world a better place? How many dead Afghans for every dead American? How many dead women and children for every dead man? How many dead mojahedin for each dead investment banker?

As we watch mesmerized, Operation Enduring Freedom unfolds on television monitors across the world. A coalition of the world's superpowers is closing in on Afghanistan, one of the poorest, most ravaged, war-torn countries in the world, whose ruling Taliban government is sheltering Osama bin Laden, the man being held responsible for the September 11 attacks. The only thing in Afghanistan that could possibly count as collateral value is its citizenry. (Among them, half a million maimed orphans. There are accounts of hobbling stampedes that occur when artificial limbs are airdropped into remote, inaccessible villages.)

Afghanistan's economy is in a shambles. In fact, the problem for an invading army is that Afghanistan has no conventional coordinates or signposts to plot on a military map—no big cities, no highways, no industrial complexes, no water treatment plants. Farms have been turned into mass graves. The countryside is littered with land mines—10 million is the most recent estimate. The American army would first have to clear the mines and build roads in order to take its soldiers in.

Fearing an attack from America, one million citizens have fled from their homes and arrived at the border between Pakistan and Afghanistan. The UN estimates that there are eight million Afghan citizens who need emergency aid. As supplies run out—food and aid agencies have been asked to leave—the BBC reports that one of the worst humanitarian disasters of recent times has begun to unfold. Witness the infinite justice of the new century. Civilians starving to death while they're waiting to be killed.

In America there has been rough talk of "bombing Afghanistan back to the stone age." Someone please break the news that Afghanistan is already there.

And if it's any consolation, America played no small part in helping it on its way. The American people may be a little fuzzy about where exactly Afghanistan is (we hear reports that there's a run on maps of the country), but the U.S. government and Afghanistan are old friends.

In 1979, after the Soviet invasion of Afghanistan, the CIA and Pakistan's ISI (Inter Services Intelligence) launched the largest covert operation in the history of the CIA. Their purpose was to harness the energy of Afghan resistance to the Soviets and expand it into a holy war, an Islamic jihad, which would turn Muslim countries within the Soviet Union against the communist regime and eventually destabilize it. When it began, it was meant to be the Soviet Union's Vietnam. It turned out to be much more than that. Over the years, through the ISI, the CIA funded and recruited almost 100,000 radical mojahedin from 40 Islamic countries as soldiers for America's proxy war. The rank and file of the mojahedin were unaware that their jihad was actually being fought on behalf of Uncle Sam. (The irony is that America was equally unaware that it was financing a future war against itself.)

In 1989, after being bloodied by 10 years of relentless conflict, the Russians withdrew, leaving behind a civilization reduced to rubble. Civil war in Afghanistan raged on. The jihad spread to Chechnya, Kosovo and eventually to Kashmir. The CIA continued to pour in money and military equipment, but the overheads had become immense, and more money was needed. The mojahedin ordered farmers to plant opium as a "revolutionary tax." The ISI set up hundreds of heroin laboratories across Afghanistan. Within two years of the CIA's arrival, the Pakistan-Afghanistan borderland had become the biggest producer of heroin in the world, and the single biggest source of the heroin on American streets. The annual profits, said to be between $100bn and $200bn, were ploughed back into training and arming militants.

In 1996, the Taliban—then a marginal sect of dangerous, hard-line fundamentalists—fought its way to power in Afghanistan. It was funded by the ISI, that old cohort of the CIA, and supported by many political parties in Pakistan. The Taliban unleashed a regime of terror. Its first victims were its own people, particularly women. It closed down girls' schools, dismissed women from government jobs, enforced Sharia laws under which women deemed to be "immoral" are stoned to death, and widows guilty of being adulterous are buried alive. Given the Taliban government's human rights track record, it seems unlikely that it will in any way be intimidated or swerved from its purpose by the prospect of war, or the threat to the lives of its civilians.

After all that has happened, can there be anything more ironic than Russia and America joining hands to redestroy Afghanistan? The question is, can you destroy destruction? Dropping more bombs on Afghanistan only shuffles the rubble, scramble some old graves and disturb the dead.

The desolate landscape of Afghanistan was the burial ground of Soviet communism and the springboard of a unipolar world dominated by America. It made the space for neocapitalism and corporate globalization, again dominated by America. And now Afghanistan is poised to become the graveyard for the unlikely soldiers who fought and won this war for America.

And what of America's trusted ally? Pakistan too has suffered enormously. The U.S. government has not been shy of supporting military dictators who have blocked the idea of democracy from taking root in the country. Before the CIA arrived, there was a small rural market for opium in Pakistan. Between 1979 and 1985, the number of heroin addicts grew from next to nothing to a massive number. Even before September 11, there were millions of Afghan refugees living in tented camps along the border.

Pakistan's economy is crumbling. Sectarian violence, globalization's Structural Adjustment Programs and drug lords are tearing the country to pieces. Set up to fight the Soviets, the terrorist training centers and madrassas, sown like dragon's teeth across the country, produced fundamentalists with tremendous popular appeal within Pakistan itself. The Taliban, which the Pakistan government has supported, funded and propped up for years, has material and strategic alliances with Pakistan's own political parties. Now the U.S. government is asking (asking?) Pakistan to garrote the pet it has hand-reared in its backyard for so many years. President Musharraf, having pledged his support to the U.S., could well find he has something resembling civil war on his hands.

India, thanks in part to its geography, and in part to the vision of its former leaders, has so far been fortunate enough to be left out of this Great Game. Had it been drawn in, it's more than likely that our democracy, such as it is, would not have survived. Today, as some of us watch in horror, the Indian government is furiously gyrating its hips, begging the U.S. to set up its base in India rather than Pakistan.

Having had this ringside view of Pakistan's sordid fate, it isn't just odd, it's unthinkable, that India should want to do this. Any third world country with a fragile economy and a complex social base should know by now that to invite a superpower such as America in (whether it says it's staying or just passing through) would be like inviting a brick to drop through your windshield.

In the media blitz that followed September 11, mainstream television stations largely ignored the story of America's involvement with Afghanistan. So, to those unfamiliar with the story, the coverage of the attacks could have been moving, disturbing, and perhaps to cynics, self-indulgent. However, to those of us familiar with Afghanistan's recent history, American TV coverage and the rhetoric of the International Coalition Against Terror is just plain insulting. America's "free press," like its "free market," has a lot to account for.

Operation Enduring Freedom is ostensibly being fought to uphold the American Way of Life. It'll probably end up undermining it completely. It will spawn more anger and more terror across the world. For ordinary people in America, it will mean lives lived in a climate of sickening uncertainty: will my child be safe in school? Will there be nerve gas in the subway? A bomb in the cinema hall? Will my love come home tonight? There have been warnings about the possibility of biological warfare—smallpox, bubonic plague, anthrax—the deadly payload of innocuous crop-duster aircraft. Being picked off a few at a time may end up being worse than being annihilated all at once by a nuclear bomb.

The U.S. government, and no doubt governments all over the world, will use the climate of war as an excuse to curtail civil liberties, deny free speech, lay off workers, harass ethnic and religious minorities, cut back on public spending and divert huge amounts of money to the defense industry.

To what purpose? President George Bush can no more "rid the world of evil-doers" than he can stock it with saints. It's absurd for the U.S. government to even toy with the notion that it can stamp out terrorism with more violence and oppression. Terrorism is the symptom, not disease. Terrorism has no country. It's transnational, as global an enterprise as Coke or Pepsi or Nike. At the first sign of trouble, terrorists can pull up stakes and move their "factories" from country to country in search of a better deal. Just like the multinationals.

Terrorism as a phenomenon may never go away. But if it is to be contained, the first step is for America to at least acknowledge that it shares the planet with other nations, with other human beings who, even if they are not on TV, have loves and griefs and stories and songs and sorrows and, for heaven's sake, rights. Instead, when Donald Rumsfeld, the U.S. defense secretary, was asked what he would call a victory in America's new war, he said that if he could convince the world that Americans must be allowed to continue with their way of life, he would consider it a victory.

The September 11 attacks were a monstrous calling card from a world gone horribly wrong. The message may have been written by bin Laden (who knows?) and delivered by his couriers, but it could well have been signed by the ghosts of the victims of America's old wars. The millions killed in Korea, Vietnam and Cambodia, the seventeen thousand killed when Israel—backed by the United States—invaded Lebanon in 1982, the tens of thousands of Iraqis killed in Operation Desert Storm, the thousands of Palestinians who have died fighting Israel's occupation of the West Bank. And the millions who died, in Yugoslavia, Somalia, Haiti, Chile, Nicaragua, El Salvador, the Dominican Republic, Panama, at the hands of all the terrorists, dictators and genocidists who the American government supported, trained, bankrolled and supplied with arms. And this is far from being a comprehensive list. For a country involved in so much warfare and conflict, the American people have been extremely fortunate. The strikes on September 11 were only the second on American soil in over a century. The first was Pearl Harbor. The reprisal for this took a long route, but ended with Hiroshima and Nagasaki. This time the world waits with bated breath for the horrors to come.

Someone recently said that if Osama bin Laden didn't exist, America would have had to invent him. But, in a way, America did invent him. He was among the jihadis who moved to Afghanistan in 1979 when the CIA commenced its operations there. Bin Laden has the distinction of being created by the CIA and wanted by the FBI. In the course of a fortnight he has been promoted from suspect to prime suspect and then, in the lack of any real evidence, straight up the charts to being "wanted dead or alive."

From all accounts, it will be impossible to produce evidence (of the sort that would stand scrutiny in a court of law) to link bin Laden to the September 11 attacks. So far, it appears that the most incriminating piece of evidence against him is the fact that he has not condemned them. From what is known about the location of bin Laden and the living conditions in which he operates, it's entirely possible that he did not personally plan and carry out the attacks—that he is the inspirational figure, "the CEO of the holding company."

The Taliban's response to U.S. demands for the extradition of bin Laden has been uncharacteristically reasonable: produce the evidence, then we'll hand him over. President Bush's response is that the demand is "non-negotiable."

(While talks are on for the extradition of CEOs—can India put in a side request for the extradition of Warren Anderson of the U.S.? He was the chairman of Union Carbide, responsible for the Bhopal gas leak that killed 16,000 people in 1984. We have collated the necessary evidence. It's all in the files. Could we have him, please?)

But who is Osama bin Laden really?

Let me rephrase that. What is Osama bin Laden?

He's America's family secret. He is the American President's dark doppelganger. The savage twin of all that purports to be beautiful and civilized. He has been sculpted from the spare rib of a world laid to waste by America's foreign policy: its gunboat diplomacy, its nuclear arsenal, its vulgarly stated policy of "full-spectrum dominance," its chilling disregard for non-American lives, its barbarous military interventions, its support for despotic and dictatorial regimes, its merciless economic agenda that has munched through the economies of poor countries like a cloud of locusts. Its marauding multinationals who are taking over the air we breathe, the ground we stand on, the water we drink, the thoughts we think.

Now that the family secret has been spilled, the twins are blurring into one another and gradually becoming interchangeable. guns, bombs, money and drugs have been going around in the loop for a while. (The Stinger missiles that will greet U.S. helicopters were supplied by the CIA. The heroin used by America's drug addicts comes from Afghanistan. The Bush administration recently gave Afghanistan a $43m subsidy for a "war on drugs.")

Now they've even begun to borrow each other's rhetoric. Each refers to the other as "the head of the snake." Both invoke God and use the loose millenarian currency of good and evil as their terms of reference. Both are engaged in unequivocal political crimes.

Both are dangerously armed—one with the nuclear arsenal of the obscenely powerful, the other with the incandescent, destructive power of the utterly hopeless.

The fireball and the ice pick. The bludgeon and the axe. The important thing to keep in mind is that neither is an acceptable alternative to the other.

President Bush's ultimatum to the people of the world—"If you're not with us, you're against us"—is a piece of presumptuous arrogance.

It's not a choice that people want to, need to, or should have to make.

PART 2:
VIOLENCE AND MOURNING

Power, or force, is that which makes a thing of anybody who comes under its sway. When exercised to the full, it makes a thing of a man in the most literal sense, for it makes him a corpse . . . For deadly force so crushes whomever it touches that it appears finally no less external to him who doles it out than to him who suffers it. . . . The vanquished soldier is the scourge of nature; possessed by war, he, as much as the slave, although in quite a different manner, is become a thing. Such is the nature of might. Its power to transform man into a thing is double and it cuts both ways; it petrifies differently but equally the souls of those who suffer it and those who wield it.

—SIMONE WEIL (1909–1943),
French writer and humanist, Jewish by birth and Catholic
by conviction, author of the classic antiwar work *The Illiad: Poem of Force* (translation by D. G. Luttinger)

*It is organized violence at the top which creates individual violence
at the bottom.*

—EMMA GOLDMAN (1869–1940),
Russian Jewish American writer, orator, and activist, one
of history's most profound advocate for women's and labor rights
and opponent of war

TSAI WEN-JI

From Song of Pathos and Wrath *and* Eighteen Verses in Hun's Flute Melody

Tsai Wen Ji's (162–239) given name was Tsai Yeng. She chose to rename herself Wen-Ji, meaning, "Noble Woman of Literature," and indeed, she was considered "the Pearl on the Palm of the history of Chinese literature. Tsai Wen-Ji was the daughter of Tsai Yong, a leading scholar of the East Han Dynasty of China who revised the six most important classics of Chinese literature. As a young woman, she was gifted in music as well as poetry and famous for her beauty and virtue. Nevertheless, she was exiled with her father for twelve years when he dared to offend the court. During her exile, her literary life came to fruition. Traveling with her scholarly father enriched her knowledge, broadened her vision, and deepened her love for the land and people of China. Her brief marriage ended when both her husband and her father died in the political turmoil of war. During the cross-fire of civil war and the Hun invasions, she was captured by the Tartar cavalry in a rampage and taken beyond the Great Wall to Inner Mongolia. In her epic poem entitled *Song of Pathos and Wrath*, she described the unimaginable conditions during the war. After she arrived in Mongolia, she was forced to wed the Tartar king Zo Xie. In twelve years of captivity, she bore two sons. She wrote, "Not that I yearn to live / Or fear to die / My wish is to return to my native land / So that my bones can rest in peace forever." She was finally released after the new Chinese regime paid gold and jade for her ransom, but she had to leave her children behind. She expressed her anguish in verse. Her famous "Eighteen Verses in Hun's Flute Melody" created a new style of music and poetry for China—a cross-cultural flower blossoming from the tears and blood of war. Suffering from remorse and longing for her children, she dedicated her aging years to reciting and writing in calligraphy the many books that she could remember by heart. Without her effort, these numerous volumes would have been forever lost.

■

FROM SONG OF PATHOS AND WRATH

. . . Tong Zho vowed to murder our emperor
and snatch the throne.
He persecuted the good and the capable,
ran them out of town.
The new lord became Tong Zho's puppet
to hide his own ambition.
All brave men rebelled,
declaring to fight evil to the end.
When Tong Zho's army headed east,
their shiny armor outshone the sun.
Our men of the plains were soft and civilized.
while the mercenary Tartars hired
by the Huns were brutal.
They pillaged towns and cities,

and faced no resistance.
These barbarians slaughtered our people,
sparing no one in sight.
Corpses clustered and leaned
upon one another.
On the sides of the barbarians' horses,
our men's heads dangled;
Behind the horses' tails,
our women were dragged in chains.
As captives, we were marched beyond our Great Wall,
mournfully looking back at our misty roads.
The roads ahead wound with danger,
and were lined with dead bodies
exposing rotting livers and putrid guts.
By tens of thousands we slaves walked in silence.
Families were forbidden to speak with their children.
Under threat of sword,
death was constantly bestowed.
It's not that I cherished my life,
but that I could not bear the verbal abuse.
Often, they bludgeoned us;
pain and sorrow were our company.
We marched crying in day;
we sat sobbing at night.
Death was too much to ask for;
living was too hard to bear.
The people of my old village
were innocent indeed.
How could this catastrophe befall them?

. . . . .

. . . It was time to rejoice,
when my countrymen came
to ransom me.
I was liberated,
yet I had to abandon my sons
fathered by the enemy.
Although Heaven links
our hearts together,
there will be no more reunion for us.
Like Life in Death we were parted;
how could I stand bidding farewell?
My son approached me and caressed my head.
"People say you will leave me!
When are you coming back, Mother?

You have always been kind to me.
Why are you cruel now?
I'm still a child.
Please think it over?"
The scene broke my heart.
My sadness turned into madness.
I caressed him as we wept bitterly.
No sooner had I departed,
than I regretted going.

FROM EIGHTEEN VERSES IN HUN'S FLUTE MELODY

My leaving was not for my withering life,
but for returning to my homeland.
The Chinese ambassadors escorted me
on four galloping horses.
Who could hear me sobbing?
The sun had lost its radiance.
I wished I could send a bird
with strong wings to carry my sons
back with me.
This is the Third Verse.
My zither plays rapid beats
as if stabbing my heart.

My body has returned home,
but my heart hangs hungrily.
Though seasons change,
my sorrow stays forever.
The mountains are high;
the earth is wide,
and there is no date when I will see you,
my son. Sometimes at night,
you come in my dream.
I hold your hands in joy with sorrow.
After waking, my sick soul will not rest.
This is the Fourth Verse.
I play it as tears cross my face.
My mind is filled with thoughts as deep
as a river flowing . . .

Translation by Pwu Jean Lee with Daniela Gioseffi

AL-KHANSA

⌐ Elegy for My Brother

Al-Khansa (circa 575–646) Tumadir bint 'Amr (bint means "daughter of") is usually called Khansa, which means "gazelle." She was one of the major poets of pre-Islamic Arabia in the era called the Jahiliya, and daughter of the famed poet Zuheir. Her *diwan* (poetry collection) was carefully preserved by Islamic scholars who needed to study seventh-century Arabic in order to explicate the Qur'an. Khansa was a member of the Sharid clan of the Banu Sulaim people and was therefore part of a powerful family of west-central Arabia, near Mecca and Medina. Most of her poems are about her brothers, Sakhr and Muawiya, killed in tribal battles predating Islam. Part of a woman poet's role was to mourn the dead in elegies performed for the tribe in public oral competitions; Khansa's laments made her famous throughout the Arab world. She met Muhammad in 629 and fervently converted to Islam. She had four sons, whom she willingly sacrificed to battle, believing in their immortality as martyrs for her faith. Even the Holy Prophet of Islam admired her verses. The lament she wrote on the death of her brother is regarded as one of the best elegies in Arabic. It is impossible to fully translate the mood and musicality of her poem.

■

How have we offended you, Death,
to make you treat us so?
Every day, you claim another trophy:
one day a soldier;
the next a president!
You select the best
as well as the least different from you, Mighty Death.
I wouldn't weep and whine
if you were fair and kind,
but you take the valiant ones most deserving of life
leaving blunderers behind.

Translation adapted by Daniela Gioseffi with Emira Omar

DIODATA SALUZZO

The War of 1793

Diodata Saluzzo (1774–1840) was born into a large Italian family of noble Piemontese origins. She wrote her first collection of enduring poems in 1796. Her refined talents and ability at composing, in various metric poetic styles, in a society in which the women were usually educated merely to sing and recite, but not to write or compose, caused her to be applauded as if she were a new Sappho. Her father, a distinguished scientist, recognized and encouraged the talent of his daughter, pushing her to publish her work. In 1789, when Diodata was only fifteen years old, her father organized a scientific and literary academy for children in his home with Diodata's siblings and other young friends, whom he taught with inspiring passion. In 1802, she became the first woman to be admitted to the Academy of Sciences of Turin. She published many works, of which the most extensive was her collection of verses, in four volumes, published in 1816–17. She also published novels and story collections. In the last years of her life, made bitter by the choice not to have a family, she wrote pieces that mourned her childlessness. In order to fill the void she felt, she traveled extensively, cultivating literary friendships around the world until her death in 1840. Here she writes of the annexation of Savoy by France in 1792 and the invasion of the Piedmont region in 1793. Two of her brothers were killed in the war.

■

Dark, dark is the night, now it wholly
Covers my native hillock; alone
The tiny stream flees away weeping
Within the green-leaved secret valley.
A song like the murmuring of the brook.
Shall I sing; from these boughs a thin
Moonbeam through pallid wisps
Of hair reaches me, falls on my lyre:
Sad is the beam, sad as I now feel
My whole soul to be. A baleful cloud
Covers my country's fate. Ah me! Silent,
Abandoned stand paternal walls
Bereft of sons; always, always at my side
Is Melancholy, sacred to the heart of poets,
Sublime mother of images born
Deep within the breast. Unknown, I am
Virgin still upon the Alps; the age of song
Has barely risen within me. One day I shall be
The Alps' noble bard, and noble verses from my lyre
Heroes shall hear: only to arouse pity
Now sing I, an unknown maiden
Dwelling among wild mountains.

Translation by Muriel Kittel

LOUISA MAY ALCOTT

From Hospital Sketches ✓ *his civil war*

Louisa May Alcott (1832–1888) was born in Germantown, Pennsylvania, but moved at an early age with her family to Boston. Her father, Bronson Alcott, was well known for his controversial and progressive teaching methods and his radical, anti-puritan belief that children should enjoy learning and be allowed to question authority. In 1840, the family moved to the center of American literary life at the time, Concord, where the transcendentalist thinker Ralph Waldo Emerson helped the family to set up residence. Louisa visited the Emerson home often and took nature walks with Emerson's protégé, Henry David Thoreau. In 1843 the Alcott family took part in a communal settlement known as the Fruitlands. The experimental village failed, and the family returned to Concord in 1845, then back to Boston in 1849, where Louisa began to feel more responsible for her family's always troubled finances. She took many jobs, from reading to the elderly to teaching small children, mending, and doing laundry. In 1852 she published her first poem, and began a long writing career. Her first big success came in 1863 with the publication of *Hospital Sketches,* from which this excerpt is taken, a book based on letters she wrote for soldiers while serving as a nurse during the Civil War. She supplemented the family's income for years by publishing popular Gothic tales under pseudonyms. Her 1868 novel, *Little Women*, became one of the best-loved books of generations of young women. Alcott achieved great success and traveled in Europe before settling again in Boston to raise the daughter of her younger sister, who had died, and remained there until her own death at the age of fifty-six.

■

The first thing I met was a regiment of the vilest odors that ever assaulted the human nose . . . and the worst of this affliction was, everyone has assured me that it was a chronic weakness of all hospitals, and I must bear it. I did, armed with lavender water, with which I so besprinkled myself and premises, that, like my friend, Sairy, I was soon known among my patients as "the nurse with the bottle" . . . I progressed by slow stages up stairs and down, till the main hall was reached, and I paused to take breath and a survey. There they were! "our brave boys," as the papers justly call them, for cowards could hardly have been so riddled with shot and shell, so torn and shattered, nor have borne suffering for which we have no name, with an uncomplaining fortitude, which made one glad to cherish each as a brother. In they came, some on stretchers, some in men's arms, some feebly staggering along propped on rude crutches, and one lay stark and still with covered face, as a comrade gave his name to be recorded before they carried him away to the dead house. All was hurry and confusion; the hall was full of these wrecks of humanity, for the most exhausted could not reach a bed till duly ticketed and registered; the walls were lined with rows of such as could sit, the floor covered with the more disabled, the steps and doorways filled with helpers and lookers on; the sound of many feet and voices made that usually quiet hour as noisy as noon; and, in the midst of it all, the matron's motherly face brought more comfort to many a poor soul, than the cordial draughts she administered, or the cheery words that welcomed all, making of the hospital a home.

The sight of several stretchers, each with its legless, armless, or desperately wounded occupant, entering my ward, admonished me that I was there to work, not to wonder or weep; so I corked up my feelings, and returned to the path of duty, which was rather "a hard road to travel" just then. The house had been a hotel before hospitals were needed, and many of the doors still bore their old names; some not so inappropriate as might be imaged, for my ward was in truth a *ball-room*, if gunshot wounds could christen it. Forty beds were prepared, many already tenanted by tired men who fell down anywhere, and drowsed till the smell of food roused them. Round the great stove was gathered the dreariest group I ever saw—ragged, gaunt and pale, mud to the knees, with bloody bandages untouched since put on days before; many bundled up in blankets, coats being lost or useless; and all wearing that disheartened look which proclaimed defeat . . . I pitied them so much, I dared not speak to them, though, remembering all they had been through since the rout at Fredericksburg, I yearned to serve the dreariest of them all. Presently, Miss Blank tore me from my refuge behind piles of one-sleeved shirts, odd socks, bandages and lint; put basin, sponge towels and a block of brown soap into my hands, with these appalling directions:

"Come, my dear, begin to wash as fast you can. Tell them to take off socks, coats, and shirts, scrub them well, put on clean shirts, and the attendants will finish them off, and lay them in bed."

Anna Akhmatova

The First Long-Range Artillery Fire on Leningrad

Anna Akhmatova (1889–1966) is one of the best known and loved Russian poets of the twentieth century. Born in Odessa, she later lived in the areas of St. Petersburg and Kiev. Like many of her contemporaries, she led a long struggle for freedom of expression. Her husband, Nikolai Gumilev, was executed in 1921, and Akhmatova herself was silenced as a poet for eighteen years during the reign of Stalin. She lived with the Mandelstam family when Osip Mandelstam was arrested and disappeared into the death camps. For a time she was restored to the Writers Union, but in 1946, she was politically attacked and her son arrested. Finally, her son was released and during her last years, she was admitted again to the Writers Union and again published. Many younger poets counted themselves among her followers, including Nobel laureate Joseph Brodsky. Akhmatova's long poem "Requiem" much admired and translated throughout the world, combined a lyrical statement with a lament and a national political conscience.

■

A mottled crowd bustled about,
and suddenly all was totally transformed.
It wasn't the usual city racket.
It came from a strange land.
True, it was akin to some random claps of thunder,
but natural thunder heralds the wetness of fresh water,
                              high clouds
to quench the thirst of fields gone dry and parched,
a messenger of blessed rain,
but this was as dry as hell must be.
My distraught wits refused
to believe it, because of the insane
suddenness with which it sounded, swelled, and hit,
and how casually it came
to murder my child.

Translation by Daniela Gioseffi with Sophia Buzevska

Helen Zenna Smith

From Not So Quiet . . .

Helen Zenna Smith (b. 1896–1985) is the pseudonym for Evadene Price, a novelist, journalist, playwright, and children's author. She is best known for her novel about World War I , written in 1930, from which this excerpt comes. *Not So Quiet . . .* was awarded the Prix Severigne in France as the novel most calculated to promote international peace. It chronicles the experience of a corps of six young upper-class Englishwomen as they drive field ambulances of wounded men rescued from the front lines of battle in France in 1918. Through their war experience, it portrays the utter ugliness and insanity of battle. Its message is that there is no glory in war, which only leaves the body and spirit broken in its wake. The novel is one of loss and suffering, not triumph, as it tells the truth of lives wrecked and devastated by the war that destroyed a generation of

Europe's young men. This excerpt begins with the loss of a comrade affectionately called "The Bug," because of her dread of the lice and vermin suffered by the women's ambulance unit.

■

I am afraid of going mad . . . of being discovered one morning among the boulders at the foot of a rocky hillside as The Bug the day following on the air-raid that smashed the station and the convoy train to matchwood . . . a night of smashings, though none so cruelly smashed as The Bug. She had lost her way and missed her footing in the darkness, said the powers-that-be. This on the brightest night in a season of moonlit nights.

An accident. . . . So The Bug rests alongside Tosh in the bleak cemetery in the shadow of the Witch's Hand.

An accident . . . drivers walking about with sullen eyes, and whisperings that are not pleasant listening . . . and I, in the hours after the midnight convoy, sitting thinking things that are best not thought . . . my fingers tight against Commandant's thick, red throat, gloating in the ebbing strength of that squat, healthy body until I am sick and faint with murderous longing.

The impulse has gone . . . but in its place has come something worse. I am haunted now as The Bug was haunted. Whenever I close my aching red eyes a procession of men passes before me: maimed; men with neither arms nor legs; gassed men, coughing, coughing, coughing; men with dreadful burning eyes; men with heads and faces half shot away; raw, bleeding men with the skin burned from their upturned faces; tortured, all watching me as I lie in my flea-bag trying to sleep . . . an endless procession of horror that will not let me rest. I am afraid. I am afraid of madness. Are there others in this convoy fear-obsessed as I am, as The Bug was . . . others who will not admit it, as I will not, as The Bug did not . . . others who exist in a daily hell of fear? For I fear these maimed men of my imaginings as I never fear the maimed men I drive from the hospital trains to the camps. The men in the ambulances scream, but this ghostly procession is ghostly quiet. I fear them, these silent men, for I am afraid they will stay with me all my life, shutting out beauty till the day I die. And not only do I fear them, I hate them. I hate these maimed men who will not let me sleep.

Oh, the beauty of men who are whole, who have straight arms and legs, whose bodies are not cruelly gashed and torn by shrapnel, whose eyes are not horror-filled, whose faces are smooth and shapely, whose mouths smile instead of grinning painfully . . . oh, the beauty and wonder of men who are whole. Baynton, young and strong and clean-limbed, are his eyes serene and happy now as they were the afternoon of the concert in the prisoners' compound . . . or are they staring up unseeingly somewhere in No Man's Land, with that fair skin of his dyed an obscene blue by poison gas, his young body shattered and scattered and bleeding? Roy Evans-Mawnington . . . is he still smiling and eager-faced as on the day he was photographed in his second-lieutenant's uniform . . . or has the smile frozen on his incredulous lips?

Oh the beauty of men who are whole and sane. Shall I ever know a lover who is young and strong and untouched by war, who has not gazed on what I have gazed upon? Shall I ever know a lover whose eyes reflect my image without the shadow of war rising between us? A lover in whose arms I shall forget the maimed men who pass before me in endless parade in the darkness before the dawn when I think and think and think because the procession will not let me sleep?

What is to happen to women like me when this war ends . . . if it ever ends. I am twenty-one years of age, yet I know nothing of life but death, fear, blood, and the sentimentality that glorifies these things in the name of patriotism. I watch my own mother stupidly, deliberately, though unthinkingly—for she is a kind woman—encourage the sons of other women to kill their brothers; I see my own father—a gentle creature who would not willingly harm a fly—applaud the latest scientist to invent a mechanical device guaranteed to crush his fellow-beings to pulp in their thousands. And my generation watches these things and marvels at the blind foolishness of it . . . helpless to make its immature voice heard above the insensate clamour of the old ones who cry: "Kill, Kill, Kill!" unceasingly.

What is to happen to women like me when the killing is done and peace comes . . . if ever it comes? What will they expect of us, these elders who have sent us out to fight? We sheltered young women who smilingly stumbled from the chintz-covered drawing-rooms of the suburbs straight into hell?

What will they expect of us?

We, who once blushed at the public mention of childbirth, now discuss such things as casually as once we discussed the latest play; whispered stories of immorality are of far less importance than a fresh cheese in the canteen; chastity seems a mere waste of time in an area where youth is blotted out so quickly. What will they expect of us, these elders of ours, when the killing is over and we return?

Once we were not allowed out after nightfall unchaperoned; now we can drive the whole night to the station . . . I do not see Commandant . . . I am in the train at last . . . Etta Potato waving farewell from the platform. . . .

My war service is ended.

I am going home.

Darkened stations . . . endless cold waits . . . soldiers in khaki . . . wounded soldiers in blue . . . V.A.D.'s . . . nurses . . . grey, uninteresting landscapes . . . bare trees . . . camps, camps, camps, . . . tin huts, wooden huts . . . marching troops . . . desolation . . . cemeteries of black crosses . . . hospitals . . . and everywhere mud, mud, mud.

I am going home.

The train stops, starts again, stops; I change to another, on and on and on. . . .

I am going home.

Why am I so calm about it?

Boulogne at last. Why do I not shout and laugh and dance? How often have I pictured this Channel crossing, my wild exhilaration, arriving under the chalk cliffs of England, the white welcoming chalk cliffs of England.

The sweetness of England . . . England, where grass is green and primroses in early springtime patch the earth a timid yellow . . . where trees in bud are ready to leaf on the first day of pale sunshine. . . . England, England, how often have I promised to throw myself flat upon your bosom and kiss the first green blade of grass I saw because it was English grass and I had come home?

But now I am coming home . . . and I do not care.

I have pictured arriving at Charing Cross. Perhaps it would be raining, but it would be English rain and I would hold my face up to its drops. Father and Mother would meet me . . . drive me though familiar places—Piccadilly, Regent Street . . . as it grew dusk lights would reflect warmly on the wet, shiny pavements . . . London and then out through the innumerable streets of toy villas towards home. . . .

Home, home . . . and I do not care.

I do not care. I am flat. Old. I am twenty-one and as old as the hills. Emotion-dry. The war has drained me dry of feeling. Something has gone from me that will never return. I do not want to go home.

I am suddenly aware that I cannot bear Mother's prattle-prattle of committees and recruiting-meetings and the war-baby of Jessie, the new maid; nor can I watch my gentle father gloating over the horrors I have seen, pumping me for good stories to retail at his club to-morrow. I cannot go home to watch a procession of maimed men in my dainty, rose-walled bedroom. It is no place for a company of broken men on parade. . . .

The wounded are trying to staunch one another's blood. A few are shell-shocked. One scales the side of the shelter frantically, scrabbling and digging her toes into the earth like a maddened animal, then runs shrieking into the night. In the distance the buzz of the planes grows fainter and fainter. The raiders have been beaten off at last.

I tie Blimey's arm. She nearly fights me as I tear strips from her petticoat to bind the artery. At last voices are heard. Soldiers from the camp rush on the scene, cursing and blaspheming at the sight of the mangled women.

The role is called. The casualties are heavy. Ten dead, two missing, twenty-four injured. Four are unhurt, and of these three are shell-shocked. I am the only woman out of forty to escape.

The ambulances are coming. The dead are lying neatly in a row. The wounded lie beside them. Soldiers are trying to dress their wounds. Blimey is unconscious from the loss of blood. Her Burberry will never be any use again. Misery and Cheery lie at my feet. Misery is clasping her unfinished crochet bedspread. Cheery looks curiously naked without her right hand. The stump of the arm is still shielding her face.

A soldier comes over to where I am sitting on the side of the trench.

"Well, you wasn't meant to die to-night," he says.

I turn my head in his direction and begin to laugh softly. He is alarmed.

"Can't get you a drink, can I? You're not hysterical nor nothing?" I tell him no. I have never felt less hysterical in my life.

. . . . . .

Her soul died under a radiant silver moon in the spring of 1918 on the side of a blood-splattered trench. Around her lay the mangled dead and the dying. Her body was untouched, her heart beat calmly, the blood coursed as ever through her veins. But looking deep into those emotionless eyes one wondered if they had suffered much before the soul had left them. Her face held an expression of resignation, as though she had ceased to hope that the end might come.

SIMONE DE BEAUVOIR

From All Said and Done

Simone de Beauvoir (1908–1986) is one of France's most distinguished contemporary writers. Her best-known book, *The Second Sex*, was an early, revolutionary work of gender theory and had a profound influence on the worldwide feminist movement. She was the longtime partner of Jean-Paul Sartre, and herself authored many philosophical works, including *The Ethics of Ambiguity*, one of the finest books to come out of the French existential movement. She also completed a multivolume autobiography, beginning with *Memoirs of a Dutiful Daughter*. A lifelong activist, she supported the Resistance during World War II, and later actively opposed French colonialism in Algeria and American intervention in Vietnam. These brief excerpts are from a long chapter in a later volume of her memoirs, *All Said and Done* (1972), on de Beauvoir's participation in the Vietnam War Tribunals. Modeled on the Nuremberg trials, these tribunals were organized by Lord Bertrand Russell in order to focus world attention on the brutal conflict in Southeast Asia. Commissions of inquiry were sent to Vietnam, and distinguished intellectuals from around the world were invited to preside at a series of hearings and judge whether the United States was guilty of war crimes in Vietnam. Here she describes a session of the tribunal held in Copenhagen in November 1967.

■

Three questions were on the agenda this session:

Had the American forces used or tried out new weapons forbidden by the laws of war?
Were Vietnamese prisoners subjected to inhuman treatment forbidden by the laws of war?
Had there been acts tending towards the extermination of the population and coming within the legal definition of acts of genocide?

We were much concerned by this third question. If our answer was to be *no*, then it would be better not to put the question. And when we considered Hitler's extermination of the Jews we hesitated to liken the war in Vietnam to genocide. At the beginning of the session we had many private conversations on this problem; but we did not reach a decision. The first days the press said we were marking time. But in fact we were not. On Thursday a Japanese delegate brought forward a fresh subject, and he handled it in a most striking manner: this was the subject of defoliation. On the pretext of ensuring the army's safety along the roads and depriving the guerillas of shelter and of food, the Americans were spraying poisonous substances not only on the forests but also on the fields of rice, sugar-cane and vegetables. The operation in fact consisted in destroying the vegetation and poisoning the population. It was a direct and efficacious form of genocide.[1]

From that moment on our interest never slackened. Gisèle Halimi had been to America; the left wing provided her with important documents—newspapers, magazines, and a book on the village of Ben-Suc, which the Americans razed to the ground after having killed some of the men and deported all the inhabitants—and she passed on their contents to us. She had also recorded the evidence of American ex-servicemen. Taken as a whole, her material formed a crushing indictment. What is more, she brought three witnesses, and in the course of the following days they gave their evidence before the court.

The first, Martinsen, was studying psychology at Berkeley University; he had belonged to the "special services"—that is to say he had taught Vietnamese government troops the art of torturing, and he himself had tortured prisoners. He was twenty-three and he was quite good-looking. At first he was very tense and even inhibited. Gradually he relaxed. He seemed to be in the throes of a very serious psychological conflict and to be easing his conscience by speaking out. "I am an average American student and I am a war-criminal," he said in an anguished tone. His evidence lasted an entire afternoon. The Americans claimed that only the government soldiers tortured and that all this was a matter between "yellow men"; but this was "just lies—pure falsehood"; he had beaten up prisoners himself; and he had seen American officers torture them by thrusting pieces of bamboo under their nails. It was usually enlisted men who did it, but always in the presence of a lieutenant or a captain, and the senior officers knew all about it. The victims often died. Martinsen gave a list of the methods used in interrogation. Everyone in the hall listened in tense, horrified silence.

The second witness was a young black named Tuck. He had not himself inflicted torture but he had been present both at torture sessions and massacres. On the orders of an officer he had killed a woman who had not joined the group gathered on the village square quickly enough: if he had disobeyed he would have been shot at once. He described the "interrogations." He had seen one prisoner thrown from a helicopter and he told us how the wounded were finished off. "Our officers think the only good Vietnamese is a dead Vietnamese." He also said, "Another very common thing was that if we were fired on from a village we had our 'crazy moment'—the tanks and machine-guns blazed away for quite a while, firing at everything in the village, living or not." He was asked how many of these "crazy moments" he had witnessed, and he replied, "I've seen them so often! A great many times—it was what you might call quite usual." He also spoke of those camps of deportees the Americans call "strategic villages." "All the people I saw looked as though they were starving, and they were all in rags."

After that we heard the evidence of Duncan, a "green beret" and the author of *New Legions,* a book in which he exposed a great many American war-crimes. He was working for *Ramparts,* a magazine based on Christian principles and actively opposed to the war. First he described the training of the young recruits: on the pretext of teaching them to hold out against torture, they are shown all the different ways of inflicting it. He asserted that the Americans massacred all prisoners in Vietnam except for the officers, who were "questioned." They were then handed over to the government forces, who sent them to death camps. After this he gave us a long account of the "strategic hamlets": he called them "garbage dumps." There are no beds or bedding, no water, no latrines. The stench is abominable. One third of the population in the south has been taken to them. The people have nothing to do. The women and old men just lie on the ground all day; the children beg and filch what they can from the American soldiers; the young women and even the little girls prostitute themselves for food.

All this evidence was extremely painful to hear: these men had actually seen the horrors they described, and this brought them tragically close to us. Their different accounts repeated one another in many points, and there was something both wearing and at the same time cruelly convincing about this reiteration. Even the journalists were impressed, and they gave full reports of these sessions. Martinsen in particular became very popular. At a press-conference he most ably explained the reasons for his presence at Roskilde. Pictures of him were to be seen everywhere.

Bardolini, a French journalist, also spoke of the hell of these "strategic hamlets," and he showed us a film in colour—huge red tents with old men, women and children crowded into them. They were to be seen there in the doorway, sitting listless, quite despairing and bewildered. Theft and prostitution: this entire peasant population, accustomed to a strict code, had been torn away from all that had made up their lives, and they were losing not only their culture but also their code of ethics. It was a positive moral murder.

We also listened to the evidence of two Vietnamese women who had been tortured. One was an "intellectual": she was a pharmacist very well known in Saigon, and this had meant that she was tried before being condemned to life-imprisonment, whereas so many others were executed without any process of law; it was thanks to her wide-spread reputation that she was released after seven years. In her dark blue velvet national dress she was very beautiful and she spoke with great dignity and restraint. She had been appallingly flogged; her chest and belly had been trampled upon; the soles of her feet had been beaten; she had been subjected to the "trip in a submarine," a variation of the mediaeval torture of the funnel; she had been hung up by her wrists; and one day they had tied her half naked to a tree swarming with ants whose slightest bite causes intolerable burning pain and swellings. She also described the treatment inflicted upon other victims: when she spoke of the sufferings of one of her uncles her eyes filled with tears. She was sent to the notorious death-camp of Pulo-Condor. Among other forms of maltreatment, one day she had a bowl emptied over her head—a bowl full of pus, the expectoration of consumptives, vomit, and water in which the lepers had washed: I found this episode even more revolting than all the torture: one's imagination fails to encompass physical pain, whereas disgust can be relayed. The judges asked a great many questions and we admired the way in which she weighed her replies and declined to assert anything that she had not observed herself. The second witness was a Communist who had been burnt with red-hot irons and tortured to the point of becoming an epileptic. But she was less interesting than the other, because she read from a report that she had obviously not written herself.

Of all the evidence we heard, the fullest and most satisfactory was that of Dr. Wolff: he had come straight from Hué, where he had been working as a surgeon in a hospital for the last two years. He was a West German: triangular face, fair hair, broad forehead, blue eyes, a cool unemotional air. In January

1966 he had sent *Les Temps modernes* a remarkable unsigned article on the Americans in Vietnam. He spoke for an hour and he answered all our questions with striking precision and wealth of detail. He began by describing the appearance of the country seen from a plane—it was like the skin of a smallpox patient: eruptions everywhere, vast areas devastated by chemicals, a landscape of dust and ashes. He told us about the military sweeps and searches—the young men taken off by helicopter to interrogation centres, tortured and flung into prison, where they died. Whole territories were completely emptied of their inhabitants: there were four million "re-located" Vietnamese in the South. Then he spoke of the wounds, the burns and the mutilations inflicted on civilian populations by the various anti-personnel weapons such as fragmentation bombs, napalm and phosphorus. He told us how, to amuse the nurses they were pursuing, American officers would take them "hunting Viets" in a plane or a helicopter: all they did in fact was to machine-gun peasants.

This testimony was confirmed by an appalling film that Pic showed us: most of it had been shot by American soldiers themselves.[2] He used two screens, the one to show the moving pictures and the other to show the stills. Both were almost unbearable. In a hospital we saw the faces of adults and children literally melted, seared away, by napalm—faces in which the eyes, staring with horror, were the only remaining human features. Charnel-houses. Bulldozers destroying whole forests. Big leering Americans killing the little Liberation Front soldiers by kicking them in the genitals, shooting them in the back of the neck or, just for laughs, in the anus. And others cheerfully setting fire to straw huts.

Our unanimous decision was that the Americans did make use of forbidden weapons, that they did treat prisoners and civilians in an inhuman manner, contrary to the laws of war, and that they were committing the crime of genocide. We also unanimously condemned their aggression against Laos and the complicity of Thailand and the Philippines. Three members of the tribunal considered that Japan helped the USA but that it was not an accomplice in the aggression against Vietnam. When the replies to all the questions had been delivered there was applause in the hall and on the platform, and people embraced one another.

I retain a lively recollection of this session. As at Stockholm, there was the pleasure of working as a team and that of keeping our friendships up to date; and we learnt even more than we had at the earlier meeting. The distressing side of it all was that because of the negligence of the press there were so few of us to profit from the impressive collection of documents, evidence and explanations. The essence was summed up in two paperbacks published by Gallimard, but too few people read them. American public opinion was overwhelmed by the revelation of the My Lai massacre in March 1968. But Tuck had already spoken of the "crazy moments" that were "ordinarily" allowed the soldiers. The number of victims at My Lai—567, including 170 children—was certainly very much higher than the average; but these murders still formed part and parcel of a routine system: GI's had been fired on from the village; one had been killed; thereupon they had charged and wiped out the population. It was no doubt because these methods were so wide-spread that Nixon had the man responsible for the massacre of My Lai absolved—among so many war-criminals why choose him as a scapegoat rather than another?

Notes

1. On 1 January 1970 *Le Monde* reported: "American scientists have recently called upon the Pentagon to stop the use of certain defoliants that cause malformations in the foetus. According to a Saigon journalist quoted by the *New Haven Register* of 1 November 1969 the South Vietnamese government is trying to keep public opinion in ignorance of the increasing number of babies who are born deformed. The American administration has just banned certain potentially dangerous defoliants in the USA, but they continue to be used in Vietnam. So although it has all the scientific information the White House accepts the risk of employing defoliants that may cause malformations in Vietnamese babies."

2. Pic had obtained photographs and films when he was in the USA.

Translation by André Deutsch

MARGUERITE DURAS

From The War

Marguerite Duras (1914–1996) is a contemporary French novelist and author of many internationally renowned books. She was born at Gia Dinh, in the French colony of Indochina, in the suburbs of Saigon, in 1914, a few weeks before the outbreak of World War I. She wrote of the war crimes of World War II in her critically acclaimed 1985 memoir, *The War*, from which this excerpt comes. The book offers insight into what is often women's lot during times of war, as they wait in tense anxiety in suspended lives for soldiers or loved ones to return from the front lines or prison camps, carrying on lives in which all normalcy has been destroyed. It is based upon Duras's own life and marriage in 1939 to the poet Robert Antelme, and events in Paris under the Occupation. Duras's husband was arrested along with her sister-in-law, Marie-Laure, who died in deportation. Antelme survived and was brought back from Dachau close to death by future French president François Mitterrand, who also introduced Marguerite to the Resistance. After the Liberation, Duras joined the French Communist Party, as many did in reaction to the Nazi Holocaust; she subsequently left the party after the Prague Uprising. By the age of thirty, in the stir of creativity of the postwar period, Duras became an eminent figure among the Paris intelligentsia. A filmmaker as well as a writer, she won renown for such films as *Hiroshima, Mon Amour* (1960), and such novels as *The Lover* (1984), all characterized by her distinctive, unadorned language.

■

There's an awesome amount of murdered people. There's really monumental numbers of dead. Seven million Jews have been exterminated—carried in cattle cars, then gassed in specifically engineered death factories, then burned in specially built ovens. In Paris, people don't talk about the Jews as yet. Their babies were handed over to female officials responsible for strangling Jewish infants and experts in the art of execution by putting pressure on the carotid arteries. They smiled and said it was painless. This new countenance of death has been invented in Germany—organized, rationalized, manufactured before it met with outrage. You're amazed. . . . Some people will always be overcome by it, inconsolable. One of the grandest civilized nations in the world, the age-long capital of music, has just systematically murdered eleven million human beings with the absolute efficiency of a national industry. The whole world looks at the mountain, the mass of death dealt by God's creature to his fellow humans. Someone quotes the name of some German man of letters who's been very upset and become extremely depressed and to whom these matters have given much fodder for thought.

If Nazi crime is not seen in world terms, if it isn't understood collectively, then that man in the concentration camp at Belsen who died alone but with the same communal soul and class cognition that made him undo a bolt on the railroad one night somewhere in Europe, without a leader, without a uniform, without a witness, has been betrayed. If you give a German and not a collective interpretation to the Nazi horror, you reduce the man in Belsen to regional dimensions. The only possible answer to this crime is to turn it into a crime committed by *all* humanity. To share it. Just as the idea of equality and brotherhood. In order to bear it, to digest the idea of it, we must share the crime.

Translation by Daniela Gioseffi with L.B. Luttinger

NATALIA GINZBURG

The Son of Man

Natalia Ginzburg (1916–1999) was an internationally known Italian author of such books as *All My Yesterdays, Family Sayings,* and *It's Difficult to Speak About Myself.* Born in Palermo, Sicily, she lived in Rome for many years before escaping to a small village in Abruzzo to live during World War II. Her husband, a Resistance fighter, was imprisoned, tortured, and finally murdered by the Nazis. In this personal essay, written in 1946, she explains what it was like to live through that war and the indelible mark it has left on the lives of those who survived it. The piece is taken from an all-new edition of Ginzburg's selected essays, entitled *A Place to Live* (2000), translated by the accomplished feminist author Lynn Sharon Schwartz for Seven Stories Press in New York.

■

There was the war, with so many houses collapsing all around us, and now people no longer feel safe and secure in their own houses, as once we did. Some things are incurable, and though years go by, we never recover. Even if we have lamps on the tables again, vases of flowers and portraits of our loved ones, we have no more faith in such things, not since we had to abandon them in haste or hunt for them in vain amid the rubble.

It is useless to think we can recover from twenty years of what we went through. Those of us who were persecuted will never again rest easy. For us the insistent blare of a doorbell in the middle of the night can mean only the one word, "police." And there's no use telling ourselves over and over that nowadays the word "police" may mean friendly faces we can call on for protection and help.

For us this word will always trigger suspicion and fright. I can watch my sleeping children and think with relief that I won't have to wake them in the middle of the night and run away. But it is not a deep or utter relief. I always have the feeling that someday we'll have to jump up at night and run away again, leaving everything behind, quiet rooms and letters and clothing and mementos.

The experience of evil, once suffered, is never forgotten. Anyone who has seen houses collapse knows all too well how fragile vases of flowers, paintings and white walls really are. He knows all too well what a house is made of. A house is made of bricks and mortar and it can crumble. A house is nothing very solid. It can crumble from one moment to the next. Behind the serene vases of flowers, behind the teapots, the rugs and the waxed floors, is the other, the true face of the house, the horrible face of the crumbled house.

We will never be cured of this war. It is useless. We are people who will never feel at ease, never think and plan and order our lives in peace. Look what has been done to our houses. Look what has been done to us. We can never rest easy again.

We have known reality in its most somber guise and are no longer repelled by it. Some still complain that the writers use bitter, violent language and tell of hard, sad things, that they present reality in its most desolate terms.

We cannot lie in books and we cannot lie in anything else we do. This may be the one good that has come out of the war: not lying and not tolerating the lies of others. This is who we young people are now, this is our generation. Our elders are still under the spell of lies, of the veils and masks shrouding reality. Our language saddens and offends them. They cannot understand the way we see reality: we are right up against the essence of things. This is the one benefit the war has brought, but only to the young. To those who are older it has brought nothing but insecurity and fear. We young people are afraid too, we too feel unsafe in our houses, but we are not defenseless against our fear. We have toughness and a strength that those who came before us have never known.

For some the war began simply with the war, with the crumbling houses and the Germans, but for others it started earlier, in the first years of Fascism, so that their sense of insecurity and perpetual danger is all the greater. For many of us it began long years ago—the sense of danger, of needing to hide, of suddenly having to leave the warmth of bed and home. It crept into our childhood games, it followed us to our desks at school, it taught us to see enemies everywhere. It was like that for many of us in Italy and elsewhere; we trusted that one day we would be able to walk the streets of our city in peace, but now that we can, perhaps, walk in peace, we realize we haven't gotten over the damage we suffered. And so we are constantly forced to seek new strength and new toughness to confront whatever reality might bring. We are compelled to seek an inner peace that rugs and vases of flowers cannot yield.

There is no peace for the son of man. Foxes and wolves have their dens, but the son of man has nowhere to lay his head. We are a generation of human beings, not a generation of foxes and wolves. We all long to lay our heads down somewhere, we long for a warm, dry little den. But there is no peace for the sons of men. All of us, at some point in our lives, were deluded into thinking we could lull ourselves to sleep somewhere or other, could seize upon some certainty, some faith, and finally rest our bones. But all the old certainties have been wrenched from us, and faith, in the end, has never been a place to take one's ease.

And we have no more tears. What moved our parents has no power to move us. Our parents and the older generations reproach us for the way we raise our children. They would like us to lie to our children the way they lied to us. They would like our children to play with plush dolls in pretty pink rooms with little trees and rabbits painted on the walls. They would like us to swaddle their childhood in veils and lies and keep reality in its true essence carefully hidden from them. But we cannot do it. We cannot do it with children we woke in the dead of night and dressed frantically in the dark, either to run or hide, or because the sirens were lacerating the skies. We cannot do it with children who have seen fear and horror on our faces. We cannot make ourselves tell these children that we found them under cabbages or that someone who has died has gone on a long trip.

There is a bottomless abyss between us and earlier generations. Their dangers were trivial and their houses rarely collapsed. Earthquakes and fires were not common or frequent occurrences. The women knitted and told the cook to get dinner ready and received their friends in houses that didn't collapse. They pondered and planned and expected to order their lives in peace. It was another era and maybe they were fortunate. But we are bound to this our anguish and glad, at heart, of our destiny as human beings.

Translation by Lynn Sharon Schwartz

FADWA TUQAN

Face Lost in the Wilderness

Fadwa Tuqan (b. 1917), born in Nablus, Palestine, is considered to be a major voice for her people and one of the finest writers of the Arab world. Sister of Ibrahim Tuqan, a well-known Palestinian poet of the 1930s and 1940s, she spent her youth in Nablus when it was still part of Jordan. Though her earlier poems were love poems, after the war of 1967, known as the Six-Day War, she turned to the serious and tragic subject of Israeli occupation of the West Bank, which has caused terrible loss and suffering on both sides of the continuing conflict. Fadwa also describes Palestinian resistance in the years before the Intifadah in her many works of prose and poetry. Here she is translated by the accomplished Arab American poet Naomi Shihab Nye with Salma Khadra Jayyusi, also a Palestinian. Tuqan still lives in Nablus.

■

Do not fill postcards with memories.
Between my heart and the luxury of passion
stretches a desert where ropes of fire
blaze and smoulder, where snakes
coil and recoil, swallowing blossoms
with poison and flame.

No! Don't ask me to remember. Love's memory
is dark, the dream clouded;
love is a lost phantom
in a wilderness night.
Friend, the night has slain the moon.
In the mirror of my heart you can find no shelter,
only my country's disfigured face
her face, lovely and mutilated,
her precious face . . .

How did the world revolve in this way?
Our love was young. Did it grow in this horror?
In the night of defeat, black waters
covered my land, blood on the walls
was the only bouquet.
I hallucinated: "Open your breast,
open your mother's breast for an embrace
priceless are the offerings!"
The jungle beast was toasting in the
tavern of crime; winds of misfortune
howled in the four corners.
He was with me that day.

I didn't realise morning
would remove him.
Our smiles cheated sorrow
as I raved: "Beloved stranger!
Why did my country become a gateway
to hell? Since when are apples bitter?
When did moonlight stop bathing orchards?
My people used to plant fields and love life.
Joyfully they dipped their bread in oil.
Fruits and flowers tinted the land
with magnificent hues—
will the seasons ever again
give their gifts to my people?

Sorrow—Jerusalem's night is silence and smoke.
They imposed a curfew; now nothing beats in the
heart of the City but their bloodied heels
under which Jerusalem trembles
like a raped girl.

Two shadows from a balcony
stared down at the City's night.
In the corner a suitcase of clothes,

souvenirs from the Holy Land—
his blue eyes stretched like sad lakes.
He loved Jerusalem. She was his mystical lover.
On and on I ranted, "Ah, love! Why did God abandon
my country? Imprisoning light, leaving us
in seas of darkness?"
The world was a mythical dragon standing
at her gate. "Who will ever solve this mystery,
beloved, the secret of these words?"

Now twenty moons have passed,
twenty moons, and my life continues.
Your absence too continues. Only one memory remaining:
The face of my stricken country filling my heart.

And my life continues—
the wind merges me with my people
on the terrible road of rocks and thorns.
But behind the river, dark forests of spears
sway and swell; the roaring storm
unravels mystery, giving to dragon silence
the power of words.

A rush and din, flame and sparks
lighting the road—
one group after another
falls embracing, in one lofty death.

The night, no matter how long, will continue
to give birth to star after star
and my life continues,
my life continues.

Translation by Salma Khadra Jayyusi with Naomi Shihab Nye

DORIS LESSING

From The Wind Blows Away Our Words

Doris Lessing (b. 1919) was born Doris May Taylor in Persia (now Iran). Both her parents were British. In 1925, lured by the prospect of getting rich through maize farming, the family moved to Southern Rhodesia (now Zimbabwe). The thousand-odd acres of bush her father had bought failed to yield any wealth. Lessing has described her childhood as a mixture of pleasure in nature and much pain. Lessing's formal education ended at age thirteen, but she became a self-educated intellectual. Feeding her mind with books ordered from London, Lessing also spent her early years absorbing her father's bitter memories of World War I. "We are all of us made by war," Lessing has written, "twisted and warped by war, but we seem to forget it." In 1949, after various odd jobs and two marriages, Lessing moved to London with her young son and published her first novel, *The Grass Is Singing*. After writing the *Children of Violence* series (1951–1959), Lessing broke new ground with *The Golden Notebook* (1962), a narrative experiment, in which the multiple selves of a contemporary woman are rendered in detailed depth. Criticized for being "unfeminine" in her story of female anger and aggression, Lessing responded, "Apparently what many women were thinking, feeling, experiencing came as a great surprise." Lessing's other important novels include *The Good Terrorist* (1985) and *The Fifth Child* (1988), and she has completed two volumes of an acclaimed autobiography. In 1995, she visited South Africa—her first visit since being deported in 1956 for her progressive political views. Her 1987 book on the Soviet war in Afghanistan, *The Wind Blows Away Our Words*, illustrates how religious beliefs of indigenous peoples can be manipulated by opposing political forces and how interventionism, east and west, reigns with terror and confusion in the lives of innocent civilians, especially powerless women, around the globe. It takes on new resonance fifteen years later.

■

Coming out of Pakistan it was as if a clamour suddenly fell silent. In Peshawar I was meeting Afghans all the time, refugees and fighters, and each one had a plea, implicit or very explicit indeed: a terrible anguish of need. If I had been able to bring myself to say: "Every day on the television screens we in the West see suffering, like yours, from several parts of the world," the reply would certainly have been, "Yes, but it is we who are fighting for you against a common enemy." They cannot understand why we do not help them. They are, all the time, surprised at our short-sightedness. They are also reproachful, incredulous, astonished, silent with hurt pride. A few of them have been driven to beg, needing to feed families—but not many, for Afghan pride is strong. Some demand, because they feel aid is their right. They expostulate. They reason with you.

And then, suddenly, the indifference of the West—silence. Even if you have expected it, it is a shock. Painful.

In *The Times* of 22 November 1986 was a small piece saying that 60,000 Afghans were fleeing to Pakistan, because the Russians had destroyed crops (they burn them in the fields). As Pakistan is no longer registering refugees for food and aid, many of these 60,000 people will die. Many of the previous outflows of refugees have died—are dying now. This piece of news was on an inside page. Information about Afghanistan is always relegated to that part of a newspaper which is reserved for secondary and unimportant news.

It is a good deal that the information is there at all. Two years ago I was in Toronto, and the *Wall Street Journal* asked to interview me. The young woman who came said she would like to talk about what interested me. Impressed by this novel approach by a journalist, I said I would like to talk about Afghanistan, which had been fighting the Russians for five years, with little or no assistance from the outside world. Her face showed she was already losing interest. I said it was unprecedented for a war to be fought for five years by a virtually unarmed people against a super power, while the world took virtually no notice. She murmured, at once, "Vietnam"—as I expected she would. I said that the Vietnamese had been armed, equipped. I said that a million Afghan civilians had been murdered by the Russians. There were five million Afghans in exile—it was as if a third of the population of the United States had taken refuge from an aggressor in Canada. At this she announced that it was all very hard to believe. The interview then continued on all too familiar lines. When it was printed, there was no mention of Afghanistan. Since then, the *Wall Street Journal* has been, as we say, "very good" about Afghanistan. But anyone involved in this business knows that there is a wall of indifference, both in Britain and in the United States, and this is so strong, so irrational, one has to begin asking why.

There are "about" ten million refugees in the world, and half of them are Afghan. You never see figures of Afghan refugees as a headline, but very often indeed the headlines, "So and so many thousand refugees in Sudan/Ethiopia."

What determines the newsworthiness of a catastrophe? Why has the horror of Afghanistan never been considered important? To answer such questions, it seems to me, would explain a good deal of the assumptions and prejudice that govern our organs of information.

The articles I wrote about what I saw in the refugee camps in Pakistan, about what I heard from the Afghan fighters, have been refused by all the American and European newspapers they were sent to. By the *Washington Post.* By *Newsweek.* By the *New Yorker.* And the *New York Times* magazine section wanted something "more personal."

I take the liberty of believing that had these articles been on another topic not subject to this mysterious inhibition, this ukase, they would have been printed. . . .

How many of the muhjahidin, how many of the people fleeing from the Russians, how many of the people still living inside, will die this winter and spring? I expect to see, tucked away on the back pages of *The Times,* or the *Independent,* or the *Guardian:* "It is estimated that hundreds of thousands of Afghans have died of starvation in the winter and spring months." While on the front page there are headlines about famine in Africa.

It is hard to get figures for deaths from starvation in Africa. Impressed by that engaging young man Bob Geldof's shout to the world "Twenty-two million people are starving to death in Africa," I tried to track down the real figures. According to Peter Gill's book, recommended by Oxfam, *A Year in the Death of Africa,* 200,000 people certainly died of famine in 1984-5. According to expert foreign relief officials, the total figures "may have" reached a million.

Why are these 200,000 or a million Africans so much more deserving of headlines than the equivalent number of Afghans?

It is because, for some reason or another, we are sensitized to Africa.

A month ago, a friend trying to get contributions for Afghan Relief in Kent was told by a woman that, "We have our own charities, nearer home, to think about." Asked if she had contributed to Ethiopian famine relief, she said, "Of course."

There are some standard responses to the situation in Afghanistan. It was discouraging coming home, experiencing such a narrow range of push-button responses.

"Afghanistan is the Soviet Union's Vietnam." Well, when you analyze it, no it isn't, except that in both cases "underdeveloped" (or if you like, "Third

World") people opposed, oppose, powerful world powers. For one thing, the Vietnamese had all kinds of weapons, training, aid. For another, the war was fought in a blaze of publicity, it was a televised war. We watched it progress, on our television screen, night after night.

"Did you know that the Russians have tied living people together, poured petrol over them, and set fire to them?" I asked.

Judiciously: "Like the Americans did in Vietnam."

"Well, actually, no. They did not."

"They used napalm, that comes to the same thing."

"Well, that's all right then, isn't it? I suppose one could say."

From a nurse in a hospital, who asked where I had been, "Where's that?"

From another, an Irishwoman, told that half the world's refugees are Afghans: "The trouble with these people is that they have so many children."

On the radio, a journalist who had interviewed a fundamentalist guerilla leader and disagreed with certain of his attitudes: "Why are we supporting such people?" Then, in a light humorous voice: "I suppose to bash the Russians."

Listening to the tones of voice people use when discussing Afghanistan is revealing. A light, humorous voice is common: the one always used, deliberately or unconsciously, on the media to signal to listeners or viewers that the matter isn't serious.

The radio again: The United Nations Commissioner for Refugees was asking for forty million pounds because the conditions for refugees everywhere was worsening. Two examples were given. The second was that certain work programmes in Pakistan for Afghan refugees were being cut. The commentator was in a hurry to get to something more interesting, and he spoke in a light, casual voice, thrown away . . . you'd never guess we were talking about people who might die without these work programmes. . . .

The Gorbachev claim: "There will be an early end to the Afghan War," is yet another clever ploy by clever propagandists.

Reporting on the negotiations for concluding the Afghan War, a new note is being struck. One of the obstacles—so we are being told—to the Soviet agreement to conclude the war, is its dislike of Islamic Fundamentalism. They do not dislike Fundamentalism. They are working very closely with Khomeini's Iran, supplying arms, experts, and advisers, technology, machinery. I heard high-level Afghans describe Iran as a Soviet satellite. But they know that we very much dislike and fear Islamic Fundamentalism. They are deliberately playing on this dislike, this fear.

Why do we fall for it, again and again? And again.

The reason is deep in our psychology, is rooted in attitudes which are taken for granted, largely unexamined. Unexamined certainly by those in whom they are the strongest.

There is a reluctance to criticize the Soviet Union. After all that has happened, all the information we have had about the place, an inhibition persists and is cleverly manipulated by the Russians.

It is almost impossible to raise this subject without being accused of being "reactionary"—so polarized have our responses become, and I feel a sort of despair even trying. There is a web, or spectrum, of attitudes, highlighted at one end by the court case at this moment going on in Australia, over exactly how many Soviet agents there have been in high places in this country: how much treachery has been going on, to use a quaint old-fashioned term. The other end of the spectrum is precisely this reluctance to criticize the Russians for anything, this readiness to excuse them. So, if the Soviet Union, at Chernobyl, releases radioactivity that poisons its own waters and soil, and will causes the deaths of no one yet knows how many of its citizens, that poisons crops and soil all over Europe, with still unknown long-term results, then in no time at all we will be reading and hearing Chernobyl and Three Mile Island equated—Three Mile Island which killed no one, and did not poison food, animals and soil. It means that if the Soviet Union shoots down a civilian airliner with the loss of everyone on board, almost at once this will be in some way proved to be the fault of the U.S., and very soon the incident will be lodged in people's minds as equally the fault of the Soviet Union and the U.S. It turns out that, in fact, the evidence seems to show that the United States was not at fault. But whether it was or not will make no difference: there is a need to think it is.

The United States' (to my mind, mistaken) policy in Nicaragua is relentlessly criticized at the top of everybody's voice, vituperously, endlessly—but the Soviet policy in Afghanistan is excused, softened.

This complex of attitudes is fascinating the psychologists, and will fascinate the historians even more.

How, they will ask, did it come about that the most brutal, cynical regime of its time, was so much admired, excused, by people describing themselves as humanist, humanitarians, democrats, and long after its true nature was thoroughly exposed?

Perhaps there are hints, suggestions we can study.

For instance: recently, a Russian said on television that a remark from a critic to the effect that the Soviet regime had murdered ten times as many people as Hitler, had been censored out of a programme, "because it would hurt the feelings of us Russians." Which must remind people of my generation of a remark made by a certain female Russian party apparatchik who, faced with Khrushchev's speech at the Twentieth Congress, said daintily that she didn't think it ought ever to have been made, because it isn't very nice for us, is it?

Well, no, none of it was very nice for those of us who went along (for whatever length of time it was) with the Soviet "dream."

Which murdered so many . . . how many?

Oh these estimates! "It is estimated that . . ."

Was it *seven million* or *nine million* deliberately murdered during the forcible collectivization of the peasants in the Soviet Union? By Stalin. As it is put: "Stalin murdered . . ." as if he did it with his own hands alone. But it was with enthusiastic and efficient co-operation of hundreds of thousands of devoted Communist Party members.

Apparently it was not *twenty million* Russian soldiers who died in the last war, but *eight million*—as Stalin himself said. The *twenty million* now cited (by the West too, following the Russians' lead) includes all those murdered by Stalin (with the enthusiastic and efficient co-operation of Party members) in the Gulag.

These figures are themselves in question—not the *eight million* who died in the war (if Stalin is to be believed) but the *twelve million* murdered. According to Victor Suvorov (the pseudonym of a Soviet officer who defected), the Soviet demographers say that the population should have reached 315 million in 1959, but the census showed only 209 million. Where, he asks, are the missing hundred million? (Hitler, he says, is estimated to have "executed" twenty million.)

What's twenty million? Or even a hundred million, these days? When I read that, during The Great Leap Forward in China, between twenty and forty million had died, I thought this must be the apotheosis of statistical whimsicality, until a short time later came the news that "between twenty and eighty million had died during the Cultural Revolution." (Both campaigns, of course, were conducted with the enthusiastic and skilled co-operation of devoted comrades.) Mind you, this cavalier attitude to the deaths of millions of Chinese probably derives from the Chinese themselves. Mao Tse Tung, addressing a crowd of around a million people in Bei Jing, shouted that it would not matter if the West did drop nuclear weapons on his people and kill half the population because there would be plenty of Chinese left. The crowd, I was told by a friend who was present, roared approval.

Statistics are tricky for other reasons than the *amour propre* of murderers, or the round figures of a statistician. When I told the *Wall Street Journal* woman two years' ago that there were two and a half million refugees in Pakistan, I was scaling it down, because of the enormity of it: the figure was already supposed to be three and a half million.

On this trip we heard various estimates, ranging from three and a half to four and a half million refugees in Pakistan; between half a million and two million in Iran. The wide divergence of figures in Iran seems to me a bad thing: an indication of worse than indifference, perhaps a cover-up.

Exiles from Afghanistan are always visualized as the people in the camps. But in addition there are hundreds of thousands in exile in London, Paris, Canada, the USA, and Australia. These are mostly middle class—the educated members of the population who were not murdered, who are not still in prisons in Afghanistan. These refugees are never mentioned.

In a world where we can accept as normal "Between twenty and eighty million were killed . . . I suppose five million Afghan refugees are hardly worth mentioning. And the million Afghan civilians murdered by the Russians? This figure, it is estimated, is now much higher—is growing larger all the time.

The people murdered by the Khmer Rouge, two million of the population, were not mentioned either. At the time no one demonstrated for them, the humanitarians were not protesting, circulating petitions. But then they were murdered by a communist dictator—(with the energetic co-operation of the young comrades) so the automatic inhibition came into action: rather bad taste, really, to mention it.

What has happened is that we have been conditioned to see Hitler's Germany, which lasted for thirteen years, a very short time, as the archetype of evil for our time; have accepted this continual hammering on one nerve. Several times a week we read, or hear, versions of this: "So and so is the worst butcher since Hitler." This pattern of thinking ignores Stalin, Mao Tse Tung, Pol Pot, the invaders of Afghanistan.

It has probably often happened in the past that a terrible atrocity has become the symbol or shorthand for other, lesser or greater, atrocities, so that they become forgotten. Our minds seem to work like this. We may observe how they work watching the changes in how we refer to the murder of six million Jews. When the news was fresh, we said, "the six million Jews murdered in the gas chambers by Hitler." This became shortened to "the six million Jews murdered by Hitler." While our minds cannot really take in the enormity of the six million, at least this is a number, a figure, standing for people, for human beings; but now there is a catch-phrase, The Holocaust, because of a television programme. The humanity of the murdered people is diminished by the slogan. Soon we may forget how many people were killed. We have already forgotten, because of this way of making Hitler stand for the evils of our time, the Jews murdered by Stalin who, in the few years just before he died (referred to then as "The Black Years") were systematically killed in the newly occupied countries of Eastern Europe and in the Soviet Union itself. It is on record that medieval tortures, medieval methods of killing, were brought out of museums and used. These poor victims are not mentioned now. How many were there of them? Hundreds of thousands? A million? Who knows! Are they ignored because there were comparatively few of them? I don't think there are any memorials to them anywhere.

We consider some forms of murder worse than others. Why should the murder of the six million Jews be worse than, say, the deliberate killing, by starvation, as a matter of policy, of seven to nine million, mostly Ukrainian peasants? If one were to ask this—and it certainly needs temerity to ask—the reply would be, "Because it was a deliberate, racial murder, qualitatively different because of the use of the gas chambers." But this "six million"—the Holocaust—has itself been simplified. Hitler also killed, on racial grounds, "about" one million gypsies. Many of them in the gas chambers. They died because they were gypsies, and—Hitler said—racially inferior. These people are never mentioned. There are no books written by the victims, no television or radio programmes, no memorial services, no memorials to the "approximately" one million gypsies murdered by Hitler. (And, of course, by his party members.) Do we share Hitler's view that gypsies do not matter? Of course not: it is just that this enormity has been swallowed up by something greater—in number. But if six million Jews are a Holocaust, then are not one million gypsies one sixth of a Holocaust? Should we not put aside this word, Holocaust, and use language that shows some thought, and care, for the dead?

Not only the gypsies have been forgotten. Hitler is supposed to have murdered, in Germany and in the countries occupied by Germany, "about twelve million people. Six million Jews, one million gypsies—that makes seven million, and leaves five million. Who were they? Before the murder of the "racially inferior" Jews and gypsies began, many Germans resisted Hitler and were killed.

Hitler's Germany murdered German communists, socialists, trade unionists, and ordinary decent people. The wound made by the killing of the Jews in the extermination camps is so deep that it has been almost impossible to concede any humanity to the Germans of that time. But surely at some point we should start looking at the whole business more coolly? Who were these other five million murdered by Hitler? How many of them were German? Is it not time that the Germans who were the first to fight Hitler (and they must have felt themselves the loneliest, the most isolated people in the world, for no one then was standing up to Hitler)—is it not time they were counted, and honoured, their story at last told? Until we do this I believe we shall be poorer for it, as we are when we allow ourselves black and white judgments, pattern thinking, oversimplification.

We ourselves are the prisoners of these numbers, these figures, the statistics—the millions; and millions upon millions. Is it possible that our careless, our casual, use of these "millions" is one of the reasons for brutality, for cruelty?

Writing this, I have been haunted by some words of the Russian poet Osip Mandelstam who died in the Gulag:

"and only my own kind will kill me."

ANDRÉE CHÉDID

Death in Slow Motion

Andrée Chédid (b. 1921) is of Lebanese-Syrian-Egyptian descent. She grew up in Egypt impressed with its ancient mythology. As a child she often spent holidays in France. At the American University in Cairo, she wrote her first poems, using English and a pen name to see if she could attract readers. She met and married a medical student, Louis Chedid, and they went to Paris to live and raise a family. Though Chedid is an expatriate by choice, her work is permeated with her love for the cultures of the Middle East. Her themes involving war and violence show the devastation of love perpetuated by such horrors. Her novel *A House Without Roots* (1985) ends tragically when a sniper's bullet during a women's peace march in Beirut destroys all loving ambitions. "Death in Slow Motion" first appeared just after the start of the Lebanese war and is from her collection *Modes Miroir Magies* (1988)—the lead story of which portrays the life of a maimed child, victim of war. Her collection of selected poems is entitled *Fugitive Suns*.

■

The young woman felt the point of impact of the bullet in her back. A brief, sharp pain. She continued walking as if nothing had happened; but the illusion did not last. Around her: uprooted trees, the street torn up, charred and gaping rectangles of buildings, proved clearly that the fighting had been violent; and the truce, once more precarious. M. had just been hit by a sudden blast of which she was not the target; but her wound was quite real.

She didn't wish to know more. The pain had left her; what counted at that moment, more than her very life, was to reach the place where someone was waiting for her; at the head of the bridge, in the angle of the parapet.

The clear light illuminated a deserted environment, shone upon her faces, clothed her thirty-year-old body. It would move forward, her body; she would force it to move. She *will* use all her strength, she *will* hold on. She *will* get through the quarter of an hour which separates her from the meeting.

The street wavers, darkens; all at once the air thickens and the sky is shrouded over. An infinite slowness governs the motions of M., her sensations weaken. Only the pressing desire to arrive in sight of the bridge still stabs her.

Pushing her hands, her arms straight before her, she looks to each of them in turn, to draw forward her body which has grown heavy, her legs which are stuffed with cotton-wool. The anguish in case she does not arrive in time is eating into her more savagely than the bullet.

Where and why fix the boundaries of this place? A succession of names come to mind. In the mud of rice fields, on the asphalt of cities, imprisoned in a crowd which is destroyed or dying in solitude, the massacred ones, the refugees, those shot or tortured converge at once into this place, into someone. Into this living woman, wounded to death. Violences pile upon each other, horror over-lying horror, bloody faces, faces drained of blood, a haemorrhage of men . . . What does the place matter? Everywhere humanity is involved, and the pageant is without end. In each body struck down all bodies groan and founder, blown by blind forces, into the same hell.

M. has counted too much upon her own strength; now seeking help around her, her eyes find nothing. She drags herself toward the wall; her hands grope, they cling to its roughness. She struggles again, persists, her head and shoulders draw-ing themselves upwards, but her feeble knees buckle, dropping her to the ground.

M. calls. Her voice catches in her throat, merely inflames her temples, becomes a murmur brushing her lips and then dies out. For a second time a smarting pang pierces her body from one point to another. A warm flow seeps between her shoulder blades, making her shirt sticky.

Now the young woman stops resisting her body, but tries rather to go along with it. Avoiding sudden movements, she accompanies her flesh, its whirling, its rotation; she does not struggle against the shaking head or the waving arms which raise themselves up, beat at the air, or even grasp for support. Husbanding her breath in the hope of surviving until the coming of a passer-by to whom she can entrust the message, M. lets herself be manoeuvred, with-out losing herself from view.

Twisted, she twists again, is bent over, pivots slowly, as in the movies, through the length of a heavy fall, until she gradually lands on the pavement where she finds herself huddled in the foetal position.

Her cheek to the ground, her eyes watching, clinging desperately to the remaining glimmers of awareness, the young woman panics at the disappear-ance of the sunlight behind a thin cloud. But, quickly again, the sun reappears. She experiences a real comfort in that. Not far away, a window creaks. The smell of coffee reaches her.

M. drives away the memories which flow over her in waves; she does not want anything to exist but the present moment, nothing other than the portion of the future which she is still seeking to save. Taking infinite precautions, she succeeds in drawing a coloured postcard from her pocket, and a stub of pencil. The end is near, so near, but to live on a bit was still possible, wasn't it? Death overhangs her tiny territory which, minute by minute, is shrinking. She sees once more—with its large brownish wings—the kite which planes endlessly above the buildings of her native city before swooping down majestically on a morsel of food placed upon the ledge of a balcony.

On her left, some distance away, a *port-cochère* has just been opened. Before venturing into the street, an old couple carefully observe the roofs on which sharpshooters are often positioned. The man carries a suitcase crudely tied with twine. Once outside they straighten and hold hands. M. drinks them in with her eyes, takes refuge between the two palms so gently joined; she poses, like the old woman, her head upon the chest of her companion, receives the same kiss upon her hair . . .

From the depth of her silence, M. cries out towards them and desperately seeks to draw their attention. Why did she put on this grey dress which blends in so with the stony ground?

Neither of them notices her. They speak in hushed tones to each other; then they start off in the opposite direction.

Just as she goes forward, the old woman turns one last time towards her abandoned lodgings. There, down there, she makes out a body stretched on the pavement.

"Stop. Look." Quickly they turn back. Supporting each other, they cross the road as quickly as their legs will allow.

The old man kneels down, examines the wounded woman, realises that the situation is grave, fatal. Suddenly, overcome with indignation, with "Why?" his eyes fill with anger and with tears; while the woman cries out, knocks upon doors, tries to arouse the neighbours. No response. Most of the buildings are empty, their inhabitants have fled to the country. After the recent sporadic gunfire the rest of the population goes into hiding, fearing that the fighting is going to begin again.

With an unexpected effort M. raises her head, with trembling fingers offers a card. The man takes the picture, looks at it, turns it over; the back is covered with writing in brown ink.

"I can't see well. You read it."

Drawing her silver-rimmed glasses from the case suspended around her neck, the old woman reads aloud. The face of the young woman appears to relax.

"I'll go."

"Alone?"

"You can see very well that we can't just leave her alone."

He agrees. Tucking in her elbows, going as fast as she can, she runs up the middle of the street, exposed on all sides to hostile fire, impetuous as always! He watches her, growing smaller as he watches, and he follows her with his eyes, anxious at heart. He sees her again . . .

But this time it is in the past. She is the same age as the young woman dying. To rejoin him from the other side of the boulevard, she hurls herself into the crowd, she runs towards him, she appears bigger, charging between the vehicles, cheeks flushed . . . her hair flying wildly, reckless as always!

Seated upon the parapet at the turn of the bridge, he was just putting his foot on the ground. The evening before he had just discovered the address of the young woman and knew that she would have received his card. The city, he was thinking, had been granted peace once again, and M. was punctuality itself. The waiting had been too unbearably long; surely she would not be coming.

From a distance, because of the same blue sweater he was wearing in the photo, the old woman recognised him. Waving the card in her extended hand she tried to make a sign to him; then a loaded bus honked so stridently behind her that she jumped on to the pavement to let it pass; it grazed her slightly and continued on its way.

A moment later, she saw the young man grasp an arm extended from the vehicle. Hooking himself on, he leapt on to the running-board and was swallowed up in its interior . . . The old woman shouted in vain, the rumbling of the machine smothering her words. In a few seconds, the bus vanished behind a cloak of dust.

Crushed, she leant back against the parapet; let several minutes pass before reading and rereading the message on the card. With each word a shred of her own youth was torn from her. Shuddering at the thought that he who was going away, without knowing anything at all, could have been her own companion, she had but one intention: to get back to her man at once. Swiftly, she again took the road against the traffic, muttering to herself by heart the words on the card:

Destruction, horror and hate have gripped the faces of everyone. In whom, in what can we believe from now on? Since daily I live with death all seems mad, useless—except true love. We love each other, M., whatever may have taken place. I shall wait for you the day after tomorrow at one in the afternoon at the turn of the great bridge, as at our first meeting (six years ago). A friend will bring you this word. I will be certain that you have received it. If you do not come, it is because all will have been definitely broken off.

Just below, the young woman had written in wavering letters in pencil: "I was coming . . ."

The old woman kneeled down, put her arm around the shoulders of her husband, told him of the failed meeting, adding: "One day, we must, we must find him again." In turn, in a low voice, the old man whispered that a passer-by had gone in search of an ambulance; but he had known from the very start there was no hope of saving the young woman.

The young woman no longer moved and hardly breathed at all. The old woman bent over her, swept the wan cheek with her warm breath and brushed the temple with her lips. Then she drew back the hair, freed the ear, and taking care with each syllable, carefully poured out one word after the other.

"He was waiting for you at the turn of the great bridge. I have seen him, little one. I have spoken to him."

A sigh from M. urged her to go on. "He is on his way. He is coming."

Raising her face towards the old man she met his glance of comradeship. Soon he took the delay: "he is at the end of the street and he is coming towards us. I recognise his blue sweater."

The old woman echoed, "There he is!"

"He approaches . . ."

Their voices came together. Waves flowed through the veins of the young woman, spread throughout her frame, a surge of joy broke through her features; from her breast there arose a sigh greater than the seas.

A giddiness of joy and distress, of despair and calm overtook the old couple. The absurdity and the meaning of things intermingled in their minds. Their hands sought each other, to form but a single hand.

A single hand which placed itself like a cloak of tenderness over the young motionless hand. The hand which was not yet completely chilled.

Translation by David Bruner

GUENI ZAIMOF

The Star Obscure

Gueni Zaimof (b. 1922), a Bulgarian poet with a degree from the National Academy of Music in Sofia, is a planetary spirit, having lived in exile from her native land, but proud of its cultural accomplishments. She has published many volumes of verse in Bulgarian, Italian, and English. To present poetry on themes of world peace, she has attended numerous international conferences. This verse, from a collection by the same name, explains the pain of the exiled who live between East and West, whose lives were stunted by the Cold War, which divided humanity into armed camps of nuclear destruction.

■

Atrocity . . . And with the star obscure
alone, with no one close, so far the homeland.
My Vladimir? . . . War took him and for sure
the sun got cold forever. In this torment,

I'm neither poet, nor a woman, but
blood and tears, scream and hatchet.
The air hisses.
My soul in the last minutes still rebutes.
Smashed to bits on the iron curtain.

VESNA PARUN

The War

Vesna Parun (b. 1922) is a celebrated poet of the former Yugoslavia. She has published numerous volumes of poems widely read throughout her native Croatia. From a collected volume of her works published in Zagreb, simply entitled *Poems*, comes this verse, chronicling the chaos set in motion by World War II and contrasting it with the pristine peace of ordinary life. Ivana Spalatin, the translator, is a scholar of the Croatian language, a poet, and an art historian born in Zagreb, and now living in Texas.

■

My grandfather sits in front of the house as leaves fall.
　　　　He looks at the figs that dry on the stone,
while the sun, very orange, vanishes behind the small vineyards
　　　　I remember from childhood.

The voice of my grandfather is golden, like the melody of an old clock,
and his dialect is rich, his words filled with restlessness.
The legend of "Seven Lean Years" follows right after the "Our Father,"
　　　　short and eternal.
One day, there was no more fishing.
Now, there is war.
The enemy surrounds the port for miles around.
The whole tiny island trembles in eclipse.
All her sons disappeared in search of war wages
a long time ago.
Canada,
Australia . . .
They'll board them next for Japan.
It's possible they'll stay forever peeking amidst the bamboo.
This is the second winter they've marched nonstop.
Even the fish sound gloomy in their chase.
One grandson is handsome and good, yet we'll find him in the snow one day
when the mountains are tired.

The girls sing as they prepare the picnic soup.
The children squat on the floor, very frightened
of the boots of the elegant old man.
One mother thinks of the sons and father who became a Malayan.

Strange, how this family has been scattered over four continents.
These big brawny people sound like children in their letters.

My grandfather stares at the red sun in the vineyard,
worn to silence, because death approaches the old fisherman of the sea.
Foreign greed; strange hunger. Freedom is a bit of bread crust.

Ah, tell the earth that watermills should run faster!
A storm took the leaves away; whatever's right shall be.

So, the young boys die, and the old men warm up their sorrows
　　　　　　　　staring at the horizon.

Translation by Ivana Spalatin with Daniela Gioseffi

MITSUYE YAMADA

From Camp Notes

Mitsuye Yamada (b. 1923) was born in Kyushu, Japan. She is the author of *Camp Notes and Other Writings*, published by Rutgers University Press in 1998 (a new edition combining *Camp Notes and Other Poems*, originally published by Shameless Hussy Press in 1976, and *Desert Run: Poems and Stories*, published by Kitchen Table: Women of Color Press in 1988). These poems come from a series in her first collection written during her incarceration in a U.S. internment camp during World War II. Her other writings focus on her bicultural heritage, women, and human rights issues. She has taught at the University of California, Irvine. A former board member of Amnesty International USA, she has served on the Committee on International Development, which promotes and funds development of human rights work in Third World countries. She has also been actively involved in Interfaith Prisoners of Conscience Project, and is founder and coordinator of MultiCultural Women Writers.

■

EVACUATION

As we boarded the bus
bags on both sides
(I had never packed
two bags before
on a vacation
lasting forever)
the Seattle Times
photographer said
Smile!
so obediently I smiled
and the caption the next day
read:
Note smiling faces
a lesson to Tokyo.

ON THE BUS

Who goes?
Not the leaders of the people
Combed out and left
with the FBI.
Our father
stayed behind
triple locks.
What was the charge?
Possible espionage or
impossible espionage.
I forgot which.

Only those who remained
free in prisons
stayed behind.

The rest of us went to
Camp Harmony
where the first baby
was christened

Melody.

HARMONY AT THE FAIR GROUNDS

Why is the soldier boy in a cage
like that?
in the freedom of the child's
universe
the uniformed guard
stood trapped in his outside cage.
We walked away from the gate and
grated guard
on sawdusted grounds
where millions trod once
to view prize cows
at the Puyallup Fair.

They gave us straws to sleep on
encased in muslin ticks.
Some of us were stalled under grandstand
seats
the egg with
parallel lines.

Lines formed for food
lines for showers
lines for the john
lines for shots.

IN THE OUTHOUSE

Our collective wastebin
where the air sticks
in my craw
burns my eyes

I have this place to hide
the excreta and
the blood which
do not flush down
nor seep away.

They pile up
fill the earth

I am drowning.

CLARIBEL ALEGRÍA

Evasion

Claribel Alegría (b. 1924) was born in Esteli, Nicaragua, and grew up in Santa Ana, El Salvador. She
is one of Central America's most respected writers. She attended college in the United States, earning
a degree in philosophy and literature from George Washington University. She has since lived in
Managua and Mallorca and has visited and read her work often in the United States. Throughout her
life as a writer and poet, Alegría has always emphasized her commitment to nonviolent resistance. She
is part of "la generacíon comprometida" (the committed generation), born out of a desire of the intellectual classes to achieve social and political justice for their less privileged compatriots. She has been
closely associated with the Sandinista National Liberation Front (FSLN), the movement that overthrew the much hated dictator, Anastasio Somoza Debayle, and took control of the Nicaraguan government in 1979. She is a prolific poet and novelist whose work is widely translated and renowned.
Alegría published *Flowers from the Volcano*, translated by the U.S. poet Carolyn Forché. Other books
include *Poetry Lives* and *Luisa in Reality Land*. Alegría has won many distinguished prizes for her
work and is best known in the United States for her much translated poem, *A Small Country*, concerning the suffering in El Salvador.

■

for Otto René Castillo

We were discussing Siva
birds
Barthes
you stepped blamelessly
between us
and we kept on talking
suddenly
at a pause
you interrupted the crochet
of our sentences
abruptly
opened the window
and pointed to Claudio

lying in his own blood
there was silence
everything stopped
you closed the blinds
and Graciela
taking up the knitting needles again
announced:
I have to undo a whole row
I slipped two stitches.

Translation by Lynne Beyer

NGUYET TU

Eyes of an Afghan Child

Nguyet Tu (b. circa 1925) was born in the central Vietnamese province of Ha Tinh. As a young woman she joined the resistance against French colonialism. A poet, writer, and journalist, she is the author of three biographies, several translations, collections of short stories, and books of poetry. Nguyet Tu is the retired director of the Women's Publishing House, which was established more than forty years ago. She lives in Hanoi with her family and grandchildren, and is now writing full time.

■

For my friend Tam, who lost two children
during the bombing of Ha Noi, Giang Bien Village,
18 December 1972

Your eyes stare at me
You neither cry nor wail
Yet you steal my heart.
Your mother, father, sisters, brothers
entombed in the abyss of a gaping crater
Behind your back, a rag of flowered bridal gown—
A sister's, an aunt's, a fellow villager's
First intimate touch of happiness
Terror bursting down
Splattering corpses in the sand.
Then today, another sister
Buried four children
Before she fled, a refugee.
The deaths, the deaths . . .
Defy calculation in figures.
Your eyes stare at me
You neither cry nor wail
            War!

Stop it!
Stop the bombing—stop the shooting
My country is becoming a desert!
Your eyes stare at me
The reflection can never be extinguished.

Translation by Lady Borton and Nguyet Tu

TOYOMI HASHIMOTO

Hellish Years After Hellish Days

Toyomi Hashimoto (b. 1925) is one of many victims who survived the U.S. nuclear attack on the civilian populations of the Japanese cities of Hiroshima and Nagasaki at the end of World War II. This personal account from *Cries for Peace*, an oral history project of Japanese youth, published in Tokyo, is only one of many such harrowing testimonies by victims of the atomic bombings that killed and maimed many tens of thousands. The United States remains the only nation ever to use nuclear weapons, and on large civilian targets. The bombing of Hiroshima at once ushered in the nuclear age, the Cold War, and a new and terrifying kind of warfare, in which the population of a city—or a planet—could be destroyed in moments. Stories like Hashimoto's bring such unimaginably vast destruction down to a heartbreakingly personal level.

■

Though at each anniversary the skies over our city are blue and peaceful, the memory of that day in 1945 still troubles my body and soul.

In spite of the wartime conditions, my husband and our little son and I lived a happy life. Many of our neighbors envied us. On the morning of August 9, 1945, I walked to the gate to see my husband off to work. My three-year-old boy, Takahsi, went out to play with some of his little friends. I was alone in the house and relieved that the air-raid alarm had just been lifted.

Then, in the distance I heard an approaching airplane. "Japanese?" I wondered. I stepped outside to see my son running to me, calling, "Airplane! Airplane!" The moment we reentered the house, there was a blinding flash followed by a tremendous explosion. The roof of the house caved in, pinning us under a mountain of debris.

Hours passed. I do not know how many. Then I heard my son crying softly and calling for mother and father. He was alive. I tried to reach for him, but a huge beam immobilized me. I could not break free. Though I screamed for help, no one came. Soon I heard voices calling names of neighbors.

My son was bravely trying to crawl from under a heap of clay that had been one of the walls. His back was turned to me. When he faced me, I saw that his right eye was obliterated with blood. Once again, I tried to move, but the beam would not budge.

I screamed so loud and long that I must have lost my voice. I called to the people I could see scurrying about, but they did not hear me. No one answered until the lady next door finally pulled my son out of the wreckage.

Happy that he was at least temporarily safe, I suddenly became aware of a sharp pain in my breast, left hand, stomach. With my free right hand I grabbed a piece of roofing tile and scraped away the dirt covering my breast. I could breathe more easily. As I tried again to crawl out, I saw that a huge nail was stuck in my stomach.

"Fire! Fire!" I could hear people shouting around me. It was either break free or burn to death. With a violent wrench, I pulled myself from under the beam. In doing so, I ripped the flesh of my stomach. Blood spurted from an agonizing gash in my body.

I was at last out of the ruined house. Still, my son was nowhere to be seen. Perhaps the kind lady next door had led him to safety. I had to search for him, but I could only limp slowly because of the pain in my stomach.

I decided to go to a nearby hill, which was open and might offer some security. As I crept slowly along, people more seriously injured than I clutched at my stomach and pleaded for help and water. Among the piteous cries I heard loud voices shouting, "Leave the old people! Help the children first." I wanted to help, but I was in grave need of assistance myself. All I could do was promise to come back with water, if it was possible.

On my way to the hill, I met a neighbor and friend. Looking long and intently at me, she finally said, "It is Toyomi, isn't it? I knew that my dress was in tatters and that I was bloody and dirty. But now, stopping to examine myself for the first time, I learned worse. One of my ears had been cut nearly off. It and my whole face were caked with congealed blood.

"Thank heaven you're alive!" I heard a familiar voice saying. Turning, with intense happiness, I saw my husband, who was holding our son in his arms. We climbed to the top of the hill together, walking among countless corpses.

On the hilltop, a kind man gave us bed sheets, candles, sugar, and other useful things. At once we began to try to do something for Takashi, who had lost consciousness. After a while, as we dripped sugar water into his mouth, he awakened.

He had already lost the sight of his right eye. Myriad slivers of glass were embedded in his head, face, body, arms, and legs. An air-raid alarm, still in effect, prohibited lighting candles. In the pitch darkness, my husband and I picked out as many pieces of glass from his body as we could find. So full of life and energy until that moment! Now blind in one eye and covered in blood and dirt! Still he bore everything bravely and only asked, "Am I being a good boy?" Pride at his courage and grief for his pain forced us both to weep quietly.

I made bandages from the bed sheet. Placing some boards over two large rocks, I made us a shelter. We were fortunate to be together. In the dark, we could hear people calling the names of their loved ones. I wondered what had happened to my younger and elder sisters.

The light of dawn showed us a hell. Corpses, some burned to cinders, others only partly roasted, lay everywhere. Barely living, faintly breathing, others rapidly drew toward death. A horrible stench filled the air.

In a few days we were taken to a bomb shelter where, in spite of a food shortage, we managed to live for a month. I was in such pain that it was excruciating to carry my son to the toilet. Nonetheless, he and I went daily to a nearby clinic for treatment. As days passed, my hair began falling; and blood oozed from my gums. My husband was too ill to walk. We began hearing rumors that the bomb that had destroyed Nagasaki was of the same kind as the one that had fallen on Hiroshima. People who had not been injured in the blast began to die, one after another. We waited for our turns to come.

Near the well from which we had to draw all our water corpses were cremated. On our way to the well, we had to pick a ghoulish way through a field of human bones. Often in the morning there would be a dead body by the well that had not been there the evening before. I wondered who would take care of our corpses when we died.

But we did not die. In September, my two drafted brothers returned from the war. My younger and elder sisters turned up, safe and well. In October, we rented the house in Oura where I live with my family today.

In about a year, I began noticing purple spots on my body. I tired easily and suffered occasional sharp pains in the head. I learned that my white-blood-corpuscle count had dropped drastically. Aware that all these symptoms characterized the atomic diseases, I became apprehensive about my future. My husband was so ill that he could not work. By the time Takashi entered primary school, it was becoming difficult for us to make ends meet. Nor was our son's lot in school easy. Cruel neighborhood children hurt him deeply when they jeered and called him a one-eyed devil.

A single bomb had wrecked a peaceful and happy family. True, my husband had not gone to the battle front, but we were nonetheless as much victims of the war as the survivors of soldiers who had died fighting. The government offered financial assistance to such people, but none to our kind. With rising anger, I often asked myself why they discriminated in this way.

To all these trials was soon added my husband's total desperation and determination to kill himself and our son so that I could try to find happiness on my own. I had to guard him constantly. Even so, he succeeded in making a number of attempts to strangle himself and our son. When, in 1948, he was taken to the police by a neighbor who found him trying to hang himself in the garden, he collapsed on the floor, crying, "Let me die. I can't stand the agony of living any more."

Since he could not work, I had to support the family by serving in restaurants, nursing the sick, and doing whatever odd jobs I could find. Over the years, my determination to keep going on was strengthened by the births of two more children. Still, sometimes I too weakened and contemplated suicide. My work was arduous, and I was weak. Occasionally I fainted on the job.

But even this was not to be the limit of what I was to witness and endure. In 1952, four months after his birth, I noticed something queer about one of my fourth son's eyes. I took him to an opthalmologist, who diagnosed the case as cancer of the eye. Very rare. One case in ten thousand. He added that unless the eye was removed at once, the cancer would spread; the eye would eventually pop from its socket; and my son would die, withered like a blasted tree. I was too shocked and terrified to cry.

The same doctor recommended that I take my child to a university hospital for treatment. At first I hesitated. We had no money to pay for such care. But

I could not sacrifice my son's life. Resolving to scrape together the funds somehow, I took him to a university clinic where the first doctor's diagnosis was confirmed and where I learned that without immediate surgery there was grave danger that the cancer would spread to the other eye. Even in the light of this knowledge, however, I could not consent to having my child's eye removed.

About fifteen months later, this same child began to cough in an odd way. I wanted to take him to a nearby hospital but could not: I owed them money. Instead, I took him to a smaller hospital some distance from our home. The doctor at first said it was only a neglected cold. But when the child got no better and I took him to the hospital again, I was told that it was diphtheria and that he would have to be hospitalized at once at the Nagasaki Hospital. Where was I to get the money?

I asked the elder brother's wife for aid, but she was too short of funds. Nevertheless, she offered to lend me her own son's health insurance policy. Her boy was three, or about a year and a half younger than my fourth son. Though terrified that our insurance fraud would be discovered, I had no choice but to accept her proposal.

Now my son was able to have good medical treatment. Vaccines were tried for a while, but they soon failed to have effect. The doctor insisted on surgery. Though the operation was a success, it had been necessary to install a respiratory device in my son's throat. The device was covered with thick gauze, which had to be kept constantly moist. If it dried, phlegm would accumulate and strangle the boy.

Since there was no money to spend on private nurses, I had to stay by his bedside constantly. My younger sister offered to help me, but a few days of the grueling routine exhausted her and made her ill. Late at night when the doctor made his rounds, he would try to cheer us: "Keep it up. You're doing a good job."

Finally, my child's condition improved. To my delight, he was to be released from the hospital. The time had come to remove the respiratory device. But the doctor who was in charge made a mistake and cut an artery in the throat. The day before he was to have come home, my son died, strangled on his own blood.

The doctor knelt by the bed, groaning for forgiveness. I blamed him. But recriminations would not bring my boy back to life. I had falsified the insurance papers and had no alternative but to remain silent. Upon arriving in the hospital room, my husband collapsed. Weeping bitterly, he blamed himself for being unable to earn money to support the family.

My fourth son died on May 10, 1945. On the nineteenth of the same month, I was given work as a scrub woman in the university hospital. My pay, five hundred yen a day, was barely enough for survival and left nothing for luxuries. When our eldest son was in the sixth grade, penury threatened to deprive him of the chance to participate in the school excursion marking the end of primary and the beginning of middle school. After consideration of our condition, his school allowed him to go on the trip free of charge. But because of my work, I could not see him off. Our next-door neighbor was kind enough to do it for me.

My happiness at the birth of our fifth son, in June, 1956, was to be short-lived. I had hoped he would be a reincarnation of the baby I had lost. And in the most tragic and ironic way, he inherited the same eye disease that had afflicted his dead elder brother.

Why? My husband was a good, kind, gentle man. No one could speak ill of him. I had done no one wrong. I had always tried to be kind to the weak and the elderly. I was considered an excellent mother and housewife. Why, among my five brothers and sisters, had I been singled out for this suffering? My frequent and repeated prayers at Buddhist temples and Shinto shrines had no effect. The white film covering my son's eye was permanent. So deep was our physical and spiritual desolation at the time that the whole family agreed to commit suicide if it should become necessary to hospitalize this little boy.

My husband did not wait for the rest of us. His final suicide attempt left him ill and broken. Once again, there was no money. I pleaded with municipal officials, telling them how my husband's weakened physical state prohibited his working. I explained his history to them and said that I earned only the smallest income as a scrub woman. Finally, they agreed to provide him free hospital care and to put our family on government relief. Our condition had improved a little. But after about three months in a hospital bed, quietly, peacefully, my husband died in his sleep.

Though we did not know it then, our worst trials were over. My eldest son, limited by partial blindness, could not choose an occupation freely. He apprenticed himself to a shoemaker. I continued to work hard in the hope of providing a better future for the other children. Almost before I knew it, three years had passed; and I had been given a chance to remarry.

My second husband, who is crippled in both legs, is a skilled carver of tortoise-shell ornaments. As my children grew up, they earned money and contributed to the general fund so that little by little we were able to buy electrical appliances and ultimately to live an average family life on my husband's earnings alone.

Takashi, my oldest child, in spite of the loss of an eye, now works for a transport company and is the father of two lovely children. Immediately before he entered primary school, a doctor who gave him a physical examination told me that my fifth son's eye cancer had stabilized and would spread no farther. At the time of writing this, he was a senior in high school.

Though we have suffered, our family has, at least in part, survived. There are many others for whom the atomic-bomb sickness remains a constant source of pain and despair or an ever-present threat. Only people who suffer from this kind of illness can know its full terror. Even doctors do not always diagnose it accurately.

Young people today have been fortunate enough to never experience war. But they must not forget. It is the duty of those of us who have lived through the hells of the atomic bombings and the years of agony following them to proclaim our experiences so that war and its evils can be recognized for what they are and abolished from the earth.

Tra Thi Nga and
Wendy Wilder Larsen

Viet Minh *and* Famine

Tra Thi Nga (b. 1927) is a contemporary Vietnamese poet-novelist who lived through the war years in her shattered country, as Vietnam was occupied first by the French and then by the Americans. A bookkeeper in her husband's firm in Saigon, she met Wendy Larsen, an American teacher who traveled with her journalist husband to Vietnam to live and teach there during the war. The two women, fleeing the fall of Saigon, were reunited in New York after the war. They collaborated on a critically acclaimed book, *Shallow Graves: Two Women and Vietnam*, which tells, with startling clarity and insight, the devastating affects of war on those who do not fight on the battlefields.

■

Viet Minh

The war between the French and the Viet Minh
came nearer and nearer.
One day, going to school,
I heard an explosion and ran to a ditch
already filled with people.
I lay outside in the ditch
watching people run by me
shouting and crying through the smoke.

I did not move until the all-clear signal.
Then I saw people lying on the ground
blood everywhere
hands and legs hanging in a tree.

I yelled and fainted.
When I woke up,
I was in a strange house.
Bao was looking down at me
trying to wipe my face with a handkerchief.

We began to whisper more and more
about arrests.
Many anti-French leaflets
were passed out at school.
Teachers left. My best friend, Dung,
did not come to school.
At first I thought she was sick.
Then I found out she had been arrested.
When friends were arrested,
we were never to speak of that person again.

FAMINE

Worse for us than the bombs
was the famine.
We had money,
but there was no rice to buy.
People ate grass.
We read that out in the countryside
peasants were stealing from landlords.
Father told us the French and Japanese
had overstocked rice in the warehouses.
Tons and tons of rotted grain
had to be dumped into the Red River.

When Father tried to fire our servants,
they begged to stay.
They had been loyal.
Where would they go?
How could they eat?
In the end he let them stay
gave them what he could.

When Father had his high position
teachers bought him gifts—
baskets of fruit
lichee and longan.
We stored them in giant vases in the hall,
cut the mooncakes into pieces to be eaten later.
Now he ordered us to eat less rice.
We made rice balls from what we saved
to give to the people outside the walls.

One day when I opened the gate
for Father to go out,
there were corpses collapsed against the wall.

I fainted.
Father offered soldiers money to remove the corpses.
Sometimes they took bodies that were still alive.
People would call from the carts,
"Don't take me. Don't take me.
I'm not dead yet."

MARIA ROSA HENSON

From Comfort Woman

Maria Rosa Henson (1928–1996) was one of many thousands of Filipina, Korean, Chinese, Taiwanese, and Indonesian women to suffer sexual slavery at the hands of the Japanese armies in World War II. In December 1991, a Manila-based nongovernmental organization, the Asian Women Human Rights Council (AWHRC), held a conference in Seoul on the issue of sexual trafficking in Asian women. At this conference, some Korean participants raised the issue of "comfort women." Prominent Filipina feminist activists, including Indai Sajor and Nelia Sancho set up an organization called Task Force on Filipino Comfort Women (TFFCW). The task force grew to fifteen member organizations from various countries, and Maria Rosa Henson was the first to respond to its fact-finding mission, in September 1992. In her simply told, but powerfully moving, autobiography, Henson first recalls her happy childhood as the daughter of a wealthy landowner, before she launches into the hideous ordeal she suffered from the tender age of fifteen, beginning in 1943, when she was abducted and raped by Japanese soldiers occupying the Philippines. Henson was held for nine months as a sex slave before she managed to escape. Her triumph against all odds was an example for many comfort women who came forth, later, to tell their own stories and enter the lawsuit brought before the World Court. The United States was the only nation to vote with Japan against reparations for these horribly abused women in the trials held by the United Nations.

■

One morning in April 1943, I was asked by my Huk comrades to collect some sacks of dried corn from the nearby town of Magalang. I went with two others in a cart pulled by a carabao. One comrade sat with me in the cart, the other rode on the carabao's back. It was the height of the dry season. The day was very hot.

We loaded the sacks of corn into the cart and made our way back to our barrio. As we approached the Japanese checkpoint near the town hospital of Angeles, the man beside me whispered, "Be careful, there are some guns and ammunition hidden in the sacks of corn." I froze. I did not know till then what we were sitting on were guns. I became very nervous, fearing that if the Japanese soldiers discovered the weapons, we would all get killed.

I got off the cart and showed the sentry our passes. At that time, everyone in the barrio needed to have a pass to show that he or she lived there. The sentry looked at the sacks of corn, touching here and pressing there without saying anything.

Finally, he allowed us to pass, but after we had gone thirty meters from the checkpoint he whistled and signaled us to return. We looked at each other and turned pale. If he emptied the sack, he would surely find the guns and kill us instantly. The soldier raised his hands and signaled that I was the only one to come back, and my companions were allowed to go. I walked to the checkpoint, thinking the guns were safe but I would be in danger. I thought that maybe they would rape me.

The guard led me at gunpoint to the second floor of the building that used to be the town hospital. It had been turned into the Japanese headquarters and garrison. I saw six other women there. I was given a small room with a bamboo bed. The room had no door, only a curtain. Japanese soldiers kept watch in the hall outside. That night, nothing happened to me.

The following day was hell. Without warning, a Japanese soldier entered my room and pointed his bayonet at my chest. I thought he was going to kill me, but he used his bayonet to slash my dress and tear it open. I was too frightened to scream. And then he raped me. When he was done, the other soldiers came into my room, and they took turns raping me.

Twelve soldiers raped me in quick succession, after which I was given half an hour to rest. Then twelve more soldiers followed. They all lined up outside the room waiting for their turn. I bled so much and was in such pain, I could not even stand up. The next morning, I was too weak to get up. A woman brought me a cup of tea and breakfast of rice and dried fish. I wanted to ask her some questions, but the guard in the hall outside stopped us from saying anything to each other.

I could not eat. I felt much pain, and my vagina was swollen. I cried and cried, calling my mother. I could not resist the soldiers because they might kill me. So what else could I do? Every day, from two in the afternoon to ten in the evening, the soldiers lined up outside my room and the rooms of the six other women there. I did not even have time to wash after each assault. At the end of the day, I just closed my eyes and cried. My torn dress would be brittle from the crust that had formed from the soldiers' dried semen. I washed myself with hot water and a piece of cloth so I would be clean. I pressed the cloth to my vagina like a compress to relieve the pain and the swelling.

Every Wednesday, a Japanese doctor came to give us a check-up. Sometimes a Filipino doctor came. The other women could rest for four or five days a month while they had their period. But I had no rest because I was not yet menstruating.

The garrison did not have much food. We ate thrice a day, our meals consisting of a cup of rice, some salty black beans and thin pieces of preserved radish. On rare occasions, we had a hard-boiled egg. Sometimes there was a small piece of fried chicken. Sometimes we also had a block of brown sugar. I would suck it like candy or mix it with the rice, and I was happy. I kept the sugar in my room.

A soldier always stood in the hall outside the seven rooms where we were kept. The guard gave us tea every time we wanted some to drink. Once, he told me to wash my face with tea so that my skin would look smooth. He was kind to all the women there.

We began the day with breakfast, after which we swept and cleaned our rooms. Sometimes, the guard helped. He fixed my bed and scrubbed the floor with a wet cloth and some disinfectant. After cleaning, we went to the bathroom downstairs to wash the only dress we had and to bathe. The bathroom did not even have a door, so the soldiers watched us. We were all naked, and they laughed at us, especially me and the other young girl who did not have any pubic hair.

I felt that the six other women with me also despised the Japanese soldiers. But like me, there was nothing they could do. I never got to know them. We just looked at each other, but were not allowed to talk. Two of the women looked Chinese. They always cast their gaze downward and never met my eye.

The only time I saw them was when we were taken for our daily bath and when, twice a week, we were taken out to get some sun. After bathing, we went back to our rooms. I would hang up my dress to dry and comb my long hair. Sometimes I sat on the bamboo bed, remembering all that had been done to me. How could I escape or kill myself? The only thing that kept me from committing suicide was the thought of my mother.

At around eleven, the guard brought each of us our lunch. He returned an hour later to collect our plates. Then a little before two in the afternoon, he brought us a basin with hot water and some pieces of cloth.

At two in the afternoon, the soldiers came. Some of them were brought by truck to the garrison. My work began, and I lay down as one by one the soldiers raped me. At six p.m., we rested for a while and ate dinner. Often I was hungry because our rations were so small. After thirty minutes, I lay down on the bed again to be raped for the next three to four hours. Every day, anywhere from ten to over twenty soldiers raped me. There were times when there were as many as thirty: they came to the garrison in truckloads. At other times, there were only a few soldiers, and we finished early.

Most of the soldiers looked so young, maybe they were only eighteen years old. Their hair was cut short, only half an inch long. Most of them were clean and good looking, but many of them were rough.

I lay on the bed with my knees up and my feet on the mat, as if I were giving birth. Once there was a soldier who was in such a hurry to come that he ejaculated even before he entered me. He was very angry, and he grabbed my hand and forced me to fondle his genitals. But it was no use, because he could not become erect again. Another soldier was waiting for his turn outside the room and started banging on the wall. The man had no choice but to leave, but before going out, he hit my breast and pulled my hair.

It was an experience I often had. Whenever the soldiers did not feel satisfied, they vented their anger on me. Sometimes a soldier took my hand and put it around his genitals so I could guide him inside me. I soon learned that was the quickest way to satisfy the men and get the ordeal over with. But there was a soldier who did not like this. When I put my hand on his groin, he slapped me. He was very rough, poking his penis all over my genitals, even my backside, because he could not find my vagina. He kept pressing against my clitoris which got so swollen that I was in pain for three days. Even the hot water compress I made could not relieve the pain.

Some soldiers punched my legs and belly after they had ejaculated prematurely, staining their pants with their semen. One soldier raped me, and when he was finished, ordered me to fondle his genitals. He wanted to rape me a second time, but he could not get an erection. So he bumped my head and legs against the wall. It was so painful. As he was hitting me, the soldiers outside started knocking impatiently on the wall. Through the thin curtain, I could see their impatient figures huddled in the hall.

Every day there were incidents of violence and humiliation. These happened not only to me, but also to the other women there. Sometimes I heard crying and the sound of someone being beaten up as there was only a partition made of woven bamboo that divided my room from those of the others.

When soldiers raped me, I felt like a pig. Sometimes they tied up my right leg with a waist band or belt and hung it on a nail on the wall as they violated me. I was angry all the time. But there was nothing I could do. How many more days, I thought. How many more months? Someday we will be free, I thought. But how?

I thought of my guerrilla activities and my comrades. I regretted passing the sentry where the Japanese soldiers saw me. Did my comrades know that I was still alive and undergoing such horrible suffering? Maybe not. Was there anything they could do, I wondered. Sometimes I lost all hope.

I was in the hospital building for three months. Afterwards, in August of 1943, we were transferred to a big rice mill four blocks from the hospital. The mill was on Henson Road, named after my father's family, who owned the land where it stood. We found seven small rooms ready for us. The daily routine of rape continued. All throughout my ordeal, I kept thinking of my mother. Did she know I was still alive? How could I get in touch with her?

DIANA DER-HOVANESSIAN

Songs of Bread *and* An Armenian Looking at Newsphotos of the Cambodian Deathwatch

Diana Der-Hovanessian (b. circa 1930), born in New England, is an accomplished Armenian American poet who also translates Armenian literature into English. The author of nineteen books of poetry and translation, she has won awards from the National Endowment for the Arts, PEN, the National Writers Union, *American Scholar,* and the Paterson Poetry Center. She was Fulbright professor of poetry at Yerevan State University. Her latest book is *The Burning Glass* (Sheep Meadow Press, 2002). She was winner of the Barcelona Peace Prize in 1985 for one of the poems presented here: "Songs of Bread" is the title of a group of poems written in prison in 1915 by the venerable and martyred Armenian poet, Daniel Varoujan, whose persona Der Hovanessian assumes.

■

SONGS OF BREAD

You think I wrote from love.
You think I wrote from ease.
You imagine me singing as I walked
through wheat praising bread.
You imagine me looking from my window
at my children in the grass, my wife
humming, my dog running, my sun still
warm. But this notebook is drenched
in blood. It is written in blood
in a wagon rolling past yellow, amber,
gold wheat. But in the dark, in

the smell of sweat, urine, vomit.
The song of blue pitchers filled
with sweet milk, the song of silver
fountains welcoming home students,
the song of silo, barn, harvest,
tiller and red soil, all written
in the dark. The Turks allowed it.
What harm in a pen soon to be theirs,
a notebook to be theirs, a coat
theirs, unless too much blood splattered.
You read and picture me in
a tranquil village, a church, on
the Bosporus, on a hillside, not
in anguish, not in fury, not wrenching
back the dead, holding the sun still
for a few more hours, making bread
out of words. This notebook you ransomed
dear friend, postponed, delayed my storm.
You see only its calm.

AN ARMENIAN LOOKING AT NEWSPHOTOS OF THE CAMBODIAN DEATHWATCH

My sack of tiny
bones, bird
bones, my baby
with head so large
your thin neck bends,
my flimsy bag of breath,
all my lost cousins
unfed
wearing your pink flesh
like cloth
my pink rag doll
with head that grows
no hair,
eyes that cannot close,
my unborn past,
heaving your dry tears.

JAYA MEHTA

The Enemy Army Has Passed Through *India*

Jaya Metha (b. 1932) was born in Saurashtra and grew up in Bombay. Both she and her older sister had to oppose patriarchal attitudes to acquire an education. As a young woman she was not allowed out of the house without her head covered with a sari, but as time went on she was able to adopt the freer styles of Western ways. Mehta had to work her way though college by teaching and doing research. Her first published collection of poetry, *One Day* (1982), demonstrates her involvement with language and her struggle to achieve accurate expressiveness. She sees poetry as an attempt to find one's way from the person to the universal. Though she is a professed atheist, her poetry is imbued with the mythos and legend of her native Gujarti culture. She received the Gujarat State Shitya Academy Award for her collection of poetry *Venetian Blind* (1978). Other published books are *The Stars Are Silent* (1985), and *Hospital Poems* (1987), in which the following poem appears.

■

The enemy army has passed through
The city is deserted
Stupified the tree stands
Leafless and gray in an unseasonal autumn.
Amid the debris of the fallen house
The walls sag, exhausted.
One's breath rebounds
Like the echoes in a ravine.
The man takes the unblinking child in his arms
Four silent eyes drip
Into the woman's empty lap.

Translation by Shirin Kudchedkar

CHAILANG PALACIOS

The Colonization of Our Pacific Islands

Chailang Palacios (b. 1933) is a Chamorro woman from Saipan, in the northern Mariana Islands of Micronesia. She is a public health education worker. In March 1985, she traveled to Britain for a monthlong tour to speak out for Women Working for a Nuclear Free and Independent Pacific. As a child, she lived through World War II in the Pacific and has been a local witness to the devastation caused by nuclear testing among her island people. Monstrous birth defects from radiation poisoning are at the highest rate in the world in the Pacific Islands. The U.S. testing, in collusion with the French, has continued in this part of the world into the new century.

■

Micronesia was colonised by the Spanish in the fifteenth century. When the Spanish soldiers came, so did the missionaries. Hand in hand. They landed in Guam and spread out over the Marianas, then all over Micronesia. The missionaries together with the soldiers began to Christianise our ancestors. They were very scared and ran away—they hadn't seen a white person before. It was hard for us to embrace Christianity. The Spanish missionaries were blessing all the soldiers while the soldiers were cutting my ancestors into half, killing our men, raping our women.

When they arrived we were about 40,000. And we ended up 4,000 because they killed everyone who didn't want to embrace Christianity, which was the Catholic faith. So the Spanish stayed over 100 years. They came to do good work. And they did it very well, because today we are 97 percent Catholic.

Another nation came, which is the Germans. Both the Spanish and Germans came for their economic purposes. The Germans again, the same story—killing our men, raping our women. They took our land. The Germans brought their own missionaries, who tried to teach us the Protestant religion. And this started making us, the indigenous group, fight amongst ourselves over who was more Protestant and who was more Catholic. That is always the way: when white nations come to conquer us, to colonise us, they divide us. And it is still happening. But the Germans didn't stay very long. They took off.

And then there is this nation just like an octopus. The octopus that goes very slowly, very slowly, and suddenly it gets you. That is like the Japanese. They came and were exactly the same. They want us to join their religion, Buddhism. They like our islands so much they stayed. They took our land for sugar plantations, for pineapple plantations. They again made my ancestors their slaves, together with the Korean and Okinawa people, paying them five cents for the whole day.

Then the Japanese and the USA sat down planning to have war. We, the Micronesian people, were the victims of that war—World War II. We suffered all over the Marianas. It was heavily damaged because it was a big military place for the Japanese. So, once again, my ancestors suffered. After stripping them of their culture, their language, their land, the Japanese forced my ancestors up into the mountains. They made us dig a hole just in case the Americans and the Japanese fought. We would be safe in the hole. But it didn't happen like that. It was Sunday morning when the war came. Everyone was far away from their holes, visiting grandparents, relatives, friends. All of a sudden—bombs from the sky and the ocean. The people were crushed fifty to one hundred in one hole because there was no way they could get back to their own hole to hide. There was no water for those people. It was so hot, so dark, bombs all over. A lot of people died. Children died because their mothers' breasts dried up. No food.

You have heard it, and I have heard it too, from the older generation: "Oh, we are so grateful that the Americans won the war. They saved us from the communists, from Russia." Yet right after the war the Americans came, like the early missionaries, in the name of God, saying, "We are here to Christianize you, to help you to love one another, be in peace." We still have the Bible while the missionaries and their white governments have all the land. . . .

For some years we were "off limits." No one could come in and no one could go out unless you were CIA or military American. The whole reason for that is that the U.S. had planned to take over mainland China. So all these nationalist

Chinese were in my islands learning how to fight. In time of peace children would be crying at night: there was big bombing and it could be heard all over the island. And the house started to shake. The only thing I remember is my parents saying, "Pray that there will be no war." So next day I said, "Why do you pray and say 'No more war'?" And she just held me and said, "Oh my daughter, I feel so sorry for your generation because probably I will not see the next war. But the next war will be so terrible that you won't need to hide." I think I was only 11 or 12 years old. I looked at her and I didn't understand. Naturally my mother died. She was not an educated woman, but with her terrible memories of World War II she just *connected*. "You won't need to hide." Those were her words. I never forget them. . . .

ANI PACHEN AND ADELAIDE DONNELLEY

From Sorrow Mountain

Ani Pachen (b. 1933) was born in Tibet, and now lives in Dharamsala, India, near the Dalai Lama and his Tibetan government in exile, where she devotes her time to her spiritual practices as a Tibetan nun. She also continues to promote the cause of a free Tibet. Pachen is one of the few women who fought as a resistance fighter in defense of her faith and homeland. She spent twenty-one years in prison under almost constant torture by the Chinese. In *Sorrow Mountain*, published in 2000, she shares the story of her harrowing adventures and tragic life, a story of courage and survival. Adelaide Donnelley of Berkeley, California, is a psychologist and photographer, as well as a writer who has spent much time in India collaborating with Ani Pachen on her memoir. It is now a half-century since the Chinese Communists invaded Tibet, beginning the brutal massacres and occupation that are here described through the eyes of a child.

■

The night was windless and still. In the distance, the faint rumbling of thunder drifted toward me. Or was it a plane? I turned over to stare at the sky. The stars were in a swarm overhead, and on the horizon a sliver of moon was beginning to rise.

I pulled the sheepskin tighter around me. Behind me, the crest of the hill curled, dark and inhospitable. The place seemed filled with sadness, and no matter how I turned or where I looked, a tangle of images drifted in front of my eyes. A hand on the ground, ripped off at the wrist. A face caved in. A child curled next to his mother.

A bird cried, and a dark shape passed overhead. I watched as its wings rose and fell, and listened to the whirring of air through its feathers. If only I could fly. Away from this wretched place to some other world. I lay staring at the sky. In the darkness, I thought I saw Gyalsay Rinpoche's face looking down at me, his eyes filled with tenderness. *Om Mani Peme Hum*, I prayed. *Blessed Rinpoche guide me on the path.*

"Yesterday many were killed." The sad voice of the Prince of Derge spread through the crowd. "We've seen the danger in traveling in such a large group. Despite our vow to stay together, we must break into smaller groups and go separate ways."

He gestured to several of the other leaders. "People from Lingkha Shipa will go via Zayul. People from Gonjo and Derge will go on to Pelbar in hopes of meeting Chushi Gangdruk. The Chinese are close behind us—we can't risk waiting. We will decide later whether to go on to Lhasa. Gather what belongings you have left, and set out now."

Confusion broke out as people began to move in every direction. Children called for their mothers, animals wandered lost. Dekyong pushed through the crowd. When she reached me I could she was crying. She threw her arms around me. We held on to each other, but we knew there was nothing we could do. She had her family to look after, I had mine. We had to go with our separate groups—there was no possibility of staying together. It seemed a cruel fate to be parting so soon after reuniting.

"Ashe Pachen!" My mother gestured frantically to come.

I took a gold ring from my finger and slipped it onto Dekyong's. I held on to her hand as if it were a lifeline. We were both crying.

"Ashe!" My mother called again.

I squeezed her hand and, avoiding her face, ran toward my mother. I turned once and saw her standing where I'd left her, her face in pain. But people passed between us and she soon disappeared.

That day we traveled north toward Rewoche, a town near Chamdo. My throat was tight from holding back tears. I had to struggle to keep them from spilling down my face with each step Shindruk took; with each step, Dekyong's eyes were always in front of me.

As we continued toward Rewoche, I noticed the terrain was familiar. It was some consolation to know we were still traveling through Khampa land, land still part of my home. For some reason it made me less lonely. Mostly we traveled at night so as not to be seen, but whenever it seemed safe to do so, we also traveled by day. Each time we got to a place where the direction was uncertain, we asked Khaley Rinpoche to cast a divination. Whatever he said, we followed without hesitation. Traveling in this way, we were able to avoid the Chinese, though we were never totally free from their presence.

"A massacre!" a man shouted.

In front of us, we saw the scene of an earlier battle. Tents ripped apart, bodies strewn over the ground.

As we approached I could see huge vultures picking over the dead, pieces of flesh in their beaks. On some of the bodies, the flesh was cleared to the bone. At the edge of the camp a few starving dogs ate limbs they had pulled to the side. Everywhere scraps of bloody clothing were blown by the wind.

Haunted by what we'd seen, we traveled much of the night. Tormented, hoping to forget, I closed my eyes and let Shindruk carry me. I soon fell asleep.

When I awoke the others were nowhere in sight.

The night was dark and windless, the moon already set. Nearby I heard the breaking of twigs. The figure of a soldier crouched down. I held my breath, but nothing moved. I looked closer; it was only a bush.

In the distance, the howling of wolves. I flicked the reins and urged Shindruk on. A shape loomed toward us and I saw glistening teeth, a foaming mouth. I jerked to the side. But the shape was merely a rock.

We stepped over branches strewn on the ground that looked like human limbs, passed rocks jutting out that looked like half-crazed dogs. Wherever we went, I couldn't erase the images of the day from my mind.

Luckily Shindruk sensed the direction the others had gone and moved ahead on his own. After a time we caught up. By then, I had calmed.

We joined the others at a small wooden bridge suspended over a gorge. It was short but unsteady, and hung like a frail web over a river far below. Following the others, I started across. With each step the bridge sprang up and down, on either side a dizzying view. Afraid of slipping underneath the handrail, I kept my eyes focused ahead.

When I was almost across, I heard the shriek of a horse. The bridge began buckling and rippling under my feet. I held the guardrail and glanced back to see that a mule had panicked and kicked the horse behind. The horse reared up, its pack coming loose. I watched the pack tumble through the air and crack open on rocks far below. Watching the pack's contents fly in every direction, I felt that was happening to my life: pieces tearing apart, scattering to the winds.

Off and on throughout the day I heard the shriek of the horse and saw the pack tumbling down. Slowly, slowly. Cracking open, flying apart.

That night, eager to reach our goal as quickly as possible, we pressed on toward the plains of Shothalhosum halfway between Chamdo and Lhasa. At one point, the night was so dark we had to get off our horses and feel with our feet, sliding them along the ground to be sure we were still on the trail. It lightened a bit as we came into a clearing, and from the sound of gurgling water, we could tell we were near a small stream. We stopped to stretch for a moment, exhausted. Several young boys went in search of wood for a fire.

Just as we'd finished our meal, we heard the sound of an airplane not far away. "The Chinese," Thupten whispered, "searching for us!"

"Quick!" someone called. "Put out the fire!" A man came running with a pot of water from the river and threw it onto the flames. They hissed and flickered, then went out. We sat, not daring to move. The air had a damp, burned smell, and mixed with the chill of the night, it made my stomach churn.

After a few moments when the plane had passed, we took the reins of our horses and continued up a narrow valley, one foot sliding after another in the darkness. All night we crept slowly through the hills. By daybreak I was so exhausted I could barely see straight. But intent on getting Mama, Ani Rigzin, and Granny to the safety of a larger group, I kept walking.

As we crossed the last hill and rode down toward the plains of Shothalhosum, we could see several thousand people spread out across a vast area. By midmorning we reached the first group of tents and learned that the plane we'd heard in the night was American, not Chinese. "There is no need to escape to India," a young man told us. "American troops have come to help take back our country!" We were overjoyed at the news. "Perhaps now we will be able to go home," Mama said. The thought was in all of our minds, but no one else dared say it. There was still much to overcome.

We soon got used to the sound of planes overhead. Each night air drops were made in the middle of the night, before we went to sleep. First a red light appeared far away in the sky. Then we heard the humming sound we'd heard the night before. Several men marked a place with many small fires to indicate where we were.

Dark shapes fell out of the sky. They floated down, suspended from large pieces of cloth. There were thirteen men, and box after box of weapons, clothing, gold coins, and food. "Stay away from the boxes," we were told. "They are being taken to the center of camp."

The men who fell from the sky were Tibetans who had been taken by the CIA to be trained in America. A couple of them were from Amdo, but the majority came from Kham. I later found that I knew some of them. Sey Donyo, Raru Yeshe, and Buchay of Derge, Yeshi Raur and Yeshi Wangyal from Markham, Bugyal from Dugur. Also men from the households of Phurba Tsang and Drakpa Lama in Markham.

The day after the first drop, three of these men called a meeting. They distributed arms to each of our groups. "Take as many as you can use," one said, "enough for each able-bodied man in your family."

So many weapons came down that those left over were stockpiled. There were eight-rounders, or Mis as they called them, pistols, grenades, and radio sets. We already had two kinds of Tibetan guns: a Bura, which could take one bullet at a time, and a Kha-dum, which had a short muzzle. With the additional American weapons, we were well equipped.

I took two eight-rounders. I gave one to a man from Gonjo and put the other one on the side of my saddle. I carried my pistol tucked into the belt of my chupa.

The air drops happened perhaps eight or nine times over the next several months. After each drop there were distributions of food and meetings to plan strategies.

A distant cousin from Markham was among the men parachuted in. He often came to talk with my mother and me, but never about the training or their mission. "We are not allowed to tell what we know," he told me. "That way, if you're caught, you'll have nothing to tell. Everything is strictly confidential." I nodded my head and asked him no questions.

From time to time, I would see him go to the top of the hill and set up a wireless radio. I never knew what he heard or said, but suspected it had something to do with the air drops, for he always seemed to know when they were about to happen.

For the next four months thousands of us lived scattered through the area of Shothalhosum surrounding the village of Pelbar. Some were camped in the valley, some in the open land. Though we received provisions from the air drops, food was still scarce. Rice and vegetables were particularly difficult to get. Horses didn't have fodder, and at times we had to feed them bushes usually used for incense. Since there wasn't enough food or grass for the animals in any one place, we had to keep moving.

At first my family stayed in the house of a friend in Pelbar, but soon food in that area ran out and we rode to an area not far away, called Dadho. We stayed at each place for over three months. During that time, people continued to arrive almost daily from the towns of Gapa, Nangchen, Karu, and Naru.

One day I recognized a few familiar faces in a group that had just arrived into camp. As I approached to welcome them, I saw that one of them was Lhamo. A young girl clutched at her chupa, and when I reached her I realized the young girl was her daughter, transformed from the infant I'd held several years before into a toddler. I felt sad to see how Lhamo's face had aged in the years we'd been apart. The skin around her eyes was puffed, as if she hadn't had much sleep. Her body, once lean, had widened, and her belly seemed unusually round.

"It's been a long time," I said. "Your child is already walking." "And a second one is coming," she replied. She gestured around and shrugged her shoulders, as if to say, *Can you imagine . . .*

As we stood talking, her little daughter came up to me and held out her hand. I remembered the crying baby and my frustrated attempts to calm her, but now she had grown and her face was smiling and cheerful. I looked into her outstretched hand and saw a small beetle crawling across her palm.

"For me?" I asked. She nodded and looked up with trusting and innocent eyes. At that moment she won my heart.

After that, each day when she saw me coming, she ran toward me with her arms held up. "Pema," I'd say, bending down to rub her forehead, "look what I've brought." Swooping her up, I'd let her reach into the front of my chupa for treats I'd hidden inside. Once a small frog. Sometimes a piece of sweet cheese.

The day settled into a routine. There was much conversation around the fire. Some, like me, spent time chanting prayers; others played games with sho dice. Always there was a search for food; occasionally messengers arrived with news.

One day a young man arrived who had been part of Chushi Gangdruk, with news that Chushi Gangdruk had been defeated and most of its forces fled to India. We gathered around him, eager to hear what had happened.

"A year ago, we were a force to be reckoned with," he said, gesturing proudly. "One of our fiercest battles, on the banks of the River Nyemo, lasted three days. At the time, the nearby fields and houses were swarming with Chinese armed with cannons, automatic weapons, and grenades. As the buglers in our camp sounded the signal to attack, our leader, Tashi Andruktsang, led seventy horsemen onto the field. Galloping at full speed we charged the enemy like wild animals, fighting them hand to hand. The Chinese were unable to resist our attack and withdrew to a nearby village. We shot the doors and windows of the houses. We eventually burned them down. It was the only way we could destroy the Chinese.

"But not long after that, losses began to happen," he said, looking down at the ground with sadness. "The loss of Tsona, our main base, was particularly difficult. The will to continue weakened. It was then that we realized the current situation was impossible. We decided to save ourselves for a future struggle and retreat for the time to India. It was with great sadness that our leader Tashi Andruk-tsang handed over our weapons to the Indian authorities and went into exile."

We were despondent after hearing the story, and wondered if we should follow them to India.

Several days later, the Chinese attacked from every direction. There wasn't even time to open boxes from the last air drop, the attack was so unexpected.

It was early morning. I was on my way to the pastures to check on the animals when I heard shooting in the camp below. Whirling around, I ran back toward our camp. As I came into it soldiers ran toward us from the camp below.

I called, "Mama! Granny! Ani Rigzin!" We grabbed our horses and began to run. Ahead of us I could see Lhamo holding Pema in her arms and struggling to run. Suddenly I heard her cry. Pema was hit. Dropping the reins of my horse, I rushed over and helped her open the little girl's robes. The bullet had torn open her chest and blood was pouring out. She was moaning with pain and I could see that she was dying. Lhamo stood paralyzed, her eyes large and clouding over. "Come!" I begged, but she didn't move. I tried to pull her after me, but she slumped to the ground, a trickle of blood seeping out of her mouth. From the look in her eyes I knew she was dying.

I heard shouts of the soldiers behind and looked frantically for Mama, Ani Rigzin, and Granny. They were running just ahead. I had no other choice but to follow. I felt a terrible sadness as I left.

We took refuge in the thick forest in the hills beyond camp with eight others from Lemdha. We crouched behind trees, our hearts still racing, and waited for night.

I leaned against the trunk of a fir tree and prayed. *Om Mani Peme Hum Om Mani Peme Hum.*

As I prayed, Lhamo's face hovered before me. No matter where I turned, I couldn't get away from her eyes. One moment they were looking at me, the next moment they were blank. It happened so fast.

All night it haunted me. It was as if she had been part of my body, as if a part of my being had died. Later, when the Chinese fired flares into the sky from an opposite hill, lighting the whole area as bright as day, I thought for a moment that her spirit had followed us.

"What is it?" Mama whispered as the lights shot into the sky. "It's Lhamo," I said. She looked at me quizzically but didn't say anything.

We pressed our bodies flat into the earth and waited for darkness.

Several days later, after we had fled farther into the hills, we heard that the fighting had gone on for three days and at the end the Chinese had taken possession of Pelbar and the surrounding area of Shothalhosum.

GÜLTEN AKIN

It's Not the Fear of Shivering

Gülten Akin (b. 1933) is Turkey's leading woman poet. After receiving her law degree from the University of Ankara, she worked as a teacher and practiced law in several Anatolian towns, where her husband served as a provincial administrator. In addition to eight collections of poems, she has published several short plays. In 1965 one of her poetry books won the coveted prize of the Turkish Language Society in Ankara. Here she admonishes those who give up love for war, even as she pities their defeat.

■

We are the tired warriors worn down by
    defeat after defeat
Too timid or ashamed to enjoy a drink
Someone gathers all suns, keeps people
    waiting for them
It's not the fear of shivering but warming up
We are the tired warriors, so many loves
    frightened us off

They have held the mountain roads
The arrows are shot, the traps are set
Someone forgives our ugliness
In the name of friendship
We set out on the flat roads again without
    arrows or rabbits
We are the daunted warriors, so many loves
    frightened us away

Translation by Talat Sait Halman

MAIRE MHAC AN TSAOI

Hatred   *Ireland*

Maire Mhac an tSaoi (b. 1935) is also known as Maire Cruise O'Brien. She created this poem in her native Irish and then translated it into English. What she writes here follows well on what other poets have offered in terms of the hate engendered by colonial oppression—in this case, the ancient wars of genocide committed upon the Irish people, and the civil strife that has continued to take lives in Northern Ireland. The poet takes a male point of view in her ironic poem.

■

May we never taste of death nor quit this vale of tears
Until we see the Englishry go begging down the years,
Packs on their backs to earn a penny pay,
In little leaking boots, as we went in our day.
[Folk verse]

i

What hatred demands is long suffering and a long fuse,
What hatred demands is the non-recognition and the blindness of patience,
What hatred demands is a steady finger on the trigger of the rifle—
And don't fire till you see the whites of their eyes like white-of-egg in your
   sights!

ii

When hatred shall come to flower they will fight on street trenches
And they will spread broken glass in the galloping path of police horses—
But in the meantime this hatred makes good manure for a garden
On a sand-bank between two tide-marks—where dwell our wives and
Our children!

✓ JUNE JORDAN

The Bombing of Baghdad

June Jordan (1936–2002) was a contemporary Jamaican American poet and educator. Both a distinguished author and an activist, Jordan authored more than twenty-three books of verse, essays, and criticism, and received the Lila Wallace–Reader's Digest Writer's Award and PEN West Freedom-to-Write Award. Jordan taught at Yale, Sarah Lawrence College, Connecticut College, the State University of New York at Stonybrook, and most recently the University of California at Berkeley. All of Jordan's work reflected a deep commitment to the protest against social injustice and a strong international sensibility. This timely poem appears in *Naming Our Destiny, New and Selected Poems* (1989), and refers to bombing raids on Iraq several years prior to the Gulf War.

■

I

began and did not terminate for 42 days
and 42 nights relentless minute after minute
more than 110,000 times
we bombed Iraq we bombed Baghdad
we bombed Basra/we bombed military
installations we bombed the National Museum

we bombed schools we bombed air raid
shelters we bombed water we bombed
electricity we bombed hospitals we
bombed streets we bombed highways
we bombed everything that moved/we
bombed everything that did not move we
bombed Baghdad
a city of 5.5 million human beings
we bombed radio towers we bombed
telephone poles we bombed mosques
we bombed runways we bombed tanks
we bombed trucks we bombed cars we bombed bridges
we bombed the darkness we bombed
the sunlight we bombed them and we
bombed them and we cluster bombed the citizens
of Iraq and we sulfur bombed the citizens of Iraq
and we napalm bombed the citizens of Iraq and we
complemented these bombings/these "sorties" with
Tomahawk cruise missiles which we shot
repeatedly by the thousands upon thousands
into Iraq
(you understand an Iraqi Scud missile
is *quote* militarily insignificant *unquote* and we
do not mess around with insignificant)
so we used cruise missiles repeatedly
we fired them into Iraq
And I am not pleased
I am not very pleased
None of this fits into my notion of "things going very well"

II

The bombing of Baghdad
did not obliterate the distance or the time
between my body and the breath
of my beloved

III

This was Custer's Next-To-Last Stand
I hear Crazy Horse singing as he dies
I dedicate myself to learn that song
I hear that music in the moaning of the Arab world

IV

Custer got accustomed to just doing his job
Pushing westward into glory
Making promises
Searching for the savages/their fragile
temporary settlements
for raising children/dancing down the rain/and praying
for the mercy of a herd of buffalo
Custer/he pursued these savages
He attacked at dawn
He murdered the men/murdered the boys
He captured the women and converted
them (I'm sure)
to his religion
Oh how gently did he bid his darling fiancé
farewell!
How sweet the gaze her eyes bestowed upon her warrior!
Loaded with guns and gunpowder he embraced
the guts and gore of manifest white destiny
He pushed westward
to annihilate the savages
("Attack at dawn!")
and seize their territories
        seize their women
        seize their natural wealth

V

And I am cheering for the arrows
And the braves

VI

And all who believed some must die
they were already dead
And all who believe only they possess
human being and therefore human rights
they no longer stood among the possibly humane
And all who believed that retaliation/revenge/defense
derive from God-given prerogatives of white men
And all who believed that waging war is anything
        besides terrorist activity in the first
        place and in the last
And all who believed that F-15's/F-16's/"Apache"
        Helicopters/

B-52 bombers/smart bombs/dumb bombs/napalm/artillery/
battleships/nuclear warheads amount to anything other
than terrorist tools of a terrorist undertaking
And all who believed that holocaust means something
     that happens only to white people
And all who believed that Desert Storm
     signified anything besides the delivery of an American
     holocaust against the peoples of the Middle East
All who believed these things
they were already dead
They no longer stood among the possibly humane

And this is for Crazy Horse singing as he dies
because I live inside his grave
And this is for the victims of the bombing of Baghdad
because the enemy traveled from my house
        to blast your homeland
        into pieces of children
        and pieces of sand

And in the aftermath of carnage
perpetrated in my name
how should I dare to offer you my hand
how shall I negotiate the implications
      of my shame?

My heart cannot confront
this death without relief
My soul will not control
this leaking of my grief
And this is for Crazy Horse singing as he dies
And here is my song of the living
who must sing against the dying
sing to join the living
with the dead

CYNTHIA ENLOE

From Maneuvers

Cynthia Enloe (b. 1938) is professor of government at Clark University and author of *The Morning After: Sexual Politics at the End of the Cold War* (1993), *Bananas, Beaches, and Bases: Making Feminist Sense of International Politics* (1990), and her now-classic *Does Khaki Become You?* (1988). Perhaps more than any other U.S. author of our time, Enloe has analyzed issues of war's impact on women—and she has done so with a spirited view full of ironic wit. She approaches the gender oppression structured into militarized societies, demonstrating how a militarized economy and political institutions shape women's identities and their lives. She also demonstrates how demilitarization can come through concrete acts and resistance, often initiated by women. In this excerpt from her 2000 book *Maneuvers: The International Politics of Militarizing Women's Lives*, she addresses an important issue often overlooked: the sexual abuse of war-besieged refugees, mostly women, by the very peacekeepers and refugee workers who are meant to protect them.

■

Prostitution and Peacekeeping

When the Vietnamese troops withdrew from Cambodia, UN peacekeeping soldiers arrived. It was the task of the United Nations Transitional Authority in Cambodia (UNTAC) to restore peace and to create an environment for the democratization of Cambodia public life. A daunting mission. Yet along with land mines removal and voter education, UNTAC brought an upward spiraling of prostitution. UNTAC did not supply the pimps, but it did supply the customers. By 1994, an alliance of women and men working in the country for relief agencies and other nongovernmental organizations (NGOs) had concluded that senior UN officials were not taking responsibility for the sexually exploitative, "no rules, anything goes" behaviors of peacekeeping personnel. The newly formed Women's Development Association estimated that the number of women working in prostitution in Cambodia grew from 6,000 in 1992 to more than 25,000 in late 1994.[1] The NGO staff workers in Phnom Penh decided, therefore, to publish an open letter to the head of the UN mission in Cambodia:

> Cambodian and other Asian women are the victims of stereotyping and often are forced into subservient roles. . . .
>
> Inappropriate behaviour by some male UNTAC personnel often leave women with a sense of powerlessness. . . . Women have little access to redress when they experience such behaviour.
>
> There has been a dramatic increase in prostitution since UNTAC's arrival and a noticeable absence of condoms and education about their use. It is not surprising that HIV has reached an "emergency" level of at least 75 percent among blood donors.[2]

Many of the women—and increasingly girls as young as twelve—recruited into Cambodia's prostitution industry have been ethnic Vietnamese, either members of Cambodia's long-resident Vietnamese minority community or migrant women drawn across the border from Vietnam by the chance to find work. Some Cambodian politicians tried to use ethnic Vietnamese women's visibility in the expanding prostitution trade as a basis for mobilizing a Cambodian brand of parochial nationalism. Despite the ongoing antagonism toward ethnic Vietnamese, this particular political ploy did not seem to meet with success.[3]

However, popular and international alarm at the prostitution industry's growth fueled by peacekeepers' presence did intensify. And, as so often has happened, once seeded by military consumers, the industry gained a foothold hard to dislodge, even when the foreign military's presence diminished. As the

UN forces were reduced in the mid-1990s, a new influx of civilian men arrived in the impoverished, sexualized Cambodia. Some were drawn there by the Internet's "World Sex Guide," which in 1996 enthused, "six-year-old is available for $3."[4]

Did the highly masculinized version of the UN presence in Cambodia foster the abuse of local women? UNTAC's presence did open up spaces for the UN's own women's advocates, staff members of UNIFEM, as well as for nongovernmental groups to extend support to Cambodian women and to nurture local women's own autonomous political organizing. Nonetheless, one report, authored by the UN Division for the Advancement of Women, noted that all fifteen of the UN Cambodian operation's civilian directorships were held by men and that, in general, "UNTAC was predominantly a male peace-keeping operation in which women held no decision-making positions."[5] Although "a few women" served in certain governments' military peacekeeping units—the Australian, Canadian, and Dutch—in May 1995 the proportion of women in the Cambodian peacekeeping mission was zero.[6]

Women activists inside the United Nations also argued that when peacekeeping was conceptualized as a militarized operation it became most masculinized. By contrast, when UN headquarters' officials see missions as not chiefly military operations (as was the case in the UN's 1989–1990 operation in Namibia), not only are women more likely to gain posts with influence but also the entire UN field *modus operandi* becomes less masculinized.[7]

Many future military peacekeeping operations will look like the peacekeeping missions launched in Cambodia in 1992–1994, in Bosnia in 1996–1998, and in Kosovo in 1999: "victory" will be elusive; a variety of governments will contribute soldiers of their own, many of them trained to be combat troops; the UN Secretariat's own Peace Keeping Organization (UNPKO) will be able to run military training programs, but only for officers and only for those officers whose governments have the funds and the will to pay for their officers' UNPKO training; coordination between governments and the UN will be delicate; NATO will be directly involved; civilian businesses will win contracts to provide support services for the troops; humanitarian aid agencies will be trying to operate without being too reliant on militaries and too deeply sucked into militarized cultures; rival domestic politicians will be competing in the rearranged public arena; local residents will be trying to recover from war-produced trauma while at the same time creating political organizations to compete in the postwar public space; pro-democracy activists will be seeking lasting reforms. Each of these processes will be gendered, will be shaped by how femininity and masculinity are imagined and deployed.

There is nothing inherent in international peacekeeping operations as currently structured that makes their soldiers immune to the sort of sexism that has fueled military prostitution in wartime and peacetime. As in every other military operation conducted by every other government, the extent of future military peacekeeping operations' reliance on the prostitution of some women will be determined by decisions made at the top and in the middle of military organizations.

In January 1996, a group of human rights' and women's organizations sent a letter to the U.S. ambassador to the United Nations, Madeleine Albright. They called on her to press for UN human rights training of peacekeeping troops. Specifically, they called on troops to be formally trained to respect local women. These organizations wanted to ensure that the behavior of some peacekeepers toward Cambodian women was not repeated in Bosnia or in future sites of international peacekeeping.[8]

Child prostitution gained greater visibility inside the bureaucracy of the UN secretariat in late 1996. In a report to the UN secretary general written by Mozambique's education minister, Grace Machel, child prostitution was cited as a principal product of international peacekeeping not only in Cambodia, but in the former Yugoslavia, Mozambique, and Rwanda.[9] This report thereafter provided feminists working as officials in UNICEF, UNIFEM, and other UN agencies to take on the distorted genderings of peacekeeping as a topic within their own policy realms.[10]

Notes

1. Sandra Whitworth, "Gender, Race, and the Politics of Peacekeeping," in *A Future for Peacekeeping,* ed. Eddie Moxon-Brown (London: Macmillan.) The Cambodian Women's Association (P.O. Box 2334, Phnom Penh, Cambodia) has published their own study of prostitution in Cambodia: *Selling Noodles, The Traffic in Women and Children in Cambodia* (Phnom Penh, Cambodia: Cambodian Women's Association, 1996).

2. "Letters: An Open Letter to Yashushi Akashi"(head of the UN operation in Cambodia in 1994), *Phnon Penh Post,* 4 October 1994. I am grateful to Liz Bernstein, one of the letter's signers, for sending me a copy of this letter. In 1995, a survey by the French humanitarian aid group Medicins Sans Frontiere revealed that, out of 200 prostitutes or sex workers tested in the northwest province of Cambodia, 92 percent were HIV positive. See Kari Hartwig "Women's Health in an Age of Globalization" (keynote address of the conference on Women's Health in an Age of Globalization sponsored by Payap University and McCormick Faculty of Nursing, Chiang Mai, Thailand, 6 February 1995), 10. See also Gayle Kirshenbaum and Marina Gilbert, "Who's Watching the Peacekeepers?" *Ms.,* May/June 1994, 10–15.

3. Penny Edwards, "Imaging the Other in Cambodian Nationalist Discourse before and during the UNTAC Period," *in Propaganda, Politics, an Violence in Cambodia,* ed. Steve Heder and Judy Ledgerwood (Armonk, N.Y. M. E. Sharpe, 1996), 62-63. See also Judy Ledgerwood, "Politics and Gender: Negotiating Conceptions of the Ideal Woman in Present Day Cambodia," *Pacific Viewpoint* 37, no. 1 (August 1996): 139–52.

4. "Virgin Territory," *The Economist,* 2 March 1996, 37. One of the organizations working to end the trafficking in women in Asia has published the following proceedings: The Coalition against Trafficking in Women in Asia, "Women Empowering Women" (proceedings of the Human Rights Conference on the Trafficking of Asian Women, Ateneo di Manila University, Quezon City, Philippines, April 1993). Cambodian human rights advocates welcomed the new Cambodian government's passage in January 1996 of a new law making illegal the trafficking of people, but have criticized Cambodian policy makers and courts for failing to prosecute those involved in prostitute procurement. See Debra Boyce, "Rescued Prostitutes Present Theater of Their Lives," *Bangkok Post,* 28 August 1996.

5. United Nations Division for the Advancement of Women and the Department for Policy Coordination and Sustainable Development, "The Role of Women in United Nations Peacekeeping," *Women 2000,* (December 1995): 8. This journal is published by the UN Division for the Advancement of Women, New York.

6. Ibid.

7. Gayle Kirshenbaum, "In UN Peacekeeping, Women Are an Untappep Resource," *Ms.*, January/February 1997, 20–21. See also Judith Hicks Stiehm, "United Nations Peacekeeping: Men's and Women's Work," in *Gender Politics in Global Governance*, ed. Mary K. Meyer and Elisabeth Prug (Lanham, Md.: Rowman and Littlefield, 1999), 41–57.

8. Barbara Crossette, "When Peacekeepers Turn into Troublemakers," *New York Times*, 7 January 1996.

9. "U.N. Focuses on Peacekeepers Involved in Child Prostitution," *New York Times*, 9 December 1996.

10. I am grateful to several UN officials who asked to remain anonymous for sharing their thoughts on peacekeeping with me in conversations from May 1997 through May 1998.

11. Lillian A. Pfluke, "Direct Ground Combat in Bosnia: Clear as Mud," *Minerva's Bulletin Board*, Spring 1996, 10.

DANIELA GIOSEFFI

"Don't Speak the Language of the Enemy!" *and* The Exotic Enemy

Daniela Gioseffi (b. 1941) is a poet, novelist, editor, literary critic, and activist who has taught and lectured widely. In 1988, she published the first edition of *Women on War*, which won an American Book Award. Her many books include several volumes of poetry, as well as a novel, *The Great American Belly;* short fiction; and essays. She received two award grants for poetry from the New York State Council on the Arts in 1971 and 1979, and a PEN Syndicated Fiction Award in 1990. In 1993 she published a second critically acclaimed anthology, *On Prejudice: A Global Perspective*. She edits the award-winning Web site www.PoetsUSA.com. Gioseffi's activism of more than forty years began with the Civil Rights movement in the early 1960s, and includes work with such groups as National Peace Action and the Writers and Publishers Alliance for Nuclear Disarmament. The Ploughshares Fund, an independent peace foundation, awarded her grants for Women's Leadership Development, which helped to make this book possible. In her story "The Exotic Enemy," from her collection *In Bed with the Exotic Enemy* (1997), she assumes the male persona. Her poem "Don't Speak the Language of the Enemy" appeared in her most recent volume of poetry, *Symbiosis* (2002), and is part of a national touring exhibit concerning the little-recognized internment of Italian immigrants in the United States during World War II.

■

"DON'T SPEAK THE LANGUAGE OF THE ENEMY!"

reads the poster at the end of a grey alleyway of childhood
where the raggedy guineas of Newark
whisper quietly in their dialects on concrete steps
far from blue skies, olive groves or hyacinths.
Bent in a shadow toward the last
shafts of sunlight above tenement roofs,
Grandpa Galileo sadly sips homemade wine
hums moaning with his broken mandolin.
Children play hide-and-seek
in dusty evening streets as red sauce simmers,

hour after hour, on coal stoves,
garlic, oil, crushed tomatoes blended
with precious pinches of salt and *basilico*—
a pot that must last a week of suppers.
The fathers' hands wear blackened finger nails,
worn rough with iron wrought,
bricks laid, ditches dug, glass etched.
Wilted women in black cotton dresses
wait in quickening dark,
calling their listless children
to scrubbed linoleum kitchens.
In cold-water flats with tin tables,
stale bread is ladled with sauce, then baked
to revive edibility. Clothes soak in laundry-tubs,
washboards afloat. Strains of opera caught in static
are interrupted by war bulletins.
The poster on the fence at the end of the block
streaked with setting sun and rain reads:
"Don't speak the language of the enemy!"
But, the raggedy guineas can speak no other,
and so they murmur in their rooms
in the secret dark frightened
of the government camps where people like them
have been imprisoned in the New World.
They teach English to their children by daylight,
whispering of Mussolini's stupidity—
stifling the mother tongue, wounding the father's pride,
telling each other, "We are Americans. God bless America!"

THE EXOTIC ENEMY: A STORY

We could invent love until the sea closed in. That's all a guy like me was sure of in 1936 in Greenwich Village. Those were gloomy dark years in New York City. My father already knew what Stalin and Hitler were up to, even if a lot of others didn't. Us kids felt a vague threat hanging over us. I dreamed of being a revolutionary poet, when I wasn't dreaming of Molly—my pretty, plump and graceful, Greek-Jewish girlfriend. She had a skinny brother, called "Nebby," who was nervous and unattractive to females. No one remembered that Nebby didn't get his nomer from "nebbish," but from the first part of his name, Nebekovski. Nebby was always worried about the way he looked because girls paid no attention to him. To become a big hero so the girls would want him, he intended to run away and join the Spanish Loyalist Army—but he was afraid of guns and didn't know a thing about shooting one. Molly made me promise to teach him how.

I was ashamed of any nebbishy guys of my ethos who were scared of guns, scared of the woods, scared of worms when you took them fishing. Being good at guns and fishing made me very suspect among my friends in the city, but I fared well in the country compared to most of the guys who were studying at Stuyvesant High School. My father, a Turkish Jew, had made a point of teaching me to hunt in the woods and fish. He believed that every man ought to know how to defend himself with a gun. He expected that at any time a workers' revolution or German troops might arrive in New York Harbor.

"Wars are fought to save rich people's money! People like us are often killed by their own governments!" my father would bellow. After Stalin's purges were known and after Hitler started World War II, he would say the same thing—with more conviction and even louder oratory. "So, why should only the government soldiers have guns? When the Secret Police come for your family, you got to be ready! When the whole world is one country, one race, one religion, one class, then you can be a pacifist!" He would hold forth as he taught me to aim and fire the rifles he bought me on my birthdays. He gave me two hunting rifles—just like his.

"You always need a spare—just in case—and you hide them in different places—one easy to find, the other impossible! You're not going to be a Socialist like these nebbishes in New York—always expecting a workers' revolution and scared even to kill a chicken! A gun's like a poisonous snake to them! They scream like girls if they only see one. They can't put a worm on a hook without throwing up! What kind of man is that?"

I felt sorry for Nebby. I always thought of him when my father talked like that. I befriended him—mostly because of his sister, but I called him Nebby too. He was in no great position to protest anything anyone called him. I was proud, too, of being the tallest guy at Stuyvesant High School—the top public school for science and math in New York City—especially, it seemed to me, taller than the guys who were scared of worms, guns and girls—the ones the German guys who hung around the park drinking beer called "sissies." The Jewish guys to get back at them, called them "Krauts," and "Beer bellies." Then the Germans would retaliate with "Kikes" and "Jewbagels" Everyone was calling the Italians "guineas," or "greaseballs," the Englishmen "fruits" or "limeys," and the blacks, "schvartzes" or "niggers." Me? I was called the "Crazy Turk" because I liked guns and hunting. But no one messed with me.

"I'm gonna to be a hero when I get back from this war!" Nebby told me. "You'll see! Then all the girls in the Party will love me and pay attention to me."

The main girl who was paying attention to me, and I to her, was Nebby's voluptuous sister Molly. I was crazy about her. She had the exotic looks of her pretty, Greek mother who was a nurse, and the brains of her Jewish father—a busy doctor who tended poor people's kids for nothing and taught courses in medicine at New York University. Just like my father did. Molly and I were from a liberal socialist group that was not at all sexually repressed like most of the other kids at school. Molly's mother had—on the insistence of her father—supplied her with birth control devices. We used to read Emma Goldman's and Margaret Sanger's essays and discuss Free Love as a high and mighty ideal—like Alexandra Kollantai of Russia! Molly and I became totally obsessed with each other. I was in the throes of the hottest love affair I'd known since discovering the difference between men and women. We lived in Washington Square. My father was a physician who had written declamatory articles for Emma Goldman's magazine, *Mother Earth*. He supplied me with all the birth control I needed, too, so I wasn't scared of making girls pregnant or catching diseases like some of the other kids at school. Ours was the only house in the square owned by radicals and we had a tendency to shock the neighborhood. I felt like a man of the world—taking Nebby's sister into the attic of my parents' house as often as I could. Molly and I were living a life of nubile bliss—but Nebby felt very left out of all the fun in our crowd and Molly started distracting me from our love-making with worry about him.

"Please help Nebby learn to shoot a gun," she pleaded with me. "I'm afraid he can't defend himself. He swears he's really going to run away to join the Spanish Loyalist Army—and he's threatened to tell my parents all about us cutting school to come up here if I tell on him. I'm worried, because he's never seen a gun in person for real."

Molly was absolutely beautiful to me—with her blond curls and the roundest softest breasts and thighs and orgastic sighs in my universe.

So, I did and it wasn't easy. Nebby tried hard, but he was just too nervous and scared of the thing. It made too big a bang and hurt his skinny shoulder when it kicked back. Whenever we finished practicing with my rifle, he claimed he had a terrible headache and had to rest. Still, I did my best to teach him—poor, haunted, scrawny guy, dying for the girls to notice him, aching to be a big hero with a medal on his chest!

To mine and everyone's surprise, he really disappeared one day, and Molly got a letter from him a few days later saying he'd joined the Spanish Loyalist Army and was about to become a real hero. One night, when Molly was supposed to meet me for a trip to the attic, she called instead. She was crying hysterically.

"I can't see you tonight or ever. I don't want to see any boys. We heard today that my brother's dead. I'm going to stay home every night after school to be with my parents, because they are crying all the time. They said I should have told them what Nebby was planning to do. I don't feel like making love anymore—because Nebby never will get to."

I'm telling you this story to make a little memorial to Nebby, I mean, Nevin Nebekovski, because now I'm sixty-six, and I still remember Molly. I remember wanting her for so many years, not being able to have her.

How deep the fascination with the exotic other goes—no sentiment about it—this passion with the blood of the other which stains our hands and tongues—this desire to poke at the fruit until its juices run, to tear the rose from its stem, scatter petals to the wind, to pluck the butterfly's wings for the microscope's lens, to plunge a fist into a teetering tower of bricks, watch the debris sail, explode fireworks until all crumbles to dust and is undone, open to the curious eye. Does this or that creature die as I die, cry as I cry, writhe as I would if my guts were ripped from the walls of my flesh, my ripe heart eaten alive?

Always the probing questions of sacred exploration—as if science can be progress without empathy. Does a penis feel as a clitoris feels? Do slanted eyes see as I see? Is a white or black skin or sin the same as a red one? Is it like me? Does it burn, does it peel, does it boil in oil or reel in pain? The obsession to possess the other so completely that her blood fills the mouth and you eat of her flesh from its bone and then know if she, if he, feels as you feel, if your world is real.

Maybe, Molly was exotic to me—we were different—she a Greek, me a Turkish Jew, or maybe because she was a blond with pale skin and blue eyes, and I'm olive-skinned with dark brown ones. Even after I had white hair, she remained a kind of obsession that no woman—not my wife of thirty years—no woman—and I tried many before I got married—could erase. I still have dreams about her.

Her mother decided to go to church again after Nebby, her only son, was killed, and her father, a Socialist, didn't approve. It broke his heart when Molly entered a convent and decided to become a nun. Thank goodness she changed her mind and left the convent for college! Her father, by then, had given up his medical practice here and moved to Israel. A few years later, her mother left the Village to look for him. I heard they got back together again over there, and Molly, when she finished college, joined them in Tel Aviv. That's where she taught school for forty years.

Yes, I'm sixty-six, and I can't forget Molly, and I know now that erotic ideas are like flashy lights turning on in heads that echo from mouths and shine up secret places, and people can be greedy in their groins and ugliness can come even from the beauty of nubile bliss. Sex can be ripped from the blood as if the body were not a house of green moss, a vase of kindness, a space for greed set alight from the dark by the glow of hand on hand.

And there are still the word wounds, like roots of mushroom clouds that could rise from the pockmarked earth: *guinea, dago, spic, nigger, polack, wasp, mick, chink, jap, frog, russkie, red bastard, kike, fag, bitch, macho pig, gimp, dyke!* The stench of flesh could follow the sprayed dust of children's eyes melted from wondering sockets, animal skin, thighs, men's hands, women's sighs roasted in a final feast of fire beasts caught like lemmings in a leap to Armageddon—false resurrection! Word wounds could rise from visions of charred lips, burnt books, paper ashes, crumbled libraries, stones under which plastic pens and computers are fried amidst the last cried words, smoke to pay lip service as all dust onto dust returns. . . .

I'm old enough to know, now, that the head is fickle like history. An orchard, the body is free and soul invents itself in smile and song. I had a letter from Molly. I tried writing to her about a year ago—a love poem of our youth, and she finally answered me.

A letter came in the mail this morning from Tel Aviv. She's been a widow now for three years, like me. She said she's coming to New York to visit her grandson next month and she'll call me. We can have dinner and a talk, she says. She thought of me often through these many years. So many long years ago when we were young! Nebby never got to be a hero—just a casualty of machismo—like me. She's worried, she says, about her grandchildren and the threat of nuclear end. . . . It would be worse than Hitler or Stalin, worse than anything right or left, she says!

Yes, we'll invent love until the sea dries up or tides flood over or the bombs explode human blossoms to dust, and poets are only madmen talking crazy and making sense.

ELLEN NDESHI NAMHILA

From The Price of Freedom

Ellen Ndeshi Namhila (b. 1941) left Namibia at the age of twelve and returned nineteen years later. Her autobiographical novel *The Price of Freedom* tells her story of exile, loss, and return to her homeland. The book is dedicated to her late husband, Billy Charles Matengu, who worked hard for the liberation of Namibia and died in the struggle. Her novel, published in Namibia in 1997, is a testimony to a people who fought for their freedom, on and off, for nearly a century, first against German colonialists and later against the brutal South African occupying armies.

■

Going into Exile

I saw white policemen for the first time in 1972. There was a gathering at Omamwandi near our school at Ondobe. The reason for the meeting was to talk about the veterinary service they received from the colonial government. Some people wanted to know why they were being charged for veterinary services and where the money was going. They wanted to know why their cattle were being vaccinated and with what.

I and other children from the school went to the meeting out of curiosity. We wanted to hear what the adults were discussing. The gathering had been going on for 30 minutes when suddenly several police vans started arriving. There were shots into the air. The man who had been speaking fell to the ground. Then there was pandemonium as the shooting continued. People were killed and injured. Some were arrested. I ran for my life. When I got home I was speechless. In the village, people mourned their dead in silence. No questions were asked for fear of reprisals.

After this incidence there was more unrest and arrests. More and more South African police came to the village in their strange-looking vehicles. The police cars were called *otjaatjaa* because they did not make much sound. People could not hear them from a distance so that there was no time to hide themselves or run away.

When I was ten years old I watched my uncle being arrested by the police. First they set their dogs on him. This scene was such a terror that I still have nightmares. As soon as the dogs stopped biting and pulling, the police dragged him out of our homestead and drove away with him. Two days later, he was returned home beaten half dead and the whole body swollen. I was afraid of him, his fingers were big, his head was big, I have never seen a human with a swollen body like that. I do not know what they did to him. I could only see that when he was returned his body was swollen head to toe. My aunt asked me to help her give my uncle a hot steam towel. I could not bear the scene of my uncle's body lying helplessly on the floor, a man who was my protector, provider and security. Now he could not even feed himself. The echo of his voice "auu" every time we put a steaming towel to his body was torturing me because I do not like to see people suffer. I was also afraid that my uncle might die. Although we got enormous support from the neighbours and relatives, it was my uncle who was dying, who was in pain; it was my family that was in trouble. Although his body eventually got healed, the experience was traumatic and the pain was very personal and to this day I cannot recover from my fear of dogs.

Around 1972 I saw a helicopter for the first time in my life. It came to arrest tate Haimbala ya Shixungileni. His brother Kambo was one of the founder members of SWAPO, who went into exile in the 1960s, although rumour had it that he and other guerrillas ate at his home every night. Tate Haimbala had been arrested several times and beaten severely by the police during interrogation regarding his brother's whereabouts. The families of people who went into exile often suffered at the hands of the South African police.

Living in Constant Terror

At the beginning of 1976 I was accepted at Eenhana Secondary School. In the center of Eenhana village a South African army base was established towards the end of 1975. This base was very close to the school and the residential areas. We saw soldiers with guns every day. There was a curfew imposed upon local residents. People were not allowed to move outside their homes between seven in the evening and seven in the morning. This was very difficult for most people in the village as they did not use watches or the clock for time.

Like most children in the village, I did not understand what the state of emergency was all about. There were many things we did not understand about the soldiers. We did not understand why they were there, who asked them to settle in our village, and why they imposed a curfew on us. We were not even informed about this curfew, we only learned by seeing that those who were found moving outside their homes after seven in the evening and before seven o'clock in the morning were shot at or arrested. Cooking meals after seven o'clock in the evening was also prohibited. Those found cooking their meals after seven were accused of preparing food for SWAPO and were severely terrorized.

Looking back now I realize our parents had the answers to some of these questions but were too afraid to talk or do anything about them, as my experience that nearly cost me my life will show.

One day as I was cycling from a friend's home in the evening I suddenly saw several army trucks driving towards me. And then I heard a gunshot. I ignored the vehicles and the shooting, thinking that the soldiers were shooting at the birds which were often in the trees around the nearby dam. The next thing I was rolling with my bicycle down the road. I had been shot in the arm and leg and was bleeding. The military vehicles had stopped and the white soldiers were asking me several questions which I did not understand.

I was in pain and terrified by my bleeding injuries. I was all alone and surrounded by white soldiers with guns and military uniforms. They were unfriendly and spoke to me in a foreign language. I was frightened as I also did not know what else they would do to harm me. One of the soldiers put some red liquid on my wounds and bandaged them. They asked me where I lived, then they threw me into the military car, dumped me near my home and drove away.

I was so traumatized that my body started feeling as if I was already dead. I was not accustomed to seeing white people, let alone soldiers with guns. No single white person lived in my village. The missionaries visited our village about once a year and we only saw them from a distance. They were not angry; they also spoke our language and they were always in the company of local priests or some other local people we trusted. I could not understand why the soldiers shot me because I did them no harm. I do not know whether they thought I was a bird or they were just having fun shooting and frightening me.

For a whole month I was an outpatient at the hospital and I had to attend school with bandages on my arm and leg. I had a feeling that no-one really wanted to know what I was going through. I was afraid and frightened. In the village, no-one tried to find out who shot me and for what reason. I tried to ask adults why the soldiers were in the village and what they were doing, but all I met with was complete silence.

While I was still recovering, warlike soldiers came to our school. Two of them came into our class armed, just walking up and down as our teacher continued his teaching. They looked at us very suspiciously. Our teacher stopped teaching and protested against the presence of armed soldiers in the class and against being observed while teaching. He was grabbed with his arms held at the back and head down. When he tried to free his arms, the soldiers were on him. They thrashed him to the ground and kicked him badly until he stopped saying anything. They threw him into their car and drove away with him.

As good Christians we were taught to love our enemies and to do unto them as we would like them do unto us. The whole school was so shocked by the arrest and the soldiers' brutality that it had to close early that day. We could not understand how the army could humiliate a teacher in front of his pupils. We could not understand how these white men could treat a teacher, a highly respected figure in the society, like that. The teachers did not want to talk about this incident, and everyone remained silent.

The brutality continued in the school and also in the village. The soldiers paid the school another visit. This time they took away bigger boys and went away with them. Again, the teachers stood by and watched helplessly with us as the pupils were taken away.

We lived in constant fear and we started wondering who would be next. What was most frightening was that teachers and parents did not want to talk about these things with their children out of fear for their own lives. Some adults thought that if they answered our questions they would encourage us to get involved in social and political problems. Unfortunately they achieved the opposite effect, because it was partly this unexplained brutality that forced most of us to look for answers and seek for alternatives by going into exile.

As a child I always felt secure in the presence of adults—parents or teachers. It terrified me to realize that adults were no longer a source of security. I did not like to live in fear, surrounded by people who posed this fear threat to me. So I decided to leave the country. Although I did not know what life in exile was really like, I knew of people who had gone there, including one of my uncles and two cousins. I thought that as soon as I got there I would immediately join them because I had imagined that all those who went into exile lived in one big village. . . .

When I decided to leave Namibia I did not realize the full implication of my move. I did not give it much thought. All that mattered was that I had to leave. It never occurred to me that I would get homesick. I was already in exile when I realized that leaving Namibia meant leaving my family, friends and country, probably never to see them again. It meant leaving my food, my language, my culture and traditions. The fear of going into the unknown world was overridden by what was happening at home.

When I left I was driven by fear of the white man. I thought I was going to where there were no white men. Soon I learned white men were everywhere and I possibly could not run away from them. I was already on the run when I started hearing about countries where the police did not shoot, arrest and beat up people for no apparent reason. And even if it was true that in some countries there were still cannibals, anything was better than living under the state of emergency. Little did I know that it would be a solid 19 years before I could set foot in my country again. Because one day we just left.

ELIZABETH NUNEZ

From Beyond the Limbo Silence

Elizabeth Nunez (b. 1942) grew up in Trinidad and then immigrated to New York, where she is currently a distinguished professor of English at Medgar Evers College of the City University of New York. She received a B.A. degree in English from Marian College in Wisconsin, and an M.A. and Ph.D. (1977) in English from New York University. She is the author of four novels, *When Rocks Dance* (1986); *Beyond the Limbo Silence* (1998), which won a 1999 IPPY Award–Independent Publishers Book Award in the multicultural fiction category; *Bruised Hibiscus* (2000), which won an American Book Award in 2001; and *Discretion* (2002). Nunez is the co-editor of the collection of essays *Defining Ourselves: Black Writers in the 90s.* Her essays and short stories have appeared in many anthologies and magazines. Nunez is the director of the National Black Writers Conference, sponsored by the National Endowment for the Humanities.

■

On the Sunday before I left Trinidad, already feeling nostalgia for the landscape that I would not see for years, my father drove me through the mountains north of Port-of-Spain to Maracas Bay, on the other side of the island. He wanted to say his good-byes to me, give me his last words of advice on the price of gifts.

Along the road he reminded me that this too, the freshly paved road on which we traveled, was a gift from the Americans to the Trinidad colonial government.

"They built it after the war," he said, spitting out the word war between clenched teeth, as he always did, as if merely voicing the word threatened to release an anger in him he had chosen to stifle. His older brother, George, obsessed by a sense of obligation to his mother country and deluding himself perhaps into believing that as a British subject he was a British person, had enlisted in that war.

Sometimes my father would boast about how his brother had learned to fly the British bomber planes in six months. "Just imagine," he would say in wonder, "one day before that, he'd never ever been in the insides of a regular plane."

At other times my father would grow morose and speak bitterly of the war that had taken his brother's life and the lives of the best of the young men in the colonies, and had given nothing back. But not so the Americans, he would tell me. They knew how to repay debts.

By then, I knew more about the Americans than I had as a child, and America had already begun to lose its fairy tale quality. A military air base at Walter Field stretched across central Trinidad; the farmers just rolled their belongings into bundles and left their lands when the British told them to move. And the naval base in Chaguaramus: the fishermen simply had to find new waters and there would be no more family picnics on Sundays on the beach at Teteron Bay. All for fifty battered American destroyers when the mother country was afraid Germany would become their father country. And no one asked us anything, my father would shout.

Now I was barely listening to him, smelling the wind full of the sea, fishy and salty. Now my mind spun circles. Could I live without this in Wisconsin? Could I live on prairie lands whose borders touched only land and more land thousands of miles from the sea?

I pressed my face against the car window, greedy for the forests of fat-trunked trees, the clutter of leaves and vines on their tops, sifting the sun, the sudden surprise of precipices that plunged from dizzying heights from the edge of the road as we curled around the tight bends up the mountain to the sea.

"For ninety-nine years," my father was saying to me. I shut out his words with the roar of the white surf crashing onto the huge rocks below us. I didn't want to feel his anger, not then, not when I was etching in my mind, for Wisconsin, white, frothy mists hugging mountain peaks, sparkling jewels reflected in the sun.

"Even the Americans knew that they had taken too much," my father said, and then mercifully, like me, he grew quiet, silenced by the beauty of the landscape.

I knew the rest of what he would have said. Even the Americans realized that the best seaports in Trinidad, Sunday picnic beaches, acres of cocoa fields and farmlands and anything else they wanted on the other islands, were too much to pay for fifty old destroyers when no one asked the people if they minded paying. And for ninety-nine years. It was too much. But when our car skated down the last stretch of road from the mountaintop and the bay appeared shimmering blue against the sunlit sky, its edges skirted with cotton white surf and then ivory brown sand, I was ready to forget. The road the Americans had built, giving Maracas Bay to us—though only to those of us in the middle class who had cars—eased the resentment of ninety-nine years. I was ready to filter out my father's words, his anger about discarded fuel and debris snaking down from the huge military ships in Chaguaramus, soiling our waters in Carenage Bay. Fishermen's sons, naked and brown like the earth, splashing in oil-drenched waters, wondering later about the eczemas that grew on their legs, pustulant and ugly.

AMA ATA AIDOO

Certain Winds from the South

Ama Ata Aidoo (b. 1942) is one of Ghana's most distinguished writers. Her books include *Anowa, Changes: A Love Story, The Dilemma of a Ghost, Our Sister Killjoy, Someone Talking to Someone*, and *The Girl Who Can Run*. This story comes from her 1970 collection of short stories *No Sweetness Here*. In her powerful and often witty fiction, Aidoo explores life in postcolonial Ghana in both urban and rural areas, where women and men struggle not only to survive in a world that offers little in the way of "sweetness," but also to sort out their identities in a changing culture. True to the spirit of traditional African storytelling, Aidoo's characters come to life through their distinct voices and speech. Much of the following story is told through the words of an aging rural widow, for whom present events trigger a memory of the overwhelming loss she suffered during World War II—a war that had nothing to do with her own life, fought by the colonial powers which at that time still controlled most of Africa.

■

M'ma Asana eyed the wretched pile of cola-nuts, spat, and picked up the reed-bowl. Then she put down the bowl, picked up one of the nuts, bit at it, threw it back, spat again, and stood up. First, a sharp little ache, just a sharp little one, shot up from somewhere under her left ear. Then her eyes became misty.

"I must check on those logs," she thought, thinking this misting of her eyes was due to the chill in the air. She stooped over the nuts.

"You never know what evil eyes are prowling this dusk over these grass-lands—I must pick them up quickly."

On the way back to the kraal, her eyes fell on the especially patchy circles that marked where the old pits had been. At this time, in the old days, they would have been full to bursting and as one scratched out the remains of the out-going season, one felt a near-sexual thrill of pleasure looking at these pits, just as one imagines a man might feel who looks upon his wife in the ninth month of pregnancy.

Pregnancy and birth and death and pain; and death again. . . . When there are no more pregnancies, there are no more births and therefore, no more deaths. But there is only one death and only one pain . . .

Show me a fresh corpse my sister, so I can weep you old tears.

The pit of her belly went cold, then her womb moved and she had to lean by the doorway. In twenty years, Fuseni's has been the only pregnancy and the only birth . . . twenty years, and the first child and a male! In the old days, there would have been bucks and you got scolded for serving a woman in maternity a duicker. But these days, those mean poachers on the government reserves sneak away their miserable duickers, such wretched hinds! Yes, they sneak away even the duickers to the houses of those sweet-toothed southerners.

In the old days, how time goes, and how quickly age comes. But then does one expect to grow younger when one starts getting grandchildren? Allah be praised for a grandson.

The fire was still strong when she returned to the room. . . . M'ma Asana put the nuts down. She craned her neck into the corner. At least those logs should take them to the following week. For the rest of the evening, she set about preparing for the morrow's marketing.

The evening prayers were done. The money was in the bag. The grassland was still, Hawa was sleeping and so was Fuseni. M'ma came out to the main gate, first to check up if all was well outside and then to draw the door across. It was not the figure, but rather the soft rustle of footsteps trying to move still more lightly over the grass that caught her attention.

"If only it could be my husband."

But of course it was not her husband!

"Who comes?"

"It is me, M'ma."

"You Issa, my son?"

"Yes, M'ma."

"They are asleep."

"I thought so. That is why I am coming now."

There was a long pause in the conversation as they both hesitated about whether the son-in-law should go in and see Hawa and the baby or not. Nothing was said about this struggle but then one does not say everything.

M'ma Asana did not see but she felt him win the battle. She crossed the threshold outside and drew the door behind her. Issa led the way. They did not walk far, however. They just turned into a corner between two of the projecting pillars in the wall of the kraal. It was Issa who stood with his back to the wall. And this was as it should have been, for it was he who needed the comforting coolness of it for his backbone.

"M'ma, is Fuseni well?"

"Yes."

"M'ma please tell me, is Fuseni very well?"

"A-ah, my son. For what are you troubling yourself so much? Fuseni is a new baby who was born not more than ten days. How can I tell you he is very well? When a grown-up goes to live in other people's village . . . "

"M'ma."

"What is it?"

"No. Please it is nothing."

"My son, I cannot understand you this evening. Yes, if you, a grown-up person, goes to live in another village, will you say after the first few days that you are perfectly well?"

"No."

"Shall you not get yourself used to their food? Shall you not find first where you can get water for yourself and your sheep?"

"Yes, M'ma."

"Then how is it you ask me if Fuseni is very well? The navel is healing very fast . . . and how would it not? Not a single navel of all that I have cut here got infected. Shall I now cut my grandson's and then sit and see it rot? But it is his male that I can't say. Mallam did it neat and proper and it must be alright. Your family is not noted for males that rot, is it now?"

"No, M'ma."

"Then let your heart lie quiet in your breast. Fuseni is well but we cannot say how well yet."

"I have heard you, M'ma . . . M'ma . . ."

"Yes, my son."

"M'ma, I am going South."

"Where did you say?"

"South."

"How far?"

"As far as the sea. M'ma I thought you would understand."

"Have I spoken yet?"

"No, you have not."

"Then why did you say that?"

"That was not well said."

"And what are you going to do there?"

"Find some work."

"What work?"

"I do not know."

"Yes, you know, you are going to cut grass."

"Perhaps."

"But my son, why must you travel that far just to cut grass? Is there not enough of it all round here? Around this kraal, your father's and all the others in the village? Why do you not cut these?"

"M'ma, you know it is not the same. If I did that here people will think I am mad. But over there, I have heard that not only do they like it but the government pays you to do it."

"Even still, our men do not go South to cut grass. This is for those further north. They of the wilderness, it is they who go South to cut grass. This is not for our men."

"Please M'ma, already time is going. Hawa is a new mother and Fuseni my first child."

"And yet you are leaving them to go South and cut grass."

"But M'ma, what will be the use in my staying here and watching them starve? You yourself know that all the cola went bad, and even if they had not, with trade as it is, how much money do you think I would have got from them? And that is why I am going. Trade is broken and since we do not know when things will be good again, I think it will be better for me to go away."

"Does Hawa know?"

"No, she does not."

"Are you coming to wake her up at this late hour to tell her?"

"No."

"You are wise."

"M'ma, I have left everything in the hands of Amadu. He will come and see Hawa tomorrow."

"Good. When shall we expect you back?"

" . . . "

"Issa . . . "

"M'ma."

"When shall we expect you back?"

"M'ma, I do not know. Perhaps next Ramaddan."

"Good."

"So I go now."

"Allah go with you."

"And may His prophet look after you all."

M'ma went straight back to bed, but not to sleep. And how could she sleep? At dawn, her eyes were still wide-open.

Is his family noted for males that rot? No, certainly not. It is us who are noted for our unlucky females. There must be something wrong with them. . . . Or how is it we cannot hold our men? Allah, how is it?

Twenty years ago. Twenty years, perhaps more than twenty years . . . perhaps more than twenty years and Allah please, give me strength to tell Hawa.

Or shall I go to the market now and then tell her when I come back? No. Hawa, Hawa, now look at how you are stretched down there like a log! Does a mother sleep like this? Hawa, H-a-a-w-a! Oh, I shall not leave you alone. . . . And how can you hear your baby when it cries in the night since you die when you sleep?

. . . Listen to her asking me questions! Yes, it is broad daylight. I thought you really were dead. If it is cold, draw your blanket round you and listen to me for I have something to tell you.

Hawa, Issa has gone South.

And why do you stare at me with such shining eyes? I am telling you that Issa is gone south.

And what question do you think you are asking me? How could he take you along when you have a baby whose navel wound has not even healed yet?

He went away last night.

Don't ask me why I did not come to wake you up. What should I have woken you up for?

Listen, Issa said he could not stay here and just watch you and Fuseni starve.

He is going South to find work and . . . Hawa, where do you think you are getting up to go to? Issa is not at the door waiting for you. The whole neighborhood is not up yet, so do not let me shout . . . and why are you behaving like a baby? Now you are a mother and you must decide to grow up . . . where are you getting up to go? Listen to me telling you this. Issa is gone. He went last night because he wants to catch the government bus that leaves Tamale very early in the morning. So . . .

Hawa, ah-ah, are you crying? Why are you crying? That your husband has left you to go and work? Go on weeping, for he will bring the money to look after me and not you. . . . I do not understand, you say? May be I do not. . . . See, now you have woken up Fuseni. Sit down and feed him and listen to me . . .

Listen to me and I will tell you of another man who left his newborn child and went away.

Did he come back? No, he did not come back. But do not ask me any more questions for I will tell you all.

He used to go and come, then one day he went away and never came back. Not that he had had to go like the rest of them . . .

Oh, they were soldiers. I am talking of a soldier. He need not have gone to be a soldier. After all, his father was one of the richest men of this land. He was not the eldest son, that is true, but still, there were so many things he could have done to look after himself and his wife when he came to marry. But he would not listen to anybody. How could he sit by and have other boys out-do him in smartness?

Their clothes that shone and shone with pressing. . . . I say, you could have looked into any of them and put khole under your eyes. And their shoes, how they roared! You know soldiers for yourself. Oh, the stir on the land when they came in from the South! Mothers spoke hard and long to daughters about the excellencies of proper marriages, while fathers hurried through with betrothals. Most of them were afraid of getting a case like that of Memunat on their hands. Her father had taken the cattle and everything and then Memunat goes and plays with a soldier. Oh, the scandal she caused herself then!

Who was this Memunat? No, she is not your friend's mother. No, this Memunat in the end ran away South herself. We hear she became a bad woman in the city and made a lot of money. No, we do not hear of her now—she is not dead either, for we hear such women usually go to their homes to die, and she has not come back here yet.

But us, we were different. I had not been betrothed.

Do you ask me why I say we? Because this man was your father. . . . Ah-ah, you open your mouth and eyes wide? Yes my child, it is of your father I am speaking.

No, I was not lying when I told you that he died. But keep quiet and listen. . . .

He was going South to get himself a house for married soldiers.

No, it was not that time he did not come back. He came here, but not to fetch me.

He asked us if we had heard of the war.

Had we not heard of the war? Was it not difficult to get things like tinned fish, kerosene and cloth?

Yes, we said, but we thought it was only because the traders were not bringing them in.

Well yes, he said, but the traders do not get them even in the South.

And why, we asked.

O you people, have you heard of the German-people? He had no patience with us. He told us that in the South they were singing dirty songs with their name.

But when are we going, I asked him.

What he told me was that that was why he had come. He could not take me along with him. You see, he said, since we were under the Anglis-people's rule and they were fighting with the German-people . . .

Ask me, my child, for that was exactly what I asked him, what has all that got to do with you and me? Why can I not come South with you?

Because I have to travel to the lands beyond the sea and fight . . .

In other people's war? My child, it is as if you were there. That is what I asked him.

But it is not as simple as that, he said.

We could not understand him. You shall not go, said his father. You shall not go, for it is not us fighting with the Grunshies or the Gonjas. . . . I know about the Anglis-people but not about any German-people, but anyway they are in their land.

Of course his father was playing, and so was I.

A soldier must obey at all times, he said.

I wanted to give him so many things to take with him but he said he could only take cola.

Then the news came. It did not enter my head, for there all was empty. Everything went into my womb. You were just three days old.

The news was like fire which settled in the pit of my belly. And from time to time, some would shoot up, searing my womb, singeing my intestines and burning up and up and up until I screamed with madness when it got into my head.

I had told myself when you were born that it did not matter you were a girl, all gifts from Allah are good and anyway he was coming back and we were going to have many more children, lots of sons.

But Hawa, you had a lot of strength, for how you managed to live I do not know. Three days you were and suddenly like a rivulet that is hit by an early harmattan, my breasts went dry. . . . Hawa, you have a lot of strength.

Later, they told me that if I could go South and prove to the government's people that I was his wife, I would get a lot of money.

But I did not go. It was him I wanted, not his body turned into gold.

I never saw the South.

Do you say oh? My child I am always telling you that the world was created a long while ago and it is old-age one has not seen but not youth. So do not say oh.

Those people, the government's people, who come and go, tell us trade is bad now, and once again there is no tinned fish and no cloth. But this time they say, this is because our children are going to get them in abundance one day.

Issa has gone South now because he cannot afford even goat flesh for his wife in maternity. This has to be, so that Fuseni can stay with his wife and eat cow-meat with her? Hmm. And he will come back alive . . . perhaps not next Ramaddan but the next. Now, my daughter, you know of another man who went to fight. And he went to fight in other people's war and he never came back.

I am going to the market now. Get up early to wash Fuseni. I hope to get something for those miserable colas. There is enough rice to make *tuo*, is there not? Good. Today even if it takes all the money, I hope to get us some smoked fish, the biggest I can find, to make us a real good sauce. . . ."

MINERVA SALADO

Report from Vietnam for International Woman's Day

Minerva Salado (b. 1944) is a contemporary Cuban poet and journalist. She graduated from the University of Havana with a degree in journalism. Her first book, *At the Closing*, won the Premio David Prize, a top literary award of her country. She has gone on to publish several more critically acclaimed books of poetry, and has worked as a correspondent for many international journals.

■

A woman is aflame.
She is twenty-one years old
and her flesh is on fire.
Her womb trembles;
her erect breasts are consumed by fire.
Her hips contort.
The muscles of her thighs boil.
Anh Dai's flesh is ignited by flames,
but she does not burn with passion.
It is napalm.

Translation by Daniela Gioseffi with Enildo García

MAVIS SMALLBERG

"The Situation in Soweto Is Not Abnormal"

Mavis Smallberg (b. 1945) is a poet and teacher who lived and wrote in South Africa during the most violent years of apartheid. Under apartheid's system of racial classification, which assigned people's rights and privileges based solely upon race, Smallberg was designated "Coloured," the category reserved for people of mixed African and European ancestry. Smallberg's works were banned in South Africa under the apartheid regime, and were published in small underground journals. In this poem, she ironically contrasts what the government newspapers report on August 27, 1986, with the realities faced by the people in the streets.

■

Everything's normal in Soweto today.
We reasonably killed eleven.
They were making a fuss in the street
You know us,
We don't stand any fuss
Not us
So we typically killed eleven
And wounded an average sixty-two
And you?

Went on a regular patrol to a school.

Some children were breaking a rule.
They burned their identity cards.
White kids don't carry 'em
Don't need to, you know
Black kids don't carry 'em
Don't want to, you know
The whole thing was just about to erupt,
When we routinely went to beat them up.
Cornered a few of 'em and rained down the blows
Split one's head. She's dead,
But nobody knows.
Naturally the children ran all around
So we just shot down those that we found.
Bullets, birdshot, buckshot,
What the hell? It's all run-of-the-mill!
Saw this "comrade" walking alone,
Shot him down before he got home.
Ja, he died.
You should've seen the ones that we fried.

What a fire! What a blaze!
Children crying, people dying.
One woman got shot in the hip
That really shut up her lip!
Now she can't walk. Mmm, there was some talk.
Ja, the situation in Soweto is not
Abnormal today.

What's abnormal, anyway?
What's monstrous, deviant, abhorrent,
weird about gassing a baby
Shooting a child, raping a mother
or crippling a father?
What's odd about killing the people we fear?
No, the situation in Soweto
is quite normal today.

Karen Alkalay-Gut

Friend and Foe
and To One in Beirut

Karen Alkalay-Gut (b. 1945) is an Israeli author who teaches poetry at Tel Aviv University and chairs the Israel Association of Writers in English. Born in London, she grew up in the United

States, but began writing when she moved to Israel in 1972. Since then she has published more than eighteen books and has appeared in numerous multimedia projects. These poems were written to a Lebanese friend during the 1982 bombings of Beirut by Israel.

■

FRIEND AND FOE

Skyhawks fly over my city
on the way to bomb yours.
We are awakened by the noise
and I fall asleep restlessly
dreaming of you and your daughters.

"If anything happens to my girls,
I'll hold you personally responsible."
April 25, Israel is bombing Beirut.
You and I stick to wine with our
lamb casserole in Cyprus
and discuss politics.

Spinning the dial now—from BBC
to the Israel Army Channel—
I don't know what to believe.
The thin voice of an 18-year-old soldier
telling how a Lebanese
kissed him when he jumped out
of his tank is muddled with the British
accents of the newsmen estimating
half a million homeless
in southern Lebanon.

Minutes after the ceasefire in Beirut
CBS photographs antiaircraft fire
From a small apartment building.
(Is that where you live? Then
who lives with you?) The Skyhawks
go down on the city again.

Friend! My husband is in civil defense,
and my sons are too small for the army. You
have daughters and are old and alcoholic.
We can't fight this war.
But both of us are in it
and responsible.

To One in Beirut

Not a day goes by without my thinking of you . . .
as in a clandestine affair I am reminded
by the newspapers, the sounds in the air,
that you are there, and I in Tel Aviv.

Today brings a letter, postmarked Princeton,
sent through Jounieh to Larnaca on its way here.
You are well, as of the sixteenth of July, 1982,
and today is the 30th. Last night
on the news, we were still pounding the city.

As long as we kept from politics, we were friends
strolling down a sea road of an Austrian town,
shocking the guide with our nationalities
and talking poems, sex, divorce, food, wine.

How our lives would be fine
now, if that were all there was
to talk of. But where we live
we speak only of death and think
of somewhere else.

GIOCONDA BELLI

The Blood of Others

Gioconda Belli (b. 1948) is a renowned Nicaraguan poet. She won the prestigious Marino Fiallos Gil Prize for Poetry of the Universidad Autonoma of Nicaragua in 1972 for *Sobre la Grama*, her first book. *Linea de fuego* won the Casa de las Americas prize in 1978, and *Amor insurrector* was published in 1984. The poems in *Linea de fuego* reflect revolutionary fervor as well as frank expressions of sexual desire and fulfillment. Belli's characteristics features are found again in *Truenos y arco iris* (1982), primarily a compilation of pieces previously prohibited. In 1987 she published *De la costilla de Eva*—published in translation as *From Eve's Rib* in the United States in 1989. In 2002, she published her memoir of the years of the Sandinista resistance and revolution.

■

I'm reading the poems of the dead,
I who am alive.
I who lived to laugh and cry
and shout *Patria Libre o Morir*
while riding in a truck
the day we reached Managua.

I'm reading the poems of the dead,
watching ants on the grass,
my feet bare,
your hair straight,
back bent over the reunion.

I'm reading the poems of the dead
and feeling that this blood we love each other with
doesn't belong to us.

Translation by Elinor Randall

SAVYON LIEBRECHT

Morning in the Park Among the Nannies

Savyon Liebrecht (b. 1948) was born in Germany in 1948 and moved to Israel as a small child. Liebrecht, who writes in Hebrew, is the author of four collections of short stories and a novel. A volume of her selected stories was published in English by the Feminist Press in 1998 as *Apples From the Desert*. In her foreword to the volume, Grace Paley writes, "Savyon Liebrecht's stories are written by a woman who knows she is living in a country occupied by two nations. . . . She tells her stories with domestic irony. . . . The stories are elegantly understated and movingly personal—but they are also fierce pleas for understanding and justice." Many of Liebrecht's stories touch upon the personal costs of the Israeli-Palestinian conflict. The child of Holocaust survivors, she also writes often about the inhumanities faced by the victims of the Nazi regime, as in this story.

■

When you showed up in the playground in the public park, I recognized you at once. It had been decades since I last saw you and still—the restrained tremor behind a curtain of languor, the unmistakable gait, the feet almost dancing, the peculiarly erect head with the neck thrust forward as if you were seeking the horizon, the quick glance lashing and sailing past. You were pushing a child's stroller on the dirt path leading to the farthest bench by the water fountain when you passed me. I saw clearly the beauty that had withstood time's wrecking powers, the sky blue eyes encircled by shadowy lines, the noble forehead arching back into the roots of your hair. I couldn't take my eyes off you as you parked the stroller in the shade of a tree, walked to the sandbox, bent down, gathered a handful of sand, and raised it to your eyes to examine it.

"She's counting the microbes," the Bulgarian nanny chuckles, and the two nannies sitting with her burst out laughing. Every so often a new nanny appears in the park and becomes the butt of the Bulgarian's mordant humor, especially if she chooses the farther benches. The others watch the impending duel with glee, hoping to fill another hour with giggles. But today I don't join their hilarity. As soon as I recognize you, the scenes we witnessed together simmer inside me like poison. Few people saw those sights and lived.

For years, you know, I saw you in my dreams, always dressed in the Chinese silk kimonos, or in those lace blouses I made for you. I saw you coming down the palace stairs with your floating gait, or standing by the window in the upper room looking at the garden, a sapphire necklace always around your neck and your hair braided on your nape like twined gold ingots nested in a fine net. In the distance, even in my dream, the Germans laughed thickly or sang their songs, or ran up and down in the black marble stairs, now and then cracking a whip with the flick of the hand. In the background, like a nightmare melody, the girls screamed and cried and wailed day and night—but not you. You maintained your dark silence.

"That's the child of the heart specialist," the Bulgarian chuckles. "They interviewed two hundred women before they picked this one. She looks more like a lady than the professor's lady."

Even in my dreams you never looked me in the eye. You looked over my head with that distant, languid gaze, but I noticed that your eyelids trembled. I would wake from those dreams as if escaping from a fire, suddenly recalling scenes much worse than the dreams: the girls bitterly crying in their first nights, very softly, almost unheard in the rustling of the beds, and sometimes a shriek, ringing in my ears for a long time, like an echo in the desert. And the next day, their eyes were worn out with weeping, shadows creeping on their faces, and in the days that followed the spark of life slowly faded from their eyes.

A few weeks later the eyes were already dead, drained of tears, the lovely bodies wilting, and then the eyes would take on a puzzled expression, refusing to understand the surrounding reality.

In the cellar where I live with my sewing machine, I would prick up my ears to hear the loud thud in the back garden, learning to distinguish it from the other sounds of the house: one of the girls had reached the end of her endurance, climbed steadily to the rooftop or to a windowsill, and hurled herself down. I would close my eyes and recite the only verse I remember from the Kaddish prayer my father used to say on my grandmother's grave: *Yisgadal veyiskadesh shmaia rabba* . . .

Now you are vigorously shaking the grains of sand from your fingers and turning your head to the toddler strapped into the stroller.

"How fast she counted the microbes," the Bulgarian grins. "I bet she won't put her in the sand. God forbid the professor's dress should get soiled."

The day the German thrust you into my room and ordered me to find you a blue silk dressing gown, I stared at you as if hypnotized. The girls who were brought into my room were all pretty. But you—there was a fatal darkness about your beauty. Your glance flicked around the room and you did not ask anything. Did you already know what kind of place it was? Were you wary of me? You stood erect and regal when I dressed you, like a proud bride in her wedding gown.

You slap your palms together and walk resolutely to the shaded bench. Your body is still amazingly supple, your legs handsome, unblemished by the years, and your narrow waist shows clearly when you bend down to loosen the little girl's strap. I am watching you openly. Now that the initial shock is over, my eyes are drawn to you as they were then. I see your iron hand gripping the child like a clamp, your fingers closing on the tiny fluttering hand. The sight awakens my hostility toward you and the sights that have been buried inside me for decades without respite. The time that passed hasn't softened your heart, you damned woman. The black light in your eyes shook me from the start.

Outside, the German snorted with laughter, calling to one of his friends, "I've brought you a present—a rabbi's daughter!" I looked at you and said to myself, trying to shield you from what I had seen, "Soon she will be found dead. Obviously she has no idea where she is, and when she understands she will want to die."

The little girl squirms in the prison of your arms and you shake and scold her. I was not wrong about you, as I hoped. You understood quite well when you stood in front of the mirror in my room. How did you guard your soul in that place?

One of the nannies runs around with the carousel, panting, shouting, "If you don't eat the apple right now, I'll give it to Michael. You want Michael to grow up big and strong, and you'll be little and weak? He'll never let you go on the swing; is that what you want?"

At night, you remember, the girl with the auburn braid used to sing. She had the sweet voice of a schoolgirl. When she sang, the weeping in the room would cease. One night a new girl was brought to the room. The night before, she told us, she had married her beloved. In the camp to which they had been transported from the ghetto, two kerchiefs had been tied together to form a canopy and a rabbi had performed the ceremony. The girl with the braid sang bridal songs for her: "The voice of mirth and the voice of gladness, the voice of a bride and the voice of a groom . . ." Later, at night, the two would sing Sabbath songs and hymns.

One morning the two girls were found lying hand in hand by the fountain in the garden, the blood flowing from their wrists. A few days later I asked you about them and I noticed your fingers did not tremble as you smoothed your hair.

A child jumps from the carousel and bursts out crying when his knee hits a stone. The nanny pounces on him: "Why do you jump without looking? Don't you remember we couldn't go out for three days because last Monday you jumped and hurt yourself? It was awful at home—you behaved terribly. Now you're jumping again? You think I want to be cooped up with you again in prison?"

It was for you that the German wanted those exquisite Chinese kimonos. I wondered where they got them in such quantities. In my room you preened yourself as though you were going to a ball. You alone, of all the girls, were an enigma: girls came and went, tore out their hair, howled like wolves—you alone kept your head up. Week after week I observed you and saw no change in you, unlike the other girls—the clear skin, the rosy tinge fading into the neck, the dark halos around the limpid blue irises, the wide, rounded forehead turning to the high temples, the red lips, the proud chin, the sculptured body, rounded shoulders, slender waist, narrow feet, the waist-length hair, the supple body movements, the dancing gait.

Once I saw you being dragged from the parlor by an officer. Another time, when you left my room, I heard the laughter of the drunken men greeting you outside. And one day, when by chance I went through the hallway to wash the filth from the carpet at the foot of the stairs, I saw you on the floor—the Chinese kimono all awry, your hair wound around your face like roots, your hands tied with rope between your knees. At night you staggered like a drunk down the stairs, your bleeding arms groping along the railing. The next morning you stood serenely, looking out the window, pieces of a broken vase at your feet, sipping soup, quietly sucking up the thick liquid, putting down the bowl, and without looking, picking up a chunk of salami and biting into it noisily; and all the while your eyes gazed at the lilac bush and your right hand held the drapes. I picked up the pieces of the broken vase, my eyes drawn to your mutilated arm holding the drapes: fingernail marks like furrows plowed in your arm, on the back of your hand. And on your elbow, like a drawing, were three flower-shaped burns.

The girls aged overnight: their complexions became ashen, their eyelids swelled, their hair lost its sheen, their bodies lost their vitality. You alone never changed, as if accustomed to vicissitudes and knowing that nothing goes on forever. And I watched in amazement as the injuries on your arms healed and your lovely skin triumphed.

The Bulgarian nanny jumps to her feet, dashes forward, and threatens, "Yuvali, get down this minute. Don't climb up from the bottom. Can't you see there's a girl ready to slide down? Do you want such a fat girl to fall on your head? Go to the ladder and slide down after the fat girl like you did before. See how she hit the bottom—kerplunk! Lucky for you I noticed her, or you'd be on your way to the first-aid station."

The night the girl from the Lodz ghetto told us about Passover Eve you were the only one who stayed in bed. All the others gathered around the girl, who told us in whispers how she and her mother had been left alone in the cellar where they were hiding. The week before her elder brother had gone out to look for food and never came back. The mother picked up some bread crumbs and flattened them into squares, which she moistened with water, and before she went out of her mind and ran screaming out into the street, calling for her sons, began to lay the Seder table, putting stones on the table in place of wine bottles, plates for fish, soup, and meat, put down the squares of bread crumbs for matzo. She walked around and sang: "How is this night different from all other nights? That on all nights we eat . . ." The whole time she was telling us about the ghetto I didn't take my eyes off you. You sat with your back to us, motionless, as if you were a piece of furniture. Did you know, as I did, that the very next day the girl from Lodz would collapse and the Germans would throw her out at noon?

"Why did you hit her?" The nanny's voice rises shriller than the children's. "I saw you hitting her. Don't lie to me. Why is she crying then? Just because you don't know how to play on the monkey bars you have to come here and hit?

Aren't you ashamed to play with girls anyway? Look at all the other kids playing nicely. Only you go looking for trouble. You think you're so smart picking on little girls? Where is your nanny anyway? What's she being paid for?"

Often I wondered if you would have triumphed over the place if it weren't for the senior officer who took you under his wing and kept the others away from you. For a while we were both protected—I with my sewing skills and you ensconced in your benefactor's room.

We both regarded the others as if their fate did not touch us. Do you remember the three girls who were taken out one night for an orgy? The Germans were drunker than ever. At dawn two of them crawled back, their bodies bruised all over. The third girl had been rolled up in a carpet, her long hair hanging out of one end, dragged out into the garden and set on fire. The drunken Germans stood and watched the hair, flaring up readily, and the smell of burnt flesh filled the rooms until the wind blew. One of the girls told us, before she was taken to the doctor and never returned, that the Germans had strangled her friend while violating her body. In the morning the other girl began to spew blood. She came to my room for shelter and showed me the fist marks on her lower abdomen.

Sometimes, when I sit here on the park bench with the nannies, listening to them bickering and chattering, watching the toddlers playing in the sandbox under the trees, I am reminded more and more of the trees at that house: the linden tree tops converging above the fountain, the thick foliage, the somber shade, the goldfish swimming among corals gleaned from ocean depths, the dew stored in the grass, the sky on clear nights. What are they doing now, those girls who sat on the Germans' knees, who wallowed on the floors? Are they living their lives, carrying the memories from night to day, from day to night? I try to figure out how old they would be today, and the thought alarms me.

Do you remember that time, at a party, when our eyes met over the back of a girl crouching on all fours, her forehead touching the pulled-off boots and licking the bare feet of the officer who stood like an artist's model, a hand on his hips, his trousers down and his underpants sagging around the pillars of his legs? His companions laughed. One of them said, "Not many of them can brag that they've caught a German officer with his pants down." What was the girl thinking of, crouching there in the noisy room? Her mother? Her father? The boy who peeped at her from behind his prayer shawl? What were you thinking of?

A young woman is dragging a weeping girl to an adjacent bench. "Tell his nanny, dear heart. Don't cry, sweetie. There, there. I'll tell her! Your kid spat at her. Is that how you teach him? Sure you're responsible. You sit here chatting about wages and gossiping about your employers while he's spitting at other kids. Some nanny! Come to the faucet, my heart, I'll wash your dress."

You were beautiful in those days. You must have found some makeup somewhere, or else your benefactor gave you some. You put on mascara, rouged your cheeks for him, and I, who knew your features like the back of my hand, noticed a new sparkle in your eyes. You braided your hair and searched in the jewelry box in my room and took out a necklace of sapphires to put around your neck. You examined yourself in the mirror and waited for his arrival.

Once, when you were in his room, the two of you came out on the little balcony. He hung his jacket around your shoulders and you talked the whole night long. I saw you from my window, talking earnestly. What did you tell him, sitting so erect, wrapped in a German officer's jacket? What did he tell you?

In the spring the garden suddenly burst into my cellar in all its glory: the spring azure of the Polish sky, the light clouds, the air laden with buds and pollen, heavy clusters of chestnut blossoms peering through curtains of leaves, young leaves thickening the treetops day by day, the gurgling of the fountain in the garden, the row of white lilac bushes along the fence like ornate gowns lined up for a fashion show. In the middle of the garden stood the palace itself, where a prince used to live before the Germans came, with huge murals, molded doors, embroidered tapestries, inlaid cupboards, lion-footed armchairs, heavy silverware, crystal chandeliers—and at rare hours, a profound silence between the walls, when the screams of the women and the stomping of jackboots on the marble stairs subsided. In that silence I could sense the staring eyes, the quivering flesh, the nameless fear. And one morning, in the sweet lilac fragrance, I lingered by the wall in one of the rooms and noticed little dabs of blood behind a chest of drawers, the dabs forming letters: Shifra daughter of Shimon. What possessed Shifra to leave her father's name in that accursed place?

"You get down this minute! We're going home now! You want to tear your pants again? Your mother won't buy you a new pair so soon. All right, just a little more, only get off those bars and come play in the sand. Better play with the girls."

On exceptionally fine summer nights the Germans would sit in the big garden, drinking beer from huge mugs, singing with their heads thrown back, sometimes amusing themselves by sitting a girl on their knees and bouncing her from lap to lap around the circle. From my low window I followed you with my eyes. Your German had seated you on a chair by his side and offered you a drink, but you declined. Gently he caressed your cheek. I was shaken. In that place the sight of endearment was intolerable. You said something to him and he immediately bent his head to you to catch it, nodding attentively. You both rose and walked down the path to the end of the garden. A few minutes later shots were heard from that corner, and the Germans jumped to their feet. The girl they had played with remained sitting like a statue. It quickly became clear that your officer was only showing off his marksmanship to you. Loud laughter rose from the edge of the garden.

You make sure the bench is meticulously clean. You pick out cigarette butts and popsicle sticks from the sand and put them in a trash can nailed to a tree trunk. Then you spread a napkin on the bench beside you and feed the child, wiping her mouth constantly, picking crumbs from her blouse—and all the while your back is straight, your thighs pressed together, like an actress in a movie.

In the days that followed you were protected, sleeping in the officer's distant, overheated room. Sometimes you stood by the window, watching the summer showers fall on the garden. Every day, by your master's orders, your food was brought to you on a tray, and you received it like the mistress of the house, sitting in an armchair and gazing at a painting over my head while I changed the sheets on your bed. Unlike the other girls, you never asked me anything. Did you not want to understand more than you had to? I knew more about the Germans than about you.

The nanny beside me pulls a crying child to her bosom. "And his father is a doctor! Can you believe it—a big doctor, with such a stupid son? Always sticks his head where he'll get hurt. Why don't you watch your head? Ask your father, he'll tell you how important it is to watch your head."

One night the house was suddenly empty and silence fell on the lawn and on the grove behind the palace. The girls, made tense by the unwonted silence, gathered like sleepwalkers in the parlor. Some lay on the sofas and on the carpets, eating candy from ornate boxes, drinking wine, whispering. One burst into tears and couldn't stop. In the morning we were woken by the stomping boots of the returning Germans, and it turned out that the officers had been summoned to a special conference. In the afternoon it was discovered that the golden-haired girl who had been brought the day before from Majdanek had taken advantage of the commotion and disappeared. They sent the dogs after her and found her hiding in the bushes, under the porch columns. We saw the dogs dragging her to the bottom of the garden.

On the morning when your officer was found dead in his bed, you were no longer in the room. The doctor was called in and suddenly there was panic in the palace—people dashing to and fro, exchanging short phrases like a secret language, passing each other on the stairs. Through the door I could see him lying in bed like a mountain, his neck red even in death. The doctor declared that his heart had given way. When the body had been removed, covered in a velvet blanket, the others pounced on you in your upper room. All that day and night the Germans kept going to your room one by one, to do to you what they had been prevented from doing while your protector was alive. In the morning I saw you staggering on the doorstep. I recognized you by the kimono.

You take no part in the general hubbub in the park. The child, too, keeps her distance from the other children; she only pushes her stroller in circles around your bench. Her pretty sandals sink into the sand. For a moment your eyes seem to focus on the baby sitting on my lap. Did you recognize me? Your hand seems to have lost control; your fingers grope along the bench, grabbing the metal edge of the board. Your body maintains its calm, your back is erect, there is only the tremor of your whitened fingers clutching the metal.

One morning the Germans were suddenly gone. They left in haste, but still took two girls with them. We got up in the morning—seven girls—to a new silence. The doctor's daughter from Lublin was the first to realize what had happened. She climbed to the fourth floor and opened all the rooms one by one, her roar growing louder the farther she went. Leaning on the top floor railing she shouted, "The swine are gone!" She shouted in Yiddish, defiantly, and a shiver went through me at the sound of those words. The girl who had been the last to arrive, her pallor glaring in the dark room, started rocking to and fro, raising her eyes to the high painted ceiling and chanting, "Blessed art thou, our God, Lord of the universe . . ." A moment later another one burst out laughing and started destroying the paintings on the wall with her bare hands.

The Bulgarian, who is as easily overcome by compassion as by cruelty, cries, "Look what a heart of gold he has! Every day he gives his chocolate milk to the cat. I tell his mother he shouldn't be so softhearted. When he grows up the girls will make his life miserable. You know what girls are like when they get hold of a nice guy—they ruin him."

We still didn't know that the Russians were already in town. We were still delirious, roaming through the rooms. You were the first to leave. You cocked the beret on your head, packed a small suitcase, broke into my room, opened the jewelery box, scooped up a fistful of jewels and put them in the bottom of my suitcase, chose two dark sweaters and a gray woollen skirt, packed them quickly, and left. At the main gate the vicious dog leapt at you, and you bent down, picked up a rock, and threw it at his head. As soon as you left, all hell broke loose, as if you had given the signal for a new life.

You gather your things, harness the child in her carriage, rise, and turn to the park gate. Once again, when you are a pace away from me, I see the icy eyes surrounded by black halos. The nannies fall silent, following you with their eyes as you pass by. For a moment I seem to feel your glance lashing at me. Have I awakened a memory in you? An echo of German voices? The touch of flesh against your flesh? The fluttering of silk against your skin? The smell of the chestnuts? Have you succeeded in forgetting? The girl who had aged in days, the one who wiped the marble tiles, who removed the soiled sheets and spread fresh ones, who sewed the glamorous dresses, ironed and stitched, and never took her eyes of you all, lovely daughters of Israel. How they gathered all that beauty and then destroyed it—were you able to forget?

Suddenly the steely eyes are on my face. And you say in a dull voice devoid of wonder, "What sandals?"

I reply, "The little girl's."

You look directly at me: "I don't know. I didn't buy her the sandals. Her mother did." And you propel the carriage onto the gravel path and walk away.

I stumble back to my seat on the bench. The Bulgarian makes room and peers into my face, concerned.

"What's wrong, dear heart? Come, sit down." She pats my back amiably and smiles. "How you ran after that lady! As if in her you'd found Cinderella's slipper that she lost at the palace."

And they all join in her laughter.

Translation by Marganit Weinberger-Rotman

SVETLANA ALEXIYEVICH

From Boys in Zinc

Svetlana Alexiyevich (b. 1948) is a dissident Belarusian writer and journalist who has been supported by PEN International and the Soros Foundation. Her documentary history, *A Plea for Chernobyl*, published in English as *Voices from Chernobyl* (1999), is not available in Belarus, where the majority of fallout from the 1986 Chernobyl disaster occurred, destroying 485 villages. (One in five Belarussians still lives in contaminated territory.) Equally controversial are Alexiyevich's books on women and war. *War's Unwomanly Face* (1985), which gives voice to women who fought in World War II, contradicts the official mythologies of the glorious Soviet army. Another collection of wartime oral histories, *Boys in Zinc* (1989), chronicles the impact on ordinary people of the Soviet war in Afghanistan—often called "Russia's Vietnam." The book was met by a lawsuit brought by military authorities, who demanded compensation for "loss of pride and honor." It also brought death threats against its author. This excerpt in English was published in the journal *Granta*. The title *Boys in Zinc* refers to the zinc coffins in which dead soldiers were returned home.

■

In 1986 I had decided not to write about war again. For a long time after I finished my book *War's Unwomanly Face* I couldn't bear to see a child with a bleeding nose. I suppose each of us has a measure of protection against pain; mine had been exhausted.

Two events changed my mind.

I was driving out to a village and I gave a lift to a schoolgirl. She had been shopping in Minsk, and carried a bag with chickens' heads sticking out. In the village we were met by her mother, who was standing crying at the garden gate. The girl ran to her.

The mother had received a letter from her son Andrey. The letter was sent from Afghanistan. "They'll bring him back like they brought Fyodorina's Ivan," she said, "and dig a grave to put him in. Look what he writes. 'Mum, isn't it great! I'm a paratrooper . . .'"

And then there was another incident. An army officer with a suitcase was sitting in the half-empty waiting-room of the bus station in town. Next to him a thin boy with a crew-cut was digging in the pot of a rubber plant with a table fork. Two country women sat down beside the men and asked who they were. The officer said he was escorting home a private soldier who had gone mad. "He's been digging all the way from Kabul with whatever he can get his hands on, a spade, a fork, a stick, a fountain pen." The boy looked up. His pupils were so dilated they seemed to take up the whole of his eyes.

And at that time people continued to talk and write about our internationalist duty, the interests of state, our southern borders. The censors saw to it that reports of the war did not mention our fatalities. There were only rumours of notifications of death arriving at rural huts and of regulation zinc coffins delivered to prefabricated flats. I had not meant to write about war again, but I found myself in the middle of one.

For the next three years I spoke to many people at home and in Afghanistan. Every confession was like a portrait. They are not documents; they are images. I was trying to present a history of feelings, not the history of the war itself.

What were people thinking? What made them happy? What were their fears? What stayed in their memory?

The war in Afghanistan lasted twice as long as the Second World War, but we know only so much as it is safe for us to know. It is no longer a secret that every year for ten years, 100,000 Soviet troops went to fight in Afghanistan. Officially, 50,000 men were killed or wounded. You can believe that figure if you will. Everybody knows what we are like at sums. We haven't finished counting and burying all those who died in the Second World War.

In what follows, I haven't given people's real names. Some asked for the confidentiality of the confessional, others I don't feel I can expose to a witch-hunt. We are still so close to the war that there is nowhere for anyone to hide.

One night I was asleep when my telephone rang.

"Listen," he began, without identifying himself, "I've read your garbage. If you so much as print another word . . ."

"Who are you?"

"One of the guys you're writing about. God, I hate pacifists! Have you ever been up a mountain in full marching kit? Been in an armoured personnel carrier when the temperature's seventy centigrade? Like hell you have. Fuck off! It's ours! It's got sod all to do with you."

I asked him again who he was.

"Leave it out, will you! My best friend—like a brother he was—and I brought him back from a raid in a cellophane bag. He'd been flayed, his head been severed, his arms, his legs, his dick all cut off . . . He could have written about it, but you can't. The truth was in that cellophane sack. Fuck the lot of you!" He hung up; the sound in the receiver was like an explosion.

He might have been my most important witness.

A Wife

Don't worry if you don't get any letters," he wrote. "Carry on writing to the old address." Then nothing for two months. I never dreamed he was in Afghani-stan. I was getting suitcases ready to go to see him at his new posting.

He didn't write about being in a war. Said he was getting a sun-tan and going fishing. He sent a photo of himself sitting on a donkey with his knees in the sand. It wasn't until he came home on leave that I knew he was in a war. He never used to spoil our daughter, never showed any fatherly feelings, perhaps because she was small. Now he came back and sat for hours looking at her, and his eyes were so sad it was frightening. In the mornings he'd get up and take her to kindergarten; he liked carrying her on his shoulders. He'd collect her in the evening. Occasionally we went to the theatre or the cinema, but all he really wanted to do was to stay at home

He couldn't get enough loving. I'd be getting ready to go to work or getting his dinner in the kitchen, and he even grudged that time. "Sit over here with me. Forget cutlets today. Ask for a holiday while I'm home." When it was time for him to get the plane he missed it deliberately so we would have an extra two days. The last night he was so good I was in tears. I was crying, and he was saying nothing, just looking and looking at me. Then he said, "Tamara, if you ever have another man, don't forget this."

I said, "Don't talk soft! They'll never kill you. I love you too much for them to be able to."

He laughed. "Forget it. I'm a big lad."

We talked of having more children, but he said he didn't want any more now. "When I come back you can have another. How would you manage with them on your own?"

When he was away I got used to the waiting, but if I saw a funeral car in town I'd feel ill, I'd want to scream and cry. I'd run home, the icon would be hanging there, and I'd get down on my knees and pray, "Save him for me, God! Don't let him die."

I went to the cinema the day it happened. I sat there looking at the screen and seeing nothing. I was really jumpy. It was as if I was keeping someone waiting or there was somewhere I had to go. I barely stuck it out to the end of the programme. Looking back, I think that it must have been during the battle.

It was a week before I heard anything. All of that week I'd start reading a book and put it down. I even got two letters from him. Usually I'd have been really pleased—I'd have kissed them—but this time they just made me wonder how much longer I was going to have to wait for him.

The ninth day after he was killed a telegram arrived at five in the morning. They just shoved it under the door. It was from his parents: "Come over. Petya dead." I screamed so much that it woke the baby. I had no idea what I should do or where I should go. I hadn't got any money. I wrapped our daughter in a red blanket and went out to the road. It was too early for the buses, but a taxi stopped.

"I need to go to the airport," I told the taxi driver.

He told me he was going off duty and shut the car door.

"My husband has been killed in Afghanistan."

He got out without saying anything, and helped me in. We drove to the house of a friend of mine and she lent me some money. At the airport they said there were no tickets for Moscow, and I was scared to take the telegram out of my bag to show them. Perhaps it was all a mistake. I kept telling myself if I could just carry on thinking he was alive, he would be. I was crying and everybody was looking at me. They put me on a freight plane taking a cargo of sweetcorn to Moscow, from there I got a connection to Minsk. I was still 150 kilometres from Starye Dorogi where Petya's parents lived. None of the taxi drivers wanted to take me there even though I begged and begged. I finally got to Starye Dorogi at two o'clock in the morning.

"Perhaps it isn't true?"

"It's true, Tamara, it's true."

In the morning we went to the Military Commissariat. They were very formal. "You will be notified when it arrives." We waited for two more days before we rang the Provincial Military Commissariat at Minsk. They told us that it would be best if we came to collect my husband's body ourselves. When we got to Minsk, the official told us that the coffin had been sent on to Baranovichi by mistake. Baranovichi was another 100 kilometres and when we got to the airport there it was after working hours and there was nobody about, except for a night watchman in his hut.

"We've come to collect . . ."

"Over there," he pointed over to a far corner. "See if that box is yours. If it is, you can take it."

There was a filthy box standing outside with "Senior Lieutenant Dovnar" scrawled on it in chalk. I tore a board away from where the window should be in a coffin. His face was in one piece, but he was lying in there unshaven, and nobody had washed him. The coffin was too small and there was a bad smell. I couldn't lean down to kiss him. That's how they gave my husband back to me. I got down on my knees before what had once been the dearest thing in the world to me.

His was the first coffin to come back to my home town, Yazyl. I still remember the horror in people's eyes. When we buried him, before they could draw up the bands with which they had been lowering him, there was a terrible crash of thunder. I remember the hail crunching under foot like white gravel.

I didn't talk much to his father and mother. I thought his mother hated me because I was alive, and he was dead. She thought I would remarry. Now, she says, "Tamara, you ought to get married again," but then I was afraid to meet her eye. Petya's father almost went out of his mind. "The bastards! To put a boy like that in his grave! They murdered him!" My mother-in-law and I tried to tell him they'd given Petya a medal, that we needed Afghanistan to defend our southern borders, but he didn't want to hear. "The bastards! They murdered him!"

The worst part was later, when I had to get used to the thought that there was nothing, no one, for me to wait for anymore. I would wake up terrified, drenched with sweat, thinking Petya would come back, and not know where his wife and child live now. All I had left were memories of good times.

The day we met, we danced together. The second day we went for a stroll in the park, and the next day he proposed. I was already engaged and I told him the application was lying in the registry office. He went away and wrote to me in huge letters which took up the whole page: "Aaaaargh!"

We got married in the winter, in my village. It was funny and rushed. At Epiphany, when people guess their fortunes, I'd had a dream which I told my mother about in the morning. "Mum, I saw this really good-looking boy. He was standing on a bridge calling me. He was wearing a soldier's uniform, but when I came towards him he began to go away until he disappeared completely."

"Don't marry a soldier. You'll be left on your own," my mother told me.

Petya had two days' leave. "Let's go to the Registry Office," he said, even before he'd come in the door.

They took one look at us in the Village Soviet and said, "Why wait two months. Go and get the brandy. We'll do the paperwork." An hour later we were husband and wife. There was a snowstorm raging outside.

"Where's the taxi for your new wife, bridegroom?"

"Hang on!" He went out and stopped a Belarus tractor for me.

For years I dreamed of us getting on that tractor, driving along in the snow.

The last time Petya came home on leave the flat was locked. He hadn't sent a telegram to warn me that he was coming, and I had gone to my friend's flat to celebrate her birthday. When he arrived at the door and heard the music and saw everyone happy and laughing he sat down on a stool and cried. Every day of his leave he came to work to meet me. He told me, "When I'm coming to see you at work my knees shake as if we had a date." I remember we went swimming together one day. We sat on the bank and built a fire. He looked at me and said, "You can't imagine how much I don't want to die for someone else's country."

I was twenty-four when he died. In those first months I would have married any man who wanted me. I didn't know what to do. Life was going on all around me the same as before. One person was building a dacha, one was buying a car; someone had got a new flat and needed a carpet or a hotplate for the kitchen. In the last war everybody was grief stricken, whole country. Everybody had lost someone, and they knew what they had lost them for. All the women cried together. There are a hundred people in the catering college where I work and I am the only one who lost her husband in a war the rest of them have only read about in the newspapers. When I first heard them saying the war in Afghanistan had been a national disgrace, I wanted to break the screen. I lost my husband for a second time that day.

A Nurse

Every day I was there I told myself I was a fool to come. Especially at night, when I had no work to do. All I thought during the day was "How can I help them all?" I couldn't believe anybody would make the bullets they were using. Whose idea were they? The point of entry was small, but inside, their intestines, their liver, their spleen were all ripped and torn apart. As if it wasn't enough to kill or wound them, they had to be put through that kind of agony as well. They always cried for their mothers when they were in pain, or frightened. I never heard them call for anyone else.

They told us it was a just war. We were helping the Afghan people to put an end to feudalism and build a socialist society. Somehow they didn't get around to mentioning that our men were being killed. For the whole of the first month I was there they just dumped the amputated arms and legs of our soldiers and officers, even their bodies, right next to the tents. It was something I would hardly have believed if I had seen it in films about the Civil War. There were no zinc coffins then: they hadn't got round to manufacturing them.

Twice a week we had political indoctrination. They went on about our sacred duty, and how the border must be inviolable. Our superior ordered us to inform on every wounded soldier, every patient. It was called monitoring the state of morale: the army must be healthy! We weren't to feel compassion. But we did feel compassion: it was the only thing that held everything together.

I skip along to the cemetery as if I'm on my way to meet someone. I feel I'm going to visit my son. Those first days I stayed there all night. It wasn't frightening. I'm waiting for the spring, for a little flower to burst through to me out of the ground. I planted snowdrops, so I would have a greeting from my son as early as possible. They come to me from down there, from him.

I'll sit with him until evening and far into the night. Sometimes I don't realize I've started wailing until I scare the birds, a whole squall of crows, circling and flapping above me until I come to my senses and stop. I've gone there every day for four years, in the evening if not in the morning. I missed eleven days when I was in the hospital, then I ran away in the hospital gown to see my son.

He called me "Mother mine," and "Angel mother mine."

"Well, angel mother mine, your son has been accepted by the Smolensk Military Academy. I trust you are pleased." He sat down at the piano and sang.

> Gentlemen officers, princes indeed!
> If I'm not first among them,
> I'm one of their breed.

My father was a regular officer who died in the defence of Leningrad. My grandfather was an officer too. My son was made to be a military man—he had the bearing, so tall and strong. He should have been a hussar with the white gloves, playing cards.

Everyone wanted to be like him. Even I, his own mother, would imitate him. I would sit down at the piano the way he did, and sometimes start walking the way he did, especially after he was killed. I so much want him always to be present in me.

When he first went to Afghanistan, he didn't write for ages. I waited and waited for him to come home on leave. Then one day the telephone rang at work.

"Angel mother mine, I am home."

I went to meet him off the bus. His hair had gone grey. He didn't admit he wasn't on leave, that he'd asked to be let out of hospital for a couple of days to see his mother. He'd got hepatitis, malaria, and everything else rolled into one but he warned his sister not to tell me. I went into his room again before I went off to work, to see him sleeping. He opened his eyes. I asked him why he was not asleep, it was so early. He said he'd had a bad dream.

We went with him as far as Moscow. It was lovely, May weather, and the trees were in bloom. I asked him what it was like over there.

"Mother mine, Afghanistan is something we have no business to be doing." He looked only at me, not at anyone else. "I don't want to go back to that hole. I really do not." He walked away, but turned round, "It's as simple as that, Mum." He never said "Mum." The woman at the airport desk was in tears watching us.

When I woke up on 7 July I hadn't been crying. I stared glassily at the ceiling. He had woken me, as if he had come to say goodbye. It was eight o'clock.

I had to get ready to go to work. I was wandering with my dress from the bathroom to the sitting room, from one room to another. For some reason I couldn't bear to put that light-coloured dress on. I felt dizzy, and couldn't see people properly. Everything was blurred. I grew calmer towards lunch-time, towards midday.

The seventh day of July. He had seven cigarettes in his pocket, seven matches. He had taken seven pictures with his camera. He had written seven letters to me, and seven to his girlfriend. The book on his bedside table was open at page seven. It was Kobo Abe's *Containers of Death*.

He had three or four seconds in which he could have saved himself. They were hurtling over a precipice in a vehicle. He couldn't be the first to jump out. He never could.

From Deputy Regimental Commander for Political Affairs, Major S. R. Sinelnikov. In fulfillment of my duty as a soldier, I have to inform you that Senior Lieutenant Valerii Gennadievich Volovich was killed today at 1045 hours.

The whole city already knew all about it. In the Officers' Club they'd put up black crêpe and his photograph. The plane bringing his coffin was due at any minute, but nobody had told me a thing. They couldn't bring themselves to speak. At work everybody's faces were tear-stained. I asked, "What has happened?"

They tried to distract me in various ways. A friend came round, then finally a doctor in a white coat arrived. I told him he was crazy, that boys like my son did not get killed. I started hammering the table. I ran over to the window and started beating the glass. They gave me an injection. I kept on shouting. They gave me another injection, but that had no effect, either; I was screaming, "I want to see him, take me to my son." Eventually they had to take me.

There was a long coffin. The wood was unplaned, and written on it in large letters in yellow paint was "Volovich." I had to find him a place in the cemetery, somewhere dry, somewhere nice and dry. If that meant a fifty rouble bribe, fine. Here, take it, only make sure it's a good place, nice and dry. Inside I knew how disgusting that was, but I just wanted a nice dry place for him. Those first nights I didn't leave him. I stayed there. They would take me off home, but I would come back.

When I go to see him I bow, and when I leave I bow again. I never get cold even in freezing temperatures; I write my letters there; I am only ever at home when I have visitors. When I walk back to my house at night the streetlamps are lit, the cars have their headlamps on. I feel so strong that I am not afraid of anything.

Only now am I waking from my sorrow which is like waking from sleep. I want to know whose fault this was. Why doesn't anybody say anything? Why aren't we being told who did it? Why aren't they being put on trial?

I greet every flower on his grave, every little root and stem. "Have you come from there? Do you come from him? You have come from my son."

Translation by Arch Tait

SLAVENKA DRAKULIČ

From S. : The Camps—Bosnia

Slavenka Drakulič (b. 1949) is a journalist and novelist who was born in Riejka in the former Yugoslavia of Italian and Croatian ancestry. Her other books include *How We Survived Communism and Even Laughed, The Taste of a Man, Marble Skin, Holograms of Fear, The Balkan Express: Fragments from the Other Side of War,* and *Café Europa: Life After Communism.* She has contributed articles to the *New York Times,* the *Nation,* and the *New Republic.* This excerpt from her 1999 novel *S.* about the "women's room" of a prison camp tells of the unspeakable crimes the character S. endured. In telling her compelling story, S. ultimately tells a story of survival that-depicts one of the most horrifying aspects of any war, the rape and torture of civilian women by occupying forces. The flashback memories of war torn Bosnia-Herzegovia take place in 1992, during the height of the Bosnian invasion by brutal Serbian and Bosnian Serb forces.

■

There is a stickiness to time that day; it drags slowly. A soldier walks into the warehouse in the early afternoon. She first sees him standing in the doorway, sees only his black outline, a dark shadow blocking the only source of light in the warehouse. The soldiers sometimes come by during the day looking for E. She usually goes with them either to the men's camp or to the administration building to treat one of their people. They would usually call out to her from the courtyard because they did not feel like walking all the way to the warehouse in the heat. Now this man is standing in the doorway. He does not move. He is waiting. He is waiting for his eyes to adjust to the semi-darkness. *Ti!* You, he shouts, you! Over here! S. thinks how stupid his order sounds without a verb. E. gets up, takes her doctor's bag and heads toward him. Not you, her! He can only mean S. because apart from the sick woman, she is the only other person in the warehouse at the moment.

E. persists. She walks over and tries to explain something to him. She tells him that she is a nurse, that she is the one they probably need, not S., it is a mistake, it is she they always call to the administration building. Her words ricochet off the soldier as if he was made of steel. Wordlessly, he pushes her aside. Just as he makes no effort to use verbs, he makes no move to go and get S. He simply extends his hand. Or a finger, straight and ominous. And that pronoun, spoken in the tone of a command. *Ti.* You. He stands there blocking out the sun. Waiting.

S. wipes her hands on her skirt, the way housewives do when someone catches them in the middle of making lunch. Or like very old women who wipe their hands on their aprons before shaking hands with an unknown visitor who finds them at the stove. Her hands are clammy. All she can feel are the palms of her hands and her throat. Suddenly she cannot swallow her own saliva.

Finally, S. takes a step. She walks towards that shadow at the other end of the warehouse. She remembers him as being huge. She walks, her throat dry, unaware of her automatic movements. Her legs carry her in spite of her will, as if they have a life of their own. She can hear her steps echoing strangely against the concrete floor, as if they are not hers. She thinks she hears somebody crying. The wings of a bird flutter under the warehouse roof. As she walks by, she sees E.'s white face and fixed stare. She thinks she has never seen such big eyes before.

She walks very slowly, at least it seems to her. Her head is a void. She feels pressure in her temples and in her chest. And a kind of tautness, as if her veins will burst and her blood spill out. She will collapse dead, right here in the middle of the warehouse.

Then she sees his face, close up. His skin is young and tight. His eyes are dark and completely opaque. There is no expression on this face, no grimace. He says not a word. He just watches, gravely. He searches her face. His eyes slide down to her breasts and then lower still.

S. remembers his hot, searching male stare as they walk together across the courtyard.

She has that same feeling of surprise and immobility that she had that morning when the young man burst into her kitchen. Suddenly her body feels so heavy that she can hardly budge. Her movements are sluggish and hesitant, her brain is drained. She wants to scream. To shout. But her mouth is dry, not a single word finds its way through her constricted throat. She wants to run away; she really would run if only she could step away; if only she had the will to do so. S. notices that she no longer has a will of her own, it has been replaced by something else, as if a robot has taken control of her body, making it move and react in her stead. Again, it is happening to someone else and to her at the same time.

It seems a long and tiring way from the warehouse to the building at the end of the courtyard. With the sun behind her, S. can now see her shadow stretch out before her, first over the concrete and then over the gravel. As his boots crunch the gravel, the soldier's shadow overtakes hers.

They stand in front of the door. The soldier kicks it open. They enter a room, an office. The linoleum on the floor is torn and tatty. A cheap office desk stands in the middle of the room. The walls are painted to the halfway mark in a shiny grey. One man is seated, two are standing. They are soldiers, dressed in camouflage uniforms with some sort of insignia sewn on to their sleeves and epaulettes. The window is closed, the air full of cigarette smoke. All three men are smoking and S. thinks to herself how they must be sweltering in those uniforms. The tall soldier who brought her in departs, closing the door behind him.

A man with beady little eyes walks up to her. He looks dangerous. He removes the belt from his trousers. He is going to hit me, I know he is going to hit me, S. thinks to herself feverishly, shutting her eyes in anticipation of the blow. She raises her arms in self-defence. But nothing happens. Another man, the one sitting down, gets up and removes his belt as well. S. is still holding her arms up over her face, but he does not hit her either. The two men stand there holding their belts in their hands and then the tallest of the three walks up to her. He tells her to undress.

S. tries to unbutton her blouse. Three pairs of men's eyes watch her movements as her trembling fingers fail to find the buttons. It is not that she does not want to obey their order. On the contrary, she is in a hurry to do so. At that moment she cannot even think about doing anything else, there is no chance of her not obeying them. As she stands there unbuttoning her top, her intention must be clear to them, but S. no longer controls her fingers. She is betrayed by her hands which lack the strength even for such a small, simple movement.

Then one of them loses patience. With a practiced hand he pulls out a knife and presses it against her throat. Hurry up, he hisses through clenched teeth, hurry up! At that same instant she is again struck by their inability to express themselves in normal sentences; they use only monosyllabic words, as if they have forgotten how to speak. *And perhaps they have. Perhaps that happens to people in wartime, words suddenly become superfluous because they can no longer express reality. Reality escapes the words we know, and we simply lack new words to encapsulate this new experience.*

A second soldier is not so "gentle." He neither threatens nor speaks, he simply walks up to her and rips her blouse off.

Now she is standing naked in the office, leaning against the wall. She is surrounded by hunters. Their eyes are on her breasts. She can feel them crawl all over her. They are wet, slimy, hot as they climb her neck, as they touch her nipples and descend over her belly to her loins. This is perhaps the worst thing that will engrave itself on her memory: the eyes of strange men revelling in their trophy just before the moment of attack. She knows they are going to attack her. She knows she has been caught in a trap like a wild beast, and there is no escape. The pounding of her heart drowns out all sound. The cigarette smoke stings her eyes. Tears shut out their faces like a curtain.

She does not know how long she has been standing there, leaning against the wall. Finally, two of them take her to the desk. They tie her arms and legs with their belts. She resists only briefly. In a last, vain attempt to break free, her body arches instinctively, and then suddenly falls limp, as if dead.

When the first of the three men penetrates her, S. feels momentary pain. Later she feels nothing more than a thrust, which pushes the desk ever closer to the window. She turns her head to the wall. A greenbottle fly paces up and down the wall nervously, as if it has lost something. For a long time it stands still, rubbing its legs together. Then it flies up to the ceiling. S. follows it with her eyes. And at that moment she sees her own legs and a man's head poking out between them. The man has his eyes closed and mouth open.

She looks for the fly again. Now it is sitting on the light bulb. The bulb is slowly swaying. When she looks down, she sees that her legs are still there but now another man's head is between them. These are her legs, of course. S. tells herself that these are her legs, but she does not actually feel them. As if I am not here, she thinks. As if I am gone. All she can feel is the hard surface of the table under her back as it inches closer and closer to the window. She can already see the courtyard through the dirty windowpane and several guards relaxing by the fence. It is a lovely sunny day. A summer afternoon.

Their grunting fills the small room. Perhaps they are even saying something. Cursing, yes, they are cursing her mother. One of them is trying to look her in the face. He turns her face his way, yelling that she will remember him, that she has to remember him. He reeks. Yes, she will remember his breath, that she will remember. But not his face His face blurs with the ceiling and with the fly, which is still idly swinging on the lightbulb.

The legs of the desk keep sliding across the linoleum from his rough thrusting. The wooden desk creaks. If only that creaking would stop, and that groaning and panting, that noise which rises over her and covers her like a lid.

S. feels no pain. Something inside her has snapped in two. She is completely at peace, completely outside herself. She is lying on the floor. Her hands are untied. Her lips sting. She touches them. There is a faint trace of blood on her fingers. She still does not fully feel her body, merely this cut on her lip which stings ferociously.

Then there is the boot on her chest. The dull pain forces the breath from her lungs. Open your mouth! S. opens her mouth. There is a long stream of urine. Swallow, he orders, I'll teach you obedience. She tries to swallow. The urine is warm and salty and makes her want to vomit. She coughs and throws up at the same time. He slaps her. Now she swallows it obediently as a child but he keeps on hitting her as if this gives him particular pleasure. He hits her with the flat of his hand. He hits hard and her head reels from one side to the other but still nothing hurts. By now it is all the same to her, whatever he does.

Being hit is the last thing she remembers, how one of the soldiers keeps slapping her again and again and again. Then she loses consciousness.

Translation by Marko Ivić

URVASHI BUTALIA

From The Other Side of Silence

Urvashi Butalia (b. 1952) is director and co-founder of Kali for Women, India's first feminist publishing house. She has been an active participant in India's women's movement for more than two decades. She holds the position of reader at the College of Vocational Studies at the University of Delhi and is among those responsible for a blossoming in Indian women's literature. This excerpt is from an extensive collection of oral histories, subtitled *Voices from the Partition of India*, regarding the convulsive division of the land of India into two countries, Hindu-dominated India and Muslim-dominated Pakistan, by the British as they left India after two centuries of ruinous colonial rule. Within a space of two months, in 1947, more than twelve million people were displaced. A million died. More than 75,000 women were abducted and raped. Countless children disappeared. Homes, families, villages and hamlets were destroyed. More than a half century later, too little is remembered and known about the horror of this massive dislocation, one of the largest displacements in human history. The world still reaps the tensions today in Kashmir, on the border between India and Pakistan, which have both become nuclear powers.

■

[Mangal Singh's] legendary status in his neighborhood came from the fact that, at Partition, he and his two brothers were said to have killed the women and children of their family, seventeen of them, before setting off across the border. I found this story difficult to believe: how could you kill your own children, your own family? And why? At first Mangal Singh was reluctant to speak to me: "What is the use of raking all this up again? he asked. But then, after talking to his family, he changed his mind—they had, apparently, urged him to speak. They felt he had carried this particular burden for too long. I asked him about the family that was gone. He described them thus: "We were people of substance. In those days people had a lot of children—so we had many women and they had many children . . . there were children, there were girls . . . nephews and others. What a wonderful family it was, whole and happy."

Why, then, had he and his brothers thought fit to kill them? Mangal Singh refused to accept that the seventeen women and children had been killed. Instead, he used the word "martyred":

> After leaving home we had to cross the surrounding boundary of water. And we were many family members, several women and children who would not have been able to cross the water, to survive the flight. So we killed—they became martyrs—seventeen of our family members, seventeen lives . . . our hearts were heavy with grief for them, grief and sorrow, their grief, our own grief. So we travelled, laden with sorrow, not a paisa to call our own, not a bit of food to eat . . . but we had to leave. Had we not done so, we would have been killed, the times were such . . .

But why kill the women and children, I asked him. Did they not deserve a chance to live? Could they not have got away? He insisted that the women and children had "offered" themselves up for death because death was preferable to what would almost certainly have happened: conversion and rape. But could they really have offered themselves? Did they not feel any fear, I asked him. He said, angrily:

> Fear? Let me tell you one thing. You know this race of Sikhs? There's no fear in them, no fear in the face of adversity. Those people [the ones who had been killed] had no fear. They came down the stairs into the big courtyard of our house that day and they all sat down and they said, you can make martyrs of us—we are willing to become martyrs, and they did. Small children too . . . what was there to fear? *The real fear was one of dishonour. If they had been caught by the Muslims, our honour, their honour would have been sacrificed, lost. It's a question of one's honour . . . if you have pride you do not fear.* (my italics)

But who had the pride, and who the fear? This is a question Mangal Singh was unwilling to address. If accounts such as his were to be believed, the greatest danger that families, and indeed entire communities, perceived was the loss of honour through conversion to the other religion. Violence would be countered, but conversion was somehow seen as different. In many ways their concern was not unfounded: mass and forcible conversions had taken place on both sides. Among the Sikhs particularly, the men felt they could protect themselves but they were convinced that the women would be unable to do so. Their logic was that men could fight, die if necessary, escape by using their wits and their strength, but the women had no such strength to hand. They were therefore particularly vulnerable to conversion. More, women could be raped, impregnated with the seed of the other religion, and in this way not only would they be rendered impure individually but through them the entire community could be polluted, for they would give birth to "impure" children. While the men could thus save themselves, it was imperative that the women—and through them, the entire race—be "saved" by them.

A few years after I had spoken to Mangal Singh I began to look at newspaper reports on Partition, searching for similar accounts of family violence. On April 15, 1947, *The Statesman*, an English daily newspaper, had carried the following story:

> The story of 90 women of the little village of Thoa Khalsa, Rawalpindi district . . . who drowned themselves by jumping into a well during the recent disturbances has stirred the imagination of the people of the Punjab. They revived the Rajput tradition of self-immolation when their men folk were no longer able to defend them. They also followed Mr. Gandhi's advice to Indian women that in certain circumstances, even suicide was morally preferable to submission.
>
> About a month ago, a communal army armed with sticks, tommy guns and hand grenades, surrounded the village. The villagers defended themselves as best as they could . . . but in the end they had to raise the white flag. Negotiations followed. A sum of Rs 10,000 was demanded . . . it was promptly paid. The intruders gave solemn assurances that they would not come back.
>
> The promise was broken the next day. They returned to demand more money and in the process hacked to death 40 of the defenders. Heavily outnumbered, they were unable to resist the onslaught. Their women held a hurried meeting and concluded that all was lost but their honour. Ninety women jumped into the small well. Only three were saved: there was not enough water in the well to drown them all.

The story referred to incidents of communal violence in Punjab which had actually begun some months before Partition, in March 1947. Early in this month, a number of Sikh villages in Rawalpindi district were attacked, over a period of eight days (March 6–13, although in some places sporadic attacks continued up to 15 March). The attacks themselves were said to be in retaliation for Hindu attacks on Muslims in Bihar; also the Sikh political leader, Tara Singh, is said to have made provocative statements in Lahore to which Muslim political leaders had reacted. It is futile to speculate whose was the primary responsibility: the reality is that once it became clear that Partition would take place, both communities, Muslim and Hindu, started to attack members of the other. In Rawalpindi district, in the villages of Thamali, Thoa Khalsa, Mator, Nara and many others, the attacks ended on the 13th of March, when the army moved in and rescued what survivors were left. In many villages the entire population was wiped out; in others, there were a few survivors.

A small community of survivors from these villages lives in Jangpura and Bhogal, two middle-class areas in Delhi. It was from them that I learnt a little more about the "mass suicide" in Thoa Khalsa described above. Because they could lay claim to this history, survivors from Thoa Khalsa, even today, seemed to have a higher standing among the Rawalpindi community, than the others. People spoke of them, as they had done of Mangal Singh, in tones of awe and respect. Conversely, the two brothers from a neighboring village who had lost their sisters to abductors were spoken of as if they were the ones who were somehow at fault. Clearly the women's "sacrifice" had elevated their families, and their communities, to a higher plane. The first person from whom we heard the story of Thoa Khalsa was Basant Kaur, a tall, upright woman in her seventies. According to her, she was one of the women who had jumped into the well, but because it was too full she did not drown. I reproduce below a long excerpt from her interview.

BASANT KAUR:
"I keep telling them these stories . . ."
My name is Basant Kaur. My husband's name was Sant Raja Singh. We came away from our houses on March 12, and on the 13th we stayed out, in the village. At first, we tried to show our strength, and then we realized that this would not work, so we joined the morcha to go away. We left our home in Thoa Khalsa on the 12th. For three or four days we were trapped inside our houses, we couldn't get out, though we used to move across the roofs of houses and that way we could get out a bit. One of our people had a gun, we used that, and two or three of their people died. I lost a brother-in-law. He died from a bullet they fired. It hit him and he died. So we kept the gun handy. Then there were fires all around, raging fires, and we were no match for them. I had a jeth, my older brother-in-law, he had a son, he kept asking, give me afim (opium), mix it in water and I will take it. My jeth killed his mother, his sister, his wife, his daughter, and his uncle. My daughter was also killed. We went into the morcha inside the village, we all left our houses and collected together in the center of the village, inside the sardaran di haveli, where there was also a well. It was Lajjawanti's house. The sardar, her husband, had died some time ago, but his wife and other women of the house were there. Some children also. They all came out. Then we all talked and said we don't want to become Musalmaan, we would rather die. So everyone was given a bit of afim, they were told, you keep this with you . . . I went upstairs, and when I came down there was my husband, my jeth's son, my jethani, her daughters, my jeth, my grandsons, three granddaughters. They were all killed so that they would not fall into the hands of Musalmaans. One girl from our village, she had gone off with the Musalmaans. She was quite beautiful, and everyone got worried that if one has gone, they will take all our girls away . . . so it was then that they decided to kill the girls. My jeth, his name is Harbans Singh, he killed his wife, his daughter, his son . . . he was small, only eight days old. Then my sister-in-law was killed, her son and her daughter, and then on the 14th of March we came to Jhelum. The vehicles came and took us, and we stayed there for about a month and then we came to Delhi.

In Delhi there were four of my brothers, they read about this—the camp—in the papers and they came and found us. Then, gradually, over a period of time the children grew up and became older and things sorted themselves out. My parents were from Thamali. Hardly anyone survived from there. You know that family of Gurmeet's, they had two sisters, the Musalmaans took them away. It's not clear whether they died or were taken away but their bodies were never found . . . Someone died this way, someone that, someone died here and someone there, and no one got to know. My parents were burnt alive.

That whole area was like jungle, it was village area. One of my brothers survived and came away, one sister. They too were helped by a Musalmaan, there were some good ones, and they helped them—he hid them away in his house—and then put them into the vehicles that came, the military ones. The vehicles went to Mator and other places. In Mator, Shah Nawaz made sure no harm came to them. People from Nara managed to get away, but on the way they were all killed. Then my brothers read the papers and got to know. My husband, he killed his daughter, his niece, his sister, and a grandson. He killed them with a kirpan. My jeth's son killed his mother, his wife, his daughter, and a grandson and granddaughter, all with a pistol. And then, my jeth, he doused himself with kerosene and jumped into a fire.

Many girls were killed. Then Mata Lajjawanti, she had a well near her house, in a sort of garden. Then all of us jumped into that, some hundred . . . eighty-four . . . girls and boys. All of us. Even boys, not only children, but grown-up boys. I also went in, I took my two children and then we jumped in—I had some jewellery on me, things in my ears, on my wrists, and I had fourteen rupees on me. I took all that and threw it into the well, and then I jumped in, but . . . it's like when you put rotis into a tandoor, and if it is too full, the ones near the top, they don't cook, they have to be taken out. So the well filled up, and we could not drown . . . the children survived. Later, Nehru went to see the well, and the English then closed it up, the well that was full of bodies. The pathans took out those people who were at the top of the well—those who had died, died, and those who were alive, they pulled out. Then they went away—and what was left of our village was saved, except for that one girl who went away. . . .

Now I sit at home and my children are out working and I keep telling them these stories . . . they are stories after all . . . and you tell them and tell them until you lose consciousness . . .

MAREVASEI KACHERE

From A Girl Soldier's Story

Marevasei Kachere (b. 1961) was born in Uzumba, Zimbabwe, and served throughout much of the 1970s as a child soldier in the bloody conflict in which black people overthrew the minority white government of what was then the former British colony of Rhodesia. Thousands of men, women, and children joined the struggle. Women fought and worked side by side with the men, often also caring for the wounded. Kachere's story portrays her life as a child soldier and describes the suffering in the camps from hunger, sickness, and enemy attacks. It does not describe the sexual abuse suffered by women in military camps, which has since been well documented through the work of women's groups within Zimbabwe. Eighteen years after independence, Kachere's expectations of the 1970s remained unfulfilled, and the small payment for her service she finally received, "too late," made little difference in her life. Her account appears in a book of oral testimonies by women in the liberation struggle, published by Zimbabwe Women Writers.

■

My name is Marevasei Kachere and I was born at Uzumba in Murewa District in 1961, the last in a family of eight children. I went to school at Chidodo when I was eight years old and stayed there up to grade seven. All the children in our family went to school but none of us progressed beyond grade seven, the top class of the primary school. My parents were unusual, as, unlike most parents in our village, they chose to send their daughters to school. This may have been due to the fact that my father had been an only child and so had not experienced discrimination against girls in his family. My education was brought to an end by the Liberation War. I didn't even see the results of my grade seven examinations since we had to leave our home before the results were available. When I eventually came back after the war, I was told that all the school records had been burnt.

Each day, after school, I had to look after the cattle and work in the fields, sometimes helping my father and one of my brothers to plough. I would lead the plough oxen so that they kept on the right course. As with schooling, there was no discrimination in our family between boys and girls as far as work was concerned. Any of us could do anything that had to be done. For instance, my brothers often used to fetch water from the well, something that is considered to be a girl's job. We lived very simply. It was only on special occasions that I was able to eat the food that I loved best—bread and eggs—and that, of course, disappeared along with our hens when we were forced by the Rhodesian soldiers to move into the keep or protected village.

In the early 1970s I used to hear the old people talking about a war and about terrorists, but at first I didn't understand what this meant. Then, round about 1972, when the war was getting hot in the Mt. Darwin area, we heard stories that told of terrorists who were invisible. If the Rhodesian soldiers came anywhere near them, they would see only their hats but not the actual people.

We just heard these stories without, as I say, understanding them. Understanding what war was came to us when the soldiers arrived in our district. When they first came they questioned people about the presence of terrorists, and I think that at that period only a few people had had any contact with them, bringing them food and other necessities. But then we were told that on such and such a date we were going to be moved into a keep, although we had no idea what a keep was. So on the appointed day in 1975 the soldiers came and, going from house to house in our village, forced the people at gun point to leave with everything they could carry. Anyone who refused to move was shot. And then the soldiers burnt all our houses.

There were no houses in the keep and, at first, people made simple grass shelters to stay in—with no roofs—until they managed to build huts. A whole family was crowded into each of these shelters, but in my case, I was lucky since my brothers and sister had married and I was the only one staying with my parents.

The keep was a large area surrounded by a very high barbed-wire fence. It was so high that one couldn't possibly climb over it and the wires were placed so close together that no one was able to squeeze through it. There were no two ways about it—when the soldiers said that we had to stay inside we had no choice. They were afraid that if we were allowed to go freely in and out we would carry food to the "terrorists" as they called them. Of course people had to be allowed to go out at set times to fetch water and to tend the vegetable gardens, and on these occasions everyone who went out was searched to see if the container he or she carried held food. And on coming back, if you were carrying a bucket of water the guards would stir it with a stick to see if there were any explosives in it. You had to make quite sure that you had brought in enough food and water for the family for if the gate was kept closed, as it sometimes was, then there was nothing you could do but go hungry. And if you came back late, after being outside, you would be shot.

Our school was also inside the fence, and every morning we had to go to school. The soldiers used to come to check the register to make sure that every child was present. If anyone was absent the rest of us were beaten with a length of hosepipe—every one of us—by the soldiers who were trying to get us to say where such and such a child had gone. We never did say for we believed that if they found out where the child had gone that child would be killed.

I was not invited by anyone to join the Liberation Struggle, but I was forced into going by the intolerable circumstances in which we lived. The soldiers used to come and take us to a place called Mashambanhaka where they put us in drums full of water and beat us almost to death. This painful routine went on for some time. Even old people suffered in the same way. Indeed, anybody who was suspected of having fed the guerrillas was taken out and beaten and then locked in the keep again. I was tired of being beaten and so I decided I would go out to join the Liberation Struggle. Doing that, I thought, might lead to my death, but as far as that was concerned I was under a constant threat of death in the keep, so it was all one whether I stayed or went. On balance I thought it better to go.

While I was still in the keep some guerrillas arrived at a base called Birimhiri and a message came that we should prepare *sadza* and take it to the comrades. We cooked the sadza, and on that day we were lucky for the soldiers had gone off to read their newspapers, and the DA's were holed up in a strong point fortified with sandbags which was called *zvimudhuri*, so we slipped out carrying the food, and I never came back. I was with a friend called Kiretti and we just walked saying nothing to each other for there was nothing to say; I mean we had no idea what to expect when we arrived at where we were going. This was all done in a moment, completely unplanned. I had not even told my mother that I was going.

That was my first day to meet the comrades. They were just ordinary people, quite visible, wearing uniforms some of which were plain khaki and some camouflage, and carrying their guns which, I noticed, they never let go of since they might have to fight at any moment. We were a bit afraid at first but soon got used to them. There were ten of them altogether. When they had eaten and were about to leave we told them we were going with them; that we wanted to go to Mozambique because we were tired of being beaten. At first they refused to take us and said they were taking boys only, and that though they had taken girls before, they did not encourage those who were very young to go. But we insisted that we were not going back to the keep to be beaten to death or to be injured, as my hearing had been impaired through the punishment I had received. And eventually they agreed.

When we left there were four girls and quite a number of boys from our keep in the group. We did not know what to expect but I did not regret what I had done. We started our journey at night, around eight o'clock, and travelled to Karimimbika which is still in the Uzumba District. Another group of comrades joined us there and we went on, travelling always by night, going via Mudzi and Area 6, and then straight on to the border between Rhodesia and Mozambique. My tennis shoes were soon worn out, and I had to make do with the one dress I had been wearing when I left the keep.

After we had crossed into Mozambique we camped at a base called Mubhanana where we stayed for some time, carrying supplies of arms for the comrades who came from Chambere. Then we moved to Zhangara Camp where there were about seven hundred people, including two hundred who were my age. At one stage there were more women than men in this camp, but in my age group there were more boys than girls, and there were no old people. At Zhangara, as in other camps, we were taught politics. Our instructors told us about the war and its origins and said that we should not think of returning home since we had chosen to come and fight for our country's independence.

For my part I never wanted to go back while things were as they were. Yes, I missed my parents, but I was in a large group of young people, all of whom were in the same boat, and that made it easier to forget about your own problems. Most of the time I was happy because I had friends—Ebamore, Tarisai, Mabhunu and Shingirai. We sang together in the choir; in times of hardship we comforted each other; we plaited our hair and mended our clothes. If we were lucky enough to have needles we made small bags in which to keep personal things out of our old dresses. Discipline was fairly strict in the camp. Girls were separated from boys and we never had boyfriends. If a girl did leave camp to meet a boy and was caught she was punished. It wasn't easy to get out of the camp because the exits were guarded. Pregnancies were rare, but girls fell pregnant when they left camp to perform military duties like carrying arms and ammunition. The most common offence for which one was beaten or made to carry ammunition was escaping from the camp to barter clothes for food in the surrounding villages. Beatings were not carried out in the open and we only saw people being called to report for a beating. In all the time I stayed at this camp, I never broke the rules, except on one occasion: my friends and I missed a meal because we had stayed too long at the river where we were getting rid of the lice in our hair. Luckily we were not punished for that. . . .

We also did some training with "arms," wooden guns that we ourselves had made. Being educated was a big advantage in the camp, and it was the educated ones who were usually the first to be selected to become trainers. I wasn't considered to be educated but I was good at physical activities so I was asked to help with military training. After we had finished the initial training we were allowed to handle real guns, and were given lessons on the different parts of a gun and on how to dismantle and load them. All this time boys and girls were taught together, and we had both male and female instructors. These lessons gave us confidence and a sense of power, so different from how we felt when we were untrained and unarmed.

The most distressing episode in this part of my life was when Tembwe was bombed on November 25, 1977. On that day people were carrying out their duties as usual but another girl and I hadn't gone to work because we were sick. I had an extensive burn on my leg as a result of an accident in the kitchen. Shingi and I had been to the clinic and on our way back we spotted a plane. We were heading for the kitchen, an area of shelters and large drums on fires in which to cook sadza, but before we got there this plane dropped a bomb right in the middle of it. All those on duty in the kitchen were killed—some by the explosion and others by the porridge from the drums. We ran to the river and hid among the reeds but then soldiers appeared and began shooting towards us and I thought I was going to die. I was hit, and the bullet wounds on my leg were deep, but I survived, though it was three months before my injuries healed.

I had never thought of the possibility of dying in a battle before. During my training I had imagined an exchange of gunfire, but nothing more. I had never seen a dead person, but now I saw so many. As we ran to the river I had stepped on the bodies of those who had died, and the thought of that experience horrified me. People die in war and I knew it then all too fearfully.

Soon after the attack on Tembwe I was sent with other survivors to Maroro where I completed my military training. I was then chosen, together with five girls and nine boys, to carry arms—what we called caches—to the comrades who were in the field. These arms—grenades for instance—were packed into sealed bags, and with these we crossed the border into Rhodesia, protected by an armed guard who knew the way. We entered the Mutoko area in July 1978 and went straight to the traditional healer in that area who gave us the go-ahead to operate there. We had been instructed not to seek confrontation with the Rhodesian security forces, and to hide if we came across any. My one experience of action in the field was in Area G. We were having a meal of sadza when we were attacked. We ran away. But four of our comrades were killed by the enemy in this engagement.

In December 1979 a cease-fire was declared. . . . [W]e celebrated Zimbabwean Independence on April 18, 1980. We talked about the fact that we had liberated our country and that now no one would be a beggar in his or her own land. We believed that every person in the country would get enough food and a place to stay, and yes, I expected to get a job that matched my education and training. We had great expectations. At that time our leaders told us that what we expected would come true.

As it worked out, some of us were sent to schools, but then the schools were closed. The leaders came and asked for those who wanted jobs, but only the highly educated were taken and given jobs in, for instance, the police force. I stayed behind in that camp while others went off to work, and on top of that they said I was too short to join the police.

Meanwhile, a cousin of mine had come looking for me, as relatives did in those days when family members who had long been lost were returning to these assembly points. As a result I went to see my parents and we wept on one another's neck when we met. They were poor. They had lost everything in the war, and they couldn't help me, nor I them at that time. After staying with them for a short time I went back to Manyene. My hope lay in the promise of jobs that had been made, and I was anxious to get back because I did not want to miss out. . . .

Eighteen years after independence most of the promises made to us remain unfulfilled. We were all promised houses and jobs and a good life, regardless of one's standard of education, but this has not happened.

The hard conditions in the camps in Mozambique have affected my health badly. I think I picked up diseases there from which I have never fully recovered. I would never recommend my daughter to follow my example if such a situation arose again.

The major change of the last couple of years has been the $50,000 payout and the $2,000 monthly pension. I managed to buy a plough, a cart and two oxen, and I was given land to use. I don't have to dig my field with a hoe anymore. But I think the money is too little. I suffered for too long and the money came too late.

Transcribed by Grace Dube
Translation by Chiedza Musengezi

JEAN KADALIKA UWANKUNDA

The Impact of Genocide on Women

Jean Kadalika Uwankunda (b. 1966) is the director of the organization Profemme (Twese Hamwe) in Rwanda. Her testimony is found in a 1999 book by John A. Berry and Carol Pott Berry entitled *Genocide in Rwanda: A Collective Memory*. Carol Pott and John Berry were residents in Kigali when the genocide began in April 1994. They managed to be evacuated home to the United States, but Carol's experience of hiding a Rwandan family in her home while the army militias murdered scores of civilians in the streets was published in the *Washington Post* and other newspapers, helping to bring some needed attention to the horrors. Since 1994, the couple have returned often to train United Nations human rights workers and to search for surviving friends and colleagues. The firsthand accounts of Rwandans like Jean Kadalika Uwankunda, who have experienced the unimaginable horror of the situation in this African country, is offered with analysis of the historical and political context of the disaster. The women widowed, displaced, and abused by the war are the very people now rebuilding the nation and most responsible for its painful and slow reconstruction.

■

Rwanda has just lived through a tragedy that caused more than a million deaths and provoked the massive movement of refugees and displaced persons. For reasons that are largely sociocultural, the massacres specially targeted men. In Rwanda, as in many African countries, it is men who have the right of inheritance and who pass on their name, their family heritage, and their ethnicity to their children. The struggle for possessions (land, houses, furnishings) and for power has therefore been primarily the concern of men and of male children. It is they who are given the right to property and to power.

A traditional expression in Rwanda states that "the hen does not crow in the presence of a cock." Because of this tradition, the women of Rwanda were powerless in their suffering during the genocide. In Rwanda before the war, everything that was done was done without the participation of women. Women did not have a role in the decision-making process. It is, above all, because of this tradition that women were powerless to resist the genocide.

Even if today many women are alone, widowed or abandoned by their husbands, even if they are poor, even if they are traumatized, even if they were raped, they are now more than ever the prime actors in the process of reconciliation and reconstruction in Rwanda. We believe that the women of Rwanda must convince themselves of this role. Women have certain advantages in this regard and should help other women to show their strength in the current crisis.

Today, the social fabric, as well as the traditional moral values of respect, tolerance, self-respect and dignity, have been destroyed. Women have always been considered as the heart of Rwandan society, as those who reconcile, as those who unify the family. Women were considered as *Nyampinga*, "the ones who welcome those who are tired." Women had the power to prevent their children, whatever their age, from taking part in crimes such as those we have just witnessed in Rwanda. But if one considers the participation of youth in the massacres, one realizes that stronger forces were working against this traditional power of women. In addition to other social factors, politicians, the media, and decision-makers manipulated the youth of Rwanda to the point that women were powerless witnesses to the massacres committed by their children, their husbands, their brothers, their relatives.

When one closely analyzes the conflict of Rwanda, one realizes the extent to which the inequality of social relations between the sexes can be a barrier to peace. Above all, one realizes the heavy consequences this barrier has on the development of the country when huge numbers of women are left on their own to manage their families, the basis of society. It is women in particular in Africa who feel the terrible consequences of genocide, massacres, and war. They are largely unprepared to assume all the new responsibilities that fall on their backs. This is why it is particularly important to reconsider the role of women in the new society that is being built in Rwanda.

The difficult times that Rwanda experiences on a political, economic, social, and cultural level require vigilance and rationalism more than ever before. Women's organizations, as intermediaries between grass-roots initiatives and governmental programs, are called to commit themselves to the resolution of the problems of women in order to build a society that is better able to support lasting development. Those involved in the development of the country have the responsibility to seriously consider the best way to maximize the involvement of women in the development of the new Rwanda.

Today these constraints are greatly accentuated, and women who were widowed, left alone, displaced, or made refugees as a result of the genocide are particularly affected. These women, as earlier noted, represent an enormous percentage of the women in Rwanda. New and urgent problems require a quick and efficient response on the part of women's associations:

- Psychological trauma caused by the loss of direct and indirect family members, rape, and its resulting unwanted pregnancies and the fear of sexually transmitted diseases
- Physical trauma resulting from wounds, rape, and malnutrition
- Lack of housing owing to destruction, occupation, or lack of money for rent
- Increase in the number of widows or woman-headed households with many children or orphans
- Problems of inheritance, especially for women who were in common-law marriages
- Increase in poverty levels due to lack of employment in refugee and displaced persons camps, loss of a spouse or other family member who assured a subsistence-level income, and a general reduction in economic activity
- Increased risk of exposure to HIV/AIDS through rape or promiscuity, especially among abandoned young girls.
- A decline in sanitary conditions due to malnutrition, poor conditions in the camps, and lack of health care facilities in rural communities
- Lack of basic household necessities
- Women held hostage in the camps by their husbands, who prevent them from making decisions for themselves and for their children

In a global sense, the women of Rwanda are traumatized by the genocide, by rape, and by destruction of all sorts. They regret that they did not have the means or the ability to prevent such events from occurring. Those women living in the camps remain the victims of a persuasive campaign of false information by militias and former soldiers, preventing them from returning to their homes. Yet in the camps, the lack of basic necessities (food, clothing, health care) is overwhelming. The death toll among children and mothers is very high. The lack of living space, of schools, of sanitation prevents women from ensuring even an adequate standard of living for their children.

Women who have suffered through the war show a disturbing level of defeatism and despair in face of the future. As a whole, the women of Rwanda fear tomorrow. Nonetheless, with numbers of people dependent on them (their own children, family members, and others who escaped the genocide), women show a certain will to struggle to overcome these multiple constraints. This, once again, points out the necessity for women's associations and other development agencies to commit themselves without reserve to supporting women in the heavy task of reconstructing and rehabilitating themselves and the country.

PART 3:

COURAGE AND RESISTANCE

Let it be understood, soberly and rationally between us, that you are fighting to gratify a sex instinct which I cannot share; to procure benefits which I have not shared and probably will not share; but not to gratify my instincts, or to protect either myself or my country. For, the outsider will say, in fact, as a woman, I have no country. As a woman I want no country. As a woman, my country is the whole world.

—VIRGINIA WOOLF (1882–1941),
famed British Modernist and feminist writer, in an essay from *Three Guineas*
(1938)

Peace may have become too much of a pious cliché. We must make it into a vigorous movement, anti-war and anti-militarism, by getting public opinion mobilized in all kinds of local groups. People must be made "propaganda proof."

—ALVA MYRDAL (1902–1985),
Swedish activist for women's rights, human rights, and nuclear disarmament,
director of UNESCO, and 1982 winner of the Nobel Peace Prize

Among the most striking changes in the last decade has been the growing popular awareness that we live in a world economy guided by corporate entities that span the globe, lacking loyalty to any polity. The implications are enormous. . . . We must demonstrate how government can be reclaimed as a vehicle through which we can act on our deepest values, rather than remain an instrument of authoritative or corrupt control.

—FRANCES MOORE LAPPÉ (b. 1944),
co-founder of Food First and the Institute for Food and Development Policy,
author of *Diet for a Small Planet*

ADELAIDE-GILLETTE DUFRESNOY

The Deliverance of Argos

Adelaide-Gillette Dufresnoy (1765–1825) acquired much fame and success in Parisian artistic circles at an early age. After her husband was financially ruined as a result of the French Revolution, she began to write for a living. Her work included verse, plays, and novels, as well as translations from English. After the restoration of the monarchy, she stayed outwardly loyal to the royalists, though her salon was a center of liberal protest. Several Romantic poets have credited her as an inspiration to their work. Here in the Romantic mode, she uses Classical Greek mythology to tell a symbolic story of female victory and courage.

■

In days of old, a woman emulating Tyrtheus,
And, like him, moved by a heroic ardor,
Avenged the citizens of Argos, lyre in hand.
They owed salvation to this young beauty
    Whose noble courage
Rivaled the valor of Greece's heroes.

Sounds of arms resound; warring legions
Have broken the walls of weak Mycenae;
The troubled waters of Inachus run with blood,
And with speed the attackers forge ahead;
    The ancient breed
Of Pelops groans from deep within his grave.

You who were proud of your lofty destiny,
Whose pale warriors now scatter and flee,
City of Agamemnon, ill-starred city!
The ashen ghost of the king of kings
    Can defend you no longer,
And your protective gods now desert your ramparts.

Sparta besieges you; where is your refuge?
But suddenly heaven summons Telesilla;
She runs, shuddering with shame and pain.
Apollo's daughter she is; inspired by the god,
    She takes up sword and lyre,
And by her songs revives the Argoan valor.

"Alas! Forgetting the ancestral bravery,
These frightened soldiers throw away their lance,

Our hopes dashed by their shameless flight!
My comrades, come, dare to follow my path,
    Put on your armor,
And may a warrior's helmet bind your locks.

"Venus is not only a goddess by her charms;
In Sparta she's a warrior: she bore arms.
Mars' companion must follow his fate,
Proud and timid sex that man so often insults,
    He owes you his courage;
Your arm's less sinewy, but stronger your heart.

"Let us send back fear to the foreign flags;
In vain does Sparta claim magnanimous Hercules;
Pelops is also Jupiter's progeny.
When the Greeks readied the conquest of Ilion,
    We headed the march;
Argos herself was Sparta's main support.

"People of Argos, my voice recalls you to honor;
Close ranks, press on, raise your glittering swords!
Drive the javelins home with intrepid hands.
My lute will sing no more but hymns of war
    Until the day our land
Has soaked up the waves of enemy blood.

"The Muses I serve do not have savage hearts.
There where Inachus peacefully flows,
I sang verses as gentle as its shores.
But then my country's woes aroused my soul;
    And my inflaming god
Fills my chords with fierceness yet unknown.

"O lyric mountains, ramparts of my native land!
Fountains! sacred woods! dear to my revery;
Sweet Argos! Must I forsake you now forever?
Will the gods suffer that a conquerer profane you?
    May Apollo and Diana,
Armed with avenging darts, protect your summits.

"I see that my prayer has finally reached them;
A formidable rainbow glitters in the clouds above:
They give the signal, they march before us.
March on, let's fear no more the sons of Hercules:
    Now Sparta retreats,
And her affrighted sons fall beneath our blows.

"Never will Eurotas see me captive;
Never will he hear me, on my plaintive lyre,
Fill the echoing plains with our misfortunes.
No; let Telesilla fall in the field of honor,
  Let her gravestone say:
'Death she preferred to the shame of chains.'"

It was thus the inspired priestess sang.
She triumphs; Argos is soon delivered from her foes.
For their immortal help her voice blessed the gods.
That day her sex had the honor of the victory;
  And to preserve her glory,
There they built an altar to Venus triumphant.

Translation by Dorothy Backer

IDA B. WELLS-BARNETT

A National Crime

Ida B. Wells-Barnett (1862–1931) was the daughter of Mississippi slaves. She was a fiercely out-spoken activist, journalist, and teacher who worked against racial discrimination and championed women's. Wells-Barnett began a national crusade against lynching in 1892, when one of her closet friends was lynched by a mob during a race riot. Such lynchings have been common throughout the world during and after ethnically or racially charged conflicts. In the following 1909 address to the National Association for the Advancement of Colored People, Wells assails the insanity that condones lynchings and other forms of "mob" justice. Such mob lynchings of African Americans, as well as Jews, Italians, Japanese, and others, continued well into and throughout the twentieth century in the United State of America.

■

The lynching record for a quarter of a century merits the thoughtful study of the American people. It presents three salient facts: First, lynching is a color-line murder. Second, crimes against women is the excuse, not the cause. Third, it is a national crime and requires a national remedy.

Proof that lynching follows the color line is to be found in the statistics which have been kept for the past twenty-five years. During the few years preceding this period and while frontier law existed, the executions showed a majority of white victims. Later, however, as law courts and authorized judiciary extended into the far West, lynch law rapidly abated, and its white victims became few and far between. . . .

During the last ten years, from 1899 to 1908 inclusive, the number lynched was 959. Of this number, 102 were white, while the colored victims numbered 857. No other nation, civilized or savage, burns its criminals; only under that Stars and Stripes is the human holocaust possible. Twenty-eight human beings burned at the stake, one of them a woman and two of them children, is the awful indictment against the American civilization—the gruesome tribute which the nation pays to the color line.

Why is mob murder permitted by a Christian nation? What is the cause of this awful slaughter? This question is answered almost daily: always the same shameless falsehood that "Negroes are lynched to protect womanhood." Standing before a Chautauqua assemblage, John Temple Graves, at once champion of lynching and apologist for lynchers, said, "The mob stands today as the most potential bulwark between the women of the South and such a carnival of crime as would infuriate the world and precipitate the annihilation of the Negro race." This is the never-varying answer of lynchers and their apologists. All know that it is untrue. The cowardly lyncher revels in murder, then seeks to shield himself from public execration by claiming devotion to woman. But truth is mighty and the lynching record discloses the hypocrisy of the lyncher as well as his crime.

The Springfield, Illinois, mob rioted for two days, the militia of the entire state was called out, two men were lynched, hundreds of people driven from their homes, all because a white woman said a Negro assaulted her. A mad mob went to the jail, tried to lynch the victim of her charge, and, not being able to find him, proceeded to pillage and burn the town and to lynch two innocent men. Later, after the police had found that the woman's charge was false, she published a retraction, the indictment was dismissed, and the intended victim discharged. But the lynched victims were dead, hundreds were homeless, and Illinois was disgraced.

As a final and complete refutation of the charge that lynching is occasioned by crimes against women, a partial record of lynchings is cited; 285 persons were lynched for causes as follows: unknown cause, 92; no cause, 10; race prejudice, 49; miscegenation, 7; informing, 12; making threats, 11; keeping saloon, 3; practicing fraud, 5; practicing voodooism, 2; bad reputation, 8; unpopularity, 3; mistaken identity, 5; using improper language, 3; violation of contract, 1; writing insulting letter, 2; eloping, 2; poisoning horse, 1; poisoning well, 2; by white capes, 9; vigilantes, 14; Indians, 1; moonshining, 1; refusing evidence, 2; political causes, 5; disputing, 1; disobeying quarantine regulations, 2; slapping a child, 1; turning state's evidence, 3; protecting a Negro, 1; to prevent giving evidence, 1; knowledge of larceny, 1; writing letter to white woman, 1; asking white woman to marry, 1; jilting girl, 1; having smallpox, 1; concealing criminal, 2; threatening political exposure, 1; self-defense, 6; cruelty, 1; insulting language to woman, 5; quarreling with white man, 2; colonizing Negroes, 1; throwing stones, 1; quarreling, 1; gambling, 1.

Is there a remedy, or will the nation confess that it cannot protect its protectors at home as well as abroad? Various remedies have been suggested to abolish the lynching infamy, but year after year, the butchery of men, women, and children continues in spite of plea and protest. Education is suggested as a preventative, but it is as grave a crime to murder an ignorant man as it is a scholar. True, few educated men have been lynched, but the hue and cry once started stops at no bounds, as was clearly shown by the lynchings in Atlanta, and in Springfield, Illinois.

Agitation, though helpful, will not alone stop the crime. Year after year statistics are published, meetings are held, resolutions are adopted. And yet lynchings go on. . . . The only certain remedy is an appeal to law. Lawbreakers must be made to know that human life is sacred and that every citizen of this country is first a citizen of the United States and secondly a citizen of the state in which he belongs. This nation must assert itself and protect its federal citizenship at home as well as abroad. The strong men of the government must reach across state lines whenever unbridled lawlessness defies state laws, and must give to the individual under the Stars and Stripes the same measure of protection it gives to him when he travels in foreign lands. Federal protection of American citizenship is the remedy for lynching. . . .

In a multitude of counsel there is wisdom. Upon the grave question presented by the slaughter of innocent men, women and children there should be an honest, courageous conference of patriotic, law-abiding citizens, anxious to punish crime promptly, impartially, and by due process of law, also to make life, liberty, and property secure against mob rule.

Time was when lynching appeared to be sectional, but now it is national—a blight upon our nation, mocking our laws and disgracing our Christianity. "With malice toward none but with charity for all," let us undertake the work of making the "law of the land" effective and supreme upon every foot of American soil—a shield to the innocent; and to the guilty, punishment swift and sure.

OLIVE SCHREINER

From Women and Labour: Women and War

Olive Schreiner (1855–1920), South African author and feminist, was born in Cape Colony and spent much of her life working as a governess. Her first acclaimed novel, *The Story of an African Farm*, was published in 1883 under the pseudonym Ralph Iron. This autobiographical novel, an intense portrayal of two children living in the African plains, stirred controversy for its feminist ideals and its exposure of colonial and Christian hypocrisy. Schreiner's long treatise "Women and War" appeared in her 1911 book, *Woman and Labour*. Schreiner believed that women's experience as givers and nurturers of life made them far more aware than men of the true costs of war, and thus its natural opponents. She also saw women's lack of enfranchisement as a cause of war.

■

It may then be said [of women]: "What of war, that struggle of the human creatures to attain its ends by physical force and at the price of the life of others: will you take part in that also?" We reply: Yes; more particularly in that field we intend to play our party. We have always borne part of the weight of war, and the major part. It is not merely that in primitive times we suffered from the destruction of the fields we tilled and the houses we built; or that in later times as domestic labourers and producers, though unwaged, we, in taxes and material loss and additional labour, paid as much as our males towards the cost of war; nor is it that in a comparatively insignificant manner, as nurses of the wounded in modern times, or now and again as warrior chieftainesses and leaders in primitive and other societies, we have borne our part; nor is it even because the spirit of resolution in its women, and their willingness to endure, has in all ages again and again largely determined the fate of a race that goes to war, that we demand our controlling right where war is concerned. Our relation to war is far more intimate, personal, and indissoluble than this. Men have made boomerangs, bows, swords, or guns with which to destroy one another; we have made the men who destroyed and were destroyed! We have in all ages produced, at an enormous cost, the primal munition of war, without which no other would exist. There is no battlefield on earth, nor ever has been howsoever covered with slain, which it has not cost the women of the race more in actual bloodshed and anguish to supply, than it has cost the men who lie there. *We pay the first cost on all human life* . . .

There is, perhaps, no woman, whether she have borne children, or be merely a potential child-bearer, who could look down on a battlefield covered with the slain, but the thought would rise in her, "So many mothers' sons! So many bodies brought into the world to lie there! So many months of weariness and pain while bones and muscles were shaped within; . . . so many baby mouths drawing life at woman's breasts;—all this, that men might lie with glazed eyeballs and swollen bodies, and fixed, blue, unclosed mouths, and great limbs tossed—this, that an acre of ground might be manured with human flesh" . . . No woman who is a woman says of a human body, "It is nothing!" . . .

In a besieged city, it might well happen that men in the streets might seize upon statues and marble carvings from public buildings and galleries and hurl them in to stop the breaches made in their ramparts by the enemy . . . not valuing them more than if they had been paving stones. But one man could not do this—the sculptor! He, who, though there might be no work of his own chisel among them, yet knew what each of these works of art had cost, knew by experience the long years of struggle and study and the infinitude of toil which had gone to the shaping of even one limb, to the carving of even one perfected outline, he could never so use them without thought of care. . . . Men's bodies are our women's works of art. Given to us power to control, we will never carelessly throw them in to fill up the gaps in human relationships made by international ambitions and greeds. . . .

War will pass when intellectual culture and activity have made possible to the female an equal share in the governance of modern national life; it will probably not pass away much sooner; its extinction will not be delayed much longer.

It is especially in the domain of war that we, the bearers of men's bodies, who supply its most valuable munition, who not amid the clamour and ardour of battle, but, singly, and alone, with a three-in-the-morning courage, shed blood and face death that the battle-field may have its food, a food more precious to us than our heart's blood; it is we especially, who in the domain of war, have our word to say, a word no man can say for us. It is our intention to enter into the domain of war and to labour there till in the course of generations we have extinguished it.

GABRIELA MISTRAL

Finnish Champion

Gabriela Mistral (1889–1957) was the first poet of South America to win the Nobel Prize for Literature, in 1945. Her passionate poetry had become legendary throughout South America, passed from country to country by word of mouth. Mistral was born in Vicuña, a high Andean village in Chile. She worked as a teacher and, in addition to poetry, wrote articles for several Latin American journals. A restless spirit, Mistral traveled widely, to Mexico, the United States, Spain, Switzerland, and Italy. In 1926, she came to Paris as the Chilean delegate to the League of Nations Committee for Intellectual Cooperation and was able to promote the works of Latin American authors throughout Europe. In 1951, in her nineties, she served as delegate to the United Nations Commission on the Status of Women and as a member of the Committee for Women's Rights, and during her last years she worked as an advisor to UNESCO. She believed that the artist's life must be dedicated to the good of the people, and wrote and spoke out all her life for human rights and social justice. On her tomb, her favorite axiom is transcribed: "What the soul is to the body is what the artist does for her people." Here she commemorates all who died in the Finnish resistance to a massive invasion by Soviet forces during World War II. Despite heavy losses, Finland succeeded in retaining its autonomy.

■

Finnish Champion, you are stretched out
in the burnished light of your final stadium,
red as the pheasant in life and in death,
stitched with wounds, drained as a gargoyle spout
of your blood.
You have fallen in the snows of your childhood,
among blue edges and steely mirrors,
crying No! to the North and the East,
a No! that compresses profusion of snow,
hardens the skis to diamonds,
stops the war tank like a wild boar.
Swimmer, ball-player, runner,
let them burn your name and call you "Finland."
Hallowed be your final course,
hallowed the meridian that took your body,
hallowed the midnight sin that granted your final
                              miracle.
You denied the invader the draught of your lakes,
your paths, the life-thread of your reindeer,
the threshold of your home, the cube of your arena,
the rainbow of your Virgins and Christ,
the baptized foreheads of your children.

Translation by Doris Dana

AGNES SMEDLEY

From Portraits of Chinese Women in Revolution: The Women Take a Hand

Agnes Smedley (1892–1950) was a feminist activist and writer. A self-made woman, Smedley drew her inspiration from the lessons of her own poverty-stricken background. Her parents' hard life—her father was a miner and her mother a laundress—and her mother's early death from malnutrition and exhaustion were tragedies that shaped her view of the world. Her best-known book, *Daughter of the Earth* (1929) is a gritty autobiographical novel of her early life. As a journalist, she went beyond "facts-and-figures"; she had the instincts of a storyteller and a moralist, and she featured the authentic voices of the people she interviewed. Smedley was instrumental in exposing prison conditions in the United States; worked to establish birth control clinics in New York, Germany, India, and China; and raised funds for the Indian resistance movement against the British. She lived and worked in China starting in 1928 and witnessed war and revolutionary turmoil ; she is buried in Beijing beneath a gravestone inscribed, "Friend of China." *Portraits of Chinese Women in Revolution* is a collection of Smedley's writings published by the Feminist Press in 1976.

■

When I first met old Mother Tsai, she had already emerged as a leader of the women in the valley. She was unusually tall for a "south Yangtze Valley" woman; her skin was brown, and the veins on her old hands stood out like ridges on a hillside. She was thin and hard, and when she spoke, her voice was firm and almost harsh. Her hair, touched with white, was drawn back at the nape of her neck. As a peasant woman and the mother of many sons, she had suffered bitterly all her life, but of this she never spoke. Her white cotton jacket was neatly buttoned up close around her neck and her dark cotton trousers always seemed to have just been washed. Though none of these people ever ironed their clothing, hers must somehow have been pressed beneath some weight. She was the embodiment of dignity and staunchness.

It was difficult to believe that she was sixty-eight, for she seemed much younger. She was, she told me, a widow with four children. Of her three sons, the two elder were in the New Fourth Army, and the younger, a boy of fifteen, helped her and her daughters-in-law till the fields.

Before the war, life in the villages had been drab and monotonous. But when the New Fourth Army had marched into the valley the year before, the world had seemed to enter with it. Many girl students had joined the Political Department of the Army; when they went knocking on the doors of the village women, the old world had crumbled. The ladies of the gentry had refused to receive them, sending their menfolk instead, and thus suggesting that the girls were prostitutes. But when the girls knocked on Mother Tsai's door, she looked into their eyes and knew they were not bad. She invited them in, placed bowls of tea before them, and called her daughters-in-law and neighbor women to come and sit with them. And in this way the Women's National Salvation Association was born in the valley. It grew until it had over a hundred members.

Mother Tsai's lean, tall figure could often be seen walking along the paths from village to village, urging women to join literacy classes, and attend discussion groups to learn what the war was about and how they could help. After the day's work was done, women could be seen sitting on their doorsteps, cutting out pieces of cloth and sewing. When I asked them what they were doing, they replied: "Making shoes for the Army."

More and more women took over the field work previously done by the men. The younger men had joined the Army and the older men and boys helped in the fields or carried supplies to the battlefield and brought back the wounded. On every festival day members of the Women's Association would go to the hospital to "comfort the wounded" with gifts of food, sing songs, and talk with the soldiers. It was always Mother Tsai who delivered the speeches in the wards, telling the wounded that they were all her sons and the sons of the Women's Association. And she never closed a speech without telling them about women's rights, or urging them to induce their womenfolk to join the Association. Some men had never heard such talk before and they listened with respect. About such matters Chinese men everywhere seemed much more civilized and tolerant than Occidental men, and only a few ever opposed the new movement.

The women had become particularly confident after Army women had conducted classes. One of these classes covered Japanese espionage and sabotage methods in the war zones and it urged women to become the "eyes and ears of the Army," to combat defeatism, watch everywhere for spies or traitors, and boycott Japanese goods. One phrase covered all such activities: "Guarding the rear of our Army." After that they never just sat and listened while their menfolk dispensed wisdom; they took part in conversations, conducted propaganda about almost everything on earth, went to mass meetings, and questioned every stranger who passed through the valley about his family and his family's family down to the tenth generation.

Now and then a man rose to protest against the "new women." There was, for instance, the merchant Chang, who declared that, when the women got going, they wore out men and exhausted horses. Mother Tsai was the worst of all, he said and an idea in her head rattled like a pea in an empty gourd. She had become particularly obnoxious to him since she had discovered that he was buying up all the small white beans from the lah tree. The people made candles from these beans, but Chang had begun cornering them and selling them in Wuhu. Now, the city of Wuhu had been occupied by the Japanese, and the women soon wanted to know just why any person traded in it. How was it, they asked, that Merchant Chang could pass through Japanese lines, month in and month out, without difficulty? And why had the wax beans of the valley suddenly found such a big market? Perhaps the Japanese made oil from them! No one respected Merchant Chang anyway, for everyone knew that he had a hand in the valley's new opium-smoking den, where the village riff-raff and even some family men had begun squandering their money.

Mother Tsai one day walked straight into Chang's shop and put the questions to him. With withering contempt, the merchant asked her if *she* wanted to buy his beans. This was not only an insult, but it mocked the poverty of the old lady and of every peasant family in the valley. Merchant Chang soon learned what it meant to despise the will of the people. Not a soul would buy or sell him anything, and when he passed through the streets people looked the other way. Once a little boy threw a stone at him and called out: "Traitor." And one day as he passed a farmhouse, he distinctly heard a dog being set on him.

At last Merchant Chang went in anger to the local government official. The official called in Mother Tsai for a friendly talk. The old lady went, but not alone. The entire membership of the Women's Association escorted her to the official's door, and her son, her daughters-in-law, and several relatives accompanied her right into his home. Other villagers trailed along and it looked as if the whole village was waiting outside the official's residence. The official himself was not a bad fellow. In fact, he was patriotic and liberal-minded. But when he saw the crowd, he became more liberal-minded than ever. He asked Mother Tsai to explain her talk with Chang, and she told him about the traffic with Wuhu and about the opium and gambling den. The opium, she pointed out, came from some corrupt officers in a provincial Chinese army farther to the west. There had never before been an opium-smoking den in the valley, and the Women's Association asked that it be closed down.

The official admitted the evil of opium and gambling, but said there was no law against either. A new opium-smoking law was expected soon; until then he urged the women to argue with the men "with love in their hearts." Old Mother Tsai replied: "We women have already argued with love in our hearts. The men will not listen. They tell us to go back to our kitchens and not interfere with men's affairs."

Mother Tsai ended the interview by announcing to the amazed official: "We women have risen. We will not allow the rich men to despise the will of the people."

Nor could the official do anything about Merchant Chang. There was no proof that he traded with the Japanese. True, he replied, men had seen him in the streets of Wuhu. But he might have slipped through the Japanese lines like other men. There was no law against this.

March 8 brought matters to a crisis. This was always celebrated throughout China as International Women's Day and the valley buzzed with preparation for a mass meeting in the great courtyard of an old ancestral temple. Men leaders had been invited to say a few words of greeting, but it was a woman's day. All the front seats in the temple courtyard were reserved for women, while soldiers, officers and civilian men were invited to sit in the back. The faces and names of the women scientists, writers and revolutionary leaders of many nations shouted at us from scores of posters. A number of them called on the women to "revive the spirit of Florence Nightingale."

On this morning Mother Tsai led the entire Women's National Salvation Association to the Army hospital to present gifts to the wounded. Before going to the wards, they called to present me with ten eggs and a chicken. Mother Tsai at very straight and asked me to tell Western women how the women of China had struggled to emancipate themselves. "You," she said, "express the high spirit of womanhood by your willingness to eat bitterness with us." I was deeply affected by her tribute.

I went with the women to the hospital wards and watched them bring in great bamboo baskets filled with eggs, cakes and half a slaughtered hog. Their husbands proudly carried the gifts down the aisles for the wounded to see and exclaim over. And when this was done, all the women gathered and sang the *Consolation for the Wounded* song, telling the soldiers, "O men of honor," that they had "suffered the wounds of war for millions of women and children."

It was a beautiful and moving scene. After it was finished, I talked with Mother Tsai and her followers. They wished to know what else they could do to help the wounded, and I proposed that they make pillows and pillow-cases, embroidering each case with such slogans as "Hero of the Nation" or "Toward the Final Victory." They accepted the idea eagerly and I started the campaign with a donation of money for cloth and silk thread, assuring them that they must not thank me, that this was my fight as well as theirs.

The mass meeting that afternoon was a tremendous success. Mother Tsai had an attack of stage fright, but conquered her fear and went on to speak of women's rights and their part in the war. Before finishing, she announced that her Association was going to root out all evils in the valley, including gambling and opium and idleness. In concluding she revealed that news had just reached her that one of her own sons had been wounded at the front. It was an honor to be the mother of a man who had suffered in such a cause, she said, and it made her own duty so much the greater.

She was about to leave the stage, but halted to stare. For all the soldiers and commanders had risen and were holding their rifles high in the air. To the stirring strains of the *Volunteer Marching Song* the old lady moved slowly off the stage.

A few days later one of the Army doctors called me out to the out-patient clinic of the hospital, and to my amazement I found old Mother Tsai lying injured on a stretcher. As I bent over her, she began in a weak voice to tell me what had happened. It was all about the opium and gambling den, she said. The Women's Association had argued with the men to close it down, and when they had refused, she and the other women had stalked into the place and peremptorily ordered the men to go home. The ruffians had shouted abuse at them. Finally Mother Tsai had brought a big stick down across the table, scattering all the money and mah-jong cubes around the room. Other women had started to follow suit, the men had fought them, and there had been a great row. Almost every woman had been beaten—Mother Tsai worst of all.

For days the valley was in an uproar. Fathers, husbands and sons, soldiers and commanders stalked about in a fury. Mother's Tsai's bed was surrounded by a crowd of women, every one of them with some sort of bruise, but all of them chattering happily. For the opium den had been closed down and Merchant Chang and every man who had beaten a woman had been jailed. "A great victory—a great victory," the women kept saying.

Old Mother Tsai appealed to me:

"Now, American comrade, write to the American Women's National Salvation Association and tell them about this. Tell them about our victory and tell them that without sacrifice there can be no victory."

I think my voice trembled a little as I said I would do that, but I sat thinking of American women—women well clad and well cared for, convinced by movies that "love" was the solution of all problems. I doubted whether many of them could appreciate the conditions under which Chinese women lived and struggled.

It was a few weeks before Mother Tsai was back on the field of battle. One day I glanced up from my desk and found her standing in the door, a small group of young women behind her—all smiling. I went outside with them and found men, women, and children carrying pillows. Each pillow-case was embroidered with flowers and birds, and across each stretched such a slogan as I had suggested. Later the women went from bed to bed, presenting each man with a pillow. The surprise and pleasure of the patients was payment enough.

There were too few pillows, however, for several wounded men had just come in, including two Japanese prisoners of war. Promising to make others for them, Mother Tsai induced two Chinese soldiers to surrender their pillows to these Japanese. With the presentation, she delivered a speech about the rights of women. The Japanese gazed up at her with amazed and embarrassed smiles.

"It's grand, simply grand," I exclaimed to a doctor. "The old lady has the Japanese on their backs, and they can't do a thing but lie there and listen to her talk about the equality of women. What a dose for them! Just what they deserved!"

MARINA TSVETAYEVA

From Verses to Chekia

Marina Tsvetayeva (1892–1941) is among the finest poets of modern Russia; Pasternak, among others, offered praise for her passionate work. Though she declared that art was for her apolitical, she wrote many verses in a spirit of opposition to the terrible era of oppression and purges under Stalin's dictatorship. She led a tragic life, caught between her husband's political loyalties to the White Russian Army and the Bolshevik revolution, and much of her life was disrupted by wars and political turmoil. Tsvetayeva lost her youngest daughter to starvation during the Moscow famine of 1919, and suffered great despair when her husband was accused of being a Soviet agent. Later, she and her family were suspected of working against the Soviet government. Her daughter and son-in-law were arrested, and Marina was exiled to Yelabuga. In 1941, in total desolation, she committed suicide by hanging herself. In the following poem, which refers to the Nazi invasion of what is today the Czech Republic and Slovakia, she portrays the eternal greed of invaders throughout history.

■

They grabbed fast, they grabbed big,
grabbed the mountains and their innards.
They grabbed our coal, and grabbed our steel
from us. They grabbed our lead and crystal.

They grabbed the sugar, and they grabbed the clover.
They grabbed the North and grabbed the West.
They grabbed the hive and grabbed the haystack.
They grabbed the South from us and grabbed the East.
They grabbed Vary and grabbed Tatras.

They grabbed the near at hand and the far off.
But worse than grabbing heaven on earth from us,
they won the fight for our native land.
They stole our bullets from us. They stole our rifles.
They grabbed our minerals and our loved ones, too.
But while our mouths hold spit,
the entire country remains armed.
Such weeping now fills our eyes,
crying with anger and passion.
Chekia's weeping.
Spain lying in its own blood,

and what a dark mountain
now shades the earth from light.
Now's the time, now's the time, now's the time
to give the billet back to God.

I decline to exist in the crazy house
of the inhuman.
I decline to go on living
in the marketplace of wolves.

I won't howl,
among the sharks of the field.
I won't swim beneath
the waves of squirming backs.
I have no need of holes for hearing
or seeing eyes.
To your crazed world there's
only one answer: No!

Translation by Daniela Gioseffi with Sophia Buzevska

SYLVIA TOWNSEND WARNER

The Drought Breaks

Sylvia Townsend Warner (1893–1978) was born and brought up at Britain's Harrow School, where her father taught history. She received no formal schooling after kindergarten, but the influence of her father developed her gifts of intellect to a high degree and made her one of the most original writers of her time. After a ten-year career in musicology, she published her first collection of poems in 1925. Her first novel, *Lolly Willowes* (1926), concerns a woman who turns to witchcraft as the only way to assert herself in the world of men. Townsend Warner published four other novels, most with historical/political themes, as well as poetry and many volumes of short stories, a form at which she excelled. Her thirty-nine-year relationship with the poet

Valentine Ackland, with whom she made her home in Dorset, is told in the volume of their collected love letters. Townsend Warner's work reflected her long involvement in revolutionary politics. She and Ackland went to Barcelona to work with the Red Cross during the Spanish Civil War in 1936, and were delegates at the Second International Writers Conference in Madrid. In this piece, she reflects the point of view of an ordinary Spanish woman, a supporter of the Republican cause, in a town that has been taken over by Franco's forces.

■

Rafaela Perez went a step or two into the street, pulling her shawl closer around her. A drizzing rain fell out of the winter sky, by midnight that rain would be snow. A cat came along, nosing in the gutters. It would not find much there, this was a poor street and the poor had no food to throw away.

In the rich quarter there was feasting and waste. The German soldiers, the Italian soldiers, were eating as they had not eaten for years. Last week a German lieutenant, tipsy, very affable, had said to her in his halting, clumsy syllables, "Spain, fine country. Much eating, much wine. Pouf!" And he had distended himself, and thumped his stomach, smiling candidly, showing his bright young teeth. "*De nada*," she had said—"It's nothing"—the conventional phrase with which one puts off a thanks or a commendation. For it did not do to give no answer at all, one must at all costs seem civil to these invaders. And she had gone on scrubbing the floor of the café, wringing out the cloth stinking of chloride of lime.

Now the cat was licking up rain-water. It would not find anything else, drink water if one can fill the belly no other way. Curious to think at all about a cat, curious to be so attentive to a grey cat slinking through the grey dusk. Ah, but life was so empty, so hideously empty, one would think of anything now, of a cat, of a cobweb.

Two days after the town was taken by the Nationalists her husband had been shot. They had not even troubled to find the gun in the chimney, the bullets padded in the mattress. His Trades Union card had been enough. One glance at it, and they were driving him out of the house, up the narrow street towards the church. A dozen other similar groups converged thither: a man, struggling, or walking in silence (Diego had walked demurely, without a word, without a glance back), and about him the soldiers and Civil Guards, and trailing after, a woman, two women, and a woman with her children. There, by the church, the firing squad was waiting, trim and powerful. And so—and so—the men were lined up against the wall, and the word was given to fire.

The bloodstains were still on the church wall and the flies buzzing round them when the church was solemnly re-sanctified. New confessionals, new hangings, new pictures and images, arrived in furniture vans and were carried in. Then had come the procession, soldiers and choir-boys, the bishop under a canopy, priests and gentlefolk and more soldiers. They, the people of the quarter, must kneel on the cobbles while the procession went by. Inside the church everything was smart and fresh, there was a smell of incense and of flowers and of varnish from the new confessionals. Outside there was the stain of blood and the smell of blood. And now, more than ever, it was impossible to escape them, impossible to say them nay, whether they came demanding alms or children.

If one's husband had been shot, then one's children must be taken also.

"Holy Church," said the Reverend Mother, her black robes seeming to fill the room, her eyebrows bristling, "Holy Church will not leave these innocents where they can be contaminated. You have three children, I think. See that they are ready by eight to-morrow morning."

The convent was far away, at the other end of the town, a heavy building with barred windows, a garden surrounded by a high wall topped with spikes. For many days the mothers of the lost children haunted there, hanging about, watching the barred windows and the spiked wall; for though there was no chance of seeing the children one might perhaps hear a voice on the other side of the wall. But there were never any voices. Twice a day one could hear a clatter of small feet, marching, marching. And so, after a time, one lost hope, did not go so often, did not go at all.

Every week the nuns came round to collect the money. They knew to a peseta how much one earned. "Your children are well. They want no other mother than the Mother of God. But they cannot be kept for nothing. We ask you in the name of the Lord and his little ones." Then the hand would glide out of the sleeve and the downcast eyes would scan the pesetas.

From the loud-speaker further up the street came the accustomed sound of the hour. A drunken vaunting voice, Queipo de Llano's, saying that Madrid would fall in a couple of days, that Valencia had been bombed, that the Catalans would not fight, that everywhere the Reds were falling back, without food, without arms, without hope. Then would come the singing, and the shouts of *Arriba España!*

It was four months and twenty-one days since the children had been taken away, and now she was standing in the rain, looking at a cat—no, looking where the cat had been, for it had long ago sneaked on its way. The street was dark and silent, as though dead. Indeed, it was half-dead, depopulated. This neighbour dead, that neighbour in prison, that neighbour gone off. People would be there in the evening, and in the morning they would have disappeared, leaving no word, no trace.

The wireless brayed on, presently there would be the national music, humstrum of guitars, snap of castanets. In the cafés of the rich quarter the foreigners would lean back in their chairs, wag their heads, stir their haunches, eye the prostitutes trailing past, say to themselves, "We are in Spain."

Later still, a noise not broadcast, there would be cries, hooting laughter, rattle of a volley. Every night, even now, they were shooting in the prisons.

In the Calle de Rosas no one stirred. Those who were left in the tall houses sat, cold and scattered, like the last leaves on a winter tree. The houses were so much colder, being half-empty: no steps on the stairs, no smells of cooking, never a laugh or a song, not even a quarrel to liven up the air.

She shook her head and sighed. Like an echo there came the noise of the wind awakening in the mountains.

The voice on the wireless bragged on. Madrid had again been bombed, a sally of the Reds had been wiped out with great slaughter, five hundred prisoners had been taken on the Basque front, an ammunition dump had blown up.

One did not listen, but yet one heard. One did not look at the placards, but yet one saw. One pulled one's shawl over one's ears, turned away one's eyes; yet through one's mind marched the newly-arrived battalions, one saw their grand equipment, one heard their strong marching and the words of command shouted in foreign tongues. A scrap of newspaper, wrapped round a bit of salt fish or a handful of olives, jabbed at one's eyes with a threat or a sneer.

And yet Diego had said that it was good to know how to read, good to take an interest in the affairs of the country.

Sometimes out of her stagnating cold misery a flash of rancour would explode like marsh-gas. If Diego had been content to work and to eat, like other men!—then, though this had come, though there had been hunger and cold and terror, there would still have been husband and children, a clue to living; and the church wall would have been only what it had been, a wall much thicker than those of the flimsy tenements around it.

The wind was rising, desolate among the stone crags. *Arriba España!* chorused the voices on the wireless, a wolfish pack-howling. Overhead a window opened softly, a head peered out.

"Rafaela! Is that you? What is it, what are you waiting for?"

"Nothing."

Without comment the head withdrew, the window was closed again. There was nothing to wait for. She must go in, chew her slow supper, lie down cold on the bed. The wind blew stronger, its voice among the mountains trembled with intensity, it was like a wild singer. The wind throbbed, came closer with its throbbing voice.

Ah! What was that?—that rending crash of sound, and after-rattle, and another and another crash? What were these jarring wings over the city? Windows opened, doors opened, the street was full of voices. Blind Adela was wailing. "It's them! Mother of God, it's them! They're going to bomb us now!"

"No, It's us, it's us! They're *ours!*"

She tore off the dripping shawl, waved it upwards in greeting, turning up her face, her heart, to the death falling from the air, as though to a greeting from life.

All around were voices, voices hushed, broken, excited; gasps, cries caught back, questions and exclamations. It was like the noise of earth, thirsty with long drought, clucking with parched lips as it drinks the rain.

LENORE MARSHALL

Political Activism and Art

Lenore Marshall (1899–1971), an American poet, essayist, and fiction writer, was known for her work in the international peace movement. She helped to found the National Committee for a Sane Nuclear Policy, popularly known as SANE, which later merged with the Nuclear Freeze Campaign to become today's National Peace Action. In this piece, written in the early 1980s, Marshall makes an eloquent statement of the need for artists to commit themselves to humanistic political activism.

O why do we write? For fame? for power? prestige? Sometimes, whether in love, in hate, in compulsion, there should still be a further reason. What are we trying to do in this world? The serious writer wants to impose his order on chaos. He has a direction, a goal, to give shape, to form an entity which is his, which represents himself. But today what order is possible? Is it realistic to believe we can shape this chaos, is it honest to set out as though what we have to say will bring clarity or hope or change, do we dare to believe or pretend that our word will be significant, faced as we are by unmanageable disorder everywhere while the great question, overshadowing all others, is the survival of the human race?

Sometimes there is an agonizing conflict for the writer who takes part in a movement in which [she] believes. . . . One wonders sometimes who one is when one feels torn limb from limb between the inner and outer lives, for one can't help it, if one believes passionately in a thing, one has to commit oneself to it. We hear about searching for our identities these days—identity crisis. Perhaps we now have to have more than one identity or perhaps the different sides really do compose into one. Who are we really? we ask. We would like to pursue a direction that is simple and clear and to arrive at our life's work. But our idea of our self-hood and the fact of it are complex. What about the writer, the poet and novelist? SANE was born in my living room in 1957. That is what I think of when I talk about political matters, of the poet (or artist) as peace worker or of the writer's divided life or the divided writer's life or the writer as activist. SANE started really through a conversation with a friend who was as concerned as I at that time about the madness of the arms race and the growing possibility of the destruction of our civilization. . . . The difference between the period in which we founded SANE and now, between yesterday and today, is that there was very little support for a peace movement then. We were considered kooks, cranks, nuts. Just one step above the Commies because, they said, if you believed in peace, that could help the enemy, so obviously you couldn't believe in peace.

At any rate, when I asked some of my writer friends to join SANE, or in some way speak out against the arms race or nuclear weapons, they would say to me, your job is to write your books. You shouldn't be engaged in these activities. Start your new novel. Of course, it was just what I was doing and wanted to do all the time. Now there are people everywhere who agree with the peace movement. Formerly there was very little to read on the subject. Now there is a large literature. Now people inform themselves about the issues. In the past, the youth generation was silent. Now there is a youth generation that *leads*, and the best of them are the best young people that we've ever had.

MURIEL RUKEYSER

Käthe Kollwitz

Muriel Rukeyser (1913–1980) was a widely respected American poet, much admired as a writer who combined exquisite craft with political commitment. A longtime advocate of women's rights, civil rights, and human rights, she served as a president of the PEN American Center and traveled to Hanoi in protest of American bombings and involvement in the Vietnam War. This poem, only one of many she composed on such themes, celebrates the life and legacy of the famed German antiwar activist and artist Käthe Kollwitz. Kollwitz lost her son in World War I and her grandson in World War II. The suffering of civilians—and especially women—in wartime is a frequent subject of her work. The first woman to hold the directorship of the German Academy of Arts, Kollwitz later had much of her work destroyed by the Nazis.

■

I

Held between wars
my lifetime
                among wars, the big hands of the world of death
my lifetime
listens to yours.

The faces of the sufferers
in the street, in dailiness,
their lives showing
through their bodies
a look as of music
the revolutionary look
that says   I am in the world
to change the world
my lifetime
is to love to endure to suffer the music
to set its portrait
up as a sheet of the world
the most moving the most alive
Easter and bone
and Faust walking among the flowers of the world
and the child alive within the living woman, music of man.
and death holding my lifetime between great hands
the hands of enduring life
that suffers the gifts and madness of full life, on earth, in our time,
and through my life, through my eyes, though my arms
     and hands
may give the face of this music in portrait waiting for
the unknown person
held in the two hands, you.

II

Woman as gates, saying:
"The process is after all like music,
like the development of a piece of music.
The fugues come back and
                            again and again
interweave.
A theme may seem to have been put aside,
but it keeps returning—
the same thing modulated,
somewhat changed in form.
Usually richer.
And it is very good that this is so."

A woman pouring her opposites.
"After all there are happy things in life too.
Why do you show only the dark side?"
"I could not answer this. But I know—
in the beginning my impulse to know
in the working life
                    had little to do with
pity or sympathy.
              I simply felt
that the life of the workers was beautiful."

She said, "I am groping in the dark."

She said, "When the door opens, of sensuality,
then you will understand it too. The struggle begins.
Never again to be free of it,
often you will feel it to be your enemy.
Sometimes
you will almost suffocate,
such joy it brings."

Saying of her husband: "My wish
is to die after Karl.
I know no person who can love as he can,
with his whole soul.

Often this love has oppressed me;
I wanted to be free.
But often too it has made me
So terribly happy."

She said: "We rowed over to Carrara at dawn,
climbed up to the marble quarries
and rowed back at night. The drops of water
fell like glittering stars
from our oars.

She said: "As a matter of fact,
I believe
          that bisexuality
is almost   a necessary factor
in artistic production; at any rate,
the tinge of masculinity within me
helped me
          in my work."

She said: "The only technique I can still manage.
It's hardly a technique at all, lithography.
In it
      only the essentials count."

A tight-lipped man in a restaurant last night saying to me:
"Kollwitz?   She's too black-and-white."

III

Held among wars, watching
          all of them
          all these people
          weavers,
          Carmagnole

Looking at
          all of them
          death, the children
          patients in waiting-rooms
          famine
          the street
          the corpse with the baby
          floating, on the dark river

A woman seeing
          the violent, inexorable
          movement of nakedness
          and the confession of No
          the confession of great weakness, war,
          all streaming to one son killed, Peter;

even the son left living; repeated,
    the father, the mother; the grandson
    another Peter killed in another war: firestorm;
    dark, light, as two hands,
    this pole and that pole as the gates.

What would happen if one woman told the truth about her life?
    The world would split open

IV / *Song: The Calling-Up*
    Rumor, stir of ripeness
    rising within this girl
    sensual blossoming
    of meaning, its light and form.

    The birth-cry summoning
    out of the male, the father
    from the warm woman
    a mother in response.

    The word of death
    calls up the fight with stone
    wrestle with grief with time
    from the material make
    an art harder than bronze.

V / *Self-Portrait*
    Mouth looking directly at you
    eyes in their inwardness looking
    directly at you
    half light   half darkness
    woman, strong, German, young artist
    flows into
    wide sensual mouth mediating
    looking right at you
    eyes shadowed with brave hand
    looking deep at you
    flows into
    wounded brave mouth
    grieving and hooded eyes
    alive, German, in her first War
    flows into
    strength of the worn face
    a skein of lines
    broods, flows into
    mothers among the war graves

bent over death
facing the father
stubborn upon the field
flows into
the marks of her knowing—
Nie Wieder Krieg
repeated in the eyes
flows into
"Seedcorn must not be ground"
and the grooved cheek
lips draw fine
the down-drawn grief
face of our age
flows into
Pieta, mother and
between her knees
life as her son in death
pouring from the sky of
one more war
flows into
face almost obliterated
hand over the mouth forever
hand over one eye now
the other great eye
closed

NADINE GORDIMER

The Artist's Rebellious Integrity

Nadine Gordimer (b. 1923) was born an English-speaking Jew in South Africa, where from an early age she resisted the pressure to conform to the white supremacist beliefs embodied in the system of apartheid. She has been politically active most of her life, and has often written about the relationships among white radicals and liberals and black people in South Africa. Her large body of internationally known works include such novels as *The Conservationist* (1974) and *Burger's Daughter* (1979), and she also excels in the short story form. In 1991 she was awarded the Nobel Prize for Literature. The excerpt comes from her Nobel acceptance speech.

■

In a period when it would be unheard of for countries such as France, Sweden and Britain to bring such charges against freedom of expression, there has risen a force that takes its appalling authority from something far more widespread than social mores, and far more powerful than the power of any single political regime. The edict of a world religion has sentenced a writer to death.

For more than three years, now, wherever he is hidden, wherever he might go, Salman Rushdie has existed under the Muslim pronouncement upon him of the *fatwa*. There is no asylum for him anywhere. Every morning when this writer sits down to write, he does not know if he will live through the day; he does not know whether the page will ever be filled. Salman Rushdie happens to be a brilliant writer, and the novel for which he is being pilloried, *The Satanic Verses*, is an innovative exploration of one of the most intense experiences of being in our era, the individual personality in transition between two cultures brought together in a post-colonial world. All is re-examined through the refraction of the imagination; the meaning of sexual and filial love, the rituals of social acceptance, the meaning of a formative religious faith for individuals removed from its subjectivity by circumstance opposing different systems of belief, religious and secular, in a different context of living. His novel is a true mythology. But although he has done for the postcolonial consciousness in Europe what Günter Grass did for the post-Nazi one with *The Tin Drum* and *Dog Years*, perhaps even has tried to approach what Beckett did for our existential anguish in *Waiting For Godot*, the level of his achievement should not matter. Even if he were a mediocre writer, his situation is the terrible concern of every fellow writer for, apart from his personal plight, what implications, what new threat against the carrier of the word does it bring? It should be the concern of individuals and above all, of governments and human rights organizations all over the world.

With dictatorships apparently vanquished, this murderous new dictate invoking the power of international terrorism in the name of a great and respected religion should and can be dealt with only by democratic governments and the United Nations as an offense against humanity. I return from the horrific singular threat to those that have been general for writers of this century now in its final, summing-up decade. In repressive regimes anywhere whether in what was the Soviet bloc, Latin America, Africa, China—most imprisoned writers have been shut away for their activities as citizens striving for liberation against the oppression of the general society to which they belong. Others have been condemned by repressive regimes for serving society by writing as well as they can; for this aesthetic venture of ours becomes subversive when the shameful secrets of our times are explored deeply, with the artist's rebellious integrity to the state of being manifest in life around her or him; then the writer's themes and characters inevitably are formed by the pressures and distortions of that society as the life of the fisherman is determined by the power of the sea.

There is a paradox. In retaining this integrity, the writer sometimes must risk both the state's indictment of treason, and the liberation forces' complaint of lack of blind commitment. As a human being, no writer can stoop to the lie of Manichean "balance." The devil always has lead in his shoes, when placed on his side of the scale. Yet, to paraphrase coarsely Márquez's dictum given by him both as a writer and a fighter for justice, the writer must take the right to explore, warts and all, both the enemy and the beloved comrade in arms, since only a try for the truth makes sense of being, only a try for the truth edges towards justice just ahead of Yeats's beast slouching to be born. In literature, from life,

we page through each other's faces
we read each looking eye
... It has taken lives to be able to do so.

These are the words of the South African poet and fighter for justice and peace in our country, Mongane Serote.

The writer is of service to humankind only insofar as the writer uses the word even against his or her own loyalties, trusts the state of being, as it is revealed, to hold somewhere in its complexity filaments of the cord of truth, able to be bound together, here and there, in art: trusts the state of being to yield somewhere fragmentary phrases of truth, which is the final word of words, never changed by our stumbling efforts to spell it out and write it down, never changed by lies, by semantic sophistry, by the dirtying of the word for the purposes of racism, sexism, prejudice, domination, the glorification of destruction, the curses and the praise-songs.

MAYA ANGELOU

And Still I Rise

Maya Angelou (b. 1928) is one of the most widely known African American women writers. Angelou wrote of her childhood amid the poverty and racism of segregated Arkansas in her most famous work, *I Know Why the Caged Bird Sings*. She has authored several subsequent volumes of memoir, screenplays, and many books of poetry, including *Just Give Me a Cool Drink of Water 'fore I Diiie, O Pray My Wings Are Gonna Fit Me Well,* and *And Still I Rise,* from which this selection comes. Much of her work is concerned with struggles for social justice, and she brings an accessible lyricism to such themes.

■

You may write me down in history
With your bitter, twisted lies,
You may trod me in the very dirt
But still, like the dust, I'll rise.

Does my sassiness upset you?
Why are you beset with gloom?
'Cause I walk like I've got oil wells
Pumping in my living room.

Just like moons and like suns,
With the certainty of tides,
Just like hopes springing high,
Still I'll rise.

Did you want to see me broken?
Bowed head and lowered eyes?

Shoulders falling down like teardrops,
Weakened by my soulful cries.

Does my haughtiness offend you?
Don't you take it awful hard
'Cause I laugh like I've got gold mines
Diggin' in my own back yard.

You may shoot me with your words,
You may cut me with your eyes,
You may kill me with your hatefulness,
But still, like the air, I'll rise.

Does my sexiness upset you?
Does it come as a surprise
That I dance like I've got diamonds
At the meeting of my thighs?

Out of the huts of history's shame
I rise
Up from a past that's rooted in pain
I rise
I'm a black ocean, leaping and wide,
Welling and swelling I bear in the tide.

Leaving behind nights of terror and fear
I rise
Into a daybreak that's wondrously clear
I rise
Bringing the gifts that my ancestors gave,
I am the dream and the hope of the slave.
I rise
I rise
I rise.

MARGARET RANDALL

Memory Says Yes

Margaret Randall (b. 1936) is an international writer of conscience whose life and work have focused on social justice and human rights. American by birth, Randall has lived in Nicaragua, Cuba, and Mexico and traveled in Vietnam, Peru, and Chile, writing often of the situation of women in these countries. Her books include *From Witness to Struggle: Christians in the Nicaraguan Revolution, Cuban Women Now, Spirit of the People: Women in Vietnam, Sandino's Daughters*, and *Inside the Nicaraguan Revolution*. She has done a good deal of translation from the

Spanish and edited the respected literary magazine *El Corno Emplumado*. Among her current works is a memoir of her life and travels.

■

All last week you preened before the mirror
viewing emerging breasts, then covering them
with gauze-thin blouse
and grinning: getting bigger, huh?
The week before you wore army fatigues
leveling breasts and teenage freckles,
tawny fuzz along your legs.
A Woman. Beginning.
Today you don fatigues again.
Today you pack, knapsack and canteen,
lace boots over heavy socks
and answer the call Reagan and Haig have slung
at your 12 years.
Yours and so many others . . .
kids, 14, 15, 18, so many others who will go
and some of them stay, their mothers shouting
before the Honduran Embassy: "Give us
our son's bodies back, give us back their bodies!"
At least that.
All last week you preened before the mirror,
moving loose to new rhythms
long weekend nights, Junior High math. Sunday beach.
Today you went off to the staccato of continuous
                    news dispatches
and I, in my trench, carry your young breasts
in my proud lonely eyes.

TONI MORRISON

From Sula

Toni Morrison (b. 1931) won the Nobel Prize for Literature in 1994. Her many award-winning novels include *The Bluest Eye* (1969), *Song of Solomon* (1977), *Beloved* (1987), and *Paradise* (1998). She is also the author of several volumes of literary criticism and social commentary, most recently *The House That Race Built* (1998). She has taught widely, and is currently a distinguished professor at Princeton University. Morrison employs harsh realism, compassion, wit, and exquisitely crafted prose in portraying the lives and history of African Americans. In this excerpt from the novel *Sula* (1973), she tells of a shell shock victim of World War I—a living casualty whose insanity seems in some ways a sane response to the madness he has witnessed on the battlefields.

■

Except for World War II, nothing ever interfered with the celebration of National Suicide Day. It had taken place every January third since 1920, although Shadrack, its founder, was for many years the only celebrant. Blasted and permanently astonished by the events of 1917, he had returned to Medallion handsome but ravaged, and even the most fastidious of people in the town sometimes caught themselves dreaming of what he must have been like a few years back before he went off to war. A young man of hardly twenty, his head full of nothing and his mouth recalling the taste of lipstick, Shadrack had found himself in December, 1917, running with his comrades across a field in France. It was his first encounter with the enemy and he didn't know whether his company was running toward them or away. For several days they had been marching, keeping close to a stream that was frozen at its edges. At one point they crossed it, and no sooner had he stepped foot on the other side than the day was adangle with shouts and explosions. Shellfire was all around him, and though he knew that this was something called *it,* he could not muster up the proper feeling—the feeling that would accommodate *it.* He expected to be terrified or exhilarated—to feel *something* very strong. In fact, he felt only the bite of a nail in his boot, which pierced the ball of his foot whenever he came down on it. The day was cold enough to make his breath visible, and he wondered for a moment at the purity and whiteness of his own breath among the dirty, gray explosions surrounding him. He ran, bayonet fixed, deep in the great sweep of men flying across this field. Wincing at the pain in his foot, he turned his head a little to the right and saw the face of a soldier near him fly off. Before he could register shock, the rest of the soldier's head disappeared under the inverted soup bowl of his helmet. But stubbornly, taking no direction from the brain, the body of the headless soldier ran on, with energy and grace, ignoring altogether the drip of brain tissue down its back.

When Shadrack opened his eyes he was propped up in a small bed. Before him on a tray was a large tin plate divided up into three triangles. In one triangle was rice, in another meat, and in the third stewed tomatoes. A small round depression held a cup of whitish liquid. Shadrack stared at the soft colors that filled these triangles: the lumpy whiteness of rice, the quivering blood tomatoes, the grayish-brown meat. All their repugnance was contained in the near balance of the triangles—a balance that soothed him, transferred some of its equilibrium to him. Thus reassured that the white, the red and the brown would stay where they were—would not explode or burst forth from their restricted zones—he suddenly felt hungry and looked around for his hands. His glance was cautious at first, for he had to be very careful—anything could be anywhere. Then he noticed two lumps beneath the beige blanket on either side of his hips. With extreme care he lifted one arm and was relieved to find his hand attached to his wrist. He tried the other and found it also. Slowly he directed one hand toward the cup and, just as he was about to spread his fingers, they began to grow in higgledy-piggledy fashion like Jack's beanstalk all over the tray and the bed. With a shriek he closed his eyes and thrust his huge growing hands under the covers. Once out of sight they seemed to shrink back to their normal size. But the yell had brought a male nurse.

"Private? We're not going to have any trouble today, are we? Are we Private?"

Shadrack looked up at a balding man dressed in a green-cotton jacket and trousers. His hair was parted low on the right side so that some twenty or thirty yellow hairs could discreetly cover the nakedness of his head.

"Come on. Pick up that spoon. Pick it up, Private. Nobody is going to feed you forever."

Sweat slid from Shadrack's armpits down his sides. He could not bear to see his hands grow again and he was frightened of the voice in the apple-green suit.

"Pick it up, I said. There's no point to this . . ." The nurse reached under the cover for Shadrack's wrist to pull out the monstrous hand. Shadrack jerked it back and overturned the tray. In panic he raised himself to his knees and tried to fling off and away his terrible fingers, but succeeded only in knocking the nurse into the next bed.

When they bound Shadrack into a straitjacket, he was both relieved and grateful, for his hands were at last hidden and confined to whatever size they had attained.

Laced and silent in his small bed, he tried to tie the loose cords in his mind. He wanted desperately to see his own face and connect it with the word "private"—the word the nurse (and the others who helped bind him) had called him. "Private" he thought was something secret, and he wondered why they looked at him and called him a secret. Still, if his hands behaved as they had done, what might he expect from his face? The fear and longing were too much for him, so he began to think of other things. That is, he let his mind slip into whatever cave mouths of memory it chose.

He saw a window that looked out on a river which he knew was full of fish. Someone was speaking softly just outside the door . . .

Shadrack's earlier violence had coincided with a memorandum from the hospital executive staff in reference to the distribution of patients in high risk areas. There was clearly a demand for space. The priority or the violence earned Shadrack his release, $217 in cash, a full suit of clothes and copies of very official-looking papers.

When he stepped out of the hospital door the grounds overwhelmed him: the cropped shrubbery, the edged lawns, the undeviating walks. Shadrack looked at the cement stretches: each one leading clearheadedly to some presumably desirable destination. There were no fences, no warnings, no obstacles at all between concrete and green grass, so one could easily ignore the tidy sweep of stone and cut out in another direction—a direction of one's own.

Shadrack stood at the foot of the hospital steps watching the heads of trees tossing ruefully but harmlessly, since their trunks were rooted too deeply in the earth to threaten him. Only the walks made him uneasy. He shifted his weight, wondering how he could get to the gate without stepping on the concrete. While plotting his course—where he would have to leap, where to skirt a clump of bushes—a loud guffaw startled him. Two men were going up the steps. Then he noticed that there were many people about, and that he was just now seeing them, or else he had just materialized. They were thin slips, like paper dolls floating down the walks. Some were seated in chairs with wheels, propelled by other paper figures from behind. All seemed to be smoking, and their arms and legs curved in the breeze. A good high wind would pull them up and away and they would land perhaps among the tops of the trees.

Shadrack took the plunge. Four steps and he was on the grass heading for the gate. He kept his head down to avoid seeing the paper people swerving and bending here and there, and he lost his way. When he looked up, he was standing by a low red building separated from the main building by a covered walkway. From somewhere came a sweetish smell which reminded him of something painful. He looked around for the gate and saw that he had gone directly away from it in his complicated journey over the grass. Just to the left of the low building was a graveled driveway that appeared to lead outside the grounds. He trotted quickly to it and left, at last, a haven of more than a year, only eight days of which he fully recollected.

Once on the road, he headed west. The long stay in the hospital had left him weak—too weak to walk steadily on the gravel shoulders of the road. He shuffled, grew dizzy, stopped for breath, started again, stumbling and sweating but refusing to wipe his temples, still afraid to look at his hands. Passengers in dark, square cars shuttered their eyes at what they took to be a drunken man.

The sun was already directly over his head when he came to a town. A few blocks of shaded streets and he was already at its heart—a pretty, quietly regulated downtown.

Exhausted, his feet clotted with pain, he sat down at the curbside to take off his shoes. He closed his eyes to avoid seeing his hands and fumbled with the laces of the heavy high-topped shoes. The nurse had tied them into a double knot, the way one does for children, and Shadrack, long unaccustomed to the manipulation of intricate things, could not get them loose. Uncoordinated, his fingernails tore away at the knots. He fought a rising hysteria that was not merely anxiety to free his aching feet: his very life depended on the release of the knots. Suddenly without raising his eyelids, he began to cry. Twenty-two years old, weak, hot, frightened, not daring to acknowledge the fact that he didn't even know who or what he was . . . with no past, no language, no tribe, no source, no address book, no comb, no pencil, no clock, no pocket handkerchief, no rug, no bed, no can opener, no faded postcard, no soap, no key, no tobacco pouch, no soiled underwear and nothing, nothing nothing to do . . . he was sure of one thing only: the unchecked monstrosity of his hands. He cried soundlessly at the curbside of a small Midwestern town wondering where the window was, and the river, and the soft voices just outside the door . . .

Through his tears he saw the fingers joining the laces, tentatively at first, then rapidly. The four fingers of each hand fused into the fabric, knotted themselves and zigzagged in and out of the tiny eyeholes.

By the time the police drove up, Shadrack was suffering from a blinding headache, which was not abated by the comfort he felt when the policemen pulled his hands away from what he thought was a permanent entanglement with his shoelaces. They took him to jail, booked him for vagrancy and intoxication, and locked him in a cell. Lying on a cot, Shadrack could only stare helplessly at the wall, so paralyzing was the pain in his head. He lay in this agony for a long while and then realized he was staring at the painted over letters of a command to fuck himself. He studied the phrase as the pain in his head subsided.

Like moonlight stealing under a window shade an idea insinuated itself: his earlier desire to see his own face. He looked for a mirror; there was none. Finally, keeping his hands carefully behind his back he made his way to the toilet bowl and peeped in. The water was unevenly lit by the sun so he could make nothing out. Returning to his cot he took the blanket and covered his head, rendering the water dark enough to see his reflection. There in the toilet water he saw a grave black face. A black so definite, so unequivocal, it astonished him. He had been harboring a skittish apprehension that he was not real—that he didn't exist at all. But when the blackness greeted him with its indisputable presence, he wanted nothing more. In his joy he took the risk of letting one edge of the blanket drop and glanced at his hands. They were still. Courteously still.

Shadrack rose and returned to the cot, where he fell into the first sleep of his new life. A sleep deeper than the hospital drugs; deeper than the pits of plums, steadier than the condor's wing; more tranquil than the curve of eggs.

The sheriff looked through the bars at the young man with the matted hair. He had read through his prisoner's papers and hailed a farmer. When Shadrack awoke, the sheriff handed him back his papers and escorted him to the back of a wagon. Shadrack got in and in less than three hours he was back in Medallion, for he had been only twenty-two miles from his window, his river, and his soft voices just outside the door.

In the back of the wagon, supported by sacks of squash and hills of pumpkins, Shadrack began a struggle that was to last for twelve days, a struggle to order and focus experience. It had to do with making a place for fear as a way of controlling it. He knew the smell of death and was terrified of it, for he could not anticipate it. It was not death or dying that frightened him, but the unexpectedness of both. In sorting it all out, he hit on the notion that if one day were devoted to it, everybody could get it out of the way and the rest of the year would be safe and free. In this manner he instituted National Suicide Day.

On the third day of the new year, he walked through the Bottom down Carpenter's Road with a cowbell and a hangman's rope calling the people together. Telling them that this was their only chance to kill themselves or each other.

At first the people in the town were frightened; they knew Shadrack was crazy but that did not mean that he didn't have any sense or, even more important, that he had no power. His eyes were so wild, his hair so long and matted, his voice was so full of authority and thunder that he caused panic on the first, or Charter, National Suicide Day in 1920. The next one, in 1921, was less frightening but still worrisome. The people had seen him a year now in between. He lived in a shack on the riverbank that had once belonged to his grandfather long time dead. On Tuesday and Friday he sold the fish he had caught that morning, the rest of the week he was drunk, loud, obscene, funny and outrageous. But he never touched anybody, never fought, never caressed. Once the people understood the boundaries and nature of madness, they could fit him, so to speak, into the scheme of things.

Then, on subsequent National Suicide Days, the grown people looked out from behind curtains as he rang his bell; a few stragglers increased their speed, and little children screamed and ran. The tetter heads tried goading him (although he was only four or five years older than they) but not for long, for his curses were stingingly personal.

As time went along, the people took less notice of these January thirds, rather they thought they did, thought they had no attitudes or feelings one way or another about Shadrack's annual solitary parade. In fact they had simply stopped remarking on the holiday because they had absorbed it into their thoughts, into their language, into their lives.

Someone said to a friend, "You sure was a long time delivering that baby. How long was you in labor?"

And the friend answered, "Bout three days. The pains started on Suicide Day and kept up till the following Sunday. Was borned on Sunday. All my boys is Sunday boys."

Some lover said to his bride-to-be, "Let's do it after New Years, 'stead of before. I get paid New Year's Eve."

And his sweetheart answered, "OK, but make sure it ain't on Suicide Day. I ain't 'bout to be listening to no cowbells whilst the weddin's going on."

Somebody's grandmother and her hens always started a layering of double yolks right after Suicide Day.

Then Reverend Deal took it up, saying the same folks who had sense enough to avoid Shadrack's call were the ones who insisted on drinking themselves to death or womanizing themselves to death. "May's well go on with Shad and save the Lamb the trouble of redemption."

Easily, quietly, Suicide Day became part of the fabric of life up in the Bottom of Medallion, Ohio.

SANDRA MORTOLA GILBERT

The Parachutist's Wife

Sandra Mortola Gilbert (b. 1936) is an accomplished poet as well as a distinguished academic and literary critic. A pioneer in feminist scholarship, she is co-author with Susan Gubar of the ground-breaking book on women's writing, *The Madwoman in the Attic*, and its sequel, *No Man's Land*. Her nine volumes of poetry include *The Ghost Volcano* (1995), *Kissing the Bread: New and Selected Poems* (2000), and *Inventions of Farewell: A Book of Elegies* (2001). This poems offers a seldom acknowledged perspective on war—the complex feelings of the woman left behind in domestic duty.

■

Six men turned to smoke in the next square
of air, their plane became wind.
You were twenty-three. Hands over your ears, a roaring
in your veins, a silence
on the radio.

Flak

knocked twice at the cockpit,
dull knuckles, thumping:
Let me in,
            let me in.

You knew you had to
give yourself to the sky the way we
give ourselves to music—no knowing
the end of the next bar, no figuring
how the chord will fall.

The clouds were cold, the plane trembled.
You pulled the cord and the chute
"bloomed like God's love," a heavenly
jockstrap anchoring you in air.

You were happy, you say, you were
never happier than that day, falling
into birth: the archaic
blue-green map of Europe glowed before you.

You were going to camp, you were
going to be free of death.
The pull of the harness, the swaying,
the ropes creaking—it was so peaceful up there,

like a page of Greek or
an afternoon in a Zen monastery
or a long slow stroll around
somebody's grandfather's garden.

I'm quiet in my kitchen, I won't
bail out, I don't think it would be the same
for me, I think if I
fell like that the hands of flak
would strip me as I
swung from the finger of God, I'd

offer myself as a bright idea
and a chorus of guns
would stammer holes in my story, nothing

would lift me over the black fangs
of the Alps, I'd dangle
like bait and the savage

map of Europe would eat me up.
I stick like grease to my oven, I wear
a necklace of dust,

my feet root in green stone.
You've forgotten I'm here!
But every morning

there are crystals of ice in my hair
and a winter distance glitters
in the centers of my eyes.

I don't need to stroll through the sky
like a hero:
in my bone cave

I marry the wind.

Darlene Keju-Johnson

Nuclear Bomb Testing on Human Guinea Pigs

Darlene Keju-Johnson (b. 1936) was born on Ebeye Island in the Marshall Islands and grew up on the northern islands, which are downwind of Bikini and Enewetak. Since her days as a graduate student in public health, she has spoken in many countries on the devastating effects of nuclear testing among the peoples and lands of the Pacific Islands. She bears witness to the evacuation of Regelap and Utirik after the people were contaminated by radioactive fallout from the 1954 explosion of a U.S. hydrogen bomb more than a thousand times stronger than the Hiroshima bomb.

■

One important date that I never forget was in the year 1946. In that year the navy official from the U.S. government came to Bikini Island. He came and told the chief Juda—and I quote—"We are testing these bombs for the good of mankind, and to end all world wars."

In 1946 very few of us Marshallese spoke English or even understood it. The chief could not understand what it all meant, but there was one word that stuck in his mind and that was "mankind." The only reason why he knows the word "mankind" is because it is in the Bible. So he looked at the man, the navy official, and he says, "If it is in the name of God, I am willing to let my people go."

When the navy official came, it was too late. There were already thousands of soldiers and scientists on the atoll and hundreds of airplanes and ships in the Bikini lagoon. They were ready to conduct the tests. The Bikinians had no choice but to leave their islands, and they have never returned. The navy official did not tell the chief that the Bikinians would not see their home again. Today Bikini is off limits for 30,000 years. In other words Bikini will not be safe for these Bikinian people ever again.

The Bikinians were promised that the United States only wanted their islands for a short time. The chief thought maybe a short time is next week, maybe next month. So they moved to Rongerik.

Rongerik is a sandbar island. There are no resources on it. It was too poor to feed the people. We live on our oceans—it's like our supermarket—and from our land we get breadfruit and other foods. But on Rongerik there was nothing. The United States put the Bikinians on this island and left them there. After a year they sent a military medical official to see how they were. When he got there he found out that they were starving. Imagine; move someone else from their own home, by your power. Dump them on a little sand. And don't even bother to go back and see how they are doing for a year.

The people of Bikini have been moved, or relocated, three times. The people of Enewetak Atoll were also relocated. You cannot imagine the psychological problems that people have to go through because of relocation.

In 1954 the United States exploded a hydrogen bomb, code named BRAVO, on Bikini. It was more than 1,000 times stronger than the Hiroshima bomb. The Marshallese were never told about this bomb. We were never even warned that this blast was about to happen on our islands. Instead we experienced white fallout. The people were frightened by the fallout. The southern area of our islands turned yellow. And the children played in it. But when the fallout went on their skins, it burnt them. People were vomiting.

The people of Rongelap and Utirik were not picked up until three days after the explosion. It was horrible. Some American soldiers came and said, "Get ready. Jump in the ocean and get on the boat because we are leaving. Don't bring any belongings. Just go in the water." That's your home and you have to decide, with your husband and children, whether you are going to leave or not. But there was no time. People had to run fast. There was no boat to get the people, not even the children and the old people, to the ship. People had to swim with their children. It was very rough. When they got to the ship each family was given one blanket. Some families had 10 or 12 children, and they had to share one blanket.

They were taken to Kwajalein. It took one night to get there. They didn't even give people a change of clothing, so it meant they had to sleep in their contaminated clothing all the way. You imagine. They are burnt, they are vomiting. When they got to Kwajalein they were given soap and were told to wash in the lagoon. The soap and salt water was supposed to wash off the radiation. They were not told what happened, why it had happened, what was wrong with them. Their hair was falling out, their fingernails were falling off . . . but they were never told why.

The people of Rongelap and Utirik were on Kwajalein for three months before they were moved again. The people of Utirik went back to their contaminated island. The people of Rongelap didn't return to Rongelap for three years: it was too contaminated.

Twenty-eight American men who were on Rongerik monitoring the tests and the crew of a nearby Japanese fishing boat were also contaminated. We are in touch with one of these men who were studying the test. He has told us that the United States knew that the wind was blowing towards islands where people lived, but that they went ahead and tested anyway. It was not a mistake. It is interesting that the United States government moved the Marshallese in the 1940s when the small bombs were being tested, and then when the biggest bomb ever was tested the Marshallese were not even warned. This is why we believe that we have been used as guinea pigs.

Since the testing there has been a tremendous increase in health problems. The biggest problem we have now, especially among women and children, is cancers. We have cancers in the breast. We have tumour cancers. The women have cancers in their private places. Children are being deformed. I saw a child from Rongelap. It is an infant. Its feet are like clubs. And another child whose hands are like nothing at all. It is mentally retarded. Some of the children suffer growth retardation.

Now we have this problem of what we call "jellyfish babies." These babies are born like jellyfish. They have no eyes. They have no heads. They have no arms. They have no legs. They do not shape like human beings at all. But they are being born on the labour table. The most colourful, ugly things you have ever seen. Some of them have hairs on them. And they breathe. This ugly "thing" only lives for a few hours. When they die they are buried right away. A lot of times they don't allow the mother to see this kind of baby because she'll go crazy. It is almost too inhumane.

Many women today are frightened of having these "jellyfish babies." I have had two tumours taken out of me recently and I fear that if I have children they will be "jellyfish babies" also. These babies are being born not only on the radioactive islands but now throughout the 35 atolls and five islands of the Marshalls. I've interviewed hundreds of Marshallese women in the northern islands and this is their story I am telling you. The health problems are on the increase. They have not stopped.

It is not just the people who have been affected but also our environment. . . .

The United States is only leasing the islands but can you imagine if it owned them? That is why in 1982 the people of Kwajalein decided to take direct action. They sailed in to take over eleven off-limits islands and lived there for four months. A thousand people. They were saying to the United States, "You are not going to treat us like second-class citizens in our own islands!" They shut the base down. The missile testing was stopped.

The United States government, after all these years, has never conducted an epidemiological survey. The Department of Energy sends their medical team. But they will only go to the two islands that the United States recognizes as affected by the fallout from the 1954 bomb—Rongelap and Utirik. But there are many others. And it is interesting that they will not check the children. They will only check those people who were on Rongelap and Utirik in 1954. . . .

Marshallese are fed up with the DOE and the United States government. We are asking for an independent radiological survey. We want to do it outside of the United States government.

This is what happened with the Rongelap people. They said, "We have had enough! You are not going to treat us like animals, like nothing at all! We are moving." So they moved from Rongelap with the Greenpeace ship, *Rainbow*

Warrior. The whole island, 350 people, moved to live on Mejato, which is a small island in Kwajalein Atoll. Kwajalein landowners gave them that island. But the United States wouldn't help. Instead they did a campaign to discredit the Rongelapese.

By doing this the Rongelap people said that they don't want to be part of this whole nuclear craziness. And that their bottom line is, "We care about our children's future." Because they know that they are contaminated. They had to come to a very hard decision. Leaving your island in the Marshalls is not easy. So they decided to that their children came first. They know they'll be dying out soon. They are dying now—slowly.

We are only small—very few thousand people out there on tiny islands, but we are doing our part to stop this nuclear madness. And although we are few we have done it! Which means you can do it too! But we need your support. We must come together to save this world for our children and the future generations to come.

LUISA VALENZUELA

I Am Your Horse in the Night

Luisa Valenzuela (b. 1938), the celebrated Argentine author, published her first novel, *Hay que sonreír*, at the age of twenty, and her first collection of stories at twenty-one. Since then she has written for numerous journals and published many books. Her work was introduced to the American reading public with *Clara* (1976). Other works published in English include *The Censors* (1992), *Bedside Manners* (1995), and *Black Novel with Argentines* (2002). Julio Cortazar has called Valenzuela "a woman deeply anchored in her conditions; she is conscious of the still horrible discriminations of our continent, yet she is filled with a joy of life." This story, from *Other Weapons*, is one of many concerning the terror and torture experienced in Argentina during the worst of the Perón years, and in many other nations of South and Central America.

∎

The doorbell rang: three short rings and one long one. That was the signal, and I got up, annoyed and a little frightened; it could be them, and then again, maybe not; at these ungodly hours of the night it could be a trap. I opened the door expecting anything except him, face to face, at last.

He came in quickly and locked the door behind him before embracing me. So much in character, so cautious, first and foremost checking his—our—rear guard. Then he took me in his arms without saying a word, not even holding me too tight but letting all the emotions of our new encounter overflow, telling me so much by merely holding me in his arms and kissing me slowly. I think he never had much faith in words, and there he was, as silent as ever, sending me messages in the form of caresses.

We finally stepped back to look at one another from head to foot, not eye to eye, out of focus. And I was able to say Hello showing scarcely any surprise despite all those months when I had no idea where he could have been, and I was able to say

I thought you were fighting up north

I thought you'd been caught

I thought you were in hiding

I thought you'd been tortured and killed

I thought you were theorizing about the revolution in another country

Just one of many ways to tell him I'd been thinking of him, I hadn't stopped thinking of him or felt as if I'd been betrayed. And there he was, always so goddamn curious, so much the master of his actions.

"Quiet, Chiquita. You're much better off not knowing what I've been up to."

Then he pulled out his treasures, potential clues that at the time eluded me: a bottle of cachaça, and a Gal Costa record. What had he been up to in Brazil? What was he planning to do next? What had brought him back, risking his life, knowing they were after him? Then I stopped asking myself questions (quiet, Chiquita, he'd say). Come here, Chiquita, he was saying, and I chose to let myself sink into the joy of having him back again, trying not to worry. What would happen to us tomorrow, and the days that followed?

Cachaça's a good drink. It goes down and up and down all the right tracks, and then stops to warm up the corners that need it most. Gal Costa's voice is hot, she envelops us in its sound and half-dancing, half-floating, we reach the bed. We lie down and keep on staring deep into each other's eyes, continue caressing each other without allowing ourselves to give in to the pure senses just yet. We continue recognizing, rediscovering each other.

Beto, I say, looking at him. I know that isn't his real name, but it's the only one I can call him out loud. He replies:

"We'll make it someday, Chiquita, but let's not talk now."

It's better that way. Better if he doesn't start talking about how we'll make it someday and ruin the wonder of what we're about to attain right now, the two of us, all alone.

"A noite eu so teu cavalo," Gal Costa suddenly sings from the record player.

"I'm your horse in the night," I translate slowly. And so as to bind him in a spell and stop him from thinking about other things:

"It's a saint's song, like in the macumba. Someone who's in a trance says she's the horse of the spirit who's riding her, she's his mount."

"Chiquita, you're always getting carried away with the esoteric meanings and witchcraft. You know perfectly well that she isn't talking about spirits. If you're my horse in the night it's because I ride you like this, see? . . . Like this. . . . That's all."

It was so long, so deep and so insistent, charged with affection, that we ended up exhausted. I fell asleep with him still on top of me.

I'm your horse in the night.

The goddamn phone pulled me out in waves from a deep well. Making an enormous effort to wake up, I walked over to the receiver, thinking it could be Beto, sure, who was no longer by my side, sure, following his inveterate habit of running away while I'm asleep without a word about where he's gone. To protect me, he says.

From the other end of the line, a voice I thought belonged to Andrés—the one we call Andrés—began to tell me:

"They found Beto dead, floating down the river near the other bank. It looks as if they threw him alive out of a chopper. He's all bloated and decomposed after six days in the water, but I'm almost sure it's him."

"No, it can't be Beto," I shouted carelessly. Suddenly the voice no longer sounded like Andrés: it felt foreign, impersonal.

"You think so?"

"Who is this?" Only then did I think to ask. But that very moment they hung up.

Ten, fifteen minutes? How long must I have stayed there staring at the phone like an idiot until the police arrived? I didn't expect them. But, then again, how could I not? Their hands feeling me, their voices insulting and threatening, the house searched, turned inside out. But I already knew. So what did I care if they broke every breakable object and tore apart my dresser?

They wouldn't find a thing. My only real possession was a dream and they can't deprive me of my dreams just like that. My dream the night before, when Beto was there with me and we loved each other. I'd dreamed it, dreamed every bit of it, I was deeply convinced that I'd dreamed it all in the richest detail, even in full color. And dreams are none of the cops' business.

They want reality, tangible facts, the kind I couldn't even begin to give them.

Where is he, you saw him, he was here with you, where did he go? Speak up, or you'll be sorry. Let's hear you sing, bitch, we know he came to see you, where is he, where is he holed up? He's in the city, come on, spill it, we know he came to get you.

I haven't heard a word from him in months. He abandoned me, I haven't heard from him in months. He ran away, went underground. What do I know, he ran off with someone else, he's in another country. What do I know, he abandoned me, I hate him, I know nothing.

(Go ahead, burn me with your cigarettes, kick me all you wish, threaten, go ahead, stick a mouse in me so it'll eat my insides out, pull my nails out, do as you please. Would I make something up for that? Would I tell you he was here when a thousand years ago he left me forever?)

I'm not about to tell them my dreams. Why should they care? I haven't seen that so-called Beto in more than six months, and I loved him. The man simply vanished. I only run into him in my dreams, and they're bad dreams that often become nightmares.

Beto, you know now, if it's true that they killed you, or wherever you may be, Beto, I'm your horse in the night and you can inhabit me whenever you wish, even if I'm behind bars. Beto, now that I'm in jail I know that I dreamed you that night; it was just a dream. And if by some wild chance there's a Gal Costa record and a half-empty bottle of cachaça in my house, I hope they'll forgive me: I will them out of existence.

Translation by Deborah Bonner

ILEANA MALANCIOIU

Antigone

Ileana Malancioiu (b. 1940) received a doctorate in philosophy from Bucharest University, has worked for Romanian television, and has been an editor with the monthly literary magazine *Viata Romaneasca*. One of the most prolific of contemporary Romanian poets, she has published more than ten volumes of poems since 1967, and won the poetry prize of the Writers' Union in 1970. This poem starkly depicts an eternal tragedy through the use of an ancient story: while the "mighty emperors" make war, it is most often the women who are left to mourn and bury their dead with dignity.

■

A frozen mound, white body of a dead man
fallen in hard battle and left above the Earth.
Hungry dogs come to bite the treacherous snow
and another winter comes, too, to take its bite.

Let a pure woman appear to break the command,
to wrench the unbelievable hill from the dogs
and hide it as a dear brother
while those near her wash their hands of it

and allow her to be buried alive in the earth
clothed in unreal white,
for as the emperor lost his great battle
she wept and buried her frozen mound.

Translation by Daniela Gioseffi with Ivana Spalatin

ISABEL ALLENDE

From The House of the Spirits: The Hour of Truth

Isabel Allende (b. 1942) is a Chilean novelist and one of the most renowned contemporary Latin American authors. She was born in Lima, Peru, and has lived outside Chile since the assassination of her uncle, President Salvador Allende, in a U.S.-supported coup in 1973. Her fiction is marked by its lush imagery and storytelling, as well as its political and feminist themes. Her books include *Of Love and Shadows* (1984), *Eva Luna* (1987), *The Infinite Plan* (1991), *Paula* (1995), *Aphrodite: A Memoir of the Senses* (1998), *Daughter of Fortune* (1999), *Portrait in Sepia* (2001), and *City of Beasts* (2002). *The House of the Spirits* (1982), from which this excerpt comes, is her best-known novel. It tells the story of a Chilean family over three generations—including, as here, the human rights abuses under the dictatorship of General Augusto Pinochet. In a gripping translation by the accomplished American writer Magda Bogin, Allende vividly re-creates the climate of terror and violence in which so many people live.

■

Alba was curled up in the darkness. They had ripped the tape from her eyes and replaced it with a tight bandage. She was afraid. As she recalled her Uncle Nicolás's training, and his warning about the danger of being afraid of fear, she concentrated on trying to control the shaking of her body and shutting her ears to the terrifying sounds that reached her side. She tried to visualize her happiest moments with Miguel, groping for a means to outwit time and find the strength for what she knew lay ahead. She told herself that she had to endure a few hours without her nerves betraying her, until her grandfather was able to set in motion the heavy machinery of his power and influence to get her out of there. She searched her memory for a trip to the coast with Miguel, in autumn, long before the hurricane of events had turned the world upside down, when things were still called by familiar names and words that had a single meaning; when people, freedom, and *compañero* were just that—people, freedom, and *compañero*—and had not yet become passwords. She tried to relive that moment—the damp red earth and the intense scent of the pine and eucalyptus forests in which a carpet of dry leaves lay steeping after the long hot summer and where the coppery sunlight filtered down through the treetops. She tried to recall the cold, the silence, and that precious feeling of owning the world, of being twenty years old and having her whole life ahead of her, of making love slowly and calmly, drunk with the scent of the forest and their love, without a past, without suspecting the future, with just the incredible richness of that present moment in which they stared at each other, smelled each other, kissed each other, and among the trees and the sound of the nearby waves breaking against the rocks at the foot of the cliff, exploding in a crash of pungent surf, and the two of them embracing underneath a single poncho like Siamese twins, laughing and swearing that this would last forever, that they were the only ones in the whole world who had discovered love.

Alba heard the screams, the long moans, and the radio playing full blast. The woods, Miguel, and love were lost in the deep well of her terror and she resigned herself to facing her fate without subterfuge.

She calculated that a whole night and the better part of the following day had passed when the door was finally opened and two men took her from her cell. With insults and threats they led her in to Colonel García, whom she could recognize blindfolded by his habitual cruelty, even before he opened his mouth. She felt his hands take her face, his thick fingers touch her ears and neck.

"Now you're going to tell me where your lover is," he told her. "That will save us both a lot of unpleasantness."

Alba breathed a sigh of relief. That meant they had not arrested Miguel!

"I want to go to the bathroom," Alba said in the strongest voice she could summon up.

"I see you're not planning to cooperate, Alba. That's too bad." García sighed. "The boys will have to do their job. I can't stand in their way."

There was a brief silence and she made a superhuman effort to remember the pine forest and Miguel's love, but her ideas got tangled up and she no longer knew if she was dreaming or where this stench of sweat, excrement, blood, and urine was coming from, or the radio announcer describing some Finnish goals that had nothing to do with her in the middle of other, nearer, more clearly audible shouts. A brutal slap knocked her to the floor. Violent hands lifted her to her feet. Ferocious fingers fastened themselves to her breasts, crushing her nipples. She was completely overcome by fear. Strange voices pressed in on her. She heard Miguel's name but did not know what they were asking her, and kept repeating a monumental *no* while they beat her, manhandled her, pulled off her blouse, and she could no longer think, could only say *no, no,* and *no* and calculate how much longer she could resist before her strength gave out, not knowing this was only the beginning, until she felt herself begin to faint and the men left her alone, lying on the floor, for what seemed to her a very short time.

She soon heard García's voice again and guessed it was his hands that were helping her to her feet, leading her toward a chair, straightening her clothes, and buttoning her blouse.

"My God!" he said. "Look what they've done to you! I warned you, Alba. Try to relax now, I'm going to give you a cup of coffee."

Alba began to cry. The warm liquid brought her back to life, but she could not taste it because when she swallowed it was mixed with blood. García held the cup, guiding it carefully toward her lips like a nurse.

"Do you want a cigarette?"

"I want to go to the bathroom," she said, pronouncing each syllable with difficulty with her swollen lips.

"Of course, Alba. They'll take you to the bathroom and then you can get some rest. I'm your friend. I understand your situation perfectly. You're in love, and that's why you want to protect him. I know you don't have anything to do with the guerrillas. But the boys don't believe me when I tell them. They won't be satisfied until you tell them where Miguel is. Actually they've already got him surrounded. They know exactly where he is. They'll catch him, but they want to be sure that you have nothing to do with the guerrillas. You understand? If you protect him and refuse to talk, they'll continue to suspect you. Tell them what they want to know and then I'll personally escort you home. You'll tell them, right?"

"I want to go to the bathroom," Alba repeated.

"I see you're just as stubborn as your grandfather. All right. You can go to the bathroom. I'm going to give you a chance to think things over," García said.

They took her to a toilet and she was forced to ignore the man who stood beside her, holding on to her arm. After that they returned her to her cell. In the tiny, solitary cube where she was being held, she tried to clarify her thoughts, but she was tortured by the pain of her beating, her thirst, the bandage pressing on her temples, the drone of the radio, the terror of approaching footsteps and her relief when they moved away, the shouts and the orders. She curled up like a fetus on the floor and surrendered to her pain. She remained in that position for hours, perhaps days. A man came twice to take her to the bathroom. He led her to a fetid lavatory where she was unable to wash because there was no water. He allowed her a minute, placing her on the toilet seat next to another person as silent and sluggish as herself. She could not tell if it was a woman or a man. At first she wept, wishing her Uncle Nicolás had given her a special course in how to withstand humiliation, which she found worse than pain, but finally she resigned herself to her own filth and stopped thinking about her unbearable need to wash. They gave her boiled corn, a small piece of chicken, and a bit of ice cream, which she identified by their taste, smell, and temperature, and which she wolfed down with her hands, astonished to be given such luxurious food, unexpected in a place like that. . . .

The third time they took her in to Esteban García, Alba was more prepared, because through the walls of her cell she could hear what was going on in the next room, where they were interrogating other prisoners, and she had no illusions. She did not even try to evoke the woods where she had shared the joy of love.

"Well, Alba, I've given you time to think things over. Now the two of us are going to talk and you're going to tell me where Miguel is and we're going to get this over with quickly," García said.

"I want to go to the bathroom," Alba answered.

"I see you're making fun of me, Alba," he said. "I'm sorry, but we don't have any time to waste."

Alba made no response.

"Take off your clothes!" García ordered in another voice.

She did not obey. They stripped her violently, pulling off her slacks despite her kicking. The memory of adolescence and Miguel's kiss in the garden gave her the strength of hatred. She struggled against him, until they got tired of beating her and gave her a short break, which she used to invoke the understanding spirits of her grandmother, so that they would help her die. But no one answered her call for help. Two hands lifted her up, and four laid her on a cold, hard metal cot with springs that hurt her back, and bound her wrists and ankles with leather thongs.

"For the last time, Alba. Where is Miguel?" García asked.

She shook her head in silence. They had tied her down with another thong.

"When you're ready to talk, raise a finger." He said.

Alba heard another voice.

"I'll work the machine," it said.

Then she felt the atrocious pain that coursed through her body, filling it completely, and that she would never forget as long as she lived. She sank into darkness.

"Bastards! I told you to be careful with her!" she heard Esteban García say from far away. She felt them opening her eyelids, but all she saw was a misty brightness. Then she felt a prick in her arm and sank back into unconsciousness.

A century later Alba awoke wet and naked. She did not know if she was bathed in sweat, or water, or urine. She could not move, recalled nothing, and had no idea where she was or what had caused the intense pain that had reduced her to a heap of raw meat. She felt the thirst of the Sahara and called out for water.

"Wait, *compañera*," someone said beside her. "Wait until morning. If you drink water, you'll get convulsions, and you could die."

She opened her eyes. They were no longer bandaged. A vaguely familiar face was leaning over her, and hands were wrapping her in a blanket.

"Do you remember me? I'm Ana Díaz. We went to the university together. Don't you recognize me?"

Alba shook her head, closed her eyes, and surrendered to the sweet illusion of death. But she awakened a few hours later, and when she moved she realized that she ached to the last fibre of her body.

"You'll feel better soon," said a woman who was stroking her face and pushing away the locks of damp hair that hid her eyes. "Don't move, and try to relax. I'll be here next to you. You need to rest."

"What happened?" Alba whispered.

"They really roughed you up, *compañera*," the other woman said sadly.

"Who are you?" Alba asked.

"Ana Díaz. I've been here for a week. They also got my *compañero*, Andrés, but he's still alive. I see him once a day, when they take him to the bathroom."

"Ana Díaz?" Alba murmured.

"That's right. We weren't so close back then, but it's never too late to start. The truth is, you're the last person I expected to meet here, Countess," the woman said gently. "Don't talk now. Try to sleep. That way the time will go faster for you. Your memory will gradually come back. Don't worry. It's because of the electricity."

But Alba was unable to sleep, for the door of her cell opened and a man walked in.

"Put the bandage back on her!" he ordered Ana Díaz.

"Please . . . can't you see how weak she is? Let her rest a little while. . . ."

"Do as I say!"

Ana bent over the cot and put the bandage over her eyes. Then she removed the blanket and tried to dress her, but the guard pulled her away, lifted the prisoner by her arms, and sat her up. Another man came in to help him, and between them they carried her out because she could not walk. Alba was sure that she was dying, if she was not already dead. She could tell they were walking down a hallway in which the sound of their footsteps echoed. She felt a hand on her face, lifting her head.

"You can give her water. Wash her and give her another shot. See if she can swallow some coffee and bring her back to me," García said.

"Do you want us to dress her?"

"No."

Alba was in García's hands a long time. After a few days, he realized she had recognized him, but he did not abandon his precaution of keeping her blindfolded, even when they were alone. Every day new prisoners arrived and others were led away. Alba heard the vehicles, the shouts, and the gate being closed. She tried to keep track of the number of prisoners, but it was almost impossible. Ana Díaz thought there were close to two hundred. García was very busy, but he never let a day go by without seeing Alba, alternating unbridled violence with the pretense that he was her good friend. At times he appeared to be genuinely moved, personally spooning soup into her mouth, but the day he plunged her head into a bucket full of excrement until she fainted from disgust, Alba understood that he was not trying to learn Miguel's true whereabouts but to avenge himself for injuries that had been inflicted on him from birth, and that nothing she could confess would have any effect on her fate as the private prisoner of Colonel García. This allowed her to venture slowly out of the private circle of her terror. Her fear began to ebb and she was able to feel compassion for the others, for those they hung by their arms, for the newcomers, for the man whose shackled legs were run over by a truck. They brought all the prisoners into the courtyard at dawn and forced them to watch, because this was also a personal matter between the colonel and his prisoner. It was the first time Alba had opened her eyes outside the darkness of her cell, and the gentle splendor of the morning and the frost shining on the stones, where puddles of rain had collected overnight, seemed unbearably radiant to her. They dragged the man, who offered no resistance, out into the courtyard. He could not stand, and they left him lying on the ground. The guards had covered their faces with handkerchiefs so no one would ever be able to identify them in the improbable event that circumstances changed. Alba closed her eyes when she heard the truck's engine, but she could not close her ears to the sound of his howl, which stayed in her memory forever. . . .

One day Colonel García was surprised to find himself caressing Alba like a lover and talking to her of his childhood in the country, when he would see her walking hand in hand with her grandfather dressed in her starched pinafores and with the green halo of her hair, while he, barefoot in the mud, swore that one day he would make her pay for her arrogance and avenge himself for his cursed bastard fate. Rigid and absent, naked and trembling with disgust and cold, Alba neither heard nor felt him, but that crack in his eagerness to torture her sounded an alarm in the colonel's mind. He ordered Alba to be thrown in the doghouse, and furiously prepared to forget that she existed.

The doghouse was a small, sealed cell like a dark, frozen, airless tomb. There were six of them altogether, constructed in an empty water tank especially for punishment. They were used for relatively short stretches of time, because no one could withstand them very long, at most a few days, before beginning to ramble— to lose sense of things, the meanings of words, and the anxiety of passing time— or simply, beginning to die. At first, huddled in her sepulcher, unable to stand up or sit down despite her small size. Alba managed to stave off madness. Now that she was alone, she realized how much she needed Ana Díaz. She thought she heard an imperceptible tapping in the distance, as if someone were sending her coded messages from another cell, but she soon stopped paying attention to it because she realized that all attempts at communications were completely hopeless. She gave up, deciding to end this torture once and for all. She stopped eating, and only when her feebleness became too much for her did she take a sip of water. She tried not to breathe or move, and began eagerly to await her death. She stayed like this for a long time. . . .Word went out that she was dying. The guards opened the hatch of the doghouse and lifted her effortlessly, because she was very light. They took her back to Colonel García, whose hatred had returned during these days, but she did not recognize him. She was beyond his power.

Translation by Magda Bogin

RUTH ROSEN

Blind, Unpredictable Terror

Ruth Rosen (b. 1945) is professor emerita of history at the University of California, Davis, where she co-founded the women's studies program. She is author *The World Split Open: How the Modern Women's Movement Changed America* (2001) and *The Lost Sisterhood: Prostitution in America, 1900–1918* (1983) and editor of *The Maimie Papers: Letters from an Ex-Prostitute* (1979). In addition to producing many scholarly articles, Rosen is an editorial writer and columnist at the *San Francisco Chronicle*, where this article first appeared shortly after September 11, 2001.

■

As the days grow shorter, I leave work in the dark, attuned to dangers that don't arrive in envelopes. I get off the train, walk through dark streets, tightly gripping my keys and whistle (my weapon of choice). The night, I am reminded, belongs to those who terrorize women with rape. Just one serial rapist can terrorize half of the population.

Most women know of what I speak. If we thought about it too much, we'd be paralyzed by fear. So we stride with purpose, take precautions, go about our lives and hope for the best. This is just one type of terror that we, as a society, have come to accept as a regrettable but normal part of our daily life.

Terror, unfortunately, is not new in America. For more than a century, African Americans in the South endured the daily threat of lynchings and fire-bombings by white terrorists committed to defending Southern apartheid. Today, in poor neighborhoods across the country, frantic parents face the threat of stray bullets hitting their innocent children. Every morning, abortion providers—longtime targets of homegrown terrorists—slip on protective bullet-proof vests once reserved for riot police. Every year, some unknown number of wives and girlfriends are battered—and then murdered—by the inexplicable rage of a husband, ex-husband or boyfriend.

Some Americans have never encountered such stomach-churning terror. They are the lucky ones, whose lives have not been upended by domestic violence, rape, drive-by shootings, firebomb attacks, a life-threatening disease, or some other close encounter with death. They are also among the newly stricken, who suddenly feel the icy shiver of fear. They worry about opening their mail. They're afraid of flying. They avoid tall buildings, underground trains and long, arching bridges. To them our hearts should open, for terror has seized their spirit as they realize, perhaps for the first time, that they, too, are mortal.

At the same time, these newly frightened folks have a unique opportunity to empathize with those who live with relentless fear. Just look around. Terror surrounds us. On the corner is a mentally ill, homeless woman. She lives in sheer terror. Voices haunt her waking hours; nightmares shatter her sleep. In a doctor's office, someone silently confronts a diagnosis of a life-threatening disease. In thousands of homes, the newly unemployed worry how they will care for their families. In New York, dazed children and bereaved spouses fear the future. In mail rooms, workers are terrified to do their jobs. In distant countries, parents fear land mines will maim or kill their kids playing on old battlefields. In a Pakistan refugee camp, a woman must decide which child to feed.

These are tough times. But please don't forget the ordinary terror that people endure every day. And for heaven's sake, don't look to our current political leaders for inspiration. If you want to tame your fears, watch those who live with blind, unpredictable terror. They know how to transcend their fears—with courage and humor—so that they wake and face another day.

MICHELE NAJLIS

They Followed Us into the Night

Michele Najlis (b. 1946) is a citizen of Nicaragua. She was one of the founders of the literary political publication *Ventana*, and has published several volumes of poetry, including *El Viento Armado* and *Augurios*. Her work demonstrates a strong solidarity with the Sandanista revolution of the 1970s, and all struggles against oppressive and unjust governments. In this poem, she defiantly asserts the determination of ordinary people in the face of nearly unimaginable brutality.

■

They followed us into the night,
they trapped us,
leaving us no defense
but our hands
united with millions of hands.
We were flogged and made to spit up blood.
Our bodies were filled with electric shocks
and our mouths with lime.
For whole nights
we were left out in the wild,
or thrown into timeless cells.
Our nails were torn out,
our blood
splattered on walls,
even on their faces,
but still,
our hands
are united with millions of hands.

Translation by Amina Muñoz-Ali

ALENKA BERMUDEZ

Guatamala, Your Blood

Alenka Bermudez (b. circa 1950) was born in Santiago, Chile, but settled in her husband's homeland, Guatemala, and has also worked in Nicaragua representing the Guatemalan Cultural
Workers Association. One of her sons was killed in combat in Guatemala during the long popular resistance to the country's military regime. Like Michele Najlis, she writes eloquently of the
people's endurance in the face of crushing poverty and oppression.

■

". . .why doesn't your poetry
talk to us about dreams, leaves,
the huge volcanos of your native land?
Come look at the blood in the streets.
—Pablo Neruda

Where is the word that will fill in for hunger
and what name can you give to this daily wanting
how to describe the empty table the abysmal eyes
little bellies swollen   forheads deformed
by weights   the endless burden of centuries
horizons of smoke   burned-up mattresses
no frying pan
scarcity in the stew that's left over because of scarcity
what substantive to use
how to name a finger cut off to get the insurance
what adjective for the holocaust
in what tense do you conjugate the verb to kill
what predicate what future what pluperfect

and when they plunder the roots and change the course of rivers
and they inundate the riverbeds with poison and everything
dies everything dies
when the sap in the trees is threatened crouching hidden
and seeing that death doesn't have gender or case
that it installs itself multiplies and scatters itself
indiscriminate unlimited specialized and computed
which quartet or triplet will it fit into
in which precious alexandrine
ineffable hendecasyllabic mysterious elegy of nothingness

I reserve the right to use the Spanish word
to tell you: death to death
and victory to life
and combat and battle and machetes to life

and courage and tenderness to life
I reserve the right of the precisely exact
Spanish word
to name death and to name life
as long as the blood holds itself suspended
in our trees.

Translation by Sara Miles

CAROLYN FORCHÉ

Return

Carolyn Forché (b. 1950), born in Detroit, Michigan, is a passionate poet, essayist, and human rights activist whose political concerns and experiences deeply inform her writing. She spent time as a journalist in El Salvador from 1978 to 1980, and was among the first U.S. writers to expose the horrors going on there during the bloody civil conflict in which U.S.-supported death squads terrorized the population. This poem exemplifies her insistence that artists must bear witness to such atrocities. Forché is the author of several books of poetry, including *The Angel of History* (1994), *The Country Between Us* (1982), and *Gathering the Tribes* (1976). She is also the editor of *Against Forgetting: Twentieth-Century Poetry of Witness* (1993). Among her translations are Claribel Alegría's *Flowers from the Volcano* (1983) and Robert Desnos's *Selected Poetry* (with William Kulik, 1991). Her honors include fellowships from the Guggenheim Foundation, the Lannan Foundation, and the National Endowment for the Arts. In 1992, she received the Charity Randall Citation from the International Poetry Forum. Forché teaches in the MFA Program at George Mason University in Fairfax, Virginia.

■

—For Josephine Crum

Upon my return to America, Josephine:
the iced drinks and paper umbrellas, clean
toilets and Los Angeles palm trees moving
like lean women, I was afraid more than
I had been, even of motels, so much so
that for months every tire blow-out
was final, every strange car near the house
kept watch and I strained even to remember
things impossible to forget. You took
my stories apart for hours, sitting
on your sofa with your legs under you
and fifty years in your face.
        So you know
now, you said, what kind of money
is involved and that *campesinos* knife
one another and you know you should

not trust anyone and so you find a few
people you will trust. You know the mix
of machetes with whiskey, the slip of the tongue
that costs hundreds of deaths.
You've seen the pits where men and women
are kept the few days it takes without
food and water. You've heard the cocktail
conversation on which their release depends.
So you've come to understand why
men and women of good will read
torture reports with fascination.
Such things as water pumps
and co-op farms are of little importance
and take years.
It is not Che Guevara, this struggle.
Camillo Torres is dead. Victor Jara
was rounded up with the others, and José
Martí is a landing strip for planes
from Miami to Cuba. Go try on
Americans your long, dull story
of corruption, but better to give
them what they want: Lil Milagro Ramirez,
who after years of confinement did not
know what year it was, how she walked
with help and was forced to shit in public.
Tell them about the razor, the live wire,
dry ice and concrete, grey rats and above all
who fucked her, how many times and when.
Tell them about retaliation: José lying
on the flat bed truck, waving his stumps
in your face, his hands cut off by his
captors and thrown to the many acres
of cotton, lost, still, and holding
the last few lumps of leeched earth.
Tell them of José in his last few hours
and later how, many months later,
a labor leader was cut to pieces and buried.
Tell them how his friends found
the soldiers and made them dig him up
and ask forgiveness of the corpse, once
it was assembled again on the ground
like a man. As for the cars, of course
they watch you and for this don't flatter
yourself. We are all watched. We are
all assembled.

Josephine, I tell you
I have not rested, not since I drove
those streets with a gun in my lap,
not since all manner of speaking has
failed and the remnant of my life
continues onward. I go mad, for example,
in the Safeway, at the many heads
of lettuce, papayas and sugar, pineapples
and coffee, especially the coffee.
And when I speak to American men,
there is some absence of recognition:
their constant Scotch and fine white
hands, many hours of business, penises
hardened by motor inns and a faint
resemblance to their wives. I cannot
keep going. I remember the American
attaché in that country: his tanks
of fish, his clicking pen, his rapt
devotion to reports. His wife wrote
his reports. She said as much as she
gathered him each day from the embassy
compound, that she was tired of covering
up, sick of his drinking and the loss
of his last promotion. She was a woman
who flew her own plane, stalling out
after four martinis to taxi on an empty
field in the *campo* and to those men
and women announce she was there to help.
She flew where she pleased in that country
with her drunken kindness, while Marines
in white gloves were assigned to protect
her husband. It was difficult work, what
with the suspicion on the rise in smaller
countries that gringos die like other men.
I cannot, Josephine, talk to them.

And so, you say, you've learned a little
about starvation: a child like a supper scrap
filling with worms, many children strung
together, as if they were cut from paper
and all in a delicate chain. And that people
who rescue physicists, lawyers and poets
lie in their beds at night with reports
of mice introduced into women, of men
whose testicles are crushed like eggs.

That they cup their own parts
with their bedsheets and move themselves
slowly, imagining bracelets affixing
their wrists to a wall where the naked
are pinned, where the naked are tied open
and left to the hands of those who erase
what they touch. We are all erased
by them, and no longer resemble decent
men. We no longer have the hearts,
the strength, the lives of women.
Your problem is not your life as it is
in America, not that your hands, as you
tell me, are tied to do something. It is
that you were born to an island of greed
and grace where you have this sense
of yourself as apart from others. It is
not your right to feel powerless. Better
people than you were powerless.
You have not returned to your country,
but to a life you never left.

HANNAH SAFRAN AND
DONNA SPIEGELMAN

If Someone Else Is Suffering:
An Interview

Hannah Safran (b. circa 1960) of Israel served as the coordinator of Isha L'Isha, the Haifa Feminist Center, between 1987 and 1996, and was involved in creating the hotline and emergency shelter for battered women. Since 1996, she has been the coordinator of the women's studies program at Haifa University, where she recently completed her Ph.D. dissertation on the history of feminism in Israel. She is a co-founder of the Israeli Coalition of Women for a Just Peace, a coalition of nine Israeli women's peace groups working to end the Israeli occupation and bring about a just and peaceful solution to the Israeli-Palestinian conflict. She recently visited Boston, and spoke at New Words Bookstore in Cambridge in an evening co-sponsored by Boston Women in Black, Jewish Women for Justice in Israel/Palestine, *Sojourner* magazine, and New Words. There she was interviewed by Donna Spiegelman (b. 1955), who is co-coordinator of Boston Women in Black and a member of the Organizing Committee of Brit Tzedek v'Shalom: Jewish Alliance for Justice and Peace, a new national organization of U.S. Jews. The interview appeared in *Sojourner* in May 2002.

■

DS: What organizations do you work with?

HS: At this time, I'm mainly involved with Women in Black in Haifa, which is a vigil that takes place once a week. We hold signs against the occupation, and we are now located in seven or eight places around Israel. The vigils started in 1988, when the first Intifada began, and the number of vigils has grown significantly ever since. In an historical perspective, Women in Black has had a significant moral impact on Israeli society. On the other hand, it's sometimes very difficult when you live in Israel not to do more, because you are so angry about what Israel is doing in the occupied territories. So we decided to form a coalition of women the Coalition of Women for a Just Peace and that coalition brought together nine different organizations, including Bat Shalom, a Jerusalem-based organization; Women in Black; WILPF, the Israeli branch of the Women's International League for Peace and Freedom; and TANDI, which is a Palestinian-Israeli peace movement. We thought that if we worked together, then we could organize larger events, get money from U.S. supporters, including Jews, of course, see our activities publicized in the media, and so on. We were able to do it, and I became very active in the coalition. Lately, a group of us lesbian/gay people who call ourselves Black Laundry marched in the last pride parade, in Tel Aviv with signs against the occupation. This was very unusual within the parade, very political.

DS: In so many situations here in the United States in the lesbian and gay movement, there are people who don't want to bring up other issues because they might lose their credibility on lesbian and gay rights. And on the other hand, the same sort of thing exists in the peace movement: if there are too many out lesbians there's a fear that there's a hidden agenda, say, that the lesbians really are concerned about lesbian rights, not about peace. Or that it's going to scare away people who are homophobic from even joining the movement. Does that come up for you?

HS: If we liberate ourselves as gay people, as lesbians, but we still live in a society that oppresses others, then what does our own liberation mean? The next day, it will be gone. I really believe if you are here to resist oppression, you have to be much wider in scope. And if you think that by talking about more than one oppression you may lose your battle, I think you are fooling yourselves. Violence is violence is violence, whether against lesbian and gay people, women, or Palestinians. It's much better to work together. Then we are bigger and might achieve our goals earlier. If you really have a peaceful society in your head, and you really want to achieve that, you have to connect to what is in your heart, peace and love and compassion. Otherwise, there's no point.

DS: Maybe you can tell us a little bit more about the Israeli occupation; what is the occupation and what is the problem with it?

HS: The problem with it is that you conquer a land inhabited by other people whose language you don't speak, who do not want you there, and then you bring your settlements over, you take the water, you take the land, you take everything. Israeli policy since 1993 was to build roads that cut the West Bank into pieces, preventing people from going from one place to another, preventing them from entering Jerusalem. It's totally evil because when you take away another people's freedom, what's left? Israel should restore the borders of the 1967 war. It will leave the Palestinians with a very small state, only 22 percent of the original Palestine in 1947, before Israel's independence. Still, there are enough people in Palestine and Israel who are ready to accept this solution. But there is a very extreme group of people, who believe that the entire Israel, greater Israel, should belong to the state of Israel. They do not recognize the Palestinians as human beings.

DS: But aren't they a minority, these people?

HS: They are a very vocal minority, they have an influence on the government, and I have a feeling that even Sharon thinks like that. What else could it mean when Sharon says that he would like to see Arafat killed? Arafat is the symbolic hero of Palestinians, like Herzl or Ben-Gurion for the Zionists. So it's none of Sharon's business who the Palestinians elect as their national hero or leader.

DS: You have said that Israel should withdraw to the pre-1967 borders. What if the Israeli settlers refuse to return to Israel?

HS: They can stay there. They can be Palestinian citizens. Twenty percent of Israeli citizens are Palestinian, so I don't mind if 20 percent of Palestine is composed of Israelis or Jews. If they choose to be Palestinian citizens, I'm sure they will be treated as well as Israeli Arabs are here—as second-class citizens. [*laughter*]

DS: You said earlier that the occupation is something we Israelis have to end for ourselves. That the occupation is our problem. Can you elaborate on that?

HS: I do not agree to any single policy of Israel since 1967. And I do not agree to the occupation. I will not stop resisting Israeli policies until Israel restores the pre-1967 borders and lets Palestinians decide what they want in their own country, what sort of government, who their leader will be. If you have conquered another people and these people resist, then it is your problem to withdraw from those territories and let them live their own lives. Because if you remain there against their will, and you try to impose your own way of life and your own occupation, your own army, and so on, then you keep on doing something that will destroy you in the long run. Because if you are doing something immoral, then your society will not be one in which you can live a decent life.

DS: But can't people just put their heads in the sand and almost not know?

HS: Most of us do. Because it's so devastating. Once you are aware, you find yourself asking, "What can I do?" And many, many people cannot get organized or get up and demonstrate.

DS: But then I wonder, how could people not know?

HS: Well the whole society is run in a way that allows people not to know. Not everybody has a son or husband in the army. Not every soldier is in the occupied territories. My son is in the army and he's never been in the occupied territories. On top of everything, newspapers and other media will not tell you what is actually going on.

DS: Is there some way that all of this has also corrupted the fabric of Palestinian morality, in that parents are allowing their children to participate in the Intifada?

HS: You cannot control your children when you're so hungry you cannot offer them food, you cannot offer them work or a future or even running water in your home. And we did the same thing in Israel with our young people when we were fighting for a state. But I am not an expert about Palestinians. I'm really concerned about the future of Israel. And I'm convinced that the well-being of Palestinians is the only way for Israel to live as a peaceful and normal society.

DS: And what about Jerusalem?

HS: It should not be divided; it should be the capital of [both] the Palestinians and the Israelis. It should have a joint police force, joint water authority, electricity everything. And if people insist on having something separate, then it's fine with me. You can have two different mayors both women, of course [*laughter*]. This vision of a border with Jerusalem will take time. You need to build it in stages. And these had been our hopes for the Oslo agreement, that it would create the stages necessary in order to achieve peace. But, unfortunately, the Oslo agreement did not really go deep enough into peace education. Peace means something much more than the absence of war. It means educating for peace. It means all our kids learning Arabic. It means undoing racism. It means demilitarizing Israeli society. It means sharing water with the Palestinians. It means a million and one things that Israel has not done since the Oslo agreement. So, the whole idea of the Oslo agreement actually and practically did not work, and we are now suffering the results. Two years ago, before the Intifada started, the Palestinians in most of Palestine did not have running water for more than two or three days a week. At the same time, their Jewish neighbors in the settlements did have water not only in their tubs but in the garden, and sometimes even in a swimming pool. So of course you become angry. If you see your neighbors freely traveling to Jerusalem to go shopping, to the movies, or to the hospital and you cannot, then of course you're angry. If you have 60 percent unemployment and your neighbors in Israel are enjoying the good life, of course you're angry. So obviously the Intifada was inevitable, because how long can you suffer?

DS: Some people don't want to make statements condemning violence, because they say people have the right to self-defense and to wage a struggle of liberation for their own freedom that sometimes needs to involve violent means.

HS: I do not support Palestinian violence. I support a peaceful solution. I can, at the same time, both condemn violence and demand that Israel withdraw from the occupied territories and give the Palestinians full rights to self-determination, a national state, and so on.

DS: And what about the Palestinian refugee issue?

HS: About how many Palestinian refugees are there? There are approximately 3.6 million Palestinian refugees registered with the United Nations Relief and Works Agency. About one-third live in the West Bank and Gaza, slightly more than one-third in Jordan, 17 percent (700,000) in Syria and Lebanon, and 15 percent spread equally among other Arab countries and the West. Israel should agree to say out loud that there are Palestinian refugees, that Israel is responsible for these refugees as much as anyone else. That is very important, the very act of recognizing the fact that there are Palestinian refugees and they were living in what is today Israel before 1948 or 1967.

DS: We were taught in the Jewish communities we grew up in that Israel or Palestine was this empty land waiting for the Jews to come back and redevelop it after its being neglected for thousands of years. For some of us here, it's been a very painful realization that it was a place where there were many people living and agriculture and cities and so on. Were Israelis taught the same thing?

HS: Yes.

DS: When did you find out it wasn't empty? Because that's a shocking realization, and it's shocking to me to discover that Israelis living right there on the land would be unaware of its recent history!

HS: Eventually people like Rabin published his memoirs [in 1979]. He tells the story about the 1948 war when they conquered Ramle and looted and expelled the people. So it's not a secret anymore that Israel was not only populated by Palestinians, but that Israel itself expelled people from their homes in the 1948 war. And everybody knows about Deir Yassin, the village near Jerusalem where the entire [Arab] population was murdered by the Irgun, an armed Jewish underground organization founded in 1931. So we also had our own terrorists called terrorists by other Jewish people. After the war, Israel did not allow even one single Palestinian refugee to return to her or his own land, even if those refugees still lived inside Israel. We are suggesting five different options for the refugees and their children. First, some may want to be compensated financially for their property. Some may want to immigrate, to go to Canada, the United States, England, or Australia. Let's ask these countries to provide quotas for those Palestinians to immigrate there; that would be the second option. Some refugees would like to return to Israel and live as Israeli Palestinians. But not all of them will come, because, first of all, they'll soon discover that their original homes no longer exist. Some may discover that their original homes are occupied by other people, so they cannot enter them. Some will not choose to live in Israel as second-class citizens. Say 100,000 people still insist on coming back. Each year 20,000 can come back, and then the following year, another 20,000. Some of them would like to come back to the occupied territories, to the new Palestine. Some of them will not want to accept anything, like the Jews who didn't want to accept the reparation payments from Germany.

DS: What about this issue of the Jewish character of Israel, if Palestinian refugees are invited to return to Israel in anything more than a token number?

HS: Since 1992 one million people immigrated to Israel from Russia, from the ex-U.S.S.R. Close to a third of them are not Jews. So now, ten years later, we have an extra million people in the state of Israel, not all of them Jewish, most of them unable to speak Hebrew because they are from Russia. Has Israel become less Jewish? Has Israel produced fewer novels in Hebrew? Have we had less poetry written in Hebrew?

DS: How do you explain the U.S.-Israel connection?

HS: The United States has interests in the Middle East, mainly oil. Nothing to do with people. Nothing to do with Jewish history. And it needs Israel as its policeman, making use of the U.S. armament. We provide the soldiers, you provide the ammunition. We fly your airplanes, your F-16s, your Apache helicopters. The U.S. needs Israel to serve as its policeman there. It needs the oil and it will do everything to keep control over those who are cooperative, and those who are not cooperative, like Iraq, will be boycotted.

DS: So you don't think that the American Jewish lobby has anything to do with this?

HS: I don't think the American Jewish lobby is distinct from the American non-Jewish lobby, from the oil industry. If Israel is a liability for the United States, the U.S. could have said plainly and forcefully, "You have to withdraw out of the territories. And if you don't do it, then we don't give you money or ammunition." Israel would withdraw the next day because it cannot do what it does without U.S. money. And if American Jewry thinks the American [Jewish] lobby does anything good on behalf of Israel, they are totally and utterly wrong.

DS: Especially in Israel, I don't see why most people don't see things the way you do, where daily life is so degraded by hatred and fear of terrorism.

HS: Our leaders have spent most of their adult life in the army. They do not know what it means to take public transportation. I would like women with a different way of thinking, with a feminist perspective of our society, women who are nonviolent, to take over. Some of what I said is directly connected to women's understanding of the oppression of women and of the other in our case, the Palestinians. You have to connect with other people, otherwise your own achievements and success are in danger and meaningless. Because what's the meaning of me enjoying my life if some else is suffering?

KIMIKO HAHN

The Bath

Kimiko Hahn (b. 1955), an award-winning American poet, is the author of six collections of poetry: *The Artist's Daughter* (2002); *Mosquito and Ant* (2000); *Volatile* (1999); *The Unbearable Heart* (1996), which was awarded an American Book Award; *Earshot* (1992), which received the Theodore Roethke Memorial Poetry Prize and an Association of Asian American Studies Literature Award; and *Air Pocket* (1988). In 1995 she wrote ten portraits of women for the MTV special *Ain't Nuthin, but a She-Thing*. She has received fellowships from the National Endowment of the Arts, New York Foundation for the Arts, and Lila Wallace-Reader's Digest Fund. The mother of two daughters and a professor in the English department at Queens College, CUNY, Hahn is working on a collection of poetry and prose, which draws on her own heritage by utilizing the classical Japanese forms *tanka* and *zuihitsu*. Here she takes on the voice of a Japanese survivor of the atomic bombing of Hiroshima.

■

—August 6, 1945

Bathing the summer night
off my arms and breasts
I heard a plane
overheard *I heard*
the door rattle
froze

then relaxed
in the cool water
one more moment
one private moment
before waking the children
and mother-in-law,
before the heat
before the midday heat
drenched my spirits again.
I had wanted
to also relax
in thoughts of my husband
when he was drafted
imprisoned—but didn't dare
and rose from the tub,
dried off lightly
and slipped on cotton work pants.
Caution drew me to the window
and there an enormous blossom of fire
a hand changed my life
and made the world shiver—
a light that tore flesh
so it slipped off limbs,
swelled so
no one could recognize
a mother or a child
a hand that tore the door open
pushed me on the floor
ripped me up—
I will never have children again
so even today
my hair has not grown back
my teeth still shards
and one eye blind
and it would be easy,
satisfying somehow
to write it off as history
those men are there
each time I close
my one good eye
each time or lay blame
on men or militarists
the children cry out
in my sleep
where they still live
for the sake of a night's rest.

But it isn't air raids
simply
that we survive
but *gold worth its weight*
in blood the coal,
oil, uranium we mine
and drill
yet cannot call our own.
And it would be gratifying
to be called a survivor
I am a survivor
since I live if I didn't wonder
about survival today—
at 55, widowed at 18—
if I didn't feel
the same oppressive August heat
auto parts in South Africa,
Mexico, Alabama,
and shiver not from memory
or terror
but anger
but anger that this wounded body
must stand *take a stand*
and cry out
as only a new born baby can cry—
I live, I will live
I will to live
in spite of history
to make history
in my vision of peace—
that morning in the bath
so calm
so much my right
though I cannot return to that moment
I bring these words to you
hoping to hold you
to hold you
and to take hold.

Molyda Szymusiak

From The Stones Cry Out: A Cambodian Childhood

Molyda Szymusiak (b. 1962) was born Buth Keo in Phnom Penh. Following the 1975 Khmer Rouge takeover, she and her family were driven out of the capital into the Cambodian country-side. Most of her immediate family was massacred or starved in the famine that accompanied the Khmer Rouge reign of terror. Along with three other surviving family members, she arrived at the Kao I Dange refugee facility on the Thai border in 1980. In 1981, they traveled to Paris, where she and two of her cousins were adopted by Polish exiles, Jan and Carmen Szymusiak. While still in her twenties, Molyda Szymusiak published her moving memoir (originally written in French) of her childhood from 1975 to 1980.

■

The war had been raging out in the countryside for a long time, but during the last two years in particular peasants had been streaming into the city, passing by our neighborhood, Tuol Svay Prey, not far from the sports stadium. My parents had long forbidden me to go walking alone. Rockets often flew over our heads when we went to school, but we hadn't gone to school for several days. One afternoon my Aunt Vathana, a young girl not yet eighteen, came to get me for a motorbike ride. I always enjoyed going off with her; the tree-lined avenues gave us the illusion of being out in the country. We were approaching the Chinese hospital when the motorbike skidded and I heard what sounded like a tire bursting. My aunt stopped short. Sitting behind her sidesaddle on the bike, I clung tightly to her belt, listening to the whistle of the shells. A man on a bicycle went past us, and I was stunned to see that he was still pedaling even though his head had been blown off! His bike crashed into the closed front gate of a high school, the Lycée du 18-Mars. A few people were sprawled on the sidewalk, and we could hear the sirens of several ambulances. We ran home terror-stricken, drag-ging the motorbike with its flat tire. Vathana went home to her mother while I slipped quietly into my parents' house. My maternal grandmother lived next door to us with her two daughters, Vathana and my Aunt Nang, the mother of my cousin Tôn Ny, who would be so close to me in the months to come.

The next day was April 16, 1975, of evil memory: the heaviest shelling I remember, fires everywhere, the sky full of smoke, and explosions in every part of the city. My family—my parents, four daughters of whom I was the second oldest at twelve, and a little four-year-old brother—had been joined by the fam-ily of my Uncle Vong, whom we called Mitia Mir, with his wife, Nang, and their nine children: the oldest, Tôn Ny, was eleven, and the youngest, Sreï Peu, was eighteen months. We spent the day together in a deep trench that had been dug at the far end of the garden. Nearby my father and uncle buried a rifle and a pis-tol, family souvenirs that had never been used. I later learned that there had been a directive ordering everyone to hand in all weapons in their possession.

The next morning, everything was calm. No one dared to go out; we were waiting for something to happen. Suddenly we heard cheering and triumphant cries: "Kampuchea is free!" Through closed windows we saw the crowd of loiter-ers and homeless people who straggled around the city all day line up on both sides of the avenue, while down the center of the pavement, in single file, were marching kids in black pants and jackets, their guns on their shoulders, wearing sandals made out of pieces of tires. Without a word or a smile, they stared straight ahead. They were heading toward the center of the city. My sister pointed out to me a jeep at the head of the line, with a white flag flying over it. My father and uncle rushed to tear up a sheet, making a white flag that they hung from the window. To go out into the street, they changed from their overly "bourgeois" trousers into a cloth they wrapped around their hips, Gandhi-fashion. Was that what liberation was all about? Suddenly I heard them run back inside the house and rummage through the bathroom for a large towel—a red one. "The red flag is up; we have to have a red flag or they'll ransack the house!" The kid soldiers didn't look as if they wanted to loot anything; they just kept coming on silently, without looking at anything or anybody. My father waved his red flag. After the young soldiers came men who seemed a little older, dressed in black like the others, but their outfits were dirty, even filthy. One of them called out to us: "We've come to save you" or "to help you," I couldn't hear too clearly. My father opened the door and seemed about to go out, but the man shouted, "Don't come out! We're going to clean up the city first, there are thieves looting the stores." We had heard, in fact, that under cover of the bombardment some people were breaking into grocery and jewelry stores.

Toward noon, we were about to have something to eat when a motorbike stopped in front of the house. My father went to see, and I followed him: it was a Khmer Rouge. "Get your things together," he said. "You have to get moving as soon as possible. You're going two or three kilometers from here, you'll be told where. We have to empty out the city. And whatever you do, don't think you can hide in the house!"

We all packed our bags, then ate a little rice and grilled fish. Our parents got the luggage ready. Father was still able to buy twenty small loaves of bread and some butter. Mother and my aunt brought out small packs wrapped in blankets to hang on both ends of the bamboo poles the adults would carry on their shoulders. Everything was collected by the front steps. Night fell; the surrounding silence was broken only by dogs howling in the neighborhood. We waited, hoping that perhaps we wouldn't have to leave after all. In any case, there wasn't any hurry. Thousands of people passed in front of our door, heading out of the city, and then nothing more. The children stayed in the house, curled up on the rugs and in the armchairs. The two men positioned themselves, with blankets, behind the front gate at the street. I huddled against the garden wall, frightened and shivering in the damp night air.

Suddenly we heard cries and banging on our neighbors' front gates: "Come out! Come out!" No one stirred. The house was apparently empty. I prayed to heaven that they wouldn't see us. They stopped in front of our gate. "Is anyone there?" No answer. Please don't let them break open the gate! No, their footsteps faded away.

We got what sleep we could, but my mother awakened us at daybreak; we had to leave after all. We redid our luggage, tied up in sheets. Everyone got a portion of rice to carry on his or her head.

The sun had just come up, and along came a Khmer Rouge: "Come on, let's go, you have to get out of here!"

"But I don't know where to go," my father said.

"Three kilometers out of town. Hurry up, we have to clean out the city. After that, you can come back, it'll take two or three days."

Small groups of people began to pass in front of our house. They seemed tired already—only the children ran from one group to another. We began to load up our bundles, but there were way too many, and we had to leave about half of them in the vestibule. If we were going to be coming back in two or three days . . . I ran quickly to see my big doll once more, patiently sitting on a straw mat. We had to leave all our beautiful things: books, paintings, statues, rugs. I did see my mother slip a few saucepans into a bundle, with some small silver articles, ashtrays, I think, and a few pieces of silk. Finally, everyone had a bundle to carry. A Khmer Rouge passed by. "Come on, hurry up! If you're not gone by nine o'clock, I'll blow up your house!"

What could we do? We left. It was already hot. The children lagged behind, the crowd was getting jammed together. We had to hang on to each other. Our dog Bobo, a young Alsatian, tried to follow us.

"No, no, that's not allowed, no dogs!"

"Go back, Bobo, we'll be home in three days."

We left him inside the front gate, but he managed to get out and slip back to us. It was impossible to catch him, so my uncle called him: "Come here, Bobo! Now go home, you have to guard the house." The dog obeyed and turned back, his tail drooping. I tried to get a last glimpse of him, but I had to watch where I was going to keep from getting lost. It was hard to move forward surrounded by people tightly packed together, bumping into each other. It was almost ten o'clock and we hadn't even gone one kilometer. At noon it was impossible to stop and fix something to eat. We would move two steps ahead, put down our luggage, then another step, then another. Hours went by. It was going to be night soon and we were only at the Phnom Boko Cinema, in the middle of the city, normally just a short trip from the house. Two of my mother's brothers joined us from the surging flood of humanity. "Where is Grandmother?" they asked. For three weeks she had been at the bedside of my cousin Sy Neang, in the hospital: he had been hit by a car while riding his bicycle and had a broken leg. In the general uproar no one had worried about them. "We have to go get them." So back my uncles went, struggling against the flow of the crowd. They returned in an hour, saying the Khmer Rouge wouldn't allow anyone to go toward the center of the city. It was beginning to be chilly, and we huddled together on the sidewalk at the edge of the steps leading up to the movie theater. We all ate a sandwich. Under the cover of darkness, my two uncles set out again into the city, returning at dawn: the hospital had been evacuated. A Khmer Rouge told them he had seen an old lady pushing a carriage with a little boy. Sy Neang was only nine years old, and his mother didn't want to go any farther until he had been found, so my two uncles went off to look for him once more. That was the last we ever saw of them.

We had to get moving again, so Sy Neang's father tried to encourage his wife, saying that his mother-in-law was an energetic woman and that she'd find a way to join up with us—and his intuition proved correct. Meanwhile, we had to move forward in tiny steps. The west wind began to bring us disquieting odors: many people had been killed over by the airport, where the fuel depot was on fire. Straight ahead we could see a thick cloud of smoke. The outskirts of Phnom Penh were in ruins. We stopped behind a stretch of wall to prepare something to eat. I collected dry leaves and old papers to start a fire and cook a bit of rice. With the heat, the dust, and the smell of decay, there were innumerable flies whirling around our heads and we had to chase them away constantly. A fire engine made its way through the crowd with two Khmer Rouge hanging on at the back, looking the crowd over as if they were searching for something. "Can we help you?" shouted my father, or maybe it was my uncle.

"Are you mechanics?"

"Yes."

"Then come with us!"

We watched them go off together, swallowed up by the crowd. We didn't dare move. After what seemed to us a very long time, a Mercedes made its way through the crowd, followed by a truck, with my uncle at the wheel. He had managed to start the broken-down truck again, and the Khmer Rouge had offered to take his family along.

"But there are two families."

"Get them in the truck!"

Without asking any questions, we tossed our baggage into the truck as it slowly moved along with the crowd. The two women climbed in first, and the children were handed up to them. We weren't really going any faster, but at least we weren't dragging ourselves along and constantly checking to see if all the children were still with us.

And yet, when I looked at all those poor people pressing in on us from all sides, I was sad and ashamed. It was as if the crowd itself were carrying us along. I would almost have welcomed their envy, but they looked at us without expression, doubtless assuming we belonged to a new class of exploiters. In the midst of the ruins, on the edges of what had been a street, I could see corpses lying here and there. Families had stopped nearby to cook their rice—there was no space anywhere else. And the waves of people went slowly by. They moved out of the way just a bit to let the truck pass through their midst. The children were silent, crushed by the heat. Our mothers were in a corner of the truck, and my father was at the back with the two Khmer Rouge.

"Why did you take us with you?" he asked them.

"We're Sihanouk Khmer," said one of them, looking at his companion.

"You're not all the same?"

"Yes, but there are different groups. We're from the East. Here, the North is in command, under Khieu Samphan."

I didn't really understand what they meant. I knew about Prince Sihanouk; my uncle was distantly related to him and used to go to receptions at the palace. We were familiar with the palace, since Father worked near it, in the official government buildings. I knew my parents weren't happy with Sihanouk's policies, but I didn't know why. At home, the adults spoke French among themselves, a language I didn't understand yet. I had been about to start school at the Lycée Descartes, where I would have learned French.

The truck moved slowly out of the city, then suddenly made a right turn down a broad avenue, leaving the crowd behind. In a huge park, many soldiers were bustling about under the trees. A vast courtyard with a building at one end came into view: the palace of President Lon Nol. We used to come here on walks, when the Prince still lived there. The place was called Cham Kamoun. Now I was horrified to see headless corpses spread out on the ground. No one paid any attention to them. Soldiers were drilling. Two young Khmer Rouge started toward the truck, but went inside to talk to the driver of the Mercedes, which had pulled up alongside. The Mercedes was transporting a shipment of medical supplies, but this wasn't its destination. We set off again.

Back in the middle of the crowd, we inched along, coming to Bar Knol—I recognized the way: it was the road we used to take every week to our house in the country. Here again there were bodies on either side of the road, with entire families weeping over their dead. We stopped for a moment; the people around us pushed ahead to get onto the bridge. Wondering if my grandmother and Sy Neang might be here, I looked for them in the crowd. On the other side of the bridge the road became wider, and we pulled off onto the shoulder. Hoping to get some rice cooked, we looked for a little space among the throngs of people. The heat was unbearable, and there wasn't one tree on that swampy terrain. From our neighbors' conversations we learned that many people had died on the other side of the river, near the silos of rice just before the bridge. They were starving and had tried to break into a silo, but the bombardments had weakened it, and it collapsed on the unfortunate people, crushing them under tons of rice in a cloud of dust.

It was time to get moving again. There was another bridge over the Mekong River to cross which put us on Highway 1, heading toward Svay Rieng. It was still very hot. My father knew this route very well and offered to take over the driving from my uncle Mitia Mir, who was exhausted and glad to hand over the wheel. He wanted to stop at our country house and wait there for events to sort themselves out, but the Khmer Rouge had told him that was impossible. "We're going to collect supplies and ammunition there for the army. The house doesn't belong to you anymore, it belongs to the Khmer nation."

"Could we stop there for just five minutes?"

"No. Make up your minds. Either you stay there on your own or you come with us."

"But where are you going?"

"To Kah Ky village. It's a reorganization center for our men."

"Okay, we'll go with you."

Two or three hours went by, and the crowd around the truck began to thin out somewhat. At the end of the afternoon we halted at the edge of Kah Ky village, finding a spot for ourselves among the people encamped everywhere. We were all stiff from the long ride, and our whole band of children had a refreshing dip in a big duck pond. My mother and aunt busied themselves fixing a meal for us.

The Khmer Rouge soldier who had been most talkative had gone off for a moment. Accompanied by a small boy, he returned with two or three jute sacks containing about twenty pounds of freshly slaughtered chickens. "Take this, you're going to need it." We couldn't believe our eyes.

The Khmer Rouge had introduced us as his family to our closest "neighbors"; his name was Sakhron. After the meal he produced a guitar from out of nowhere and played music while we danced. After sundown the truck went back to Phnom Penh, but Sakhron stayed with our group. In the cool of the evening, under a clump of trees, he told us that he had been in the forest with Pol Pot's men for ten years. "My heart is not with the Khmer Rouge," he said. "If you like, I'll take you into Prey Veng Province, on the Vietnamese border. In any case, you can't go back to your house in Prek Heng, so close to Phnom Penh."

Neither my parents nor my aunt and uncle wanted to go to the frontier. "You're wrong," Sakhron told us. "If you're related to the royal family, you won't survive here."

The next day he brought us fruit and told us it came from Prey Veng Province. "There are Sihanouk Khmer in Prey Veng, it's your only chance." My parents were doubtful and wondered if they should still have faith in the Prince. "If you don't believe me, do as you like. In the meantime, take this bag of medicine, you can always trade it for food."

One morning Sakhron announced that he was leaving for Phnom Penh. "I'll try to find out about Sy Neang and his grandmother. I'll also bring you back some sarongs and material. Wait for me here." Six days later he came back—it was impossible to get into Phnom Penh, and the Khmer Rouge guards had fired at him. He had escaped only by throwing himself into the Mekong, where he swam all night, hanging on to a big piece of mangrove root. "I'm going to report this to general headquarters in Prey Veng." He left with the Mercedes and returned that evening bringing sugar, soybeans, and other provisions for us, but he didn't tell us what authorities had said to him regarding Phnom Penh. He insisted once more that we must make a decision.

"Do you want to come to Prey Veng?"

Our parents told him no.

"Think about it some more. You don't have a chance here. I'm definitely leaving tomorrow."

Just after he left at daybreak, two young Khmer Rouge came up to us.

"You have until eight o'clock to get out of here."

"To go where?"

"Anywhere. Not here. You don't belong to this village."

Father conferred with my uncle about us all going together to our country house; Mitia Mir thought it would be better to get a bit farther away from Phnom Penh. They decided we should go to Bal Kâs, an island in the middle of the Mekong, far from the main network of roads. Our fathers found two boats to rent in the village in exchange for one sack of rice per trip and some money. We did have money—my aunt had cleaned out her bank account—but nobody wanted paper money anymore. Two kilos of sugar cost 5,000 rials, whereas a month earlier a kilo of bread had been only 5 rials. Luckily, both women had brought along some gold and jewelry.

My older sister and Tôn Ny stayed with the baggage while our fathers helped the two peasants maneuver the overloaded boats, which were taking on water. One peasant told us children, "Whatever you do, don't move!" He seemed frightened; some boats had already capsized in the swirling water, and people had drowned. It was difficult for us to sit still in the boats for half an hour, but we could see that the island was really beautiful, its shores lined with trees, flowers, and bamboo. We hoped we could stay there and grow our own food while waiting to go home. Our fathers went back to get our luggage while we found a shady spot to fix our food. Afterward we looked for a place to spend the night. The weather was so mild, all we needed was a roof of banana trees. Later on we could build a shelter for protection against the rain. I heard my father and Mitia Mir making plans; living on the island wouldn't be that easy, because other people had thought about settling there, too.

At dawn the next day, two Khmer Rouge came to tell us that no one was allowed to live on the island. "You'll go to Viel Trumph." The trip back through the rushing water was even more difficult the second time, and cost us another hundred kilos of rice and more pieces of material.

The two peasants let us off on the riverbank. We had to proceed on foot, our parents carrying the heavily laden bamboo poles on their shoulders, the children with bundles of rice and personal effects on their heads—except for Sreï Peu, the youngest, whom our parents took turns carrying. We must have stopped for a while around noon, but I no longer remember anything except our arrival in the village. We felt sick to our stomachs, since all along the river we had seen corpses floating downstream and smelled that appalling odor of rotting flesh. We set up camp under some fruit trees and took a bath in cool water, which was somewhat dangerous because the water's edge was quite muddy and you could sink deeply into the mire. You had to get out quickly by grabbing on to lianas.

We had just started to eat when three or four young soldiers dressed in black came up to us.

"What are those girls doing with long hair? You'll have to cut all that off. It's unsanitary."

"Oh sir, they're only children."

"No more 'sir,' no more 'mister.' We're all addressed as 'Met' [comrade]."

"Oh, Mâ," "Poh" for "Pâ," when we addressed our parents, and "Pou" for "Uncle," which is how we addressed strangers. Same thing for the everyday words for eating and sleeping . . .

"If you won't cut your hair, I'll cut your hair, I'll cut it myself with clippers," one soldier said. "And the rest of you, get out, this spot is reserved for someone else."

"Where do you want us to go?" asked my uncle.

"The comrade village headman will be here, he'll assign a place to you."

We had lost our appetites, but we had to eat in a hurry before the village headman arrived. He was a short man, very dark-skinned. He was called Met

Krom, and he came toward us escorted by two armed soldiers.

"You, comrade, what work did you do?" he asked my uncle.

"I'm a man of the people. I drove taxis."

"What's your name?"

"Vong." (That was the last syllable of his "city" name.)

And that's how my father came to be called Rêh; my mother, Nêm; my aunt, Nang. As for the children, they were called "girl" or "boy," using the various Khmer forms of these words.

"Met Vong, how many houses did you have, how many cars, how many bicycles?"

"I didn't have any of those things. My taxi belonged to my Chinese boss."

That was the only answer I heard. They questioned us individually, away from one another—first the parents, then the children, one by one, even the four- and five-year-olds. Met Sakhron, before leaving, had taught us carefully: "Answer as briefly as possible and always the same thing."

"Did your children go to school?"

"Of course not. We didn't have anything for them to wear."

"And those brightly colored clothes they're wearing?"

"We took those from a house before we left the city."

"It's forbidden to talk about the city. Tonight will be mild, you'll stay here under the trees. Tomorrow I'll find you a house."

The next day our two families were installed on the bare ground under a huge house built on piles, as were all the houses near the river. It was still the dry season. That night a boy who seemed pretty sharp came to our camping spot under the house and spoke to my uncle.

"You, Comrade Vong, I know you. I've seen you at the border. You were the chief customs inspector."

"Comrade son, you're dreaming. I've never been to the border."

That night the boy came back with two soldiers in black. "Met Vong, come with us, we're going to interrogate you." My uncle returned at dawn, sad and worn out. While we were cooking the morning rice, Met Krom arrived with his two men in black.

"Met Vong, you're going into the forest. There will be work for you. And you need special education: you're going to study the doctrine of Pol Pot. Don't attempt any resistance. This is for your welfare and that of your family."

"Am I supposed to take anything with me?"

"Don't ask any questions, the Angkar is watching over you."

We heard this word for the first time. We thought for a long while that it meant a new king or president, but it was a word from the new language we had to learn and referred to the supreme organization that governed the people's destiny.

My uncle followed Met Krom toward a big pagoda on a hill. We learned the next day that he had left with a group of about sixty men, all former civil servants, doctors, engineers, lawyers, and other professionals.

Translation by Linda Coverdale

REVOLUTIONARY ASSOCIATION OF THE WOMEN OF AFGHANISTAN (RAWA)

Three Poems

MEENA
I'll Never Return

Meena (1957–1987) was born in Kabul. During her school days, many students in Kabul and other Afghan cities were deeply engaged in social activism and rising mass movements. She left the university to devote herself to organizing and educating women. Meena laid the foundation of the Revolutionary Association of Women of Afghanistan (RAWA) in 1977, meant to give voice to the deprived and silenced women of Afghanistan. She started a campaign against the invading Russian forces and their puppet regime, organizing numerous processions and meetings. In 1981, she launched the magazine *Payam-e-Zan* (Women's Message) to promote Afghan women's equality and expose the oppression of fundamentalist groups. Meena also established the Watan Schools for refugee children, a hospital, and handicraft centers for refugee women in Pakistan. Her active social work and effective protests provoked the wrath of the Russians and the fundamentalist forces alike, and she was assassinated by agents of KHAD (the Afghanistan branch of the KGB) and their fundamentalist accomplices in Quetta, Pakistan, on February 4, 1987. This poem and the others in the section, in English translations, are supplied courtesy of the RAWA web site, www.rawa.org.

■

I'm the woman who has awoken
I've arisen and become a tempest through the ashes of my burnt children
I've arisen from the rivulets of my brother's blood
My nation's wrath has empowered me
My ruined and burnt villages fill me with hatred against the enemy
Oh compatriot, no longer regard me as weak and incapable,
My voice has mingled with thousands of arisen women
My fists are clenched with fists of thousands of my compatriots
To break all these sufferings all these fetters of slavery.
I'm the woman who has awoken,
I've found my path, and to bondage I will never return.

REZA FARMAND
For Meena: Our Valiant Leader, Martyred in the Struggle

Reza Farmand (b. circa 1950) is an Iranian poet and a member of RAWA. No other information is available on Farmand. Many feminist activists living in fundamentalist countries guard their identities and activities closely for the sake of safety. Farmand wrote this poem in Persian to honor Meena.

■

Blind faith of how many wild beasts are needed
To justify such gleeful, wanton human slaughter?
Is it Faith that solidifies. Turns black,

And like tombstones in the graveyard
Lies heavy on the chests of men?
Which Satan blew the sinister blare of the Trumpet
To rouse these corpses
From their graves
To thus pollute the clean air of Existence
With their murky, misty gospel?

Meena! The faith these corpses profess
Prohibits your name
Your word is banned
Your thought is banned
Your body is banned
Your love is banned.

Meena! The faith these corpses profess
Is too unfit, too unqualified,
To teach them about your glory.
But who cares?
The sun of womankind,
—This shining side of humanity—
Is emerging from the dark and cruel shadow
Of historical eclipse.

Meena! Time is now rendered clearer, purer
By your voice,
And every instant
Words are being purified from the sediments
Of blind faith.
The rusty logic and reasoning
Of these corpses—Used like obsolete weapons—
I have seen in museums.
I am confident that these corpses will return to eternal slumber
In their graves in History.
This I know because
Long since, Time
Has separated Faith from the Sword.

SHEEMA KALBASI
For the Women of Afghanistan

Sheema Kalbasi (b. circa 1965) was born in Tehran. She has traveled a good deal and lived in various countries, and she writes poems in several languages. Recently, she was a nursing student in Denmark. Kalbasi wrote her first poem at the age of eight, and is also a painter and a photographer.

■

As I walk in the streets of Kabul,
behind the painted windows,
there are broken hearts, broken women.
If they don't have any male family to accompany them,
they die of hunger while begging for bread,
the once teachers, doctors, professors
are today nothing but walking hunger houses.
Not even tasting the moon,
they carry their bodies around, in the covered coffin veils.
They are the stones in the back of the line . . .
their voices not allowed to come out of their dried mouths.
Butterflies flying by, have no color in Afghani women's eyes
for they can see nothing but blood-shaded streets
from behind the colored windows,
and can smell no bakery's bread
for their sons bodies exposing, cover any other smell,
and their ears can hear nothing
for they hear only their hungry bellies
crying their owners' unheard voices
with each sound of shooting and terror.
Remedy for the bitter silenced Amnesty,
the bloodshed of Afghani woman's life
on the-no-limitation-of-sentences-demanding help
as the voices break away not coming out but pressing hard
in the tragic endings of their lives.

"Woman, are you the brown March Violets?"
"I saw an angel in the Miramar
I carved and carved
until I freed her out."
—Michelangelo

My utopia brushed
an unusual current
turned into
autobiographical circulation of
devilish misplaced luck

as a woman today
I have
never had much fruit
much happiness

My parents' ambition is
not to see me sealing my body
to the sad painted windows

Men with unknown identity
without faces
decide for my very existence

My voice
a recorded statement
I am a hopping sparrow
. . . . Maybe tomorrow
            behind the veil
            the flesh
            dies away
            all the pain
            the sorrow
of being a woman
in Afghanistan
in the year zero, zero, zero

I tried
I tried
to pour burning oil on the crying cells
on my body
Inside
only inside
the burning oil
were the poisoned houses of wishes!

A mushroom in the city-world-of-universe
From trying to pass the dying
the head first and then dripping bread
comes

Shifting
from one age to another
Lively playing with death

I die-to-die and live to live
If I could only live
a noble life.

WOMEN IN BLACK OF BELGRADE

We Are All Women in Black
A Collective Poem Compiled by Jasmina Tesanovic

Women in Black was founded in 1988 in Israel as a pacifist, feminist peace vigil that began among both Palestinian and Israeli women, and grew throughout various war-torn countries of the world, as well as the United States. A large Women in Black group formed in the early 1990s in Serbia, in response to the Serbian nationalist wars that devastated the former Yugoslavia. The group's compelling public protests consist of simply standing, dressed in black, in the streets in silent vigils of mourning and defiance. According to Jasmina Tesanovic of Serbia (whose work appears elsewhere in the book), in an essay on the activities of the Belgrade Women in Black, "The fundamental principle of the international group is to protest sovereign governments entering into aggressive war on foreign territory. . . . The women's goal was also to spread the character of the movement beyond the national borders of one country and immediate zones of conflict." "Today," says Neda Bozinovic, eighty-two years old and participating in vigils since October 1991, "today, we are fighting against the global militarism that is destroying all of us." On October 9, 1998, upon their seventh anniversary of standing vigil, more than one hundred members of Women in Black of Belgrade wrote statements on pieces of paper, which were then compiled by Tesanovic into this collective poem. The note that follows the text of the poem is by Tesanovic.

■

OCTOBER 9, 1998—7 YEARS OF WOMEN IN BLACK

We are all Women in Black
I CONFESS:
I, Jelena, 12 years of age, confess only to life
J'accuse
That in 1991 I was against war, and I am now
I simply confess
That I will never be loyal to these authorities and
that I love Sabahet and Mira and Vjosa and Ana
To everything you wrote
That I am loyal to non-violence, solidarity, friendship and
that I am disloyal to all forms of authoritative power, vio-
lence, hate
That I can no longer stand it and that I can't take it any-
more
That I have lived two lives, one in Sarajevo and one in
Belgrade
That I did not wish for all that which happened to us, but
I could not stop it
To all the charges, I confess that I am a traitor in every
sense
That I am a traitor of the dominant militaristic values in
Serbian society
That I will protest against all forms of violence, war and
Discrimination

That I sang Bosnian songs and danced Albanian dances
throughout the whole war
That I hate war, violence and killing
I confess, but I also accuse
That violence in Kosovo cannot stop in the presence of
the Serbian police. But it can with international forces
which will allow peace and the process of negotiation
That there is no way I will go to the army. Put militarism
in the trash where it belongs
I confess that I will not give up my convictions, even if I
wind up in prison.
That from the beginning of the peace movement I have
been an active participant in all anti-war gatherings
That I will organize yet one more anti-war campaign if
you keep up this
bullshit
That I am European, a citizen of the world and that I am
an irreconcilable
opponent to this regime
That I respect the human rights of the Other and that first
and foremost I consider myself a citizen
That I do not recognize war, discrimination, criminals
and hopelessness
That for seven years I have plotted against this Nazi
regime
That I am bitter about the fact that the authorities in Ser-
bia and Yugoslavia constantly wage war
That conflicts should be resolved through negotiation
and not violence
No passaran!
That I read books, I like the theatre, I speak other lan-
gauges, I like freedom of thought
That our life is peace and creativity and that I have been
thinking about this and working on it since I learned it
from my girlfriends
To everything and even more
To everything which is written on the panel
I confess
That of this current population you have the most principles.
Thank you

Of one hundred symbolic sheets displayed with the heading I CONFESS on a
stand on Republic Square for the one-hour protest of Women in Black, all
were signed, and half of them had the above quoted texts written on them.

When I took the poem the following day to the independent daily *Nasa
Borba* to be published, uniformed police were in the office. Actually, those were

the last days of freedom of the press in Serbia, which was completely smoth-ered by the first NATO bombs and martial law after ten years of what was authentically a development of a civil society based on freedom, if not anarchy, of the press. Serbia was actually the country with the most definite potential for a free press of all the former Yugoslav republics, notwithstanding the strong hand of the dominant regime. That is all past, ten years of struggle, of tiny steps and searches, the actions of what was supposed to be a society in transi-tion, has turned into the debris of democracy and civil society, visible in the debris of bridges, buildings, traumatized people . . .

I had to hurry to finish my text and send it by e-mail, the last means of com-munication with the rest of the world, because we are told the phone lines will be bombed very soon. It was supposed to be a different essay, before the world as it is took this turn . . .

Belgrade, April 30, 1999
After a night of heavy bombing

Translation and explanatory note by Jasmina Tesanovic

PART 4:
HOPE AND SURVIVAL

Yes, it is there, the city full of music,
Flute music, sounds of children, voices of poets,
The unknown bird in his long call. The bells of peace
Essential peace, it sounds across the water
In the long parks where the lovers are walking,
Along the lake with its island and pagoda. . . .
It is there, the human place . . .

—MURIEL RUKEYSER (1913–1980),
distinguished and politically engaged U.S. poet, from the poem "It Is There"

It has been women's task throughout history to go on believing in life when
there was almost no hope. If we are united, we may be able to produce a world
in which our children and other people's children can be safe. . . . Warfare is just
an invention known to the majority of human societies by which they permit
their young men either to accumulate prestige or avenge their honor or acquire
loot or wives or slaves or grab lands or cattle or appease the blood lust, their
gods or the restless souls of the recently dead. It is just an invention, older and
more widespread than the jury system, but none the less an invention of men.

—MARGARET MEAD (1901–1978),
internationally known anthropologist who asserted the value and
complexity of all cultures

I want that there should be a belief, a faith in the possibility
of removing mountains to the side of right. If we believe that war is wrong,
as everyone must, then we ought to believe that by proper efforts
on our past, it maybe done away with.

—LUCRETIA MOTT (1793–1880),
American Quaker, leader in the abolitionist movement and the early women's
rights movement

SAPPHO

To an Army Wife in Sardis

Sappho, famed lyric poet of ancient Greece, was born on the Island of Lesbos (b. circa 610 B.C.E.) and spent some time in exile in Sicily. She was leader of a group of young women devoted to music, poetry, and the goddess Aphrodite. Many of her poems are, like this one, addressed to women, and are characterized by both passion and simplicity. Although only fragments of her work survive, it influenced poets as diverse as Catullus, Ovid, Swinburne, Tennyson, and many contemporary women poets.

■

> Some say a cavalry troop,
> others say an infantry, and others, still,
> will swear that the swift oars
>
> of our sea fleet are the best
> sight on dark earth; but I say
> that whomever one loves is.

Translation adapted by Daniela Gioseffi

JANE ADDAMS

From Peace and Bread in Time of War *Spanish American war*

Jane Addams (1860–1935), the first American woman to win the Nobel Peace Prize, grew up just after the Civil War in a Quaker family of abolitionists and reformers in Cedarville, Illinois. Her family encouraged her to realize a potential that was not restricted to the traditional roles of women. In Chicago she founded Hull House, modeled on settlement houses she had visited in London, which addressed the effects of terrible urban poverty wrought by industrialization. Addams attracted a group of able women who cared for the sick and for the children of working mothers, and fought against disease and child labor. She traveled widely, speaking on social reforms and helping to found settlement houses throughout the United States. She expanded her efforts to include support for women's suffrage and opposition to the Spanish-American War and later World War I; her pacifism was reinforced by the devastating tour of postwar Europe described in the excerpt below. Addams was often derided as unpatriotic, but her 1931 Nobel Peace Prize was acknowledgment of her role in the world disarmament movement as well as her pioneering work among the poor.

■

We had, of course, seen something of the widespread European starvation before we went into Germany; our first view in Europe of starved children was in the city of Lille in Northern France, where the school children were being examined for tuberculosis. We had already been told that forty percent of the children of school age in Lille had open tuberculosis and that the remaining sixty percent were practically all suspects. As we entered the door of a large school room, we saw at the other end of the room a row of little boys, from six to ten years of age, passing slowly in front of the examining physician. The children were stripped to the waist and our first impression was of a line of moving skeletons; their little shoulder blades stuck straight out, the vertebrae were all perfectly distinct as were their ribs, and their bony arms hung limply at their sides. To add to the gruesome effect not a sound was to be heard, for the French physician had lost his voice as a result of shell shock during the first bombardment of Lille. He therefore whispered his instructions to the children as he applied his stethoscope and the children, thinking it was some sort of game, all whispered back to him. It was incredibly pathetic and unreal and we could but accept the doctor's grave statement that only by a system of careful superfeeding, could any of these boys grow into normal men. We had also seen starved children in Switzerland: six hundred Viennese children arriving in Zurich to be guests in private households. As they stood upon the station platforms without any of the bustle and chatter naturally associated with a large number of children, we had again that painful impression of listlessness as of a mortal illness; we saw the winged shoulder blades standing out through their meagre clothing, the little thin legs which scarcely supported the emaciated bodies. The committee of Swiss women was offering them cakes and chocolates, telling them of the children at home who were waiting for them, but there was little response because there was no vitality with which to make it.

We were reminded of these children week after week as we visited Berlin, or Frankfort am Main, or the cities of Saxony and the villages throughout the Erzgebirge in which the children had been starved throughout the long period of the war and of the armistice. Perhaps an experience in Leipzig was typical when we visited a public playground in which several hundred children were having a noonday meal consisting for each of a pint of "war soup," composed of war meal stirred into a pint of hot water. The war meal was, as always, made with a foundation of rye or wheat flower to which had been added ground vegetables or sawdust in order to increase its bulk. The children would have nothing more to eat until supper, for which many of the mothers had saved the entire daily ration of bread because, as they sometimes told us, they hoped thus to avert the hardest thing they had to bear; hearing the children whimper and moan for hours after they were put to bed because they were too hungry to go to sleep.

These Leipzig children were quite as listless as all the others we had seen; when the playground director announced prizes for the best gardens, they were utterly indifferent; only when he said he hoped by day after tomorrow to give them milk in their soup did they break out into the most ridiculous, feeble little cheer ever heard. The city physician, who was with us, challenged the playground director as to his ability to obtain the milk, to which the director replied that he was not sure if he could, but that there was a prospect for it, and that the children must have something to hope for, that was the prerogative of the young. With this uncertain hope we left them to visit day nurseries, child welfare stations, schools and orphanages where the midday meal was practically the same war soup. We were told by probation officers and charity workers of starved children who stole the family furniture and clothing, books and kitchen utensils in order to sell them for food, who pulled unripe potatoes and turnips from the fields for miles surrounding the cities, to keep themselves alive.

Our experiences in the midst of widespread misery, did not differ from those of thousands of other Americans who were bent upon succor and relief and our vivid and compelling impressions of widespread starvation were confirmed by the highest authorities. Mr. Hoover had recently declared that, owing to diminished food production in Europe, approximately 100,000,000 Europeans were then dependent upon imported food. Sir George Paish, the British economist, repeated the statement when he said that 100,000,000 persons in Europe were facing starvation. All this was made much worse by the rapid decline in the value of European money in the markets of the world.

One turned instinctively to the newly created League of Nations. Could it have considered this multitude of starving children as its concrete problem, feeding them might have been the quickest way to restore the divided European nations to human and kindly relationship. Was all this devastation the result of hypernationalism and might not the very recognition of a human obligation irrespective of national boundaries form the natural beginning of better international relationships?

SIBILLA ALERMO

Yes to the Earth

Sibilla Alermo (1876–1960) was an Italian poet who was raped as a young woman and forced to marry her rapist because she was pregnant by him. Courageously, in 1902, she ran away to Rome. There, a woman alone, she wrote and published the first feminist novel of Italian literature, *Una donna*, describing the imprisonment of a wife by her husband's violent will. The novel became an international success. Alermo worked hard to alleviate the labor conditions of Roman workers. She wrote several more novels and in 1920 began to publish poetry. This poem, in its way, embodies the spirit of ecofeminism in response to oppression and destruction.

■

So shines the Earth in certain mornings' light
with its roses and cypresses
or with its grain and its olives,

so suddenly does it shine on the soul
and isolates it and makes it forget everything
even if an instant earlier the soul
was suffering to the quick or mediating, bitter,

so shines the Earth in certain mornings' light
and in its silence reveals itself,
a marvelous lump spinning from the skies,
and, beautiful in its tragic solitude, so laughs

that the soul, although not asked,
answers, "Yes," "Yes," to the Earth,
to the indifferent Earth "Yes,"

even if in an instant the skies and the roses
and the cypresses should turn dark,
or the labor of living be made more burdensome
and breathing yet more heroic,

"Yes," the subjugated soul answers the Earth,
so does it shine in certain mornings' light,
beautiful over all things and human hope.

Translation by Muriel Kittel

CH'IU CHIN

Free Women Blossoming from Old Battlefields

Ch'iu Chin (1879–1907), sometimes called the "Shakespeare of China," was a revolutionary
activist and poet whose poems are still memorized and recited by Chinese schoolchildren. After
an early marriage and the birth of her first child, she went to study in Japan, where she joined Sun
Yat-sen's democratic party and soon became a leader along with the social reformers who sought
to overthrow the despotic Ch'ing dynasty. Back in China, in 1906, she founded a Shanghai newspaper concerned with women's rights and taught in a school that served as a secret headquarters
for the revolutionary army. She was arrested by the government, that used her poems as evidence
against her in her trial, and she was beheaded five years before the overthrow of the Ch'ing
dynasty. Ch'iu Chin is venerated throughout China as a people's martyr. Her poem reflects the
hope of a future in which women are free of oppression, free to advance peace and justice.

■

How many sagacious and brave men
Have survived the dust and grime of earth?
How many lovely women have been paladins?
There were the stately and celebrated women generals
Chi'in Lian-yu and Shen Yu-yin.

Though tears spotted their shirts
Their hearts were full of blood.
The savage strokes of their swords
Trilled like dragons and wept with agony.

The balm of freedom burns in my mind
With anguish for my homeland.
When will we ever be unstained?
Sisters, I say to you,
Spare no effort, struggle ceaselessly,
That at last peace may come to our people.
Bejeweled bodices and deformed feet
Will be unbound.
And some day under the vast firmament
We'll see lovely free women,
Blooming from old battlefields flowering
And bearing bright and honorable human beings.

Translation by Daniela Gioseffi with Pwu Jean Lee

ELEANOR ROOSEVELT

In Defense of the United Nations

Eleanor Roosevelt (b. 1884–1962) was a renowned American humanitarian and one of the most active presidential wives her country has ever known. Devoted to numerous social causes, she worked to further the rights of women, people of color, and workers. She traveled widely, lecturing, observing conditions, and promoting good causes (and was much dogged by the infamous FBI director J. Edgar Hoover, who accused her of being a Communist). From 1945 to 1953, she served as U.S. delegate to the United Nations, and in 1946, she was made chair of the Commission on Human Rights, a subsidiary of the Economic and Social Council. Roosevelt was instrumental in the creation of the UN Declaration of Human Rights. In 1950, she became a leader of the liberal wing of the Democratic party. For her tireless dedication to the cause of human welfare and world peace, she is today recognized as one of America's greatest humanist leaders and as the social conscience of her era.

■

You have heard, as many of us have heard, the current saying, "What good has come from the United Nations? Hasn't the United Nations failed? It was set up to bring us peace, and we don't have peace." But that is really a most unfortunate misconception. The object that the sovereign states hoped for when they wrote the charter in San Francisco was that we could use this machinery as united nations to achieve a peaceful world. But it's only machinery, and machinery doesn't work by itself. It's the people that make it work.

We have also heard it said that the United Nations is just a debating society. Yet we have found over the years that it requires a good deal of talk for people to learn to understand one another. Even in the Congress of the United States we don't always find an immediate meeting of minds. Well, you take sixty sovereign nations, all representing peoples with different customs and habits, frequently different religions, frequently different legal systems. How can you expect them immediately—within six or seven years, that is—to arrive at a meeting of minds? True, the breach has widened between us and the

Soviets, but that breach might have broadened into a war if there hadn't been a place where we had to meet and where we were able to talk.

And if the United Nations is a debating society, do you feel that you have learned all you should about what conditions are all over the world—for instance, in India? I am sure that many of you have no conception of what it is to live in a country where there is always a famine somewhere. I know it wasn't until I went to India and saw the famine districts that I realized what it would be like if some part of my own country was always living under famine conditions. I know of no way in which we can learn these things as quickly as we are learning them from the information that comes to us through channels provided by the United Nations.

I get a lot of letters from people who say, "How can you expect the United Nations to succeed when you do not recognize God in the United Nations?" We have in the U.N. building a little room known as a prayer room to serve all devout people. From those who live according to their own religious standards I have learned a tremendous amount. I have learned to respect them, for I sometimes think that the same spirit pervades the good people in all religions. If you want others to respect your beliefs, you must in return give respect for theirs.

These are some of the things that you learn as you find yourself in close association with people from different parts of the world. It is because they are things that we all need to learn that I believe parents and teachers today have such a tremendous responsibility. They have to prepare our children for living as leaders in a world that will follow their leadership, if the world can respect it. And that will require of our children a greater knowledge of the rest of the world than any of us have ever had before. They are going to be leaders in a world where not only are there different religions and habits and customs but different races—and two-thirds of that world is made up of peoples of different colors. . . .

When all is said and done, then, what we need is to know more about the United Nations and its action groups—the specialized agencies—if only because this is machinery that we people of the different nations must use. For if we do not know about it and if we do not back it up, it isn't going to be used as well as it might be. Furthermore, I feel very strongly that with more knowledge, many of the fears we have had about the United Nations will be dispelled.

Remember, this cooperation is so new, so new in every field, that it's very hard for any of us to work together even on what we think are simple things. So we shouldn't be discouraged when we do not achieve peace all at once. Peace is not going to drop on us from heaven. It is going to have to be worked for, with the hearts and minds and wills of human beings. I believe it can be achieved, but we are going to have to work much harder. We must strengthen it, at the same time learning about the rest of the world.

This is why parents and teachers today must have courage to stand up against waves of public opinion. At present we are going through a period of what I call unreasonable fears, fears that cause great suspicion among us. Many people are afraid to say what they think because it might by chance be something that somebody else might think subversive. Yet our nation has been built on differences of opinion, stated openly. Throughout our history we have had quite a number of people who stood for almost revolutionary ideas. But we have weathered the years, and we have come to be the leading nation in the world. And now it is a question of how well we prepare the next generation to take the burden from their elders. These young people have to know much more than we knew. We had to know about our own country; they have to know about the world. They have to feel and understand things that we didn't have to feel and understand at all. . . .

We have to have unity. We have to believe in each other. We cannot be suspicious of everybody. Surely there are people among us who perhaps do not believe in the things we think essential, but I think the vast majority of us are well rooted in the beliefs of freedom.

I think we can stand up against any infiltration or propaganda, but first we must have a feeling of confidence. We must really care about bringing to the people of the world a leadership that is good, a leadership that is strong. I do not mean strong just in a military and economic way but in a spiritual and moral way. If we do have that feeling and can impart it to our young people, I believe we can do this job, the biggest job any nation has ever had. We are at the crossroads. It is up to us whether we move forward—slowly, to be sure, but step by step—to a better world or whether we fail.

What is going to happen? I do not know. If we succeed, it will be because you and I, as individuals, believe in ourselves and in the need to work with our neighbors throughout the world. I think we will hand on to our children a struggle, but a struggle that will give our nation the capacity to lead the world toward peace and righteousness and freedom.

LOLITA LEBRON

I Have All the Passion of Life

Lolita Lebron (b. 1919) is a living symbol of the struggle for survival by indigenous peoples throughout the world, especially in her native Puerto Rico. As her translator, Gloria Waldman, notes in her essay "Affirmation and Resistance: Women Poets of the Caribbean," Lebron saw her homeland confiscated and corrupted, and its people's culture and ecological beauty destroyed by U.S. multinational corporations. Lebron spent twenty-five years in the women's prison in Alderson, West Virginia, for leading and participating in a desperate act of resistance in 1954— the attack against the U.S. House of Representatives on behalf of Puerto Rican independence. Her charisma, at once mystical and political, is communicated through her frank and passionate poetry, in which she often expresses her longing for her homeland of Puerto Rico. She was released from prison in 1979 and remains a symbol of resistance for Puerto Rican nationalists everywhere. This poem was one of many written from prison to affirm life in the face of tyranny, prejudice, injustice, and colonialism.

■

I have all the passion of life.
I love the sun and the stars
and the seeds.

Everything fascinates me:
water, brooks, groves,
dew and cascades.

I adore looking at the
flowing streams: this clear
proof of beauty;
this joy in my marrow
in my sight,
this knowing about what's hidden,
and this sensation of seeing
what is clear.

Whoever denies life its joy,
the wealth of its complexity,
its rainbow-like countenance,
its downpour and its universe
of beauty, its generous giving,
the caress, the grain
with fruit and delicacies,
the bud, the flower, pain and
                       laughter;
those who deny life its measure
of joy
are the unseeing ones.
Nor have they drunk from
life's overflowing cup of passion.

I have all the rapture,
the savoring.
That's why they stare and ask:
"Lolita, what do you see of
any beauty?
What do you like? The sky?
These sterile and arid mountains,
these hours so full of ugliness
and injustice,
with endless sighs
and the pushing and the shoving?"

"Why do you sing and laugh, Lolita?
Is your face really lit up
with the joy of life?
Are you mad, Lolita?"

Translation by Gloria Waldman

MERIDEL LE SUEUR

Women Know a Lot of Things

Meridel Le Sueur (1923–1996) was the best-known woman among the "proletarian" writers of the Depression years in the United States. A lifelong activist as well as a poet, fiction writer, memoirist, and journalist, she was blacklisted during the McCarthy era, and her work fell into obscurity until it was revived by feminist scholars. During the 1970s, Le Sueur, then in her eighties, enjoyed a rediscovery and appreciation from younger women writers, who recognized her visionary work. Carl Sandburg said that Le Sueur's work is infused with "a rare quality of reverence for humanity and of intimacy and pride regarding women and motherhood." Here, from a collection of her work entitled *Ripening*, is an essay written in Minneapolis during the 1930s, in the years when Le Sueur labored hard to raise her children by herself.

■

Minneapolis

Women know a lot of things they don't read in the newspapers. It's pretty funny sometimes, how women know a lot of things and nobody can figure out how they know them. I know a Polish woman who works in the stockyards here, and she has been working there for a good many years. She came from Poland when she was a child, came across the vast spaces of America, with blinders on, you might say, and yet she knows more than anybody I know, because she knows what suffering is and she knows that everyone is like herself, throughout the whole world. So she can understand everything that happens, and moving between the shack where she lives on the Mississippi bluffs and the canning department of Armours, she feels the hunger and the suffering of Chinese women and feels as if she is in Flint with the Women's Brigade.

I was having a cup of coffee with her the day the Women's Brigade knocked out the windows so the air could get into the factory to the gassed sit-downers and she told about how they were all singing a song we knew:

> "We shall not be moved
> Just like a tree standing by the river
> We shall not be moved."

And how they were all leaning out of the windows singing this song, hundreds of them probably, with machine guns mounted on the buildings opposite and she got up and walked around the little stove that warmed her shack. She couldn't sit still.

"Imagine that," she said. "Can you believe it, them all singing that song, with the guns pointing right at them and the women, scooting in there and smashing those windows. O, say, I woulda like to have been there." And she wasn't in that shack at all, the boundaries of that shack weren't anything.

That's the way it is with women. They don't read about the news. They very often make it. They pick it up at its source, in the human body, in the making of the body, and the feeding and nurturing of it day in and day out. They know how much a body weighs and how much blood and toil goes into the making of even a poor body. Did you ever go into a public clinic to weigh your child? And you feel of him anxiously when you put his clothes on in the morning. You pick him up trying to gauge the weight of his bones and the tiny flesh and you wait for the public nurses to put him on the scales, and you look, you watch her face like an aviator watches the sky, watches an instrument register a number that will mean life and death.

In that body under your hands every day there resides the economy of that world; it tells you of ruthless exploitation, of a mad, vicious class that now cares for nothing in the world but to maintain its stupid life with violence and destruction; it tells you the price of oranges and cod liver oil, of spring lamb, of butter, eggs and milk. You know everything that is happening on the stock exchange. You know what happened to last year's wheat in the drouth, the terrible misuse and destruction of land and crops and human life plowed under. You don't have to read the stock reports in Mr. Hearst's paper. You have the news at its terrible source.

Or what kind of news is it when you see the long, drawn face of your husband coming home from the belt line and the speed up and feel his ribs coming to the surface day after day like the hulk of a ship when the tide is going down?

Or, what price freedom and the American Way so coyly pictured on the billboards, when you go up the dark and secret and dirty stairs to a doctor's office and get a cheap abortion because you can't afford another baby and wait for the fever that takes so many American women and thank heaven if you come through alive, barely crawling around for months?

A woman knows when she has to go to work and compete with other men, and lower the price of all labor, and when her children go to work, tiny, in the vast lettuce and beet fields of the Imperial Valley and Texas. She knows when she has to be both father and mother, her husband like a fine uncared-for precision machine, worn down in his prime, or eaten by acids in Textile, or turned to stone by Silicosis.

In the deeps of our own country, the deep south, Arkansas and Tennessee and Alabama women are beginning to read the news right. In the center earth of China women who for centuries have been slaves, are lifting their faces from the earth and reading a sign in the skies.

In South America, in the deepest and most inaccessible mountains, a woman walking behind a donkey, or working in the sugar cane, is preparing to vote, if she was asked, the way of her international sisters. It's the same there, wondering if there is enough meal in the sack, if watered thin, for a meal. Anxiously looking at the lank husband's body, the dark quick hungering eyes of children, measuring with eagle eye their appetites, knowing to a grain how much would send them from the table without a roving eye.

Hunger and want and terror are a Braille that hands used to labor, used to tools, and close to sources, can read in any language.

International Women's Day is the recognition of that mutual knowledge leading to the struggle of women throughout the world.

When we look at Germany and Italy we know that the coming of fascism exploits men and women alike, and takes from woman the painful civic and political gains she has bought with a century of struggle.

This year promises to be a crucial one for women, and one that will unite them in even closer bonds with the international struggle against war and fascism, those twin beasts that threaten our frail security. The cause of women will be the cause of all toiling humanity.

Men and women alike are beginning to know this. No longer does the good union man keep his woman at home to mind the kids. The Woman's Brigade at Flint was an important weapon in the strike. The Women's Auxiliary came out of the kitchen and fought side by side with the men. This is only a beginning.

Immediate in the struggle in America is the Woman's Charter. This document will draw up a Legislative plan, uniting all women against reaction which strikes at democratic rights and at the labor movement while pushing women back into the dark ages. The basic principles of this Charter are: that women should have full political and civil rights; full opportunity for education; full opportunity for employment according to their individual abilities, and without discrimination because of sex; and security of livelihood, including the safeguarding of motherhood.

This coming year will see the tide of war and fascism rising high, but it will also see the strong and invincible wall of working men and women, locked in strong formation in a party of farmers and workers everywhere, in a Farmer Labor Party, saying with the international workers, in Spain, Russia, China, FASCISM SHALL NOT PASS.

Maria Simarro, one of the young women of the Spain Youth Delegation now touring America, told me that in Spain when they gave the women the vote, everyone was nervous. Here were thousands of illiterate peasant women, held for many years in medieval ignorance and darkness, kept in subjugation to the Church, to endless toil and childbearing. What would they vote for? How could they understand international problems, the great program of the United Peoples Front of Spain and the world? It was a problem that worried everyone. They held the election in their hands. The Liberal Spanish government was afraid. These newly enfranchised women could turn the tide of the election. They needn't have worried.

The so-called ignorant peasant women of Spain were not ignorant. They voted with their hands, their feet, the knowledge bred and seeped in sun-drenched labor, in every bone and muscle, in grief in the night, and terror, of hours of walking behind the plow, their sweat dropping into the furrows, birthing children on straw with only the blessing of the priest to ease the pain.

They voted from this knowledge, solid, with one voice, one body, for the Peoples Front of Spain, voted for that democracy they later showed themselves ready to defend against the Church and the Landlords.

This is the kind of knowledge the women of 1937 must have. They are no longer negative mourners, weepers at the weeping wall, shrouded in the black of grief and defeat. The old English folk song says, "Men must work, and women must weep. . . ." No longer. The International women of 1937 will protect democracy with their lives, demanding food that can now be so abundantly provided out of the earth's rich land and factory, demanding security for loved ones—standing militant in the wheat fields, at factory gate and bench, raising her cry of—Land . . . Bread . . . and Peace.

DENISE LEVERTOV

Making Peace *and* What It Could Be

Denise Levertov (1923–1997) was a native of Great Britain who lived in the United States following World War II. Author of numerous volumes of verse and literary commentary, she wrote powerfully in opposition to the Vietnam War, and later on the threat of nuclear war. Her activist work with various peace and antiwar groups made her an example of bravery and commitment for other poets of her time, and she managed in her work to seam the personal with the political in a crafted lyricism for which she is much admired and respected. These poems from *Candles of Babylon* and *Breathing the Waters* crystallize the hope of peace.

■

MAKING PEACE

A voice from the dark called out,
     "The poets must give us
imagination of peace, to oust the intense, familiar
imagination of disaster. Peace, not only
the absence of war."
               But peace, like a poem,
it is not there ahead of itself,
can't be imagined before it is made,
can't be known except
in the words of its making,
grammar of justice,
syntax of mutual aid.
               A feeling towards it,
dimly sensing a rhythm, is all we have
until we begin to utter its metaphors,
learning them as we speak.
               A line of peace might appear
if we restructured the sentence our lives are making,
revoked its reaffirmation of profit and power,
questioned our needs, allowed

long pauses. . . .
            A cadence of peace might balance its weight
on that different fulcrum; peace a presence,
an energy field more intense than war,
might pulse then,
stanza by stanza into the world,
each of living
one of its words, each word
a vibration of light—facets
of the forming crystal.

WHAT IT COULD BE

Uranium, with which we know
only how to destroy,

lies always under
the most sacred lands—

Australia, Africa, America,
wherever it's found is found an oppressed
ancient people who knew
long before white men found and named it
that there under their feet

under rock, under mountain, deeper
than deepest watersprings, under
the vast deserts familiar
inch by inch to their children

lay a great power.
            And they knew the folly
of wrestling, wrestling, ravaging from the earth
that which it kept
            so guarded.
Now, now, now at this instant,
men are gouging lumps of that power, that presence,
out of the tortured planet the ancients
say is our mother.
            Breaking the doors
of her sanctum, tearing the secret
out of her flesh.

But left to lie, its metaphysical weight
might in a million years have proved

benign, its true force being to be
a clue to righteousness—

showing forth
the human power
not to kill, to choose
not to kill: to transcend
the dull force of our weight and will;

that known profound presence, *un*touched
the sign
providing witness,
        occasion,
        ritual
for the continuing act of
*non*violence, of passionate
reverence, active love.

NINA CASSIAN

On a Japanese Beach

Nina Cassian (b. 1924) is one of Romania's leading poets. Born in Galati, she has published more than fifty volumes of poetry, children's verse, translations, and short stories. She is also a composer of chamber and symphonic music, a journalist, and a film critic. Politically exiled, she has made her home in the United States, where she has taught at New York University and the University of Iowa and married the American author and classical actor Maurice Edwards. Some of her volumes of poetry have been translated into English, including *Lady of Miracles, Call Yourself Alive, Countdown, Cheerleader for a Funeral,* and *Life Sentence.* She is well known for her protest against the repression of the creative spirit by the Ceauşescu dictatorship, which she fled on pain of death. Her most recent collection, *Take My Word for It,* was published in English in 1998.

■

Hiroshima Memento

Blind children are brought to the beach
They bask in sunlight
And wade in waters.

Sunbeams, like a huge woman, hug them,
gentle waves kiss their eyes.
Wind combs their hair.
Sand puts slippers on their feet.

But the colors,
only the colors,

the colors can do nothing for them,
but shimmer from surface to surface,
from sand to sea,
from hand to eyelids,

and the children are orphaned by colors;
and the colors are orphaned by children.

Translation by Daniela Gioseffi with the author

RUTH KLUGER

From Still Alive: A Holocaust Girlhood Remembered

Ruth Kluger (b. 1931) was born in Vienna, and in 1942, in the year of her eleventh birthday, she was deported to the concentration camp Theresienstadt, and later to Auschwitz-Birkenau and the work camp Christianstadt. After escaping from a work detail near the end of the war, she lived for two years in occupied Germany, then emigrated to the United States in 1947, where she graduated from Hunter College; earned a Ph.D. from the University of California, Berkeley; and became a distinguished professor of German. Now professor emerita at the University of California, Irvine, she has authored five volumes of German literary criticism. The memoir from which this excerpt comes was published in 1992 in Germany, where it became a bestseller, and subsequently published in Dutch, French, Italian, Spanish, Czech, and Japanese, and in English by the Feminist Press in 2001. It has won eight German literary awards and France's prestigious Prix Memoire de la Shoah, and has been compared to the work of Primo Levi and Imre Kertész. It is both a compelling real-life horror story and a deeply philosophical work demonstrating a keen understanding of human motivation.

The excerpt here comes from the section of the memoir entitled "Death Camp."

∎

If only the war would end! During the entire Hitler period I never heard a Jew voice the opinion that the Germans could be victorious. That was a possibility which was really an impossibility, a taboo sentence, an unspeakable thought. To hope was a duty.

The word *hope* will appear several times on the next pages. In Hebrew hope is *hatikvah*, which includes the article and so means "the hope," as if there were only one, which encompasses all other, minor ones. It is also the name of a song which some of the condemned sang on the trucks that took them to the gas chambers, because it was the Zionist hymn, and today "Hatikvah" is the national anthem of Israel. There is a saying that where there is hope, there is life. Or is it the other way around: where there is life, there is hope? No matter. But if hope is the reverse of fear, I think it is fear rather than hope that can give you the impression of life, of a vibrant vitality, for fear feels like sand on your tongue and courses through your veins like an exciting drug.

Tadeusz Borowski, a talented young Polish writer who after the war gassed himself to death in his kitchen, having escaped the gas chambers, thought that only despair gives us courage, while hope makes cowards of us all. In *This Way for the Gas, Ladies and Gentlemen*, he wrote about hope in Auschwitz:

Do you really think that without the hope . . . that the rights of man will be restored again, we could stand the concentration camp for even one day? It is that very hope that makes people go without a murmur to the gas chambers, keeps them from risking a revolt, paralyses them into numb inactivity. It is hope that breaks down family ties, makes mothers renounce their children, or wives sell their bodies for bread, or husbands kill. It is hope that compels man to hold on to one or more day of life, because that day may be the day of liberation. Ah, and not even the hope for a different, better world, but simply for life, a life of peace and rest. Never before in the history of mankind has hope been stronger in man, but never also has it done so much harm as it has in this war, in this concentration camp. We were never taught how to give up hope, and this is why today we perish in gas chambers.

Come to think of it, it is odd that we weren't constantly in the grip of fear, that in a way we got used to this unholy situation. Maybe there are two types of despair, the kind that enables you to take risks, as Borowski thought, and which he held in higher esteem than hope, and then the kind of despair that makes you listless, sluggish, impassive. There was a type of prisoner who had given up, whose will to live had been destroyed, who acted and reacted as if sleepwalking. I don't know the source of the moniker *Muselmänner*, Muslims, which was used to describe them, but no racial slur was implied, since Islam wasn't an issue either for the Nazis or for the inmates of the camps. The *Muselmänner* were walking dead men who wouldn't live long, I was told. I composed poems about them and the camp with slick rhythms and rhymes which were inappropriate for the subject but good for memorizing—an important asset, since I couldn't write them down, lacking pencil and paper.

I never gave up hope, and today it seems to me that the explanation is simply childish illusion and denial of death. In my case, hope was justified as it turned out—a satisfying result, to be sure, but not one that refutes the improbability of such an outcome anymore than naming a sweepstake winner refutes the fact that most gamblers lose their stake, or that it just as unlikely that a particular player will win as it is certain that one player will. Don't make the mistake of confusing the laws of statistics with Providence, for laws don't choose and evaluate. From a statistical point of view, some of us were bound to get through alive, since the Nazis were losing the war. But to ask for the characteristics of the lucky dogs who crawled away from that murderous madness is to depart from numerical probability into a fairy tale forest of success stories. I can hear you ask: "Then why tell such a story?" Yet another dilemma, is my answer. Take old-fashioned tragedy (I think in these terms, because the study of literature is my living, and yes, my life, too), where you get the mutually related, attractive concepts of fate and necessity. The spectator can rest reassured, because whatever befalls the characters in that framework was meant to happen, for better or worse. Statistics has usurped the place formerly occupied by these tragic twins—fate and necessity—but statistics falls a little short of human interest and is not exactly prodigal with the details of individual lives. Statistics doesn't enter into our terrors and joys. And yet all human stories are about terror and joy—mine, too. All I can do is warn the reader not to invest in optimism vouchers and not to give credit, much less take credit, for the happy end of my childhood's odyssey—if indeed simple survival can be called a happy end.

DAISY AL-AMIR

The Future

Daisy al-Amir (b. 1935) is one of the more visible figures in women's fiction in the Arab world today, and her work occupies an important and unique place in contemporary Islamic literature and gender studies. Her recent stories intimately reflect women's experiences in the chaotic worlds of the Lebanese civil war and Saddam Hussein's Iraq. They shed light on an unusual Middle East refugee experience—that of a cultural refugee, a divorced woman who is educated, affluent, and alone. Al-Amir is also a poet and novelist, whose sensual prose grows out of a long tradition of Iraqi poetry. But one also finds existential themes in her works, as al-Amir tries to balance what seems fated and what seems arbitrary in the turbulent world she inhabits.

■

She paid for the dress, quickly, though she was not at all certain that it was the right size. But she was certain that it was made of a heavy cloth that would be good for spring or fall. Now it was the middle of summer, maybe there would be another fall and another spring. And yet, would they come? Would spring and fall come? Last spring and fall had not happened. Time had stood still, as it had stood still in all the four seasons of the year. But it had not stood still for the fighting which never stopped, and which assassinated every moment and every whisper and every emotion and everything . . . everything . . . She quickly hid the dress in the bag. She didn't want to admit to herself that she had committed a crime in buying this dress. The murderous war dominated everything. Two years, weeks, and months? No . . . no . . . she could no longer concentrate. She could no longer count the number of minutes and seconds, and she . . . she . . . she waited, as everyone else waited, minute by minute, for news . . . news that was not horrifying. News that did not tell of vast destruction and of absolute darkness. . . .

She had bought the dress from the house next door to one in which she lived. She had not crossed the street nor gone downstairs. The woman in the next-door house sold clothes.

The shops were still operating When she thought about buying the dress she felt as though tar was being thrown on her and her house, that burning, flaming tar which is thrown onto the houses of those of who have been disgraced, so that all passersby should know that the woman in this house had been vilified and that her hair had been cut off and her house set aflame and . . . she touched her hair with one hand and grabbed hold of the bag which hid the dress with the other.

The dress was for fall, and now it was summer. Whoever was still alive was either a prisoner of his own house, or else he was lucky not to have been caught by a sniper's bullet (either aimed or shot at random), or else he was a coward, or had not been kidnapped by the guards at the barricades, or his religious faith had not made him a martyr. Who could tell how many ways there had been, throughout history, of killing a person?

She had bought the dress at a moment when she could not even afford bread for the next few days. If those days should come, would she be able to afford fuel for heat and cooking? . . . Would there ever be a night without hunger cramps? She had bought the dress at a moment when hundreds of thousands could not find a roof over their heads. And hundreds were longing for a crust of bread, and hundreds more were lying dead.

Lebanon was dying; the fighting made headlines in the world press and broadcasts. All were trying to describe graphically this horror, this sickness for which there was no cure.

If only she had saved a little of her money. Would it not have been better not to buy the dress? If only she had kept this money in her purse? Or in her closet? If she were to put the dress in her closet with her other clothes, how could she make certain that she would not lose any of them? The whole house was exposed to burglary—possessions, money, owners—what was the difference between buying a dress and hoarding the money for its purchase? Everything might be looted. This dress she had bought, where had its seller acquired it? How had all those dresses displayed there come into her hands? Had people brought them in? How had they been paid for? And did those who sold the dresses buy them? Did they import them? Did they make them themselves? Rumors of thefts from commercial establishments, banks, offices, and privates homes were rife.

Some armed groups kill for a national cause and die gladly as martyrs; other armed groups just fight to loot. Where are the former groups? And where the latter? And who has robbed whom? And who has held on to possessions of those who are not armed? The fighters permit themselves to steal, to loot goods and souls. Where is the armed element which defends the national cause when it sees the other gang looting and plundering?

Is the national cause the looting of the nation? Is the national cause the plundering of the individual's property and his soul?

That dress was bought with dirhams earned by the sweat of her brow. And so was the dress she was wearing now. *That* purchase had not been a disgrace.

Someone else . . . someone else should be doused with hot, burning, flaming tar, and his house, too, so that all passing by should know it. The real shame must be burnt and proclaimed abroad. She rummaged through the bag to touch her dress. It was still there, all rolled up. She wanted to show it to someone else and explain that she had bought it from a shop that did not deal in stolen dresses, it was not stolen. She wanted to shout out loud: I haven't stolen . . . I haven't stolen . . . I have not and shall not steal . . . I shall wear this dress next spring or fall. Next? She was not expecting anything. She did not know what season this was, nor why thinking about the seasons following each other and waiting for the moment might be the end . . . the end . . . death.

Had she only one second left it would be enough to enjoy having bought a dress, not stolen it, and it would help diminish her rage. What matter if she never got to wear the dress? The important thing was the pleasure she derived from the act of buying it. What should she save her money for? The future? Was there a future? Would she witness tomorrow's sunrise

She wanted to feel that life continued, she wanted to feel the desire for possessions, she wanted to anticipate the coming days. And suddenly she realized that she wanted to go on living, to look forward to the future, to fall and to spring. She had a new dress to wear, she wanted to feel that she might not die at any moment. Was she trying to justify herself, to rid herself of a feeling of shame? Buying a new dress . . . while people were starving to death and rockets and grenades were exploding all around her? Death was waiting at every corner, and she held on tightly to the dress, as if by clinging to it she were clinging onto life itself.

Lebanon was dying, calling for help. And the whole world injected more deadly poison and plunged in more daggers.

The world was covering its ears, closing its eyes; it stretched out a furtive finger to steal, then sent provisions in a ship that never arrived, sent delegations to sell the truth . . . or falsehoods . . . hope, accomplishments, faith, lies. . . .

All this is happening in Lebanon, and she . . . she was buying a dress for a fall she knew would not come?

The saleswoman said she had been forced to sell dresses from her home since her husband and children had lost their jobs, and this was the way she could earn their keep. The woman was forever trying to justify her business as a means of keeping the family alive. And here she was buying a dress, for an autumn that would not come. Would it save her from starving? Would it save her from the sniper and the rockets and grenades exploding all around her? Would it light up the darkness she was so afraid of? Or could it make her wait less anxiously for the fall and the summer preceding it? She folded the bag so it should not look so large. She folded it, shrinking its size, so that she might forget that she was carrying her very own dress in that bag.

An armored car passed . . . some shots were fired to frighten her and she was not afraid.

She was used to the bullets and the cannons and the explosions and the rockets . . . and the darkness . . . and she was used to none of it.

She had not died yet with all the many dead and wounded and disfigured whom she saw and of whom she heard and did not hear, but . . . was it right that she buy a dress with the excuse that she had not yet died? Would she be able to hang on to it? Would her house not be looted? Would she be able to get a doctor? Would a doctor get to her if she became sick? If she were wounded? If she were hit? Would the guard at the barricades allow her to explain to him that she would die if she didn't get to the hospital? And the fighters? What did they care about the word Death, experiencing it at every second and hour and day and week and month throughout these two years? What did this individual matter? Or whether the number of the dead was increased tenfold or a hundredfold or a thousandfold or if he remained alive? Since when has a living individual been important in the eyes of fighters who are exposed to death all the time?

Fighters are exposed to death here, but they are protected by a barricade, there are some weapons with which they protect themselves. . . .

Weapons and fighters and leaders and presidents and parties and followers and organizers who approach and move away from each other, who support and oppose each other, who curse and praise each other, and she . . . she was this individual like so many others who do not belong to any of those; how could she get rid of fear of the moment, of the hour and of the day? Of the memories of the days gone past?

Would tomorrow come? Would there be a new day with a new sun after the long, dark night, lit only by rockets? And she? She had bought a dress suitable for fall! The saleswoman had said that it would do for spring as well as for fall. Which season was the nearest? And when would the days come when she could truly feel and see? When the whole world did not close in on her, neither the sky nor the buildings?

A grenade fell at the entrance to the building. She was not afraid, nor did she jump and run away. She stood stock still contemplating the shattered glass and listening to the screams of the terrified. Where had she got this bravery from? Was she holding on to the future in a bag that she got this bravery from? Was she holding on to the future in a bag that she was hiding under her arm? The inhabitants of the building rushed to the shelter. She stood at the top of the stairs and watched them running and screaming, carrying their little ones; she could not tell who was more frightened, the young or the old. Who among them would live another second and for whom was death waiting? And she . . . she felt the dress. Her soul was grieved to death, unable to find a justification for the purchase of a new dress.

The grenades increased, shattering the walls and windows. She went down the dark stairwell, holding on to the banister. She reached the door of the shelter. She did not know what had compelled her to stop and prevented her from running into the depths with the others.

She felt the dress and calmed down. Who could tell her at this instant why it was that she had bought the new fall dress? And if anyone saw her, how could she convey her contentment at carrying her new spring dress?

More grenades and rockets fell close by. The screaming and wailing increased and she tightened her hold on the bag. Uniformed fighters entered the building. All wore beards and carried all sorts of arms on their shoulders. One of them came rushing towards her, shouting and yelling, "Get into the shelter, can't you hear? Can't you see? Why are you standing there? The shelter is the only place that will save you from getting killed." And he lifted his Kalashnikov, shooting into the air. The panic increased and shouts rose to where she stood. She stood there as though paralyzed, and the figher's fury increased. He came closer, screaming at her, "Go down! I told you to go down to the shelter. What are you doing here? Move! What is it that you are holding on to so tightly? Are you worried about it? Give it to me and go down." And her grip on the bag with the fall/spring dress tightened. She did not answer. The shouting started again, and he screamed at her again, his bullets reverberating. He stared at her furiously and she screamed at him, "This is my future, this is for fall and for spring." She clasped it to her breast, and now his greatest fear was that she would pounce on him.

Translation by Miriam Cooke

LYNNE SHARON SCHWARTZ

The Spoils of War

Lynne Sharon Schwartz (b. 1939) is an award-winning author of several novels and volumes of stories, essays, poems, and translations. *Disturbances in the Field, Balancing Acts, Rough Strife,* and two collections of short stories, *Acquainted with the Night* and *The Melting Pot,* were among her early works. More recent work includes *Face to Face* (2000), a collection of essays; *In the Family Way: An Urban Comedy* (1999); *Ruined by Reading* (1996), a memoir; *The Fatigue Artist* (1995), a novel; *Smoke over Birkenau* (1991), a translation of Liana Millu's Holocaust memoir; and *Leaving Brooklyn* (1989), which was nominated for the PEN Faulkner Award. She recently published *In Solitary* (2002), a collection of poems, with Sheep Meadow Press, and translated Natalia Ginzsburg's essays, which are also excerpted in this book. She is the recipient of National Endowment and Guggenheim Fellowships. Her personal account, written in 1980, is the result of a teaching experience during the Vietnam War years at Hunter College in New York, where she lives.

■

He always sat in the back row, as far away as he could get: long skinny body and long face, thin curly hair, dark mustache. Sometimes his bony shoulders were hunched as he peered down at his notebook lying open on that bizarre prehensile arm that grows out of college classroom chairs. Or else he leaned way back, the lopsided chair balanced on two legs and propped against the rear wall, his chest appearing slightly concave beneath his white shirt, and one narrow leg, in jeans, elegantly stretched out to rest on a nearby empty chair.

Casual but tense, rather like a male fashion model. Volatile beneath the calm: someone you would not want to meet on a dark street. His face was severely impassive in a way that suggested arrogance and scorn.

He must have been about twenty-seven years old, an extremely thin young man—ascetic, stripped down to the essentials. His body looked so brittle and so electrically charged that I almost expected crackling noises when he moved, but in fact he slipped in and out silently, in the wink of an eye. His whole lanky, scrutinizing demeanor was intimidating. He would have no patience with anything phony, I imagined; would not suffer fools gladly.

About every fourth or fifth class he was absent, common enough for evening-session students, who had jobs, families, grown-up lives and responsibilities. I was a trifle relieved at his absences—I could relax—yet I missed him, too. His presence made a definite and compelling statement, but in an unintelligible language. I couldn't interpret him as readily as I could the books on the reading list.

I was hired in the spring of 1970. It was wartime. Students were enraged. When I went for my interview at Hunter College I had to walk past pickets into a building where black flags hung from the windows. I would use the Socratic method, I earnestly told the interviewer, since I believed in the students' innate intelligence. To myself, I vowed I would win their confidence. After all, I was scarcely older than they were and I shared their mood of protest. I would wear jeans to show I was one of them, and even though I had passed thirty and was married and had two children, I would prove that I could be trusted. I was prepared—even eager—for youthful, strident, moral indignation.

Far from strident, he was only totally silent, never speaking in class discussions, and I was reluctant to call on him. Since he had a Spanish name, I wondered whether he might have trouble with English. Bureaucratic chaos was the order of the day, with the City University enacting in microcosm the confusion in the nation at large; it was not unusual for barely literate or barely English-speaking students to wind up in an Introduction to Literature class. His silence and his blank arrogant look could simply mean bewilderment. I ought to find out, but I waited.

His first paper was a shocker. I was surprised to receive it at all—I had him pegged for the sullen type who would give up at the first difficult assignment, then complain that college was irrelevant. On the contrary, the paper, formidably intelligent, jarred my view of the fitness of things. It didn't seem possible—no, it didn't seem *right*—that a person so sullen and mute should be so eloquent. Someone must have helped him. The truth would come out in impromptu class papers, and then I would confront him. I bided my time.

After the first exam he tossed his blue book onto my desk, not meeting my eyes, and, wary and feline, glided away, withdrawing into his body as if attempting a disappearing act. The topic he had chosen was the meaning of "the horror" in Joseph Conrad's *Heart of Darkness*, the novella we had spent the first few sessions on.

He compared it to Faulkner's *Intruder in the Dust*. He wrote at length about racial hatred and war and their connection in the dark, unspeakable places in the soul from which both spring, without sentimentality but with a sort of matter-of-fact, old knowledge. He knew Faulkner better than I did; I had to go back and skim *Intruder in the Dust* to understand his exam. I do know that I had never before sat transfixed in disbelief over a student paper.

The next day I called him over after class and asked if he was aware that he had an extraordinary mind. He said, yes, he was. Close up, there was nothing arrogant about him. A bit awkward and shy, yet gracious, with something antique and courtly in his manner.

Why did he never speak in class, I asked.

He didn't like to speak in front of people. His voice and his eyes turned evasive, like an adolescent's, as he told me this. Couldn't, in fact. Couldn't speak.

What do you mean, I said. You're not a kid. You have a lot to say. You write like this and you sit in class like a statue? What's it all about?

He was in the war, he said, and he finally looked at my face and spoke like the adult that he was. He was lost for a long time in the jungles of Vietnam, he explained patiently, as if I might not know what Vietnam was, or what a jungle was, or what it was to be lost. And after that, he said, he couldn't. He just found it hard to be with people. To speak to people.

But you're so smart. You could do so much.

I know. He shrugged: a flesh-and-blood version of the rueful, devil-may-care, movie war-hero shrug. Can't be helped.

Anything can be helped, I insisted.

No, he insisted back, quietly. Not after that jungle.

Hunter had a counseling service, free. Go, I pleaded.

He had already gone. They keep asking me questions about my childhood, he said, my relationship with my parents, my toilet training. He grinned quickly, turning it on and off. But it doesn't help. It's none of that. It's from when I was lost in that jungle.

You must work, I said. Don't you have to talk to people when you work?

No, he was a meter man.

A what?

He went around checking on cars, to see if they had overstayed their time at the parking meters.

You can't do that forever, I said. With your brains!

Well, at least he didn't have to talk to people, he said sweetly. For now. Maybe later on he would get braver.

And what would he do if I called on him in class? If I made him talk?

Oh no, don't do that, he said, and flashed the wry grin again. If you did that I'd probably run out of the room.

I never called on him because I didn't want to risk seeing him run out of the room. But at least we stopped being afraid of each other. He gave up his blank look, and occasionally I would glance at his face, to see if I was still making sense or drifting off into some seductive, academic cloud of words.

I thought of him a lot this summer after I saw young men lined up at post offices to register for military service. I thought of him also when I heard Ronald Reagan and John Anderson, on television, solemnly pledge themselves to the defense of this country's shores. No candidate has pledged himself to the defense of this country's young men, to "taking every measure necessary" to "insure" that their genius does not turn mute and their very lives become the spoils of war.

ROBIN MORGAN

Ghosts and Echoes:
Letter from Ground Zero

Robin Morgan is an award-winning writer, feminist leader, political theorist, journalist, and activist. The former editor-in-chief of *Ms.* magazine, Morgan has been active in the international women's movement for more than twenty-five years. Founder of the Sisterhood is Global Institute (www.sigi.org), the first international women's think-tank, she has also co-founded and serves on the boards of many other feminist organizations in the United States and abroad. Robin Morgan has published eighteen books, including several books of poetry, volumes of fiction and essays, a memoir entitled *Saturday's Child* (2000), and the now-classic anthologies *Sisterhood Is Powerful* (1970)and *Sisterhood Is Global* (1984; 1996). Her third anthology, *Sisterhood Is Forever: The Women's Anthology for a New Millenium*, was published in 2003 by Washington Square Press. For her nonfiction work *The Demon Lover: On the Sexuality of Terrorism* (1989), Morgan traveled to Mideast refugee camps to work with and interview Palestinian women, and in her writing argues for noticing the connection between patriarchal power, religious fundamentalisms of all kinds, and the inevitability of terrorism. *The Demon Lover* gained new resonance in the wake of the September 11 attacks, and a new, updated edition in 2001 included as an afterword Morgan's letters from Ground Zero—emails she sent to friends and colleagues around the world in the days and weeks following the attacks. Morgan, who lives a mile and a half from the World Trade Center site, offers a gripping eyewitness account of the physical and emotional devastation—but also insists upon examining its larger meanings.

■

Dear Friends,

Your response to the e-mail I sent on Day 2 of this calamity has been overwhelming. In addition to friends and colleagues, absolute strangers—in Serbia, Korea, Fiji, Zambia, all acrosss North America—have replied, as have women's networks in places ranging from Senegal and Japan to Chile, Hong Kong, Saudi Arabia, even Iran. You've offered moving emotional support and asked for continued updates. I cannot send reguular reports/alerts as I did during the elections last November or the cabinet confirmation battles last year. But here's another try.

I'll focus on New York—my firsthand experience—but this doesn't mean any less anguish for the victims of the Washington or Pennsylvania calamities. Today was Day 8. Incredibly, a week has passed. Abnormal normalcy has settled in. Our usually contentious mayor (previously bad news for New Yorkers of color and for artists) has risen to this moment with efficiency, compassion, real leadership. The city is alive and dynamic. Below 14th Street, traffic is flowing again, mail is being delivered, newspapers are back. But very early this morning I walked east, then south almost to the tip of Manhattan Island. The 16-acre site itself is closed off, of course, as is a perimeter surrounding it controlled by the National Guard, used as a command post and staging area for rescue workers. Still, one is able to approach nearer to the area than was possible last weekend, since the law-court district and parts of the financial district are now open and (shakily) working. The closer one gets the more one sees—and smells— what no TV report, and very few print reports, have communicated. I find myself giving way to tears again and again, even as I write this.

If the first sights of last Tuesday seemed bizarrely like a George Lucas special-effects movie, now the directorial eye has changed: it's the grim lens of Agnes Varda, juxtaposed with images so surreal they could have been framed by Bunuel or Kurosawa.

This was a bright, cloudless, early autumnal day. But as one draws near the site, the area looms out of a dense haze: one enters an atmosphere of dust, concrete powder, and plumes of smoke from fires still raging deep beneath the rubble (an estimated 2 million cubic yards of debris). Along lower 2nd Avenue, 10 refrigerator tractor-trailer trucks are parked, waiting; if you stand there a while, an NYC Medical Examiner van arrives—with a sagging body bag. Thick white ash, shards of broken glass, pebbles, and chunks of concrete cover street after street of parked cars for blocks outside the perimeter. Handprints on car windows and doors—handprints sliding downward—have been left like frantic graffiti. Sometimes there are messages finger-written in the ash: "U R Alive." You can look into closed shops, many with cracked or broken windows, and peer into another dimension: a wall-clock stopped at 9:10, restaurant tables meticulously set but now covered with two inches of ash, grocery shelves stacked with cans and produce bins piled high with apples and melons—all now powdered chalk-white. A moonscape of plenty. People walk unsteadily along these streets, wearing nosemasks against the still particle-full air, the stench of burning wire and plastic, erupted sewage; the smell of death, of decomposing flesh.

Probably your TV coverage shows the chain-link fences aflutter with yellow ribbons, the makeshift shrines of candles, flowers, scribbled notes of mourning or of praise for the rescue workers that have sprung up everywhere—especially in front of firehouses, police stations, hospitals. What TV doesn't show you is that near Ground Zero the streets for blocks around are still, a week later, adrift in bits of paper—singed, torn, sodden pages: stock reports, trading print-outs, shreds of appointment calendars, half of a "To-Do" list. What TV doesn't show you are scores of tiny charred corpses now swept into the gutters. Sparrows. Finches. They fly higher than pigeons, so they would have exploded outward, caught midair in a rush of flame, wings on fire as they fell. Who could have imagined it: the birds were burning.

From a distance, you can see the lattices of one of the Towers, its skeletal bones the sole remains, eerily beautiful in asymmetry, as if a new work of abstract art had been erected in a public space. Elsewhere, you see the transformation of institutions: The New School and New York University are missing persons' centers. A movie house is now a rest shelter, a Burger King a first-aid center, a Brooks Brothers™ clothing store a body parts morgue, a record shop a haven for stranded animals. Libraries are counseling centers. Ice rinks are morgues. A bank is now a supply depot: in the first four days, it distributed 11,000 respirators and 25,000 pairs of protective gloves and suits. Nearby, a mobile medical unit housed in a McDonald's has administered 70,000 tetanus shots. The brain tries to process the numbers: "Only" 50,000 tons of debris had been cleared by yesterday, out of 1.2 million tons. The medical examiner's office has readied up to 20,000 DNA tests for unidentifiable cadaver parts. At all times, night and day, a minimum of 1,000 people live and work on the site.

Such numbers daze the mind. It's the details—fragile, individual—that melt numbness into grief. An anklet with "Joyleen" engraved on it—found on an ankle. Just that: an ankle. A pair of hands—one brown, one white—clasped together. Just that. No wrists. A burly welder who drove from Ohio to help, saying softly, "We're working in a cemetery. I'm standing in—not on, *in*—a graveyard." Each lamppost, storefront, scaffolding, mailbox, is plastered with homemade photocopied posters, a racial/ethnic rainbow of faces and names: death the great leveler, not only of the financial CEOs—their images usually formal, white, male, older, with suit-and-tie—but the mailroom workers, receptionists, waiters. You pass enough of the MISSING posters and the faces, names, descriptions become familiar. The Albanian window-cleaner guy with the bushy eyebrows. The teenage Mexican dishwasher who had an American flag tattoo. The janitor's assistant who'd emigrated from Ethiopia. The Italian American grandfather who was a doughnut-cart tender. The 23-year-old Chinese American junior pastry chef at the Windows on the World restaurant who'd gone in early that day so she could prep a business breakfast for 500. The firefighter who'd posed jauntily wearing his green shamrock necktie. The dapper African American midlevel manager with a small gold ring in his ear who handled "minority affairs" for one of the companies. The middle-aged secretary laughing up at the camera from her wheelchair. The maintenance worker with a Polish name, holding his newborn baby. Most of the faces are smiling; most of the shots are family photos; many are recent wedding pictures. . . .

I have little national patriotism, but I do have a passion for New York, partly for our gritty, secular energy of endurance, and because the world does come here: 80 countries had offices in the Twin Towers; 62 countries lost citizens in the catastrophe; an estimated 300 of our British cousins died, either in the planes or the buildings. My personal comfort is found not in ceremonies or prayer services but in watching the plain, truly heroic (a word usually misused) work of ordinary New Yorkers we take for granted every day, who have risen to this moment unpretentiously, too busy even to notice they're expressing the splendor of the human spirit: firefighters, medical aides, nurses, ER doctors, police officers, sanitation workers, construction-workers, ambulance drivers, structural engineers, crane operators, rescue worker "tunnel rats". . . .

Meanwhile, across the U.S., the rhetoric of retaliation is in full-throated roar. Flag sales are up. Gun sales are up. Some radio stations have banned playing John Lennon's song "Imagine." Despite appeals from all officials (even Bush), mosques are being attacked, firebombed; Arab Americans are hiding their children indoors; two murders in Arizona have already been categorized as hate crimes—one victim a Lebanese-American man and one a Sikh man who died merely for wearing a turban. (Need I say that there were not nationwide attacks against white Christian males after Timothy McVeigh was apprehended for the Oklahoma City bombing?)

Last Thursday, right-wing televangelists Jerry Falwell and Pat Robertson (our home-grown American Taliban leaders) appeared on Robertson's TV show *The 700 Club*, where Falwell blamed "the pagans, and the abortionists, and the feminists and the gays and lesbians, . . . the American Civil Liberties Union, People for the American Way," and groups "who have tried to secularize America" for what occurred in New York. Robertson replied, "I totally concur." After even the Bush White House called the remarks "inappropriate," Falwell apologized (though he did not take back his sentiments); Robertson hasn't even apologized. (The program is carried by the Fox Family Channel, recently purchased by the Walt Disney Company—in case you'd like to register a protest.)

The sirens have lessened. But the drums have started. Funeral drums. War drums. A State of Emergency, with a call-up of 50,000 reservists to active duty. The Justice Department is seeking increased authority for wider surveillance, broader detention powers, wiretapping of persons (not, as previously, just phone numbers), and stringent press restrictions on military reporting.

And the petitions have begun. For justice but not vengeance. For a reasoned response but against escalating retaliatory violence. For vigilance about civil liberties. For the rights of innocent Muslim Americans. For "bombing" Afghanistan with food and medical parcels, NOT firepower. There will be the expectable peace marches, vigils, rallies. . . . One member of the House of Representatives—Barbara Lee, Democrat of California, an African American woman—lodged the sole vote in both houses of Congress against giving Bush broadened powers for a war response, saying she didn't believe a massive military campaign would stop terrorism. (She could use letters of support: email her, if you wish, at barbara.lee@mail.house.gov.)

Those of us who have access to the media have been trying to get a different voice out. But ours are complex messages with long-term solutions—and this is a moment when people yearn for simplicity and short-term, facile answers.

Still, I urge all of you to write letters to the editors of newspapers, call in to talk radio shows, and, for those of you who have media access—as activists, community leaders, elected or appointed officials, academic experts, whatever— to do as many interviews and TV programs as you can. Use the tool of the Internet. Talk about the root causes of terrorism, about the need to diminish this daily climate of patriarchal violence surrounding us in its state-sanctioned normalcy; the need to recognize people's despair over ever being heard short of committing such dramatic, murderous acts; the need to address a desperation that becomes chronic after generations of suffering; the need to arouse that most subversive of emotions—empathy—for "the other"; the need to eliminate hideous economic and political injustices, to reject *all* tribal/ethnic hatreds and fears, to repudiate religious fundamentalisms of every kind. Especially talk about the need to understand that we *must expose the mystique of violence,* separate it from how we conceive of excitement, eroticism, and "manhood"; the need to comprehend that violence differs in degree but is related in kind, that it thrives along a spectrum, as do its effects—from the battered child and raped woman who live in fear to an entire populace living in fear. . . .

Meanwhile, we cry and cry and cry. I don't even know who my tears are for anymore, because I keep seeing ghosts, I keep hearing echoes.

The world's sympathy moves me deeply. Yet I hear echoes dying into silence: the world averting its attention from Rwanda's screams . . .

Ground Zero is a huge mass grave. And I think: Bosnia. Uganda.

More than 6,300 people are missing and presumed dead (not even counting the Washington and Pennsylvania deaths). The TV anchors choke up: civilians, they say, my god, *civilians.* And I see ghosts. Hiroshima. Nagasaki. Dresden. Vietnam.

I watch the mask-covered mouths and noses on the street turn into the faces of Tokyo citizens who wear such masks every day against toxic pollution. I watch the scared eyes become the fearful eyes of women forced to wear the *hajib* or *chodor* or *burka* against their will . . .

I stare at the missing posters' photos and think of the Mothers of the Disappeared, circling the plazas in Argentina. And I see the ghosts of other faces. In photographs on the walls of Holocaust museums. In newspaper clippings from Haiti. In chronicles from Cambodia. . . .

I worry for people who've lost their homes near the site, though I see how superbly social-service agencies are trying to meet their immediate and longer-term needs. But I see ghosts: the perpetually homeless who sleep on city streets, whose needs are never addressed. . . .

I watch normally unflappable New Yorkers flinch at loud noises, parents panic when their kids are late from school. And I see my Israeli feminist friends like Yvonne, who've lived with this dread for decades and still (even yesterday) stubbornly issue petitions insisting on peace. . . .

I watch sophisticates sob openly in the street, people who've lost workplaces, who don't know where their next paycheck will come from, who fear a contaminated water or food supply, who are afraid for their sons in the army, who are unnerved by security checkpoints, who are in mourning, who are wounded, who feel humiliated, outraged. And I see my friends like Zuhira in the refugee camps of Gaza or West Bank, Palestinian women who have lived in precisely that same emotional condition—for four generations.

Last weekend, many Manhattanites left town to visit concerned families, try to normalize, get away for a break. As they streamed out of the city, I saw ghosts of other travelers: hundreds of thousands of Afghan refugees streaming toward their country's borders in what is to them habitual terror, trying to escape a drought-sucked country so war-devastated there's nothing left to bomb; a country with 50,000 disabled orphans and two million widows whose sole livelihood is begging; where the life expectancy of men is 42 and women 40; where women hunch in secret whispering lessons to girl children forbidden to go to school, women who risk death by beheading—for teaching a child to read.

The ghosts stretch out their hands. *Now you know,* they weep, gesturing at the carefree, insulated, indifferent, golden innocence that was my country's safety, arrogance, and pride. *Why should it take such horror to make you see?* the echoes sigh, *Oh please do you finally see?*

This is calamity. And opportunity. The United States—what so many of you call America—could choose now to begin to understand the world. And join it. Or not.

For now my window still displays no flag, my lapel sports no red-white-and-blue ribbon. Instead, I weep for a city and a world. Instead, I cling to a different loyalty, affirming my un-flag, my un-anthem, my un-prayer—the defiant un-pledge of a madwoman who also had mere words as her only tools in a time of ignorance and carnage, Virginia Woolf: "As a woman I have no country. As a woman I want no country. As a woman my country is the whole world."

If this is treason, may I be worthy of it.

In mourning—and in absurd, tenacious hope,

Robin Morgan
New York City

LADY BORTON

A Forgiving Land

Lady Borton (b. 1942) has lived and worked in Vietnam, helping to rebuild the war-torn land, for more than thirty years. She is the author of *Sensing the Enemy: an American Woman Among the Boat People of Viet Nam* (1984) and *After Sorrow: An American Among the Vietnamese* (1995, Vietnamese edition, 1996). Borton is international affairs representative for the Quaker American Friends Service Committee in Hanoi and adjunct professor at Ohio University's Center for Southeast Asian Studies. She is currently working with the Vietnamese Women's Press to edit and translate a volume of Vietnamese women poets for publication by the Feminist Press. Lady Borton has devoted her life to the service of peacemaking by increasing understanding between the American and Vietnamese peoples, as exemplified by her story here.

■

"Hands up, American!" Second Harvest said in Vietnamese. She poked my ribs. "You're under arrest!"

Barefoot, I lifted my sandals over my head. In the moonlight, the tiger cactuses along the rice paddy loomed like phantoms with bizarre, prickly limbs.

"Forward!" Second Harvest said in a teasing voice. "You can't run away now."

She was leading me into Ban Long, a village of 8,000 people in the Mekong delta southwest of Ho Chi Minh City. During the "American War," as Vietnamese call the Viet Nam War, U.S. bombers had attacked Ban Long, blasting houses into craters, families into corpses. Agent Orange had stripped the earth of green.

Now, in 1989, fourteen years after the war, the green had returned. Dense foliage obscured the moon. The air smelled sweet with the fragrance of frangipani. An owl called out, *cu cu, cu cu;* two frogs croaked while, all around, cicadas buzzed in an insistent chorus.

As I walked on through the darkness, I could feel the path of packed mud with my toes. I paused when we came to a moonlit clearing. Nearby, gold and white frangipani blooms lifted like trumpets, their fragrance triumphant.

Amazing, I thought: The earth has forgiven us.

During the war, I'd worked in South Viet Nam with Quaker Service as a health administrator. Ten years later, in 1980, I lived in Malaysia's largest refugee camp for Boat People who had fled Viet Nam. Now, I wanted to know Vietnamese who had chosen to stay.

"We'll stop at my father's," Second Harvest said, pointing.

I turned; my toes gripped the path. I couldn't move. Frail kerosene light defined the shadowy outline of a wooden house in a grove of trees. A ladder of light from the slat siding spread across fresh water urns under the thatch eaves. Its source, a tiny kerosene lamp, illuminated a welcoming doorway. But between me and that doorway stood a creek and, spanning the creek, a "monkey bridge"—a lone and graceless palm trunk greased with muddy footprints.

"*Chet roi,*" I muttered, using Vietnamese slang for the insurmountable, literally "Dead already."

Second Harvest stepped onto the bridge. She was stocky for a Vietnamese and wore her peasant over-blouse and loose black satin trousers with the ease of middle age. Her round face was open like a lotus blossom at midday. She reached for my hand. In the darkness, braced by this former revolutionary, I edged across.

At that time, I was and would remain for years the only foreigner whom the Vietnamese allowed to live with peasants in the countryside. Curious villagers stared wherever I went: I was the circus come to town.

"A giant!" the kids announced. They stepped on my heels, they petted my arms. "She's furry! Like a monkey!!"

"Look," one boy whispered, surprised that hair could be curly. "It's like dead vines!"

"The giant is as timid as a toddler," a girl observed as I teetered across a monkey bridge.

These children had never seen an American. Even teen-agers couldn't remember the war. In contrast, during his eighty years, Second Harvest's father had known only a few years of peace.

I called Second Harvest's father "Senior Uncle," the same title the Vietnamese use for Ho Chi Minh, founder of the modern Vietnamese state. Senior Uncle was a tiny man with huge hands. He could swing among the water apple trees, gathering the translucent dimpled fruit as nimbly as his grandsons. His mind was equally keen. Yet with me Senior Uncle repeated himself, as if to make up for the years we had missed knowing each other.

"My Child," Senior Uncle said each evening as we rinsed our bowls in the creek, "always save rice for tomorrow. Who knows? Tomorrow you may have nothing to eat. Never drink from the creek, Child. Drink from the rain-water crocks under the eaves. . . ."

"Father . . ." Second Harvest worried I might find Senior Uncle boring. She hovered, tending me as if I belonged to an endangered species. During the American War, Second Harvest had commanded one hundred guerillas. In those days, she loaded her canoe with weapons, concealing the contraband with water-palm leaves. Then she slipped along sluices and creeks. When helicopters appeared, she jumped overboard.

"Always keep these two holes above water," Second Harvest told me, touching her nostrils.

"We were rats," her father said. "We lived underground, in tunnels. Slept by day, prowled at night. Our feet knew the way! But we were different from rats." He chuckled. "We were smarter!"

During the war, Senior Uncle had organized Ban Long's literacy campaign. To his lifetime collection of books—a Confucian primer, a book on Lenin, a volume of Ho Chi Minh's poetry—he now added the photo book of the United States my father had sent with me. Senior Uncle showed the photo book to every neighbor who visited.

"Do you have a water buffalo on your farm in Ohio?" one woman asked me.

"Do you eat milk fruit?" a second said, cutting the top off a fruit that looked like a Granny Smith apple but tasted like thick, vanilla custard.

"Do you fish in a bomb crater?" Fifth Brother asked.

"You don't grow rice?!" his mother, Third Sister, exclaimed. She'd lost three sons during the war. Toothless, she mashed her betel nut in a U.S. shall casing. "Then, how do you eat?"

One day, Third Sister laughed so hard she couldn't finish her betel nut. Eight women had come to visit. Middle-aged, they looked like a bridal party posing for a silver wedding anniversary photo. All wore over-blouses in varying hues and the traditional loose black satin trousers. They had asked about American bridal dress.

"What!?" Third Sister said at my description. "No trousers?" The women rollicked at this immodest thought.

As with everything else, the villagers watched me harvest. Second Harvest chuckled as I stepped off the paddy dike.

"Please!" said an old woman bent like a walking cane. "Don't take your pretty white legs into the paddy muck!"

I sank to mid-calf in mud and slogged toward the row of women harvesting. The ooze sucked me off balance.

"What's wrong with her?" the old woman asked. "Did she drink rice wine?"

The harvesters cut the tall rice with sickles and set the grasses aside on the stubble. They cut and set, cut and set, moving together in a long line as if choreographed. Sickle in hand, I joined them.

"Hold the grass farther down," Second Harvest yelled.

I slid my left hand down.

"No! Five plants at once."

I sliced the grass.

"No, no, farther up."

I set the grasses aside.

"Lay the stems even!"

I felt like a dancing bear. I'd had days of this. I was tired of Second Harvest telling me when to shake out my grass mat, how many bowls of rice to eat, when to wash my feet. I stood up, sickle in hand, fuming.

"Didn't Uncle Ho say, 'Eat with the people, live with them, work with them?'"

"Yes—."

"When did Uncle Ho say, 'Stand on the paddy dike, give orders'?"

Second Harvest's face wilted.

I was horrified. I'd been incredibly rude.

"Forgive me," I said in Vietnamese.

"Hello?" Second Harvest said in English. To get me to smile, she tried all the English phrases I'd taught her. "O.K.?" "Thank you?" Then she herded the watchers down the paddy dike, her laughter reaching back across the mud and stubble.

My last evening, the harvesters came to visit. They brought milk fruit, water apples, breadfruit, and dried tamarind. "Please," they said, "take these gifts to the women in the U.S."

After they left, Senior Uncle approached me. In his huge hands he cradled a tiny photograph. "This is the only picture of me young," he said. "Give it to your father. Tell him to come live with me in Ban Long. I'll take care of him in his old age."

It's even more amazing, I thought: The people have forgiven us.

Later that evening, Second Harvest and I swung together in the hammock. She worried about her teen-age son, who ran with a fast crowd in town; she couldn't keep him in bicycle brakes. And she worried about her father alone in the countryside; recently he'd fallen from a water apple tree.

"Older Sister—," I said when the conversation lulled, thinking I would at last ask a question I'd long wondered. "Are you a communist?"

Her fingers fluttered, No.

"Senior Uncle?"

"No, no! Father fought the French colonizers for thirty years before he ever heard of communists."

A canoe passed, a woman paddling bow, a man in the stern. Between them, three little boys slept curled around each other like bananas from the same stalk. The cicadas buzzed; a tree frog chortled. Somewhere in the distance, an owl called out, "*cu cu*," sounding its Vietnamese name.

"Don't you understand?" Second Harvest said, gesturing toward the creek and the canoe and her father's house with its ladder of light lying on the fresh water urns under the thatch eaves. "Can't you see? This is all we wanted."

XUAN QUYNH

My Son's Childhood

Xuan Quynh (1942–1988) is considered Vietnam's most famous modern woman poet. She was born in the northern province of Ha Tay and died with her husband (Vietnam's most famous modern playwright) and their twelve-year-old son (Vietnam's most famous child poet) in a car accident in 1988. She wrote "My Son's Childhood" in 1969, at the height of the Vietnam War.

■

What do you have for a childhood
That you still smile in the bomb shelter?
The morning wind comes to visit you
The full moon follows you
The long river, the immense sea, a round pond
The enemies' bomb smoke, the evening star.
At three months you turn your head, at seven you crawl!
I long for peace every day, every month for a year.
For a year, you toddle around the shelter.
The sky is blue, but way over there
The grass is green far away on the ancient tombs.
My heart is a pendulum
Pounding in my chest, keeping time for the march.
The small cricket knows to dig a shelter
The crab doesn't sleep: it, too, fears the bombs.
In the moonlight, even the hare hides.

The black clouds hinder the enemy's sight.
Flowers and trees join the march
Concealing troops crossing streams, valleys, villages.
My son, trenches crisscross everywhere.
They're as long as the roads you'll someday take.
Our deep shelter is more precious than a house.
The gun is close by, the bullets ready
If I must shoot.
When you grow up, you'll hold life in your own hands.
Whatever I think at present
I note down to remind you of your childhood days.
In the future, when our dreams come true,
You'll love our history all the more.

Translation by Phan Thanh Hao with Lady Borton

ANN SNITOW

Holding the Line at Greenham Common: On Being Joyously Political in Dangerous Times

Ann Snitow (b. 1943) is a writer, educator, and activist living in New York City. She co-edited *Powers of Desire: The Politics of Sexuality* and has taught women's studies and literature at Eugene Lang College of the New School for Social Research. Long involved in the women's movement, she has been especially active in working with feminist groups from the former Eastern bloc. Greenham Common Peace Encampment in Great Britain, about which she writes here, became a worldwide symbol in the 1980s of women's action in opposition to nuclear armaments and the nuclear death machine. It inspired other women's peace camps to take root in West Berlin, Japan, Scotland, northern Germany, Norway, Sweden, Arizona, Wisconsin, South Carolina, Washington State, and upstate New York.

■

Back in 1981 when I first heard about the women's peace camp at Greenham Common, I was impressed but a little worried, too. Here was a stubborn little band of squatters obstructing business as usual at a huge military base. But the early media reports celebrated these women as orderly housewives and mothers who would never make this vulgar noise just for themselves but were naturally concerned about their children, innocent animals, and growing plants.

My feminist reaction was: not *again*. I had joined the women's liberation movement in 1970 to escape this very myth of the special altruism of women, our innate peacefulness, our handy patience for repetitive tasks, our peculiar endurance—no doubt perfect for sitting numbly in the Greenham mud, babies and arms outstretched, begging men to keep our children safe from nuclear war.

We feminists had argued back then that women's work had to be done by men, too: no more "women only" when it came to emotional generosity or trips to the launderette. We did form women-only groups—an autonomous women's movement—but this was to forge a necessary solidarity for resistance, not to cordon off a magic femaleness as distorted in its way as the old reverence for motherhood. Women have a long history of allowing their own goals to be eclipsed by others, and even feminist groups have often been subsumed by other movements. Given this suspiciously unselfish past, I was uneasy with women-only groups that did not concentrate on overcoming the specific oppression of women.

And why should demilitarization be women's special task? If there's one thing in this world that *won't* discriminate in men's favor, it's a nuclear explosion. Since the army is a dense locale of male symbols, actions, and forms of association, let men sit in the drizzle, I thought; let *them* worry about the children for a change.

But even before going to Greenham I should have known better than to have trusted its media image. If the women were such nice little home birds, what were they doing out in the wild, balking at male authority, refusing to shut up or go back home? I've been to Greenham twice now in the effort to understand why many thousands of women have passed through the camps, why thousands are organized in support groups all over Britain and beyond, why thousands more can be roused to help in emergencies or show up for big actions.

What I discovered has stirred my political imagination more than any activism since that first, intense feminist surge 15 years ago. Though I still have many critical questions about Greenham, I see it as a rich source of fresh thinking about how to be joyously, effectively political in a conservative, dangerous time. Obviously this intense conversion experience is going to take some explaining.

When, in the summer of 1981, a small group of women from Cardiff in Wales decided to use their holidays to take a long walk for peace, they could choose from a startlingly large number of possible destinations. Unobtrusive, varying in size and purpose, more than 100 U.S. military facilities are tucked away in the English countryside, an embarrassment of military sites available for political pilgrimage.

One U.S. base distinguished itself as particularly dreadful. Enormous, centrally located, but quietly carrying on incognito, the site was Greenham Common, outside the town of Newbury, where the U.S. air force was then preparing for 96 ground-launched cruise missiles to be deployed in the fall of 1983. The cruise, along with the Pershing II missile, is the centerpiece of NATO's new European arsenal. Because it is small and deployed from mobile launch points on sea or land, and because it flies low, the cruise is hard to detect—transparently a first-strike weapon. . . .

To protest this new step in the arms race, the Welsh women set out to walk 120 miles due east to Newbury, only 60 miles out from London. They were a varied bunch, mostly strangers to each other—36 women from very different class and political backgrounds, four men in support, and a few children. Their nine-day walk, which was ignored by the press, filled them with excitement and energy, and they were greeted warmly in the towns along the way.

By the time they reached Greenham, however, the media silence had become galling. Four women decided to chain themselves to the main gate of the base to force the world to take notice. This act of protest has had children and grandchildren undreamed of by the original, quite humble, and politically inexperienced Greenham marchers. Teachers, farmers, nurses, and—yes— housewives, they had no intention of staying at Greenham. But first the media took their time; then tents had to be set up and people informed. A few days spent in support of the chained women lengthened to a week, then two. Some campers had to leave, but others were just arriving.

The summer days began to give way to the chill damp of English winter. Perhaps it felt callow to give up protesting against nuclear disaster just because the afternoons were drawing in. Gradually, as the peace camp persisted—a small cluster of tents and caravans at the main gate of the base—one fact became plain: Greenham was tapping a great, hidden energy source for protest. There were enough women who were willing to give bits of time stolen from the work-that-is-never-done to keep a campfire perpetually burning on Greenham Common.

After initial amusement and tolerance, the missile base took alarm. Winter came but the women did not go away. On January 20, 1982, the nearby town of Newbury served notice on the camps of its intention to evict.

If ever the women had considered packing it in, this evidence that they were a real thorn in the side of the American military and its English support systems must have clinched matters. Prime Minister Margaret Thatcher told the world the women were irresponsible; she didn't like them one bit. The women began telling reporters, "We're here for as long as it takes"—the "it" left menacingly specific. Some may have meant only the local rejection of U.S. cruise missiles. But by this time even the opposition Labour party was beginning to consider the far more ambitious goal of unilateral disarmament as a serious English option.

The long-threatened eviction didn't come until late May 1982, when the camp was nine months old. By this time the women's community was firmly entrenched. Individual women came and went, but the camp endured. The shifting population made even honest generalizations about the women difficult, while the press had long ended its romance with docile housewives and now made more insulting efforts to stereotype them (just middle-class ladies, just lesbians, just green-haired punks). The women themselves refused self-definition, other than to say that they were unified by their double commitment—to nonviolence and to direct action. Since they eschewed leaders as well as generalizations, there was no spokesperson to mediate between the world and the spontaneous acts of the group.

It is no doubt this very amorphousness that had made evicting the women so difficult. The police are taught to arrest the ringleader, but here there is none. Campers evicted from the Common land simply cross over to Ministry of Transport land, a strip alongside the road, or to Ministry of Defense land. Evicted from there, they move back to council land. Constant evictions— sometimes daily—have become a central, shaping reality of Greenham life. Since no location there is legal, even the smallest acts of persistence acquire special symbolic weight. For anyone, just visiting Greenham Common, sitting down on an overturned bucket at a campfire for a chat and tea, is an act of civil disobedience.

During my first visit, a two-day stay, I assumed that it was with grisly irony that the women had named the gates the colors of the rainbow. My time at Indigo was absurdly bleak and monochromatic. We struggled to keep the fire going; Maria (who, it turned out, was from Spain) performed a vegetarian miracle on a tiny, precariously tilted grill; we talked to the guards five feet from us on the other side of the fence about war, peace, men, women, weather, money; we slept in an ingenious but soaking handmade teepee, while outside an ever-changing pair of guards patrolled with growling dogs under giant arc lamps, which sizzled in the rain and lit up our dreams.

Greenham seemed mainly a passive test of endurance, though it was obvious too, that instead of destroying the encampment, the stream of evictions has become a source of solidarity, resistance, and imagination. Where once gardens were planned, now a few flowers grow in a pram, easily rolled away at a moment's notice. Where once elaborate circus tents were pitched, now a cup on a stick holds up a makeshift roof. Those unprepossessing huddles of plastic I saw on my arrival were actually full of women, sheltering from the rain. These "benders" can look squashed and ugly from the outside; but the bent branches that support the plastic are often still covered with leaves, making the inside a bower. When the bailiffs come with their big "chompers," they get a pile of soggy polyethylene, while the campers carry their few possessions across the road to safety. As soon as the bulldozers are gone, up go the plastic shelters once more.

Familiar domestic collages of blackened tea kettles, candles, corn flakes, bent spoons, chipped plates (never paper ones) lie around as if the contents of a house had been emptied into the mud, but here the house itself is gone. The women have left privacy and home, and now whatever acts of housekeeping they perform are in the most public of spaces up against the fence or road. Greenham is the ultimate housewife's nightmare: the space that can never be swept clean, ordered, sealed off, or safe. But as the mud blackens hands and the wood smoke permeates clothes and hair, the women of Greenham give up gracefully. (With thick irony I was offered the following suggestions: "Wood smoke is a pretty good deodorant." "Try washing dishes in boiling water; it loosens things up a bit, under the fingernails.")

The evictions have further clarified the situation—this is life *in extremis*, life carried on where authority and custom do not mean it to be lived. There is only one source of water for all the camps. Only small and portable Robinson Crusoe contrivances have a chance. Greenham shreds the illusion of permanence and pushes those who live there into a naked, urgent present.

It is hard to imagine a better intellectual forcing ground for people struggling to grasp the full reality of the nuclear threat. Sitting at the fire, we discussed the postindustrial society, postimperialist England, whether or not one should eat meat, the boundary between useful and irresponsible technical advances. Strewn around us were mixtures of very old technologies (how to make a fire with nothing but damp wood; how to cook everything on that fire—there is no electricity *anywhere* in the camps; how to build a shelter from bracken) and useful new ones (plastic protects everything; some women have fancy Gore-Tex sleeping bags or jackets because, though waterproof, they "breathe").

I told one woman who had lived at Greenham for two years that sometimes the camps looked to me as if World War III had already happened, as if we were rehearsing for life after the bomb, in a flat landscape where there will probably be plenty of bits of plastic and Velcro, but no clean water, no electricity, nowhere to hide. She looked at me pityingly: "Greenham is a holiday camp next to what things would be like if these bombs go off."

Of course, of course. Still, Greenham is a grim reminder of how much effort the simplest acts of maintenance take once one has removed oneself from the house, the town, the city. People there are experimenting with self-governance in small communities; they are living with less, seeking new definitions of comfort and satisfaction. . . .

Part of what makes the daily exhaustion of Greenham endurable for so many different kinds of women—and in such large numbers—is that contrary to first appearances, the place is a magnificent, exotic stage set for effective political gestures. Unlike the political demonstrations I have known, peace camps are permanent frames that can give form to hundreds of individual acts of resistance. Energy flows like light—because of the immediacy of everything, the constant, imminent possibility for self-expression and group solidarity.

You are not only joining something larger than yourself but something that is continuously, inexorably taking its stand of militant witness and rebuke, even while you're sleeping, even when you're fed up and go off to spend a night in town, even when you're angry, confused, or at a political loggerheads with every other woman in the place. Greenham is a springboard from which actions that would usually take months of laborious planning can be dreamed, discussed, and performed between night and morning.

Ideas for Greenham action can come from anywhere—something read in the paper, an image someone shares at the fire—and one such action made Greenham internationally famous, the "embrace the base" demonstration of December 12, 1982. The precipitating image—borrowed from the U.S. Women's Pentagon Action—was of women encircling the fence, surrounding it with feelings of power and love. No one knew if enough women would come to stretch around the nine-mile perimeter, so the nervous few who had set the idea in motion told everyone to bring long scarves to use as connectors, just in case.

Somewhere between 30,000 and 50,000 came, more than enough to embrace the entire round. (Whatever the press says, the women are always uncountable: Greenham has no center, no check-in point, no higher ground for surveying the scene. It is forced—by geography and police—to be scattered; it is elusive and invertebrate by choice.) The women festooned every inch of fence with symbols, paint, messages. To those who were there and the millions more who heard about it, the action seemed a miracle. The next day, 2,000 women blockaded the base, and two weeks later, on New Year's dawn, 44 climbed the fence and began an hour's dance on the half-completed missile silos.

On the anniversary of "embrace the base" the women tried another, more hostile image of encirclement. Again 50,000 came, this time with mirrors they held up to the fence, reflecting its own dreary reality back on itself. At yet another carefully planned action, the women locked the soldiers inside the base by securing all the gates with heavy-duty bicycle locks. The increasingly frantic soldiers couldn't cut their way out and, finally, had to push one of their own gates down.

But it is a distortion of Greenham activism to mention only these large and well-known events, which required an unusual amount of advance planning. In fact, nothing was more maddening for an old new leftist like me than the effort to figure out where a Greenham action comes from—rather like trying to find out how a drop of dye travels though a gallon of water. Women told me: Well, this one had this idea. And we all had a meeting. (Who is "all"? "Whoever wanted to do an action.") Then some of us didn't like it. And we kept talking about it. We changed it a bit. We agreed to ask all our friends and their friends, by phone, by chain letter. We have a big network. . . .

Most direct action at Greenham is generated not from the larger network but within small affinity groups. An idea or image travels around the gates like wildfire. "Let's have a vigil at the gate at sunset and call the names of the people who wanted to be here but couldn't." "Let's confuse them by blockading the road a mile from the gate and creating such a traffic jam that they can't get to us to arrest us." Once, at Easter: "Let's dress up like furry animals and cover ourselves with honey, and break into the base." (No one arrested the women who did this one—maybe because they were too sticky?)

Or take the fence, that always present reminder of an "outside" versus "inside," a raggle-taggle band of colorful women who sing and dance and watch versus a gray-and-brown squad of soldiers who march and drill and watch. My first impression of this fence as something final and authoritative left me entirely unprepared for the women's view of it: they have simply rejected it as a legitimate boundary. Slipping under or cutting doors through the wire, they enter the base constantly, exploring, painting, filching frighteningly bureaucratic memos about nuclear war—symbolically undermining the concept "security." Hundreds have been arrested for criminal damage to the wire, yet women continue to enter the base routinely, in large numbers.

Certainly Greenham's effectiveness is hard to measure. The powers that be—from Margaret Thatcher to NATO and even as far as the Kremlin—profess to be paying no attention to the women, nor to the mass European peace movement in general. But the women don't accept the powers that be, a stance that has earned them a grudging respect among their compatriots.

As early as the 1950s, Winston Churchill warned the British that they were letting their island become an "unsinkable aircraft carrier" for the United States. Successive governments of both parties ignored these warnings, preferring to think of England as maintaining some measure of old empire through its "special relationship" with the world's greatest power.

But, in order to keep up these costly prerogatives, to have an independent nuclear force and colonial clout in farflung places like the Falklands, the British government has allowed its own soil to be colonized. Britain has quietly become a client state. . . .

To turn around an arms race so richly fed by capital investment, a mass movement is essential, but what sort of *mass*? Greenham's effectiveness must be measured not only by the role it plays in mobilizing large numbers but also by the kind of political culture it has to offer those numbers. . . .

These women bring to the fire values forged in a variety of movements: they absolutely reject any leadership (like the anarchists, or like the feminist consciousness-raising groups some of them came from); they insist on nonviolence (like the pacifist, Quaker, or other Christian groups some of them came from). They are ecologists, trade unionists, Labour party members, and, frequently, Campaign for Nuclear Disarmament (CND) activists. A wide variety of left politics also fertilizes Greenham; in England, left paradigms are taken more for granted than in the United States. . . .

The Greenham women I talked to take great pains to point out that the purpose of Greenham is not to exclude men but to include women—at last. Though a few women there might still tell you women are biologically more peaceful than men, this view has been mostly replaced by a far more complex analysis of why women need to break with our old, private complicity with public male violence. No one at Greenham seems to be arguing that the always evolving Greenham value system is inevitably female. The women recognize their continuity with the Quakers, with Gandhi, with the entire pacifist tradition, and with the anarchist critique of the state. At the same time, women, the Greenham campers believe, may have a separate statement to make about violence because we have our own specific history in relation to it. . . .

A whole activist generation is being forged at Greenham, not of age but of shared experience. These women are disobedient, disloyal to civilization, experienced in taking direct action, advanced in their ability to make a wide range of political connections. The moveable hearth is their schoolroom, where they piece together a stunning if raffish political patchwork.

Before visiting Greenham, I had feared that its politics would prove simple-minded, that those absolutes, life and death, would have cast more complex social questions in the shade. How, for instance, could the old question What do women want? survive when the subject is Mutual Assured Destruction (MAD, U.S. military slang for nuclear deterrence). As Brenda Whisker wrote in *Breaching the Peace,* an English collection of feminist essays criticizing the women's peace movement, "I think that stopping the holocaust is easier than liberating women." Hard words, certainly, but understandable, solidified through bitter experience. While women and children are first, feminism continues to be last. . . .

I wonder if women are having to learn at Greenham—with a difference—what men learn too early and carry too far: the courage to dare, to test reaction, to define oneself *against* others. Nonviolent direct action takes great courage. The big men on their horses or machines are doing as ordered—which is comfortable for them. In contrast, it can be truly terrifying to refuse to do what an angry, pushing policeman tells you do do. For women particularly, such acts are fresh and new and this cutting across the grain of feminine socialization is a favorite, daring sport of the young at the fence. Such invitations give women a revolutionary taste of conflict, lived out fully, in our own persons, with gender no longer a reliable determinant of the rules. . . .

Certainly it is no use for women to turn self-righteous, as I had found myself doing—claiming a higher moral ground than men. On that ground we are admired but ignored. As Dorothy Dinnerstein has argued in *The Mermaid and the Minotaur*, emotional women have traditionally been treated like court jesters that the king keeps around to express his own anxieties—and thus vent them harmlessly. A woman's body lying down in a road in front of a missile launcher has a very different symbolic resonance for everyone from that of a male body in the same position. Greenham's radical feminist critics wonder just what kind of peace a female lying down can bring. Won't men simply allow women to lie in the mud forever because the demonstrators themselves only underline men's concept of what is female (passivity, protest, peace) and what is male (aggression, action, war)?

Before I came to Greenham, I shared these worries. But at Greenham at its best, women's nonviolent direct action becomes not another face of female passivity but a difficult political practice with its own unique discipline. The trick—a hard one—is to skew the dynamics of the old male-female relationships toward the new meanings, to interrupt the old conversation between overconfident kings and hysterical, powerless jesters. This will surely include an acknowledgement of our past complicity with men and war making and a dramatization of our new refusal to aid and assist. (I think of a delicious young woman I heard singing out to a group of also very young soldiers: "We don't find you sexy anymore, you know, with your little musket, fife, and drum.")

Perhaps some of the new meanings we need will be found buried in the old ones. If women feel powerless, we can try to share this feeling, to make individual men see that they, too, are relatively powerless in the face of a wildly escalating arms race. Naturally, this is a message men resist, but the women at Greenham are endlessly clever at dramatizing how the army shares their impotence: The army cannot prevent them from getting inside the fence or shaking it down. It cannot prevent them from blockading the gates. It cannot prevent them from returning after each eviction.

Or, rather, it could prevent all this, but only by becoming a visibly brutal force, and this would be another kind of defeat, since the British armed services and police want to maintain their image of patriarchal protectors; they do not want to appear to be batterers of nonviolent women. Greenham women expose the contradictions of gender: by being women they dramatize powerlessness but they also disarm the powerful. . . .

When I describe Greenham women—their lives in these circumstances—

I often get the reaction that they sound like mad idealists, detached from a reality principle about what can and cannot be done, and how. In a sense this is true. The women reject power and refuse to study it, at least on its own terms. But the other charge—that they are utopian dreamers who sit around and think about the end of the world while not really living in this one—is far from the mark. . . .

Greenham women see a kind of fatalism all around them. They, too, have imagined the end, and their own deaths, and have decided that they prefer to die without taking the world with them. Nothing makes a them more furious than the apathy in the town of Newbury, where they are often told, "Look, you've got to die anyway. So what difference does it make how you go?" These are the real millenarians, blithely accepting that the end is near.

In contrast, the women are very hardheaded, very pragmatic. They see a big war machine, the biggest the world has known; and, rather than sitting in the cannon's mouth hypnotized, catatonic with fear or denial, they are trying to back away from the danger, step by step. They refuse to be awed or silenced by the war machine. Instead they say calmly that what was built by humans can be dismantled by them, too. Their logic, clarity and independence are endlessly refreshing. Where is it written, they ask, that we must destroy ourselves?

ALICE WALKER/ZORA NEALE HURSTON

Only Justice Can Stop a Curse

Alice Walker (b. 1944) is a renowned African American author best known for the widely read novel *The Color Purple*. She has received both Guggenheim and National Endowment for the Arts Fellowships and a prize from the National Institute of Arts and Letters for her writing. Walker is also credited with being instrumental in the rediscovery of the pioneering African American writer and folklorist Zora Neale Hurston. During the 1920s and 1930s, Hurston traveled through the South recording the richness of traditional black oral literature. This "curse," paraphrased here, and blended with oaths from other folk literature, was found by Hurston in her travels and resurrected by the work and efforts of Alice Walker. Walker is a supporter of many humane causes, including several organizations in the peace and social justice movement.

■

"To the Man God: O Great One, I have been sorely tried by my enemies and have been blasphemed and lied against. My good thoughts and my honest action have been turned to bad actions and dishonest ideas. My home has been disrespected, my children have been cursed and ill-treated. My dear ones have been backbitten and their virtue questioned. O Man God, I beg that this that I ask for my enemies shall come to pass:

"That the South wind shall scorch their bodies and make them wither and shall not be tempered to them. That the North wind shall freeze their blood and numb their muscles and that it shall not be tempered to them. That the West wind shall blow away their life's breath and will not leave their hair grow, and that their

fingernails shall fall off and their bones shall crumble. That the East wind shall make their minds grow dark, their sight shall fail and their seed dry up so that they shall not multiply.

"I ask that their fathers and mothers from their furthest generation will not intercede for them before the great throne, and the wombs of their women shall not bear fruit except for strangers, and that they shall become extinct. I pray that the children who may come shall be weak of mind and paralyzed of limb and that they themselves shall curse them in their turn for ever turning the breath of life into their bodies. I pray that disease and death shall be forever with them and that their worldly goods shall not prosper, and that their crops shall not multiply and that their cows, their sheep, and their hogs and all their living beasts shall die of starvation and thirst. I pray that their house shall be unroofed and that the rain, the thunder and lightning shall find the innermost recesses of their home and that the foundation shall crumble and the floods tear it asunder. I pray that the sun shall not shed its rays on them in benevolence, but instead it shall beat down on them and burn them and destroy them. I pray that the moon shall not give them peace, but instead shall deride them and decry them and cause their minds to shrivel. I pray that their friends shall betray them and cause them loss of power, of gold and of silver, and that their enemies shall smite them until they beg for mercy which shall not be given them. I pray that their tongues shall forget how to speak in sweet words, and that it shall be paralyzed and that all about them will be desolation, pestilence and death. O Man God, I ask you for all these things because they have dragged me in the dust and destroyed my good name; broken my heart and caused me to curse the day that I was born. So be it."

This is a curse-prayer that Nora Zeale Hurston, novelist and anthropologist, collected in the 1920s. And by then it was already old. I have often marveled at it. At the precision of its anger, the absoluteness of its bitterness. Its utter hatred of the enemies it condemns. It is a curse-prayer by a person who would readily, almost happily, commit suicide, if it meant her enemies would also die. Horribly.

I am sure it was a woman who first prayed this curse. And I see her—Black, Yellow, Brown or Red, *"aboriginal"* as the Ancients are called in South Africa and Australia and other lands invaded, expropriated and occupied by whites. And I think, with astonishment, that the curse-prayer of this colored woman— starved, enslaved, humiliated and carelessly trampled to death—over centuries, is coming to pass. Indeed, like ancient peoples of color the world over, who have tried to tell the white man of the destruction that would inevitably follow from the uranium mining plunder of their sacred lands, this woman—along with millions and billions of obliterated sisters, brothers, and children—seems to have put such enormous energy into her hope for revenge, that her curse seems close to bringing it about. And it is this hope for revenge, finally, I think, that is at the heart of People of Color's resistance to any anti-nuclear movement.

In any case, this has been my own problem.

When I have considered the enormity of the white man's crimes against humanity. Against women. Against every living person of color. Against the poor. Against my mother and my father. Against me. . . . When I consider that at this very moment he wishes to take away what little freedom I have died to achieve, through denial of my right to vote. . . . Has already taken away education, medicine, housing and food. . . . That William Shockley is saying at this moment that he will run for the Senate of my country to push his theory that Blacks are genetically inferior and should be sterilized. . . . When I consider that he is, they are, a real and present threat to my life of my daughter, my people, I think—in perfect harmony with my sister of long: *Let the earth marinate in poisons. Let the bombs cover the ground like rain. For nothing short of total destruction will ever teach them anything.*

And it would be good, perhaps, to put an end to the species in any case, rather than let white men continue to subjugate it, and continue their lust to dominate, exploit and despoil not just our planet, but the rest of the universe, which is their clear and oft-stated intention, leaving their arrogance and litter not just on the moon, but on everything else they can reach.

If we have any true love for the stars, planets, the rest of Creation, we must do everything we can to keep white men away from them. They who have appointed themselves our representatives to the rest of the universe. They who have never met any new creature without exploiting, abusing or destroying it. They who say we poor and colored and female and elderly blight neighborhoods, while they blight worlds.

What they have done to the Old, they will do the New.

Under the white man every star would become a South Africa, every planet a Vietnam.

Fatally irradiating ourselves may in fact be the only way to save others from what Earth has already become. And this is a consideration that I believe requires serious thought from every one of us.

However, just as the sun shines on the godly and the ungodly alike, so does nuclear radiation. And with this knowledge it becomes increasingly difficult to embrace the thought of extinction purely for the assumed satisfaction of—from the grave—achieving revenge. Or even of accepting our demise as a planet as a simple and just preventative medicine administered to the Universe. Life is better than death, I believe, if only because it is less boring, and because it has fresh peaches in it. In any case, Earth is my home—though for centuries white people have tried to convince me I have no right to exist, except in the dirtiest, darkest corners of the globe.

So let me tell you: I intend to protect my home. Praying—not a curse—only the hope that my courage will not fail my love. But if by some miracle, and all our struggle, the Earth is spared, only justice to every living thing (and everything is alive) will save humankind.

And we are not saved yet.

Only justice can stop a curse.

NANCY MOREJON

Black Woman

Nancy Morejon (b. 1944) is a celebrated Afro-Caribbean poet and feminist of Cuba. She earned her diploma as a teacher of English and was graduated from Havana Institute with a degree in art in 1961. She has said, "As a black woman, I would not be a poet at all if it were not for La Revolución." Morejon has won the top prizes of Cuba for her poems and has published several poetry collections, as well as an ethnic history, *The Tongue of a Bird,* about the mining town of Nicaro where peasant laborers were exploited by American corporations.

■

I can still smell the foam of the sea I was forced to cross.
Neither I or the ocean remember that night.
But I can't forget the first bird I saw in the distance.
The clouds were high like innocent witnesses.
Perhaps, I haven't forgotten my lost coastline or my ancestral tongues.
They dragged me here and here I've lived.
And because I was made to work like a beast here,
here I was born again.
I was forced so many times to remember my Mandingo origins.

I became disobedient.

You, master, bought me in the square.
I embroidered your coat and gave birth to your son,
but my son had no name.
And you, master, died in the arms of an impeccable British Lord

I walked far.

This is the land where I suffered the stocks
            and the whip.
This is the land where I flow through many rivers,
            and under its sun planted seed.
This is the land where I harvested
            but reaped no food.

As a home, I had a prison.
I myself carried the stones to build the barracks.
I sang the national anthem composed by your national birds.

I rebelled.

In this same land, I touched fresh blood and rotting bones
            of others enslaved by this land like me.
and I never again dreamed of the road home to Guinea.

But, was it Guinea? A Benin? Was it Madagascar?
            Or Cabo Verde?

        I worked even harder.

I composed my own song infused with my African memories.
Here, I built my own world.

        I fled to the mountains.

My true independence was a shelter in the highland jungles.
where I learned to mount a horse among the soldiers of Maceo's troops.
Only in a century much later,
next to my descendents
from the azure mountain,
            I came down from La Sierra
to be finished with exploiters and usurers,
with generals and slave owners.
Now, I exist: only today do we have and create our own.

        Nothing is alien to us.
Ours is the land!
Ours, is the sea and sky!
Ours, the magic of dreams!
I am equal among the people. Here, I dance with them
among fruit trees we have planted to share among ourselves,
our communal harvest!
The prodigal wood already resounds!

Translation by Daniela Gioseffi with Enildo Garcia

MAIREAD CORRIGAN MAGUIRE

Letter to an Iraqi Woman

Mairead Corrigan Maguire (b. 1944) won the Nobel Peace Prize in 1976 with her comrade in nonviolent activism, Betty Williams. The two "housewives" risked their lives to lead many peace protests in the streets of Northern Ireland. The year 2001 marked the one hundredth–anniversary celebration of the institution of the Nobel Peace Prize, and thirty-four of the thirty-nine living Nobel Peace laureates assembled in Oslo to participate in the events. Maguire's presentation took the form of this open letter from the Peace People of Northern Ireland to Ms. Umm Reyda. Maguire had met Umm Reyda during a visit in 1999 to the remains of the Ameriyah refugee shelter in Baghdad, which was destroyed, along with its hundreds of civilian inhabitants, by American bombs during the Gulf War. It was published on the Web site of Voices in the Wilderness, a nongovernmental peace group that works to alleviate the suffering of Iraqi civilians caused by economic sanctions on Iraq. An estimated half-million Iraqi children, as well as thousands of adult civilians, have died because of the lack of food, medicine, and water prohibited to them by the sanctions.

■

Dear Umm Reyda,

I hope you receive this letter. We met three years ago on a Sunday in March, 1999, when Kathy Kelly of Voices in the Wilderness and Fr. John Dear, International Fellowship of Reconciliation, an American peace initiative, brought an international delegation, including Adolfo Perez Esquivel (Nobel Peace Prize winner) and myself, to visit the site of the Ameriyah shelter in Baghdad.

How are you keeping, Umm Reyda? Well, I hope, in spite of the ongoing suffering and hardship.

When we met, you were living in a little Portacabin on the site and acting as a guide for visitors to the shelter. You told us that one night during the Gulf war many hundreds of people had gathered in the shelter to celebrate the end of Ramadan. (This happened to be the same day as Christians were remembering Ash Wednesday, the beginning of 40 days of repentance, prayer and fasting). That night the shelter was struck by two American bombs. Of the hundreds present, only 14 people survived the inferno. Your son, your daughter Reyda, and thirteen of your relatives were among the dead. We were moved to tears when we saw the photographs of the victims, most of whom were women and children. You told us that you had worked since that day to keep the truth alive—for them and for the world. I remember so well your passionate plea for the story to be told about what happened and your call for "no more wars." How much we need to hear your voice in our world today.

Since then, I am haunted by the memory of the burnt imprints of bodies, fused into the concrete walls. In the shelter, overwhelmed with grief, I remembered another time when sorrow had paralysed my soul. It was January 1988, when at the invitation of Elie Wiesel, I walked through the horror chambers of the concentration camp in Auschwitz. I cried at what those who called themselves Christians had done to their Jewish brothers and sisters. That day my hope and strength lay in my belief that God loves, and lives, in each one of us. It is not God who kills. It is human beings who are blinded by hate and fear.

Auschwitz and the Ameriyah shelter. How much suffering can the human family bear without drowning in a collective sea of despair and hopelessness? But suffering can also be a positive force. It can water the seeds of compassion and motivate us to speak truth to power.

Umm Reyda, your words challenge each of us not to harden our hearts or fall into despair, but to begin a journey of repentance and forgiveness together which can lead to reconciliation and to a celebration of life itself.

Your gift to me that day was your gentle presence and witness to truth. The truth that each person's life is precious and unique. You have suffered so much, yet your dignity as a woman and as a mother was shining from within. You remind us that even in our brokenness and vulnerability, the human spirit is magnificent. Together with millions of men and women around the world, you are a source of hope and an inspiration for all of us to practise forgiveness in the search for justice. You give us the courage to believe in ourselves and in each other. When I see you in my mind's eye, standing in front of the shelter by your Portacabin, I think that you are living proof of the transforming power of love.

It is now Ramadan, a month of penance and purification for Muslims. It is also a special time for Christians, as we prepare for Christmas during the season of Advent. It is a time for us to repent for the wrongs we have done to others.

On this occasion, I would like to apologise to you, Umm Reyda, for the terrible injustice being inflicted upon the Iraqi people by the misguided policies of my government. I am ashamed to witness the continuing imposition of economic sanctions, a silent bomb, which cost the lives of thousands of Iraqi children. I understand your increased fear at the present moment by the threats, being made openly, that your country will again be targeted because of the war in Afghanistan. I want you to know that I am, just as openly, opposed to these threats, and will continue to work in a peaceful way to prevent these becoming a reality. And not just in Iraq, but in so many countries, children are suffering because of our life styles and policies.

Fear is at the root of many problems. Fear can blind us from seeing the image of God in each other, in all of creation, and stops us from loving our neighbour as ourselves.

In December, in the Christian tradition, we celebrate the birth of Jesus, who was born two thousand years ago in Bethlehem. Today, in Bethlehem, as in so many places around the world, children continue to suffer from violence and war. It was in the awareness of the need to build a better future for children, that the Nobel Peace laureates launched a campaign which has culminated in the declaration by the UN General Assembly of the Decade for a Culture of Peace and Non-violence for the Children of the World (2001–2010). This decade gives us all hope.

Everyone, especially children and youth, can bring their imagination and creativity to building this new culture. They can take inspiration from others in the past such as Mahatma Gandhi, Abdul Ghaffar Khan, Martin Luther King, Dorothy Day, Takashi Nagai, and Abraham Joshua Heschel. People who loved humanity and strived to overcome prejudice and discrimination to build the "beloved community."

Recent developments in Northern Ireland also give hope. With its deep social and political problems resulting in almost 30 years of "troubles" it is an example that complex relational and structural issues cannot be solved by military or paramilitary means, but only by building a peace process through dialogue at all levels. The new all-inclusive, power-sharing government now in place will allow the Northern Irish people to begin healing past wounds and to engage in a genuine process of reconciliation. I believe that the lessons we have learned in Northern Ireland could be of help to other communities emerging from years of violent conflict, encouraging them to explore new nonviolent alternatives in the search for peace.

In this regard, I am full of hope for humanity. I believe we can, we must, we will overcome violence and war. Many will think I am naïve in saying this, but I believe you will understand me, Umm Reyda.

I wish you peace. Peace also to my Iraqi brothers and sisters, whose kindness I remember with a smile. I hope someday to visit you again, to share your friendship, and savour once more the beauty and mystery of your people and their desert land.

Salaam,
Mairead

PETRA KELLY

Women and Ecology

Petra Karin Kelly (1947–1992) was a West German political scientist who became an internationally known leader of the Green party. When Kelly's ten-year-old sister died of cancer, she founded the Grace P. Kelly Association for the Support of Research into Children's Cancer, which includes in its work an investigation of the causes of cancer in children living in the vicinity of chemical and nuclear installations. In 1972, she joined the West German Association for Environmental Protection Actions Groups and in 1979 helped to found the Greens, becoming their leading national candidate. Following the West German elections in 1983, Petra Kelly was one of the twenty-seven Greens elected to the Bundestag. There she was elected one of the Greens' three parliamentary speakers. She was awarded the Alternative Nobel Prize, established by Jahob von Uexkull, in Stockholm, in 1982. In 1983, the Women's Strike for Peace, a U.S. organization, named her Peace Woman of the Year. She wrote several books and articles on feminism, children's cancer, disarmament, and Hiroshima, the best known being the collection entitled *Fighting for Hope* (1984), the source of this excerpt. Many German peace activists suspect foul play in her strange and untimely death, deemed a joint suicide with her companion, a former Nazi soldier who had also become a committed peace activist.

∎

While women have increasingly discovered their own oppression in Western Europe, in the United States, in Australia, and elsewhere, they have also learned to organise themselves and to speak out against the oppression of others—particularly the victims of militarisation and nuclearisation.

There has been much consciousness raising among the new brave women in a "brave new world." Political issues become personal, and personal issues become political. I have been with many women, whether I marched alongside them in Sydney or Hiroshima or Whyl, whether I sat in a tent on a windy Irish day at Carnsore Point, or spoke to them at the UN Plaza during the Disarmament March, or during my campaign trail for the European Elections as head of the German Ecological List.

I have hope for the world, although it is ten minutes before Doomsday. Women all over the world are rising up, and infusing the anti-nuclear and peace movements with a vitality and creativity never seen before. Women stand up in courtrooms and explain the differences between natural and artificial radiation; they stand up at demonstrations and non-violent occupations of nuclear sites. They are the genuine ombudsmen of children to come. Like Dr. Helen Caldicott, a children's doctor from Australia, they firmly believe that each of us must accept total responsibility for the earth's survival.

We are discovering how commercial and military technologies impose unacceptable risks to health and life. To defeat these technologies, we must begin to shape world events.

World expenditure on the arms race is over $1,000 million per day. Countless children are condemned to illiteracy, disease, starvation and death by the massive diversion of resources (natural and human) to the arms race. The cost of one tank would supply equipment for 520 classrooms and the cost of one destroyer could provide electrification for three cities and nineteen rural zones. Women who have opposed the military base enlargement in Larzac, women who do not buy toy guns at Christmas, know that the accumulation of weapons today constitutes much more of a threat than a protection. There have been over 900 nuclear explosions on the surface of the earth by the end of 1978 and it is estimated that the number of soldiers in the world today is twice the number of teachers, doctors and nurses.

Woman must lead the efforts in education for peace awareness, because only she, I feel, can go back to her womb, her roots, her natural rhythms, her inner search for harmony and peace, while men, most of them anyway, are continually bound to their power struggle, the exploitation of nature, and military ego trips. Our timidity must end, for the earth has no emergency exit.

The conditions are being created for a police state, centralized uncontrollable energy systems, and increasing mechanization, all led by the silicon chip which Japanese manufacturers claim achieves circuits in which there are only thirty failures in one billion hours of operation. Increasing numbers of persons will become unemployed and superfluous—already in 1970, in a report to the World Bank, Robert McNamara spoke of such persons as "marginal men." It is estimated that by 1980, there will be one billion of them. The huge corporations that make human beings marginal can sell, make and break governments, and decide whether a non-nuclear nation like Ireland will have to go nuclear. And the same big companies now even begin to dominate the solar industry in the West. According to UN reports, a new form of so-called solar monopoly could mean further Third World dependence on a handful of corporations. Already production of large solar-based electricity generating plants is mainly restricted to gigantic companies like Northrup, McDonnell-Douglas and Mobil Oil. The Ford Motor Corporation, Philips and General Motors dominate small-and medium-sized solar power plants. Firms are attempting to restrict access to this technology—awaiting the time when they need areas of *cheap* labour before moving production out to the Third World.

We are often told that the experts and the big firms do not know how to deal with the problems which threaten worldwide disaster, "that all the facts are not in," that more research must be done, and more reports written. This is simply an excuse for endlessly putting off action. We already know enough to begin to deal with all our major problems: nuclear war, over-population, pollution, hunger, the desolation of the planet, the inequality among peoples. The present crisis is a crisis not of information, but of policy. We cannot cope with all the problems that threaten us, while maximising profits.

As things stand now, the people, especially women and children of the Third World, are to perish first. They have already begun to starve; all that is asked of them is to starve quietly. The plight of women in the Third World is one that touches me deeply. There are now about 100 million children under the age of five always hungry. Each year 15 million children die from infection and malnutrition. There are about 800 million illiterates in the world; nearly two-thirds of them are women.

The number of women unable to read and write is about half a billion. In the Third World, 40-70 per cent of agricultural labour is female—they plant the seed, haul the water, tend the animals, strive to keep their families alive—but all the while they are socially inferior. Men in the Third World are lured into the cities to work for one of the many Western companies or join Third World armies, supplied with guns and tanks sold by the same companies. The women left behind on the land, usually infibulated and circumcised (bodily and sexually mutilated), are not taught the use of new irrigation systems and immediate small-scale alternative technology. Instead they learn to buy Nestle's Lactogen Milk Powder to mix with dirty brown water. The result: many babies die with bloated stomachs. Women in the Third World are further exploited through various forms of prostitution—whether through "rent-a-wife" schemes, as in Vietnam, or though international finance companies developing hotel brothels and promoting tourism through sexist advertisements.

The developed nations are armed to the teeth and mean not only to hold on to what they have, but to grasp anything they still can. Look at the uranium mines in Namibia, look at what we, the Europeans, are doing to the soul and culture of the Aborigines in Australia; look at the plight of the Navajo Indians in North America dying from the radon gases. And as the great famines occur, the grain and other agricultural produce is either rotting away in EEC silos or is fed to cattle to supply the rapidly increasing demand for meat in affluent countries. The suffering people of this world must come together to take control of their lives, to wrest political power from their present masters, who are pushing them towards destruction.

This is also a plea to all women to join those sisters who have already risen up—who have helped to shape the ecological revolution. Together we can overthrow all the imposed structures of domination.

Even in the affluent parts of the world the same patterns of sexual inequality may be seen. Equal pay and equal treatment in all areas of schooling, training, promotion and working conditions have not, in reality, been won. Women in South Italy, and in the West of Ireland, lead lives of desperation and humiliation. Battered women and children take refuge from husbands and fathers and women increasingly get cervical cancers and other abnormalities from the Pill of the pharmaceutical giants. Women who stay on hormones poison their cells, saturate their bile and risk birth defects in later children. Every eighth child in Germany is born handicapped in some way.

The story of thalidomide, commercially available for years after it should have been outlawed, is just one of the many. The pitiful caricatures of adults, living reminders of an unconcerned pharmacology, show how lethal the policies of male researchers and male politicians have been—industries have falsified data, bought off scientists, posited ridiculous risk-benefit ratios and threshold levels. This has resulted in a cancer rate that qualifies as "epidemic." The total economic impact—including health care and lost productivity due to cancer—has been estimated at $25 billion a year.

The earth has been mistreated, and only by restoring a balance, only by living with the earth, by employing soft energies and soft technologies can we overcome the violence of patriarchy. Although the masculine ego and capitalist consciousness have made advances in science and technology, they have lost touch with the earth in setting out to conquer nature. The desire for power has left in its wake a terrible path of destruction. There is at the same time a danger of women being seen in the subservient role from which they hope to rise. Some of the ecological, communal and human potential movements are deeply infected by a type of romantic escapism which could all too easily recreate woman's role as the servant of male culture. As an English feminist once said, "We don't want an ecological society where men build windmills and women silently listen, bake bread, and weave rugs."

In recent years, I have also observed that some women have sought to overcome their inferior role by becoming part of the masculine world (Mrs. Thatcher, Indira Gandhi, etc.) When women fight for equal status with men, they run the risk of joining the ranks in times of war. We are so conditioned by masculine values that women often make the mistake of imitating and emulating men at the cost of their own feminism. When I assess the world of male values, it is clear to me that I do not want this kind of "equality."

Recent court-martial proceedings in the USA have indicated that a large group of guardsmen responsible for nuclear missiles are using and distributing illegal drugs. Armed guards had used marijuana, cocaine and LSD while on duty and carrying a loaded pistol. Another example of wanton disregard for life is provided by the French electricity generating board, which recently decided to bring into operation two new nuclear power stations while admitting that there are certain cracks in key reactor components. While governments all over the world are faced with escalating nuclear research bills (bills which private industry will *not* pick up), and while workers repair nuclear accidents with pencils and paper clips (as was recently the case in a nuclear station in Virginia) a young woman is shot dead by the police in an antinuclear demonstration in Spain; policemen denounce women as "whores" during pro-abortion demonstrations and there are still investigations going on to discover what really happened to Karen Silkwood.

. . . the police states foreseen by Orwell—all in the name of secure nuclear societies. Women must lose all fear of speaking up and demanding what is theirs and their children's. Only if we begin to rediscover our own nature, can we discover new ways of wholeness, balance, and decentralisation—can we forge a bond with the Earth and the Moon, living with cooperation, gentleness, non-possessiveness and soft energies.

LINDA HOGAN

Black Hills Survival Gathering, 1980

Linda Hogan (b. 1947) was born into the Chickasaw Nation, a tribe indigenous to what is now known as Oklahoma. Hogan, a poet and environmentalist, now lives in the Colorado mountains with her family. Her work has appeared in such magazines as *Ms.*, *American Voice*, and the *Denver Quarterly*. She has published several award-winning volumes of poetry, including *Power*, *Solar Storms*, *Book of Medicines*, and *Mean Spirit*. This poem comes from a volume entitled *Eclipse*, but first appeared in a volume of Native American poems entitled *Songs from This Earth on Turtle's Back*, edited by Joseph Bruchac of the Laguna Nation, the well-known poet and founder of the Greenfield Press.

■

Bodies on fire
the monks in orange cloth
sing morning into light.

Men wake on the hill.
Dry grass blows from their hair.
B52s blow over their heads
leaving a cross on the ground.
Air returns to itself and silence.

Rainclouds are disappearing
with fractures of light in the distance.
Fierce gases forming,
the sky bending
where people arrive
on dusty roads that change
matter to energy.

My husband wakes.
My daughter wakes.
Quiet morning, she stands
in a pail of water
naked, reflecting light
and this man I love,
with kind hands
he washes her slim hips,
narrow shoulders, splashes
the skin containing
wind and fragile fire,
the pulse in her wrist.

My other daughter wakes
to comb warm sun across her hair.

While I make coffee I tell her
this is the land of her ancestors,
blood and heart.
Does her hair become a mane
blowing in the electric breeze,
her eyes dilate and darken?

The sun rises on all of them
in the center of light
hills that have no boundary,
the child named Thunder Horse,
the child named Dawn Protector
and the man
whose name would mean home in Navajo.

At ground zero
in the center of light we stand.
Bombs are buried beneath us,
destruction flies overhead.
We are waking
in the expanding light
the sulphur-colored grass.
A red horse standing on a distant ridge
looks like one burned
over Hiroshima,
silent, head hanging in sickness.
But look
she raises her head
and surges toward the bluing sky.

Radiant morning.
The dark tunnels inside us carry life.
Red.
Blue.
The children's dark hair against my breast.
On the burning hills
in flaring orange cloth
men are singing and drumming
Heartbeat.

FLORA BROVINA

A New Dawn in Town

Flora Brovina (b. 1949) is an Albanian poet, doctor, and peace activist of Kosovo. She was active in the resistance movement against the regime of President Slobodan Milosevic, who revoked Kosovo's status as an autonomous republic and imposed increasingly brutal Serb military rule on the region. When Serb forces marched into Kosovo to suppress the opposition, Brovina was fired from her post at a Pristina hospital, joining many Albanians dismissed from key positions. Her involvement in the ensuing struggle was prompted by a massacre in Likosane, a small village in central Kosovo: "I saw pictures of an entire family that had been slaughtered," she said. "I saw helpless children had been gunned down." She founded and became president of the Women's League of Kosovo, a movement that mobilized mass support against violence. At one point, twenty thousand Albanian women gathered in Pristina, waving sheets of blank white paper symbolizing that nothing was written down, and that a peaceful solution could still be negotiated. Brovina also established a clinic and refuge for women and children in Pristina, as well as an orphanage for children who had lost their parents to the civil war. When the NATO bombings began, Brovina's son e-mailed the writers' association PEN to report that his mother had been arrested by masked Serb paramilitaries; she was released many months later, after the end of the NATO campaign.

■

The streets are stirring early.
All's quiet in town.
I observe the silent steps of a new beginning.
People pass, walking to somewhere,
Optimism on their lips offering
a greeting of "good morning."

Their footsteps ring on the washed sidewalks
Like factory mallets or typewriters.
The morning passes briskly.
The streets have awakened early.
There's the newspaper editor,
There the shoe-shine man, the milk man:
Passersby, simply walking, walking some place,
And a woman with a baby in her arms.

Translation by Daniela Gioseffi and Ivana Spalatin

DAISY ZAMORA

Song of Hope *and* When We Go Home Again

Daisy Zamora (b. 1959) was director of programming for the radio station of the Sandanista National Liberation Front during the years that it struggled to free the Nicaraguan people from the long dictatorship of Anastasio Somoza. After the Sandanistas took power in 1979, she served as vice president of culture for many years. Her poems, published internationally, have won the National Poetry Prize of her homeland.

SONG OF HOPE

Some day the fields will be always green
and the earth will be black, sweet and damp.
On it, our children will grow tall,
and the children of our children.

And they will be free, like the trees
of the mountain, like the birds.
Every morning they will wake up happy
to be alive, and they will know that the earth
was reconquered for them.

Some day . . .

Today, we cultivate parched fields,
but every furrow is dampened with blood.

Translation by Jane Glazer and Elizabeth Linder

WHEN WE GO HOME AGAIN

When we go home again to our old land
the one we never knew
and we talk of all those things
that have never happened

We'll go on our way leading by the hand
children that have never existed

We'll listen to their voices and we'll live
the life we've talked about so much
and have never lived.

Translation by Miriam Ellis

ANA ISTARÚ

A Time of Cannons Comes Flying

Ana Istarú (b. 1960), a playwright and actress, has won high acclaim in Costa Rica and Spain for her theatrical work. She has been a Guggenheim fellow and received her first prize in poetry at the age of fifteen. Since then, she has published six collections of poetry in Spanish. Her poems appear in anthologies published in Europe, Latin America, and the United States. Istarú's *Death and Other Ephemeral Wrongs* was translated into English by Zoë Anglesey, an award-winning U.S. poet who has played a pivotal role in introducing English-speaking readers to the work of women poets of Central America.

■

Your hand goes to mine
it is the unexpected touch i wait for
the ultimate vestige of what's eternal
a human juncture
that thing that links me to the universe
the irrefutable proof.
Your betrothed hand.
We are together.
But there is a yellow fang, left behind.
It deposits its larva its green pomp
its sticky and undesirable puncture.
A time of cannons comes flying
history's savage affliction.
Over this land the phantom spore
putrefaction
the raucous war destroys
peace, its porcelain
the fragile and ashen flower
we want to survive unnoticed
and transparent to the bullets.
This country that wanted to be invisible
be in another spot on the planet
so as not to hear the bone as it breaks
nor the mouth calling up an inner scream
piety for the gums,
the velvet genitals between the legs
ground to mincemeat. This country
thought it could float immaculately
above the blood.
It said: *My chastity*
my straight and narrow trajectory
I do not live in that stinking hell hole.
They aren't my kin.
But the war connives
to get its garlands.
Doesn't choose to promise peace, has a loose criteria:
it comes to my country and imposes
its little trickle of salt, waits and waits,
watches hate and its abscess grow
spits a sick spit
into sealed ink

leaves the accords vilified.
Therefore, the population does not support itself
sucks in
the toxic print that falsifies,
UPI and AP and. The stingy pig
putting on the docile mug of a North American
goes to a podium and gives a press conference
to infect the transmission to dailies,
and by daybreak it's been quickly turned
into verbose crap.
The population, my compatriots,
the people whom I'm inspired by
and aim
my imperturbable love
don't know they don't know
that fascism grabs them at the neck,
is a fascinated voyeur who spies
until they are down and out
unkempt and fall into oblivion,
thinking about other things other than
peace, peace, the peace, the sovereign
peace proven overwhelmingly to be affectionate.
The general population begins to hate, mumbles,
fabricates humiliating stories against one another,
withdraws, slithers off, goes blank inside.
Oh who can possibly hear me
who as an act of faith for each eardrum.
A time comes of loathing and of cannons
of horror set in motion.
I am here
linked to every existing thing. I love people
they who don't know and face change, who give in
to the living conditions, who fall in the struggle.
My people are not a nation nor a race.
Their plight is because of borders.
Meanwhile your hand is the ultimate
vestige of what's eternal
gripping a world among worlds:
your hand multiplied
one in another's linked to other hands of the people
who know certain they know,
and bestow their hard-won love to the planet
who pledge their faith, their resolute devotion,
and hope
at gale force

comes flying
to resist a time of cannons.

Translation by Zoë Anglesey

MICHELLE CHIHARA

Tough Love

Michelle Chihara (b. 1974) is a senior writer at AlterNet.org, an important nonprofit, progressive media source known within the peace and social justice movement for its accuracy. She has worked as a reporter and online editor on both coasts and in Brazil. Her work has appeared in a variety of newspapers and Web sites, including Fox.com, the *Boston Globe,* and the *Houston Chronicle.* AlterNet and similar sites were an important source of alternative news and opinions in the United States in the months following September 11, 2001, when this piece appeared.

■

I'm a patriot—always have been, always will be. My patriotism isn't new, and it isn't nice. But it's deep. It doesn't translate easily into bumper stickers. That doesn't diminish its strength.

I inherited my love of country from my parents, particularly from my father. He was born in this country, the son of a Japanese immigrant, in 1932. Following President Roosevelt's Executive Order 9066 in 1942, he and his entire family were placed in an internment camp in Minidoka, Idaho. He was shipped there at age 10. He left two and a half years later, a year before the war ended.

The camps were a gross violation of America's Constitution. The U.S. government has since apologized to Japanese Americans and offered $20,000 per survivor, in reparation for property and livelihood lost during the internments. The money, generous though it was, works out to less than 10 cents on the dollar of what Japanese Americans lost.

But despite it all, my Japanese-American forefathers passed down no resentment toward this country, no sense of bitterness about one of the U.S. government's gravest mistakes. Instead, I inherited an immigrant's gratitude for America's freedom and an immigrant's appreciation of just how fragile that freedom can be. Patriotism, as I grew up understanding it, means constant vigilance.

If we've learned anything from history, it's that during times of crisis we most need to keep watch over our government's actions.

On September 11, I watched the twin towers crumble in real time on cable TV, while standing in a hotel in Quito, Ecuador. Desperate to get to New York (I was scheduled to fly on September 13), traumatized, grieving, I couldn't stand to hear criticisms of America for a few days. At one point, I ran into an American in a bookstore in Quito who asked me if I had been watching CNN. I began reeling off the latest headlines. And this young American responded by complaining about U.S. television coverage. She seemed to be saying that Americans shouldn't take so much television news at face value. "I wish Americans would just think more," she said.

I turned and walked away. For once in my life, I just couldn't listen to anything critical of America or Americans. If there was ever a piece of news to be taken at face value, I felt, it was the stark, inescapable image of the twin towers falling.

My reaction, at that moment, was understandable. On September 13, the missing count was still rising, and the planes were still unable to fly to New York. I was grieving, and not yet ready to take a step back and critique the media coverage.

But my reaction—a need to grieve first and analyze later—wasn't patriotism, and my compatriot was tactless, not unpatriotic. One of the most obvious perks of living in the U.S. is that you are always allowed to trash it. Even when people around you get offended, patriotism must always involve passionate and constructive critiques of the U.S. By speaking out against policies or trends I disagree with, I'm trying to hold the U.S. to the highest standards of excellence, to everything that I believe it stands for.

My time in Ecuador came at the end of a year-long stay in South America. Most of that time I spent living in Brazil, in Rio de Janeiro. Rio is a beautiful, vibrant, amazing place to live. But it gave me a newfound appreciation for a host of blessings we North Americans often forget to count. For one thing, in Brazil I had to buy a phone line on the black market. For another, in Brazil it seemed like the dogged news magazine *Veja* could dig up a whopping political scandal every week. Brazilians watched crooked senators siphon millions of taxpayer dollars into Swiss bank accounts and luxury properties. Then they watched the millions stay gone, even after the scandals had hit the press. In the U.S., we like to complain about voter apathy. In Brazil, *Veja* called on its readers to fight voter helplessness.

In Brazil, I heard people compare believing in honest Brazilian politicians to believing in Santa Claus. But honest Brazilian politicians do exist, in significant numbers, and they're fighting to exorcise corruption in their government. Activists and lawyers are fighting to reform the Brazilian justice system. Reformers are fighting to reduce the gaping abyss between the rich and poor, which just about everyone in Brazil recognizes as its primary concern. The Brazilians who must love their country, it seemed clear to me, were the ones working for change.

We live with a level of transparency and accountability in this country that we sometimes take for granted. But that transparency takes upkeep, that accountability means nothing if we don't actively hold our officials accountable. We have so much to be thankful for. Take it for granted, and we might watch it disappear.

Now, in the mainstream media, any difference of opinion on how we should wage the war on terrorism is being set up as a straw man in opposition to patriotism. Alessandra Stanley of the *New York Times* glibly wrote that the public finds all voices questioning America's war in Afghanistan "loopy and treasonous." *Time* magazine reports that "for the eternal skeptics, whose views were defined by Vietnam and its aftermath, the new patriotism represents a kind of homecoming."

For most Americans, however, patriotism doesn't mean blind acceptance, and it's not a release from post-Vietnam, or any other brand, of skepticism. Most Americans can recognize the absurdity and atrocity of various U.S. policies, past and present, at the same time that we recognize that the United States has come closer to creating a just and equal society than any other nation in the history of the world.

I say that despite a host of other nations that might challenge that claim. But they have small, relatively homogeneous states. The U.S. created a tide that raised the standard of living for millions upon millions of people. It has absorbed wave after wave of immigrants, from every ethnicity and country in the world. That doesn't mean that each new wave hasn't had to fight for equal access to the American dream—they have. But given the challenges we've faced, we've come closer to the free and open ideal than anyone else. We only get closer to that ideal through the patriotic efforts of reformers, activists, and critics of all stripes. And we can only take pride in how far we've come if we understand that the fight isn't over.

It took a long time for Japanese American activists to obtain redress for the camps. But in the 1980s, the Supreme Court finally ruled the internment camps unconstitutional. In 1982, President Reagan's Commission on Wartime Relocation and Internment of Civilians published the following conclusion: "Executive Order 9066 was not justified by military necessity. The broad historical causes . . . were race prejudice, war hysteria and failure of political leadership." The American government apologized, and paid reparations to living internees.

Who, then, were the patriots in 1942? The people who said nothing as their neighbors lost their lives' work, who bought their fishing boats for a pittance, because they knew the Japanese Americans had no choice? Or the handful of Americans, many of them Jesuits and Quakers, who spoke out against the order and for the Constitution?

My issei grandfather came to this country when he was 14 years old, in search of the American dream (issei is the Japanese word for the first to arrive in America, nisei means the first generation born here). He spoke no English and had an 8th grade education. He worked on the railroads, and then in hotels, until he finally saved enough money to open his own general store. In 1941, he'd been living in the U.S. for 24 years as a legal immigrant, but was prevented by race-based laws from obtaining citizenship. He was a father of four.

The day after Pearl Harbor, my grandfather was taken into custody as a "dangerous alien." The primary allegations against him were membership in a Japanese fencing association (he taught kendo, the martial art where you fight with sticks) and a friendship with a former Japanese Navy officer. My grandmother was left by herself to round up her kids, pack up and abandon the store and their house, and take only a suitcase per person to Minidoka. My grandfather wasn't paroled and allowed to rejoin his family there until 1943.

But my family remained staunchly American. In the camp, my father tells me, "we celebrated all the usual American holidays, such as Christmas, New Year's and Thanksgiving. We listened to the radio and heard all the pop songs (that you know so well). Saw American movies when we could. We played American sports—football, baseball. In short, camp was not a breeding ground for turning us into citizens of Japan."

My uncle tells me that my grandmother dressed up my youngest uncle, only four at the time, in a tiny general's uniform. "The amused issei women referred to him as 'Ma Ca Sa,'" my uncle says, "for General McArthur—who was leading the U.S. campaign against the Japanese."

"There was the feeling in the camp that we would all be representatives someday of Japanese Americans," my father says. At the end of the war, when other families were hesitant to return to American society, my grandfather was one of the first to take his family out of Minidoka. Many Japanese were wary of a society that had rejected them, and (legitimately in some cases) worried about hate crimes. Not my grandfather. "I suspect that he thought we should leave because he believed that his children would be better off in the outside world," my father says.

The family landed in Spokane, Washington. "We were the only Japanese family in the parish," my father says. "I don't know how I might have turned out if I had been shunned by everyone in my class as an enemy, but, as it turned out, the kids were great. I was accepted as a classmate by everyone. I played on the football team for two years, I went camping with my classmates and in general had great times there. I even went to dances. The nuns treated me as they did every other student. In such a milieu, it is no wonder that I felt I was an American."

Score one for Spokane, and for all-American acceptance.

Before and after the injustice of the camps, the U.S. managed to do enough right not to alienate the Japanese American community. Despite racist laws preventing Asian resident aliens from gaining citizenship, despite laws forbidding Asian legal aliens to own land, the American system provided enough opportunity to allow hundreds of thousands of Japanese Americans to make a life for themselves before the camps. After the war, despite everything the Japanese Americans had lost, and how far they had been betrayed, Japanese Americans loved this country enough to want to reintegrate themselves. And American society proved open and tolerant enough to allow that to happen.

During the war, many Japanese Americans proved willing to go to any length to prove their loyalty to this country. When the American army came calling, 10,000 Japanese Americans volunteered for the 442nd Regimental Combat Team. Many of them volunteered from inside camps. The 442nd went on to become the most decorated combat unit in U.S. military history. More than 800 of them died in one mission to save a stranded Texas battalion of 221 soldiers. They became known as the "Purple Heart Battalion" (the Purple Heart is a medal of honor awarded to those wounded or killed in the line of duty).

My father, who was only 10 years old at Minidoka, has always been proud of the 442nd.

Immigrants now make up a sizable portion of the waves of recruits showing up at Army offices across America. Some are hard up for a job, or are trying to speed the process of becoming a citizen (the wait drops two years for members of the military). Many of them, like the men of the 442nd, probably feel they have something to prove. Most are patriots. Like converts to a new religion, immigrants are often the most zealous believers in the American way. They cherish America's opportunities and liberties because they have firsthand experience with the alternatives.

We have even more to cherish today than in the days of the 442nd. Many battles have been won against racism and for civil rights. There will be no internment camps for Arab Americans. It's been heartening to see Japanese-American organizations around the country throw their support behind the Arab-American community, organizing town meetings and talks. For every hate crime we hear about in the papers, we hear another story about people doing their best to make their Arab or Sikh or Muslim neighbors feel at ease. Lone American nut jobs have thrown Molotov cocktails at gas stations owned or run by Arab Americans, and in response, scores of American neighbors have turned out with flowers or cakes and support.

But if we let down our guard, if we don't do everything in our power to keep our government in line, if we allow today's FBI and CIA to run roughshod over immigrants' and everyone else's civil liberties, then we cannot call ourselves patriots. The president (and I reserve the right to continue ragging on him) tells us the terrorists hate our freedom. So the patriotic thing to do is to make sure America maintains those freedoms. The government made some of the same arguments for Executive Order 9066 that they are making now for the U.S.A. Patriot Act, and for the detention of over a thousand immigrants. The patriotic thing to do, here, is to keep a close watch over the detention process, and to make sure no one's constitutional rights are trampled.

American patriotism means loyalty to American rights, to a beautiful set of principles, a brilliant Constitution and a messy reality. Maybe being patriotic for the French, say, can mean pride in French food and wine, in French high culture, in the way French women pout. I've always been tempted to try and identify with other more cohesive, more homogenous cultures. But I'm not French, nor am I Japanese, and I can't locate national pride in my blood. I'm American, and American patriotism lives in the head and the heart.

My Japanese grandfather is a myth to me. I never knew him, and my family doesn't often speak of him and all that they went through. I imagine that he would probably find me strangely foreign—weird clothes, weird music. Plus, I'm Jewish. My grandparents on my mother's side were Jewish, born in this country but of Eastern European descent. When my parents announced their engagement, my Jewish grandparents were shocked and upset (primarily because my father is a goy). But they came around. I was raised celebrating both Passover and Christmas, the child of a union unlikely to have happened anywhere else. I know that everything I am, everything I have, everything I may have accomplished, is based on the road my forefathers paved, both Jewish and Japanese. My grandparents all loved America, and while I claim both of their Old Worlds as influences on my own, I can only understand myself as an American.

On September 11, my generation's age of innocence ended. But even if my patriotism is renewed, it's no different. I criticized my country before

September 11, and I'll keep carping until I feel that America is not in any danger of forgetting what she stands for.

Because if I don't, I would be letting down my grandparents, my father and everyone who ever fought or died for liberty and the American way of life.

Select Bibliography

Complete publication information on the works included in this book can be found in the following section, Sources and Permission Credits.

I . SOCIAL AND POLITICAL FACT, THEORY, HISTORY

Addams, Jane. *A Centennial Reader: Selected Writings and Speeches of the Nobel Peace Prize Winner and Founder of the Women's International League for Peace and Freedom.* Ed. Emily Cooper Johnson. New York: MacMillan, 1960.

Allen, Beverly. *Rape Warfare: The Hidden Genocide in Bosnia-Herzegovina and Croatia.* Minneapolis: University of Minnesota Press, 1996.

Alonso, Harriet Hyman. *Peace as a Women's Issue: A History of the U.S. Movement for World Peace and Women's Rights.* Syracuse, NY: Syracuse University Press, 1993.

Anderson, Bonnie S. and Judith P. Zinser. *A History of Their Own, Vol. I & II.* New York: Harper & Row, 1988.

Balch, Emily Greene. *Occupied Haiti.* New York: Garland, 1972.

Beard, Mary Ritter. *Making Women's History.* Ed. Ann J. Lane. New York: Feminist Press, 2000.

Beauvoir, Simone de. *The Ethics of Ambiguity.* New York: Random House, 1970.

———*The Second Sex.* New York: Random House, 1970.

Berkin, Carol R. and Clara M. Lovett, eds. *Women, War, & Revolution.* New York & London: Holmes & Meier Publishers, 1980.

Berube, Allan. *Coming Out Under Fire: The History of Gay Men and Women in World War Two.* New York: Free Press, 1990.

Caldicott, Helen Broinowski. *A Desperate Passion: An Autobiography.* New York: W.W. Norton, 1997.

———*If You Love This Planet.* New York: W.W. Norton, 1992.

———*Nuclear Madness: What You Can Do.* New York: W.W. Norton, revised Edition, 1994.

Caldwell, Nancy Sorel. *The Women Who Wrote the War.* New York: Arcade, 1999.

Cataldo, Mima, Ruth Putter, Byrna Fireside, and Elaine Lytel. *Women's Encampment for a Future of Peace and Justice.* Boston: South End Press, 1983.

Chang, I. *The Rape of Nanking.* New York: Penguin, 1997.

Cockburn, Cynthia. *The Space Between Us: Negotiating Gender and National Identities in Conflict.* London: Zed Books, 1999.

Cooke, Miriam. *Women and the War Story.* Berkeley: University of California Press, 1996.

Coony, Robert and Helen Michalowski. *The Power of the People: Active Non-Violence in the United States.* Philadelphia: New Society, 1987.

Cooper, Helen M., Adrienne Auslander Munich, and Susan Merrill Squier, eds. *Arms and the Woman: War, Gender and Literary Representation.* Chapel Hill: University of North Carolina Press, 1989.

Davies, Miranda. *Women and Violence.* London: Zed Books, 1994.

Deming, Barbara. *We Are All Part of One Another: A Barbara Deming Reader.* Edited by Jane Meyerding. Philadelphia: New Society, 1984.

De Pauw, Linda Grant. *Battle Cries and Lullabies: Women in War from Prehistory to the Present.* Norman: University of Oklahoma Press, 1998.

Dobkin, Marjorie H. Smyrna. *Nineteen Twenty-Two: The Destruction of a City.* Ohio: Kent State University Press, 1988.

Dolgopol, Ustinia and Snekal Parenjape. *Comfort Women: An Unfinished Ordeal.* Geneva: International Commission of Jurists, 1994.

Early, Frances H. *A World Without War: How U.S. Feminists and Pacifists Resisted World War I*. Syracuse, NY: Syracuse University Press, 1997.

Edwards, Laura F., ed. *Scarlett Doesn't Live Here Anymore: Southern Women in the Civil War Era*. Urbana: University of Illinois Press, 2000.

Ellis, Deborah. *Women of the Afghan War*. Westport, CT: Greenwood, 2000.

Enloe, Cynthia. *Does Khaki Become You: The Militarization of Women's Lives*. Boston: South End Press, 1983.

Ensler, Eve. *Necessary Targets: A Story of Women and War*. New York: Villard, 2001.

Federikse, Julie. *South Africa: A Different Kind of War*. Boston: South End Press, 1987.

Fitzgerald, Frances. *Fire in the Lake: The Vietnamese and the Americans in Vietnam*. Boston: Atlantic Monthly Press, 1979.

Florence, Mary Sargent, Catherine E. Marshall, and C.K. Ogden, eds. *Militarism Versus Feminism: Writings on Women and War*. London: Virago Press, 1987.

Forsberg, Randall and Carl Conetta, eds. *The Peace Resource Book*. Hagerstown, MD: Ballinger, 1988.

Franke, Linda Bird. *Ground Zero: The Gender Wars in the Military*. New York: Simon & Schuster, 1997.

Fuentes, Annette and Barbara Ehrenreich. *Women in the Global Factory*. Boston: South End Press, 1983.

Gavin, Lettie. *American Women in World War I*. Niwot, CO: University Press of Colorado, 1997.

George. Susan. *A Fate Worse Than Debt: The World Financial Crisis and the Poor*. Washington DC: Institute for Policy Studies, 1987.

Glendinning, Chellis. *Waking Up in the Nuclear Age: The Book of Nuclear Psycho-Therapy*. New York: William Morrow, 1987.

Goldman. Emma. *Anarchism and Other Essays*. Original 1910. Reprint Port Washington, NY and London: Kennidat Press, 1988.

Gould, Benina Berger, Susan Moon, and Judith VanHoorn. *Growing Up Scared? The Psychological Effects of the Nuclear Threat on Children*. Berkeley: Open Books, 1986.

Griffin, Susan. *The First and the Last: A Woman Thinks About War*. New York: Harper & Row, 1987.

Gruhzit-Hoyt, Olga. *They Also Served: American Women in World War II*. Secaucus, NJ: Carol Publishing Group, 1995.

Hanley, Lynne. *Writing War: Fiction, Gender and Memory*. Amherst: University of Massachusetts Press, 1991.

Hart, Janet. *New Voices in the Nation: Women and the Greek Resistance*. Ithaca, NY: Cornell University Press, 1996.

Holland, Barbara. *Soviet Sisterhood*. Bloomington, IN: The University of Indiana Press, 1994.

Honey, Maureen, ed. *Bitter Fruit: African American Women in World War II*. Columbia: University of Missouri Press, 1999.

hooks, bell. *Outlaw Culture: Resisting Representations*. New York: Routledge, 1994.

Jancar-Webster, Barbara. *Women and the Revolution in Yugoslavia, 1941-45*. Denver: Arden Press, 1990.

Jeansonne, Glen. *Women of the Far Right: The Mothers' Movement and World War II*. Chicago: University of Chicago Press, 1996.

Kaminski, Theresa. *Prisoners in Paradise: American Women in Wartime South Pacific*. Lawrence: University Press of Kansas, 2000.

Keon, Susan and Nina Swaim. *A Handbook for Women on the Nuclear Mentality: Ain't No Where You Can Run*. Women's Alliance for Nuclear Disarmament, Arlington, MA 02174, 1980.

Kollantai, Alexandra. *Selected Writings of Alexandra Kollantai, Russian Revolutionary*. Ed. Alix Holt. Westport, CT: Lawrence Hill, 1977.

Lall, Betty Gortz. *Building a Peace Economy: Opportunities and Problems of Post-Cold War Defense Cuts*. Boulder, CO: Westview Press, 1992.

Lapchick, Richard Edward. *Oppression and Resistance: The Struggle of Women in Southern Africa.* Westport, CT: Greenwood Press, 1982.

Lappe, Frances Moore. *Betraying the National Interest.* New York: Ballantine, 1987.

Larson, Jeanne and Madge Micheels-Cyrus, eds. *Seeds of Peace: A Catalogue of Quotations.* Santa Cruz, CA: New Society Press, 1987.

Luxemburg, Rosa. *Rosa Luxemburg Speaks: 16 Speeches and Articles.* Ed. Mary-Alice Waters. New York: Pathfinder Press, 1988.

Macy, Joanna Rogers. *Despair and Personal Power in the Nuclear Age.* Philadelphia: New Society Publishers, 1983.

Mansfield, Sue. *The Gestalt of War: An Inquiry into the Origin and Meaning As a Social Institution.* New York: Dial Press, 1982.

Mertus, Julie. *War's Offensive on Women: The Humanitarian Challenge in Bosnia, Kosovo and Afghanistan.* With a case study on Afghanistan by Judy A. Benjamin. West Hartford, CT: Kumarian Press, 2000.

Miller, Alice. *For Your Own Good: Hidden Cruelty in Childrearing and the Roots of Violence.* New York: Noonday Press, 1983.

Miller, Judith, S. Engelberg, and W.J. Broad. *Germs: Biological Weapons and America's Secret War.* New York: Simon & Schuster, 2001

Morehouse, Maggi. *Fighting in the Jim Crow Army: Black Men and Women Remember World War II.* Landham, MD: Voices and Visions, 2000.

Morgan, Robin. *The Demon Lover: The Roots of Terrorism.* 1989; 2nd ed. New York: Washington Square Press, 2001.

——— ed. *Sisterhood Is Global: An International Women's Movement Anthology.* 1984; reprint New York: Feminist Press, 1996.

Myrdal, Alva. *The Game of Disarmament: How the U.S. and Russia Run the Arms Race.* New York: Pantheon Books, 1982.

Nash, Mary. *Defying Male Civilization.* Denver: Arden Press, 1995.

National Conference on Crimes Against Humanity. *The Aremenian Experience: Genocide.* Chicago: Zoryan Institute, 1984.

Newark, T. *Women Warlords: An Illustrated Military History of Female Warriors.* London: Blandford, 1989.

Norton, Mary Beth. *Liberty's Daughters: Revolutionary Experience of Women, 1750-1800.* Ithaca, NY: Cornell University Press, 1986.

Norman, Elizabeth M. *We Band of Angels: The Untold Story of American Nurses Trapped on Bataan by the Japanese.* New York: Pocket Books, 2000.

Pallacios, Chilang et al. *Women Working for a Nuclear-Free and Independent Pacific: Pacific Women Speak.* London: Green Line Press, 1987.

Pearce, Jenny. *U.S. Intervention in Central America and the Caribbean.* Boston: South End Press, 1981.

Peteet, Julie Marie. *Gender in Crisis: Women and the Palestinian Resistance Movement.* New York: Columbia University Press, 1991.

Plain, Gill. *Women's Fiction of the Second World War: Gender, Power and Resistance.* New York: St. Martin's Press, 1996.

Raitt, Suzanne and Trudi Tate. *Women's Fiction and the Great War.* New York: Oxford University Press/Clarendon Press, 1997.

Reardon, Betty. *Sexism and the War System.* New York: Teachers College Press, 1987.

Reilly, Catherine, ed. *Chaos of the Night: Women's Poetry and Verse of the Second World War.* London: Virago, 1984.

Rowe, Dorothy. *Living with the Bomb.* London: Routledge & Kegan Paul, 1985.

Russell, Diana E.H. and Nicole Van de Van, eds. *International Tribunal on Crimes Against Women.* Brussels: Les Femmes Publications; California: Milbrae, 1986.

Schecter, Susan. *Women and Male Violence.* Boston: South End Press, 1982.

Schneider, Dorothy. *Into the Breach: American Women Overseas in World War I.* New York: Viking, 1991.

Schreiner, Olive. *An Olive Schreiner Reader: Writings on Women and South Africa.* Ed. Carol Barash. London: Routledge & Kegen Paul, 1987.

Seager, Joni. *The State of Women in the World Atlas.* New York: Penguin: 1997.

Sheafer, Silvia Anne. *Women in America's Wars.* Springfield, NJ: Enslow Publishers, 1996.

Sherrow, Victoria. *Women and the Military: An Encyclopedia.* Santa Barbara: ABC-CLIO, 1996.

Shiva, Vandana. *Biopiracy: The Plunder of Nature and Knowledge.* Boston: South End Press, 1999.

———*Stolen Harvest : The Hijacking of the Global Food Supply.* Boston: South End Press, 1999.

Sidel, Ruth. *Keeping Women and Children Last: America's War on the Poor.* New York: Viking-Penguin, 1996.

Simons, Margaret A., ed. *Hypatia.* Journal of socio-political and philosphical theory, founded by the Society of Women in Philosophy. Edwardsville, IL: Southern Illinois University Press, 1987.

Skaine, Rosemarie S. *Women at War: Gender Issues of Americans in Combat.* Jefferson, NC: McFarland, 1999.

———*The Women of Afghanistan Under the Taliban.* Jefferson, NC: McFarland, 2001.

Slaughter, Jane. *Women and the Italian Resistance (1943-45).* Denver: Arden Press, 1997.

Strum, Philippa. *The Women Are Marching: The Second Sex and the Palestinian Revolution.* Chicago: Lawrence Hill Books, 1992.

Stewart Talley, Rhea. *Fire in Afghanistan 1914-1929: The First Opening to the West Undone by Tribal Ferocity Years Before the Taliban.* New York: Universe Books, 2000.

Turshen, Meredith and Clotilde Twagiramariya, eds. *What Women Do in Wartime: Gender and Conflict in Africa.* London: Zed Books, 1998.

Urdang, Stephanie. *Fighting Two Colonialisms: Women in Guinea-Bissau.* New York: Monthly Review Press, 1979.

Wagner, Lilya. *Women War Correspondents of World War II.* Westport, CT: Greenwood Press, 1989.

Walker, Keith and Martha Raye, eds. *A Piece of My Heart: The Stories of 26 American Women Who Served in Vietnam.* New York: Ballantine, 1991.

Weil, Simone. *The Simone Weil Reader.* Edited by George A. Panichas. New York: David MacKay Company/Random House, 1977.

Willenz, June A. *Women Veterans: America's Forgotten Heroines.* New York: Continuum Press, 1938.

Woolf, Virginia. *Three Guineas.* 1938; reprint New York: Harcourt Brace Jovanovich, 1985.

Woodward, Susan L. *Balkan Tragedy: Chaos and Dissolution After the Cold War.* Washington, DC: Brookings Institution, 1995.

II. BIOGRAPHY, AUTOBIOGRAPHY, MEMOIR, AND ORAL HISTORY

Afkhami, Mahnaz. *Women in Exile.* Charlottesville: University of Virginia Press, 1994.

Agosin, Marjorie, ed. *A Map of Hope: Women's Writing on Human Rights: An International Literary Anthology.* New Brunswick. NJ: Rutgers University Press, 1999.

Atiya, Nayra Khul-Khaal. *5 Egyptian Women Tell Their Stories.* Syracuse, NY: Syracuse University Press, 1982.

Bacon, Margaret Hope. *Valiant Friend: The Life of Lucretia Mott.* New York: Walker & Co., 1980.

Balabanoff, Angela. *My Life As a Rebel.* New York: Harper & Row, 1938; reprint Westport, CT: Greenwood Press, 1987.

Baxandall, Rosalyn Fraad. *Words on Fire: The Life and Writing of Elizabeth Gurley Flynn, Early Twentieth Century U.S. Social Activist and Labor Organizer.* New Brunswick, NJ: Rutgers University Press, 1993.

Blaikie, Evi. *Magda's Daughter: A Hidden Child's Journey Home.* New York: Feminist Press, 2003.

Borton, Lady. *Sensing the Enemy: An American Among the Boat People of Vietnam.* New York: Dial Press, 1984.

Brian, Irene. *Lady G.I.: A Woman's War in the South Pacific.* Throndike, ME: G.K. Hall, 1998.

Brittain, Vera. *Chronicle of Youth: The War Diary, 1913-1917.* Ed. Alan Bishop. New York: William Morrow, 1981.

Brombert, Beth Archer. *Cristina.* Chicago: University of Chicago Press, 1977.

Burgess, Lauren Cook, ed. *An Uncommon Soldier: The Civil War Letters of Sarah Rosetta Wakeman, Alias Private Lyons Wakeman, 153rd Regiment, NY State Volunteers.* New York: Oxford University Press, 1996.

Busby, Margaret, ed. *Daughters of Africa.* New York: Pantheon Books, 1992.

Cantarow, Ellen with Susan Gushee O'Malley and Sharon Hartoman Strom. *Moving the Mountain: Women Working for Social Change.* New York: Feminist Press, 1980.

Carl, Ann B. *A Wasp Among Eagles: A Woman Military Test Pilot in WWII.* Washington, DC: Smithsonian Institute Press, 1999.

Chang, Jung. *Wild Swans: Three Daughters of China.* New York: Simon and Schuster, 1991.

Claiborne, Sybil. *Climbing Fences: Grace Paley.* New York: War Resisters League, 1987.

Cooke, Miriam and Roshni Rustomji-Kerns, eds. *Blood into Ink: South Asian and Middle Eastern Women Write War.* Boulder, CO: Westview Press, 1994.

———War's Other Voices: Women Writers of Lebanese Civil War. Syracuse, NY: Syracuse University Press, 1996.

Davis, Kati. *A Child's War: World War II Through the Eyes of Children.* New York: Four Walls Eight Windows, 1989.

Day, Dorothy. *The Long Loneliness.* Boston: South End Press, 1984.

Delbo, Charlotte. *Auschwitz and After.* New Haven, CT: Yale University Press, 1995.

———Convoy to Auschwitz: Women of the French Resistance. Boston: Northeastern University Press, 1997.

Duba, Ursula. *Tales from a Child of the Enemy.* New York: Penguin Books, 1997.

Durova, Nadezhda. *The Cavalry Maiden.* Translated and Annotated by Mary Fleming Zirin. Bloomington: The University of Indiana Press, 1988.

Edmonds, S. Emma. *Memoirs of a Soldier, Nurse and Spy: A Woman's Adventures in the Union Army.* Northern Illinois University Press, 1999.

El Saadawi, Nawal. *Memoirs from the Women's Prison.* Ed./trans. Marilyn Booth. Berkeley: University of California Press, 1986.

Ellis, Deborah. *Women of the Afghan War.* 1989; reprint Westport, CT: Greenwood Publishing, 2000.

Fitzpatrick, Sheila and Yuri Slezkine, trans./eds. *In the Shadow of Revolution: Life Stories of Russian Women from 1917 to WWII.* Princeton, NJ: Princeton University Press, 2000.

Florence, Barbara Moench. *Lela Secor: A Diary in Letters: 1915.* New York: Burt Franklin & Co., 1978.

Fourtouni, Eleni. *Greek Women in Resistance.* New Haven, CT: Thelphini Press, 1986.

Frank, Anne. *Anne Frank: The Diary of a Young Girl.* New York: Doubleday, 1952.

Freedman, D. and Jacqueline Rhoads, eds. *The Forgotten Vets: Nurses in Vietnam.* Austin: Texas Monthly Press, 1987.

Galicich, Anne and Samantha Smith. *A Journey from the US to the USSR for Peace.* Minneapolis, MN: Dillon Press, 1987.

Gluck, Sherna, ed. *Rosie the Riveter Revisited: Women, the War and Social Change.* New York: Twayne, 1987.

Golden, Renny. *The Hour of the Poor, the Hour of Women: Salvadoran Women Speak.* New York: Crossroad, 1991.

Goldman, Emma. *Living My Life.* Several editions, various publishers, 1960-2000.

Gonzalez, Shirley Mangini. *Memories of Resistance: Women's Voices from the Spanish Civil War.* New Haven, CT: Yale University Press, 1995.

Gordimer, Nadine. *Writing and Being.* Cambridge, MA: Harvard University Press, 1995.

Gorkin, Michael and Rafiqa Othman, eds. *Three Mothers: Three Daughters: Palestinian Women's Stories.* Berkeley: University of California Press, 1996.

Greenburg, Judith E. *Journal of a Revolutionary War Woman.* New York: Franklin Watts, 1996.

Gurewitsch, Brana, ed. *Mothers, Sisters, Resisters: Oral Histories of Women Who Survived the Holocaust.* Tuscaloosa: University of Alabama Press, 1998.

Hammond, Jenny and Druce, Nell, eds. *Sweeter than Honey: Ethiopian Women and Revolution: Testimonies of Tigrayan Women.* Trenton, NJ: Red Sea Press, 1990.

Hayton-Keeva, Sally, ed. *Valiant Women in War and Exile: Thirty-Eight True Stories.* San Francisco: City Lights Books, 1987.

Hertig, Victoria. *Flowers of Hope: A Memoir.* Troy, MI: Momentum Books, 1996.

Higgins, Marguerite. *War in Korea.* New York: Doubleday, 1951.

Hillesum, Etty. *Letters from Westerbork.* New York: Pantheon Books, 1986.

Ibarruri, Dolores. *They Shall Not Pass: The Autobiography of La Pasionaria.* New York: International Publishers, 1966.

Jacobs, Harriet (writing as Linda Brent). *Incidents in the Life of a Slave Girl.* New York: Signet Classic, 2000.

Kanafani, Fay Afaf. *Nadia, Captive of Hope: Memoir of an Arab Woman.* Armonk, NY: M.E. Sharpe, 1999.

Kazuko. Kuramoto. *Manchurian Legacy: Memoirs of a Japanese Colonist.* East Lansing: Michigan State University Press, 1999.

Kearns, Martha. *Kathe Kollwitz: Woman and Artist.* New York: Feminist Press, 1976.

Keyso, Ruth Ann. *Women of Okinawa: Nine Voices from a Garrison Island.* Ithaca, NY: Cornell University Press, 2000.

Kim, Elizabeth. *Ten Thousand Sorrows: The Extraordinary Journey of a Korean War Orphan.* New York: Doubleday, 2000.

Kollwitz, Kathe. *The Diary and Letters of Kathe Kollwitz.* Ed. Hans Kollwitz. Evanston, IL: Northwestern University Press, 1988.

Laska, Vera, ed. *Women in the Resistance and the Holocaust: The Voices of Eyewitnesses.* Westport, CT: Greenwood Press, 1983.

Ling, Ding. *I Myself Am a Woman: Selected Writings of Ding Ling.* New York: Beacon Press, 1989.

Litoff, Judy Barrett and David Smith. *Since You Went Away: World War II Letters from American Women on the Home Front.* Lawrence: University Press of Kansas, 1995.

Makeba, Miriam. *Makeba: My Story.* New York: New American Library, 1988.

McAllister, Pam. *You Can't Kill the Spirit.* Santa Cruz. California: New Society Publishers, 1988.

McCarthy, Mary Therese. *Hanoi.* New York: Harcourt Brace & Company, 1968.

Meyer, Doris, ed. *Lives on the Line: The Testimony of Contemporary Latin American Authors.* Berkeley: University of California Press, 1988.

Moore, Molly. *A Woman at War: Storming Kuwait with the U.S. Marines.* New York: Scribner, 1993.

Morhange-Beague, Claude. *Chamberet; Recollections from an Ordinary Childhood: A Child's View of the Nazis.* New York: Marlboro Press, 1988.

Mullaney, Marie Marmo. *Revolutionary Women.* New York: Praeger, 1983.

Nicholson. Mavis, ed. *What Did You do in the War, Mommy? British Personal Narratives.* Ansley (UK): F.A. Thorpe, 1995, 1996.

Nikolic-Ristanovic, Vesna, ed. *Women, Violence and War: Wartime Victimization of Refugees in the Balkans.* Central European University Press, 2000.

Opfell, Olga. S. *The Lady Laureates; Women Who have Won the Nobel Peace Prize.* Metuchen, NJ & London, Scarecrow Press, 1983.

Ritvo, Roger A. and Diane M. Potkin. *Sisters in Sorrow: Voices of Care in the Holocaust.* College Station, TX: Texas A & M University Press, 1998.

Rosenwasser. Penny. *Voices from a "Promised Land": Palestinian and Israeli Peace Activists Speak Their Hearts, Conversations with Penny Rosenwasser.* Willimantic. CT: Curbstone Press, 1992.

Sanghatana, Stree Shakti. *We Were Making History: Women and the Telangana Uprising.* London: Zed Books, 1989.

Saywell, Shelly. *Women in War.* New York: Viking Penguin, 1985.

Schneider, Karen. *Loving Arms: British Women Writing the Second World War.* Lexington: University of Kentucky Press, 1997.

Sergeant, Elizabeth Shipley. *Shadow-Shapes: The Journal of a Wounded Woman.* Boston: Houghton Mifflin, 1920.

Sheafer, Silvia Anne. *Women in America's Wars.* Springfield, NJ: Enslow Publishers, 1996.

Sheldon, Sayre P., ed. *Her War Story: Twentieth-Century Women Write About War.* Carbondale: Southern Illinois University Press, 1999.

Silko, Leslie Marmon. *Yellow Woman and the Beauty of the Spirit.* New York: Simon & Schuster, 1996.

Schomburg Library of Nineteenth-Century Black Women Writers: Six Women's Slave Narratives. Introduction by William L. Andrews. New York: Oxford University Press, 1988.

Sterling, Dorothy. *Black Foremothers.* New York: Feminist Press, 1987.

Taylor, Sandra. *Vietnamese Women at War: Fighting for Ho Chi Minh and the Revolution.* Lawrence: University of Kansas Press, 1999.

Thompson, Dorothy. *Let the Record Speak.* New York: Houghton Mifflin Company, 1967.

Turner, Karen Gottschang and Phan Thanh Hao. *Even the Women Must Fight: Memories of War from North Vietnam.* New York: John Wiley & Sons, 1999.

Uglow. Jennifer S., ed. *The International Dictionary of Women's Biography.* New York: MacMillan, 1982.

Van Devanter, Lynda and Joan A. Furey, eds. *Visions of War, Dreams of Peace: Writings of Women in the Vietnam War.* New York: Warner Books, 1991.

West, Rebecca. *The Young Rebecca: Writings of Rebecca West, 1911-1917.* Ed. Jane Marcus. New York: Viking, 1982.

Woolsey. Gamel. *Malaga Burning: An American Woman's Eyewitness Account of the Spanish Civil War.* Reston, VA: Pythia Press, 1998.

Young-Bruehl, Elisabeth. *For Love of the World: A Biography of Hannah Arendt.* New Haven: Yale University Press, 1988.

III. FICTION, POETRY AND LITERATURE

Agosin, Marjorie, ed. *The House of Memory: Stories by Jewish Women Writers of Latin America.* New York: Feminist Press, 1999.

Akhmatova, Anna. *The Poems of Akhmatova.* Boston: Little Brown,1983.

Alegria, Claribel. *Thresholds.* Willimantic, CT: Curbstone Press, 1984.

Anglesey, Zoe. *Ixok Amar-Go: Central American Women's Poetry for Peace.* Penobscot, ME: Granite Press, 1987.

Bachman, Ingeborg. *The Thirtieth Year.* New York: Holmes & Meier, 1987.

Bennett, Betty T. *British War Poetry of the Age of Romanticism.* London: Garland Publishers,1987.

De Cervantes, Lorna. *From the Cables of Genocide: Poems of Love and Hunger.* New York: Arte Publico, 1991.

Drabble, Margaret. *The Gates of Ivory.* New York: Viking Penguin, 1991.

Emecheta, Buchi. *Second Class Citizen.* New York: Braziller, 1987.

Fallaci, Oriana. *A Man.* New York: Simon & Schuster. 1980.

Fourtouni, Eleni. *Greek Women Poets.* New Haven: Thelphini Press, 1978.

Gordimer, Nadine. *Burger's Daughter.* London: Russell & Volkening. London, 1979.

Green, Rayna, ed. *That's What She Said: Contemporary Poetry and Fiction by Native American Women.* Bloomington: Indiana University Press, 1984.

Harjo, Joy: *In Mad Love and War.* Wesleyan, CT: Wesleyan University Press, 1990.

Hussein, Aamer, Mamtaz Shirin, and Jamila Hashmi, eds. *Hoops of Fire: Fifty Years of Fiction by Pakistani Women.* London: Zed Books, 2000.

Hurston. Zora Neale. *I Love Myself When I Am Laughing and Then Again When I Am Looking Mean and Impressive.* Ed. Alice Walker. New York: Feminist Press, 1983.

Jordan, June. *Naming Our Destiny: New and Selected Poems.* New York: Thunder's Mouth Press, 1989.

Kelly, A.A. editor. *Pillars of the House: An Anthology of by Irish Women from 1690 to the Present.* Dublin: Wolfhound, 1987.

Kolmar, Gertrude. *Dark Soliloquy: The Poems of Gertrude Kolmar.* New York: Seabury Press, 1975.

Kumin, Maxine. *The Long Approach.* New York: Viking Penguin, 1986.

Lessing, Doris. *The Good Terrorist.* New York: Vintage Books, 1985.

———*Landlocked.* New York/London: HarperCollins, 1965.

Levertov, Denise. *Poems.* New York: New Directions, 1973.

Lippit, Noriko Mizuta and Kyoko Iriye, Selden, trans./eds. *Japanese Women Writers: Twentieth Century Short Fiction.* Armonk, NY: M.E. Sharpe, 1991.

Macdonald, Nina. *War-Time Nursery Rhymes.* London: Routledge & Kegan Paul, 1998.

Macdonald, Sharon, Pat Holden, and Shirley Ardener, eds. *Images of Women in Peace and War: Cross-Cultural and Historical Perspectives.* Madison: University of Wisconsin Press, 1987.

Morante. Elsa. *History: A Novel.* New York: Alfred A. Knopf, 1977.

Nieh, Hualing. *Mulberry and Peach.* New York: Feminist Press, 1998.

Nwapa, Flora. *Wives at War and Other Stories.* Trenton, NJ: Africa World Press, 1992.

Paley Grace. *The Collected Stories.* New York: Farrar, Strauss & Giroux, 1999.

———*Just As I Thought: Selected Essays.* Farrar, Straus & Giroux, 2000.

Pirtle, Sarah. *An Outbreak of Peace.* Santa Cruz: CA: New Society Publishers, 1987.

Price, Alan, ed. *The End of the Age of Innocence: Edith Wharton and the First World War.* New York: St. Martin's Press, 1996.

Rich, Adrienne. *The Will to Change.* New York: W.W. Norton, 1971.

Rukuyser, Muriel. *A Muriel Rukuyser Reader.* New York: W.W. Norton, 1994.

Sachs, Nelly. *O the Chimneys.* New York: Farrar, Straus & Giroux, 1995.

Szymborska, Wislawa. *View with a Grain of Sand: Selected Poems.* New York: Harcourt Brace & Company, 1995.

Tate, Trudi. *Women, Men and the Great War.* London & New York: Manchester University Press, 1995.

Tanaka, Yukiko, ed. *To Live and To Write: Selections by Japanese Women Writers, 1913-1938.* Seattle: Seal Press, 1988.

Van Devanter, Linda and Joan A. Furey, eds. *Visions of War. Dreams of Peace: Writings of Women in the Vietnam War.* New York: Warner Books, 1991.

Walker, Alice. *Meridian.* New York: Harcourt Brace Javanovich, 1976.

Washington, Mary Helen, ed. *Invented Lives; Narratives of Black Women, 1860-1960.* New York: Anchor/Doubleday, 1960.

Sources and Permission Credits/Author Index

The editor gratefully acknowledges the following contributors, their works, and their publishers with the following copyright notices. No part or selection from this book may be reprinted or reproduced in any form including electronic, audio, or visual means, without the express written permission of copyright owners, except in the case of brief quotations for review purposes.

The following works and excerpts were reprinted with the express permission of their authors, translators, representatives, publishers, or literary estates and may be reprinted only by permission. Write directly to the copyright holders listed below for permission to reprint individual selections whose copyrights are the possession of their authors, literary estates, or publishers. All original sections of this book, including the introduction, notes, some translations, and the compilation in total are copyright 2003 by Daniela Gioseffi; for permission to quote from these sections, write to the Feminist Press at the City University of New York, The Graduate Center, 365 Fifth Avenue, Suite 5406, New York, NY 10016, Attn.: Rights and Permissions.

Every effort has been made to trace the owners of the copyrights of all works included in this anthology. Any omission is purely inadvertent and will be corrected in subsequent editions, provided written notification is given to the editor. Write to Daniela Gioseffi c/o The Feminist Press at the address above, or e-mail daniela@garden.net.

Addams, Jane (p. 293): excerpt from *Peace and Bread in Time of War* (circa 1918; reprint New York: Garland, 1972).

Aidoo, Ama Ata (p. 175): "Certain Winds from the South," © 1970 by Ama Ata Aidoo, from *No Sweetness Here and Other Stories* (New York: Feminist Press, 1995); reprinted by permission of the publisher.

Akmadulina, Bella (p. 27): "Words Spoken by Pasternack During a Bombing," translation by Daniela Gioseffi with Sophia Busevska, © 1988 by Daniela Gioseffi; used by permission of the translators.

Akhmatova, Anna (p. 107): "The First Long Range Artillery Fire on Leningrad," translation by Daniela Gioseffi with Sophia Busevska, © 1995 by Daniela Gioseffi, appeared on PoetsUSA.com and in *Symbiosis* by Daniela Gioseffi (New York: Rattapallax Press, 2002); used by permission of the translators.

Akin, Gulten (p. 157): "It's Not the Fear of Shivering," © Talat Saít Halman; used by permission of the translator.

al-Amir, Daisy (p. 307): "The Future," from *Promises for Sale* (Lebanon, 1981); translation by Miriam Cooke, © 1994, appeared in *Blood Into Ink: South Asian & Middle Eastern Women Write War*, edited by Miriam Cooke (Boulder, CO: Westview Press, 1994); used by permission of the translator.

Alcott, Louisa May (p. 105): excerpt from *Hospital Sketches* (1864; reprint Cambridge, MA: Belknap Press of Harvard University, 1960).

Alegria, Claribel (p. 135): "Evasion," translation © 1987 by Lynne Beyer, from *Ixok Amar-Go: Central American Women's Poetry for Peace*, edited by Zoe Angelsey (Penobscot, ME: Granite Press, 1987); used by permission of the editor.

Alermo, Sibilla (p. 295): "Yes to the Earth," translation © 1986 by Muriel Kittel, from *The Defiant Muse: Italian Feminist Poems from the Middle Ages to the Present*, edited by Beverly Allen, Muriel Kittel, and Keala Jane Jewel (New York: Feminist Press, 1986); reprinted by permission of the publisher.

Alexiyevich, Svetlana (p. 193): excerpts from "Boys in Zinc," translation from the Russian © 1990 by Arch Tait, from *Granta* 34, Autumn 1990; reprinted by permission of *Granta*.

Alkalay-Gut, Karen (p. 182): "Friend and Foe" and "To One in Beirut," © 1986 by Karen Alkalay-Gut, from *Mechtizaï* (Merrick, NY: Cross-Cultural Communications/Stanley Barkan, 1986).

al-Khansa (p. 104): "Elegy for My Brother," translation by Daniela Gioseffi with Amira Fatuwa, © 2002 by Daniela Gioseffi; used by permission of the translator.

Allende, Isabel (p. 255): "The Hour of Truth" by Isabel Allende, translation © 1985 by Magda Bogin, from *The House of the Spirits* (New York: Knopf, 1985); reprinted by permission of the translator.

Angelou, Maya (p. 240): "And Still I Rise," © 1975 by Maya Angelou, from *And Still I Rise*; also in *The Collected Poems of Maya Angelou,* © 1994 by Maya Angelou (New York: Random House, 1994); reprinted by permission of the publisher.

Atwood, Margaret (p. 39): "Bread," © 1983 by Margaret Atwood, from *Murder in the Dark* (Toronto: McClelland & Stewart, 1983); used by permission of the author.

Beauvoir, Simone de (p. 111): "Report from the World Tribunal on Vietnam," translation by Andre Deutsch, © 1974, from *All Said and Done* (New York: G.P. Putnam's Sons and London: Weidenfeld and Nicholson, 1974); used by permission of the translator; original French *Toute Comple Fait,* © 1972 (Paris: Gallimard, 1972).

Belli, Gioconda (p. 189): "The Blood of Others," translation © 1987 by Elinor Randall, from *Ixok Amar-Go: Central American Women's Poetry for Peace,* edited by Zoe Angelsey (Penobscot, ME: Granite Press, 1987); used by permission of the editor.

Bermudez, Alenki (p. 263): "Guatemala, Your Blood," translation © 1987 by Sara Miles, from *Ixok Amar-Go: Central American Women's Poetry for Peace,* edited by Zoe Angelsey (Penobscot, ME: Granite Press, 1987); used by permission of the editor.

Bertell, Rosalie (p. 20): Introduction to *Earth: The Latest Weapon of War,* © 2000 by Rosalie Bertell (London: The Woman's Press, 2000); reprinted by permission of the Women's Press, Ltd., 34 Great Sutton Street, London EC1V 0LQ.

Borton, Lady (p. 321): "A Forgiving Land," © 1990, 2003 by Lady Borton, first appeared in the *New York Times,* "Hers" column, 12 August 1990; also appeared in slightly different form in *After Sorrow: An American Among the Vietnamese* (New York: Viking, 1995); used by permission of the author.

Brooks, Gwendolyn (p. 10): "The Progress," © 1971 by Gwendolyn Brooks, from *The Blacks* (Chicago: The David Company, 1971); also appears in *Selected Poems* by Gwendolyn Brooks (New York: HarperCollins, 1999); reprinted by permission of HarperCollins Publishers.

Brovina, Flora (p. 346): "A New Dawn in Town," translation © 2003 by Daniela Gioseffi; original Albanian © Flora Brovina; used by permission of the translator.

Butalia, Urvashi (p. 203): excerpt from *The Other Side of Silence: Voices from the Partition of India* (Durham, NC: Duke University Press, 2000), © 2000 by Duke University Press; reprinted by permission of the publisher.

Caldicott, Helen (p. 28): excerpt from Introduction to *The New Nuclear Danger: George W. Bush's Military-Industrial Complex,* © 2002 by Helen Caldicott (New York: The New Press, 2002); reprinted by permission of the New Press, (800) 233-4830.

Cassian, Nina (p. 306): "On a Japanese Beach," translation © 1987 by Daniela Gioseffi with the author; original Romanian © 1987 by Nina Cassian; used by permission of the translator.

Chedid, Andree (p. 127): "Death in Slow Motion," translation © 1993 by Charlotte H. Bruner, from *The Heinemann Book of African Women's Writing,* edited by Charlotte H. Bruner; reprinted by permission of the publisher; original French © 1988, from *Mondes Miroirs Magies* (Paris: Editions Flammarion, 1988); used by permission of Flammarion.

Chin, Chi'iu (p. 296): "Free Women Blooming Like Flowers," translation by Daniela Gioseffi with Pwu Jean Lee, © 1988, 2003 by Daniela Gioseffi; used by permission of the translators.

Chihara, Michelle (p. 350): "Tough Love," © 2002 by Michelle Chihara, from *After 9/11: Solutions for a Saner World,* edited by Don Hazen, Tate Hausman, Tamara Strous, and Michelle Chihara (San Francisco: Independent Media Institute, 2002); used by permission of the author.

Cohn, Carol (p. 56): "Sex and Death in the Rational World of Defense Intellectuals," © 1987 by University of Chicago Press, from an article in *SIGNS* 12 (Summer 1987); reprinted by permission of the University of Chicago Press.

Cortez, Jane (p. 24): "Stockpiling," © 1984 by Jayne Cortez, appeared in *Coagulations* (New York: Thunder's Mouth Press, 1984); used by permission of the author.

Der-Hovanessian, Diana (p. 147): "Songs of Bread" and "An Armenian Looks at Newsphotos of the Cambodian Deathwatch," © 1986 by Diana Der-Hovanessian, from *Songs of Bread, Songs of Salt,* © 1990 by Diana Der-Hovanessian, (New York: Ashod Press, 1990); also in *Selected Poems of Diana Der Hovanessian* (Long Island, NY: Sheep Meadow Press); first appeared in *Graham House Review* and *Nantucket Review;* used by permission of the author.

Dufresnoy, Adelaide-Gillette (p. 217): "The Deliverance of Argos" translation © 1986 by Dorothy Backer, from *The Defiant Muse: French Feminist Poems from The Middle Ages to the Present,* edited by Domna C. Stanton (New York: Feminist Press, 1986); used by permission of the publisher.

Duras, Marguerite (p. 115): "We Must Share the Crime," from *The War,* translation © 2003 by Daniela Gioseffi with L.B. Luttinger; original French © 1985, from *La Douleur* (Paris, P.O.L Editeur, 1985); used by permission of the translator.

Drakulic, Slavenka (p. 200): excerpt from "The Camps: Bosnia," from *S.,* a novel, © 1999 by Slavenka Drakulic, translation © 2000 by Marko Ivic (New York: Viking Penguin, 1999); reprinted by permission of Viking Penguin, a division of Penguin Putnam.

Druyan, Ann (p. 53): "At Ground Zero in Hiroshima," © 1988 by Ann Druyan; used by permission of the author.

Ehrenreich, Barbara (p. 43): excerpt from "The Religion of War," *from Blood Rites: Origins and History of the Passions of War,* © 1997 by Barbara Ehrenreich (New York: Henry Holt and Company, 1997); used by permission of the author.

Enheduanna (p. 3): "Lament to the Spirit of War," translation version by Daniela Gioseffi, © 1988 by Daniela Gioseffi; used by permission of the translator.

Enloe, Cynthia (p. 161): © 1999 by the Regents of the University of California, excerpt from *Maneuvers: The International Politics of Militarizing Women's Lives* (Berkeley: University of California Press, 2000); reprinted by permission of the publisher.

Farmand, Reza (283): "Meena," from the web site of the Revolutionary Association of Afghan Women, www.rawa.org; used by permission of RAWA.

Forche, Carolyn (p. 264): "Return," © 1984 by Carolyn Forche, *from The Country Between Us* (Pittsburgh, PA: University of Pittsburgh Press, 1984); used by permission of the author.

Gellhorn, Martha (page 7): excerpt from the Introduction to *The Face of War,* © 1959, 1988 by Martha Gellhorn (New York: Atlantic Monthly Press, 1988); reprinted by permission of Grove Atlantic, Inc.

Gilbert, Sandra (p. 247): "The Parachutist Wife," © 1988 by Sandra M. Gilbert, from *Blood Pressure* (New York: W.W. Norton, 1989); first appeared in *Field;* used by permission of the author.

Ginzburg, Natalia (p.116): "The Son of Man," from *A Place to Live and Other Essays* of Natalia Ginzburg, translation © 2002 by Lynne Sharon Schwartz (New York: Seven Stories Press, 2002); reprinted by permission of the translator and the publisher.

Gioseffi, Daniela (p. 165): "Don't Speak the Language of the Enemy," © 2002 by Daniela Gioseffi, from *Symbiosis: Poems* (New York: Rattapallax Press, 2002) and "The Exotic Enemy," © 1997 by Daniela Gioseffi, from *In Bed with the Exotic Ememy: Stories by Daniela Gioseffi* (Greensboro, NC: Avisson Press, 1997); used by permission of the author.

Goldman, Emma (p. 4): "Patriotism As 'a Menace to Liberty,'" from speech given in 1934 on a lecture tour in the United States.

Gordimer, Nadine (p. 238): Nobel Laureate Lecture, © 1999 by Nadine Gordimer; used by permission of the author.

Hahn, Kimiko (p. 137): "The Bath," © 1987 by Kimiko Hahn; first appeared in *Jes'Grew*; used by permission of the author.

Hashimito, Toyomi (p. 137): "Hellish Years After Hellish Days," © 1978 by Toyomi Hashimito, from *Cries for Peace,* edited by Richard L. Gage, compiled by the Youth Division of Soka Gahkai, Antiwar Publication Committee (Tokyo: The Japan Times, Ltd., 1978).

Henson, Maria Rosa (p. 144): excerpt from *Comfort Woman: A Filipina's Story of Prostitution and Slavery,* © 1999 by Maria Rosa Henson (Oxford, UK: Rowman & Littlefield, 1999); originally published as *Comfort Woman: Slave of Destiny* (Manila: Philippine Center for Investigative Journalism, 1996); reprinted by permission Rowman & Littlefield and the Philippine Center for Investigative Journalism.

Hitchens, Theresa (p. 88): "Why Missile Defense Won't Keep Us Safe," © 2002 by Theresa Hitchens, Vice President of The Center for Defense Information, Washington. D.C.; used by permission of the author.

Hogan, Linda (p. 344): "Black Hills Survival Gathering, 1980," © 1984 by Linda Hogan, from *Eclipse* (1982); also appeared in *Songs from This Earth on Turtle's Back,* edited by Joseph Bruchac (Ithaca, NY: The Greenfield Press, 1984).

Istarú, Ana (p. 347): "A Time of Cannons Comes Flying," translation © 2002 by Zoe Angelsey, from *Ixok Amar-Go: Central American Women's Poetry for Peace,* edited by Zoe Angelsey (Penobscot, ME: Granite Press, 1987); used by permission of the translator.

Jimenez, Lilliam (p. 54): "To the Soldiers of El Salvador," translation © 1988 by Mary McAnally. Used by permission.

Jordan, June (p. 158): "The Bombing of Bagdad," © 1997 by June Jordan, from *Kissing God Goodbye, Poems 1991-1997* (New York: Anchor/Doubleday, 1997); reprinted by permission of Doubleday, a division of Random House.

Kachere, Marevasei (p. 207): "A Girl Soldier's Story," © 2000 by Zimbabwe Women Writers, from *Women of Resilience* (Harare, Zimbabwe: Zimbabwe Women Writers, 2000); also appears in *Women Writing Africa: Vol. 1, The Southern Region* (New York: Feminist Press/Women Writing Africa Series, 2002); reprinted by permission of Zimbabwe Women Writers.

Kalbasi, Sheema (p. 284): "For the Women of Afghanistan," © 2001, from the web site of the Revolutionary Association of Afghan Women, www.rawa.org; used by permission of RAWA.

Keju-Johnson, Darlene (p. 249): "Nuclear Bomb Testing on Human Guinea Pigs," © 1986, from the pamphlet *Pacific Women Speak: Why Haven't You Known?,* (Oxford, UK: Green Line, 1986); reprinted by permission of the publisher.

Kelly, Petra (p. 340): "Women and Ecology," translation by Marianne Howarth, © 1984, from *Fighting for Hope,* (Boston: South End Press, 1984); reprinted by permission of the publisher.

Kingsolver, Barbara (p. 86): "A Pure, High Note of Anguish," © 2001 by Barbara Kingsolver, first appeared in the *Los Angeles Times,* 23 September 2001; from *Small Wonder* © 2002 by Barbara Kingsolver (New York: HarperCollins, 2002); reprinted by permission of HarperCollins Publishers and the Frances Goldin Agency, New York.

Kluger, Ruth (p. 307): excerpt from *Still Alive: A Holocuast Girlhood Remembered,* © 2001 by Ruth Kluger. (New York: Feminist Press/Helen Rose Scheuer Jewish Women's Series, 2001); reprinted by permission of the publisher.

Kumin, Maxine (p. 15): "The Nightmare Factory," © 1970 by Maxine Kumin, from *The Nightmare Factory* (New York: Harper & Row, 1970); used by permission of the author.

Labra, Carilda Oliver (p. 11):"Declaration of Love," translation © 1995 by Daniela Gioseffi with Enildo Garcia, from *Dust Disappears* (Merrick, NY: Cross-Cultural Communications, Latin America Series #1, 1986); original Spanish, Letras Cubanas Havana; used by permission of author and translators.

Liebrecht, Savyon (p. 185): "Morning in the Park Among the Nannies," © 1986, 1988, 1992 by Savyon Lebrecht, translation © 1998 by Barbara Harshav, from *Apples from the Desert: Selected Stories* (New York: Feminist Press/Helen Rose Scheuer Jewish Women's Series, 1998); reprinted by permission of the publisher.

Le Seuer, Meridel (p. 301): "Women Know Alot of Things," © 1937, 1982, by Meridel Le Seuer, from *Ripening* (New York: Feminist Press, 1982); reprinted by permission of the publisher.

Lebron, Lolita (p. 299): "I Have All the Passion for Life," translation © 1984 by Gloria Waldman; first printed in *Voices of Women: Poetry by and About Third World Women* (Women's International Resource Exchange, 1984); used by permission of the translator.

Lessing, Doris (p. 120): excerpt from *The Wind Blows Away Our Words,* © 1987 by Doris Lessing (New York: Vintage, 1987); reprinted by permission of Jonathan Clowes, Ltd., London, on behalf of Doris Lessing.

Levertov, Denise (p. 304): "What It Could Be," © 1982 by Denise Levertov, from *Candles in Babylon* (New York: New Directions, 1982) and "Making Peace," © 1988 by Denise Levertov, from *Breathing the Waters* (New York: New Directions, 1987); reprinted by permission of New Directions Publishing Corp., New York.

Luxemburg, Rosa (p. 5): "Militarism As a Province of Accumulation," translation by Daniela Gioseffi with Sophia Buzevska, © 1988 by Daniela Gioseffi; used by permission of the translators.

Malancioiu, Ileana (p. 255): "Antigone," translation © 1998 by Daniela Gioseffi; used by permission of the translator.

Marshall, Lenore (p. 232): "Political Activism and the Artist" © 1985 by The Marshall Fund, Arizona, from *Invented a Person,* edited by Janice Thaddeus (New York, Horizon Press, 1985); used by permission of the author's estate.

Mac an tSaoi, Maire (p. 157): "Hatred," © 1959, 1987 by Maire Mhac an tSaoi, Dolmen Press, from *An Cion Go dli Seo Sait Seal O Marcaigh,* (Dublin: Ita, 1987); used by permission of the author.

Maguire, Mairead Corrigan (p. 337): "Letter to an Iraqui Woman," appeared on the web site of Voices in the Wilderness.

Meena (p. 283): "I'll Never Return," from the web site of the Revolutionary Association of Women of Afghanistan, www.rawa.org; used by permission of RAWA.

Mehta, Jaya (p. 149): "The Enemy Army Has Passed By," translation © 1994 by Shirin Kudchedkar, from *Women Writing in India, vol. 2: The Twentieth Century* (New York: Feminist Press, 1994); reprinted by permission of the publisher.

Millay, Edna St. Vincent (p. 6): "Earth, Unhappy Planet Born to Die," © 1934, 1962 by Edna St. Vincent Millay and Norma Millay Ellis, from *Collected Sonnets of Edna St. Vincent Millay* (New York: HarperCollins, 1988); reprinted by permission of Elizabeth Barnett, literary executor.

Mistral, Gabriela (p. 223): "Finnish Champion," translation © 1961, 1964, 1970, 1971 by Doris Dana, from *Selected Poems of Gabriela Mistral: A Bilingual Edition,* edited by Doris Dana (Baltimore: John Hopkins University Press, 1999); reprinted with permission of Joan Daves Agency/Writer's House, New York, on behalf of the proprietors.

Morejon, Nancy (p. 336): "Black Woman," translation © 1987 by Daniela Gioseffi with Enildo Garcia; original Spanish © 1985 by Nancy Morejon, Letras Cubanas, Havana; reprinted by permission of the author and translators.

Morgan, Robin (p. 315): "Ghosts and Echoes," © 2001 by Robin Morgan; from "Afterword: Letters from Ground Zero," in *The Demon Lover: The Roots of Terrorism* by Robin Morgan (New York: Washington Square Press/Simon and Schuster, 2001); reprinted with permission of the author.

Morrison, Toni (p. 242): excerpt from *Sula,* © 1973 by Toni Morrison (New York: Alfred A. Knopf, 1973); reprinted by permission of International Creative Management, Inc.

Najlis, Michele (p. 262): translation © 1987 by Amina Munoz, from *Ixok Amar-Go: Central American Women's Poetry for Peace,* edited by Zoe Angelsey (Penobscot, ME: Granite Press, 1987); used by permission of the editor.

Namhila, Ellen Ndeshi (p. 173): excerpt from *The Price of Freedom,* © 1997 by Ellen Ndeshi Namhila (Windhoek, Namibia: New Nambia Books/Gamsberg Macmillan Publishers, 1997); reprinted by permission of the publisher.

Nyguyet Tu (p. 136): "Eyes of an Afghan Child," © 2001 by Nyguyet Tu, translation © 2001 by Lady Borton with Nyguyet Tu; used by permission of the translator.

Nunez, Elizabeth (p. 173): excerpt from *Beyond the Limbo Silence,* a novel, © 1998 by Elizabeth Nunez (Seattle: Seal Press, 1998); used by permission of the author.

Pachen, Ani, and Adelaide Donnelley (p. 151): excerpt from *Sorrow Mountain: The Journey of a Tibetan Warrior Nun,* © 2000 by The Tibet Fund (New York: Kodansha America, 2000); reprinted by permission of Kodansha America, Inc.

Palacios, Chailang (p. 149): "The Colonization of our Pacific Islands," © 1986, from the pamphlet *Pacific Women Speak: Why Haven't You Known?,* (Oxford, UK: Green Line, 1986); reprinted by permission of the publisher.

Paley, Grace (p. 12): "Is There a Difference Between Men and Women" and "What If (This Week), © Grace Paley, from *Begin Again: Collected Poems of Grace Paley* (New York: Farrar, Strauss & Giroux, 2000); used by permission of the author.

Parun, Vesna (p. 131): "The War," translation © 2003 by Daniela Gioseffi with Ivana Spalatin; used by permission of the translator.

Peacock, Molly (p. 49): "Among Tall Buildings," © 2002 by Molly Peacock, from *Cornucopia, New & Selected Poems* (New York: W.W. Norton, 2002); reprinted by permission of W.W. Norton & Company, Inc.

Randall, Margaret (p. 241): "Memory Says Yes," © 1982, 1984, 1988 by Margaret Randall, from *Memory Says Yes* (Willamantic, CT: Curbstone Press, 1988) with acknowledgement to Nuke Rebuke, The Spirit That Moves Us Press, 1984; used by permission of the author.

Ratner, Rochelle (p. 49): "Borders," © 1988, 2002 by Rochelle Ratner; previously appeared in *The Minnesota Review*; used by permission of the author.

Rich, Adrienne (p. 23): sections 5 and 6 of "Six Narratives" © 1991 by Adrienne Rich, from *Dark Fields of the Republic: Poems 1991-1995* (New York, W.W. Norton, 1991); used by permission of W.W. Norton & Company.

Roosevelt, Eleanor (p. 297): speech made before the United Nations General Assembly, 1946, as chair of the Commission on Human Rights, a subsidiary of the Economic and Social Council of the United Nations.

Rose, Wendy (p. 52): "The Fifties," © 1986 Wendy Rose, from *Nuke Chronicles* (New York: Contact II Publications, 1986); used by permission of the author.

Rosen, Ruth (p. 261): "Blind, Unpredictable Terror," © 2001 by Ruth Rosen, appeared in *San Francisco Chronicle,* 29 October, 2001; used by permission of the author.

Roy, Arundhati (p. 90): "The Algebra of Infinite Justice," © 2001, 2002 by Arundhati Roy, published in *Power Politics,* 2nd edition (Boston: South End Press, 2002); first appeared in the *Guardian,* London, 29 September, 2001; used by permission of the author.

Rukeyser, Muriel (p. 234): "Kathe Kollwitz," © 1973 by Muriel Rukeyser, from *A Muriel Rukeyser Reader* (New York: W.W. Norton, 1994); first appeared in *Breaking Open* (New York: Random House, 1973); reprinted by permission of International Creative Management, Inc.

Safran, Hannah, and Donna Spiegelman (p. 267): "If Someone Else Is Suffering," Interview of Hannah Safran by Donna Spiegelman, © 2002 by Donna Spiegelman, appeared in *Sojourner: The Women's Forum,* Boston, May 2002; reprinted by permission of Donna Spiegelman.

Salado, Minerva (p. 181): "Report from Vietnam for International Women's Day," translation © 1987 by Daniela Gioseffi with Enildo Garcia; original Spanish, Letras Cubanas, Havana; used by permission of the translators.

Saluzzo, Diotata (p. 104): "The War of 1793," translation © 1986 by Muriel Kittel, from *The Defiant Muse: Italian Feminist Poems from the Middle Ages to the Present,* edited by Beverly Allen, Muriel Kittel, and Keala Jane Jewel (New York: Feminist Press, 1986); reprinted by permission of the publisher.

Sappho (p. 293) translation version © 1988 by Daniela Gioseffi; used by permission of the translator.

Schreiner, Olive (p. 221): "Bearers of Men's Bodies," from Woman and Labour, (1911; reprint London: Virago Press, 1978).

Schwartz, Lynne Sharon (p. 313): "The Spoils of War," © 1984 by Lynne Sharon Schwartz, first appeared in the *New York Times,* "Hers" column, 1984; used by permission of the author.

Shiva, Vandana (p. 69): "Bioterror and Biosafety," © 2001 by Vandana Shiva, published in *The Hindu,* New Delhi, 19 October 2001; used by permission of the author.

Smallberg, Mavis (p. 181): "The Situation in Soweto Is Not Abnormal" © 1987 by Mavis Smallberg; used by permission of the author.

Smedley, Agnes (p. 224): "The Women Take A Hand," © 1943, 1970 by Agnes Smedley, from *Portraits of Chinese Women in Revolution,* edited by Jan MacKinnon and Steve MacKinnon (New York: Feminist Press, 1976); originally published in book form in Battle Hymn of China (1943); an earlier version appeared in Vogue, April 1942; reprinted by permission of the Feminist Press.

Smith, Helen Zenna (p. 107): excerpt from Not So Quiet . . . , (1930; reprint New York: Feminist Press, 1989).

Smith, Joan (p. 70): "Crawling From The Wreckage," © 1989 by Joan Smith, from *Misogynies* (New York: Ballantine Books, 1992 and London: Faber & Faber, 1989); used by permission of the author.

Snitow, Anne (p. 320): excerpt from "Holding the Line at Greenham Common: On Being Joyously Political in Dangerous Times," © 1985 by Ann Snitow, from *Mother Jones,* February/March 1985; used by permission of the author.

Szymborska, Wislawa (p. 14): "Children of the Epoch," translation © 1986 by Austin Flint, from QRL Book Series, vol. xxii (Princeton, NJ: Quarterly Review of Literature, 1986); reprinted by permission of the publisher.

Szymusiak, Moldya (p. 274): excerpt from *The Stones Cry Out* © 1986 by Hill & Wang, a division of Farrar, Straus & Giroux, translation by Linda Coverdale (New York: Hill & Wang, 1986); reprinted by permission of Hill & Wang, a division of Farrar Strauss & Giroux, LLC.

Tesanovic, Jasmina (p. 80): "Women and Conflict: A Serbian Perspective," © 2001 by Jasmina Tesanovic, from *Me and My Multicultural Street* (Belgrade: Feministicka 94, 2001); used by permission of the author.

Townsend Warner, Sylvia (p. 229): "The Drought Breaks," appeared in *Life and Letters Today,* Summer 1937; used by permission of the Sylvia Townsend Warner/Valentine Ackland Collection and Archive.

Tra Thi Nga and Larsen, Wendy Wilder (p. 142): "Viet Minh" and "Famine," © 1986 by Tra Thi Nga and Wendy Wilder Larsen, from *Shallow Graves* (New York: Random House, 1986); used by permission of the authors.

Tsai Wen-Ji (p. 101): translation © 2003 by Pwu Jean Lee with Daniela Gioseffi; used by permission of the translators.

Tsveteyeva, Marina (p. 228): "Verses to Checkia," excerpted from "Poem of the End," translation adapted by Daniela Gioseffi with Sophia Buzevska, © 1992 by Daniela Gioseffi; original Russian text written in Prague, 1924; used by permission of the translators.

Tuqan, Fadwa (p. 118): "Face Lost in the Wilderness," translation © 1994, 2003 by Naomi Shihab Nye with Salma Khadra Jayyusi, from *Against Forgetting*, edited by Carolyn Forche (New York, W.W. Norton, 1994); used by permission of the translators.

Uwankunda, Jean Kadalika (p. 212): excerpt from "The Impact of Genocide on Women," © 1999 by Pro-femmes/Twese Hamwe B.P. 2758, Kigali, Rwanda, from *Genocide in Rwanda: A Collective Memory*, edited by John A. Berry and Carol Pott Berry (Washington, DC: Howard University Press, 1999).

Valenzuela, Luisa (p. 252): "I Am Your Horse in the Night," © 1976, 2002, by Luisa Valenzuela, translation by Deborah Bonner, from *Other Weapons* (Hanover, NH: Ediciones del Norte, 1976); reprinted by permission of Dunow & Carlson Literary Agency.

Walker, Alice (p. 333): "Only Justice Can Stop a Curse," © 1983 by Alice Walker, from *In Search Of Our Mothers Gardens: Womanist Prose* (New York: Harcourt Brace Jovanovich, 1983); reprinted by permission of Harcour, Inc.

Wells-Barnett, Ida (p. 219): "A National Crime," speech delivered in 1909 before the National Association for the Advancement of Colored People.

Women in Black of Belgrade, "We Are All Women in Black," translation and compilation © 2001 by Jasmina Tesanovic, from *Me and My Multicultural Street* (Belgrade: Feministicka 94, 2001); used by permission of Jasmina Tesanovic.

Wolf, Christa (p. 17): excerpt from "A Work Diary About the Stuff Life and Dreams are Made Of," from *Cassandra*, translation © 1984 by Jan Van Heurck; reprinted by permission of Farrar, Strauss & Giroux, LLC: original German © 1983 by Christa Wolf, Hermann Luchterhand Verlag, GmbH & Co. KG Darmstadt and Neuwied.

Xuan Quynh (p. 324): translation © 2001 by Phan Thanh Hoa with Lady Borton, appeared in *Visions of Hope, Dreams of Peace: Writings by Women in the Vietnam War*, edited by Lynda Van Devanter (New York: Warner Books, 1991); reprinted by permission of the translators.

Yamada, Mitsuye (p. 133): "Evacuation," "On the Bus," "Harmony at the Fairgrounds," and "In the Outhouse," © 1998 by Mitsuye Yamada, from *Camp Notes and Other Writings* (New Brunswick, NJ: Rutgers University Press, 1998); reprinted by permission of Rutgers University Press.

Zaimof, Gueni (p. 131): "The Star Obscure," © 1985 by Gueni Zaimof, from *The Star Obscure* (Luxembourg: International Publications, Euroeditor, 1985); used by permission of the author.

Zamora, Daisy (p. 346): "Song of Home" and "When We Go Home Again," translations by J. Glazer, Elizabeth Linder, and M. Ellis, © 1987, from *Ixok Amar-Go: Central American Women's Poetry for Peace*, edited by Zoe Angelsey (Penobscot, ME: Granite Press, 1987); used by permission of the editor.

Subject/Geographic Index

Editor's Note: The following index lists broad subjects and themes covered by the pieces in this collection. All page numbers refer to the first page of each piece addressing that theme, rather than the pages on which a specific reference may occur. (Most of these themes are also addressed in the book's introduction.) The index also lists the countries of national origin/residence of the authors included in this book. Entries indicating author's nationality appear in italics.

315, 325, 340
Germany, 17, 334
Ghana, 175
Globalization, *see* Colonialism/Neocolonialism
Great Britain, 7, 70, 107, 120, 229
Greece (ancient), 293
Guatemala, 263
Gulf War, *see* Iraq wars

Holocaust, Nazi, 17, 115, 120, 185, 307, 315, 337
Hiroshima/Nagasaki, 53, 56, 137, 272, 306, 315
HIV/AIDS, war and, 212

India, 69, 90, 149, 203
India, partition of, 203
Internment of Japanese Americans and Italian Americans, WWII, 133, 165, 350
Iran, 283
Iraq, 309
Iraq wars, 28, 86, 90, 158, 337
Ireland, 157, also see Northern Ireland
Israel, 182, 185, 267
Italy, 104, 116, 295

Japan, 137

Kosovo, 340

Labor, war and, 4, 5, 301, 315
Language/literature, war and, 17, 24, 41, 49, 56, 86, 90, 116, 165, 232, 238, 307, 315, 350
Latin America, wars/civil conflicts/dictatorships in, 54, 135, 184, 241, 252, 255, 262, 263, 264, 315, 346, 347
Lesbian and gay rights/homophobia, 267, 315
Love and personal relationships, impact of war on, 11, 23, 49, 70, 101, 104, 107, 116, 118, 127, 131, 132, 133, 149, 157, 158, 165, 182, 184, 252, 255, 267, 272, 287, 315, 321, 344, 346, 347
Lynchings of African Americans, 219, 261

Marshall Islands, 249
Media/journalism and war, 7, 24, 28, 120, 193, 267, 315, 347, 350
Memory of/and war, 7, 17, 23, 27, 49, 53, 86, 90, 116, 118, 120, 127, 131, 166, 184,

185, 234, 240, 241, 255, 272, 283, 287, 307, 315, 324
Mexico, 241
Middle East, 28, 49, 86, 90, 118, 127, 158, 182, 267, 309, 315
Militarism, 4, 5, 17, 25, 28, 29, 41, 53, 56, 70, 80, 88, 90, 158, 221, 272, 287, 315, 325, 333, 340, 350
Misogyny, war and, 17, 56, 70, 80, 144, 185, 200, 203, 315, 333
Missile-defense systems ("Star Wars"), 28, 88
Motherhood, war and, 80, 86, 101, 107, 116, 131, 137, 149, 175, 182, 193, 221, 229, 234, 267, 324, 337, 344, 346
Muslim Americans, attacks on/threats to, 90, 315, 350
Mythology, war and, 3, 17, 41, 217, 255

Namibia, 170
Native America, 52, 344
Native Americans, nuclear testing and, 52, 344
Native American genocide, 158
Nicaragua, 135, 184, 262, 346
Nonviolent activism, *see* Peace activism
Northern Ireland, 332
Northern Ireland, conflict in, 157
Northern Mariana Islands, 149
Nuclear weapons, manufacture and trade of/threat of, 7, 11, 15, 20, 24, 28, 49, 52, 53, 56, 86, 137, 149, 249, 304, 306, 325, 337, 340, 344
Nurses/medical personnel, war experiences of, 105, 107, 193

Palestine, 118
Patriotism/nationalism, 4, 10, 13, 41, 70, 80, 90, 161, 315, 350
Peace activism, 4, 5, 7, 12, 14, 17, 20, 27, 28, 53, 56, 80, 90, 120, 158, 221, 232, 234, 264, 272, 287, 293, 295, 315, 325, 337, 340, *also see* Peace activism, Women's solidarity
Philippines, The, 144
Poland, 14
Poverty, relationship of war to, 7, 39, 69, 120, 143, 263, 264, 293, 301, 315, 333, 340, 350
Prisoners of war/political prisoners, 39, 80, 133, 142, 144, 147, 151, 255
Prostitution, war and, 161, 334, also see

Rape/forced prostitution
Psychology of peace, 116, 295, 297, 299, 304, 315, 325, 333, 337, 346
Psychology of war/psychological impact of war, 7, 17, 23, 24, 41, 39, 53, 54, 56, 70, 80, 86, 90, 115, 116, 120, 157, 158, 165, 185, 212, 221, 234, 243, 264, 280, 307, 309, 313, 315, 325, 347
Puerto Rico, 299

Racial/ethnic hatred, war and, 7, 12, 41, 49, 80, 144, 158, 165, 170, 173, 181, 185, 200, 203, 212, 219, 240, 287, 313, 315, 333, 350
Rape/forced prostitution in/and war, 80, 144, 185, 200, 212, 261, 264, 315
Refugees and exiles, 7, 80, 120, 151, 170, 261, 267, 315, 346
Religion, war and, 41, 54, 70, 80, 203, 229, 315, 337
Resistance to war/injustice, 24, 54, 90, 101, 104, 149, 158, 161, 185, 193, 207, 217–290, 296, 301, 307, 313, 315, 325, 333, 347, *also see* Peace activism, Women's solidarity
Romania, 255, 306
Russia, 4, 27, 107, 193, 228
Rwanda, 212
Rwandan genocide, 161, 212, 315

September 11, 2001, 28, 49, 86, 88, 90, 261, 315, 350
Serbia, see Yugoslavia
Sex/sexuality, war and, 56, 70, 161, 185, *see also* Gender, Prostitution, Rape/forced prostitution
Sisters, impact of war on, 104, 255
Slavery, 12, 219, 240, 333, 336
Soldiers, experience of woman as, 207, 217, 224, 241
South Africa, 181, 221, 238
Southern Africa, wars of liberation in, 170, 181, 207, 238, 261
South Pacific, nuclear testing in, 149, 249
Soviet Union, see Russia
Spanish Civil War, 166, 228, 229, 301
"Star Wars," *see* Missile defense systems
Sumeria (ancient), 3

Terrorism, 28, 54, 69, 86, 88, 90, 170, 261, 315, 350
Tibet, 151

Torture, 54, 252, 255, 262, 264
Trinidad, 173
Turkey, 157

United Kingdom, see Great Britain
United Nations, 293, 297
UN Peace Keeping Organization (UNPKO), 161
United States, 4, 6, 10, 12, 15, 23, 24, 41, 49, 52, 53, 56, 86, 88, 105, 133, 147, 158, 161, 165, 219, 224, 232, 234, 240, 241, 242, 247, 261, 264, 272, 293, 297, 299, 301, 304, 307, 313, 315, 321, 325, 333, 344, 350

Venezuela, 255
Vietnam, 136, 142, 324
Vietnam War, 11, 120, 136, 142, 147, 161, 181, 274, 313, 315, 321, 324

War crimes, 7, 17, 80, 111, 115, 120, 144, 185, 200, 272, 274, 315, 337
Wives/Widows, impact of war on, 175, 193, 212, 231, 234, 247, 293
Women's solidarity, 12, 17, 20, 53, 80, 185, 200, 212, 224, 229, 255, 283, 287, 296, 301, 315, 321, 325, 333, 337, 340
World War I, 41, 70, 107, 234, 242, 293
World War II, 7, 27, 49, 52, 53, 56, 70, 115, 116, 131, 133, 144, 149, 165, 175, 185, 223, 224, 228, 234, 247, 272, 307, 315, 350

Yugoslavia, 80, 287, see also Bosnia-Herzegovina, Croatia, Kosovo
Yugoslavia, former, wars in, 80, 161, 200, 287, 315

Zimbabwe, 207

Gioseffi   Women on War